A Gentlemanly and Honorable Profession

A Gentlemanly and Honorable Profession

The Creation of the U.S. Naval Officer Corps, 1794–1815

Christopher McKee

Naval Institute Press
Annapolis, Maryland

© 1991
by the United States Naval Institute
Annapolis, Maryland

Figures by K. D. Rex

Library of Congress Cataloging-in-Publication Data

McKee, Christopher.
    A gentlemanly and honorable profession : the creation of the U.S.
naval officer corps, 1794–1815 / Christopher McKee.
        p.   cm.
    Includes bibliographical references (p.   ) and index.
    ISBN 0-87021-283-4 (alk. paper)
    1. United States. Navy—Officers—History—18th century.
    2. United States. Navy—Officers—History—19th century. I. Title.
VB313.M35   1991
359.3'32'0973—dc20   90-6232

Printed in the United States of America on acid-free paper⊗

9 8 7 6 5 4 3 2

First printing

His relations in Maryland have chosen for [Midshipman Joseph Israel] the profession of the navy, not with a view to profit or support, but because they consider it a gentlemanly, an elegant, and, with good conduct, a very honorable station.

Secretary of the Navy Robert Smith
to Commodore Edward Preble,
2 August 1803

Contents

Acknowledgments

During the more than twenty years that I have been working on this book hundreds of people have helped me in one way or another: archivists, librarians, curators, editors, student research assistants, graphic artists, grant administrators, secretaries, fellow scholars, professional colleagues, friends, and members of my family. Without the assistance of each of these generous individuals, this large undertaking could not have been completed. Two were so central to that successful outcome that they must be named: Jetta Lentz, for her astonishing mastery of the computer, her commitment to the project, and her tolerance, and Kay Wilson, whose love and belief in me made a seemingly impossible task finally possible. The only appropriate response within my means is to dedicate this book to all who aided me in whatever manner. Your support is appreciated far more than you can ever know.

After helpful people, money is the second essential for successful historical research. Critical financial sustenance was provided by Grinnell College, the Inter-University Seminar on Armed Forces and Society, the Newberry Library and the National Endowment for the Humanities, Southern Illinois University at Edwardsville, and University House of the University of Iowa. The faith these agencies had in this project, their generosity, and their long-suffering patience was exemplary.

Introduction: The Bafflement of William Jones

Constitution-Guerriere. Wasp-Frolic. United States-Macedonian. Constitution-Java. Hornet-Peacock. That arresting series of victories by the U.S. Navy in ship-to-ship combat during the six months between August 1812 and February 1813 put the American people and the nations of the Atlantic and Mediterranean worlds on notice that a highly professional new naval force was cruising the oceans. It had come about so quickly. In 1793 the United States had no part of a navy—neither warships, nor commanders, nor dockyards. How had the United States, a new nation, developed this effective fighting force in eighteen years?

Five elements composed this new national institution: ships, shore establishment, civilian administration, seamen, and officers. Among those five elements the one that made the crucial contribution to the emergence of the U.S. Navy would have to be its skillful, professional officer corps. Seamen and petty officers came and went, moving back and forth between merchant marine and navy, their commitment usually coterminous with their enlistments. The history of the Continental navy of the Revolutionary War provided abundant documentation that fine ships counted for nothing without good officers. However, the officer corps that went to war in 1812 was intimately connected with another of the five elements: the civilian administration. Together the two must be considered the organism that was the professional navy, an organism that, continually losing some members and initiating others, quickly became an institution with its own internal élan.

So far as anyone knows former secretary of the navy William Jones, who had filled that office during the War of 1812, was the first person to attempt a systematic analysis of the reasons why this officer corps had developed into a successful, professional body. Jones was puzzled by the question whether officers whose formative years as seamen had been passed in the merchant marine were more or less successful as naval commanders during that war than those who entered the navy directly as adolescents. Some time after peace had returned to the United States he made a list of the thirty-three men who either had been captains at the declaration of war in June 1812 or had attained that rank before 1 March 1815.[1] Beside the names of those he thought had acquired character-molding experience in the merchant service before entering the navy as mature men Jones placed the symbol —. Those who had been "brought up principally in the navy, but many of [whom] had, when on furlough, seen considerable service in mercantile ships" were marked ‖. Jones then placed checks (√) next to the names of captains who had been beyond Cape Horn or the Cape of Good Hope before the declaration of war, and asterisks (*) by the names of men who had won "brilliant and decisive victories" during the War of 1812. When William Jones had finished working, his list read:

—		Alexander Murray
—		John Rodgers
—		James Barron
*	—	William Bainbridge
—		Hugh G. Campbell
*	‖	Stephen Decatur
√	—	Thomas Tingey
*	‖	Charles Stewart
*	—	Isaac Hull
√	—	Isaac Chauncey
√	—	John Shaw
	‖	John Smith
	‖	John H. Dent
*	‖	David Porter
—		John Cassin
—		Samuel Evans
	‖	Charles Gordon
*	‖	Jacob Jones
*	‖	James Lawrence
*	‖	Charles Morris
	‖	Joseph Tarbell
	‖	Arthur Sinclair
*	‖	Oliver Hazard Perry
*	‖	Thomas Macdonough
*	‖	Lewis Warrington
	‖	Joseph Bainbridge
	‖	William Crane
*	‖	Johnston Blakeley
	‖	James T. Leonard
√ *	‖	James Biddle
√	‖	Charles G. Ridgely
	‖	Robert T. Spence
	‖	Daniel T. Patterson

What conclusion William Jones drew from his compilation is not known. Perhaps he decided the data were hopelessly ambiguous. True, more than five times as many navy-trained officers won "brilliant and decisive victories" as those brought up in the merchant service, even though the former outnumbered the latter by a margin of only two to one. Still, two of those "brilliant and decisive victories" had been won by men with extensive early training in the merchant marine: Isaac Hull and William Bainbridge, by universal admission among the most able and professional officers of the U.S. Navy.

Better information and additional analysis of his list might have convinced Jones that his merchant-trained/navy-trained distinction was misleading, if not false. Consider the case of Charles Stewart, categorized by Jones as navy-trained. Stewart had entered the navy in 1798 as a lieutenant, not a midshipman, unquestionable evidence that he had worked his way at least as high as mate in the merchant service before he received his naval appointment. Between early 1807 and the declaration of war in 1812, Captain Stewart was not on active duty as a naval officer. Instead, he spent the time on furlough, making merchant voyages in pursuit of private fortune. John Smith, too, entered the navy on a lieutenant's appointment, sure indication that he ought also to be labeled merchant-trained. David Porter, called navy-trained by Jones, had made three merchant voyages to the West Indies before his appointment as midshipman. An analogous record apparently holds true for Charles Gordon. Jones himself may have come to realize that distinction between the two groups was almost impossible to defend, for he concluded his analysis,

> Lieutenant Commandant [William] Burrows entered the navy when young, but had seen much private service and had just returned from India when he was put in command of the Enterprize and achieved the glorious victory over the Boxer in which he was mortally wounded.
>
> Of the numerous junior officers who distinguished themselves in subordinate stations in brilliant actions, it is impossible to discriminate between those who were brought up in the navy and those who had previously served in mercantile ships, but the great majority of the young officers have been brought up in the navy. There is, however, a laudable spirit of enterprise which stimulates them to seek active employ in the merchant service during peace, by which they become expert seamen in a short time and return to their profession with great advantage.

The pages that follow are an attempt to take up the investigation where William Jones dropped it a century and a half ago. The question remains, How did the United States, the new nation of 1794, develop an effective, professional navy in a period of eighteen years? Jones had intuitively sensed the proper course to steer when he sought the answer in the characteristics and career experiences of the officer corps; but in focusing on his merchant-trained/navy-trained division, he elected to consider too few elements in his analysis. The historian must ask a more complex series of questions concerning each officer who entered the navy between 5 June 1794 and 13 February 1815:[2]

When was he born?
Who were his parents?
Where did he live?
How had he been educated?

What career, if any, did he pursue before he entered the officer corps?

Can his political affiliation be discovered?

How did he secure his appointment in the navy?

Why did he decide to pursue a naval career?

Did he have siblings or other relatives in the officer corps? Relatives in places of power in the world of government?

How was he trained and socialized as a member of the officer corps?

If he remained in the navy, what rank or ranks did he attain?

What did his commanding officers think of him?

What characteristics did he display, what deeds did he perform, that marked him out for advancement?

If he left the navy before the end of the War of 1812, why did he do so?

The dates—5 June 1794 and 13 February 1815—are oddly precise enough to require some explanation. The earlier is that on which the first six officers of the navy, all captains, were officially notified of their appointments. At the head of that list stood the name of Revolutionary War veteran John Barry. On the evening of 14 February 1815 official word of the Treaty of Ghent, which ended the War of 1812, reached Washington. The previous day, sixteen-year-old William Barry Grove Taylor of North Carolina had been offered and accepted the appointment of midshipman. He is the last officer about whose life I have asked my series of questions.

Why stop then? The War of 1812 represents the culmination of the preceding eighteen years of the navy's history; the postwar navy was one whose mood and whose concerns were markedly different from those of the earlier organization. No longer did the officers fear, as they still did well into the War of 1812, that Congress might actually mutilate or abolish the navy. A professional body, the three-man Board of Navy Commissioners, aided the secretary of the navy in the management of naval affairs. During the first twenty-one years of its existence the new navy had fought three wars. After the brief encore of the Algerian War of 1815, it entered a long period of peace—interrupted by a campaign in the 1820s against West Indian piracy—that extended until the Mexican War of 1846–48. Before 1815 there had been enough to do to keep most of the officer corps on active duty; education and furloughs for practical training in merchant vessels had busily occupied the rest. With the coming of peace there were too many officers, not enough jobs to be done. Deprived of an external enemy to fight, one's fellow officers often became the object of one's animosity. Rapid promotion had been the expectation of the pre-1815 officer. Of the thirty-three captains on William Jones's list, twenty-one had entered the navy as midshipmen in 1798 or later. In the post-1815 years it was to take a David G. Farragut approximately as long to advance each grade in rank—midshipman to lieutenant, lieutenant to commander, commander to captain—as the fifteen years it had taken Daniel T. Patterson to run that entire course from midshipman to captain. A social history of the officer corps in the years between the War of 1812 and the Mexican War could be a fascinating book, but it would be about a different body from the one described in these pages.

I first became interested in exploring the social history of the navy's officers while writing a biography of one of them, Edward Preble. Biography of individual naval officers has long been a popular form of historical investigation;

but individual biography can raise as many questions as it answers. A host of minor figures—fellow officers, but not important historical personages—appear and disappear. Who were they? How did their lives relate to that of the "important" figure about whom one is writing? Does individual biography exaggerate the uniqueness of one man? One may sense that the individual under study is part of a social context, and is perhaps thrown into prominence by historical forces that are but dimly perceived. Individual biography is a poor tool for discovering that context and those forces. Indeed, until that larger social context is established with some certainty, the individual biography floats without fixed points of reference; it is impossible to relate the details of one particular life to any more general pattern. An equally troubling consideration: Might not an officer become the subject of individual biography because he was outstanding or atypical? Was he not, therefore, in important ways, unrepresentative of the whole corps of his fellow officers on whom the existence of the navy depended?

There is no question that in studying an entire officer corps, one loses much that makes individual biography appealing. A prosopographer cannot begin to know his group as intimately as a biographer knows one person. Lost are the mastery of every scrap of documentation, the degree of definitiveness, and the depth of psychological understanding that a biographer can achieve in relation to the individual subject. Realizing all that, it still seemed worthwhile to attempt to delineate the officer corps whole, if for no other purpose than that future biographers of individual officers might have a larger scheme to which those singular lives could be related.

This is a book about people. The navy of 1794–1815 is a superlative subject for the historian because rich documentary records survive to illuminate the lives of hundreds of its officers. Almost all of these are men who will never be the subjects of individual, full-scale biographies; but they come alive through those documents as sharply delineated and memorable personalities who deserve to be known and remembered. If a book about them is to be more than an atomistic series of vignettes, pattern must be discovered. That pattern can best be detected by using the tool of numbers. *Typical, many,* and *often* are words too vague and too slippery to be acceptable language for those who seek a sophisticated understanding of the pre-1815 navy. Were Edward Preble's officers during his 1803–1804 campaign against Tripoli *boys*? Was maritime New England home to *most* of the navy's officers? Did prize money make officers *rich*? Such questions can be answered only when one has accurate numbers and the means of comparing those numbers with the larger American society of 1794–1815, with other armed forces of the Napoleonic Wars era, or with the U.S. Navy of a later day. The pages that follow must often speak of the navy's officers in terms of numbers. Such numbers should not be intimidating. They are here presented only to provide a grid—a map, if you will—on which may be positioned human beings from the past, restored to life by the historian.

PART ONE
Building the Corps

1. At Headquarters

Prehistory

STRICTLY SPEAKING, the U.S. Navy's officer corps is older than the Navy Department itself. As early as August 1789, in the act establishing the War Department, Congress had placed under the administrative direction of the secretary of war not only the army, but the "naval forces, ships, or warlike stores of the United States" as well, even though there was not, at that moment, a single U.S. naval vessel in existence. When, in the wake of a declaration of war by Algiers, the national legislature authorized (27 March 1794) the construction of six frigates, it was the War Department that carried out this building program. Growing French hostility at sea moved Congress to legislate, July 1797, the manning and employment of three of these frigates. (Work on the others had been stopped in April 1796 upon the conclusion of peace with Algiers.) Again, it was the secretary of war who was charged with the task of getting this tiny navy to sea, just as he was expected to set in motion the process of acquiring and arming the twelve additional vessels that Congress authorized in April 1798 in further response to the French threat. Although the War Department had much to do with the building of the navy's first warships, *Constellation*, *Constitution*, and *United States*, it had small impact on the navy's human component. The 1794 legislation authorized the appointment of full complements of officers for each of the six frigates, but only six captains were actually appointed; their role was to provide professional superintendence for the frigates during construction. In the four years and three months between March 1794 and June 1798 the War Department had accumulated perhaps 350 applications for officer appointments in the new naval force.[1] Secretary of War James McHenry, working with heavy inputs from President John Adams above and Captains John Barry, Samuel Nicholson, Thomas Truxtun, and Richard Dale below, had named some fifty-nine officers[2] when the new Navy Department, which had been created on 30 April as part of the rapid naval buildup, commenced its de facto existence on 18 June 1798.

Apart from those fifty-nine officers, three frigates built and nearly ready to put to sea, materials assembled for the construction of three more frigates, four merchantmen purchased for conversion into ships of war, the 350 applications from would-be officers, a printed set of naval regulations, and a small quantity of navy-related records, the new Navy Department's principal legacy from the War Department was an established and proven administrative tradition. Three executive offices of government—the Department of War, the Department of Foreign Affairs, and the Post Office—had come into existence under the old Articles of Confederation and, with some changes of name and personnel, had continued in de facto existence to provide the structure of administrative stability that underlay the smooth transition in 1789 from the old Confederation government to the new political arrangements under the constitution.[3] When the hour came, in 1798, to break away the naval affairs component of the War Department's responsibilities, all the federal departments had time-tested and efficient methods for the transaction of their business, methods well understood by the clerks who formed the backbone of administrative continuity. By drawing on these established models and this fund of accumulated administrative lore, the new Navy Department was soon operating as normally and as efficiently as if it had been in business for several years. With minor adjustments of procedure along the way, this system continued essentially unchanged to and beyond the conclusion of the War of 1812.

Housing

During those sixteen and a half years the Navy Office, as it was commonly called, occupied at least six different homes. Until the removal of the federal government to the District of Columbia in June 1800, the department transacted its business in Philadelphia, initially at 139 Walnut Street and later at the corner of Eighth and Chestnut, but making two short-term flights to Trenton, New Jersey, to escape outbreaks of yellow fever.[4] Upon the move to Washington, the department took up temporary residence at one of the so-called Six Buildings on the north side of Pennsylvania Avenue, between Twenty-first and Twenty-second Streets, N.W., where it remained until the spring of 1801. When the British burned the government offices in August 1814, the Navy Department found temporary quarters by leasing a house at the corner of Twentieth and Eye Streets, N.W., which belonged to Joseph Mechlin, bookkeeper in the office of the accountant of the navy. It was still camped out at Mr. Mechlin's when the War of 1812 came to an end in February 1815.

These temporary wanderings aside, from spring of 1801 till late summer of 1814, Headquarters, as the navy's officers half-facetiously referred to it, was a two-and-one-half-story brick building two hundred yards west of the White House, on the site later covered by the southern portion of the Executive Office Building. The Navy Department shared this structure, known as the War Office, with the War and State Departments. Although the exact interior arrangement of the building, which measured 156 by 57 feet and contained thirty-four rooms, is not known in detail, some basics are on record. The secretary of the navy and his staff were housed on part of the second floor, while the accountant of the navy and his larger corps of clerks occupied a part of the first floor. That second-floor office suite consisted of three offices (or rooms, as they were always called), a central hallway ten feet wide running the length of the building, and a stair providing access to the accountant's complex below.[5] Above was an attic, one room of which became the inevitable storage place of the department's noncurrent records, space that a newly arrived chief clerk described, early in 1813, as "filled with books, old letters, and papers of various kinds (some important) in great disorder and dirty."[6]

Comprehension of these physical relationships is an important aid to understanding the navy's social history. At the top level of government, at least in the pre-1815 years, a high proportion of the major decisions were reached and much of the day-to-day business was transacted without the creation of a formal paper record. A document was likely to be prepared only when a compelling reason existed: a decision must be communicated to some distant person; an application had to remain on file for future consultation; an officer needed formal orders; settlement of an account required a statement from the secretary of the navy allowing certain charges; some official wanted to get his position on a disputed issue on the record. None of this is to suggest that the government's decisions were made naively, offhandedly, or unsystematically. They were not. But, if the secretary wished the accountant's opinion on who were the best pursers, the former simply invited the latter upstairs to talk the matter over in the privacy of his office. Did the secretary of war have a friend whose son's application for a midshipman's appointment he hoped to move closer to the top of the pile? The secretary of the navy's office was under the same roof, and a few minutes' conversation was readily arranged. Was the president's decision needed on some matter? His office was two hundred yards away in the White House. Easy enough for the secretary to walk over and review the pros and cons in person. If there were papers to be read and pondered, or if the matter did not require a face-to-face conversation, a brief note could be written on a scrap of paper or on the band that tied the documents together; back the scrap or the file would come with the president's "Approved" written on the same medium. The Treasury was a mere two hundred yards to the east of the White House, no more than a five minutes' walk from the Navy Office. Even though a mile and a half of Pennsylvania Avenue separated the administrative complex clustered around the White House from the Capitol, one has the impression that, during sessions of Congress, the stairs leading to the secretary's office were almost constantly creaking under the feet of congressmen and senators ascending to urge the appointment of some political ally's temporarily unemployed brother as a sailing master or to advocate the awarding of a hemp contract to an important constituent. Those who think that the telephone has impoverished the historical record do not appreciate how little of the government's crucial decision making in the pre-1815 years was actually conducted in formal, written communications.

Presidents and Secretaries

The location of the secretary of the navy's office on the second floor of the Navy Department's official home physically announced the eminence of his position as the chief executive of the department. He, of course, was appointed by, reported to, and exercised his authority in the name of the president of the United States. This meant different things in the cases of each of the four men who held the nation's highest elective office during the formative years of the navy's officer corps. Except in the selection of the first six captains, a decision in which he was a heavy player, George Washington's role in naval affairs was minimal. He left the building of the first frigates to the secretary of war, subject only to his general administrative oversight. Washington's successor,

John Adams, was keenly interested in naval affairs, and particularly in the recruitment of promising young officers; but he tended to ride certain hobbies enthusiastically, whether it was the appointment of men from the New England states, or interfering in the chain of command between the secretary of the navy and the commanders of individual ships when the ships were anchored in Boston harbor and the president was in Massachusetts, or devoting an inordinate amount of time to promoting the career of Captain Silas Talbot, a man he thought had been unfairly overshadowed by Thomas Truxtun. President Adams's enthusiasms did little to make the life of his secretary of the navy any easier, but they could be tolerated, because the president's heart was in the right place. He was an ardent and constant supporter of the navy and things naval.

Of the four presidents, Thomas Jefferson took the greatest interest in the day-to-day operations of the Navy Department. An efficient administrator and a prompt decider, Jefferson neither interfered with nor abridged his secretary of the navy's authority, but he did expect to be kept informed about all major items of departmental business on which action had to be taken. Although Jefferson was inclined to complain that Navy was the department whose affairs he understood the least, this form of self-deprecation should not be taken at face value. None of the four chief executives had a greater daily command of what was going on over at the Navy Office. James Madison took a more distant interest in the management of naval affairs than did either of his immediate predecessors. The correspondence of Presidents Adams and Jefferson with their secretaries of the navy constitutes a rich historical record of the formulation of naval policy in the ten years between June 1798 and March 1809. Madison, by contrast, seems to have been content to leave the day-to-day details of naval management to his three successive secretaries of the navy, subject to regular personal conferences that kept him informed of what was happening generally. He limited his direct involvement in naval decision making to strategic issues in the deployment of the nation's ships and to naval affairs questions that immediately affected foreign policy. Unlike Adams and Jefferson, Madison played almost no role in the development of the navy's corps of officers.

Whatever the administration, the secretary of the navy was the key man, although, as will shortly be seen, he had some crucially important assistants whose contributions to the navy's history have been inadequately appreciated.

Benjamin Stoddert, who took office when naval affairs were placed under the jurisdiction of a separate department and remained until 31 March 1801, was consumed with the task of getting a navy of some forty-nine vessels built or purchased, officered, manned, supplied, and at sea to fight the Quasi-War with France. A merchant in Georgetown, D.C., at the time of his appointment, Stoddert's most immediately relevant experience and his strongest recommendation was his year and a half's service as secretary to the Continental Board of War during the Revolution. Stoddert is a strangely colorless historical figure, one who fails to emerge as an individual from the hundreds of pages of documentation that he left. About the closest thing to a glimpse of the human being that survives is an officer's comment, after a personal interview, that the secretary "is a man of very few words."[7] For certain Stoddert was a hard-driving executive who organized a substantial provisional navy to win the undeclared naval war with France in less than three years. Under the pressure of wartime conditions he had relatively little time or energy to devote to the long-range development of an officer corps, but he did more than might have been expected in the circumstances. Beginning with the nucleus of fifty-nine officers inherited from the War Department in June 1798, Stoddert directed the expansion of that corps to some seven hundred individuals by the summer of 1800. If this rapid mobilization brought into the corps a substantial number of unsuitable individuals who later had to be excised from its ranks, it recruited an equal number of men who had long, useful, and, in some cases, distinguished naval careers. Stoddert regularized appointment and promotion procedures, which thereafter remained essentially unchanged through the pre-1815 years, and he quickly moved to establish strict standards for professional behavior by members of the officer corps. But Benjamin Stoddert always saw himself as a short-service public official. He would exert himself to his physical and psychological limits to get the navy on its feet; the first moment he could return to private life with honor, he would do so.[8] The long, patient business of shaping a truly professional officer corps was to be left to other hands.

Upon his succession to office, President Jefferson was, for some months, unable to appoint a secretary of the navy. Persons initially offered the post, apparently perceiving that they were being asked to preside over the diminution and possible extinction of the navy—not foreseeing that, in fact, the navy was about to enter upon its period of most intense professional development—gracefully sidestepped the presumed hatchet man's role. Jefferson designated Secretary of War Henry Dearborn to serve as acting secretary of the navy—the two departments were, it will be recalled, housed under the same roof by summer of 1801—and Dearborn, in turn, delegated the actual performance of many of the secretary's duties to Samuel Smith, a Republican congressman from Baltimore, who did not wish to give up his seat in the House of Representatives to accept the permanent cabinet post.

By late July, however, an acceptable candidate for the job had been found. He was Samuel Smith's brother, Robert, a Baltimore attorney who had served in the Maryland legislature and as a presidential elector, but who had not previously held any national office. Robert Smith had built an independent fortune through his law practice and, being still a vigorous man in his early forties, had expressed a wish to "retire from the busy scenes of the law" to some "honorable post" under the national government.[9] An unknown quantity when he assumed office, Smith proved to be a sleeper. The conjunction of his nearly eight-year term of office and his particular interests, abilities, and personality made him the secretary who had the single greatest influence in shaping the officer corps of the navy. If Robert Smith walks tall through the pages of this book, it is because the overwhelming majority of officers, both senior and junior, who distinguished themselves in the War of 1812 either entered the navy or received their crucial professional development during his term in office.

Not that Robert Smith necessarily made a favorable first impression. Frances Few, a young woman from New York who visited Washington in the fall of 1808, reported that "his figure is good, and he is much of a gentleman in his manners and would be handsome, if he was not disfigured by his nose"; but she added, "[The] secretary of the navy is a man of a very little sense. He is excessively fond of parade and show, and, though his origin was low, very low, he boasts of his family as well as his furniture. Mrs. Smith is a charming woman and though upwards of forty is still very handsome, rather inanimate, but her countenance is sweet and inclined to melancholy. She is much devoted to dress and displays much elegance and taste in it."[10]

The navy's officers, who knew Smith more intimately and over a far longer period of time, assessed him differently. Master Commandant Isaac Chauncey's opinion of his civilian superior could be replicated many times over, if not so eloquently, from the private correspondence of Chauncey's peers. "There is no family, that I am not particularly connected with, that I love and respect more," Chauncey wrote, "for Mrs. Smith I think is one of the most amiable women I ever knew, and Mr. Smith, although not to be surpassed in his public character as secretary of the navy, I think in private life he is still more a pattern for example and hardly to be equaled. . . . Mr. Smith's relinquishment of office would be the greatest misfortune that could happen to the navy, and I believe that I am within bounds when I say that nine-tenths of the officers think with me."[11]

Benjamin Stoddert, reviewing his successor's eight years in office, gave him high marks for his performance, and recorded only one criticism: Smith's natural inclination to be polite sometimes led him to defer to Jefferson's opinions when the country would have been better served had the secretary stuck firmly to his own.[12] All in all, the assessment of Smith the secretary that gives the best insight into his own conception of his office, his manner of filling that role, and his relations with the officers is one apparently written not too long after the War of 1812, but not made public until Smith's death in 1842 at the age of eighty-five. Although the newspaper that published the letter did not reveal its author's identity, he was clearly either an officer of the navy or a civilian official who had worked closely with Smith when the latter was in office. The prose may be a bit overwrought, and the content was for Smith's eyes; if one can push beyond these liabilities, it is to discover a valuable perspective on how a key secretary did his job:

> The unpopularity of the navy with the government and the people which you had to encounter on taking charge of the Navy Department in 1801—the solicitude which you evinced for its honor and its interests—the order and discipline you infused into it—deserve not only the thanks of the navy, but of the nation. When you assumed the control of this branch of our national forces, nothing could be more unpopular. It was desponding under the law of that year which created the naval peace establishment, and its energies seemed prostrated for ever. Under the authority of the law you pruned its excrescences, sifted the mass, and encouraged it with hope. On every occasion which presented itself you afforded an opportunity to draw it toward the public eye and thus destroyed the public prejudice.
>
> In your intercourse with the officers of the navy they were taught to know that, if their situations were not lucrative, they were highly honorable. You inculcated the principles of gentlemen, and they felt that they were such. You drew them to Washington on every proper occasion and thus became personally acquainted with them, their qualifications, and their intelligence, whereby you attained a power of discriminating their various capacities for the duties required of them which has never been surpassed—and perhaps will never again be equaled. In your office and in your house your manner and deportment were always those of the gentleman. No peevishness, petulance, or upstart pride of official station embarrassed the intercourse of the officers with you or cowarded the manly feelings of those subject to your orders and control. You at all times respected their rank and never lost sight of their merits. Your official practice

was constant and unvarying: none could be disappointed, for all knew on what they had to depend—their own merits and not the intercession of friends. If any one amongst them so far forgot himself and the principles you inculcated as to be no longer an honor to his corps, your duty enforced the laws, and he ceased to disgrace the rolls of your office. No lawless interference with your duties would arrest your practice or render pliant your principles.

The officers, in their correspondence with the department, were promptly noticed; and, if nothing further was required, the receipt of their letters was invariably acknowledged. Your fortune was not spared in rendering grateful hospitality to the navy and procuring for it a respectful attention. They could not be insensible to your efforts at the time, and their gratitude has been evinced in a manner perhaps, until now, unknown to yourself. The principles you inculcated, uniting with the duty they owed to their country and their affection for you, determined them to yield nothing, even to Britain's naval prowess, which valor, skill, and honor could accomplish. Thus, Sir, you had rendered them almost invincible. They felt that, in acquiring glory for their country, it reflected honor on you, who had so often delighted in honoring them. While you exacted rigidly the duties of the officers of the service and enforced the laws and regulations for the government of their conduct, you respected their rights under those laws and supported them in the exercise of all their functions. Under the supervision of such a gentleman, we are not astonished at the efficiency of the navy in the wars of 1802 with Tripoli, of 1812 with England, and of 1815 with Algiers.[13]

Under the best of circumstances Robert Smith was going to be a tough act to follow. President James Madison turned to South Carolina's former comptroller of finance (1800–1804) and governor (1804–1806), Paul Hamilton. Although the officer corps experienced the unavoidable apprehensions over a new secretary at the department's helm, personal contact caused these to evaporate almost immediately. "You may rest assured of one fact," William Bainbridge wrote David Porter late in Hamilton's first year in office, "that we have an excellent secretary and that he is a most zealous friend to the navy." When Porter had a chance to meet Hamilton he could only agree: "I am extremely pleased with the secretary of the navy. He is a plain gentleman and a man of great penetration and inquiry."[14] Because of Hamilton's military service during the southern campaigns of the Revolution, the corps expected him to be sensitive to the fine distinctions of professional etiquette and precedence that were points of concern to them as officers. As had his predecessor, Hamilton regarded the selection of novice officers as one of his most critical responsibilities, and to it he devoted a major portion of his official time. His concern did not end with appointment. No issue was closer to his heart than strengthening and expanding the program for the education of newly appointed midshipmen begun by Robert Smith. Throughout his tenure Hamilton stringently enforced the highest standards of personal and professional conduct by the navy's officers.

Then, when Paul Hamilton had been secretary for perhaps two years, things began to go sour. Even today it is difficult to sort out all the elements that led to the collapse of his administration of the Navy Department. The traditional explanation is that Hamilton began drinking so heavily that he became incapable of directing effectively. Convincing evidence has been mustered to support this charge, but as a single encompassing explanation it is too facile.[15] As will be seen when the time comes to explore the problem of alcohol

*Is it merely that the unknown miniaturist who painted this watercolor-on-ivory portrait
of Secretary of the Navy Paul Hamilton was not an artist of the first rank? Or does the
face—look especially at the eyes—reveal a man who was friendly and sensitive, but none
too forceful? Aware as historians are of Hamilton's political and administrative death
from self-inflicted wounds, it is tempting to read such qualities into the only unquestionably
authentic image of the man.* Gibbes Museum of Art, Charleston, South Carolina.

addiction among the officer corps, excessive drinking was widespread in the
United States of 1812, but it was also a great taboo. To claim that someone
who simply enjoyed two-fisted drinking was an alcoholic was one way to nail
him when subtler charges failed to bring him down. Arguing against the
drinking-on-the-job accusation is the fact that Hamilton's handwriting, of which
there are numerous examples, remained beautifully small, clear, and precise
right through to the end of his term of office, a phenomenon one would
scarcely expect in a man supposedly too intoxicated to perform his duties in
the latter part of the day. It is also worthy of note that in all the surviving
personal correspondence of all the naval officers who had occasional or frequent
contact with the secretary, only David Porter makes the drinking charge. If
Hamilton was increasing his alcohol intake, a trend alleged by more than one
congressional observer, he had ample provocation in the deterioration of his
financial affairs in South Carolina, where his creditors were forcing the sale of
his slaves by the tens and twenties to recover debts he could not otherwise
meet.[16]

The real cause of Hamilton's fall from power is more complex than the
drunk-all-afternoon story, but better documented. Paul Hamilton was a man
of the strictest personal integrity, one whose endearing human qualities, his
friendliness and generosity, made it difficult for his professional subordinates
to say a hard word about him, no matter how things fell apart.[17] But truth was,
drunk or sober, Paul Hamilton was no administrator. Or, to put it in the
language of the times, his "want of method had introduced irregularity and

confusion" into the operations of the Navy Office.[18] Robert Smith was not, by anyone's account, a hard-nosed executive, lashing his staff on to ever-greater prodigies of productiveness, but he did know how to get the job done and keep the office up-to-date and efficient. The momentum he had imparted to the operation kept it running smoothly, to all external appearances, during Paul Hamilton's first two years in office; but, inside the shell, Hamilton's lack of administrative skills was slowly, subtly corroding the whole operation. The chief clerk began neglecting his duties. Record keeping became more and more careless. A week after Hamilton left office, the acting secretary of the navy had to suffer the embarrassment of telling President Madison that no one could figure out, "in any reasonable time," how much of the currently appropriated funds had been spent or committed. Hamilton's successor discovered that the warmhearted but careless South Carolinian had appointed "many more" midshipmen before and during the opening months of the War of 1812 than were authorized by law.[19] James Ewell, a bankrupt doctor in need of a job with a steady salary, was appointed to a key clerkship for which he had neither the accounting skills nor the handwriting.[20] Sympathy for friends or acquaintances struggling to establish businesses or keep them afloat led Hamilton into some ill-advised and possibly illegal contracts that provided the navy with goods of inferior quality or excessive cost. In the latter regard things finally got so bad that the accountant of the navy blew the whistle on his superior and refused to approve payment for a cordage delivery that ran 43 percent over the fair market price.[21] All this while a politically motivated congressional fishing expedition, the Committee of Investigation, was assiduously trawling for documents and testimony to establish careless financial administration at the Navy Office and finding enough to keep the secretary on the defensive. In fact, the papers collected by the Committee of Investigation provided merely supporting documentation for what had already become a widespread condition in Congress: terminal erosion of confidence in Hamilton's administrative skills. Finally, the president could stand the political heat from Capitol Hill no longer; on 29 December 1812 he asked the secretary to come over to the White House where, as tactfully as possible, Madison pointed out the absolute necessity of Hamilton's resignation from office.[22]

If efficiency and administrative effectiveness were what congressmen and senators thought they wanted in a secretary of the navy, they were certain to be satisfied with William Jones, who filled the post from 19 January 1813 till 1 December 1814. If anyone thought the new secretary would also bring a Smith-like skill in human relations to the job, they were soon disappointed. Jones had impressive qualifications: Revolutionary War privateer officer under Thomas Truxtun, peacetime master mariner to India and elsewhere, Philadelphia merchant, and one-time Republican member of Congress. He threw himself into the job with energy and enthusiasm. Not since the days of Benjamin Stoddert had a secretary of the navy worked so hard. "As to exercise, it is out of the question, except the head and hands," he told his wife when he was less than two months into the job. "I rise at seven, breakfast at nine, dine at half-past four, eat nothing afterward; at dinner take about four glasses of good wine, but have not drank a drop of any kind of spirit since I have been here. I write every night till midnight, and sleep very well when I do not think too much."[23] Never one to expend much time or energy on protecting the feelings of others, Jones saw his first task as that of getting the Navy Office functioning methodically, efficiently, and correctly. Selected firings and fresh appointments quickly placed him in firm control. By 1 January 1814, with the exception of messenger Joseph Sutherland, not a single clerk who had served under any previous secretary of the navy remained on the office payroll. While Jones toiled at his self-advertised labor of cleaning up the mess in naval affairs that arose "from the corruption of self-interested men who have taken root in the establishment and, like the voracious poplar, nothing can thrive in their shade,"[24] Paul Hamilton could, and did, point out that the navy's ship-to-ship victories during the opening year of the war had all been won under his supposedly inept and lethargic administration.

William Jones was a strongly positive force in naval administration, but his long-term influence on the development of the navy's officers was restricted. Jones held office less than two years, which precluded the sustained effort required to have an appreciable effect in the shaping of the corps. Throughout those two years his primary energies had to be devoted to the immediate business of fighting. Nor is there evidence that he invested greater care in the selection of officer candidates or enforced higher standards of professional and personal behavior than had Smith and Hamilton, his immediate predecessors. One can, indeed, argue that Jones's interest in the professional development of the officer corps was far from his highest priority, because he almost immediately dismantled the educational apparatus for incoming midshipmen that had been so carefully nourished by both Smith and Hamilton.

If Jones had an effect on the officer corps at all, it was the negative one of temporary estrangement between the professionals and their civilian leader. Obedience they gave, for they were officers; but it was obedience without the enthusiastic followership that they had displayed for Smith and Hamilton. For this condition, the secretary's personality was at fault. Sure of his own abilities and opinions; haughty, reserved, and abrasive in his relations with his subordinates; Jones managed to alienate a broad spectrum of people during his less than two years in office. Few went so far as Captain Charles Stewart, who called the secretary "a fat-headed fool."[25] A more representative opinion was probably that of Oliver Hazard Perry. Jones, said he, "is a strange man. . . . *His promises* are not worth much. I do not think I shall trouble him on my own account very shortly." Or that of Purser Samuel Hambleton, commenting after a series of especially abrasive interviews: "You know the secretary is apt to take the stud—therefore I do not wish to push him too hard."[26] Even Jones's personal experience in the maritime business proved to be less than an unalloyed asset. In the field of naval architecture he fancied himself something of an expert; as chief executive of the navy's ship construction program he enforced his own opinion in matters that would have turned out more satisfactorily if they had been left to the professionals.[27] One of those administrators who are happier dealing with papers than with people, Jones tended to isolate himself in his room on the second floor of the Navy Office, where, with his door jealously guarded by the chief clerk, he quickly developed the reputation of being a most difficult man to see. Thomas B. Robertson, Republican member of Congress from Louisiana, "told me that I ought not to mind being denied an audience," wrote the disgruntled Samuel Hambleton. "It was [Jones's] way— that no man stood more in need of solitude than the secretary—that he was not capable of conceiving an idea in less than a day."[28]

Benjamin Williams Crowninshield, a copy traditionally ascribed to Robert Hinckley, after an 1816 portrait by John Vanderlyn. The face of a friendly man, well equipped to reestablish harmonious relations with an officer corps alienated by the abrasiveness and inaccessibility of his predecessor, William Jones. **Peabody Museum of Salem, Massachusetts.**

Personal financial problems imperiously demanded that Jones cut short his term in office even before the close of the war.[29] Now that the Navy Office was once again functioning efficiently, James Madison, in seeking his third secretary of the navy in an eight-year presidency, could turn to someone able to do a repair job on the human relations component of the secretarial assignment. His choice fell on Benjamin Williams Crowninshield of Salem, Massachusetts. So little of Crowninshield's term of office (16 January 1815 to 30 September 1818) occurred before the news of the end of the War of 1812 reached Washington that it was impossible for him to have any influence on the development of the officer corps that is the subject of this history. But as the war ended a new secretaryship dawned auspiciously for the navy's officers. "The secretary . . . is certainly a very different man from Mr. Jones," commented one of them. "There is a friendly affability and a conciliatory manner about him, extremely pleasing."[30]

Seconds-in-Command

It is easy for the naval historian to attach so much importance to the different secretaries that the crucial role of a second official, almost as powerful as the secretary, is lost in the shadows. That second official was the chief clerk of the Navy Department. In at least some secretary–chief clerk combinations the two officials worked so closely and so sympathetically as to make it impossible to distinguish the separate strands of opinion, of prose, or of responsibility and attribute them correctly to the secretary or to the chief clerk.

Although the working relationship and the exact mix of responsibilities differed from one secretary to the next and from one chief clerk to another, the outlines of a chief clerk's duties remained broadly the same.[31] To him were committed all the records of the Navy Department; he was responsible for their physical safety and for their accuracy. More time-consuming was his role as the principal channel of communication between the secretary and the navy's officers, and between the secretary and the other parts of the office staff. His was the responsibility for seeing that all letters, documents, and business requiring the secretary's attention reached his superior's desk each day. Once these had been examined and the necessary decisions made, back the papers would go to the chief clerk. A secretary of the navy would himself physically write and carefully revise replies only to the most important and sensitive correspondence. For the bulk of the letters reaching his desk, he would note the substance of the reply on the letter itself (the practice with Hamilton and Jones) or on a small scrap of paper (Smith's method).[32] The chief clerk would then either prepare the full reply from these notes himself—usually only in the cases of the more important letters—or hand it to one of his subordinate clerks for preparation of a response. Finished letters went back to the secretary's desk for signature or, very occasionally, were returned by the secretary, if he was dissatisfied with the reply as drafted. Once a chief clerk got acclimatized to working with a secretary, he would know how his principal was likely to respond to a particular issue, and would prepare a reply for the secretary's signature and submit it along with the original letter.[33] After the secretary had signed the outgoing mail a sheet of damp tissue paper was used to take a copy of each communication in the office's letterpress, a difficult process that often resulted in only partially legible copies. As time permitted, these tissue copies were later transcribed into tall leather-bound letterbooks by the subordinate clerks and the tissues destroyed.[34]

The system appears to have been devised to insure that the secretary would not be overwhelmed with a crushing burden of paperwork, but would have ample time to consider major questions of policy and for personal conferences with the navy's officers, applicants for navy appointments, contractors, his civilian counterparts, members of Congress, and the president. Acting as gatekeeper to the secretary's office in the face of the steady stream of visitors clamoring for the secretary's attention was another of the chief clerk's jobs,[35] as was the drafting of the often lengthy and complex reports demanded by Congress, and the preparation of the annual estimates of expenditures for the succeeding year, which estimates formed the basis of the administration's appropriation request to Congress.[36] Finally, the chief clerk served as disbursing officer for the office contingent account, which was used to pay for a wide range of goods and services, such as furniture, stationery, printing, postage, firewood and coal, feed for the messenger's horse, repairs and redecoration, scrubbing the offices, halls, and stairs, washing towels, cleaning out the privy, newspaper subscriptions, pictures, maps, and charts for the office walls, and books for the department library.[37] It was a position of potentially enormous power. No wonder that officers assiduously sought to develop good relationships with the chief clerk or seemed tainted with paranoia when they feared that he was prejudiced against them.[38]

Abishai Thomas, who held the post from 1 July 1799 till 31 March 1802 under the title *principal clerk*, was a North Carolinian and a protégé of that state's powerful Blount family, whose agent he had been in various business ventures. *Colonel* Thomas, as he was habitually known, first came to the attention of the national government in 1788 when the North Carolina House of Commons, to which he had been elected in 1787, appointed him one of the agents to settle the state's Revolutionary War accounts with the federal government. Unless some now-lost cache of Benjamin Stoddert papers comes to light, the circumstances of Thomas's appointment as principal clerk in the Navy Office will probably never be known, but he needed the job to make ends meet. For Abishai Thomas had one serious weakness. He was a compulsive gambler and was imprisoned for debt at least once. In the eyes of his contemporaries, it was this fatal character flaw that kept Thomas from attaining either financial independence or a more important federal appointment. When at last he married in the summer or fall of 1800, the one thing known about the match is that it was not financially advantageous.[39]

Surviving references leave no doubt that Colonel Thomas was a presence to be reckoned with in dealings at the Navy Office, but his position as principal clerk was compromised by the fact that Secretary Stoddert had a confidential or private assistant, Charles Washington Goldsborough, who seems to have had the closest access to his ear and his mail.[40] This awkward situation, which worked satisfactorily enough under Stoddert, endured for the first nine or ten months of Robert Smith's tenure, whereupon the latter chose to end it by naming Goldsborough as chief clerk and consolidating the duties of chief clerk and confidential clerk in one position. Reduced to just another clerk in the Navy Office, Thomas remained on the payroll till the end of 1802, performing quasi-autonomous work as secretary to the Commissioners of the Navy Pension Fund, in which capacity he had his hands full trying to discover and collect the government's share of prize money earned during the Quasi-War with France.[41] Attenuated status was too painful to be endured indefinitely, and Abishai Thomas finally resigned to face a bleak future. He is, said a fellow North Carolinian, "not able scarcely to get along. He is very poor indeed, and I fear from his character will never be in a better situation." Late in 1803 or early in 1804 he left for Darien, Georgia, where other members of his family had already settled, to make a fresh start, but died less than twelve months later. The Federalist press tried to make a political martyr of Abishai Thomas, claiming that he "was among the many old officers that was removed by Mr. *Jefferson*," but there is absolutely no evidence that partisan politics had anything to do with his departure from office.[42]

Goldsborough, who succeeded Thomas on 1 April 1802, was just a few days shy of his twenty-fifth birthday when he first sat down at the chief clerk's desk. He was soon to establish himself as the most powerful and important holder of that post in the first quarter-century of the navy's existence. As in the case of Abishai Thomas, the origins of Goldsborough's connection with the Navy Department are lost along with Benjamin Stoddert's private papers. In the absence of positive information one notes that Goldsborough was a native of Cambridge, Maryland; that he joined the Navy Office payroll on 25 June 1798, only seven days after Benjamin Stoddert assumed the duties of secretary of the navy; that he was then twenty-one years old; and that he was Stoddert's confidential secretary. From all of this one is inclined to speculate that

Charles Balthazar Julien Fevret de Saint-Mémin's profile portraits challenge the historian. Handsome as they are, it is harder to read personality in a profile than when the subject confronts the viewer directly, eyes make contact, and expression is captured as it flits across the full face. Still, for more than a dozen key figures of the pre-1815 navy, Saint-Mémin's are the only likenesses that survive. One such is his portrait of Navy Office Chief Clerk Charles Washington Goldsborough. What does one see here? The face of a skillful and determined administrator. Anything else? Perhaps a suggestion of the hauteur—or even pomposity—recorded in the caustic comments of certain contemporaries, but wholly unrevealed in his numerous private letters. These are not only a unique source for the inner history of the navy's earliest years, but a graceful and urbane record of Goldsborough's vast capacity for friendship and its nurture. National Portrait Gallery, Washington, D.C.

Goldsborough may have served an apprenticeship in Stoddert's Georgetown, D.C., countinghouse or have been otherwise known to Stoddert at the time of his initial appointment. One secret of Goldsborough's success as chief clerk was an astonishing capacity for paperwork. He was able to write easily, and with considerable rhetorical elegance, for hours on end—seemingly with little need to revise what he had written. The number of official papers that left the Navy Office in his beautifully clear handwriting on any given day would have exhausted an average clerk. On top of this Goldsborough was able to maintain an extensive private correspondence with individual officers of the navy in which much of the real business of the Navy Office was transacted without it ever appearing on the official record. No other chief clerk reveled so openly in the exercise of the authority and influence his position conferred. Goldsborough was clearly a man who loved his job.

The Goldsborough-Smith combination was an unusually effective and congenial one. The chief clerk became so skillful at expressing the secretary's ideas on paper that, save in those cases in which Smith's penchant for the subjunctive mood gives the game away, it is impossible to tell which of the two was really responsible for the contents of a particular letter, regardless of whose signature appears at the bottom of the page. That said, it is clear from the record that Smith always remained in full command at the Navy Office, never actually handing over the reins of power to Goldsborough; the latter was at no time more than a highly trusted and extremely capable deputy.

With the arrival of Paul Hamilton the situation underwent a subtle change. For one thing, Goldsborough served as acting secretary of the navy from 9 March 1809, a few days after the new administration took office, until Hamilton arrived from South Carolina on 15 May, and again from 14 August till 13

November 1809 while Hamilton went back to South Carolina for his family.[43]
Not only had Goldsborough experienced a heady taste of the top job, he also
had eleven years' experience with the inner workings of the Navy Department.
Hamilton had none, a state of affairs that was bound to make the new secretary
extremely dependent on the knowledgeable chief clerk. "Goldsborough is as
great a man as ever and appears to have quite a *new* smile," noted one officer,
following his first meeting with Smith's successor in office.[44] Hamilton was
inclined to let Goldsborough exercise more power and to take more initiatives
than Smith had ever permitted, even to the point of allowing Goldsborough to
draw up several key reports to Congress without any particular supervision
from the secretary, who was named on the reports as their author.[45] As
Hamilton's careless administrative methods became apparent, Goldsborough,
instead of keeping the department running well in spite of his chief, let his
own formidable management skills go slack and contributed to outsiders'
perception of a Navy Office badly in need of new administrative brooms.
Finally, in a mad act of self-mutilation, Goldsborough allowed himself to be
drawn into a very abusive, highly public controversy with a naval-surgeon-
turned-gunpowder-manufacturer, Dr. Thomas Ewell, a quarrel that reached
its nadir of public embarrassment when Ewell plastered Washington with a
printed broadside beginning, "THAT sense of duty which impels every man to
cry out *Mad-dog* on the approach of a rabid animal urges me to make this effort
to guard the Public against one of the most cunning scoundrels with whom I
have ever come in contact. This man is Charles W. Goldsborough, the Chief
Clerk in the Navy Department." Goldsborough immediately replied with an
equally vicious sheet—"Your kind publication of yesterday has just been handed
to me by a *friend* (although you supposed I had *none*)"—and the paper war was
on.[46] Whatever his abilities or past services to the navy or the government, by
the early days of 1813 Goldsborough had become a liability to the administration.
Moreover, a new secretary of the navy was determined to be undisputed master
of his house. Once he had gotten his bearings in the Navy Office, William
Jones gave Goldsborough his choice of resigning or being fired. The chief clerk
naturally picked the former alternative and left office on 9 March 1813.[47] In
1815 Goldsborough was able to return to the Navy Department, first as a
member of the staff of, and later as secretary to, the Board of Navy Commissioners. Admonished by the debacle of his final years in the chief clerkship,
Goldsborough worked hard for the commissioners, avoided controversy, and
died, chief of the Navy Department's Bureau of Provisions and Clothing, on
14 December 1843, "one of the oldest and most respected residents" of
Washington.[48]

In immediate need of a person at the chief clerk's desk who had no previous
connection with the Navy Department and who was, in effect, his own man,
Jones was persuaded by Secretary of State James Monroe to appoint Benjamin
Homans of Massachusetts to the post. A protégé of Vice-President Elbridge
Gerry, Homans was then in Washington trying to secure any other federal job
in preference to the consulship at Tunis, which he had been offered but did
not want. Indeed, Monroe had begun promoting Homans's candidacy for the
chief clerkship nearly a month before Jones asked for Goldsborough's resignation. A man in his late forties at the time of his appointment as chief clerk,
Homans served in that capacity from 9 March 1813 till 1 December 1823, a
few days before his death. In the 1780s and 1790s Homans had been a merchant

captain commanding ships out of Boston, but his fervent Jeffersonianism had forced him into self-imposed exile in Bordeaux during the Quasi-War with France for fear of prosecution under the federal Sedition Act. Republican victory in the election of 1800 cleared the way for Homans's return to Boston, where he pursued his merchant captain career for a year or two before coming ashore for good to experiment with careers as bookstore owner, notary public, and coroner. Evidently Homans was more effective, and probably personally happier, as a public official than as a businessman. Once having obtained the coroner's post, Homans held one government job or another for the balance of his life. He was elected secretary of the Commonwealth of Massachusetts in January 1810, holding that post until another turn of the Massachusetts political tides swept him out of office in January 1812. Bearing the twin assets of martyrdom to the Republican political cause and a reputation for bringing "system and order" to the operations of the office of the secretary of the Commonwealth of Massachusetts, and propelled by the vigorous backing of James Monroe, Homans rolled into the chief clerkship of the Navy Department without other candidates being seriously considered for the post.[49]

There is reason to think William Jones regretted letting Monroe twist his arm. Jones and Homans never established a close working relationship. Perhaps it was because their personalities were too much alike. Both were austere and had problems in dealing with people. Perhaps Jones resented Homans being pushed on him. Whatever the root cause, Benjamin Homans held the title and the duties of chief clerk, but he never had the secretary's confidence or his ear. Samuel Hambleton put it neatly: "The first mate does not know much of what passes in the cabin."[50] The person who did know was Edward W. DuVal, who joined the Navy Office as a clerk on 3 April 1813. Jones would certainly have preferred DuVal for chief clerk had he been a free agent in the choice. E.W. DuVal was an attorney by training. Even though the two men elected to spell the family name differently, Edward was the nephew and protégé of Gabriel Duvall, associate justice of the Supreme Court and former comptroller of the treasury (December 1802 to November 1811). While Uncle Gabriel had been comptroller, Edward had been at once a clerk in the comptroller's department and a law student in the uncle's private office as well. DuVal had an insider's knowledge of the workings of the federal offices; he was certainly as facile a writer and as accurate an accountant as Homans. The basis for Jones's preference for DuVal when it came to the most confidential assignments is not clear from the historical record. Perhaps it was simply that Jones found DuVal a more congenial person with whom to work closely. Be that as it may, it quickly became clear to the navy's officers, as to other contemporaries, that Edward DuVal was the man to see: "I presented your compliments to Mr. Homans and delivered your message," Samuel Hambleton wrote Oliver H. Perry from Washington in April 1814. "He promised to attend to the business. I shall mention it to Mr. DuVal, who, in my opinion, has it more in his power to be useful. In consequence of what I said to him a few days ago, he got Dr. [Usher] Parsons put on the roll for promotion."[51]

With the arrival of B.W. Crowninshield as secretary in January 1815, Benjamin Homans's fortunes took a sharp turn for the better. The two would have known each other well in Massachusetts Republican circles, and Crowninshield had a confidence in Homans's abilities that Jones never possessed. "The mate is now in favor," Hambleton noted almost a year to the day after he had reported that DuVal was the man to see.[52] The awkward state of affairs during the Jones regime, combined with the rather quarrelsome dispositions of both men, had created an atmosphere of explosive hostility between Homans and DuVal. Now, as Homans's star rose, DuVal's set, and he left the Navy Office, 8 April 1816, to become naval storekeeper at Washington. The world was at peace for the first time in a quarter-century; many of the secretary's former duties were now being eagerly performed by the Board of Navy Commissioners. Crowninshield saw himself principally as the navy's political spokesman. Present in Washington only when Congress was in session, he was content, the balance of the time, to run the department by mail from his imposing waterfront mansion in Salem, which left Homans as de facto secretary of the navy more than half of the year.[53] Thus, with the close of the War of 1812, Benjamin Homans finally came into his own as chief clerk of the Navy Department, though he seems never to have developed the close rapport with the senior officers that had been the secret of Goldsborough's success in the job. But to follow that part of Homans's story would be to travel into a period of the navy's history with which this book does not concern itself.

Workhorses

Below the secretary and the chief clerk on the Navy Office's ladder of responsibility stood the subordinate clerks. It would be wrong to think of these men as stenographers, seated on tall stools, monotonously copying out letters with quill pens all the day long. Better to see them as administrative assistants, each charged with a semi-autonomous area of responsibility, though every job did have its share of monotonous copying. These were definitely jobs for gentlemen. Two of the clerks were physicians who could not make adequate livings from their medical practices; several of the clerks held, at one time or another, prominent civil offices in the District of Columbia. Their status can best be assessed from their salaries: the chief clerk's annual compensation exceeded that of the captains who commanded the navy's frigates, while most of the subordinate clerks were the salary peers of the captains who commanded 20- to 31-gun ships or of masters commandant.

The size of the Navy Office staff fluctuated with the pressures of war and the retrenchments of peace.[54] At the height of the Quasi-War with France there were four assistant clerks in addition to Principal Clerk Abishai Thomas. With the winding down of that conflict and the reduction of the navy to what was perceived as a normal, peacetime establishment, the office force gradually shrank until, by the beginning of 1803, there were only two permanent clerks— Samuel T. Anderson and John Kilty Smith—to aid Goldsborough. Robert Smith contrived to fight the Tripolitan War to its successful conclusion with this diminutive staff. Frequently the press of business required Smith's office force to work a much longer day than its official hours of nine a.m. till three p.m. This was especially the case when a squadron was getting under way for or had just returned from the Mediterranean, or when Congress was in session and calling for frequent reports with voluminous enclosures. They were a happy, congenial group who willingly put in the extra hours at their desks, well knowing that sleepy summer days would be coming when Goldsborough could report, "We are very dull for want of business."[55] Finally, at the beginning of 1806, Smith decided that he was an ogre to expect three men to handle the volume of paper that was passing through his office, and one additional clerk was hired.[56] Although Paul Hamilton sought, as early as December 1810, to expand the office staff to four clerks in addition to the chief clerk, Congress demurred until the War of 1812 brought pressures severe enough to cause that body to fund expansion under a secretary in whose administrative abilities it had greater confidence.[57] Growth began early in 1813; by war's end the normal office complement was Chief Clerk Homans, six assistant clerks, and a seventh employed occasionally as the work demanded.

The distribution of responsibility within the office staff varied over time with the size of that staff and the special skills of the persons employed, but the parceling out of duties in force at the end of 1810 was probably not far different from that prevailing throughout the period of relative stability from mid-1801 till the declaration of war in mid-1812.[58]

Next in authority to the chief clerk was the position sometimes referred to as the register of the Navy Department.[59] This was the desk occupied by E.W. DuVal when he eclipsed Benjamin Homans. In 1810 its incumbent was Nathanael Greene Maxwell, the godson and namesake of the late General Greene of Revolutionary War fame. When Paul Hamilton served as South Carolina's comptroller of finance, Maxwell had been one of his clerks; he had subsequently gone into the commission business as a partner of one of Hamilton's close friends, George Ogier. The Embargo brought hard times for Ogier & Maxwell, so the latter sold out to his partner and accepted Paul Hamilton's invitation to join the Navy Department's civilian staff, effective 1 January 1810. As Goldsborough's troubles began to spring up around him like weeds, Maxwell saw himself as the logical successor at the chief clerk's desk. This awakened ambition produced a degree of alienation between Maxwell and his old patron, Hamilton, who was inclined to deny Goldsborough's troubles and his own.[60]

The register's title derived from his charge to keep track of the appointments, promotions, changes in duty assignments, resignations, dismissals, and deaths of all officers, which information he recorded in large volumes arranged alphabetically by the first letter of the officer's family name. Unfortunately, Maxwell was not always as careful about keeping this information as had been his predecessor, Samuel T. Anderson, who held the job during Robert Smith's tenure at the Navy Department. It is a sad day for the historian of the officer corps when the unfailingly meticulous Samuel Anderson moves on to a better job as naval storekeeper at New York in November 1809.[61] One possible reason for Maxwell's less than perfect record keeping was the volume of other work arriving on the register's desk. He was expected to fill out the officers' commissions and warrants for signature by the secretary and the president. Press copies of letters sent by the secretary to officers were handed to Maxwell for transcription in the series of large leather-bound volumes in which all such correspondence was recorded in chronological order. If that were not enough, after each incoming letter (except those relating to money matters) had been read and acted upon by the secretary or the chief clerk, these letters were piled on Mr. Maxwell's desk; he noted on the back of the letter its date, the name of the writer, the place from which it had been written, and a summary of the contents. The letters were then folded in such a way that the synopsis could be read without opening the letter itself, and the correspondence was filed away in cases near the chief clerk's desk.[62]

The only unquestionably authentic portrait of Navy Office Register Nathanael Greene Maxwell is this silhouette, which was probably cut after he had left government service to become a publisher and bookseller in Baltimore. Still, the medium can be eloquent. Maxwell's pouty lips and retreating chin suggest a man who may not have been all that uncomfortable in the atmosphere of self-serving interpersonal acrimony that characterized the navy's headquarters during the secretaryships of Paul Hamilton and William Jones. Maryland Historical Society, Baltimore.

Press copies of letters to correspondents who were not officers were handed to Conrad Schwarz for transcription into a separate series of letterbooks. Schwarz, a native of Germany, also copied into bound volumes each contract entered into by the Navy Department. Because Schwarz was a skilled draftsman, he spent a substantial part of his official time in copying ship plans and architectural drawings and in making maps and charts. It was he to whom the secretary turned for translations when the department received occasional letters in foreign languages.

Money could be disbursed neither to the officers of the navy nor to the civilian agents of the department without the authorization of the secretary of the navy. Processing requisitions for money, preparing the actual warrant for the secretary's signature, keeping track of commitments against appropriations, and copying various financial statements into the department's estimate books were the work of Samuel P. Todd, who just happened to be the nephew of Mrs. Dolly Payne Todd Madison.[63] When Samuel Todd became a navy purser in July 1812, Paul Hamilton replaced him with Dr. James Ewell, the bankrupt physician (and brother of Thomas Ewell of the Ewell-Goldsborough quarrel) with whose accounting and handwriting services William Jones was so anxious to dispense when he assumed direction of the Navy Office in January 1813.

Although this was a neat theoretical division of duties, it should not be assumed that real-life, daily operations were so compartmentalized. One clerk often had more to do than he could well manage, while another might be looking for something to keep himself occupied. Everyone pitched in to help out whoever was the busiest; often there were assignments that fell into no one's area of specified responsibility. With the possible exception of the register, who seems to have had a separate office, all the clerks wrote in a common room, under the immediate eye of the chief clerk.[64] There was a tendency for the officers and civilians waiting to be admitted to the secretary's private office to entertain themselves by visiting with the clerks, which, grumped Benjamin Homans when he was a few weeks into his new job, was "detrimental to the discharge of business." Homans wanted to move the subordinate clerks to a different room, if one could be found or created, but he admitted that "any innovation attempted on my part now would be illy received and add to the jealousy and ill-will that appear to prevail against me."[65]

One other position completed the secretary's office staff: the messenger. For all but one year of the period from June 1798 till February 1815, this job was filled by either George or Joseph Sutherland. As the title implies, the messenger was expected to spend much of his day on foot or horseback, picking up or delivering mail at the post office, carrying documents over to the White House or the Treasury, or perhaps posting off to the navy yard or the marine barracks with an urgent communiqué from the secretary or the chief clerk. He was also responsible for the physical security of the office—the department furnished him with a nearby residence—for getting the fires started on chilly mornings, for keeping track of the private mail that officers expected to receive at the Navy Office as they passed through Washington, and for affixing the department's handsome seal to commissions and other documents whereon it was required. The messenger also got stuck with all the odd and occasional jobs no one else wanted to bother about, such as finding someone to do the heavy cleaning around the office or to whitewash the walls when they got too dirty to be scrubbed.[66]

Downstairs

Thus far the tour has remained on the second floor of the War Office building, where was to be found the secretary of the navy's office with its attendant clerical staff. Downstairs, on the building's first floor, was much the larger half of the navy's civil establishment: the office of the accountant of the navy.

While the secretary of the navy was the man who authorized the issuing of money to pay the navy's bills and keep it functioning at home and abroad, it was the accountant of the navy who was responsible for seeing that the money had been properly expended by the officers and civilian agents to whom it had been disbursed. In the cases of the War and Navy Offices, Congress placed this accounting function not in the Treasury Department, as was the case with all other federal agencies, but under the administrative control of the secretary of war or of the secretary of the navy, subject to a later audit at the treasury. An examination of the day-to-day functioning of the accounting and auditing process will be deferred until the time comes to discuss the navy's pursers and the problem of debt among the officer corps, but an acquaintance with the existence of the accountant's office and with the people who worked there is essential to understanding the history of the officer corps.

The accountant of the navy was in many ways the second-ranking officer of the Navy Department, presiding over his own quasi-independent fiefdom. Of all the men who served at the Navy Office, only he and the secretary of the navy required nomination to, and confirmation by, the Senate. Only the secretary and the accountant had the franking privilege for mail. When they were both away from the office on the same day, the chief clerk had to take the day's outgoing mail down the hall to the War Department or the State

Department and have it franked by the secretary of war or the secretary of state.[67] During the entire period from the establishment of the Navy Department as a separate administrative body until the close of the War of 1812 the post of accountant of the navy was, to all intents and purposes, synonymous with one man: Thomas Turner, who served from 9 January 1800 till 15 March 1816.

For all of that, Turner was not the first man to hold the job. On 18 July 1798, two days after Congress authorized the establishment of the accountant's office, William Winder, a planter from Somerset County, Maryland, was nominated to the Senate as accountant of the navy and immediately confirmed. So far as experience and paper qualifications were concerned Winder seemed an excellent man for the post. Trained as a merchant, Winder had served, 1778–80, as a commissioner of the Navy Board of the Middle Department during the Revolution. With the approach of peace in 1782 Winder was appointed to adjust and settle the wartime accounts between the Confederation government and the state of Delaware, a task he completed so satisfactorily that his mandate was subsequently extended to include the accounts of Virginia and North Carolina as well. This successful record in public accounting aside, nothing is known concerning the exact circumstances of Winder's selection. Because the appointment was made so soon after Benjamin Stoddert took office and so quickly after the creation of the accountant's post, it seems likely that the choice of Winder was not a unilateral decision of the new secretary's, although the two men must have known one another from their simultaneous service in the national administration during the Revolution and perhaps in other connections as well. Winder may have been pressed on Stoddert by cabinet members longer in office, just as Benjamin Homans was foisted off on a subsequently resentful William Jones. Be that as it may, the only recorded objection to Winder's appointment came from hard-line Federalists in Maryland, who judged him too infected with Republicanism to be politically reliable.

Stoddert experienced considerable difficulty getting Winder on the job. Although appointed on 19 July, the new accountant did not actually arrive in Philadelphia to take up his duties until mid-September.[68] Even that achievement had required a strongly worded letter from Stoddert. Once Stoddert got Winder at his desk, he had trouble keeping him there: "Your immediate presence is necessary," the secretary wrote a year later, when Winder had once again disappeared to Somerset County, Maryland, "for I much fear your office is not in a state to afford the information which Congress will certainly require and which ought to be given at the commencement of the session. The loose accounts I believe are not yet commenced and Mr. Macdaniel [one of the clerks in the accountant's office] does not know how to commence them." Finally, after a year and a half in office, William Winder submitted his resignation, effective 8 January 1800.[69] One suspects that it had been requested. Over and above what may be surmised about Winder's lack of deep interest in the job from Stoddert's difficulties in getting and keeping him at work, Winder seems to have lacked the management skills needed to cope with the task of organizing so large and complex an operation as the accountant's office proved to be. With the establishment of the office of accountant of the navy on 16 July 1798 the accountant for the War Department, who had previously handled naval business, ceased to have any responsibility in that area. Winder dallied till mid-September in getting to Philadelphia, and all the while accounts were arriving at the Navy

*The perfect man for the job. Not only was former Georgetown mayor Thomas Turner
the most highly regarded of the long succession of individuals who attempted, with varying
degrees of success, to cope with the early-nineteenth-century navy's formidable accounting
burden, he even looked like an accountant of the navy! C.B.J. Fevret de Saint-Mémin's
engraved profile of a man notorious for his official integrity was probably taken about
1808.* National Portrait Gallery, Washington, D.C.

Office for adjustment. Flow increased as his office got off to a creaky start.
The bookkeeping system Winder attempted to establish seemed hopelessly
complex for the size of staff he had—or that Congress was likely to authorize.
A manual of instructions for pursers was begun, but languished in draft until
Winder's more efficient successor finished the job and pushed it through the
press. Most significant of all, although a veritable flood of accounts was pouring
into the office for adjustment and settlement, only a slender stream of approved
ones ran from the accountant's office to the Treasury Department for final
audit and close. In the sixteen months between September 1798 and 31
December 1799 William Winder had processed and passed on to the treasury
accounts totaling $546,918.07; his successor, Thomas Turner, in his first fifteen
months in office settled $3,123,514.68 worth of navy accounts, or roughly six
times the dollar volume. Making every allowance for the fact that Winder had
to start from scratch, Turner almost certainly did not exaggerate in saying that,
when he took over, "I found the accounts with the department dreadfully
situated—almost the whole unsettled—[and] Mr. Stoddert, the then secretary,
was extremely importunate that they should be adjusted without further
delay."[70]

There is every reason to suppose that Thomas Turner, the person selected
to put the accountant's house in order, was entirely Stoddert's choice, for they
were both residents of Georgetown, D.C., where Turner had served as mayor
during 1795. At the time of his selection as accountant, he already held a
government appointment as one of the commissioners for the valuation of
lands and houses and for the enumeration of slaves for purposes of federal
taxation under the act of 9 July 1798.[71] A point to notice about both the
accountant and his staff was their long tenure in their jobs, the lack of turnover
contrasting with the situation upstairs in the secretary's office. Once appointed,
Turner served sixteen years and two months. Although he did not attempt to
conceal his adherence to the Federalist party, no evidence exists that Turner's
removal from office on political grounds was ever contemplated. The election

of 1800, bringing the Jeffersonian Republicans to power as it did, naturally made Turner apprehensive, but he was an old friend of Samuel Smith's, who assured him, "I will do everything in my power to retain you in office, because you deserve it."[72] When William Jones succeeded Paul Hamilton as secretary in 1813 and heads began to roll on the second floor, Turner was fearful that his might be next. Benjamin Homans complained that the accountant was being standoffish in supplying him with papers and information he needed in his new job as chief clerk, attributing Turner's behavior to "the usual jealousy of office, the political antipathies of party, and the personal pride of those who feel the superiority of knowledge from long experience."[73] But Jones soon enough concluded, as had his predecessors, that he had better leave the accountant's office undisturbed. No secretary could find valid fault with either Turner's abilities or his performance, assets that were even more appreciated after his death, when Thomas Turner proved to be a hard act to follow. More important, probably, was the attitude of the Jefferson and Madison administrations, which, like their Federalist predecessors, took accounting for the public money most seriously. They regarded the accounting staffs of the federal government as professionals, immune from political removals. Fully appreciated was the cumulative knowledge that men such as Turner had acquired in their jobs, the duties of which often required them to go back to settlements made many years earlier in search of principles and rulings that applied to present cases.

Turner's health began to show signs of weakening as early as the summer of 1811. The summer following he had to spend three or four weeks at the springs in search of relief from rheumatism. A year later he was so seriously ill that he was unable to spend any extended time at the office or to work at home between mid-May and early September 1813. Thereafter Turner's health seemed, to all appearances, to be fully restored; he experienced no more extended absences from his desk until his final siege of ill health overtook him in late February 1816. Even in that instance, until the day before his death (15 March 1816) the members of Turner's staff were expecting him to recover and return to the office.[74] That the navy's accounting operation continued to function without any apparent loss of efficiency during its chief's illness-induced absences must be attributed in large measure to its principal clerk, Thomas Handy Gilliss, whose appointment by William Winder on 22 September 1798 was almost certainly the latter's greatest contribution to the future success of the accountant's office. A native of Somerset County, Maryland—and, in fact, a kinsman of Winder's by his mother's side of the family—Gilliss was just three months shy of his thirtieth birthday when he was appointed to the job he was to hold for the next fifty-one years and nine months, at which point ill health finally compelled him to resign. The secret of Gilliss's long and successful tenure in one tedious and demanding job was his personality: "He was a man of a naturally equable, systematic, affectionate, and gentle character."[75]

The seriousness with which the national administration, whether Federalist or Republican, took the responsibility of accounting for the expenditure of the public money is demonstrated by the fact that—except for the first year, when William Winder was having so much trouble getting his office on its feet, and the latter half of the War of 1812, when the big expansion of the secretary's office force took place under William Jones—Thomas Turner presided over a staff approximately twice the size of the one that supported the secretary of the navy. Wartime or peacetime, it required nearly ten people to assist the accountant in processing the navy's financial business. Midway through 1805 Turner reduced his office staff from ten to nine, so that he would have more salary money to distribute among his senior examining clerks. In so doing he put the remaining nine on notice that the higher salaries would continue only if the smaller force could absorb the same amount of work previously performed by a larger one.[76] Absorb the workload they did until the early months of 1813, when it became clear that more accounts were coming in the door from pursers, navy agents, and station commanders for settlement than were leaving the office for final audit by the comptroller of the treasury. One more examining clerk was added to Turner's staff in April 1813.[77] Still, the tide of unsettled accounts continued to rise. It is a tribute to Turner's and Gilliss's formidable administrative skills that on 6 December 1813, a year and a half into the War of 1812, there were accounts from only forty-two disbursing agents, totaling approximately $4.8 million (roughly the equivalent of the appropriation for the support of the navy and the marine corps for the year 1812) awaiting examination or in the process of settlement in the accountant's office; and that not more than eleven of these had come into the office earlier than the year 1812.[78] Even this much of a backlog was convincing to Congress; by the end of the War of 1812 the staff in the accountant's office had expanded to twelve men.

The stability and longevity characteristic of the accountant's office were in marked contrast to the situation in the secretary's domain. Although the accounting staff was nearly twice as large as the secretary's staff, a total of only twenty-seven individuals occupied desks in the accountant's office, in contrast to the thirty-four men who rotated through the much smaller number of jobs upstairs. Of the eight men employed in the secretary's office on 1 January 1815 the one with the greatest seniority was messenger Joseph Sutherland, who had started working there sometime between 31 March 1810 and 30 June 1812[79]; the next longest tenure was that of Chief Clerk Benjamin Homans, whose service—and thus whose knowledge of the workings of the office and the navy—went back only as far as 9 March 1813. The accountant's office, where twelve men were employed on 1 January 1815, presented a different tale. One of the twelve (T.H. Gilliss) traced his seniority from the very establishment of the office; four more had come on board in 1799; and three other clerks had started working there in 1800, 1805, and 1808 respectively. This stability surely reflects the government's need for long-service professionals to run its accounting operations. It is equally indicative of Thomas Turner's ability to build a congenial staff who were able to work together without the destructive interpersonal tensions that racked the secretary's staff during the days of Hamilton, Jones, and Crowninshield, even if the quarreling clerks of the secretary's office do make for more interesting history than the placid denizens of the accountant's sphere.

Late in 1810 the nine members of the accountant's staff were organized in a work pattern that changed little, if at all, during Turner's term of office. At the top of the office hierarchy sat Principal Clerk Thomas H. Gilliss; at the bottom was the messenger, Thomas J. Sutherland. Neither of their jobs needs to be described, for they were closely similar to those of their counterparts in the secretary's office. Below Gilliss in the structure of the office was George G. Macdaniel, who was responsible for examining the accounts for the receipt and expenditure of stores submitted by the navy agents and navy storekeepers.

These were absolutely the most difficult accounts to handle, which was the reason for Mr. Macdaniel's eminence on the office roster and the fact that his salary was the highest of all the office staff, save for that of T.H. Gilliss. When the store accounts were up to date, George Macdaniel was asked to serve as examiner for those unusually large or confusing accounts that required more than ordinary skill to unravel.

Joseph Mechlin of Berks County, Pennsylvania, was the bookkeeper in the accountant's office, a post he had held since February 1799, and the duties of which he would still be performing when the War of 1812 came to an end. Near the bottom of the office hierarchy, one notch above the messenger, was the copying clerk, William W. Clagett, of Montgomery County, Maryland, who spent his days entering press copies of the accountant's outgoing correspondence in the official letterbooks and making neat, attractive copies of other documents as needed. "The salary [of the copying clerk] is not large," Turner had told one of Clagett's predecessors, "nor are the duties arduous; they will, however, require your attention during office hours, from nine till three o'clock."[80]

The vital center of the accountant's staff were the four examining clerks, posts held in 1810 by John Macdaniel, Jr., of Prince Georges County, Maryland; John Craven, born in Monmouth County, New Jersey; Henry Forrest, from St. Marys County, Maryland; and Ezekiel Macdaniel, another Prince Georges native who had started his office career in Clagett's job as copying clerk.[81] Ezekiel Macdaniel was the newcomer of the four. He had joined the staff in December 1805. Forrest and John Macdaniel could trace their office careers back to mid-1800, while John Craven was a real veteran, having first appeared on the payroll in January 1799. Although the ages of none of the other clerks is known, John Craven was certainly the senior in years as well. In late 1810 he was sixty-nine years old but still highly active. Craven was, in fact, one of the mainstays of Turner's staff in terms of hard work and accounting skills. Not until he had passed his eightieth birthday, which found him still at work in his old job, would time begin to take its toll of John Craven's vigor and skills. All the business day long, these four men were busy "examining and making office statements of accounts with the department, embracing the voluminous accounts of the navy agents, pursers, commanders of gunboats, paymaster to the marine corps, etc., which require particular investigation and accurate calculation; and it is important that the clerks employed should be men of business and good accountants."[82] A typical purser's account could total as much as $35,000 or $45,000 when it came to the office for settlement.[83] The vast bulk of this total was composed of minute sums ranging from a few cents for slops to a few dollars for pay, all of which charges had to be audited and the purser's calculations checked—or even recalculated—without the aid of a single mechanical or electronic device. Realizing this, one gains some faint sense of the tedium with which an examining clerk's day was filled and feels awe for the patience and skill of these men, in a quiet office in the District of Columbia, who were required to conjure order, accuracy, and proof of payment out of records kept amid the excitement and the chaos of some of the most dramatic events of the U.S. Navy's pre-1815 history.

2. A Ranked Society

$\mathcal{A}$LTHOUGH MANY AMERICANS who lived during the two decades in which the navy's officer corps grew to maturity may have pledged intellectual allegiance to a democratic and egalitarian vision of society, at the visceral level almost all of them still lived by a view of the world according to which human beings had been perceiving themselves for hundreds of years. This way of seeing and ordering the world may have been dying, but it had so totally permeated every aspect of people's lives that the mindset could be neither quickly nor easily cast aside. That organizing principle is best captured by the term *deference*. The ethos of deference held that God (or Nature) had ordained a social and economic hierarchy in which some men were placed high and others low; that those who were placed higher had a right and a duty to command and lead; that it was the duty of those placed in subordinate stations to obey their social leaders and to be content with their lowly stations in life; and, finally, that the good of the whole social order depended on respecting this hierarchical social structure, for without that ordered ranking, anarchy, destruction, and unnameable evils would appear.

So it was in a ship of war. Its world rose in a hierarchy from the greenest landsman to the seemingly boundless authority of the captain. Indeed, life at sea could only reinforce a conviction of the essential rightness of the deference ethos. The safety of every individual on board depended in large measure on each knowing his station and his duties and in implicitly obeying those in authority over him. It is easy enough to criticize the self-serving character of a deference world view for those at the top of the social ladder; but deference had survived as a way of organizing and understanding one's life situation because it was instinctively accepted by most men and most women, on whatever rung of the ladder, as a system for insuring a measure of order and stability in an often chaotic and unpredictable world. Deference is an organizing principle to which this book will return more than once as it seeks to understand the way the pre-1815 U.S. Navy operated. To be sure, gale-force winds of democracy and egalitarianism were blowing in the larger society of 1794–1815, and not even the naturally conservative world of the ship of war could sail on unstrained by them; but throughout those years hierarchy and deference remained the bedrock principles of the naval world with which this book is concerned.

28

At the top of the ship's hierarchy or social order stood the officers, who themselves constituted but a tiny fraction of the ship's company. When *Constitution* sailed out to defeat *Java* in 1812, she carried a total complement of 436, including marines. Only 36 of these 436 men (or 8.3 percent) were officers.[1] Even this tiny elite of officers was not an undifferentiated lump. Neither was it a simple, easily understood order rising in one clean line from bottom to top. Rather, it formed four different hierarchies of status, of legal, and of social relationships. In no two of those hierarchies did all the members of the corps stand in exactly the same relationships to one another as they did in the other hierarchies. The hierarchies were defined in terms of naval ranks and stations. Because these ranks and stations will be repeatedly mentioned in the pages of this book, it will be desirable to take a brief overview of them here.

On the Ladder—or Off

The first, and the most important, distinction that has to be made among the navy's officers is between those who were eligible to ascend to the ultimate power and authority, command of a ship or squadron at sea, and those who were not. Of the ten ranks that an officer of the pre-1815 navy could occupy, only four—captain, master commandant, lieutenant, and midshipman—were on the promotion ladder.

The rank of captain is so well understood as to need no explanation here. It was the highest rank in the navy of 1794–1815, for Congress repeatedly declined to authorize the rank of admiral and would continue to do so until the Civil War. Failing the creation of admirals, commanders of squadrons had to content themselves as best they could with the courtesy title of *commodore*, which, once attained, customarily continued to be applied to the holder even after he had ceased to command a squadron at sea. Master commandant was the equivalent of the rank later called commander. That its holders were really junior captains is sufficiently indicated by the fact that masters commandant were unfailingly addressed as "captain." By law ships of 20 guns or larger had to be commanded by captains. Though captains did sometimes command ships smaller than 20 guns, brigs and sloops of war—classes that embraced such well-known War of 1812 cruisers as *Argus*, *Hornet*, and *Wasp*—were normally the bailiwick of masters commandant. Lieutenants were the captain's or master commandant's principal assistants in his command functions, taking charge of watches at sea and divisions of guns in battle. Senior, experienced lieutenants could also be found commanding cruisers smaller than those of the classes normally assigned to masters commandant. John Shaw was a lieutenant when he commanded the schooner *Enterprize*, 12. This little vessel captured six French privateers and recaptured seven U.S. merchantmen during the Quasi-War with France to make *Enterprize* one of the most successful antiprivateer vessels of the war and establish the basis for Shaw's subsequent rise to prominence in the officer corps. At the lowest rung on the promotion ladder was the midshipman. Of his life, training, and duties this book will have a great deal to say. For the moment, it will be sufficient to note that this was the entry-level or apprentice rank for those young men who aspired to climb the promotion ladder to a command at sea.

The remaining six officer ranks—surgeon, surgeon's mate, sailing master, purser, chaplain, and captain's clerk—were not on the promotion ladder. There

Almost all the portraits tell the same story: it was a young man's navy. Surgeon John Bullus, who wears the new uniform authorized in August 1802, posed for Gilbert Stuart sometime between 1803 and the summer of 1805 while Stuart's studio was located in Washington, D.C., where Bullus was stationed. Youthful as he may appear, Dr. Bullus was no novice: he had been a naval physician for not less than five years. Lawrence Park, Gilbert Stuart: An Illustrated Descriptive List of His Works (1926).

were established patterns of progression from certain of these nonpromotion ranks to other nonpromotion ranks, as well as two arduous paths by which holders of nonpromotion ranks might cross over to the promotion track.

Surgeon and surgeon's mate are two ranks whose role is obvious. The normal pattern was for a medical officer to enter the corps at the rank of surgeon's mate; then, after some years of service and (perhaps) additional formal medical education, to advance to the rank of surgeon. Throughout the pre-1815 period, it was perfectly possible, and often happened, that a physician of sufficient education and experience was appointed directly to the grade of surgeon without passing through that of mate.

If one can surmise what a surgeon or a surgeon's mate did, the rank of sailing master will have no recognition value except to those well versed in the era of sailing navies. According to the *Naval Regulations* of 1802 a sailing master was charged with navigating the ship under the direction of her commanding officer, supervising the keeping of her log, receipt and inspection of provisions and stores, stowage of the hold, maintaining the ship in her best sailing trim, and being accountable for the ship's charts as well as her navigation books and instruments. Only a minority of the men who held the rank of sailing master performed the duties defined by the *Naval Regulations,* and of that minority fewer still were competent to perform the duties well in a large or medium-size ship of war. To be the sailing master of a frigate or a sloop of war demanded seamanship of a high order. In actual practice in the pre-1815 navy the rank of sailing master was employed to bring into the service merchant

captains, somewhat older and considerably more experienced than the typical
midshipman, and thereby to provide a corps of nonpromotion-track commanders for the navy's gunboat-size units, forces on which it could not afford to
fritter away its precious cadre of commissioned lieutenants and which there
were never enough suitable midshipmen to command. Far more will be said
later about the navy's large body of sailing masters, their anomalous position
in the corps, and the heart-burnings that position induced. Suffice it to note
here that crossover from the nonpromotion-track rank of sailing master to the
promotion track at the rank of commissioned lieutenant was always a theoretical
possibility. Thereby hangs much of the masters' professional tale.

A purser may be thought of as a ship's business agent. His role was more
comprehensive than that of the latter-day paymaster, his closest equivalent. He
was, it is true, responsible for keeping the ship's pay- and muster rolls and for
paying the officers and men at the end of a cruise. In addition, his steward
issued, and the purser was accountable for, the ship's provisions. The purser
also ran a kind of ship's store wherefrom he issued, to be deducted from the
ship's company's end-of-cruise pay, essential articles of clothing and luxury
items, such as tobacco, sugar, tea, or coffee, which were not part of the ration
the men drew each day. Finally, when his ship was cruising far from major
ports, the purser might be required to purchase certain articles for her—
perhaps fresh beef or fruit. However, most major buying did not fall to his lot,
because each port habitually used by the navy had a civilian navy agent. The
latter was a patronage appointee, who acted as the Navy Department's purchasing arm for the vast bulk of all provisions and stores. As with the sailing
master, so with the purser: more will be said of his duties and of his problems,
financial and political, when the time comes to speak of money and the naval
officer.

Chaplain is almost certain to be a misleading rank, because only occasionally
during the pre-1815 years was its holder a clergyman, though the duties did
require that its holder's education be of a superior order, comparable to that
of a clergyman or an attorney. The chaplain had, according to the *Naval
Regulations*, three official duties: (1) to read divine service at Sunday muster;
(2) to perform funerals over those who died on shipboard;[2] and (3) to serve as
schoolmaster to the frigate's midshipmen. By custom, the chaplain often had
another assignment, one that must have consumed at least as much time as his
three official duties combined, that of serving as secretary to the squadron
commodore. Ships smaller than frigates were not permitted to carry chaplains.
During the Quasi-War with France and the early days of the Tripolitan War
some ships bore, at a reduced rate of pay, an officer with the title of *schoolmaster*
in place of a chaplain, but this practice appears to have died out around 1802.
Thereafter the title *chaplain* was used exclusively to designate the holders of
the post.[3] In this book no attempt will be made to distinguish between chaplains
and schoolmasters, for the duties were largely identical and the distinct ranks
soon merged into one.

Captain's clerk, the final rank on the nonpromotion track, was not a rank
in the same sense as the others that have been discussed. The register of officers
in the secretary of the navy's office contained no pages for captain's clerks;
they carried no documents of appointment signed by the president and the
secretary of the navy. To the naked eye he might look like a midshipman,
because he often wore that uniform; but, in reality, a captain's clerk was simply

a young man hired by the captain to assist him with his paperwork and serving at his pleasure.[4] There is an important reason for including this rank when one is examining the officer corps, for it was a point of entry into a professional naval career. Quite typically a young man might start out as a captain's clerk. If he proved capable, the captain might secure him a chaplain's warrant; thereafter, experience, demonstrated ability, and the powerful support of one's captain or commodore made the successful chaplain a strong candidate for a coveted post, one that often brought big financial rewards: a pursership.

Perhaps the captain's clerk might conclude that a purser's career of peddling small stores and acquiring tension headaches over the tiny columns of a payroll was not for him. Was a life more action-filled his true calling? If his captain was convinced that he had the right stuff to make a good fighting officer, the clerk could often persuade the captain to procure him a midshipman's warrant and, thereby, transfer to the promotion track. This happened to Pennsylvania-born Charles A. Budd, who later recalled,

> In July 1803 I entered with Captain [Charles] Stewart on board the Syren as his clerk, and, having been to sea three years previously in the merchant service, after doing what little writing was incumbent on me, I preferred

When Samuel Curwen Ward died in November 1817, sharp-penned Salem, Massachusetts, diarist and clergyman William Bentley summed up his life: "Sam was not without talents or wit, but embarrassed in his business, he became at last a gay companion and lost that rank in society which in more early life he maintained. He had an excellent wife and able friends, and he became content in this dependence." One of those "able friends" was Edward Preble, who gave Ward the job of captain's clerk during the frigate Essex's *pioneering voyage to Java in 1800 and who tried (unsuccessfully) to secure him a more permanent appointment as a purser. Michel Felice Corné's likeness of Ward, India ink wash and Chinese white on paper, was taken in 1803, about two years after the close of the former clerk's naval service.* Essex Institute, Salem, Massachusetts.

standing a watch and doing midshipman's duty on board than lounging below. At the first unsuccessful attempt to enter the harbor of Tripoli for the purpose of destroying the captured frigate Philadelphia Captain Stewart placed so much confidence in me as to give me command of the green cutter and seven armed men to assist at the destruction of that frigate; but, which owing to the heavy sea running at that attempt, in hoisting out, [the cutter] was unfortunately bilged by striking against one of the guns in a deep roll of the brig, which deprived me of my command, but which I remedied by volunteering myself as second [in command] with Mr. [Samuel B.] Brooke in the barge on the night of [*Philadelphia*'s] being fired.[5]

By the Senate's Advice and Consent—or Without

Officers were not simply divided into those who could be promoted and those who could not. At least three other divisions complicated life even further. The second division was purely a legal one. Some officers held their ranks by virtue of commissions. This category comprehended captains, masters commandant, lieutenants, surgeons, surgeon's mates, and (after April 1812) pursers. To hold one's rank by commission, an officer had to have been nominated to, and confirmed by, the Senate of the United States. Midshipmen, sailing masters, chaplains, and (before April 1812) pursers held their appointments by virtue of warrants, signed by the president and the secretary of the navy, but which did not require Senate approval. Captain's clerks and schoolmasters possessed neither commissions nor warrants, being appointed by the ship's captain for a particular cruise. The more distant from the District of Columbia a ship or a squadron might be, the more likely it was to have acting midshipmen, acting sailing masters, acting surgeons, acting surgeon's mates, acting chaplains, and (occasionally) acting pursers, all of whom held their offices by virtue of letters of appointment from the captain or commodore, and whose existence might not be officially known in Washington until months, or even years, after the fact.

In the pre-1815 years the commissioned/warranted distinction was of much less importance than the division into promotion and nonpromotion tracks. In theory it may have been more difficult for the Navy Office to rid itself by administrative action of an unwanted commissioned officer than was the case with a warrant officer, but in practice secretaries of the navy dismissed holders of every rank, from captains, through sailing masters and midshipmen, down to chaplains, without benefit of court martial. The Senate-approved commission's lack of clout, when it went up against the promotable/nonpromotable distinction, was redemonstrated every time the question arose whether surgeons and pursers, who were commissioned officers, were eligible to sit as members of courts martial. Such bodies were, by law, to be composed of "officers . . . ranking agreeably to the date of their commissions." Always the answer was the same—though rarely was it so baldly stated as by Secretary William Jones: "Pursers in the navy, though commissioned officers, have no rank or command and, therefore, have no common interest or feeling with those officers who have, and were not contemplated by the law as competent to sit on courts martial. Surgeons, surgeon's mates, and marine officers are commissioned, but it has not been supposed that they are competent to sit on courts martial."[6]

. . . and Gentlemen

The notion, often cited in relation to the British army and navy, that it was the possession of a commission that automatically conferred the status of a gentleman on those who did not already possess it, appears not to have prevailed in the U.S. Navy of 1794–1815.[7] Sailing masters, midshipmen, chaplains, and pre-1812 pursers would have rushed to assert that they were every bit as much gentlemen as captains, masters commandant, lieutenants, surgeons, and surgeon's mates. Although all of these officers thought of themselves as gentlemen, and although the words *gentleman* and *gentlemanly* must have been used hundreds of thousands of times in naval correspondence between 1794 and 1815, no one in the navy ever attempted to define the term. This vagueness allowed the title to be applied to those who were (or thought they were, or wished they were) at the upper end of the status spectrum of the pre-1815 United States. Calling a naval officer a gentleman did not necessarily imply birth into a clearly defined social class, or possession of inherited or earned wealth, or attainment of a carefully specified level of education. Of all the definitions of *gentleman*, the one that most closely approximates what the naval officer had in mind when he identified himself with the term is that which describes a man who does not engage in any menial occupation or in manual labor for gain, and who lives by a certain code of behavior thought appropriate to his exalted status.

There existed in the pre-1815 U.S. Navy a caste of officers who were never considered gentlemen by their contemporaries, even though they held warrants that were in no way distinguishable from those held by sailing masters, midshipmen, chaplains, or pre-1812 pursers. These were the navy's boatswains, carpenters, sailmakers, and gunners. Although they were all warrant officers, their contemporaries never regarded them as gentleman officers. Boatswains, carpenters, sailmakers, and gunners were, in the minds of the gentleman officers, relegated to a separate and inferior status category. The reason is not difficult to see. Each of these "officers" was perceived as engaged in a menial or manual occupation and could not, by definition, be a gentleman. This distinction, the third division of the officer corps, is nowhere explicitly stated in contemporary records; implicitly it is everywhere, lurking between the lines of any document referring to a holder of one of these four ranks.[8] This book concerns itself with those whom contemporaries saw as the true officers: the gentleman officers, men trained and socialized to live by a particular code of behavior signaled by words like *honor*. Boatswains, carpenters, sailmakers, and gunners were not officers in that sense.

Eating and Sleeping

One is still not done with the hierarchies by which the pre-1815 officer corps was organized. A fourth and final status was based on shipboard living arrangements. The captain (or master commandant) lived, of course, in isolated grandeur in the cabin, usually inviting his subordinate officers to dine with him in rotation, one, two, or three at a time. Those subordinates were divided into two groups, depending on where they lived in the ship. Messing together in the wardroom, and living in their diminutive but private cabins off it, were the lieutenants, the sailing master, the surgeon, the purser, the chaplain, and the marine lieutenant(s). Unless irresolvable personality conflicts destroyed

harmony, they formed a cohesive cadre of social equals, taking liberty together
ashore, dining as a group every day, inviting the captain for dinner once a
week and counterparts from other ships when opportunity and mess funds
permitted. The other cadre of social equals comprised the midshipmen, the
surgeon's mate(s), and the captain's clerk. They were relegated to the steerage,
where they kept their somewhat rowdier mess and slung their hammocks in
one common space.[9] Wardroom and steerage will be revisited later. For the
moment, one may leave their denizens, wine bottles uncorked, singing around
the mess tables, and direct attention to another face of the naval society: its
numbers.

3. Counting the Corps

*I*NDIVIDUAL HUMAN BEINGS were the ultimate components of the pre-1815 navy's officer corps. But, before examining the corps as distinct individuals, it will be helpful to look at that body in its most abstract form—reduced to numbers. A sense of scope and scale is always necessary to enable one to get one's bearings. How big was the corps? How did its size change between the Quasi-War with France and the War of 1812? Because there exist no comprehensive and accurate figures from other sources that may be hastily summarized here, such numbers must be discovered and briefly reported before the historian can proceed far into the story of the navy and its officers.

Given the prevailing lack of congressional enthusiasm for a substantial standing naval establishment during most of the years between 1794 and 1815, there were, in statutory law, surprisingly few explicit statements of the precise authorized strength of the officer corps. The original act of 27 March 1794, which marks the birth of the federal navy, and the subsequent act of 1 July 1797, providing for the manning and employment of *Constellation, Constitution,* and *United States,* both itemized the numbers of officers of every grade to be allowed to each ship. However, as naval expansion heated up in 1798 and 1799 to meet the French threat during the Quasi-War, Congress contented itself with authorizing so many ships of such-and-such rates, leaving "the number and grade of the officers to be appointed for the service of said vessels [to] be fixed by the president of the United States."[1] It was patently undesirable to impose a rigid inflexibility upon executive discretion that would have mandated a return to Congress for fresh legislation every time experience or circumstances indicated that a minor change in manning patterns was in order. Besides, Congress had other tools for limiting the size of the navy's corps of officers, if it cared to use them. In addition to the specific limitations cited in the paragraphs that follow, Congress also possessed indirect, if effective, controls over the number of officers employed through its annual appropriation for "pay and subsistence" and—at least insofar as commissioned officers were concerned—by the requirement of Senate advice and consent to all such appointments.

The Peace Establishment Act of 3 March 1801, in many ways a vague, confusing, and apparently hastily drafted piece of legislation intended to provide for the reduction of the navy upon the ending of hostilities with France, specified an officer corps of 9 captains, 36 lieutenants, and 150 midshipmen. It said nothing about masters commandant, a rank presumably abolished by the law. Neither did it speak of sailing masters, surgeons, surgeon's mates, pursers, or chaplains; their numbers were implicitly confided to the discretion of the executive. As events turned out, the Peace Establishment Act had little real effect on the size of the officer corps. Robert Smith, always one to exercise maximum administrative discretion, argued that the subsequent congressional authorization of hostilities against Tripoli, 6 February 1802, not to mention the still-later authorization of additional vessels to carry on those hostilities, superseded the Peace Establishment Act. Under this interpretation of the law, Smith concluded the Tripolitan War with an officer corps that, by his own count of December 1805, numbered 10 captains, 8 masters commandant, 73 lieutenants, and 142 midshipmen, with 9 of the last category acting as lieutenants.[2] Congress, persuaded by Robert Smith of the necessity of bringing the navy's authorized peace establishment into conformity with the nation's realistic needs for officers, on 21 April 1806 set the corps at 13 captains, 9 masters commandant, 72 lieutenants, 150 midshipmen, and "for the vessels in actual service so many surgeons, surgeon's mates, sailing masters, chaplains, [and] pursers . . . as may, in [the president's] opinion, be necessary and proper."[3]

In the dying days of the Jefferson administration, when Congress was in a rebellious mood over the Embargo and the president's policy of excessive reliance on gunboats to the exclusion of frigates and other cruising vessels, the number of authorized midshipmen was increased (31 January 1809) by 300 to provide a total authorized strength of 450 young gentlemen.[4] What is notable about this increase in the number of midshipmen is that it was the last time, within the years with which this book is concerned, that Congress specified by law the precise size of any rank in the officer corps. Thereafter, beginning with the act of 30 March 1812, Congress reverted to the Quasi War practice of authorizing the construction, purchase, or employment of so-and-so many vessels and providing, typically, that "the officers and seamen of the navy may be increased so far as may be necessary to officer, man, and equip the vessels so to be put into service, any law to the contrary notwithstanding."[5]

Clearly, then, the executive had, throughout the years 1798–1815, a substantial degree of latitude in setting the size of the naval officer corps. How did the Navy Department use this discretion? How big was the corps at various times in its history? The best answers that the historian can provide appear in Table 1. This presents a census of the actual numbers of officers holding the various ranks at certain critical moments in the corps' history, including men serving on acting appointments from ship, squadron, or station commanders of whom the Navy Office was officially unaware, but whose existence can be documented from other sources. The reasons for selecting the seven points at which to take a census of the corps require explanation. By 1 July 1800 the navy was fully mobilized for the Quasi-War with France. Reduction of the Quasi-War officer corps under the Peace Establishment Act was substantially complete by 1 February 1802. Figures for 1 January 1805 reveal the corps at its fullest mobilization during the Tripolitan conflict. By 1 June 1807 the provisions of the Peace Establishment Act as amended by the law of 21 April 1806 had been fully implemented, but the size of the corps had not yet been affected by the repercussions of the *Chesapeake-Leopard* incident of 22 June

1807. A count has been taken as of 1 January 1810 to show the corps' strength at roughly the midpoint in the cold war with Britain that stretched from the *Chesapeake* incident to the declaration of war five years later. By 1 January 1813 the substantial expansion of the corps carried out by Paul Hamilton in the months preceding and following the 18 June 1812 declaration of war had been completed. A final column presents the strength of the officer contingent as it stood on 14 February 1815, the day the news of the end of the War of 1812 reached Washington.[6]

Save for the ranks of captain, master commandant, and (perhaps) lieutenant, no claim of absolute accuracy can be made for Table 1. As will be seen in a later chapter some officers died, resigned, or simply dropped out of the navy at dates that cannot now be established with precision, and some of which were uncertain at the time. Only with a pay- or muster roll in hand for each ship and each shore station during the pre-1815 years could one be reasonably certain to have identified every acting midshipman, acting sailing master, acting surgeon, acting surgeon's mate, chaplain, or captain's clerk appointed by the local ship, squadron, or station commander during those years. Because of the destruction of a substantial portion of these rolls, such absolute accuracy is forever impossible. To take only the most obvious example, the number of identified captain's clerks for the Quasi-War years can only be a fraction of the number who must have served in that conflict's forty-two oceangoing ships of war, even if not every vessel carried one. Any attempt to estimate the number of now-unknown acting officers could only be an exercise in fantasy, because there exists no factual basis on which to ground the estimate. Certainly the number of unknown officers is not large enough to affect in any real way the general accuracy of this history of the corps.

In the first two years of the Quasi-War with France the officer corps expanded from virtual nonexistence to a peak size of some seven hundred individuals by midsummer 1800. Implications and consequences of such headlong expansion will be explored more than once in the pages that follow. This luxuriant growth was pruned by two-thirds under the Peace Establishment Act of 1801. Between the closing months of 1801 and the months immediately preceding the declaration of war in 1812, the officer corps remained a relatively stable organization, always growing in size, but never at a pace faster than that at which new members could be recruited, trained, and employed. The most striking evidence of this is to be found in the number of midshipmen. Although the act of 31 January 1809 authorized an increase of the corps of midshipmen to a total of 450 young gentlemen, that strength was not actually reached (and passed) until November or December 1812. By that date, however, a sufficient cadre of experienced officers existed to permit a rapid and effective expansion of the officer corps during the War of 1812. The corps entered that war numbering more than twice the men it had counted on the eve of the *Chesapeake* affair of 1807 and ended the war almost four times as large, but the expansion had been accomplished without the severe growing pains that accompanied the Quasi-War's explosive development.

Numerically the heart of the officer corps was always the three ranks of lieutenant, midshipman, and sailing master. Together they never accounted for less than three-fourths of the entire corps; sometimes they constituted more than 80 percent of the total number of enrolled officers. Although small in numbers, captains and masters commandant were critically important to the history of the corps because of their conspicuous leadership roles; but the sheer numbers of lieutenants, midshipmen, and sailing masters demand that they, together with the captains and masters commandant, should occupy center stage in any history of the navy's officers. Two other small groups will not be overlooked in these pages: chaplains, because of their central role in the education of the navy's midshipmen, and pursers, men who highlight in a special way the question of money and the naval officer.

4. Places Much Sought

*F*ROM MARCH 1794, when Congress authorized the construction of the U.S. Navy's first frigates, until the last shot of the War of 1812 was fired in the remote waters of the East Indies in 1815, there were always more men and boys who wanted to be naval officers than there were openings to be filled. No surprise, perhaps, in periods, such as the War of 1812, when the nation's unexpectedly successful navy enjoyed wide popular support and Secretary of the Navy William Jones could report that there were ten applicants for every vacancy in the corps; but the eager scramble for appointments was just as characteristic of years when the navy's public and congressional fortunes appeared to be at their nadir and even the navy's continued existence seemed open to question. "The places of midshipman are so much sought that (being limited) there is never a vacancy," President Jefferson told a friend in November 1802.[1] The absolute desirability of naval appointments is in no way better documented than by the congressman who might one day be a vigorous critic of naval expenditures on the floor of the House, but on another could be found climbing the stairs to the secretary's office to solicit a midshipman's appointment for his son.[2]

Mechanics

It was, then, never a question of the navy having actively to recruit its officers; the concern was one of choosing among the many apparently qualified men who sought to join the corps. That process always began with a letter of recommendation, often (but not invariably) accompanied by a letter of application from the would-be officer himself: "The present serves to enclose you the letter of the father in favor of his son from Mr. Charles Boarman, [Sr.], addressed to me, and a letter from the son himself stating his wish to procure the place of midshipman in the navy," Robert Brent, the mayor of Washington and paymaster of the army, wrote Paul Hamilton in August 1811.

> The son is not personally known to me. The father has been for a great number of years a preceptor of youth in Maryland and in this district and has sustained the best possible character. He would not, I persuade myself from

his character, recommend even a son u[pon?] the terms that he has, unless he had merit to authorize such recommendation. The son, you will observe by his letter which is somewhat singular, has promised much should he be honored with the situation which he solicits at your hand.

If Hamilton could restrain his curiosity to read the son's "somewhat singular" letter, he would next have opened the father's appeal to Mayor Brent:

> At the repeated solicitations of my son Charley to procure him a berth as a midshipman in the navy, I take the liberty to address you the following lines, requesting you will be pleased to interest yourself in my son's behalf with Mr. Hamilton, so as to procure him the midshipman's berth in some of our frigates. Mr. Hamilton, I am sure, is a gentleman of great merit and of superior discernment in his department; consequently will duly appreciate the merits of a youth stepping forward in defense of his country. Though he is only sixteen years old, as a parent I can with confidence say [that] my son is of an engaging, aspiring disposition by nature, regardless of those little difficulties and trials that generally retard and dishearten those of his age in the pursuit of their favorite object. He has been educated for some years in Georgetown College and, consequently, has studied the languages for a certain space of time and is as well versed in arithmetic as most of his age generally are.

Now, at last, the secretary could unfold the aspiring midshipman's own letter of application:

> Washington, August 13, 1811
>
> Robert Brent, Esqr.
> Sir:
> I am happy to find my father has applied to you, as a friend, to procure me a berth as a midshipman in the navy. Should I succeed in my wishes, at your request, my greatest ambition shall at all times be to merit the confidence reposed in me and to prove thereby, Sir, my gratitude to you. Though sixteen years old, I already begin to think myself a man! And why not? Alexander, it is said, was a little man, yet fame gives him the credit and honor of possessing a great soul! May not, Sir, great feats be performed by a little David as well as by a Goliah? Methinks I already hear the roaring of the cannons, and my soul, impatient of delay, impetuously hurries me on to the scene of action!—there—there to prove the innate courage that characterized on the rolls of fame the immortal and intrepid Major Boarman on the first occupying this happy land. With many thanks for your kind offer, I am, dear Sir, your very obedient and greatly obliged humble servant,
>
> CHARLES BOARMAN

Most midshipman applicants, it should be emphasized, did not seek to persuade the secretary of the navy of their merits by comparing themselves with Alexander the Great or with the future Hebrew king, David. Neither did they customarily indulge in Charley Boarman's other rhetorical flourishes. If Paul Hamilton had any misgivings, they can only have been momentary; the day after he received Brent's letter of recommendation, Hamilton noted "To be appointed" on young Boarman's application. The latter was off on a successful naval career that would eventually lead, before his death in 1879, to the rank of rear admiral on the retired list.[3]

As the applications and recommendations came into the Navy Office they were read by the secretary or the chief clerk, one or the other of whom might occasionally endorse the papers, "Keep this in view"; "Special consideration";

"Entitled to particular attention"; "N.B. When appointments are made the secretary's attention to be called to this application particularly"; "This among the early appointments"; "To have the first appointment."[4] They were then turned over to the register, who assigned each applicant's papers a file number and entered in a book his name, the appointment sought, his place of residence, and the name or names of the person or persons recommending him.[5] With the rare exception of a politically prominent father who sought a midshipman's warrant for his son,[6] neither the applicant nor his recommenders could expect any acknowledgment of the receipt of the application, any interim report on its status, or any word that it had been passed over or rejected. If the application were successful, the appointee would be informed by letter, often sent through the hands of his principal recommender. If otherwise, the rule was silence.[7] Of course there are always ways to circumvent rules. If an applicant or his supporters had entrée to a member of Congress or other public official in Washington, that person might be persuaded to walk or ride over to the Navy Office, where the secretary or the chief clerk would orally reveal the application's status and perhaps allow himself to be politely lobbied on behalf of the would-be officer. Not only were applications never formally rejected, they remained permanently on file. It was far from unknown for an aspirant to keep adding letters of support to his dossier year after year until persistence or the discovery of a recommender with the requisite clout led to ultimate success. Such was the case with William Paul Zantzinger of Lancaster, Pennsylvania, who first applied for a purser's warrant at least as early as 1808, but did not finally receive one till the summer of 1813.

Unless, say, a sailing master were immediately needed for a vessel that was about to be placed in commission, normal practice in the Navy Office was to wait until a number of vacancies had accumulated. Then the secretary reviewed the file of pending applications and selected those persons he wished to appoint. Precisely how the actual selection was made is not known; the closest one can come is Robert Smith's statement that "the preference is given to those who are the best recommended."[8] Presumably he sought the applicants whose substantive recommendations were the strongest, but it is conceivable (though unlikely) that he meant those whose recommenders held the highest status in the secretary's eyes.

Who was doing the recommending was important. Other qualifications being apparently equal, the more prominent one's recommenders, the more likely one was to obtain an appointment. Nor was this strange. The pre-1815 United States was a hierarchical society; it was expected by appointer and aspiring appointee alike that the recommendations of those who stood highest should carry the most weight. Equally important, the secretary needed to know the degree of reliance that could be placed on the truthfulness of the recommendations. This was easier to assess when the name at the bottom of the recommendation was that of a prominent man, perhaps even one personally known to the secretary. So candidates who came forward bearing letters of recommendation from members of Congress, senior naval officers (one of the most potent recommendations a would-be midshipman could get), cabinet-level and other Washington-based officeholders, collectors of customs, federal and state judges, navy agents, governors of states, the president (very occasionally, except in the case of the active John Adams), or persons of high standing in private life (merchants or attorneys known to the secretary, college professors, prominent clergy) were those who stood the strongest chance of securing the coveted berths in the corps of officers.[9] Those applicants whose letters of support were not signed with names possessing instant recognition value were not necessarily excluded from selection. In such cases the secretary often turned for help to the applicant's state congressional delegation for insight into the reliability of the recommendation.[10]

A handful of the young gentlemen whose names were recorded in the register of applicants were in a much more exclusive category. Their names also appeared on a piece of paper referred to as the "private list" or "special list," presumably kept in either the secretary's or the chief clerk's desk.[11] These were the young men whose claims upon appointments, either on the basis of their own merits or because of the clout—or *interest*, the term then in use to denote the same concept—of their backers, were so strong that their applications took precedence over all others and were, in effect, assured of success. Here might be found the name of the son of one of the navy's captains, that of the brother of a highly regarded senior lieutenant, or one identified as the nephew of a cabinet member.[12]

Searching for the Ideal

As the secretary sat skimming the dozens upon dozens of letters of application and recommendation that it was necessary to read before making a handful of appointments, what special things was he looking for, other than the signature at the bottom of the page, that would help to determine which one applicant in ten would get the coveted vacancy? First of all, the application had to fulfill four formal requirements. Far and away the most important of these requirements was *personal knowledge of the applicant by the recommender*. On no subject could Robert Smith be more eloquent than on this absolute condition. New York City's mayor, De Witt Clinton, brought forward the name of Peter Quackenbos for a midshipman's warrant on the grounds that "his father is a respectable and opulent burgher; the enclosed certificate from two of [the] professors of Columbia College [in behalf of Peter Quackenbos] may be relied on." That was definitely not enough for Smith: "From your recommendation of him you appear to have no personal knowledge of him," he replied.

> Therefore, I must candidly tell you that your recommendation is insufficient in this case. I wish to introduce into the navy none but young gentlemen of perfectly fair and honorable characters and entreat my friends to recommend none but such as they personally know to be of this description. I have often been under the necessity of dismissing from the service young gentlemen (either from their being wholly unqualified for the stations they held [or] from some improper conduct) who have been introduced by some of my best friends. This has been a painful duty which I am anxious to avoid in future. I need not tell you that a young man may be extremely amiable and respectable yet unqualified for the navy service, which requires strong constitution of body and mind, a high love of character, and passion for glory. Recommend to me such young men as known to you, and I shall be happy to notice your recommendations.

Although young Quackenbos eventually obtained his midshipman's warrant, the event proved the wisdom of Smith's skepticism. Quackenbos resigned after making his first and only voyage to sea.[13]

The requirement of personal knowledge of the applicant by the recommender held for all appointments at whatever rank. The second formal requirement, *parental consent to the application*, applied only to minors seeking appointments as midshipmen.[14] The navy had no wish to be involved in legal confrontations with hurt and angry parents trying to reclaim runaway minor sons. Even if the parents were unwilling to assert their full legal rights, the occasional case that slipped by caused enough distress to demonstrate the wisdom of the rule. Shortly after the Fourth of July 1806 Robert Smith received a letter from Ferdinand Fairfax and George Hite of Charles Town, Virginia, in which those two gentlemen were compelled to admit a keen embarrassment: "As we were amongst those who recommended David Wark as a midshipman, we deem it proper to say that we did so under the impression that his parents were consenting to the measure; but we are sorry also to inform you that, since the arrival of his commission, they have declared an invincible reluctance to part with their son; in consequence whereof he cannot with propriety enter the public service." By the time Smith received this letter he had been placed in a position in which two ethical imperatives—the rights of the parent and the code of the gentleman—were in conflict; for, by the same mail that brought their letter "I also received Mr. Wark's acceptance of his appointment. Mr. Wark . . . having received [his warrant] and accepted his appointment, I cannot now recall it without doing violence to his rights as an officer and his feelings as a gentleman; but, should he resign, I will accept his resignation. You will judge whether it will be proper for you to have a conference with Mr. Wark upon this subject." Exactly what happened next is unknown, but David Wark did not resign his warrant. Bitter indeed must have been his parents' feelings when he died of yellow fever on active duty thirteen months later.[15]

Beyond the recommender's personal knowledge of his recommendee and parental consent lay a third formal requirement of the appointment process: *fair geographical distribution of appointments*. The secretary of the navy had a clear idea of what each state's fair share should be. He tried to fill that share insofar as there were qualified applicants from the state, although one would be wrong to suppose that the Navy Office worked with a mathematically precise formula that allotted so many new appointments to each state or region. Fair geographical distribution was not simply a negative limitation. It also implied an active attempt to encourage applications from states and regions that might be underrepresented in the corps.[16]

The final formal requirement for appointment was that *absolute preference would be given to applications by citizens of the United States*. One model by which the fledgling U.S. Navy could have developed its corps of qualified officers would have been to appoint experienced, but unemployed, officers of foreign navies to certain key posts and thus transmit their professional training and accumulated knowledge to the larger mass of American officer recruits. The idea was by no means alien to the mindset of the late eighteenth century, as witness the number of British officers serving in the Imperial Russian Navy.[17] Nearer home, the collective American memory honored those French and German officers who had served with and trained the Continental army of the Revolutionary War. Prominent, too, were the examples of John Paul Jones, an admiral in the navy of Catherine the Great, or Joshua Barney, who—unhappy with his relative seniority among the first six captains nominated for the federal navy in 1794—declined the job and found employment instead as a *capitaine de vaisseau* and *chef d'escadre* in the navy of revolutionary France. From the beginnings of the federal navy this course was, with a tiny number of exceptions, explicitly rejected. Building the new American navy would be the work of the country's native sons.[18]

Determining whether a particular applicant met the formal requirements for appointment was normally not too difficult. Discovering from a few pieces of paper which men had the personal qualities to become good or even outstanding officers was much more of a quest after the perpetually elusive. Recognizing this, many applicants from states surrounding the District of Columbia, as well as those from farther afield who could afford the cost of the trip, traveled to Washington. Their hope was that giving the secretary of the navy a chance to meet them face to face—an interview often arranged by the applicant's congressman or senator or some family friend in power—would prove the decisive factor in winning a coveted appointment. "Young Mr. [Thomas W.] Freelon is desirous of obtaining a midshipman's warrant," Republican congressman Samuel L. Mitchill wrote Paul Hamilton from New York. "Although I have informed the candidate that, a few weeks before I left Washington, the berths were full, yet he has determined upon a trip to Washington that he may personally present himself to the Navy Department, where I know he will be kindly received and liberally treated."[19] Fifteen-year-old Thomas Freelon already knew how to go about getting what he wanted. He made such a favorable impression on Hamilton that the secretary granted him a midshipman's warrant on the spot. By his death in May 1847 Freelon had risen to the rank of commander.

Of what personal characteristics was the secretary of the navy seeking clues when he sat down with a pile of applications or when he visited with the aspiring officer and his congressman? In the case of midshipmen, the one that was most easily identified and measured was age. Every secretary of the navy from Benjamin Stoddert to Benjamin Crowninshield who expressed an opinion on the matter agreed that midshipmen ought not to be younger than twelve or older than eighteen at the time they received their warrants.[20] "Gentlemen who enter the navy above eighteen frequently resign after wasting one or two years in the experiment," Robert Smith wrote in rejection of one aspirant's application. "It was but on Monday last that I accepted the resignation of a midshipman under these very circumstances." The resignation in question was that of John Fendall, whose precise age has not been discovered, but who wrote from *Hornet* at Charleston, South Carolina, at the end of two and a half years' experience as a midshipman (and uniformly unfavorable fitness reports by his commanding officers), "After all my strict application to acquire a knowledge fit for such a profession, I find I have no turn for a sailor. Besides these things, I entered the service at too advanced an age." Fendall's commanding officer forwarded the resignation on to Washington with enthusiasm: "There is little hopes of his ever coming forward in the navy as a seaman and officer."[21] Beyond eighteen young men's personalities were too fully developed, and habits—good, bad, or merely inappropriate—too deeply rooted, to be educated and socialized into naval officers. Or so the prevailing wisdom held.

To state the rule is immediately to encounter the exceptions. In almost all cases the only information the secretary had on an applicant's age was what the applicant or his recommenders told him. Age might be stated equivocally, concealed, or deliberately misrepresented.[22] As often, the secretary might be persuaded to bend his own rules. A particular applicant's age, Robert Smith told Governor Daniel D. Tompkins of New York, "which you state at nineteen years, is too far advanced to give him a prospect of success in the navy service, unless he has already obtained a considerable knowledge of the practical part of the profession in the merchant service. Should this be the fact (which you will have the goodness to inform me) I will with pleasure give his application a respectful attention whenever appointments in the corps of midshipmen shall be made."[23]

Beyond seeking would-be midshipmen who were of an age at which it was supposed they were still sufficiently malleable to be trained into effective naval officers, the secretary went looking for a range of other qualities, some of which pertained especially to midshipmen, some to officers generally, and all of which were more elusive and more difficult to measure than simple chronological age. Benjamin Stoddert summed these up neatly when he said that he sought "sprightly young men of good education, good character, and good connections."[24] This concise sentence captures all the qualities sought as the secretary read through a file of applications, but one may still ask, What did the secretary mean by each of his phrases?

Stoddert's *sprightly*, a favorite word of his in describing midshipmen, was perhaps better defined by Robert Smith (in his previously quoted letter to De Witt Clinton) when he said that a naval career "requires strong constitution of body and mind." The navy had no use for the dull-witted or for young men of feeble health or physical handicaps who could not endure the rigors of an apprentice officer's life. *Good connections*, elsewhere cited by Stoddert as "reputable connections," referred both to the applicant's immediate family and to a more extended network of kin by blood or marriage: uncles, cousins, brothers-in-law. The reference was not only to their social and economic standing in the community, but also to the moral and ethical esteem in which they were held. Because the successive secretaries of the navy and almost all those who had occasion to write to them in support of applications shared a view of the world in which each understood what was meant by the code phrases *good connections* and *reputable connections*, no secretary of the navy ever experienced the need to define these terms. Determination of the precise social realities that the words expressed will be deferred until a later chapter. A similar lack of definition is encountered with the phrase *good education*. These code words, too, expressed a shared, if perhaps elastic, standard, the nature of which will shortly be discovered.

By contrast, on the question of what was embraced by the phrases *good character* or *good principles*, the secretaries spoke out more than once by way of definition and elaboration. At the most basic level the navy sought as its officer the young man of "correct habits," who could present "the strongest recommendations as to his morals"; that is to say, the person with a sound foundation of ethical behavior and one who was not addicted to debilitating vices such as excessive consumption of alcohol. To these he needed to unite "the honorable and manly feelings of a gentleman."[25] A successful naval officer required personal qualities above and beyond these basic ones. Two that Robert Smith had identified in his letter to De Witt Clinton were "a high love of character and passion for glory." Had Smith been writing with more precision, he would have called *passion for glory* by another name: *passion for fame*. For educated middle- and upper-class Americans who lived during the years between the

Revolution and the War of 1812 the pursuit of fame was a highly esteemed motivating force in giving definition to one's life, a motivation that had the capacity to transform man's base egotism and avaricious self-aggrandizement into a passion for distinction through public service:

> To be famous or renowned means to be widely spoken of by a man's contemporaries and also to act in such a way that posterity also remembers his name and his actions. The desire for fame is thus a dynamic element in the historical process; it rejects the static complacent urge in the human heart to merely *be* and invites a strenuous effort to *become*—to become a person and force in history larger than the ordinary. The love of fame encourages a man to make history, to leave the mark of his deeds and his ideals on the world; it incites a man to refuse to be the victim of events and to become an "event-making" personality—a being never to be forgotten by those later generations that will be born into a world his actions helped to shape. . . . The audience that men who desire Fame are incited to act before is the audience of the wise and the good in the future—that part of posterity that can discriminate between virtue and vice—that audience that can recognize egotism transmuted gloriously into public service. The love of fame is a noble passion because it can transform ambition and self-interest into dedicated effort for the community, because it can spur individuals to spend themselves to provide for the common defense.[26]

Unless this search for fame—that is, a laudable motivation to exert oneself to and beyond the limits of one's capability—is recognized as a primary element in the ethical air breathed by the naval officers of 1794–1815, a true understanding of that corps is as impossible as if one lacked the basic data on ranks and numbers. It is as key a concept as deference. None could guarantee that even the most skillful and deserving naval officer's career would lead to fame. Events beyond his control might bring adversity or defeat. To serve the nation well in such circumstances demanded Smith's "high love of character," which may be defined as the psychic strength and personal and professional integrity to meet such situations.

When Secretary Stoddert described his ideal officer he used words such as *zeal, activity, enterprise,* and *energy.* "Men who suffer trifling difficulties to interpose between them and their duty are unfit for public service. . . . If our officers cannot be inspired with the true kind of zeal and spirit which will enable us to make up for the want of great force by great activity, we had better burn our ships and commence a navy at some future time when our citizens have more spirit." "A spirit of enterprise and adventure cannot be too much encouraged. . . . We have nothing to dread but inactivity." "Men of energy should be selected for our navy officers." As important as restless energy in his eyes was courage: "Bravery is a quality not to be dispensed with in the officers. Like charity, it covers a great many defects." But blind energy and courage were not all-sufficient for those destined to the highest commands. Such men also needed superior judgment: "The captains of our larger vessels should possess good sense and real bravery—and, of our smaller vessels, bravery at least. . . . Some indifferent men have already crept into command in our navy. It will prove worse than worthless if it should be badly commanded."[27]

In this list of qualities that went to make up the ideal officer candidate, nothing has been said about nautical skill or experience at sea. For would-be midshipmen such a requirement was largely irrelevant. It was helpful when a future midshipman had some sea experience, but the possession of such experience or the lack of it was rarely a significant factor in determining which young gentlemen were selected for warrants. The navy preferred to find Stoddert's "sprightly young men of good education, good character, and good connections" for midshipmen. It could teach them seamanship.[28] With the other great class of entry-level officers, the sailing masters, the requirement was different. As might be anticipated from the posts they were called to fill, masters were expected to be complete seamen, as well as to possess all the other qualities the navy sought in its officers. The sailing master, said Robert Smith, "ought to be a skillful, experienced seaman . . . an officer, and a gentleman; he should possess skill, bravery, activity, and a fair, irreproachable reputation."[29]

By Other Doors

Such was the way the appointment process normally worked; such was the way it had been intended to work from the beginnings of the navy. It was the system used in other federal offices—at the War Department for selecting army officers, at the Treasury Department in filling major vacancies in the customs houses and the revenue cutters. There were, however, two deviations from normalcy that were substantial enough that they must be included in any examination of the appointment process. One was the rapid mobilization during the Quasi-War with France; the second was the practice of acting appointments throughout the pre-1815 years.

The necessity of expanding the navy's corps of officers from fifty-nine in June 1798 to seven hundred in July 1800 was beyond the capabilities of the centralized system of officer selection just described unless Secretary Stoddert and his principal assistants seriously neglected other aspects of their responsibilities. Applications and recommendations continued to roll into the Navy Office. Many appointments, based on such dossiers, were made by Stoddert throughout the Quasi-War. But this method could neither produce sufficient officers nor produce them quickly enough. One alternative was to exercise as much care as possible in selecting the commander for each vessel, then to allow the commanding officer to compile a list of nominations for most or all of the remaining officer berths in his ship's company. In principle, all such persons nominated by commanding officers had to be approved by Stoddert and President Adams, and—in the case of commissioned officers—confirmed by the Senate. In reality, to be selected by the commanding officer meant the selectee got the job.[30]

This system possessed the great advantage that the captain was going to have to sail and fight his ship with his choices. Self-interest strongly dictated that he make the best possible selections. Once a ship had been either built or purchased in a particular port, its captain was often appointed from the immediate geographical area, its crew recruited in that and neighboring towns, and local applicants given the preference for officer berths. (This practice did not continue beyond the end of the Quasi-War with France.) The captain, in nominating his subordinate officers, was usually selecting from among men he knew personally or about whom he could learn by asking well-placed questions locally. All things being equal, such a system should have been more likely to lead to better men being chosen than the one that had Secretary Stoddert sitting in Philadelphia reading dossier after dossier of glowing testimonial. Alas, it possessed a congenital weakness. Success depended on the skill of the commanding officers as judges of men and on their ability to lay aside any emotional blinders. "I advise you," Congressman Christopher G. Champlin told his fellow Rhode Islander Christopher Raymond Perry in the same letter in which he reported the latter's appointment as a captain in the navy, "not to be led *from motives of friendship* to recommend any man to serve as an officer under you who is not in every respect qualified for the appointment he solicits. You will doubtless have many applications made to you of the kind I allude to."[31]

Sound advice but, as the following months were to prove, easier for wise heads to give than for Perry and many of his fellow captains to follow. Consequently, Stoddert turned not only to those commanding officers whose selection skills he could trust, but to certain civilians he trusted as much or more. In one extreme case in which the captain's judgment was distrusted, Stoddert sent Virginia congressman Josiah Parker a list of the officer appointments to be filled, telling him to "select proper characters for these appointments" and to consult the captain only in the choice of a sailing master and a sailing master's mate. When Parker became ill, leaving the captain a clear field to pick whom he pleased, Stoddert's unhappiness was great indeed: "We had better have no navy than have it commanded by indifferent men," he lamented. "And it shall be my study to rid the service of such men as fast as possible."[32] Although navy-oriented congressmen such as Parker might occasionally be used in the officer-selection process, Stoddert's favorite recourse, next to the commanders themselves, was his patronage appointees, the civilian navy agents in the different ports. "Permit me," he wrote Messrs. Gibbs & Channing of Newport, "to claim your assistance so far as to recommend two persons fit to be lieutenants, if you go no further. You may rely that you will never be questioned on the subject by any person who may be disappointed. I enclose a list of persons recommended from your state for different appointments. I should be glad of your comments on each."[33]

In addition to using commanding officers, navy agents, and members of Congress as resources in officer selection, Stoddert also had to deal with certain special cases. These were the committees of "citizens"—principally well-off merchants, successful ship captains, and established master craftsmen with investment capital—who, under the authority of an act of 30 June 1798, built ships for the government in return for stock of the United States bearing 6 percent interest on the total sum invested. Under such circumstances the gentlemen of the committees came armed with great clout when they politely stated their expectation of naming the ship's officers from among local sons who followed the sea. "The president being in Massachusetts, I cannot at this moment obtain his consent that the captain to command the ship and all the officers shall be appointed by the gentlemen who contribute to the expense," Stoddert wrote Senator Benjamin Goodhue, spokesman for the citizens of Salem who were to build the frigate *Essex*. "But this is a measure so obviously right, and affords so infinitely the best chance of having the ship well officered, that I am sure I risk nothing in undertaking for his cheerful and hearty concurrence in it."[34]

Quasi-War appointments departed from customary practice not only in the suspension of the principle of centralized selection of all officers by the secretary of the navy, but also in the appointment of men to promotion-ladder berths higher than the entry-level rank of midshipman. In 1798 the nation needed an officer corps for its navy, but its only officers were three captains and a handful of acting appointees at lower ranks. The sole way to get lieutenants, masters commandant, and more captains was to appoint men from civilian life directly to those ranks. From the outset the practice was regarded as, at best, a necessary evil. Whether in military or civilian life, no greater stimulus to superior performance exists than the hope of advancement to a higher rung on the ladder. Every time a direct appointment was made of a captain, a master commandant, or a lieutenant, it meant that a promotion had been denied to someone on the next rung lower—resulting, at best, in resentment and lowered morale among the disappointed; at worst, in the resignations of talented men passed over. As early as August 1799 Stoddert was pointing to the desirability of terminating the practice. By late spring of 1800 all appointments to the ranks of lieutenant, master commandant, and captain were being filled by promotion.[35] From that date till the end of the War of 1812 and beyond, access to the promotion ladder was to be had only through entry-level appointments as midshipman or sailing master.[36]

The Quasi-War deviation from the practice of centralized officer selection, closely controlled by the secretary of the navy, was a short-lived phenomenon. By the summer of 1800 the urgent need for new officers had dwindled sufficiently for Benjamin Stoddert to begin reconsolidating the selection power in the secretary's office. Quasi-War practice of choosing a commanding officer and leaving it to him or to a civilian committee to pick his subordinates would not reappear in the pre-1815 navy, even in the officer corps' substantial expansion during the War of 1812. There was, however, another practice, one that flourished from the beginnings of the navy right down to the end of the War of 1812, that did significantly compromise the principle of centralized selection of new officers. This was the matter of acting appointments, particularly at the ranks of midshipman, sailing master, and surgeon's mate. When operating independently, a commanding officer had the power to make them. Theoretically this power existed so that should a vacancy occur when constraints of time, distance, or communications prevented the vacancy being reported to the Navy Office for action, the senior officer present could appoint someone to fill the vacuum. In practice, the power of conferring acting appointments was much more widely applied and liberally interpreted.

Often a station commander who had repeatedly bombarded the Navy Office with requests for new officers to fill vacancies—requests as often ignored by a Navy Office whose supply of fresh officers was at ebb tide—his patience worn to the breaking point, simply appointed somebody to get the job done. When Secretary of the Navy William Jones had to call his old friend William Bainbridge on the carpet for making such an acting appointment without Jones's prior permission, Bainbridge defended himself and his acting appointments without much display of deference:

> The sailing master of the Constitution died on his way conducting seamen to Sackets Harbor in May last. The information was given to you and another master called for. But even to this moment [it was by now 2 September] none has been ordered by the department. The services of a master is early required in the equipment and stowing a ship of war, and it became necessary to have one for the Constitution. And, as I had called for one without receiving any answer, I presumed you had left it with me to make the appointment, which I did; and, had I not done so, it is probable the ship would to this moment [have]

Persistence rewarded. New Yorker Benjamin Kissam's determined eye had long been fixed on a surgeon's appointment in the navy. A graduate of the medical program at Columbia College, Kissam put one recommendation after another on file at the Navy Office without success until he accidentally encountered Commodore John Rodgers on the first day of April 1812 and was told by the commodore that, if Kissam could join the brig Nautilus *more or less immediately as acting surgeon, the post would be his. Even with one foot in the door, it still required sixteen months and a steady barrage of recommendatory letters from the likes of John Rodgers, William M. Crane, and James Lawrence to replace the acting appointment with a commission. At war's end Surgeon Kissam had an opportunity to put his professional training to full use as* Hornet's *chief medical officer in her encounter with* Penguin. *His portrait, by an unknown artist, was probably painted not too long after the War of 1812; the landform dimly glimpsed in the background may be Tristan da Cunha, the site of* Hornet's *1815 victory.* USS Constitution Museum, Boston.

been left without a master or purser—although the services of both have been for some months indispensably necessary.[37]

It was expected that all acting appointments would, after a possible probationary period, be reported to the Navy Office for the issuance of confirming warrants, thus maintaining at least the form of centralized selection of officers by the secretary of the navy. Especially under Secretaries Paul Hamilton and William Jones adherence to this practice became exceedingly ragged. Many commanding officers, particularly those on the southern stations, neglected to report acting appointees for the issuance of warrants. The first the Navy Office might know of the existence of acting sailing master So-and-So was when the station purser's rolls arrived at the accountant's office, perhaps months or years after the fact. Even when acting appointments were faithfully reported to the department and warrants requested, the request all too often got stuck at someone's desk and languished. In September 1812, acting on instructions from Paul Hamilton, Commodore Isaac Chauncey appointed a number of acting sailing masters at New York, assured them that they would receive warrants, and took some of the best of them off with him to Lake Ontario. Fall passed, winter passed, and spring finally came to upstate New York, but the mails brought no warrants for Chauncey's acting sailing masters. In an attempt to break the bureaucratic logjam Chauncey wrote to the new secretary, William Jones, in April 1813, explaining the situation at length: "I am apprehensive from the hurry of business and from the change in the department that these gentlemen have been overlooked. . . . This I should be sorry for, as most of them are men of the first respectability in the line of their profession. It would be particularly hard upon those who volunteered with me upon this service, and have remained with me ever since, and have [suffered] many privations."

Chauncey's letter was duly received at the Navy Office, read—and filed. No warrants addressed to the expectant acting sailing masters appeared at the Sackets Harbor post office. When Chauncey returned to the subject in mid-June he was even more to the point in his expostulations with Jones: "The situation of some of these gentlemen who have served with me upon this lake since the first of October last is truly mortifying. They were assured that their appointments would be confirmed, but they begin to think now (and with reason) that I have deceived them." That letter finally got the job done. Jones endorsed Chauncey's letter, "Make out immediately and forward to Commodore Chauncey warrants for the sailing masters named within"; on 3 July 1813, ten months after the original acting appointments, warrants were at last issued for Chauncey's sailing masters.[38] The fate of warrants for acting officers whose commanders did not muster Chauncey's clout and persistence may readily be guessed.

Important as was the role of acting appointments in filling berths in the cadre of sailing masters, acting appointments for midshipmen were even more significant in the building of the officer corps. Although they did not directly subvert the principle of centralized selection of officers by the secretary of the navy, such appointments did constitute a kind of end run around the long queue of midshipman applications awaiting consideration at the Navy Office.[39] Many of these written applications to the secretary sounded alike; most came with the endorsement of potent backers. The number of applicants was large, the number of midshipman vacancies small. What if the would-be midshipman's parents or kin had access to a captain or a squadron commodore and could persuade him to take the aspirant into his ship or squadron as an acting midshipman? Then the odds became much more favorable. If, on actual trial at sea, the acting midshipman seemed to have the makings of a good officer, the captain or commodore who had given him the acting appointment could use his interest with the secretary to secure an actual midshipman's warrant— in effect moving the young man to the head of the line of applicants. Recommendations from senior officers, if vigorously pressed, rarely failed of success.

Even though the practice partially compromised the principle of centralized selection by the secretary of the navy, it possessed a decided advantage over the selection-on-the-basis-of-paper-credentials method that was not lost on the captains, and probably not on most secretaries most of the time. Midshipmen who began their careers as acting midshipmen stood a better chance of succeeding in their chosen work than midshipmen appointed directly from civilian life. The reason is not hard to discover. To obtain his commanding officer's interest in procuring the desired warrant, an acting midshipman had first to demonstrate his aptitude as a future officer. Those of patently improbable success never made it to the point at which a warrant was issued. Captain George Little of *Boston* recognized this as early as the Quasi-War with France, argued that ships should carry only acting midshipmen, and declined the midshipman's warrant offered his own son, Edward Preble Little:

Warrants given to midshipmen have been a damage to them in general. They make them idle and cause them to think so much of themselves that they scarce ever make seamen. In all navies except ours midshipmen have no warrants. They are only rated on the ship's books, which makes them more ambitious, as they know it is in the power of the commander to disrate them as well as to rate them on the books. . . . The Boston, after the first six months of her sailing, had not more than half her complement of midshipmen, and half of them not worth the salt they eat and were [but] lumber in the ship. In that case it was necessary that some acting ones should be appointed who knew how to carry on the ship's duty. I therefore appointed several active American seamen with good abilities and education.[40]

Captain Little's letter with its reference to midshipmen who were but lumber in his ship shifts the story of the selection of naval officers from the search for ideal qualities to the realities with which the navy often had to deal. It is time to ask, Who were the men actually picked to be officers of the U.S. Navy?

PART TWO
A Corps of Young Gentlemen

Who were the men actually chosen to be officers of the U.S. Navy? The historian might attempt to answer that question by recording selected facts about each of the nearly three thousand persons known to have entered the corps before the end of the War of 1812. Finding, noting, and manipulating information about so many individuals would be a formidable and enervating task. If ever completed, it must leave the historian so drained as to have little mental energy for analysis.

Fortunately it is not necessary to face so pitiless a test. The great majority of the men who entered the navy's officer corps before 14 February 1815 did so at the rank of midshipman or that of sailing master. Exceptions to this sweeping statement were those 130 individuals who were appointed directly to the ranks of captain, master commandant, or lieutenant during the Quasi-War with France, as well as those whose only appointments were as surgeons, surgeon's mates, pursers, chaplains, schoolmasters, and captain's clerks. Sailing masters differed from midshipmen; just what those differences were may be left to a later chapter. Pursers, the navy's money men, will sit for a separate portrait at the point at which the historian delves into their professional lives and business practices. Chaplains and schoolmasters, too, shall have their day in the sun when the time comes to consider the navy's in-house educational effort.[1]

That leaves midshipmen, the primary body of recruits from whom the navy developed the officers who were to climb the rungs of the promotion ladder. "A corps of young gentlemen of the best characters and standing from different parts of the union who are destined for future commands in the navy" was how President Jefferson characterized them.[2] An attempt to use the light of social history to discover the human beings behind Jefferson's sweeping generalization could fail from the sheer numbers to be investigated if all of the midshipmen who served at some time between March 1798 and February 1815 were lined up for examination. Worse yet, looking at the entire mass of the navy's midshipmen might hide as much as it revealed. There exists another method that both is more manageable in its numbers and has the advantage of detecting differences among the young men who became midshipmen at different times between the height of the Quasi-War with France and the last full year of the War of 1812. Profiles have been compiled of those midshipmen who received their appointments in the years 1800 (181 young gentlemen), 1804–1805 (121), 1809 (185), 1812 (232), and 1814 (166).[3] Although any year of the Quasi-War with France might have been chosen, the navy's surviving personnel records for 1800 are more extensive. Numbers of new midshipmen appointed in any one

57

twelve-month period between 1802 and 1808 were so small that it was necessary to combine the two years with the largest number of appointments (1804 and 1805) to collect an adequate pool to illuminate selection practices during the Tripolitan War. The year 1809 marked the beginning of a significant expansion of the corps of midshipmen; 1812, when war was declared on Great Britain, saw more new midshipmen appointed than any other similar period since 1799. Just as the classes of 1800, 1804—1805, and 1812 may enable the close observer to detect differences among the selection practices of Secretaries of the Navy Benjamin Stoddert, Robert Smith, and Paul Hamilton, that of 1814 was chosen because it was one in which William Jones alone picked the young men who were to receive warrants.

5. Geography

$\mathcal{I}$F FOR NO OTHER reason than because the Navy Office needed to know where to mail his orders, a midshipman's geographical origins were—his date of appointment aside—the piece of information about him that was the most carefully recorded by the clerks.[1] These were geographical origins in the sense of where a young man was living when he became a midshipman, which was not necessarily the place in which he had been born. So long as the new appointee was a citizen of the United States, the exact place of his birth was information of little interest or value to the pre-1815 U.S. Navy and was never systematically collected by the Navy Office.[2]

A Union of Regions

Where were they from, these young gentlemen who crowded into the steerage of the navy's ships? The answer will be most clearly seen if one thinks of the nation in terms of groups of states, that is, as geographical and political regions. The number of midshipmen appointed from some states was so small that relative proportions could easily be distorted by the absence of state-of-origin information on even a handful of appointees. By regions the numbers are less prone to distortion. Moreover, the regions exhibited real differences of politics and mindset, differences that influenced the manpower contributions they made to the navy's corps of officers.

First, a long-range snapshot of the entire 1800–1814 crew (Table 2). Across the fifteen-year period nearly two-thirds of the navy's midshipmen came from the middle section of the country, an area bounded inclusively by New York on the north and Virginia on the south. This great midsection may be split into two smaller regions: New York–New Jersey–Pennsylvania–Delaware, which contributed slightly less than one-third of the new midshipmen, and Maryland–District of Columbia–Virginia, whose share was a bit more than a third. Fewer than one midshipman in five hailed from the New England states; slightly more than one in ten came from the three states of the lower South: North Carolina, South Carolina, and Georgia. The new western states and territories—Ohio, Kentucky, Tennessee, Mississippi and Louisiana[3]—were home for roughly one in twenty. Within the regions, certain states stand out as big suppliers of midshipman recruits. In New England, Massachusetts, which embraced the present state of Maine as well, was the place of origin of more midshipmen than all the other New England states combined. New York and Pennsylvania together supplied nearly one-quarter of the navy's midshipmen. Maryland and Virginia were close rivals as the states that the greatest numbers of midshipmen called home; between them they furnished three out of every ten of the navy's apprentice officers. Among the truly southern states, South Carolina had an edge over its neighbors, though nothing like the Maryland-Virginia hegemony.

Are these regional differences mere reflections of variations in the distribution of people in the pre-1815 United States? One may compare the number of midshipmen from each of the five geographical regions with the 1810 census category "free white males of 16 and under 26 years," a category that reasonably approximates the age group from which midshipmen were drawn (Figure 1).[4] In the lower South states of North Carolina, South Carolina, and Georgia the number of young men choosing naval careers precisely parallels the presence of young men in the population. New York, New Jersey, Pennsylvania, and Delaware have a slightly higher percentage of the country's free white males, sixteen to twenty-five, than they have of midshipmen, but the difference is so small that the region's contribution to the corps can be said to mirror accurately its pool of young men. Discrepancies begin to appear when one reaches the New England states. Fewer young men seek careers as naval officers than one would expect from that region's pool of sixteen-to-twenty-five-year-olds. A similar pattern exists in the western states and territories. Most of all it is the Maryland–District of Columbia–Virginia region that should draw the eye. There far more young men sought careers as naval officers than might be expected from the region's small share of the nation's young adults. A region

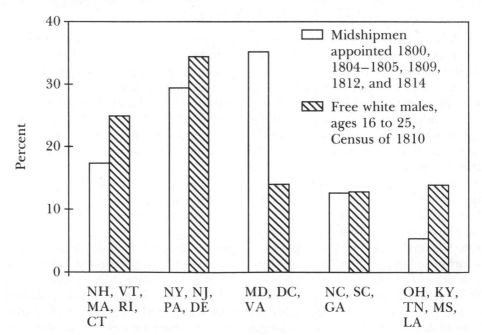

Figure 1 Population Base and Midshipman Appointments Compared

that could claim only 14 percent of the nation's free white young adult males disproportionately dominated the officer corps by supplying more than one-third (35.2 percent) of its midshipman recruits.

When one steps closer to the crowd pictured in the general snapshot and examines the midshipmen of particular years, significant variations begin to appear (Table 3). These are particularly striking in the case of New England's role in the naval establishment. In 1800, a year in which the Federalist party was in secure control of New England and of the national government, the states east of the Hudson River were supplying nearly one-quarter of the navy's midshipmen. After control of the national government passed to the Jeffersonian Republicans in 1801 the secretary of the navy's correspondence began to lament the difficulty of attracting adequate numbers of qualified New Englanders to apply for midshipman berths. The historian is always unsure how much weight to assign to a single incident as evidence of an attitude in an entire region, but a March 1809 letter from John Kittredge, collector of customs at Gloucester, Massachusetts, to Secretary of the Navy Robert Smith reported active efforts in that Embargo-wounded seaport to discourage young men from pursuing careers as officers:

> At the time of recommending the young men whose warrants I enclose there was a great desire in their parents and themselves for appointments in the U.S. Navy. Finding that they were waiting uncertain events whether to accept or not and feeling myself implicated in their temporizing, [I] called on them for a decisive answer, knowing that there had been a general effort in this place, since their recommendation, to dissuade them with threats and promises, which had so much operated on their minds as to render them unworthy [of] their appointments. I therefore requested them to return their warrants.[5]

Such subjective evidence of New England's alienation from the national government is amply confirmed by objective numbers. In 1804–1805 New England recruits drop to slightly more than one man in twenty and rise to only one in ten by 1809. Then something unexpected happens. Although the New England Federalist leadership's disaffection from the War of 1812 is a matter of historical notoriety, at the grass-roots level the onset of hostilities sees New England rejoining the union, at least if the evidence of midshipman recruitment is to be believed. Both in 1812 and again in 1814 one midshipman in five is a son of the New England states. The case of New Hampshire is noteworthy in this regard. Even in the Federalist era the Granite State had displayed a remarkable lack of interest in the navy.[6] In 1812 New Hampshire's enthusiasm for the navy suddenly comes alive; nine young men from that state are successful in their quest for midshipman warrants.

Politics was not the only factor that could cause the number of midshipmen from a particular state to fluctuate. Maryland was always a large source of midshipmen, with a share that ranged between 10 and 15 percent of all newly issued warrants. In 1804–1805 that state's portion suddenly shoots up to nearly one man in three! South Carolina's contribution is usually about one midshipman in twenty. Come 1809 it is twice that size. Pennsylvania's share hovers around one in ten in 1804–1805, 1809, and 1812, then rises sharply to one in five in 1814. Is it pure coincidence that a Marylander (Robert Smith) is secretary of the navy in 1804–1805? South Carolina's native son, Paul Hamilton, in 1809? Or Pennsylvania's William Jones in 1814? One rather doubts it. What is at work here is not merely home-state chauvinism. To be sure, each of the secretaries probably harbored an unexpressed conviction that his state really had not gotten its fair share of new midshipmen under the previous regime and went to work to set matters straight. More basically, recommenders from a secretary's home state generally had better access to him in advocacy of their protégés' merits. Because the secretaries knew the recommenders from their home states, there was an almost unavoidable bias toward trusting their recommendations to a greater degree than those of worthies from distant states whom one did not know so well. Of the secretaries, Maryland's Benjamin Stoddert alone appears to have been immune to home-state chauvinism; none was so egregious as Robert Smith, who warranted Marylanders with unblushing enthusiasm.

Here the ugly suspicion surfaces that the reason so few New Englanders were appointed midshipmen in 1804–1805 and in 1809 was because Republican secretaries of the navy denied warrants to New England and gave them instead to pro-Republican sections of the country. Might this have happened? What was the real meaning of the Navy Department's self-announced rule of a fair geographical distribution of appointments? Fortuitously, one of the registers that the Navy Office maintained to keep track of applications for appointments survives to allay the partisan suspicion and illuminate the meaning of the department's fair-geographical-distribution rule. The document, which can be dated to early 1809, records each applicant's name, the rank sought, his place of residence, and the names of the persons recommending him.[7] At the time the register was compiled there were 242 active applications for midshipman warrants on file. Of these 242 hopefuls roughly one young man out of four eventually received an appointment. Or, looked at from the perspective of the disappointed, three out of every four applicants for a midshipman's warrant were turned down. This striking evidence confirms the repeated assertions of presidents and secretaries of the navy that there was no shortage of individuals seeking naval careers. The Navy Office was in the enviable position of having an ample pool from which to select the strongest potential officers—if it could succeed in discerning the best men through the opaque glass of uniformly enthusiastic and often misleading letters of recommendation.

Taking the nation region by region, new midshipman warrants were awarded in almost exactly the same proportions as applications flowed in from that region. In some cases the congruence is so close as to be uncanny. New England submitted 13.2 percent of the applications; it received almost precisely that percentage of the midshipman appointments. Maryland, Virginia, and the District of Columbia accounted for 43.4 percent of the midshipman applications; their share of the appointments was closely parallel. Only the New York–to–Delaware seaboard states wound up with less than their "fair share" of the coveted warrants. However, some region or regions would have had to make a sacrifice of midshipman berths, because one region, the western states and territories, received preferential treatment. In fact, it was not the region as a whole, but Orleans Territory in particular that was granted favored consideration. That newly acquired territory received approximately twice as many midshipman berths as it should have gotten had the coveted warrants been doled out in strict proportion to the number of applications. If a young man wanted to be a midshipman, he definitely had an unfair advantage by living in Orleans Territory. Preferential treatment for residents there was the expression of a deliberate policy of using naval appointments to bond the new citizens of that world to the United States. Louisiana had scarcely been acquired before President Jefferson was advising Secretary Smith, "I wish some of the native French of New Orleans could be induced to put their sons into our navy, and I suspect they would readily do it if they knew the door was open." Robert Smith and his successors fully agreed.[8]

Only on a regional basis was the Navy Office concerned about geographical fairness. Less anxiety was felt to apply state quotas. Maryland might be the source of nearly one application out of every five received and be awarded nearly one-fifth of the warrants, but Connecticut could present eight hopeful young men, only to have every one of them turned down. No records survive as to why some states appeared to get their numerical quota of appointments and others did not. Lacking definite evidence one has to suppose that, once geographical quotas were satisfied on a regional basis, positive or negative decisions were made on the strength of individual applications from within those regions without too neat an attention to state-by-state balance.

A Regional Navy?

If secretaries of the navy distribute midshipman warrants to the different regions of the country more or less proportionally to the unequal demand for them from those regions and follow this policy for a number of years, the result is an officer corps more representative of particular areas than of the country at large. The pre-1815 U.S. Navy became the child of one clearly defined section of the country: the middle states. One-third (35.2 percent) of all the officer recruits came from the District of Columbia and the two adjoining states, although that same area held only 14.0 percent of the nation's population of young men. The band of states that stretched from New York on the north to Virginia on the south was home to two thirds (64.6 percent) of the navy's officers, but to less than half (18.1 percent) of the corresponding age group in the population as a whole. New England, the most maritime region in the nation, was badly underrepresented in the nation's navy by every measure. The Deep South mustered slightly more than one officer out of ten; the West one out of twenty.

Why did the navy appeal so much more strongly to the middle region and its sons than to the outlying parts of the nation? Contemporaries were bemused. "I should be much better pleased to see a due proportion of candidates for the place of midshipmen from the North," lamented President Jefferson in the summer of 1804 when Virginia and Maryland were running away with the corps. "They [the northern states] ought not to expect to reap that whereon they have bestowed no labor, nor where others have labored that they should reap the fruits. I am sorry they are not disposed to make the sacrifice of time and money necessary by which our young midshipmen qualify themselves for service and that this disposition seems confined to the Middle and South. I wonder to see so much of it in Virginia, which is so much more agricultural than nautical." Robert Smith could provide no answer:

> To me, as to you, it appears really surprising that so many applications for appointments in the navy are received from Virginia and Maryland. But the eastern states have no cause of complaint. All applications from that quarter have been duly respected by us. And if they have not been as numerous as from some of the other*states, no blame can, on that score, attach to us. The

fact is that I have frequently expressed my surprise to the eastern members of Congress that the young men of their country had not at this time more zeal for the service.[9]

When two of the brightest and best-informed contemporary observers were at a loss to explain why the officer corps was rapidly becoming the domain of men from the middle states, the historian should perhaps hesitate to rush in. If New England Federalists felt alienated from the national government after the election of 1800, there were still plenty of Jeffersonian Republicans in the region who should have experienced a correspondingly strengthened bond and who might have encouraged their sons to pursue naval careers. One is tempted to propose a psychological answer. Those states that were closest geographically to the national capital at Washington seemed to feel the greatest sense of identification with the national government and its navy; in the parts of the union farthest from the national capital—New England, the lower South, the West—one's primary identification was with one's state or one's region. It is almost certainly not an unrelated phenomenon that, in the pre-1815 years, separatist movements in the United States were most active in those same remote regions that sent relatively few sons to serve the national government in its navy.

Misleading it would be to suggest that the demand method of filling appointments was allowed to run on, lamented but unchecked. Neither Robert Smith nor Paul Hamilton seemed unduly disturbed by the prospect of an officer corps more regional than national in character. William Jones thought otherwise. Although he made no public statement of his intent, it is clear from the newly appointed midshipmen of 1814, a cohort over whose selection he had decisive control, that he acted to bring the distribution of midshipman warrants into line with the distribution of the nation's people—or at least of its free white

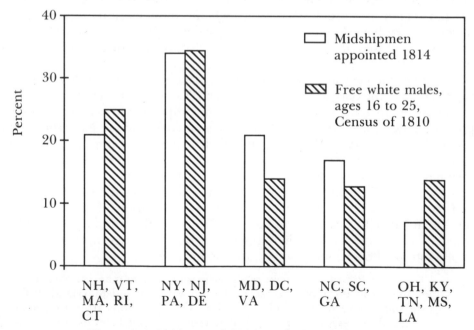

Figure 2 Midshipmen of 1814 vs. the Population Base

males (Figure 2). The Maryland–District of Columbia–Virginia hegemony was not wholly eliminated, but it definitely had been curbed. The lower South, too, was overrepresented slightly among the newly appointed midshipmen; New England and the western states were somewhat underrepresented; but there existed more congruence between the distribution of midshipman warrants around the nation in 1814 and the realities of U.S. population than at any previous point in the navy's short history. In giving credit to William Jones for a vision of a navy that was the creature of no single region, one should also recognize that his task was made easier by the enhanced sense of national identity and unity that the War of 1812 was creating. The navy had caught the country's imagination, and the flow of midshipman applications from hitherto shy parts of the union was on the rise.

Spawning Grounds

To this point the story of midshipmen's geographical origins has been told in terms of states and groups of states. This is entirely appropriate, because those were the terms in which the Navy Office thought about the mass of applications from would-be officers. Although the states of the union were in some degree shaped by natural features, they were primarily human-defined territories; that is, they were political and administrative subdivisions of the country. To examine the geographical origins of the navy's officers only in terms of the nation's states is to risk overlooking at least half of the story.

Among the 822 midshipmen whose home state at the time of appointment is known, 742 can be tracked to a specific locality (city, town, village, or county) within that state. Six cities and their immediately surrounding villages and countryside were home to four out of every ten (289 or 38.9 percent) of the midshipmen:

Philadelphia, Pa.	95 midshipmen
New York City	45
District of Columbia	43
Charleston, S.C.	41
Baltimore, Md.	38
Boston, Mass.	27

Philadelphia's status as the premier producer of midshipmen was beyond challenge. The old national capital was home to 12.8 percent of all young men recruited into the corps of midshipmen, more than double the number selected from New York City, though the populations of the two places were by no means that disproportionate. The District of Columbia, comprising the three population centers of Alexandria, Washington, and Georgetown, owed its high ranking more to the immediate proximity of would-be midshipmen to the powers that appointed them than to its relatively puny population base. Adding to the list all the other towns and cities that were home to at least ten midshipmen causes these places to appear:

Centerville and Queen Annes Co., Md.	16
Richmond, Va.	15
Providence, R.I.	13
New Orleans, La.	13
Fredericksburg, Va.	12

By themselves those eleven concentrations of population contributed nearly half of the navy's midshipmen (358 or 48.2 percent). Beyond them stretches a list of towns that were home to between five and ten midshipmen each, including Dover, Delaware, and Norfolk, Virginia (9 midshipmen apiece); Annapolis, Maryland, and Petersburg, Virginia (8); Albany, New York, Newport, Rhode Island, Williamsburg, Virginia (7); Carlisle, Pennsylvania, Frederick, Maryland, Portland, Massachusetts, Portsmouth, New Hampshire, Wilmington, North Carolina (6); and Georgetown, South Carolina, New Castle, Delaware, and Savannah, Georgia (5). By the time one reaches the end of this list of towns or small cities that contributed at least five midshipmen, the tally of city and town dwellers has reached six out of every ten midshipmen. It would rise higher if one continued the list and added the towns that were home to one, two, three, or four young men. This trend for the navy's midshipmen to come from cities and towns was not simply a reflection of where the most people lived in the pre-1815 United States. Town dwellers were disproportionately present among the new midshipmen by a wide margin. The same six cities that provided nearly 40 percent of the navy's midshipmen were home to not more than 5 percent of the nation's free white young adults.[10]

Does that mean that one should think of the navy's midshipmen as city boys? Yes and no. One runs a risk in applying nineteenth- and twentieth-century concepts called *cities* to the different world of a pre-1815 United States. Of the listed cities and towns only Philadelphia, New York, and Boston for certain, and probably Baltimore and Charleston, could really be called urban, if by that term one embraces not only density and size of population and intensity of commercial activity, but a certain mentality and style of life as well. All the rest were simply towns, larger or smaller, and certainly not without a high degree of culture and sophistication, but towns nonetheless, with all the intense awareness of surrounding rural areas that the term connotes.

If it is useful to think of the typical midshipmen as town or city dwellers, that is still not the absolutely best way to appreciate the geography of their homes. The list of towns and cities provides a clue. Only Dover, Delaware, Carlisle, Pennsylvania, and Frederick, Maryland, are not immediately adjacent to the sea or on navigable rivers leading to the sea. If town boys tended to become midshipmen in greater numbers than country boys, it was not so much that they came from towns as that the towns were ports and centers of maritime activity. Deciding whether a particular place that a midshipman called home was a maritime or an inland environment is hardly an exact science. Is Williamsburg, Virginia, located in the middle of a neck of land approximately nine miles wide between two navigable (but out-of-sight) rivers, *maritime*? Nevertheless, it is a safe generalization to say that, the inland western states aside, approximately three-quarters of all midshipmen came from maritime environments; that is, from places touching directly on salt water or on inland navigation that communicated directly with salt water. Not more than a quarter, and possibly fewer, of all midshipmen came from places that were naturally landlocked. Only in three states—Delaware, Virginia, and North Carolina—did there exist a roughly equal division between maritime and inland environments as providers of midshipmen.

Exposure to the sea and to seafaring was a key factor in determining which young men chose to become midshipmen in the nation's navy. Three among four of them lived within sight of, communicated via, traveled upon, ate from, and were at least partially supported by a watery environment in which a floating body was as familiar a means of motion as a four-legged one. If naval officers rarely spoke of this shared maritime heritage and the influence it may have had on their lives and careers, that is no surprise. As with the air they breathed, it had always been there, too much a part of their visceral lives and selves to be given much analytical thought.

6. Time

O N NO REQUIREMENT for an appointment as a midshipman did the Navy Department appear to have so clear a policy as its age threshold and age ceiling: young gentlemen appointed should be neither younger than twelve nor older than eighteen. Did the pre-1815 navy succeed in sustaining this policy? Not particularly well.

Information on officers' ages is sparser than on those same officers' geographical roots. Not until the secretaryship of William Jones did the Navy Office make a sustained attempt to collect age data on its new appointees; under his successor, Benjamin Crowninshield, a similar effort was made to ascertain the ages of serving officers. Wide variation exists in the apparent reliability of the surviving information respecting midshipmen's ages. Such information is available for only about one young man in three appointed in 1800 and in 1804–1805. Ages can be determined for slightly less than half of the novice midshipmen of 1809; in 1812 the number is nearly two-thirds; by 1814—and reflecting the Navy Office's vigorous attempt to gather the information—ages of almost nine out of every ten newly minted midshipmen are on record. When all years are combined, ages can be ferreted out for about half of the midshipmen. But whether it is a year for which only one-third of the ages are available or one for which nine-tenths are on record, the numbers are so remarkably consistent as to inspire strong faith in their reliability.[1]

If one ignores for the moment the ages of the oldest and youngest midshipmen appointed, numbers that can be misleading, the Navy Office's appointment practice as respects the age of new midshipmen was highly consistent across the entire 1800–1814 period (Table 4). The median age held steady at seventeen, save for the years 1804–1805 when, for some unaccountable reason, the number jogs upward to eighteen. With the exception of 1812, in which year it was deflected downward by some very young appointments (of which more later), the mean age remained constant at about seventeen and a half years. The pattern of the Navy Office's practice with respect to the ages of young men selected as midshipmen can be seen most clearly by creating a visual image of its appointment record (Figure 3). Fifteen, sixteen, seventeen, and eighteen were the premier ages for young men to begin careers as naval

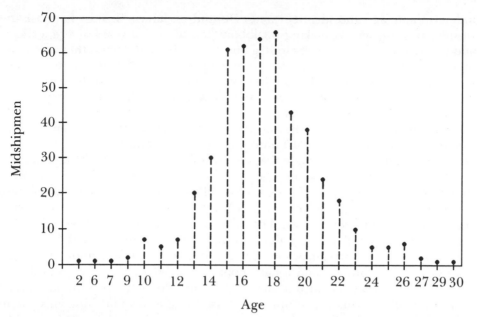

Figure 3 Number of Midshipmen of Known Ages Appointed in 1800, 1804–1805, 1809, 1812, and 1814

officers; those four cohorts embrace more than half (52.7 percent) of all the novice officers. Nineteen and twenty are the second most popular age brackets at which naval careers are begun, followed by thirteen/fourteen and twenty-one/twenty-two years of age. Two-thirds (69.6 percent) of all newly appointed midshipmen were between fifteen and twenty years of age; almost nine out of every ten (88.8 percent) fell somewhere within the age spectrum of thirteen through twenty-two.

If newly appointed midshipmen ought not to be younger than twelve or older than eighteen, how well did the Navy Office follow its self-announced criteria (Table 5)? With the partial exception of the year 1812, appointment practices or the demographic realities of the applicant pool were remarkably consistent. Year in, year out, two-thirds of the new appointments fell within the span that the navy perceived as the desirable one in which to begin a naval career; but, just as consistently, approximately one-third of all new appointees had reached or passed the age threshold at which their chances for successfully adapting themselves to careers as naval officers were thought to be sharply diminished.

Before pursuing the midshipmen whose ages fell in the middle or at the upper end of the spectrum, one must visit a hoary legend: the belief that midshipmen were essentially seagoing children, young boys of twelve or ten or even younger. There is an enormous cadre of these child midshipmen sailing and fighting their way through the pages of historical fiction. Such tales have established a probably invincible popular conviction that this was the way the pre-1815 world worked. The child midshipman is a stock character almost sure to show up in the pages of enlisted men's autobiographies as well. After describing a beating with a rope's end administered by *Constitution*'s sailing master, William Bagot, in consequence of a report by a midshipman of indeterminate age and identity, James Durand exclaims, "I must here ask the reader the propriety of making small boys, ten to twelve years of age, officers and giving them full authority to flog and abuse the men, when they are as yet unacquainted with the actual duty belonging to a ship."[2] Durand, and others like him, make it sound as though the navy's ships swarmed with these underage martinets, precocious apprentices in the pleasures of sadism at the expense of the honest, hardworking sailors.

Dismissing, until a later chapter, the likelihood that any responsible officer would have ordered corporal punishment on the whim of a ten- or twelve-year-old boy, one may conclude that the reason a very young midshipman was so well remembered was because he stood out from the crowd. Boys younger than thirteen constituted only 5 percent of all the new midshipmen. Even these few were usually the relatives or protégés of senior officers, boys who were acquiring early experience at sea. Typical was ten-year-old John Ripley Madison, the lone midshipman younger than twelve to be appointed in 1804–1805. A Massachusetts-born orphan whom Edward Preble had taken under his wing, Madison served thirteen and a half months as a boy in *Constitution* and *John Adams* before Preble obtained a warrant for him. Preble then promptly placed him in school—not on active duty—and used Madison's midshipman's pay to help defray educational costs.

The year 1812, with its eleven appointments as midshipmen of boys younger than twelve, should be seen as an aberration in Navy Department practice. Whether the blame ought to be laid on Chief Clerk Charles W. Goldsborough or on Secretary Paul Hamilton or shared by both is not clear; but in that year the intent, if not the letter, of the Navy Office's authority to issue midshipman warrants was blatantly abused. The most flagrant case was the appointment of the two-year-old son of the late Commodore Samuel Barron. Here, the motive was apparently monetary relief for the pensionless mother, a lady in far from enviable financial circumstances. Other cases were only in degree less abusive. Goldsborough's six-year-old son, Louis, was given a warrant, as was James Madison Cutts, aged seven and son of Republican congressman Richard Cutts. Ten-year-old boys of the naval chaplain Andrew Hunter and Charleston, South Carolina, navy agent Nathaniel Ingraham also received the coveted documents. Only the fact that his age is unknown prevents the inclusion of the suspicious-looking appointment of Edward Wilkinson Hamilton—son of the secretary himself—in the roll of dubious appointments. With the exception of young Ingraham, none of these boys would actually perform any service during the War of 1812; their parents simply held their warrants against a day when they would be old enough to pursue naval careers. Such 1812 child appointments need to be kept in perspective. They do not represent the Navy Department's customary way of doing business, but were one more element of the garish sunset of sloppy administration in which Paul Hamilton's tenure at the Navy Office self-destructed. With the arrival of William Jones the practice stops abruptly; in 1814 twelve again becomes the age threshold at which young men gained midshipman warrants.

The child-midshipman issue is a red herring that can lead the historian badly astray, for the real story is the relative maturity of the young men entering the corps (Figure 3). Four out of every ten new midshipmen were between eighteen and twenty-three years old when they received their warrants; eight among ten were fifteen to twenty-three. Parents of most would-be midshipmen saw twelve or thirteen as too early to begin a naval career; educations were still in progress and shipboard vices were best not encountered at so impressionable an age. Although it is appropriate to call most of these newly fledged midshipmen *young* men, it would be a mistake to assume that the behavior and attitudes of a seventeen-year-old of the pre-1815 world were necessarily the same as those of a seventeen-year-old of the second half of the twentieth century. Society—and especially maritime society—of the late eighteenth and early nineteenth centuries expected men and women to learn adult roles and (one hoped) adult behavior at a relatively earlier age. In the merchant service a young man typically began his sea career in his early teens; if he came from the right background or had the appropriate abilities, he could expect to fill a mate's berth by his late teens and attain the full responsibility of master of a small cargo-carrier on transoceanic voyages by his early twenties at the latest. The navy expected its midshipmen's psychological maturity to develop at a comparable pace.

Despite all disclaimers to the contrary, about one-third of the navy's midshipmen began their careers above eighteen, the age that the Navy Office said was the ceiling for successful integration into the corps. This suggests the possibility that some of these men may have been turning to the navy after rejecting—or being rejected by—other careers. Was the secretaries' perception that men aged nineteen and above were less likely to survive in the navy an accurate one? A definite answer may be given to the question, but that answer involves a strong dose of numbers. One can compare the career lengths of the midshipmen who entered the navy in the recommended age range, twelve through eighteen, with career endurance for those who began their lives as naval officers at nineteen or older.[3] As a group the twelve-to-eighteen-year-olds attained a median naval career of 8.1 years; their mean career length was 17.5 years. By contrast, the median length of service for entering midshipmen nineteen and older was 4.9 years and the mean 11.4 years. An immediate objection arises: midshipmen who entered the navy at a more advanced age naturally had (as a group) a shorter professional life expectancy. The answer to this objection is to repeat the calculation, but to eliminate all those who died in service, thus measuring career lengths only for men who eventually resigned or were dismissed. These categories should be especially rife with men who could not adjust to naval life. The results are similar. Among the resigned and dismissed, those who came into the navy aged twelve to eighteen had a median naval career of 3.3 years and a mean length of service of 7.7 years; for the nineteen-and-older midshipmen the corresponding figures are 1.8 and 4.4 years. By all of these measures, the Navy Office was definitely justified in regarding would-be midshipmen who had reached nineteen as career risks.

There is, however, an alternative measure of career success other than mere length of service. What proportion of each age group survived to attain that first vital promotion, the one to lieutenant? Seen from this perspective the undesirability of the nineteen-and-older midshipmen is less clear-cut. Among newly fledged midshipmen twelve to eighteen years of age, 44.8 percent attained lieutenancies. In the nineteen-and-older group, the survival-to-promotion rate was 32.4 percent. If the odds were greater that a novice midshipman in the twelve-to-eighteen group would one day make lieutenant, still the professional survival rates for the two groups were not that disparate. One doubts that any secretary of the navy ever calculated the relative survival-to-lieutenant rates for the two groups in precise mathematical terms; but some experience-derived appreciation that the nineteen-and-older group had a professional success rate not much lower than the twelve-to-eighteen crew must explain why the navy continued to admit one-third of its new midshipmen at ages by which it officially asserted their chances for fitting in satisfactorily were greatly diminished. Had the Navy Department rigidly enforced a not-older-than-eighteen policy in midshipman appointments, Stephen Decatur, Jesse Duncan Elliott, Jacob Jones, John B. Nicolson, and many another subsequently distinguished officer would have been forced to find other careers.

7. Kin

*H*ISTORIANS MAY NEVER know as much about midshipmen's parents as they might wish. Only occasionally did the Navy Department have much of a dossier on a parent. The recommender might, but often did not, mention the parent's name. More probably the recommendation would assert that the parent was a worthy or respectable citizen, a loyal member of the party in power, or a widow in less than affluent circumstances. Should the recommendation files fail to reveal the parent's identity, one can hope to find a name if the father or the mother had occasion to write to the Navy Office. Few did. Other sources present different problems. When the historian is able to pursue a midshipman to a genealogy, a town history, a volume of vital records, or a city directory, it is often to be confronted by several individuals with the same family name, any one of whom could be the parent. Sometimes acceptable inferences are possible. When the Charleston, South Carolina, city directory for 1809 lists only one adult named Kreps, and that individual is Ann Kreps, baker at 164 King Street, it is reasonable—though by no means foolproof—to infer that she is the widowed mother of Midshipman John Kreps. Even if it is possible to link father and son in a genealogy or a town history, odds are the volume will dwell lovingly on the parent's military service in the Revolution with nary a hint of how he kept bread on the family table in the quarter century after.

Then there are the problems of imbalance. Genealogies, town and country histories, and published vital statistics are more common north of the Mason-Dixon line than south of it, making it somewhat easier to identify northern parents. The occupational statuses of fathers and mothers who lived and worked in the nine or ten cities with published directories are more readily discoverable than those of their rural and small-town counterparts.[1] Finally, there is the best-known pitfall of them all: the more prominent a midshipman's parents, the more likely the historian is to identify them. Unless carefully guarded against, this bias can create the impression that most midshipmen came from the upper reaches of the social pyramid.

For all these reasons it is illusory to hope that anything like a statistically reliable profile of midshipmen's parents is here attained. (In the discussion that

73

Rembrandt Peale's 1802 portrayal of this midshipman reveals why one young Virginia woman called him "the exquisite Lewis Warrington," a description that may astonish those who know only the pictures of the heavy-jowled man who was experiencing substantial weight gain along the path to master commandant and captain. He was rumored to be the out-of-wedlock son of the Comte de Rochambeau, commander of the French forces at the battle of Yorktown in 1781, and Rachel Warrington, a young Williamsburg woman who had extended too great a degree of Southern hospitality to the military leader of America's allies. Such stories of his racy, if romantic, parentage certainly did nothing to lessen Lewis Warrington's appeal for his female contemporaries. Minneapolis Institute of Arts.

follows only one parent is counted for each midshipman, either a father or a widowed mother, as appropriate.) Among the 885 midshipmen under scrutiny, *something*—a name, whether alive or dead, occupation, Revolutionary War service—is known about the parents of 382 of them (43.2 percent). Deducting those parents concerning whom a name, and nothing more, can be learned leaves 323 midshipmen about whose parents one other fact can be discovered. In some cases among the 323 that single known fact may only be that one or both parents were dead or that the father was a Revolutionary War veteran. When these are eliminated from the calculations, there remain parents of 262 midshipmen (29.6 percent) about whose occupation and status enough is known that they may be positioned correctly on the pre-1815 U.S. social pyramid. In the pages that follow, for all the reasons outlined, parental statuses will be discussed as approximate fractions of the larger group of parents, but never as percentages. To use percentage terminology would be to create an illusion of precision about a matter that is, in fact, highly imprecise.

If a fully reliable inventory of parental status eludes, a question of importance can still be asked. Recommenders and secretaries of the navy alike agreed that a midshipman should be of *respectable* or *worthy* parentage. Because all used these terms and none felt the need to define them, there must have existed a commonly understood core meaning, even if one suspects that the words were vague and ambiguous enough to permit a spectrum of interpretations. Is it possible, from an examination of what is known about midshipmen's parents, to form some idea of those layers of the social pyramid that were encompassed by the labels *respectable* and *worthy*?

Exploring the Pyramid

The status that united more of the fathers of midshipmen than any other was death. Among the 323 midshipmen about whose parents something other than a name is known, at least 98 of the fathers were dead at the time the son sought and obtained his appointment as a midshipman. Add to these a number of cases in which the name and social standing of the father are known, but in which it is uncertain whether he was still alive when his son became a midshipman, and it is by no means unrealistic to estimate that close to one-third of all young men entering the navy came from homes in which the biological father had died before the young man gave serious consideration to choosing the navy as a career.

A second common status shared by more than one-fifth of the parents of midshipmen about whom something more than a name is known was the father's service by land or by sea on the winning side during the Revolutionary War. However brief this military experience in the Revolution, it was a talisman almost sure to be mentioned at some point in the son's application or recommendation for a midshipman's warrant. The mythic importance of this act of bearing arms in the conflict that established political independence and a distinct national identity was perceived as strong enough to confer entitlement to preference when it came to awarding midshipman warrants. Boston ship chandler Nathaniel Thayer applied for such an appointment for his son Edward Niles in 1812; the only identification of his own status he thought required was to tell Secretary Hamilton, "If my saying that I took an active part in the Revolutionary War with Commodore Manly and others will have any influence, I can refer you to the secretary at war, [William Eustis], who I am well known to."[2]

A father's having fought on the winning side in the American Revolution was obviously perceived as an asset that should be prominently mentioned when the son sought a midshipman's appointment. What weight it carried with the secretary of the navy as he began sifting through the pile of applications is wholly unknown. Certainly it never hurt anyone's chances, but neither was it an absolute prerequisite. No numbers can be given, but sons of Revolutionary War Loyalists were far from uncommon in the pre-1815 navy. If someone got mad enough at one of these Loyalist progeny, the unpatriotic heredity was likely to be whispered about or thrown in his face. Captain William Bainbridge was the most prominent son of a Loyalist father in the navy of 1794–1815, but there were others less well known. Noble W. Glen from Savannah, Georgia, served as midshipman from 1800 till he resigned in April 1804. Noble's father, John Glen (who had died about a year before his son became a midshipman), began the Revolutionary War as a prominent and enthusiastic Georgia patriot. Discouraged by the changing fortunes of war, he later took the oath of allegiance to the British Crown. John Glen suffered both loss of property and public opprobrium when yet another reversal in the fortunes of war left the former colonies victorious and independent. The passage of time, the healing of old wounds, and the emergence of former Loyalists as pillars of the Federalist party restored John Glen to his former prominence. Within the two years before his death, the elder Glen had been chosen mayor of Savannah and judge of the Georgia superior court.[3]

Being dead or having served in the land or sea forces that helped to win the Revolutionary War were special status categories that cut across social rank as it was commonly understood. How were the parents of midshipmen distributed among these more conventional social categories? Based on the information now in hand, it appears that about one-quarter of them (perhaps 64 of the 262 parents whose occupation and status are known) held some kind of elective or appointive position under the federal government. Rather surprisingly, only seven of the sixty-four were congressmen and senators. These legislators were among the best-positioned people in the country to secure midshipman appointments for their sons, had they so desired; for whatever unknown reasons, naval careers for their male children seem to have held no strong appeal.

By contrast, holders of major presidential appointments were active in seeking naval careers for their sons, accounting for twenty-three out of the sixty-four. Fathers in this group included secretaries of the federal departments, collectors of customs, postmasters, commissioners of loans, navy agents at major ports, U.S. marshals, federal judges, and district attorneys. Such positions often conferred more status and power than financial reward. John Randall, the collector of customs at Annapolis, lamented that his federal post—the collectors' jobs were among the highest-prestige national appointments—netted him but $300 per year in 1804, while he had ten children to support.[4] It is easy to understand why he was eager to procure a midshipman's warrant for his son, Henry K. Randall.

Military fathers, who accounted for twenty-four of the sixty-four parents who were federal officials or employees, were almost as anxious as presidential appointees to seek naval appointments for their sons. Seventeen of the twenty-four fathers were naval officers, men who were in an extremely favorable position to secure midshipman berths for their sons. Four other fathers were army officers; one held a marine corps commission. More noteworthy are the two midshipmen whose fathers held ranks of but moderate prestige: James William Forrest, son of Alexander Forrest, longtime sergeant major of the marine corps, and John Downes, son of *Constitution*'s purser's steward during the Quasi-War with France. Young Forrest's unhappy naval career of a little more than four years ended in a dismissal by court martial for drunkenness in 1814, but Downes rose rapidly to the rank of captain and held some of the navy's most responsible posts.[5]

Finally, one notes that four clerks in the federal offices—including Charles W. Goldsborough, chief clerk of the Navy Department, and Nathan Lufborough, chief clerk in the office of the comptroller of the treasury—secured midshipman appointments for their sons, as did two navy yard clerks, a senior mechanic at the Washington navy yard, and a minor customs official. That one-quarter of the midshipmen whose parents' occupations can be identified had fathers who held elective or appointive federal positions should come as no surprise. All of these fathers possessed excellent access, direct or indirect, to the source of midshipman's warrants; those who held appointive posts had an especially keen sense of identification, both emotional and financial, with the national government. One strong warning remains to be expressed. Just because one-quarter of the 262 parents of known status were fathers who held elective or appointive posts under the federal government, one may not rush on and assume that one-quarter of the parents of the larger group of 885 midshipmen held similar federal jobs. It is easy for the historian to identify parents who were congressmen or collectors of customs or naval officers; consequently, most of them have already been accounted for among the 262 parents. The proportion of such fathers would be much lower among the full 885.

A smaller segment of the 262 midshipmen—twenty-seven or about one in ten—had fathers who were state, county, or local officials, men who occupied a spectrum of posts ranging from state governor down to toll collector on the bridge between Charlestown and Boston. If any pattern is to be detected among these twenty-seven it is that most were court officials of one kind or another, whether they be Anne Arundel County (Maryland) register of wills John Gassaway, parent of a midshipman of the same name, or Gwyn R. Tompkins, longtime sheriff of Fayette County (Kentucky) and father of Midshipman John Tompkins. If the speculation proposed earlier when the geographical origins of the midshipmen were examined—namely, that a sense of identification with the national government was a significant factor in the choice of a naval career—is correct, that same loyalty or its absence may help to explain why parents who were holders of state, county, and local offices were less than half as numerous as parents who held federal positions; and this even though state, county, and local governments were far more pervasive in day-to-day American life than was the national government. The latter's presence was most likely to be experienced only at the post office or the customs house—or perhaps in a transient army or navy recruiting party.

What united the one-third of the midshipmen's fathers who held some kind of post under the national, state, county, or local government was the possession of an office that automatically conferred the status of *respectable* and *worthy*, just as did honorable service as an officer during the Revolution. The status gap that separated a U.S. senator from an inspector of salted provisions at Georgetown, D.C., might be enormous, but both were comfortably within the range of acceptable fathers for naval officers. Another class of fathers whose respectability and worth were unquestioned by the secretary of the navy were those who practiced what were known as the learned professions: medicine, law, and the ministry. About one-eighth (31 of the 262) of the parents of midshipmen whose occupations have been identified come under this rubric. Right away a warning flag must be run up, because among this one-eighth are counted only those fathers whose primary status was the practice of one of these professions. Many of the fathers already counted as holders of federal or state elective or appointive offices were or had been attorneys. But in their own eyes and in those of their contemporaries their standing in society was closely linked to the offices they held. Alexander James Dallas, father of a midshipman of the same name, was a lawyer, but his relative position in society was primarily determined by his federal job as U.S. attorney for the eastern district of Pennsylvania. It is as a federal officeholder, not as a practitioner of a learned profession, that he is here counted.

In day-to-day reality the secretary of the navy spent precious little time scrutinizing applications from sons of the clergy, for almost none applied to be midshipmen. Of the 262 parents being here considered, only 2 have been identified as ministers. Impressionistic evidence from the naval officer corps as a whole suggests that children of the manse were a rare, but not wholly unknown, phenomenon. For practical purposes the sons of the learned professions who sought midshipman warrants were the children either of physicians (17) or of attorneys (12). The apparent imbalance in favor of the doctors is deceptive. As noted, a number of the lawyer-fathers have been counted as officeholders. If tallied here, too, the attorneys would have a slight lead over the physicians.

Given that most midshipmen were born and grew up in a maritime geographical environment, it is surprising to learn that only one out of every fourteen midshipmen was the son of a master in the merchant service. The historian is tempted to speculate that the sons of merchant captains, having grown up with the reality of life at sea, were the less attracted to it; that experienced seamen steered their sons into other callings; or that many mothers felt as did Elizabeth Chamberlayne of King William County, Virginia, widow of a merchant captain lost at sea along with his eldest son, a lady who rejected a midshipman's warrant offered to her son on the grounds that "all my calamities and misfortunes in this world has arisen from the water."[6] The correct answer may, however, be more prosaic. Active seafaring was a young man's profession in the United States of 1794–1815. By the time they had sons who were old enough to be considered for appointments as midshipmen, fathers who may have commanded at sea in their younger days would often have moved into less physically demanding positions ashore. John Kelly, whose son John, Jr., became a midshipman in 1814, had spent many years on the quarterdeck of merchantmen. When young John was ready to seek a naval career his father was in his seventies and long since established ashore as a grocer in Philadelphia's Southwark district.

Simply looking for merchant captains among the fathers is casting too small a net. If one thinks, instead, in terms of maritime-related occupations, it is to discover that approximately one-third of the 262 midshipmen had a parent who pursued an occupation intimately involved with the sea in a nongovernmental capacity. These were occupations that ranged from merchants (38) and the already-mentioned ship captains (19), through makers of navigation instruments (4), shipbuilders, auctioneers, insurance brokers (3 of each), ship chandlers, notaries, and consuls of European nations (2 apiece), down to lone cases of a cooper and a baker of ships' bread. Because the corps of midshipmen was recruited primarily in the maritime regions of the United States, it would not be surprising, should more information on parents of naval officers be uncovered, to learn that the proportion of maritime-related occupations among them was higher than one-third. It certainly would be higher if one added the naval officers, customs officials, and other holders of maritime-related offices who have already been tallied as employees or elected officials of the federal government.

Identifying maritime-related occupations is a valid and helpful way of looking at the parents of naval officers, but this umbrella would appear to shelter individuals of highly diverse social and economic standing. John Hollins, wealthy and powerful Baltimore merchant, and Ann Kreps, baker of ships' bread at Charleston, both pursued occupations dependent on the sea. They stood on very different steps on the social pyramid. It is important to take the midshipmen's parents who engaged in some kind of business or commercial enterprise, exclude the masters of merchantmen, and examine their businesses. Such individuals amounted to nearly four out of every ten identified parents.

Far and away the largest group of these parents were the thirty-eight who called themselves merchants or brokers. The image conjured up by the word *merchant* is probably that of someone like Benjamin Leverett, the father of Midshipman George Haven Leverett and a broker with a net worth of $100,000 doing business at Boston's Exchange Coffee House. Or it might be Midshipman Adam Kuhn's father, Peter, "a prosperous and respectable merchant, principally engaged in the trade of the Mediterranean coast of Spain."[7] If that is the image the parents themselves and their genealogy-writing descendants hoped to conjure up with the merchant label, the term was vague enough to include parents in more marginal financial circumstances. Henry Geddes of Charleston, South Carolina, the presumptive father of a midshipman of the same name, has descended from merchant in the Charleston directory of 1801 to shopkeeper in a similar directory published two years later. Parent John Stratton of Norfolk, a merchant in 1801, reappears in 1806 as a measurer of customs. One can surmise that he has been glad to exchange a faltering role in business for the modest economic security of a government job.

It will be useful to divide the business and commercial parents into two groups. In the first, along with the thirty-eight self-identified merchants and brokers, may be placed those whose occupational titles were intended to mark them as members of the commercial elite. Such parents would probably include the bank officers (5), insurance brokers (3), auctioneers (3), printers and newspaper publishers (3), army contractors (3), ship chandlers (2), shipbuilders (3), and the failed entrepreneurs (3) whose sons still had to be found "respectable" niches in life.

Added together, such elite businesses account for two-thirds of the commercial parents. There is little to startle the social historian here. All of these occupations have long been recognized as being *respectable* and *worthy* in the pre-1815 American world. With the remaining third one senses that the historian is approaching the lower fringes of *respectable* and *worthy,* a sense reinforced by the fact that these are the parents whose occupations are never specifically identified in the letters of recommendation or in the genealogies, but which must be ferreted out from the city directories. The largest group among them are the ten individuals who may be lumped together as innkeepers, hoteliers, and proprietors of boardinghouses. Here one finds Samuel Richardet, proprietor of the City Tavern and Coffee House at 86 South Second Street in Philadelphia, or Benjamin Stallings, innkeeper at 28 Baltimore Street in the city of the same name. The boardinghouses are typically the domains of the widowed mothers of midshipmen, whether it be Sarah Phillips (mother of Midshipman John) with her Philadelphia boardinghouse at 139 South Fifth Street or Charleston's Hannah Crowley, maintaining a boardinghouse at 105 Broad Street and mother of Midshipman Charles E. Crowley. With these ten inn and boardinghouse parents, one should probably include an eleventh parent, Seth Johnson, Sr., proprietor of the livery stable at the Green Dragon in Boston's Union Street.

The balance of the lower-level business parents were master craftsmen or small independent business persons. At their summit, in terms of skill and prestige, were the midshipmen's fathers—including Philadelphia's Thomas Biggs, father of Midshipmen James and Joseph—who were makers of navigation and surveying instruments. Such fathers were the elite of master craftsmen and universally recognized as such. Of similar status was Midshipman John F. Howell's parent, Reading Howell, Philadelphia surveyor and draftsman. The rest were owner-operators of small and medium-size businesses: tailors and merchant tailors (2), boot- and shoemakers (2), brewers and distillers (2), coppersmiths (2), a founder, a baker, a carpenter, a cooper, and a gunsmith.

To such parents is as far down the social pyramid as it has proved possible to trace the origins of the pre-1815 navy's midshipmen. It is at this lowest layer that one finds the clearest evidence of the search for upward mobility between generations. Coppersmith John McCauley (a man whom his descendants have been anxious to pass off as a "merchant") had married Sarah Stewart, the sister of Captain Charles Stewart, U.S. Navy, a man whose own somewhat obscure origins suggest that he, too, was upwardly mobile. Two of John and Sarah's children were Charles Stewart McCauley and Daniel Smith McCauley. Uncle Charles had no difficulty in obtaining midshipman warrants for the two young men, neither of whom had cause to complain about their subsequent career success: Charles rose to the rank of captain and commodore on the retired list; Daniel left the navy in 1825, but thereafter became U.S. consul at Tripoli and, later still, consul general at Alexandria, Egypt.

If the son of a master craftsman or a small businessman or an innkeeper was smart, and self-disciplined, and (perhaps) related to someone already secure in a naval career, then an officer's profession in the navy could be a channel for upward social mobility as it was for the McCauley brothers. For young men whose parents were farther down the social pyramid such a career was out of reach—or, if they succeeded in getting a fingerhold, the pressures against retaining it were great. Too many people were stamping on their hands. Evidence of such prejudice is not abundant, but it is to be found. "I wish to see our service respectable and have no doubt, had there been a proper investigation into the merits of some of the late [midshipmen's] appointments here, that they would not have received their warrants," Commodore Alexander Murray complained from Philadelphia in March 1809. "Some are drunkards, others the sons of barbers, tailors, sailmakers, etc., etc., that I fear will not be considered as proper associates for young gentlemen of respectability, especially as their merits are as yet untried." Within the next months Murray had the undisguised pleasure of being instrumental in securing the dismissal, for various pieces of misconduct, of Midshipman Samuel Brittin—"the son of an obscure tavern keeper and perfectly uneducated, as well as an idle, worthless fellow"— and Midshipman John Runchey, "the son of a barber, quite vulgar in all respects."[8] For such young men the odds were formidable indeed.

One occupational category among the fathers of midshipmen remains as yet untallied. The pre-1815 United States was preponderately a rural country. What of the fathers who followed agricultural pursuits? Among the 262 parents with identified occupations only 1 in 15 is known to have been a farmer, and that small number is made up almost entirely of larger-scale northern farmers and of southern planters operating in a slave-labor economy. Typical among the latter was Thomas Shubrick, Revolutionary War officer and hero, quartermaster general of the South Carolina militia, landowner, master in 1810 of 254 slaves, and father of Edward, Irvine, John, and William Shubrick, all officers of the U.S. Navy.[9] One farmer/planter father in fourteen is surely too low a proportion, even given the well-established fact that the navy drew its midshipmen from the maritime fringe and the urban centers of the United States. The imbalance is intensified because many of the identifications of parents' occupations must be drawn from city directories, a source that strengthens the urban bias.

Labeling parents and placing them in occupational categories, while a task that has to be performed, is an arbitrary and a misleading one. In the United States of 1794–1815 a parent might pursue several careers alternately or simultaneously. Peleg Wadsworth, father of Midshipmen Henry and Alexander S. Wadsworth, is here counted as a Revolutionary War officer and a member of Congress. A town resident in Portland much of the year, Congressman Wadsworth was also a paternalistic country squire on his extensive landholdings at Hiram, Maine. Charles Morris, midshipman, lieutenant, and captain, was the son of a man of the same name who alternately pursued careers as merchant captain, navy purser, and farmer. Midshipman Richard Shubrick Pinckney's father, Roger, was a Charleston attorney in fact as well as in name; he was just as much a southern planter whose several properties were operated by slave labor.

The Marginal Middle Class

Such naval parents, and others like them in the records, show how foolish it is to think that a variegated human life can be reduced to a brief label: master mariner, planter, merchant, Revolutionary War veteran, maker of mathematical instruments. Worse, the effort can be misleading. Behind these convenient labels—the public faces—that the naval parents present to a later time were private realities that were often very different. The naval records occasionally enable one to peer behind the public masks.

Midshipman John Haywood Bell's father is "an old revolutionary officer"; he has also, "unfortunately for his country, as well as for his fine family of children . . . wasted a handsome estate and somewhat sunk himself in the public estimation, though without tarnishing his honor, by a too free indulgence in the use of strong drink."[10] It is a happy circumstance that Benjamin Waller Booth of Winchester, Virginia, is provided with a midshipman's appointment in the navy, a correspondent tells president-elect James Madison. His father, Mordecai Booth, had married "a Widow Travis. . . . They set out in life in very independent circumstances and, although Mr. Booth was always a very sober man and free from gambling or other dissipated causes, yet by bad bargains, bad management, and living in too expensive a style he has reduced his family to absolute beggary, for indeed they have been chiefly supported by the bounty of his friends for some time past." The elder Booth was eventually able to keep the wolf from the door by finding employment in 1811 as clerk to Thomas Tingey, commandant of the Washington navy yard.[11] Thomas Babbit, Harvard graduate, physician, sometime U.S. Navy surgeon (April 1804–April 1810), and the father of three pre-1815 naval officers—Fitz Henry, Edward, and

Charles—was remembered as the best physician and surgeon in Brookfield, Massachusetts, and the surrounding towns, "in person . . . large and dignified in manner; in conversation very pleasing and interesting." But, "he was generous to a fault and gave little attention to money matters and so acquired few means."[12] Put less elegantly, having spent all the money he made, Dr. Babbit left his family in real financial distress when he died in February 1814.

By no means are these stories isolated, curious cases. Examples could be multiplied. Perhaps the historian cannot generalize from the fathers of naval officers to pre-1815 U.S. society at large, but the evidence from such naval parents says that there was no necessary relationship between middle to high status and financial security.[13] To be sure there were many midshipmen who came from financially secure, prudently managed family backgrounds; but the more the historian pokes about in the records, the stronger the impression of the naval parents as a middle class surviving on modest means, "respectability," its wits, mutual support, and a good measure of luck. The financial breakers were dangerously close to leeward.

To see the intimate embrace among perceived high status, chronic and imminent financial disaster, and the search for more secure futures for sons through naval careers, one need look no farther than three Virginia midshipmen: Thomas ap Catesby Jones, Walter F. Jones, and Richard Lee Smith. Meriwether Jones began his adult career as an attorney, but he soon discovered that the rough and tumble of partisan political strife was what really appealed to his combative personality. In 1798 Jones founded and thereafter edited the pro-Jeffersonian Richmond *Examiner*. Neither as an attorney nor as a newspaper publisher were business skills Meriwether Jones's long suit. No sooner was his party in office than he was applying for the handsome federal patronage subsidy that would come from having the *Examiner* selected to publish the federal session laws and complaining that, "not having been educated a printer, various impositions are practiced upon me, and I find it almost impracticable to become well enough acquainted with the mechanical arrangements of an office to make my profits commensurate to the labor and expense." That letter alone should have hoisted a large red flag in someone's mind, but Jones was a party wheelhorse and when, in 1804, a new U.S. commissioner of loans was needed for Virginia, Jones was given the job, although the nomination cleared the Senate by only a narrow margin and after serious foot dragging by the senators.[14] Meanwhile, Meriwether Jones's brother Catesby and his wife Lettice had both died, leaving Meriwether with an additional anxiety and drain on his finances in the person of a young nephew, Thomas ap Catesby Jones, who had to be provided for along with his own son, Walter. Fortunately, by the fall of 1805 young Catesby was eager to get into the navy; with a strong assist from President Jefferson, the elder Jones soon extracted the desired warrant from Robert Smith and thereby launched his fifteen-year-old nephew on one of the more famous and colorful careers in the nineteenth-century navy.[15]

If there was a sense of urgency in Meriwether Jones's efforts to secure a naval appointment for nephew Thomas, he had good cause. Already Meriwether's body, naturally thin, was beginning to waste away under the impact of a slow, relentless illness that finally claimed his life at Warm Springs in Bath County, Virginia, on 9 August 1806.[16] The Jones family fortunes had struck the rocks. With the settlement of the estate came the discovery that Meriwether

Jones's debts amounted to at least ten times his total assets and that he was in default to the United States in his capacity as commissioner of loans for the sum of $17,072. Even before his death Jones had lost suits over debts; if these earlier judgments were ruled to have priority over the federal claims against the estate, the United States would be lucky to recover 3 cents on the dollar for the money Jones owed as commissioner of loans.

As with all federal appointees responsible for large sums of money, Meriwether Jones had been required to post a surety bond for $10,000. One of his two sureties was a fellow attorney named George William Smith. When the treasury called in the surety bond to cover the Jones default it discovered that Mr. Smith was equally unable to pay up. His entire assets consisted of a house in Richmond, a few house slaves, three hundred acres of non-income-producing land in Hanover County alleged to be worth $2,500, and an interest in some additional land in Mason County to which Smith's title was in dispute. So much for the assets. Several years earlier Smith had endorsed a friend's note; the friend had died without paying his debt; and now Smith was about to be sued for more than $1,200. What kept Smith afloat? Only his income as a practicing attorney. To make matters even more complicated, George Smith, himself a widower with children, had married the Widow Jones. He now had Meriwether Jones's son, Walter, as well as Meriwether's debts to worry about.

Like his late friend, George W. Smith was a politician; in 1811 he was elected governor of Virginia. Fortunately for the governor, the federal authorities were not pushing recovery on the Jones surety bond vigorously; with sufficiently skillful legal maneuvering Smith might be able to hold them at bay indefinitely. Unfortunately for these hopes, however, Governor Smith was one of the victims of the tragic Richmond theater fire of 26 December 1811.[17] Now the Smith family fortunes were on the rocks, too, for with the governor's death, income from his law practice as well as his salary came to an abrupt end. Things looked grim indeed for widow Lucy Smith. Both Smith and Jones offspring must be provided for; about her only means would be the help she might get from friends and relatives. One group of these got busily to work and arranged a midshipman's appointment for George Smith's son, Richard Lee Smith, but eighteen-year-old Richard found that he needed to pursue some line of work more lucrative than a midshipman's if he was going to help out at home, and he resigned within a few months.[18] Walter Jones was more fortunate. He found patrons who supported him till he finished his education, whereupon he, too, entered the navy as a midshipman under a warrant dated 11 June 1814. Although Walter Jones earned excellent fitness reports and appeared to be headed for a fine future as a naval officer, he elected to resign late in 1821 in order to marry and pursue a none too lucrative attorney's career.[19]

There is no need to pursue the subsequent history of the Jones-Smith financial debacle or the later lives of the three midshipmen, the origins of whose naval careers, brief or extended, were so directly linked to it. The concern here is only to show the shaky financial underpinnings of men who occupied positions as high and as powerful as U.S. commissioner of loans and governor of the State of Virginia. Opportunity to escape from such financially treacherous waters and achieve a reliable, if modest, measure of security could be a powerful motivating force in the choice of a naval career.

Extended Families

Parents, whether secure or financially imperilled, were not the only relatives a midshipman might possess. There could be brothers, sisters, uncles, aunts, brothers-in-law, sisters-in-law, cousins, not to mention more exotic possibilities such as the eighteen-year-old-midshipman with an older nephew already in the navy. The ground of the historian's interest in these relationships is a suspicion— certainly not without solid foundation, as many a page of this book will reveal— that these relatives were looking out for one another's interests in the navy. For the historian with a penchant for the conspiratorial view of history, the navy, and especially its personnel decisions, becomes a puzzle that can be solved only by linking up the kinfolk in and out of uniform.[20]

What a feast such historians can have with Commodore Thomas Tingey, whose life stretched from 11 September 1750 till 23 February 1829. On 30 March 1777 in the island of St. Croix young Captain Tingey, for he was then a master in the merchant service, married twenty-six-year-old Margaret Murdoch of Philadelphia. By this marriage Tingey acquired a brother-in-law, one John Murdoch, a silversmith who died in 1786, leaving a family of six children. Captain Tingey had a knack for making and holding onto money, so it was only to be expected that he would take the fatherless Murdochs under his wing and get them started in life. When he sailed for India in 1795 in command of *Ganges* his ship's company included three Murdoch boys: James as third officer, John as clerk, and William as ordinary seaman. After Tingey received his commission as captain in the navy in 1798 he continued to look out for the Murdochs. James came in as lieutenant and another boy, Joseph, began a midshipman's career under Uncle Tingey in that same *Ganges*, now transformed into the navy's first seagoing warship.

Joseph died in 1802 and Captain Tingey was unable to keep James from being one of the lieutenants discharged in the reduction of 1801, but this was not the end of the Murdoch connection. Margaret (Murdoch) Tingey had an older sister, Mary, who had married one George Beale; the Beales in turn had children, three of whom are of present interest. Mary Beale, the daughter,

Thomas Tingey by C.B.J. Fevret de Saint-Mémin. Icon of a man conscious of his place in the navy, in Washington society, and in his family. Ideally, one's demeanor should correlate well with one's roles. National Portrait Gallery, Washington, D.C.

Tunis Craven, by C.B.J. Fevret de Saint-Mémin. A sensitive and pleasant young man, age about twenty-four; hardly the face of an aggressive businessman equipped to survive in the turbulent economy of the early-nineteenth-century United States. Capable and secure as a federal accountant, Craven discovered the level of his incompetence when he left government service to establish his own business in Alexandria. After the traumas of bankruptcy and loss of a naval pursership when the ink was barely dry on his commission, Craven eventually found financial security through his thirty years' service as naval store-keeper first at Portsmouth, New Hampshire, and later at Brooklyn, New York. National Portrait Gallery, Washington, D.C.

married a Philadelphia sea captain named John Kelly and bore, among other children, John Kelly, Jr., who entered the navy as a midshipman in 1814 with the assistance of his great-uncle, Thomas Tingey. George and Mary (Murdoch) Beale also had sons: George II settled in Norfolk, Virginia, as an auctioneer and had a son, George Beale III, who became a purser in the navy in 1812, presumably with the assistance of his great-uncle. Meanwhile, the younger brother of George Beale II and uncle of George Beale III, one Thomas Tingey Beale, had been appointed a midshipman in 1800, but had resigned three years later.

Thus far the genealogical fun is only beginning! Thomas and Margaret Tingey had children of their own. One of them, Hannah Tingey, married a government-clerk-turned-businessman named Tunis Craven. When Craven's hardware business went bankrupt, taking some of father-in-law Tingey's treasured capital down with the ship, Captain Tingey, who had been superintendent of the Washington navy yard since January 1800, was able to persuade Paul Hamilton that the failed Tunis Craven would make an excellent purser. He was so appointed in August 1812. That was more than William Jones was prepared to swallow; he relieved Craven of his purser's commission in 1813, though Jones was soon thereafter persuaded to allow him to assume the less sensitive post of storekeeper at the Portsmouth, New Hampshire, navy yard. Hannah and Tunis were busy having their own children, two of whom became naval officers and established a service dynasty; but the Craven children's naval careers began after 1815 and are not of immediate concern here. The historian is not yet done with the Cravens. When Tunis's "relation," Ishi (presumably a cousin, but the connection cannot be traced), grew weary of clerking in Tunis's prebankruptcy store, Captain Tingey obligingly helped him secure a midshipman's warrant. Ishi's naval career lasted only a few months in 1809 and ended in an unexplained resignation. One might here pause to recollect that Tunis's uncle, John Craven, held a sensitive and responsible job in the office of the accountant of the navy.

Margaret (Murdoch) Tingey was dead. Her loss, in April 1807, was a severe psychological blow to Captain Tingey, but after five years as a widower, thoughts of remarriage seemed less like desecration of Margaret's memory. The sixty-two-year-old captain took as his second bride Ann Bladen Dulany, twenty-seven, daughter of Alexandria planter and country gentleman Benjamin Tasker Dulany. Commented William Jones to Mrs. Jones: "I have seen Tingey's wife, and she is really a comely, genteel, and youthful woman, while he is a withered, tremulous old man."[21] How had this June–November match come about? The answer is not far to seek: Tingey's daughter, Sarah Ann, had married Ann Dulany's brother, Daniel French Dulany, back in April 1811.

Through his own marriage to Ann Dulany and his daughter's marriage to Ann's brother, Thomas Tingey had acquired a whole flock of additional naval relatives. For one, there was his new brother-in-law, Bladen Dulany, who had become a midshipman in 1809. Then there were the two Forrest lads, Dulany and French, sons of Ann's older sister, Elizabeth, and her none too financially secure husband, Joseph Forrest. Finally, there was yet another Dulany sister, Rebecca, who had married, 7 March 1811, former naval purser Timothy Winn. While documentary evidence is lacking, one strongly suspects the hand of Thomas Tingey in Paul Hamilton's attempt to have Winn named navy agent for the District of Columbia. The navy agent had such a close working relationship with the commandant of the navy yard, including various opportunities for not quite illegal mutual financial advantage, that the proposed appointment was too incestuous for the Senate to swallow. Winn failed to secure the required confirmation, one more casualty of Paul Hamilton's vanishing clout and credibility. He eventually returned to the roll of the navy's pursers in May 1815.

Happiness did not smile on the Thomas Tingey–Ann Dulany marriage. Seventeen months later the bride was dead at the age of twenty-nine. Thomas Tingey was not a man equipped to enjoy the single life. After three years of mourning for his lost Ann, the captain went looking for a new wife, whom he found in the person of his son-in-law's thirty-year-old sister, Ann Evelina Craven. They were married at the Craven family home in Hunterdon County, New Jersey, on 19 May 1817. There Thomas Tingey's genealogical saga ends. He and Ann Evelina had no children. She outlived him many years, dying in the first summer of the Civil War, in which her Craven nephews were to play prominent parts.[22]

Having related this genealogist-boggling maze of intermarriage, the de-mythologizing social historian must rap the table loudly to get everyone's attention and firmly make the point that such tangled webs of relationship were highly *un*typical of the pre-1815 navy. There were, in fact, only two other (and less elaborate) extended kinship networks: the Stockton-Hunter connection and Commodore Samuel Nicholson, his sons, and his nephews. The Nicholsons, though numerous, were for the most part rather marginal naval officers, never truly in the corps' mainstream. Such clans, colorful though they may be, can easily be inflated all out of proportion to their real impact on the life of the navy. What do the records of the 885 midshipmen here tracked show about the role of kinship in building the officer corps?

The key relationship was that of brother to brother. Among the 885 midshipmen no fewer than 101 had one or more brothers who served in the pre-1815 navy. This number almost certainly slightly understates the reality, for there are a small number of cases in which brother relationships can be suspected—the same family name from the same geographical locality—but not proved. (Brothers-in-law were the functional equivalents of brothers in many cases. It has not been possible to obtain an accurate count of the number among the 885 midshipmen who could claim one or two brothers-in-law in the pre-1815 officer corps. Between ten and twenty appears a likely estimate, based on known examples.) By far the most common configuration, 70 out of the 101 cases, was that of two brothers: John and George W. Rodgers, Isaac and Wolcott Chauncey, David and John Porter. The list could be extended, much of it made up of names at least noddingly familiar to anyone with a modest knowledge of U.S. naval history. Not all the brother pairs served simultaneously in the navy. James Bryden, Jr., was appointed a midshipman in 1800 and lost a few weeks later in *Insurgente*; his brother John B. Bryden did not become a midshipman until 1812. Even though such siblings did not always serve simultaneously, it is clear from the surviving documents that a sense of family tradition had been established.

The two-brother pattern had strong, if negative, reinforcement from the Navy Office. "You have already two sons in the navy," Paul Hamilton advised solicitous parent William Caton of Annapolis, "and the applications are very numerous. Hence, I cannot encourage you to expect an appointment for a third son."[23] In spite of this policy, cases of three or more brothers shoehorning their way into the corps of naval officers were far from unknown. Among the 885 midshipmen, 22 had two brothers in the pre-1815 navy, 7 had three brothers, and there are at least 2 instances of five-brother constellations. Oliver Hazard Perry had to work hard to achieve his goal, but he did eventually launch his three brothers—Raymond Henry Jones Perry, Matthew Calbraith Perry, and James Alexander Perry—on successful naval careers.[24] Knowledge of kinship is vital to this degree: brothers absolutely did help brothers. Here is the same Oliver Hazard Perry writing from Norwalk, Connecticut, to David Porter in early December 1814:

> I have met my brother [Lieutenant Raymond H.J. Perry] thus far on his way to New York in consequence of my letter requesting him to come on. The secretary's [William Jones's] conduct in respect to our brothers appears to be strange. If you will get your brother [Lieutenant John Porter] clear from [Isaac] Chauncey, I will give him one of my five vessels and, should you not go out yourself, if you see no impropriety, I beg you will do something of the kind for mine.[25]

Seventeen of the 885 midshipmen were the sons of serving or former officers in the U.S. Navy. To these seventeen father-son combinations should be added the twenty midshipmen who had one or more uncles in the navy, for uncles were as active and effective in promoting the careers of nephews as fathers were in working for their sons. Although Charles Morris was the son of one navy purser, it was his uncle, Purser Noadiah Morris, who did the most to help him make his way in the navy.[26] In this case their respective ages made Noadiah (ten years the elder) and Charles, Jr., more like an older brother–younger brother team than uncle-nephew.

Beyond the brothers and the brothers-in-law, the fathers and the sons, the uncles and the nephews, there is little, if any, evidence that other relationships had much bearing on naval careers. Cousins were far less common than the mythology would lead one to suppose. Although some naval cousins have certainly eluded the present historian, only 34 of the 885 midshipmen here tracked could count one or more cousins in the navy's corps of officers. More to the point, officers did not seem to spend much effort looking out for cousins. Such energy was husbanded for closer relatives. The level of concern a naval officer manifested over cousinage was perhaps most neatly captured in Charles Gordon's offhand remark at the end of a highly critical word-portrait of Commodore Alexander Murray: "He is a cousin of mine, I believe."[27] So much for cousins!

8. School

*N*OTHING ABOUT THE navy's midshipmen is so poorly recorded as their prenaval education. To investigate the 885 young men whose backgrounds are here being tracked is to discover that for only one among nine of them has any educational information—from the vaguest to the most specific—been found, either in the navy's records or in other sources. Because most U.S. colleges whose history extends back to the late eighteenth or early nineteenth century have compiled lists of their alumni, much of the knowledge that can be gleaned on the prenaval education of midshipmen is heavily slanted in favor of college attendees, a group who were a small minority of the corps. For education below the collegiate level, enrollment records are far less accessible than for college attendance. Archives, such as they may have been, of too many of the institutions that taught these young men have vanished along with the institutions themselves.[1] The navy, its officer-selection process, and the papers created by that selection process were little concerned with the specifics of schooling. While a rare recommender might supply precise details about educational attainment, most were content with general statements. Would-be midshipman Harrison Henry Cocke "has had a pretty good English education and perhaps a little smattering of Latin." Seventeen-year-old Joshua Sands is "a youth of a very liberal education."[2]

Is there a way, other than drawing possibly misleading conclusions from the experiences of an atypical minority of college-educated midshipmen, to learn something of the kinds of schooling young men brought to their naval careers? There is, and one discovers thereby that the seemingly vague statements of the recommenders actually encode specific information about the educational attainments of the young men recommended. Historian Lawrence Cremin's investigation of the American educational experience provides a useful framework on which one can position the references to formal education scattered among the navy's appointment dossiers and recombine those fragments into a consistent whole.[3] For Cremin the concept of education is broader than mere time spent in school. Rather, it is "the deliberate, systematic, and sustained effort to transmit or evoke knowledge, attitudes, values, skills, and sensibilities."[4] During the years in which the pre-1815 officer corps was formed, Cremin discovers this effort being carried out by four institutions: the family, the church, the school and college, and the newspaper. What contribution families, churches, or newspapers made to the education of future naval officers passes unrecorded in the sources on which this book is based. To pursue these themes would lead into the realm of speculative inference, an endeavor inappropriate to a history that aims to reconstruct a lost world insofar as that world can be known from surviving factual data. Under the remaining rubric—formal education—Cremin identifies four classes of schools that bear on the prenaval education of future officers.

The English school was the most basic. Customarily a single building with a single teacher, the English school enrolled students ranging between two or three and fourteen years of age. Here the future naval officer and his male and female peers learned reading, spelling, penmanship, grammar, basic composition, arithmetic, geography, and history. Many a dreary hour was spent practicing the Italian cursive script in which the hundreds of thousands of pages of surviving naval records are written, though for some naval officers, Jesse D. Elliott and David Porter being flagrant examples, handwriting degeneration seems to have set in almost as soon as they left the shadow of the schoolhouse for the last time. Even if nowhere explicitly stated, it is clear that the completion of English school was a universally accepted minimum requirement for appointment as a midshipman. When former secretary of war Henry Dearborn sought (successfully) to have his none too promising grandson, George Hobart, then serving as an ordinary seaman in *Constitution*, promoted to midshipman, Hobart's commanding officer, Charles Stewart, reported that the young man had "received a plain English education." Stewart thereby signaled to the Navy Office that Mr. Hobart just met the minimum educational requirement for the requested promotion.[5] If a young man did not know how to read fluently, to write legibly, grammatically, and with a certain style, and to perform basic arithmetic calculations, and did not possess at least the foundation of general culture, there was no place for him in the navy. Midshipman John Homer More is "very smart in his duty on board ship," reported Lieutenant Arthur Sinclair, "but he has been sent to sea too young (and at first as a servant boy), which has deprived him of an opportunity to acquire an education and the dignity necessary to make a good officer." If More was to continue his naval career, said Sinclair, further education was absolutely essential.[6]

The Latin grammar school built on the work begun by the English school. Boys generally enrolled in a Latin school at nine or ten years of age and pursued the course of study there for perhaps four or five years. To enroll in a Latin school the student would be expected to read and write English and to possess some knowledge of English grammar. With this foundation assumed, the Latin school concentrated on building basic skills in Latin and Greek, supplemented by work in history, geography, and mathematics. Geometry, algebra, and trigonometry were the branches of mathematics that the student was expected to master in the Latin school. Except in the case of the Boston Public Latin School, some nineteen or so of whose alumni served in the pre-1815 navy at one or another officer rank, the surviving records contain scarcely any direct references to attendance at Latin schools by future midshipmen. There is ample indirect evidence that many of them must have done so. Admission to a college demanded the ability to pass examinations in basic Latin and Greek. Any midshipman who attended a college, however briefly, necessarily must have pursued his prior education through the equivalent of a Latin school. (This easy assumption is, as will be seen in a moment, complicated by the existence of another, somewhat parallel, type of educational institution.) When Boston ship chandler Nathaniel Thayer applied for a midshipman's warrant for his son, fifteen-year-old Edward Niles, and reported that "he has been educated for the University at Cambridge [i.e., Harvard, but] he declines going through the college and has a disposition for the navy," young Thayer's general level of educational attainment would have been clear to the secretary of the navy: the basics of Latin and Greek, history, geography, and mathematics, as well as a strong command of English language and composition.[7] He was, in fact, a product of Boston's Public Latin School. The same assumption would have been made about any midshipman applicant whose sponsors asserted that he had been "fitted to enter college."[8]

If, unlike Edward Niles Thayer, the future midshipman did actually enter college, he faced an arduous four-year curriculum that included intensive and extensive mastery of Greek and Latin; courses in rhetoric and oratory; higher mathematics, including its practical application to navigation; physics, astronomy, and perhaps other natural sciences; logic, moral philosophy, and theology. Future naval officers attended colleges that extended from lately established Bowdoin and comparatively ancient Harvard in Massachusetts, through Brown in Rhode Island, Yale in Connecticut, Columbia and Union in New York, Princeton's College of New Jersey, the University of Pennsylvania at Philadelphia and Dickinson at Carlisle (Pennsylvania), St. Mary's at Baltimore and St. John's at Annapolis (Maryland), century-old William and Mary in Virginia, and North Carolina's new state-sponsored university, to Cumberland College (Tennessee) and Transylvania (Kentucky) beyond the mountains.[9]

It would be a mistake to assume that all college educations were equal or even that the phrase *college-educated* always represented a closely similar educational attainment. Harvard, Yale, or the College of New Jersey offered highly structured four-year programs culminating in the award of the bachelor of arts degree. Williamsburg's College of William and Mary, alma mater of Lewis Warrington, Arthur Sinclair, and other prominent and obscure naval officers, gave a strong education, but did not have a structured program leading to a degree; the collegian studied until he and his professors judged him prepared to enter a profession or a career. One would be hard-put to measure the quality gap that must have existed between an education at well-established Harvard and at Tennessee's shaky Cumberland College; one would be naive to suppose the gap did not exist. Georgetown in the District of Columbia and St. Mary's in Baltimore, though commonly referred to as colleges and counting significant numbers of future midshipmen among their students, did not offer a structured four-year course of study leading to the bachelor's degree. As institutions, they ought perhaps to be classed with the academies, a breed of which more will be said shortly. This is not to denigrate them. St. Mary's especially enjoyed an enviable academic reputation and attracted many students, such as the two sons of Commodore Richard Dale, whose families had no affiliation with the Roman Catholic Church but chose St. Mary's for its strong educational program.

A minuscule number of naval officers of the 1794–1815 years pursued a college education far enough to earn a diploma. Of the 885 midshipmen whose prenaval careers are here surveyed, only 6 held the bachelor's degree. Even if one includes the self-styled colleges that might better be counted as academies, the number of future naval officers who had enrolled at one time or another in a college was perhaps eight or nine times the number of college graduates. Here was the crux of the matter: the navy was seen as a career for which a completed college education was not considered necessary or perhaps even desirable. Not every bright young man was equipped with the temperament necessary to become a scholar; even when he had the intellectual capacity to achieve a classical education, the tolerance for tedium and sedentary discipline needed to survive the four-year process might not be present. If a future midshipman actually entered college, he or his parents sooner or later concluded that a more active career option might be the wiser choice. "When the Tripolitan War broke out I panted to assist in setting my countrymen free and accordingly sacrificed my education at Dickinson College when having nearly completed my studies," was the way former midshipman Robert Smith Steele chose to remember, eight and a half years after the fact, his decision to leave college.[10] However much Steele and others like him may have wished to think they had nipped opportunities in the bud through selfless sacrifice for the nation, the reality was that an action-oriented career had seemed much more attractive than continued enrollment in college. The important thing was to get one's start in a profession that might support one for life. With the right prospects in view, additional schooling could be sacrificed. As soon as the future captain Arthur Sinclair's family thought they had the promise of a midshipman's appointment for him in the newly formed navy, "I was immediately taken from college [at William and Mary] and put on board a London trader in order to qualify for the naval service."[11]

One would be incorrect in assuming from all this college leaving and college avoidance that naval officers were poor students, underequipped in their general cultural attainments, and shunted into careers at sea because they lacked what it took to make good on land. In the pre-1815 United States true colleges educated only a tiny minority of the American population. No particular handicap or stigma attached to the lack of a college degree; the highest ranks of society could be attained without one, while the possession of a college education was no guarantee of respect, financial security, or more than just-get-by competence in one's later career.[12] Most of the navy's officers, like most of their fellow citizens whose jobs and places in society demanded skills that a classroom education conferred, were the products of a different type of school from the college, a type that had its heyday in the eighteenth and nineteenth centuries.

It is comfortable to think of the progression English school to Latin school to college, because it appears to correspond to a familiar sequence: elementary school, high school, college. It is also sadly misleading, for education in the pre-1815 United States was hardly that structured and tidy. In fact, the English-Latin-college sequence was experienced by only a small minority of the school-educated. Paralleling this idealized track, and serving the greatest part of the nation's advanced education needs, was a fourth type of school, the academy.[13] No scholar has yet succeeded in producing a neat, clear definition of an academy. The curriculum therein covered might range from the upper end of the one appropriate to the English school, through that of the Latin school, and overlap in part with the subject matter taught in the four-year, degree-granting college. Corresponding to the wide net cast by the curricular offerings was the age range of students enrolled at any one time. At New Hampshire's

Phillips Exeter, where at least 4 of the 885 midshipmen obtained their educations, the age spread of currently enrolled students in the year 1812 was ten to twenty-eight. Just as alien to a later mindset was the wildly erratic pattern of enrollment; students did not necessarily arrive at the same time and proceed together through something labeled an academic year. There was a slow but continual turnover in the student body. Neither was it at all uncommon for a student to quit the academy to work for a season, then return for another short, intensive spell of schooling. A student or his parents called an academy education complete when the student had acquired the knowledge needed to pass the entrance examination for college or to commence a career—or when the money ran out. Nothing better illustrates the sporadic, wandering character of an academy education than this brief passage in a nearly contemporary biographical sketch of Lieutenant William Howard Allen, who was born, 8 July 1790, at Hudson, New York, son of a master in the merchant service:

> For a year and a half preceding February 1798 he was at a boarding school in London. On returning home, his studies were continued in his native city until the fall of 1800, when he sailed for Calcutta. At the end of a year he resumed his studies again and pursued them in the academy at Hudson and at Williamstown College, down to May 1805. At this time his family removed to the state of Pennsylvania for a short period, and he was sent to Doylestown College where he remained until the fall of 1807, when he again went to sea. . . . He received a midshipman's warrant in January 1808.[14]

Most academies were small operations, a detached building or even a single room, with a master and perhaps one or more assistants. Typically the impetus for an academy's creation was local: a population concentration, even in near-frontier areas, with a desire to provide for the higher schooling of at least its elite male children. Once established, some academies became magnets, attracting students from a distance who boarded in local homes while in attendance. Future midshipman Henry Wadsworth, a native son of Portland, in the District of Maine, attended Phillips Exeter in New Hampshire. Others stayed close to home. Midshipman Joel Abbot, born and raised in Westford, Massachusetts, received his final prenaval education at the local Westford Academy. Some of the academies at which future naval officers were educated have survived as well-known private schools: Phillips Exeter, Governor Dummer. A few— Washington Academy in Lexington, Virginia, for one—academies when they educated pre-1815 midshipmen, would evolve into degree-granting colleges. Most—like Forest Hill Academy in Jessamine County, Kentucky, where at least 3 of the 885 midshipmen obtained their final educations and which was essentially a high-quality private school run by Samuel Wilson at his home— have long since vanished.

"Perhaps the most that can be said of any given academy is that it offered what its master was prepared to teach, or what its students were prepared to learn, or what its sponsors were prepared to support, or some combination or compromise among the three," writes Cremin.[15] The quality of the education offered must have varied spectacularly from the best academies to the weakest. But, one-man shows that they were, even the most evanescent of these academies could, and many assuredly did, offer excellent education when the master was a well-trained, highly motivated, and skillful teacher. What was the specific content of that education? How were teaching and learning experienced? These are the hardest questions to answer, owing to scanty sources. At the more rigorous academies, those that saw their primary mission as college preparation or grooming for one of the learned professions, the structured curriculum customarily embraced the Latin, Greek, and French languages; English grammar, composition, and rhetoric; history, with emphasis on Greece and Rome, as well as ancient and modern geography; arithmetic and geometry, often algebra and trigonometry; astronomy and an introduction to the physical sciences. Such was certainly the curriculum pursued by a Henry Wadsworth at Phillips Exeter or a Melancthon Woolsey at Flatbush, one that equipped the latter midshipman with a passable knowledge of conversational French. At academies where college preparation was not the chief business, emphasis shifted toward the English language as a written and spoken medium and to the applied aspects of mathematics and science, whether they were bookkeeping, navigation, or surveying. Typical, perhaps, of study at the latter sort of academy was the experience of Midshipman Thomas Henry Bowyer of Fincastle, Virginia, who wrote from Lexington in January 1812 to advise Secretary Hamilton that he had received his warrant, but requested that a few weeks might elapse before he was called to active duty: "Having heretofore entered as a student at the Washington Academy for the present session and being now engaged in the study of navigation and the French language, I could wish to remain and pursue those studies."[16] At either end of the spectrum the business of the academy was the mastery of basics. Teaching methods emphasized the acquisition of mental self-discipline through the commitment to memory of rules and texts and the demonstration of their mastery in recitation. Intellectual curiosity and independent study were nourished as well, most particularly by autonomous student debating and literary societies. These existed alongside the formal curriculum, supplementing it by providing forums in which the students explored texts and topics of contemporary literary and political interest. All that said, pitifully little is known about the subjects or the methods—about the business of teaching and learning—of the nation's pre-1815 academies, most especially of the life that a charismatic teacher could impart to the most abstractly forbidding of subjects.

For future midshipmen, as for almost all pre-1815 Americans who called themselves educated or were by others labeled as educated, academy instruction was the terminal experience of formal schooling. Academy educations of only a handful of individuals (18 out of 885) have been traced to specific institutions. If one can no longer identify the academies where the great majority of midshipmen obtained this terminal schooling, one can assess the results. True, the navy had its problems with badly educated and undereducated midshipmen, such as John Homer More, not to mention those who were just plain ignorant. In fact, however, the badly educated call attention to themselves because they stand out from the crowd. It is easy to be snide about both the pedagogy and the content of education in the pre-1815 years: the emphasis on drill, memorization, recitation; the classical languages; the seemingly skimpy attention to physical science. Look, instead, at the results. What impresses the historian, and what can be verified by the thousands of quoted words in the pages of this book, is that young men whose highest formal schooling was an academy or a brief exposure to college were, as a body, able to write English prose (and occasionally poetry) clearly, correctly, readably, and often with eloquence. Let the private diaries of Melancthon T. Woolsey or Henry Wadsworth or William

Boerum stand as a measure of what could be attained through an excellent academy education. Strong foundations in history, geography, and the classics enabled naval officers to travel the world, informed about what they were seeing and recording their observations in diaries, letters home, and formal publications.[17] Most of all these prenaval educations had been successful because, while they had equipped their subjects with the tools for the future, they had also left the better of them with an awareness that education was never complete; that curiosity, reading, careful observation, and written reflection were an integral part of an entire active lifetime.

9. Work

ISCOVERY THAT one-third of all newly appointed midshipmen were nineteen or older aroused the suspicion that a substantial number of them may have tried other careers before turning to the navy. The suspicion is reinforced by the widespread practice, just mentioned in the story of William Howard Allen's schooling, of interspersing education with work. Unfortunately, the illumination shed by the navy's records is only partial. One cannot be sure what is lost in the shadows. Among the 885 midshipmen whose backgrounds are under examination, evidence can be uncovered for earlier work experiences for 155. This is a number about which it is wise to be cautious. Just because the records are silent about possible prenaval work experience by the other 730 midshipmen, it does not necessarily follow that they lacked such experience. Here is what history knows about the premidshipman work experience of 155 young men—that is all one can say with conviction. Even this information is probably distorted by an unavoidable bias. Recommenders and applicants were most likely to mention work experience at sea, however brief, in the hope that it might give the application a competitive edge; there was no such self-serving motivation to mention an abortive career start as a law student or a merchant's clerk.

Working by Land

Ten of the 155 had begun studying for admission to one of the learned professions. Two had stuck a toe in the waters of medicine; a like number had commenced professional apprenticeship study in architecture. More common among future midshipmen was the study of the law, an endeavor that six young men said they had tried and rejected. No great significance should be attached to these numbers. Certain it is that many others among the 885 must have explored—or been encouraged by parents to explore—these career paths. The important thing was the exploration and the rejection. Perhaps it was a case of the mentor advising the pupil to look for a different line of work better suited to his native abilities; possibly it was the student deciding he really did not like either study or the subject. Thomas Russell Gerry, son of Elbridge Gerry, vice-president of the United States, graduated from Harvard in 1814 and immediately began to study law in the office of his brother-in-law, James T. Austin. When Vice-President Gerry died in late November 1814 his son was almost immediately awarded a midshipman's warrant. Had his father's death deprived Thomas of the financial means to continue his legal studies? Possibly. But some way of going ahead might have been found. The speed with which the warrant was issued suggests that entering the navy was a long-harbored ambition—this was, after all, the middle of the War of 1812—an ambition previously thwarted by a father's wishes for a son's career.[1]

William Lewis, from Fredericksburg, Virginia, began the study of medicine, then allowed "a little incident, trifling in itself," to turn him against the healer's profession. Next he turned his hand to law, only to discover he liked that career no better. Finally he sought and obtained a midshipman's warrant (August 1802) and settled at last into a profession that he was to pursue with notable success until he was lost at sea in August 1815. William Lewis had few illusions about himself; neither did he excuse what he saw when he looked inward. "My dear Aunt," he wrote when he was a little more than a year into his new naval career:

> You know the fruitless attempts I have made at acquiring a profession which would have subsisted me in the world. The time I lost in making those attempts had nearly ruined me, by leaving me in the prime of life without a source of future maintenance and with habits of indolence almost confirmed on me. I deem it the most fortunate circumstance in my life that I obtained a situation in the navy, which would have been still more fortunate if it had happened at an earlier time. It will be the means of forcing a profession on me, for I fear I never should acquire one if left to myself. I possess a fickleness of disposition which would always be an effectual bar to a steady pursuit of any object, provided the regulation of my time was left in my own direction. As it is, I am obliged to conform to the orders and rules of the service, in doing which I shall, of course, acquire a knowledge of seamanship and naval tactics sufficient to insure my promotion. In that event, my fortune is made.[2]

For how many naval officers, less introspective or less articulate, did William Lewis speak?

Nine midshipmen reported that they had been trained in business. By this they meant that they had entered a merchant's countinghouse where they learned to copy important letters and draft routine ones, draw up invoices and accounts current, master the intricacies of bookkeeping and exchange rates among currencies. These skills well honed, they would be ready for their first ventures as supercargoes in one of the merchant's trading vessels. It is hard to know where to draw the line between the nine who said they had been trained for business and the six who reported being clerks in stores before electing a naval life. The frontier was so obscure as to be largely a question of which terminology one elected to use. Reasons why the business career was abandoned for the navy probably ranged all the way from Overton Carr's, who had completed his training and was prepared to set out on his own but could not pull together the capital for a start, to Richard Brashears's, who simply grew tired of clerking in a store.[3]

One group of midshipmen about whom less is known than one could wish were those whose initial training had pointed them toward careers as skilled artisans or master craftsmen. Evidence has been found of only five with this specialized training. But, because master craftsmen were well represented among the fathers of midshipmen, more of the future naval officers than can now be identified must have received training as manual workers. Joseph Smith's father was a shipwright; the young admiral-to-be had learned the basics of his parent's trade. Winlock Clark of Dover, Delaware, mastered the tanner's art before he decided to pursue a military commission. An army appointment eluded him, just possibly because of his craftsman training.[4] Clark was more successful with his naval application. He had risen as far as lieutenant when he drowned at the age of thirty-one. Twenty-four-year-old William H. Mott of Georgetown, D.C., began his working life as a coach painter. Lured away from paint and coach bodies by the appeal of the sea, he made two or three voyages in the merchant service, then decided to seek a career in the navy. Through the support of several of Georgetown's master craftsmen, Mott was able to meet Georgetown worthy and prominent Republican John Mason of Analostan Island; Mason in turn presented Mott to Paul Hamilton, who granted the ex-painter a warrant the same day. Although Mott had one brief spell of disciplinary difficulty, he made lieutenant in normal progression—about six years—and remained in the navy till his death in 1823.[5]

What is notable is that in every case in which the historian can identify a midshipman who began his working life with the intention of becoming a master craftsman, that midshipman had a successful naval career and remained an officer until death. It was a rate of professional survival most atypical of the corps as a whole. One suspects these former craftsmen entered the navy both with greater maturity than the average midshipman and with a self-disciplined determination to improve their status, or, as they would have put it, to rise in the world.

Working by Sea

Status is largely in the eyes of the beholder. The social gradation between an established master craftsman on land and the typical master or mate in the merchant service was so indistinct as to be almost impossible to define. In a typical workday both of them got their hands dirty. Far and away the most common work experience claimed by entering midshipmen—90 out of the 155—was in the merchant service. Even admitting that there were self-interested reasons for midshipman applicants to emphasize sea backgrounds in preference to other types of work, the geographical and social roots of the corps predict that for those midshipmen with previous work experience, the merchant service would constitute the greatest part of that experience. It might be a single voyage to the coast of Brazil, on to Calcutta, and back home again, as was reported by Seth B. Alby when he sought a midshipman's warrant. Or it might be the eight years in the merchant service, "mostly on South Sea voyages," claimed by Alexander B. Pinkham.[6] Desirable as it would be to summarize this merchant service in statistical language—to say that this percentage of the midshipmen had more than this many years of service at sea before they joined the navy—it cannot be done. While some midshipmen's self-reports are explicit in this regard, many others are too vague—"several voyages," "considerable" experience at sea—to admit of reduction to numbers. Moreover, because previous sea service was perceived as lending weight to one's application, there was a natural tendency to inflate truth to its limits. Twenty-five months at sea could be called "between two and three years."

Even allowing for this, the historian still must be impressed by the amount and the quality of the previous sea experience that those entering midshipmen who had been at sea at all brought with them to the navy. There were successful naval officers who had never spent a day at sea before they received their midshipman warrants; but green hands among the midshipmen may have seized a larger place in the historian's imagination than they occupied in life. As novices to the sea they were the young men most likely to maintain the diaries and write the detailed letters home through which the historian recaptures the experience of being a midshipman. Among the ninety midshipmen with merchant service experience, at least thirteen had been at sea long enough and were sufficiently well trained to have served as mates, that is, to have had the responsibility of commanding a watch at sea; two more had even held the ultimate responsibility of master. The greatest number, however, were something better than landsmen, but not yet skillful enough to be mates.

What was the quality of the experience that these future midshipmen gained in the merchant service? It has become fashionable for historians to see the pre-1815 American maritime world as the mirror of a stratified Anglo-American society. In this vision ships' crews were seagoing proletarians, trapped by economic exploitation in their roles as deckhands. Among their ranks— slumming, so to speak—were a select cadre from higher social origins. These latter were only gaining some hands-on experience before moving to the quarterdeck and a mate's cabin, advancement that was off-limits to the mass of workaday mariners. There is some truth here; when a young man's parents apprenticed him to a merchant captain, it was with the expectation that he would gain the skills needed one day to command a ship. But the sharply defined status categories imagined by some historians seem hardly to have been as rigid as they propose. Like many another naval officer, Captain Robert T. Spence was proud to point out that he had entered seafaring life through the hawseholes, not through the cabin windows.[7] What he and his peers meant was that they gained their experience at sea exactly as did any other working mariner: living in the forecastle; eating the less than appealing food; learning the basics of survival at sea; going aloft under the best and the worst of conditions; exposing oneself to precisely the same dangers of injury or death. From a distance it may appear easy to draw the hard-to-cross status line in the seagoing community; but to the historian who examines seafaring at the level of individual lives, the merchant service seems an opportunity-laden and democratic, if never an egalitarian, world. There is so much upward and downward mobility across the supposed frontier of status separation that eventually one loses track of the line entirely.

As for the specifics of life before the mast, one may let the experiences of sixteen-year-old John Kelly, Jr., of Philadelphia, son of a retired-merchant-captain-turned-grocer and grandnephew of Captain Thomas Tingey, stand for all of them. Young Kelly's initiation was more dramatic than some, but it was in no way untypical of others nearly as well recorded: "Thanks to the Almighty I have the pleasure of informing you of the arrival of Captain Samuel Murdoch and my John, whose first essay on the watery element has been attended with nearly all the vicissitudes incidental to a seafaring life," the elder Kelly wrote Tingey in mid-December 1812.

On the passage out he fell from the topgallant crosstrees overboard, the ship going between four and six knots, and was far astern before discovered; in about fifteen or twenty minutes [he] was picked up by the stern boat, perfectly collected. Then, homeward bound, [he was] cast away in the Straits of Sunda and robbed and plundered of every article that was worth taking by the crew of the ship of war that gave them assistance and who carried them to Batavia, and was at last impressed, with the whole of the crew, on board the British frigate Cornelia, although the commander had given his word of honor not to molest them, and with much reluctance gave up John after three days' detention. He had two severe spells of fever while at Batavia, but at last got a passage from there in a country ship to Madras, from there to Iseopaly, a port on the coast, to load salt, and from there to Calicuta, where they fortunately met the ship Francis, Captain Haskill, of Salem, just ready for sea [and] bound to Pernambuco, who in the most friendly manner gave them a passage. When they arrived [at Pernambuco] the prospect was still gloomy, as the ship was to wait for orders; but luckily the brig Squirrel . . . sent out . . . to Rio de Janeiro to stop the sailing of the Atalanta of this port [because of the declaration of war] arrived to repair the copper on her bottom. The acquaintance between Captain Murdoch and [the captain of the *Squirrel*] put an end to their peregrination, and they unexpectedly arrived the 8th instant in perfect health.

I had some hopes that so many unlucky accidents that occurred during this voyage would induce John to give up a seafaring life, but in this I am mistaken. He still perseveres but has changed ground. He now wishes to get in the navy and argues thus: If he goes in the merchant service, [he] is liable to be captured, when a prison or prison ship will be his lot—or probably may be detained on board their ships of war. Rather than encounter any of these risks, he prefers his country's service. I now, my friend, request of you to use your influence in getting him a midshipman's station in our service.

John Kelly was a young man who had a clear idea of what he wanted from life. Even with Tingey's powerful assistance he had to wait till 1814 to receive his warrant, but once in the navy he stuck to his career, eventually reaching the rank of captain. Without doubt Captain Murdoch had showed a special concern for Kelly, securing his release from *Cornelia* and keeping him with him all the way home to Philadelphia, through multiple adventures, while the balance of the ship's company seem to have been left to shift for themselves. Evidence of special status for John Kelly? Absolutely, but not one deriving from his father's place in the social order. Samuel Murdoch was the first cousin once removed of John Kelly, Jr., not to mention the fact that Samuel's brother James (a former naval lieutenant) was married to the young Kelly's sister Maria. Captain Murdoch was looking out for a relative.[8]

More remains to be said on the question of rigid classes in pre-1815 U.S. society versus opportunities for social mobility, but before doing so one should note another aspect of young John Kelly's adventures: his brief impressment in *Cornelia*. Among the ninety future midshipmen who reported work experience in the merchant service, eight said they had been impressed at some point in their merchant careers. Twenty-one-year-old Samuel Wardwell Adams from Bristol, Rhode Island, was "impressed several years since into the British service, where he remained three years, in which time he was advanced to the berth of acting midshipman." Lewis Edwards Simonds, weary of training to be an apothecary, "took a fancy to follow the sea" and, in the capacity of an ordinary seaman, sailed to various ports in Europe and Latin America until he fell foul of first Spanish and then British impressment. From the latter he was finally able to escape and make his way back to the United States, where he promptly put his family and his family's friends to work securing him a midshipman's warrant.[9]

Concerning these eight impressed Americans who subsequently became naval officers, two points are noteworthy. First, a man such as Samuel Wardwell Adams, who entered the U.S. Navy's officer corps with three years' experience in the British force, part of them as an acting midshipman, had an immense advantage over his peers fresh from school or the merchant service. In Adams's case this experience was reflected both in his favorable fitness reports and in his early promotion to acting lieutenant.[10] The second point to note are the numbers: eight men impressed into the British navy out of ninety with merchant service experience. Fewer than one man in ten. There is every reason to believe that this proportion is reasonably accurate. Any would-be midshipman who had been impressed had good reasons to mention it. There was not only the job-related-experience factor, but the sympathy factor as well. One was entitled to some preferential consideration because one had been held hostage to arrogant British seapower. The figure, eight men with records of impressment out of ninety, agrees reasonably well with the evidence compiled by James F. Zimmerman, the scholar who gave the question of the numbers of American mariners impressed into the British navy the most careful study. Although accurate estimates are extremely difficult to make, it appears that something on the order of ten thousand American mariners experienced impressment, a number substantially less than 10 percent of the American maritime workforce during these same years.[11] Apart from this independent confirmation of Zimmerman's conclusions, the numbers—eight out of ninety—remind us that, on the question of impressment, as with many a problem that becomes an emotional political issue, a realistic appraisal of the quantitative dimensions of the problem is among the first casualties. Even so well-informed a naval officer as Stephen Decatur could assert, "It is a well-known fact, Sir, that a vast majority of our seamen have, at some period of their lives, been impressed into the British service."[12] All reliable data establish that Captain Decatur's rhetoric had gotten way ahead of the facts, but he only reflected the mood of a nation too caught up in the emotions generated by the issue to be concerned with rational analysis.

Not included among the ninety future midshipmen with experience in the merchant service are the thirty-three who entered the navy at another rank and had, in effect, been promoted to midshipman. One group among them were the nine young men who began their naval careers as captain's clerks. A ship's commanding officer was free to pick whomever he wished for this post. Clerks came from exactly the same backgrounds as the mass of midshipmen. They had received good academy educations or perhaps some college training, possessed superior skills at penmanship and possibly a little basic bookkeeping picked up in a countinghouse. Some may have been disappointed applicants for a midshipman's warrant. On shipboard the clerks were expected to copy the captain's letters neatly, prepare other routine paperwork, and keep the captain's books up to date. Not even the most elaborate efforts at artistic penmanship, of which some striking examples survive, could turn this into full-time duty. The captain's clerk lived with the midshipmen. Sooner or later boredom and ambition prompted him to request permission to stand a watch with his midshipman peers, an idea that the commanding officer usually encouraged. If experience proved that the captain's clerk made a good midshipman, his commanding officer normally had little trouble in persuading the Navy Office to grant him a warrant.

More engrossing to the historian are the ten midshipmen who entered the navy at one of the enlisted ranks; these reopen the question of upward mobility from humble social origins to the higher-status profession of naval officer. If one is looking for evidence of such mobility, the results are disappointing. The ten are a mixed bag. At least four of them are clearly young men from reasonably elite origins who had run away to sea. Edward Carter, son of Nathaniel Carter, Jr., merchant of Newburyport, Massachusetts, had been serving as a seaman in the frigate *United States* since February 1810, much of that time as captain of the mizzen top. Why Edward had left home to become a before-the-mast sailor is unrecorded, but the event must have occurred in his early or middle teens, for he was rated seaman, indicating significant skill and experience, when he joined *United States* at the age of eighteen. Apparently the Carter family was not a little embarrassed at the sailor's career in which Edward seems to have taken considerable pride. His uncle, New Hampshire's Federalist senator Charles Cutts, badgered Paul Hamilton to grant a midshipman's warrant to the nephew, a request that was eventually granted, though perhaps with a certain reluctance. What kind of an officer Edward Carter might have made can never be known. He died at the naval hospital in New York about a month after his twenty-first birthday and before he had the chance to serve under his new midshipman's warrant.[13]

With the possible exception of one or two among the ten whose origins are totally obscure, none of the officers who began as enlisted men can be traced to especially humble social beginnings. Even so, having entered the navy as an enlisted man was not an auspicious beginning for a midshipman's career. Only three of the ten were successful officers. The remaining seven either soon died or were quickly eased out of the corps. Did entering the navy as an enlisted man handicap a midshipman, however respectable his social origins? It certainly appears that such may have been the case if John Homer More, one of the seven career casualties, and whose story was related in the last chapter, is any test. There the stigma of going to sea young in a menial capacity and the consequent lack of adequate education had combined to drive More from the navy.

Searching for evidence of upward social mobility among those midshipmen who began their naval lives as enlisted men is probably looking in the wrong place. A better hunting ground is among the twelve midshipmen who entered the navy at the rank of master's mate, a hazy status zone between officer and enlisted ranks. Legally master's mates were petty officers who assisted a ship's sailing master in his duties, but several career paths crisscrossed through this usefully vague terrain. The most experienced midshipmen were often made master's mates to hone their skills in preparation for acting lieutenancies. Other master's mates who were not midshipmen may have signed on in that capacity with the hope of promotion to sailing master, a not uncommon career pattern. Most significantly, master's mates could be promoted from among the ship's enlisted ranks; once the mate's rating was secured, the master's warrant was no impossible dream. Improving one's status in life is usually, and most successfully, a gradual process, not one grand leap. It looks as if the master's mate rating might have been the best back door to officer status.

What of the twelve midshipmen who came into the navy via this berth? All of them arrived as experienced seamen, some with a great deal of experience. James Terry, twenty-one years old and a native of New York State, reported "having been bred to a nautical life from my early youth and served in every capacity except master in the merchant service. I embraced the earliest opportunity to enter the navy," as master's mate in *Essex* on 25 September 1812, "when, by a declaration of war, there was a field to assert the abused rights of American seamen." Twenty-four-year-old John Greaton, appointed a master's mate in *President* on 4 December 1813, summarized his qualifications: "I have led a seafaring life for nearly eight years, six of which I have been chief mate of various vessels out of Boston, until the declaration [of] war, [when] I was hove out of that employ." But Jacob E. Gilmeyer of Maryland could claim only a more modest record—three years in the merchant service—when he entered as master's mate in *Constellation* in September 1812, just short of his twentieth birthday.[14] Three of the master's mates owed their promotions to midshipman to good conduct in battle: Hugh Sweeny and James Conner for 1812's *Wasp-Frolic* encounter and Joshua H. Justin via his performance under Thomas Macdonough's own eye at the battle of Lake Champlain in 1814. It is perhaps significant that Conner, a twenty-year-old Philadelphia County native who had been third officer of the ship *Dorothea* before the war, had sought unsuccessfully to enter the navy as a midshipman. Failing in that attempt, he took the master's mate route and received his warrant only because Jacob Jones spoke up for him after the battle.[15]

Lending credence to the idea that these master's mates who became midshipmen may have come from modest origins and were seeking to reach a higher rung on the social ladder is the fact that in only two of the twelve cases has the identity of their parents been discovered. In both of those instances the father was no more elevated in status than master in the merchant service. This is not to suggest that any of the twelve came from the very lowest rungs of the social ladder; so great a climb would have been unrealistic. But the clues certainly point to men bent on self-improvement. Whatever their ambitions, the twelve master's mates who became midshipmen fared as poorly in the officer corps as did the enlisted men who became midshipmen. Only one exceptional individual—John Percival, later famous as Mad Jack or Crazy Jack—gained promotion to lieutenant. Several soon left the navy. Should this failure to advance farther be attributed to the limitations of social origins and to educational deficiencies? Did strong prewar backgrounds in the merchant service give the master's mates who became midshipmen profitable and tempting opportunities to abandon the navy and return to that trade? A definite answer cannot be given with the information now at hand, but it appears that the former enlisted men and the former master's mates found naval officership a less congenial way to rise in the world than did the sons of master craftsmen.

10. Politics

POLITICAL ANIMOSITIES RAN HIGH, partisan debate was venomous, throughout the years when the navy's officer corps was born and grew to maturity. At least twice—at the election of Thomas Jefferson and during the War of 1812—dismemberment of the union over partisan issues appeared to be a real danger. But civil conflict did not erupt; all threats during those years to split the United States fizzled out after some initially eye-catching fireworks. The historian can well argue that the forces that held the people of the United States together as a society and as a political entity were, in fact, the basic reality; that the partisan politics were an interesting and a consuming show, dancing on the surface of more powerful currents of shared, though perhaps unarticulated, consensus concerning the basic purposes and direction of American society. Even so, given the battle-to-the-death rhetoric in which much of the nation's political dialogue was conducted, it is important to ask what role the Federalist–Jeffersonian Republican conflict may have played in the selection of officers for the nation's navy.

Very little. The evidence supports the argument that, for all the tumult, the American people of 1794–1815 were more united than divided. Among the 885 midshipmen whose prenaval backgrounds are here cut open for analysis, party affiliations can be attributed to 66, either on the stated preference of the young man himself or on that of his family; in other words, one young man in thirteen. Of the sixty-six, some fifty-four are identified as Jeffersonian Republicans. Apart from laying to rest the hoary myth that the pre-1815 naval officer corps was all but entirely Federalist in its sympathies, these numbers have no great value as indicators. The Federalist party controlled the executive branch until March 1801; then the appointment power passed to (and remained with) the Republicans through and beyond February 1815, the terminal point of this book's concern. Almost all the surviving letters of recommendation, the best and primary source of information on political affiliation, come from the years when the Republicans controlled the executive government. When the Republican party was in power it was obviously to the advantage of would-be midshipmen from families of that political persuasion to call attention to the fact, and for young men of Federalist backgrounds to see that no mention of politics appeared in their recommendations. The not surprising consequence is that, after March 1801, the only political affiliations that are identified are those of Republicans.

One cannot, however, reverse the argument; just because no political affiliation is mentioned, it does not necessarily follow that the recommendee's political background is Federalist. Neither is it necessarily true, simply because most recommendations for midshipman appointments were channeled through members of the congressional delegations who were from the same political party that controlled the administration, that the young men recommended were necessarily one in political faith with the congressman or senator who acted as intermediary. In many cases they were; but ties of kinship, friendship, business, or shared social and economic status could also claim a congressman's or a senator's support. Finally, political affiliations could always be expressed in ambivalent circumlocutions—"his political principles coincide with those of the majority of the nation"[1]—that might leave it deliberately vague just which party the applicant claimed as his own. The only valid conclusion that may safely be drawn from the numerous letters of recommendation citing Jeffersonian political beliefs is one that should have been surmised long since: the Republicans were neither so naive nor so lacking in supporters in the nation's maritime community that they were compelled to fill the vacant berths in the officer corps with young Federalists.

Those who judged they had claims to preference for midshipman appointments for themselves or their sons on political grounds were not shy about throwing those claims onto the scale. From Westford, Massachusetts, nineteen-year-old Joel Abbot reported in September 1812 that, when antiwar Federalist governor Caleb Strong proclaimed a fast day and the Reverend Caleb Blake, pastor of Westford's First Parish, was known to be preparing "a most scandalous and abusive sermon against the government and the war," Abbot and a group of his pro-war friends decided to show up at church in their militia uniforms by way of protest. In retaliation, or so young Abbot claimed, the Federalist trustees of Westford Academy voted to forbid his continuing his education under that roof, thereby depriving him of the opportunity of entering Harvard College a year later.[2] In light of Joel Abbot's difficulties with authority figures during his subsequent naval career, one suspects the trustees may have had a different perspective on these events. Be that as it may, Joel Abbot's expulsion gave Westford's Federalists and Republicans a hot local issue on which to choose up sides for a good brawl.

Republican senator Michael Leib urged the political merits of the father as a reason for appointing a son when he wrote Paul Hamilton from Philadelphia in August 1812:

> Judge [Frederick] Wolbert of this place has requested me to mention his son, Frederick Wolbert, Junr., as a midshipman. Mr. Wolbert is a veteran in our cause and has been a martyr to his principles. The people of the city and county of Philadelphia, for his services and his merits, elected him sheriff, an office worth above $10,000 a year. The late Governor McKean, after his apostasy and junction with the Federalists, refused to commission Mr. Wolbert and for no other reason but because he clung to the standard of the Republican party. Such a man is entitled to reward, and I am sure that such are your predilections for men of that stamp that you will appoint his son a midshipman. He is a smart, active youth of uncommon spirit.[3]

Was the political consideration a decisive factor insuring that Abbot and Wolbert received midshipman warrants when other applicants were turned down? Because Paul Hamilton left no record of the basis for his decisions, there is no sure way of knowing. Both did receive warrants, which is a point in favor of the political argument. Against this contention one can set the fact that both young men proved to be good officer timber. Joel Abbot rose to the rank of captain and was commander of the East India squadron at his death in 1855. Wolbert served thirteen years and earned his promotion to lieutenant. In an officer corps characterized by a high attrition rate among entering midshipmen, Abbot's and Wolbert's survival argues just as strongly that the secretary based his choice on qualities other than party loyalty.

Did party politics have a bearing on keeping an appointment and getting ahead in the navy? The evidence is hardly abundant. In mid-June 1803 Midshipman Henry Wadsworth noted in his diary,

> The commodore [Richard V. Morris] has informed me that the secretary [of the navy] in his communications mentioned my father's request that I might be removed from the Chesapeake to some other ship and that he (the commodore) might remove me to the ship most wanting midshipmen. "However," said the commodore, "you had better stay with me; for, as your father is a noted Federal character [Peleg Wadsworth was a congressman from Massachusetts], and as political principles have some influence, perhaps you might be with a commander of opposite sentiments and who would not do you justice, so that you might hang astern even after you deserved promotion."[4]

The most interesting feature of this passage is its clear statement, by a man who ought to have had accurate knowledge, that officers senior enough to command the navy's ships came in both political persuasions.[5] This is welcome ammunition to refute the oft-repeated claim that the upper ranks were solidly Federalist.* Beyond that, Morris's statement has the self-serving ring of a commanding officer trying to hang onto an able (and favorite) subordinate. Indeed, on the face of the matter, it appears that Republican secretary of the navy Smith was being highly considerate of Federalist congressman Wadsworth's efforts to promote his son's career.

---

* An astounding assertion of Federalist hegemony in the upper ranks of the officer corps from an astonishing source was made by Secretary of the Navy Paul Hamilton in the wake of an 1810 incident in which Lieutenant John Trippe accepted the apology of the commander of the British brig *Moselle* for firing into Trippe's *Vixen* rather than going into action against the more heavily armed *Moselle* to avenge the apparent insult to the U.S. flag. "I cannot describe to you how much I have been mortified" by Trippe's conduct, Hamilton lamented to Caesar A. Rodney on 27 July, "and, as God is my judge, if I could select one of our commanders in whom I could safely confide, I would have this and the Chesapeake business both balanced very shortly; but alas, they are, as I am informed, all Federal, and therefore I must observe the caution suitable to the occasion and wait for a better tone in our government—or some new insult. But, even in this latter event, I have my doubts. Our commanders either fear or love the British. The conduct of [Isaac] Phillips, [James] Barron, and Trippe is too much in support of this belief. I have ordered [David] Porter on board the Essex and given him my ideas, but behold, Porter vindicates Trippe as I have discovered. I have issued general orders which go to require that not even a 'menace or threat' shall be submitted to from a foreign vessel, but this will avail nothing if an insult is offered by [a British vessel], for I repeat that all our navy officers, of any rank, are Federalists and therefore are the friends of Britain."[6] Presumably the events of the last six months of the year 1812 enlightened Paul Hamilton on this score. Fortunately for Hamilton's relations with the officer corps he commanded, his opinions did not become public knowledge.

Then there is an obscure passage in a letter from Secretary Smith to President Jefferson, which reads in its entirety:

> I am sorry to see such an account of the midshipman. He was strongly recommended by Mr. [Philip R.] Thompson of Virginia, [Republican] member of Congress, and, from the great interest he took in procuring him the station on board the schooner, I concluded he was safe on the score of politics.

Unfortunately the surviving records do not permit absolute identification of the midshipman, neither do they provide information on how he had offended.[7] In the absence of such elaboration the evidence may be noted, but it can hardly be translated into proof of a political loyalty test for would-be midshipmen. The most likely guess is that the offending midshipman was Charles C.B. Thompson, who was then serving in the schooner *Nautilus*.[8] If so, the incident had no negative impact on young Thompson's naval career; he was promptly promoted to lieutenant when he became eligible and attained the rank of captain by the time of his death in 1832.

Thereafter the historian finds no references to the bearing of party affiliation on officer appointments until the War of 1812. Then one meets Commodores Joshua Barney at Baltimore and Jacob Lewis at New York using party membership as one criterion in selecting commanders for gunboats. These two officers were highly political men, brought into the navy "for the duration" to command harbor and inland-waters defense forces manned and officered with war-idled local mariners. Both in spirit and in law the two flotillas, and especially the Barney force, were kept distinct from the regular professional navy. Things went on within their ranks that would not have been permitted in the seagoing navy.[9]

That is the sum total of the evidence. It hardly adds up to a convincing case for the existence of a political loyalty test for admission to, or advancement in, the navy's officer corps. The most that can be argued is that Secretary Stoddert was disposed to smile benignly on applications from the sons of Federalists and that his Republican successors smiled just as broadly at the opportunity to honor their supporters' requests to place sons in the navy. But Stoddert had appointed the Republicans who commanded the ships that Richard V. Morris warned young Wadsworth to avoid. From most dossiers reaching the desks of Robert Smith or Paul Hamilton or William Jones none of those three men would have been able to ascertain with certainty the political convictions of the applicants' families. Neither did they reject applicants simply because their parents were known to be Federalists. William Jones willingly and speedily complied with the request of Philadelphia merchant Paul Beck, asking a warrant for son Samuel, even though Jones and Beck were on opposite sides of the Philadelphia political fence. "Mr. Beck is well known to be a Federalist, not however of the 'Boston Stamp,' " wrote one deeply committed Republican in seconding the younger Beck's search for a naval career.[10]

Whatever the rancor of the national political debate, surprisingly little of this animosity appeared in the ranks of the officer corps or affected the corps' relations with the national administration. Despite occasional charges to the contrary—always a good accusation to hurl when someone had been disappointed on more legitimate grounds—this historian has found no evidence of a single instance in which an officer's known or assumed political affiliation had a detrimental effect on his naval career at the hands of a secretary or a president of the opposite persuasion.[11] Certain officers can be identified as members of one or the other of the two major parties, but the doctrine that "the cloth has no politics"[12] provided a philosophical basis that enabled Republicans to pursue naval commissions vigorously during the Quasi-War with France and Federalists to fight the British with undisguised enthusiasm during the War of 1812. What this doctrine implied was that the officer's primary ideological commitment had shifted from the political party and its program to the navy and its interests, which interests he identified with those of the national government. Officers wrote hardly at all on the subject of party politics and possible conflicts with their role as military men, so William Bainbridge's elaboration of his views is especially welcome. "My religion and politics are my own," he wrote David Porter in June 1815.

> And are both such as I am proud to avow as honorable to myself and patriotic to my country. But neither of them has ever interfered, under any administration, with either church or state. I am no tool of any party, or do I meddle with the turbulent sea of politics. And I care not what the political creed of any man is, so long as I believe him honest to his country. And as for my intimates and associates, the requisites I require are those which gentlemen possess. Almost *eighteen* years have I served my country with ardent zeal, and let the records of the Navy Department test whether I have not been as faithful under the present administration as I was under the Federal. Seldom indeed do I talk on the subject of politics, but when I have occasionally done so it has often been in defense of measures of the present administration. In the late war I certainly joined heart and hand. I, however, do not pretend to be a politician, nor am I a sycophant. I am a sailor—honest and capable enough to do my duty—and I have *independence* at all times to act like a gentleman.[13]

The officer corps was able to maintain this doctrine consistently and successfully in an era of intense partisan conflict. Such success supports the view that, below the seeming battle-to-the-death of the parties, there existed a national consensus of common identity and shared values that was far stronger than might be supposed from the turmoil of the parties. It was this national consensus that enabled the United States to maintain an officer corps undivided by partisan conflict. The perception of consensus is certainly strengthened when one reads thousands of pages of letters written by naval officers during the pre-1815 years without encountering evidence of real divisions over philosophy or principle—or even much discussion of the foreign and domestic issues facing the nation. Those few references to questions of public policy that have been observed in officers' correspondence invariably discuss the issues in terms of their favorable or unfavorable impact on the navy or the writer's career. When the officer corps or its individual members entered the political arena it was in pursuit of objectives that were self-interested: rank, pay, and the promotion of the navy as a means of national defense.

11. Why

WHAT MOTIVATED YOUNG men to join the navy as midshipmen? Finding satisfactory answers to that question is doubly difficult. The Navy Department did not ask an applicant or his sponsor why the would-be officer wanted to become a midshipman, but a few applicants and a few sponsors did answer the unasked question in their letters of application or recommendation. Can the historian extrapolate from the reasons in a handful of cases to the motivation of an entire corps? Even if one fearlessly answers yes to that question, there is still a second difficulty. Motivations are often complex and multiple; they may be interactive. Is the historian qualified to unsnarl them and say that *this* was the decisive motivation? Psychohistory has properly taught investigators to be wary of dealing exclusively in conscious motives. An individual may sincerely think he or she is making a decision for a particular reason or reasons when, in fact, that individual's behavior and decision making is strongly determined by psychological factors of which the person is unaware. Naval history needs more psychological investigation than it has yet received, but the materials on which this book is based—a necessarily superficial search for common and disparate elements in a mass of men—do not provide much help in exploring unconscious motivations. The most that can here be attempted is a statement of the major threads of conscious motivation as they are found in the surviving letters of application and recommendation.

One man never had any doubt—at the time or later—why he wanted to become an officer. "Dear Uncle," fourteen-year-old George N. Hollins wrote Senator Samuel Smith in February 1814, "I saw Commodore Perry and witnessed the honors paid him. I never was so pleased with the appearance of any person. Anxious to deserve similar honors and emulate his actions, I have taken the liberty to solicit your interest to procure me a midshipman's commission in the navy."[1] Many years later, after a long career in the U.S. and Confederate navies, Hollins still remembered his motivation for that career exactly as he had stated it to his famous uncle:

> When I was about fourteen years old Perry's great victory on the lakes was the event of the day. Commodore Perry was visiting Baltimore and [was] entertained by many of the prominent citizens, besides having had a grand ball

Midshipman George Nicholas Hollins at age sixteen, two years older than he was when a meeting with Oliver Hazard Perry triggered his latent desire to become a naval officer. His face hints at a youthful anxiety Hollins suppressed or had forgotten when he wrote the autobiographical narrative of his career choice many years later. The skilled miniaturist who produced this handsome and expressive image has not yet been identified. Frick Art Reference Library, New York.

given in honor of his presence. He was entertained by my father [merchant John Hollins], and during his visit in my father's house I was called in and introduced to the gallant hero. My father asked him what kind of a midshipman I would make. The commodore said, "He will make a first-rate one, Sir. I entered the navy just at his age." My father then said, "Go and ask your mother." I remember so well [that] when I asked her she burst into tears and begged me not to go to sea. She had painful associations with the idea of any of her children going to sea. But a few years before, her second son, William, had been lost at sea, and her mother's heart shrank from trusting another one of her loved children to the treacherous element. She offered me a farm—anything—but I felt as if I were to be a man at once and my own master, so I persisted, and she finally gave a reluctant and tearful consent.[2]

No other midshipman was quite so disingenuous and seemingly uncomplicated in his motivation as George N. Hollins. But even in Hollins's case motivation is not as simple as it seems at first reading. There is his desire to look and act and be honored like Oliver Hazard Perry; but there is also a desire to be on his own, away from home, perhaps even an urgent need to escape a too protective mother. The latter force might have been smoldering—conscious, semiconscious, or unnoticed—with Perry's appearance in Baltimore and a father's astute perception of a son's anxiety providing a legitimate way of satisfying the inner demand to escape and be independent.

Most midshipmen's applications fail to provide the psychological clues to be gleaned from the Hollins autobiography. As concerns stated motivations, two major themes run through the letters; there were many variations on the way the themes might be played.

One principal theme was the desire for a more active life. Eighteen-year-old Ishi Craven has been working as a clerk in his cousin Tunis Craven's store for nearly two years, but is "tired of the inactivity of the business . . . as unsuitable to the energy of his desires."[3] A major variation on this theme is the aspiring midshipman's lack of enthusiasm, or even tolerance, for academic endeavor. "I have a son who has made up his mind to go into the navy," Massachusetts solicitor general Daniel Davis wrote Congressman Josiah Quincy early in 1808.

> He was fitted for college by Mr. Pemberton of Bellerica, but he conceived such a desire to go to sea that I thought it not prudent to attempt to *force* him into literary life. He accordingly went on board the Cordelia, not through the cabin windows (as the sailors term it), but in a voyage of eighteen months round Cape Horn to Lima he did his duty before the mast with Captain Stuart, who is one of the smartest seamen in the merchant service. Upon his return, he went again before the mast a voyage to the West Indies and, upon his return, Captain Stuart took him as his *first officer* on a voyage to Europe, where he served in that capacity eighteen months, during which time he coasted the Mediterranean upon both sides and was [in] many other ports in Spain and Portugal. This was his last voyage.[4]

When the father then went on to describe his son, William, as "of an uncommonly robust and healthy constitution" an image begins to emerge of a young man whom heredity has not particularly equipped to be happy in a classroom or any other stuck-at-a-desk occupation.

The desire for an active life needed to take the particular form of a wish for a life at sea—or at least an openness to accept that option when it was presented. "My sons having a predilection for a sea life for a long time past, I have always put them off by saying to them that when they had completed their education I would talk to them on the subject," wrote Richard Dale to fellow Philadelphian William Jones even as the father crumbled before John's and Richard's pleading to begin naval careers.[5] Given the senior Dale's distinguished record in the Continental and U.S. navies, as well as in the East Indies trade, it was natural for his sons to view the sea as a career option. But what of the young man from Pendleton Courthouse, South Carolina? His bemused sponsor wrote Paul Hamilton,

> The application, indeed, gave me no small degree of surprise, knowing that Mr. William Steele, the applicant, could have no knowledge of maritime transactions excepting such as he must have acquired by reading. . . . William Steele, Junr., has had a classical education and was considered always at school as a very promising lad of a good genius. If he was a Yankee or had been brought up in the bosom of maritime pursuits of every kind, such an ambition from him could not be thought strange. But, being brought up in the mountains in the back parts of Carolina, the desire in him is to me paradoxical.[6]

Often as the desire to go to sea was expressed as a motivation, no applicant elaborated or analyzed that desire in records that have survived. Why the sea? What about the sea? One can only speculate. Unlike William Steele, Jr., most midshipmen came from environments wherein the sea was very much a part of their and their parents' daily lives. As with George N. Hollins, going to sea was a socially acceptable way of declaring the end of one's childhood and establishing one's sense of self. Once safely at sea, going home was not an immediate option. This basic human need was reinforced by other inclinations long endemic among human beings and especially young, unattached human beings: the desire to be on the move, to see new and exotic parts of the world, to encounter experiences different from those one had known at home. For young male Americans of the early nineteenth century, going to sea was perhaps the most readily available means of satisfying such needs.

A not uncommon variation on the theme of the young man's need for a more active way of life was sounded by Sarah Connolly, the mother of midshipman-aspirant J. Mifflin Connolly. "He finds himself so amazingly independent of me that, as he is determined to be [a] sailor and I am told is very smart in that line, to indulge his inclination I believe to be right," Sarah Connolly wrote from Philadelphia in June of 1799. Thus far a familiar theme. A few lines more in a similar vein, and then comes the twist: "He is a wild boy and is beyond my management, which makes me desirous that he should not sail from this port, as I am convinced [that] whenever he comes [in] from a cruise he will always play on the softness of a mother."[7] The motivation here, and in many a similar case in the pre-1815 years, was that of the parent rather than the son. The navy was seen as an institution that might be able to discipline the wild boy and turn him into a useful citizen. (In young Connolly's case he appears to have embraced a sea life with enthusiasm, quite independent of the parent's agenda of reformation.) As will be seen in more detail later, the wild boy was as much of a problem for the navy as he was for his parents. Such young men made highly unpromising officer timber, a rule to which J. Mifflin Connolly, out of the officer corps almost as soon as he entered it, was no exception. Sons who lacked the self-discipline to conform at least minimally to the constraints of parents and of civil society were rarely equipped to meet the navy's special combination of greater temptations for misconduct and more demanding standards of discipline. Nonetheless, desperate parents continued to hope that the navy could succeed where they had not and sought warrants for their unmanageable sons. Why did the navy accept such dubious risks? Because few parents were as disingenuous as Sarah Connolly was about her son's shortcomings. Normally, the wild boy's dossier arrived on the secretary's desk in the form of glowingly enthusiastic recommendations, the reality behind which did not emerge until the first few weeks or months of active duty.

The final variation on the need for a more active life was rare, but not unknown: the search for better health. William Anderson, Jr., of Kentucky appealed to Congressman Henry Clay in June 1812 for assistance in obtaining a midshipman's berth:

> When a boy at school I was assiduous and successful in application to my studies. But, unfortunately, bad health for two or three years past had almost extinguished the flattering hopes I then conceived. I feel an energy that cannot in any way exert itself under my present circumstances. I have felt my situation unfortunate in being destitute of influential friends or in not being able to satisfy the claim my feelings persuaded me I possessed to a small appointment in the navy, a situation particularly suited to the nature of my indisposition that would at once make me master of myself and satiate that restless craving for exertion which, in my present situation, it seems impossible to satisfy.

Critical reading of Anderson's letter suggests that his bad health had a strong psychological component, that dissatisfaction with his life as a private Latin teacher and tutor was manifesting itself in physical symptoms. Whether it was the sea air or the active life, a year's service as a midshipman in the navy restored Anderson's health, physical and mental.[8]

The second great theme that runs through would-be midshipmen's statements of motivation is the economic one. When Lieutenant Arthur Sinclair succeeded in securing a midshipman's warrant for his brother-in-law-to-be, Beverley Kennon, Beverley's sister Sally (the future Mrs. Sinclair) came right to the point: "Although [Mama] is so dreadfully afraid of the water, she is so fully sensible of the advantage it will be to him as to money matters [that] she has consented to his accepting it."[9] Were visions of thousands of dollars in prize money dancing in mother Elizabeth Kennon's head? No, the lure was the assurance of a fixed salary, paid month in and month out. In the pre-1815 United States positions that offered both the expectation of long-term job security and the promise of a predictable income were few in number; almost all were in one or another form of government employment. Other careers were at the mercy of a volatile, unregulated economy in a world at war. High status was no guarantee of financial security or even solvency. When Midshipman George Haven Leverett entered the navy as a midshipman in 1812 his father, Boston broker Benjamin Leverett, claimed a net worth of $100,000. Ten years later he had lost it all and reported his net assets as zero.[10] The senior Leverett's was far from being an isolated case. Under such conditions it is no wonder that the number of highly qualified applicants for any government position—in the civil departments just as well as the navy—far exceeded the number of jobs available to be filled.

Neither the high-status ranks of society nor the comfortable middle class of the pre-1815 United States possessed the established fortunes that would provide economic security for their children. Capital loss canceled capital accumulation, and cash flow was an ever-present concern. The rising generation could not have the luxury of being cultured gentlemen of leisure; they had to expect to work for a living. Of his son Charles's decision to seek a midshipman's warrant, Christopher Ellery, former Republican senator from Rhode Island and then U.S. commissioner of loans at Providence, commented, "Accustomed from very early years to consider his advancement in life as depending wholly on his own exertions, his father having many children and but little property, he has been led to reflect upon the courses he might pursue with the best prospect of securing to himself fortune and reputation—the seeming, if not the real, sources of happiness; and, thus reflecting, he had determined, long since, to follow the seas."[11]

If such were the expectations of the sons of a highly positioned father such as Christopher Ellery, the sons of thrifty middle-class parents, who constituted the majority of the young men entering the navy as midshipmen, felt even more the keen need to find careers in which to support themselves. It is in this context that the statement of one recommender concerning a pair of brothers for whom he sought warrants should be understood: "They are poor; their characters are good; and it is from this class of society that we are to expect to find the real defenders of our country."[12] The Caton brothers did not come from backgrounds of genuine poverty and deprivation, as the historian or the social worker would understand the word *poor*. The family was certainly middle-class and surely well enough off as far as meeting day-to-day needs; but little if any capital was being accumulated, and economic well-being was dependent on the continued earning power of the father.

*Upon receiving his commission as a surgeon in April 1809 one of Dr. William P.C.
Barton's first acts was to engage fellow Philadelphian Thomas Sully to paint him in his
new uniform. The priority was symbolic. Barton's interest in a surgeon's appointment
seemed to spring more from a desire for status and a secure income than from any attraction
to naval life. He displayed a notable aversion to sea duty (and to his shipboard messmates),
but he was almost equally adept at wriggling out of shoreside assignments away from his
home in Philadelphia. Bright, able, witty, well born, and well educated, the doctor appears
to have been one of those individuals who secure special consideration more on the promise
of future achievements (ultimately unfulfilled) than for actual service and proven accomplishments.* Philadelphia Museum of Art.

Even when capital accumulation was taking place, it was essential to conserve
these resources toward the day when one's mother might be a widow or for
the support of one's female siblings. When David Porter pointed out to Paul
Hamilton that the recently deceased father of Midshipman Laurence Rousseau
of Louisiana had been "a wealthy and respectable planter with many [i.e.,
twelve] children, chiefly females," the latter would immediately have understood
young Rousseau's motivation in leaving the family plantation for a career in
the navy.[13] Although the pages of any city directory from the pre-1815 United
States will reveal that single women—perhaps unmarried, more likely widowed
or estranged from spouses—were more active as operators of independent
businesses than is commonly supposed, such women competed under many
disadvantages. Their survival had first call on family capital, such as it might
be.

Death of a male parent was a powerful motivator in determining young
men to select naval careers. Officership in the navy provided a financially
secure, high-status job that could be attained without the investment of family
funds in years of education with no offsetting income, as would be the case if

a young man elected to pursue a career in law or medicine. After the father's death funds for education, let alone venture capital to start out in business, might be scarce to nonexistent. Letters of recommendation confirm what the tally of the numbers of dead fathers among the midshipman applicants suggested. From Queen Annes County, Maryland, Richard Hall reported that his sister, who was married and had her own family to worry about, had inherited the care of their brother Benjamin's two children after the death of both Benjamin and his wife.

> [The] son . . . being now too stout for that attention she would wish to bestow on him, [my sister] is anxious to get him into the Navy of the United States and will feel herself ever grateful to you if you would endeavor to procure a midshipman's berth for him. He is very young, not more than thirteen or fourteen. But, as she intends he should continue in the navy through life, she would prefer getting him in at an early age, that by degrees he may have an idea of naval tactics and rise by grade, that when he comes to the age of manhood he may have acquired a thorough knowledge of the station he may [fill], as it will be the only means he can look forward to as a support through life.[14]

Reduced to One

Does the historian, scorning the dangers of oversimplification, dare to attempt a portrait of the typical midshipman of the pre-1815 navy? He was probably a native of tidewater Maryland or Virginia. The odds ran about one in three that his father was dead by the time the son decided to seek a midshipman's warrant; indeed, the loss of his father and the resulting decline in family income probably were a significant factor in his decision to pursue a career in the navy. While alive, the father had either been an appointed or (less likely) an elected federal officeholder or else he had owned a town-based business with a strong orientation to the maritime world. The midshipman's eventual monetary legacy from his parents was likely to be modest, if there was one at all. But his parents had been able to see that he received a strong formal education. He wrote a clear hand as well as lucid prose; his literary and mathematical training had prepared him for the task of continuing self-education that the navy would impose on him. Although he had gained sufficient mastery of Latin and Greek to enter college, he did not linger long in collegiate life, if he began it at all. His body rebelled at additional sedentary study; his spirit was restless under parental supervision. No mama's boy or stay-at-home, the future midshipman had gone to sea before the mast in a merchantman to discover the world beyond the horizon. He adapted to the sea and relished the life, but he also craved the status and financial security of a naval officer's career. A family member or a neighbor who knew the district's representative to Congress had ridden over with the would-be naval officer to ask for the congressman's help in securing a warrant. The latter inquired about the aspiring midshipman's age and nodded with approval when told it was seventeen, was pleased to note that the lad's family regularly supported him and his party at election time, and explained the steps it was necessary to take to secure a warrant. Then it was only a question of being patient to see what the mail might bring.

PART THREE
A Society within Wooden Walls

12. Eye of the Novice

*F*OR THE PROMOTION-TRACK officer in the U.S. Navy of 1794–1815, progression through the ranks provided a common grid across which the professional life course was run. But the two decades were turbulent; the tasks the nation expected its navy to perform changed in response to the turbulence of the times; the path an officer's career might take was heavily determined by the moment on that twenty-one-year time line at which he began his career. Still, there did exist, for the mass of officers, a core of shared experiences that can be partially recovered through their documentary legacy of letters and diaries.

Signing On

Those shared experiences began with the letter of appointment, a document for which the would-be officer had been waiting patiently, impatiently—or even despairingly. The text of this paper varied little during the pre-1815 years; it was early reduced to a printed form with the appropriate blanks filled in by hand. In the first days of June 1809, fifteen-year-old John Hodges Graham of New York City received from his father, attorney John Andrew Graham, a paper addressed to the young man that had come enclosed in a letter to the parent. Unfolding the sheet, John Hodges read,

> Navy Department, 2 June 1809
>
> Sir: *Herewith you will receive a warrant as a* Midshipman *in the Navy of the United States, dated* 18 May 1809. *I enclose a copy of the Navy rules and regulations and the requisite oath which you will take and return to me. This appointment must be accepted by letter, from the date of which letter your pay will commence.* You will report yourself in person to the commanding officer of the New York station. Your obedient servant,
>
> PAUL HAMILTON[1]

As Secretary Hamilton's letter instructed, young Graham had to carry out two formal, but critical, tasks. The first was to go before a judge or other magistrate and swear the oath (another printed form with blanks to be filled in by hand) required of all naval officers. In midshipman-designate Graham's

119

case, his father's status gave the son access to New York City's mayor, De Witt Clinton, before whom John Hodges appeared, placed his left hand on the Bible, raised his right, and repeated,

> *I*, John Hodges Graham, being *appointed* Midshipman in the Navy of the United States, *do solemnly swear to bear true allegiance to the United States of America, and to serve them honestly and faithfully against all their enemies or opposers whomsoever; and to observe and obey the orders of the President of the United States of America, and the orders of the officers appointed over me, and in all things to conform myself to the rules and regulations which now are or hereafter may be directed, and to the articles of war which may be enacted by Congress, for the better government of the navy of the United States, and that I will support the constitution of the United States.*

John Hodges Graham was still not officially an officer of the U.S. Navy. There remained the second task enjoined by Hamilton's letter—the task that would formally make him an officer, and from the date of which he could draw his pay. He must write a letter to the secretary actually accepting the appointment. In young Graham's case, after who knows how many rejected drafts and what parental advice as to content and form, he dispatched this, in flawless penmanship:

> New York, June the 5th 1809
>
> Respected Sir: This day I received your esteemed favor covering the warrant appointing me a Mid-Shipman in the Navy of the United States. I hasten to return you my best thanks for your kind attention and favor, and most eagerly accept of the appointment. I beg leave to assure the Honbl. the Secretary Mr. Hamilton that I never shall knowingly or wittingly abuse the confidence that may be placed in me—or disgrace the Flag of the United States.
>
> I send inclosed the affidavit as you desired, taken before the Honbl. Mr. Clinton, Mayor of this City. I remain, with the most profound respect & Consideration
>
> JOHN HODGES GRAHAM
>
> Honbl. Mr. Hamilton
> Secretary of the Navy &c. &c.[2]

For some midshipmen, as it happened with John H. Graham, orders to active duty came in the letter of appointment. Others waited a month, a year, or occasionally even longer for that first duty assignment. Whether it came soon or late, the initial shipboard cruise remained one of the most keenly remembered of the shared experiences of the officers of the pre-1815 navy. Perhaps, if the route to his first duty assignment lay through Washington and if he had a parent or sponsor of sufficient status to arm him with the appropriate letter of introduction, the midshipman made a courtesy call on the secretary of the navy at his office. There—at least during Robert Smith's tenure as secretary—the novice customarily found the navy's leader ready with a cordial welcome to the new profession and encouragement for the apprehensive. "I am very much prepossessed in favor of Mr. Smith, the secretary. He received me at first with the utmost politeness and has continued to show me great attention," reported Midshipman William Lewis of Spotsylvania County, Virginia, late in August of 1802. "I informed him that I was ignorant of navigation and expected to meet with many difficulties in consequence of it; but he replied that my situation was not singular, that a great number of midshipmen were in the same predicament, and even some of the lieutenants."[3]

Slightly protruding eyes and a beaklike nose may have made him a bit of an ugly duckling, but Midshipman Ralph Izard was a keen observer of his world, a young man whose letters to his mother are one of the most valuable records of life in the Jeffersonian navy. Miniaturist Edward Greene Malbone pictured the South Carolinian with full-frontal honesty (left).

C.B.J. Fevret de Saint-Mémin customarily posed his sitters facing to the viewer's right. By having Izard face left, the artist brought the new-fledged lieutenant's single epaulette into view (right). Honest deception! Unless the viewer is knowledgeable in subtle distinctions among naval uniforms, Saint-Mémin's positioning of his sitter creates the illusion that Izard may actually be a captain. DAR Museum, Washington, D.C.; National Portrait Gallery, Washington, D.C.

With young men of the very highest status, there were flattering possibilities of social contacts at an even more rarefied level. Commandant of the marine corps Colonel William Ward Burrows—a South Carolinian in his origins and an old family friend—escorted Midshipman Ralph Izard, Jr. (son of the former Federalist senator from that state), and Christopher Gadsden (grandson of South Carolina's Revolutionary War leader of the same name) to the White House to call on President Thomas Jefferson. Young Izard advised the folks at home that "the President's House is not as well finished by any means as my father's house on South Bay [near Charleston]; all the chimney places are of wood." But Izard found the president himself to be "a very sociable man," who asked Ralph how he liked life in the navy and inquired solicitously about Ralph's father, who had been incapacitated by a stroke several years earlier and was now out of public life. A few days later came an invitation to dinner at the president's, where Midshipmen Izard and Gadsden encountered Secretary of the Treasury Albert Gallatin for the first time. "Of all the men I ever saw," Izard continued his reports home, "I never found one who looked so much like a thief. He cannot even look a man in the face, always looking out of the corner of his eye. His wife was there likewise. I cannot [say] much for her beauty, nor her sister, Miss [Jehoiadden] Nicholson. They are both very affected."[4]

Calls on the secretary and dinners with the president might be suggestions of the social life a naval officer could lead if he persevered and succeeded in his profession; for the present, they could only cushion the new midshipman's encounter with the realities of naval life itself. Equipped with his stout chest—customarily it had a drawer for linen, a large upper compartment for woolens, books, and quadrant, and locks to keep out prying peers—a liquor case filled with brandy, gin, and wine to share with messmates, and cigars and tobacco that he told his mother were really for the sailors, the midshipman arrived on board his first ship.[5] Even if that first ship were one of the navy's largest and finest 44-gun frigates, the midshipman's new quarters were a rude surprise. "The apartment belonging to us is very confined and hot, very low, for I was obliged to stoop in it, and altogether quite disagreeable," said William Lewis of his late August 1802 arrival on board *New York*. "I expect it will go pretty hard with me at first, but think I shall soon get used to it and like the life extremely well."[6] Helping to ease that initiation and change the shock of the new into a life that one liked "extremely well" was the chief authority figure and parent-surrogate in the midshipman's professional life: the vessel's commanding officer. He moved, at an early moment, to establish his role in the minds of the officer-initiates. "On our arrival Captain [William] Bainbridge came on board, who is to command the ship," wrote fifteen-year-old Midshipman William Henry Allen from his first duty assignment, the ship *George Washington* at Philadelphia. "He appears to be a fine man, much the gentleman, and is reckoned a good seaman. Yesterday he called all the midshipmen into the cabin and recognized them as such, informed us of the number of his house, and desired us, when we came on shore, to call and refresh ourselves as we would do at our fathers'."[7]

As the midshipman began to sort out the cacophony of experiences and impressions that dinned in upon him from all sides, he found himself in a world where discipline, order, training, efficiency, and ceremony formed the fabric of daily life. Almost certainly the first person he met when he came on board was the marine sentinel in full uniform marching back and forth at the gangway with his musket. As he made his way through the ship to his new quarters he passed additional uniformed marines guarding the galley, the scuttlebutt, the fore hatchway, and the door of the captain's cabin. If he were sharp-eyed, he even noticed the well-drilled sergeant's guard, resplendent in their dress uniforms, now lounging more or less in idleness, but ready to turn out, "at a moment's warning," to man the side should the quartermaster on duty report to the officer of the watch that a boat bearing any important personage, naval or civilian, had been sighted making for the ship.[8]

On superficial glance the new midshipman may not instantly be able to distinguish between officer and seaman, for during an ordinary workday the officers, like the sailors, are apt to be dressed in duck frocks, duck trousers, checked shirts, and straw hats purchased from the purser's supply of slops, thus sparing expensive uniforms for more formal occasions.[9] But any such external equalitarianism is purely illusory. Ceremony and military ritual speak of obedience, hierarchy, and deference. Let an officer be going out of the ship on duty; check shirt and duck trousers will be speedily replaced by uniform and sword.[10] Does a junior officer address a senior? He had best be careful to commence the conversation by touching his hand to his hat, even if it be a common straw one. Whether he enters the quarterdeck from below, from the rigging, or from a boat, he fails to salute it, by touching his hat, at his peril. Neither does he intrude needlessly on its weather side, which is reserved for the captain or the officer commanding the watch. Quickly he learns that the captain is not shy about expressing his displeasure should he catch midshipmen quarreling on duty, lolling about the quarterdeck, sitting on the guns, or climbing on them the better to view whatever craft may be passing.[11]

Then, one afternoon, a special air of anticipation runs through the ship. Word has come that the president and the secretary of the navy will be visiting the frigate. All the officers, the full marine detachment, and the marine band are drawn up on the quarterdeck. Aloft, the enlisted men, dressed in blue jackets and white duck trousers, stand erect on the yards and booms, supporting themselves by lifelines and facing in the direction of the approaching boat. With exquisite precision the guns are booming out a salute. The boat with its dignitaries is alongside. At a signal the men on the yards face the quarterdeck. The president and then the secretary come through the gangway. Three drum rolls are heard, and the captain is stepping forward to receive them. The men in the rigging give three cheers, and the marine band strikes up:[12]

At Sea at Last

Such elaborate ritual might well characterize a frigate's final days in port, when the new officer's first ship was ready to sail. The midshipman, if he did not come from a maritime background, was about to encounter the sea itself. A first storm was an experience no midshipman ever seemed to forget; neither would any future gale seem quite so fierce. William Lewis, last seen as he encountered the hot, low confines of *New York*'s quarters for midshipmen, had his first sea experience on a passage from Norfolk to Gibraltar in 1802:

> We met with a severe gale of wind which lasted nearly eight days. My troubles just then commenced. I can't describe to you the terrible appearance of the sea. The tremendous waves, the furious wind and rain, lightning and thunder, altogether formed a scene horrid enough to frighten the oldest sailor, much more such a *young hand* as I was. . . . We housed the guns the first evening, and the captain [James Barron], who is one of the most experienced and able seamen in the service, endeavored as much as possible to put the ship in a state for riding out the gale; but, notwithstanding all his precaution and skill, we expected to roll away our masts and were prepared to clear the wreck in case of such an event.[13]

Midshipman Charles T. Clark of Prince Georges County, Maryland, making his trial of a sea life in *Essex* in 1811, remembered not storm but the nausea of seasickness: "I had a cold before I left Hampton Roads and that, together with seasickness, put me in a situation that made me mourn the day I applied for a midshipman's warrant. Notwithstanding my indisposition, Captain [John] Smith would not permit me to remain below, but made me do duty. However, I soon got the better of it."[14]

Slowly or quickly, they all learned to cope with life on the water. "The sea has been very high all day, and the ship rolled so terribly that it was impossible to sit at the table to dine," Midshipman William Boerum of *Hornet* confided to his journal in the closing days of the War of 1812.

> We were compelled to sit upon the deck with our plates between our knees. It would have amused any person could he have witnessed our grotesque appearance. One might have been seen bracing his foot against a cleat on the deck and another against a chest, but a second and a third, not equally fortunate in their positions, aided each other by extending their limbs and placing foot to foot in opposite directions, while the bulkheads supported them behind. Thus situated we attempted the arduous business of dining and, notwithstanding our caution, it has happened more than once that a sudden and violent roll of the ship has thrown us and our dinner into one promiscuous heap, while more solicitude has been manifested for the preservation of our food and grog than for our limbs.[15]

Then, one day or another, the first big storm subsided, the seasickness disappeared, adjustment to this new life set in, and the novice officer found himself actually enjoying it all. Novelty crowded in from all sides. At no subsequent period of his career would his mind and his senses be so alive to all that was happening within and around his ship, or his pen so ready to record such impressions, among which these from *Hornet*'s 1815 cruise are among the most eloquent that have survived:

> In the evening the moon shone with great splendor. Our crew, in great spirits as they generally are, enjoyed themselves with dancing. You probably think it strange that our men should be permitted to dance on the Sabbath, but it's a general saying among sailors that there is no Sunday in five fathoms water. . . .
>
> This morning it rained with great violence for upwards of four hours. We caught near five hundred gallons of fresh water. . . . We dined on a piece of one of the [five large] sharks that were caught yesterday, and on which we made a very sumptuous repast. . . .
>
> There was a brilliant rainbow this morning and, as we were contending with a heavy head sea, the spray continually broke over the bow and presented a rainbow wherever the sun shone. . . .
>
> In the evening a flying fish flew on board. It was an uncommon large one. I heard some of our oldest sailors say it was the largest they ever saw. It was between eighteen and nineteen inches in length. Those fish are exceeding fine when fried—something similar to perch.
>
> In the afternoon John Clark fell from the flying jibboom, whilst preparing to get it inboard. The ship was going ten knots through the water, and every exertion was immediately made to save him. Spars were thrown overboard. Four or five men jumped into the boat, and she was cut away; but by this time poor Clark was near half a mile astern. The boat pulled in the direction [in] which they had last seen him and soon discovered him as they rose on the top of the waves, which had by this time rose to a stupendous height, and whose curling tops threatened them immediate destruction. However, we shortly had the satisfaction to see him hauled into the boat; but, had they been five minutes

longer, he must have perished, for he was so exhausted that he was unable to
walk for two days after. . . .

In the afternoon saw a large shoal of sea hogs ahead of the ship, and though we were going eleven knots through the water, they crossed and recrossed our bows with astonishing velocity. . . .

After supper (as usual) we drank to our *sweethearts* and *wives*. At midnight the gale . . . had now increased to its greatest violence. The lightning streaked the sky and the thunder's roar was dreadful—yet the scene was very sublime. The sea was covered all over with luminous ridges, and the spray, as it dashed over the bulwarks, fell in showers of fire on the deck, while the lightning shed a dismal light on all around. . . . At half-past four a.m. the wind shifted from S.E. to N.N.E. The storm was lulled almost to a calm; the sky became suddenly clear and appeared of an uncommonly deep azure, while the stars shone with wonderful brilliancy. What a contrast! But an hour before all was darkness, tempest and fury. . . .

In the afternoon it died away to a perfect calm. Hoisted our boat out, and all of us that could swim jumped overboard. . . .

For the last four or five days a large whale has been sporting about the ship, particularly in the evening, near the setting of the sun, his enormous snout rising sometimes above the waves with a fountain spouting through the aperture in the skull. Sometimes his huge curved back appeared like a rock in the ocean, and at other times he would spread his tail like a fan and lie on the surface of the water for hours. He frequently comes so near the ship that he wets our decks fore and aft, spouting higher than the maintop.[16]

If day-to-day routine eventually palled, interest might be rekindled by a special occasion so memorable as to deserve a longer entry in one's journal:

About eleven a.m. [29 June 1815] we crossed the Equator. . . . As we expected a visit from Father Neptune, we shortened sail and hoisted a flag bearing the motto of "Sailors Rights and No Impressment" at the fore, the jack on the bowsprit, and our largest ensign at the gaff. Our music striking up Yankee Doodle at this time created a general huzzah throughout the ship, for triumph—of whatever kind—always brings war and combats to the mind of man. Soon after, Neptune came over the bows accompanied by his usual train of followers, with the American flag waving in his hand. As he approached the quarterdeck, with a long speaking trumpet he hailed to inquire after the captain's health and where we were from. He was answered by the captain [James Biddle], and, when informed of our capturing an enemy's sloop of war and our escape from the 74, he expressed the greatest satisfaction. He and his followers each drank a toast in their turn; Captain Biddle also drank one; and now Neptune proceeded to business. His clerk held a book in his hand (bottom upwards) and, after turning the leaves over several times, called one of the men's names and sent his guard to seek him. He was found, brought aft, and set upon a bucket. The barber then blindfolded him and, with a large brush, lathered him with tar, paint, and several other things mixed together and commenced shaving him with an *iron hoop*. After being shaved, he was lashed to the pump and obliged to take the following oaths:

First. To aid and assist Neptune on all occasions, if called upon.

Second. Never to leave the pumps till the ship was free.

Third. Never to drink water when he could get grog.

Fourth. Never to kiss the maid when he could kiss the mistress, without she was the handsomest.

Many others followed, the last of which was "Never give up the ship." Every time the poor fellow opened his mouth to answer, the barber put his brush full of lather in. After that was over he took the trumpet to hail the line and, as he opened his mouth, a bucket of water was dashed in. The bandage was then taken off his eyes, and [he] set at liberty, when another one was called, and he went on [in] the same manner till all those who had never crossed the line before had gone through with the same ceremony. Neptune now made his exit, and all hands were called to mischief. A double allowance of grog was served out, and a universal joy reigned throughout the ship. At six o'clock there was only one sober midshipman in the ship.[17]

As it happens, the "one sober midshipman" in *Hornet* was William Skiddy, who later wrote an autobiography, "The Ups & Downs of a Sea Life," and who therein related what his messmate elected to obscure behind the phrase about universal joy reigning throughout the ship:

We crossed the line. . . . It was nearly calm, the topsails were close-reefed, and all hands piped to mischief. By-the-by, it requires very little encouragement on board a ship of war to see this in perfection, and I cannot imagine how a commander can give such an order. Salt water was soon showered from aloft in every direction. It being quite calm the officers mostly left the deck. The crew drank all the whiskey they could get. The middies, boatswain, gunner, carpenter, etc., made a muster and obtained enough to get pretty well drunk and made no small noise. I was that day the only one that dined with the captain and thereby escaped being one of the party. After dinner the captain sent me down to order the middies on deck. The minute I put my head in the steerage I was pulled in. There they were all in their glory, full of all sorts of spirits, and poor Tom Tippett trying to eat a glass tumbler, the blood trickling down each side of his mouth. . . . [I] retreated on deck and informed the captain that they were not in a state to come forth. He sent again. They would not come. He ordered the sergeant and guards of marines to bring them up, but that would not do. They sent word to the captain that, if he would order the marines away, they would come up. This was done, and up they came, and a pretty set of beauties they were, some half-dressed, some bloody—having been cut with broken bottles—but all gloriously drunk. They all pleaded innocence, said they were all perfectly sober, so the captain ordered old Smoot on the starboard roundhouse, Titus on the other, Tippett on the arms chest, and in this way they were all distributed about the quarterdeck. It was very laughable to hear them all pleading. First old Smoot on his back and, as he said, perfectly innocent, disgraced by a set of rascals that ought, to do them justice, be confined in double irons; he, the oldest mid in the ship, disgraced on the eve of promotion. Then Titus would break out and address the captain (who was all this time walking the deck) in the same style until we were obliged to tie some of them to different parts of the quarterdeck. They, being fatigued, soon fell asleep and were liberated at midnight. The next day all went on as usual. The captain never said a word, as I presume he very justly blamed himself.[18]

For all of Midshipman Skiddy's after-the-fact censoriousness, one does not have to seek too far to understand the psychological roots of such rare moments of mindless abdication of responsibility or of the total delight taken in less spectacular recreations lovingly recorded in midshipmen's journals. The hair-breadth rescue of John Clark reminds that the sea was an environment of continual danger and imminent death. Without occasional resort to moments of total escape and oblivion, few could retain their psychological balance under

such conditions.* Skiddy himself well captured this ever-present peril. A few
days out from Sandy Hook, *Hornet* fell in with a Portuguese brig; Captain
Biddle sent Skiddy to bring the master and his papers on board the U.S.
warship.

> I took him back after the examination. [It] then getting dark, and a black
> squall rising in the northwest, on leaving the brig I took a small lantern that
> the ship might perceive our situation. The squall being now up with us, blowing
> violently and quite dark so that nothing could be seen, the Hornet was to
> windward, which obliged us to pull head to the sea. We made but little headway,
> and the boat was soon half-full of water and the light extinguished. While [we
> were] pulling in this critical situation, they were consulting on board whether
> to bear up and look for us or remain hove to. They were fearful we had
> swamped and could never reach the ship. Had they adopted the first plan, we
> should certainly have been all lost, as the ship would have passed by or over us
> without seeing the boat.[19]

If peril and mortality were recurring threads in the fabric of shipboard
life, so also was an extensive and institutionalized round of social exchanges.
The legend of the captain maintaining his authority and dignity by dining
alone in his cabin is simply not supported by the records. Certainly he did eat
some meals by himself, probably cheerfully welcoming the chance to be alone.
But for his midafternoon dinner his officers, whether the most senior lieutenant
or the newest midshipman, joined him in rotation at his well-laden and well-
appointed table. The wardroom officers imitated their captain's system of
rotation by inviting an inferior or two from the midshipmen's and surgeon's
mates' mess to share their dinner. Nor were such courtesies a one-way street.
Come Sunday the captain would, upon receipt of a formal written invitation
delivered week in and week out, join the wardroom officers (or, less frequently,
other officer messes) as their dinner guest.[20] Apart from its obvious recreational
aspects, all this socializing among the ship's officers served a more serious
purpose. It was a significant part of the process by which the officer recruit
was integrated into his new profession. Through dining in cabin or wardroom
the novice was expected to perfect (or acquire) the polished and elegant
manners that were essential to the successful officer, whose future career would
embrace repeated contacts with some of the loftiest echelons of American and
foreign society. Not only was that function served, but the captain—especially
if he were one who gave high priority to his role as a teacher—would often
steer table talk to officership, military life, history, naval tactics, or contemporary
affairs, using the art of good conversation as an educational device.

Let the Good Times Roll

A ship's internal social life paled beside that which took center stage when
she reached port, whether in home waters or abroad. Festivities began almost

---

* In the case of the incident censured by Skiddy, Captain Biddle permitted discipline to be
relaxed to such an extent only on *Hornet*'s second crossing of the Equator, when she was homeward
bound, and when he knew that peace between the United States and Great Britain had been signed
six months earlier. Moreover, it followed a cruise in which *Hornet* had fought a bloody battle with
Penguin and narrowly escaped capture by a British line-of-battle ship after a chase that extended
over two days.

the moment the ship reached her anchorage. When *Boston* entered the Bay of Naples in 1802, Midshipman Woolsey reported,

> We were no sooner anchored than we were serenaded by a band of music from the city who came off in a small boat and lay under our stern. Before night we were surrounded by boats, some loaded with fruit, others containing jugglers who gain their subsistence by performing sleight of hand tricks. One of them I particularly noticed. After performing several tricks with the cups and balls, either to excite our pity or surprise, I cannot say which, [he] tortured himself by running an iron skewer or pin upwards of six inches in length up his nose. He also imitated the notes of different birds in a most surprising manner.[21]

Naturally every mother's son among the officers was eager for shore leave, and the captain had to restrain their ardor by reminding them that his prior permission was required before an officer could leave the ship; that the ship must never be left with fewer than two lieutenants (or one lieutenant and the sailing master), not counting the first lieutenant; that not more than one-third or one-fourth of the midshipmen could have shore leave at the same time; and that leaves might never exceed twelve hours, nor were overnight stays ashore tolerated without special permission. To all of which regulations he might add some general exhortations on behavior: "It will be well to instill into the minds of our officers in general that no propensity for amusements must ever get the better of the duties required of them," Alexander Murray admonished his subordinates via the first lieutenant as the pleasures of a West Indian port-of-call beckoned. "Not but I wish them to enjoy themselves by rotation and in moderation, so as to avoid getting into any broils or scrapes that must tend to the discredit of the naval service as well as themselves."[22]

With such calls to virtue ringing in their heads—at least so long as they were still within earshot of the ship—the young officers were soon on their way ashore to explore novel worlds. Perhaps it was Melancthon Woolsey taking in the theater at Marseilles and making his first encounter with Empire fashions:

> There were a great number of young people of both sexes, dressed in the tip of the mode—and a ridiculous figure they made! The ladies wore tiny, short-waisted gowns, with sleeves so short that their naked arms could plainly be seen to their armpits and so low in the neck as [to] expose that part of the breasts which the more modest ladies of America endeavor to conceal. Their dress, which was very thin, was also calculated to show their elegant figures; and they appeared to possess the art of showing their shapes, too, to great advantage, especially when turning a corner suddenly, stepping across a gutter, or entering a house. The young beaux—or, more properly, *fops*—wore long pantaloons reaching to their armpits; waistcoats with two, and the longest three, buttons; and very long, narrow-backed and short-waisted coats with lapels about six inches in length. As to the ladies in this place, I must confess I saw more pretty faces and elegant figures among them than in any place into which we had been.[23]

Because the U.S. warship was herself as much of a novelty as the places she visited, she became, of necessity, the stage for entertaining, both informal and formal. On the Fourth of July 1802 the midshipmen in *Boston*, their noses out of joint because Captain Daniel McNeill had invited all the wardroom officers to dine with him in the cabin but left the midshipmen and their messmates to their own devices, decided to arrange a party. When *Boston* had finished firing a federal salute in honor of the day, and when her band had played "Yankee Doodle" more or less under the noses of the British warships anchored nearby at Valetta, Malta, the midshipmen retired to their own quarters for "a very excellent dinner," followed by sixteen spontaneous toasts: "Captain McNeill: As a brave man and a friend to his country we love him!" "Our Brave Tars: May their constant maxim be *Death before dishonor to our flag*!" "The American Fair: May they never refuse their embraces to those who undergo fatigues and perils for *their* country!" "May we never be commanded but by men of honor, valor, and patriotism!" Sixteen toasts notwithstanding, a number of the midshipmen were that evening able to make it ashore, where they encountered some of their peers from the British ship *Tigre*, arm-in-arm with whom they repaired to a nearby coffeehouse to spend the balance of the Fourth eating ice cream and drinking coffee. The evening ended with an invitation to *Tigre*'s young gentlemen to dine in *Boston* the next day, 5 July. Preparations consumed the entire morning. The guests from *Tigre* arrived around noon, were served "a very splendid dinner" by their *Boston* peers, and did not depart for their own ship till ten that night, at which time, Midshipman Woolsey reports, they were sent on their way "nearly as independent as we had been the day before."[24]

Peers from other navies might form the core of the officers' social life, but the ship was a magnet for curious civilians, too. "We had a great number of ladies and gentlemen to see the ship," Woolsey recorded at Marseilles a month later.

> I being the only one on board that could speak French (at that time) I had to muster all I was master of to pay the many civilities that French ladies naturally expect. In this doubtless I greatly fell short, as it would be next to an impossibility for an American sailor, who is used to mount on the topsail yard in gales and pull and haul whenever occasion requires, to make so graceful and easy a bow as a French petit-maitre, who perhaps has spent all his days either in a dancing school, under the tuition of his music master, or on his knees before his mistress. However, a good glass of Mount Aetna wine in the cabin perhaps made up the deficiency. In fact, I almost got myself fuddled in pledging these fine young ladies in full bumpers. They left the ship after spending about two hours with us—to appearance very much pleased, whether it was with the ship, our wine, or our American politeness I cannot tell.[25]

Before the ship left port, she and her officers had to repay in a formal manner—usually with a grand ball and supper on shipboard—the hospitality they had enjoyed. As for the events of one of these grand shipboard parties, they are best described by a guest—in this case Elizabeth Kennon, a widow, the mother of Midshipman Beverley Kennon, and mother-in-law of Lieutenant Arthur Sinclair. "I have taken up my pen to fulfill the promise I made you, in my letter to Rachel, to give you a description of the grand party we went to on board the Congress," she wrote her friend Ellen Mordecai in the spring of 1812:

> I will begin then with informing you that the quarterdeck, on which the young and gay figured in the windings of the mazy dance, was covered with an awning—the outside made of canvas, within lined with national flags—and festooned down to the bulwarks. The guns were run out so far that very little could be seen of them; and, to prevent the ladies from being injured by the night air, sails were fixed on the outside over the portholes in such a manner

that it could not be seen in the ballroom, and it produced the desired effect, for it was warm and comfortable as we wished it to be. Both the quarter- and gun decks were illuminated, the former in a very characteristic manner: muskets with fixed bayonets, cleaned until they actually glittered like silver, were placed around the capstan . . . and in the muzzle of each a lighted candle was placed. It really looked very handsome. I suppose there were not less than forty of them, which, in addition to numerous glass lanterns hung fancifully about, had a pleasing effect, and enabled the beauties of both sexes to display their charms to advantage—but the ugly ones, alas, vice versa. For those who chose to play, card tables were placed in what is called the [captain's] forward cabin. The after one, as it is styled, was given to the use of the wiser sort, who chose sociable converse. . . .

At eleven we were conducted to the supper room. This was on the gun deck, but was so judiciously enclosed with screens, signals, etc., that it looked like a handsome room, quite separate from any other place. And I will acknowledge to you that for once my vanity was tickled by the attention of a beau; for the elegant captain [John Smith] passed by a number of ladies—and some of them as old as I was—and, coming to me, said, "Will Mrs. Kennon permit me to lead her to supper?" I gave him my hand in the most graceful manner, and he conducted me to the table and seated me next to himself. . . .

The supper was elegant in the extreme. The table, by far the longest I ever saw in my life, was covered with a profusion of delicacies enough to satisfy the greatest epicure. I do not exaggerate when I tell you [that] I could not distinguish, from the place where I was, who did the honors at the foot of the table. I was told it was the first lieutenant [Lewis Warrington], with whom I was well acquainted, but the distance prevented my knowing him notwithstanding the table was brilliantly lighted. The captain himself presided at the head, and everything was conducted with the greatest propriety. . . . Instead of the common, old-fashioned way of having salvers, jellies, syllabubs, etc., in the middle of the table, there were four cakes placed in the form of a pyramid—a very large one at the bottom and the others small[er] by degrees, and beautifully less, until they ended nearly in a point at top. They were variously colored and looked very tasty. Around each, on the space which you know would be left, as one was smaller than the other, stood companies of soldiers under arms, made of sugar candy and colored naturally. . . .

After spending a most delightful evening, the company separated between one and two o'clock and returned to their respective dwellings—the young ones to dream perhaps of each other, and the old ones to sleep off their fatigue.[26]

13. Midshipman to Lieutenant

$\mathcal{S}$OCIAL LIFE—whether it was a group of off-duty midshipmen emptying a few bottles of madeira with peers from another ship or Captain Smith's grand party in *Congress*—was a significant and ongoing activity on shipboard. Still, it was just the frosting on the cake, relief from the tension and responsibility of much more serious business, specifically, the officer's growing role in the management of the ship as he gained experience at sea and moved up the promotion ladder from midshipman to lieutenant. As midshipman or as lieutenant, he participated in the same routines, the same duties, and the same shared experiences, but with one essential difference. The midshipman was an apprentice, assisting the lieutenant and learning from him. When he became lieutenant the actual responsibility would be his.

Structures

There were, the new midshipman learned, many lists—or, more properly, bills—in a ship of war, all posted under the quarterdeck for the instruction of such among the ship's company as could read.[1] Three were of paramount importance: the station bill, the quarter bill, and the watch bill.

Let all hands be turned up to moor or unmoor ship, to set or take in sail, to tack or to wear, and it was the station bill that specified precisely where each of the frigate's three or four hundred men was to report to assist in performing these evolutions. Officers as well: lieutenants to their positions of command on quarterdeck, forecastle, or gun deck; midshipmen up on the yards, or attending to sheets, tacks, braces, backstays—their hands dirty, their clothes soaking wet, and their feet half-frozen. It was only by frequent repetition that one could master all these maneuvers and be prepared to perform them automatically under stressful conditions, so the captain's regulations specified that the setting and the taking in of sail were to be practiced as often as the ship's duty would permit, whether she was at sea or in port.[2]

Pride of place among the ways in which a ship's company, that large and totally disciplined team, could be organized was the quarter bill. Assigned therein to every soul on board, from captain down to youngest boy, was his precise station and responsibilities when the ship went to quarters and cleared for action to meet an enemy. Basic to quartering the men, as the process of assigning them their roles on the quarter bill was called, was the demarcation of the ship's guns into divisions. Usually, in a frigate, there would be three divisions of ten guns apiece on the gun deck, and a fourth division on the spar deck, each division commanded by one of the ship's lieutenants assisted by one or more midshipmen.[3] (The quarterdeck guns were customarily manned by the marines and commanded by the marine officers.) Each division's paramount responsibility was to be ready to meet an enemy ship in battle. "It is absolutely necessary," Commodore John Rodgers enjoined, "that all officers, seamen, and others belonging to a man-of-war should be well skilled in the use of great guns; otherwise, the greatest ability in a commanding officer in taking positions will always be rendered abortive." To gain that skill one of the divisions drilled for three hours each morning that weather permitted. They did not, of course, cast loose the entire division of guns to practice; that would interfere too much with other ship's work. Instead, all members of the division took turns at one or two of the guns. Nor was drill confined to the big weapons. Boarding axes, cutlasses, and pistols were brought out during the divisional exercises; gun crews, especially those detailed as boarders, were carefully taught how to use these arms in an effective manner.[4]

The quarter bill not only organized the ship for battle, it was also the basis for supervising the discipline and the welfare of the enlisted men. Every evening, unless the weather was so severe as to put it out of the question, all the divisions mustered under the eyes of their officers. Fighting equipment was inspected to make sure it was in "perfect readiness for battle." As vitally important was the officers' inspection of their men to make sure that none was intoxicated, none absent, none slovenly or dirty, and that all shaved and put on clean shirt and trousers at least twice a week. Once a month or maybe twice, the divisional officers inspected every article of clothing the enlisted man owned and his bedding as well to make certain both were clean and in good repair. Was a man in need of additional or replacement garments? His divisional officers reported it to the first lieutenant, the first lieutenant to the captain, and the captain authorized the purser to make the appropriate issues. Had shore leave been granted? The enlisted man could not go over the side until he had passed inspection by his division officer to determine that he was "clean and decently dressed."[5]

In the division, too, the young officer learned to begin coping with paperwork. Not only was every midshipman expected to keep an official journal of the cruise—a document over which the captain would cast his eye once a week—he must have in his possession correct copies of the watch, quarter, and station bills, so that he might quickly determine whether all were present who ought to be and whether they were in their correct places. Moreover, he had to maintain a complete and accurate list of all the articles of clothing belonging to each enlisted man under his supervision, at least one purpose of which list was to make certain that the men were not trading clothing among themselves for liquor. To judge by the peremptory and irritable tone with which the captains repeatedly enjoined the keeping of all these lists by the divisional officers, it must have been an onerous responsibility, tempting to neglect, and one perhaps as much honored by its evasion as by its execution.[6]

The watch bill, the last of the triumvirate of lists that organized the ship as a sailing and fighting society, divided the men into two watches, which, in rotation, were responsible for the routine maneuvering of the ship by night and by day. Each of the three junior lieutenants and the sailing master was, in succession, officer of the watch; the midshipmen were customarily divided into three watches.[7] For lieutenants and midshipmen the number of hours of deck duty per twenty-four-hour period was substantially smaller than for the seamen. Midshipmen were expected to devote a major part of their day to study. With the lieutenants the shorter number of watch hours permitted the performance of other responsibilities such as gun drills. More important, shorter periods on watch assured greater alertness and attention to duty by the officer and reduced the number of hours per day each lieutenant must bear the stress of responsibility.

Shouldering the Burden

Responsibility. That is the word that best sums up the lieutenant's role as officer of the watch. True, both captain and first lieutenant were as near as their cabins should a serious situation arise; but the immediate burden for the functioning and the safety of the ship rested on the shoulders of the watch officer. He it was who must see that the ship maintained the course set by the captain; that sails were kept trimmed, rigging taut, and everything about the decks neat and properly stowed. Are the lookouts at the mastheads, the catheads, and the quarters alert and scanning the horizon for the first sign of a strange sail? Night has fallen. Are the men on their feet and in motion, performing the duties assigned them, or is anyone dozing at his post? "The officer of the watch will be held accountable for all irregularities or improprieties committed in his watch," John Rodgers warned.[8] Judging by the number of times it is mentioned in the ships' standing orders, one of the major irregularities and improprieties for which the officer of the watch had to be alert was the disappearance of midshipmen who were supposed to be on duty, whether that disappearance took the form of slipping below in the middle of the watch or standing down before a relief appeared.[9] During the day the officer of the watch had to keep a sharp eye on boats arriving alongside to make certain no liquor was smuggled on board, a task that sometimes seemed almost impossible. Was the weather blowing? His was the duty of seeing the ship pumped out every hour. Come night he had to make sure that lights were doused at nine p.m. in summer and eight p.m. in winter.[10] A few lights were still essential in case all hands must be called. These must be secure in lanterns, for fire in a wooden ship miles from land was a justly terrifying thought; that safety responsibility fell to the officer of the watch as well.[11] Fire, though fearfully dangerous, was also essential. Should the ship unexpectedly fall in with a stranger in the night, hot loggerheads must be at hand to fire the guns. A small charcoal fire was kept going in the galley all night, wherewith to light matches, if necessary; a watchful eye had to be kept on it, too.[12] As his duty drew to a close, or other quiet moment offered, the lieutenant must take a few minutes to note the courses, winds, speeds, and events of his watch in chalk on the log board for subsequent transfer to the ship's logbook—that is, if he had neglected the captain's standing order to do so "instantly" upon the hour.

Most of all the watch officer needed to be alert for signs of threatening weather, for strange ships, or for other things out of the ordinary. He needed to know, too, when the captain expected to be notified of these possible dangers.[13] Gradually—perhaps so slowly that the officer himself did not notice it—this burden of responsibility was modifying and shaping his personality. Novice midshipman William Lewis was self-aware enough and sufficiently new to the navy to observe the change in himself and in those about him:

> I am more than ever in the habit of thinking on past times. . . . This habit has been confirmed on me by the etiquette which exists on board ships of war and which prohibits any social intercourse between officers while on duty and thus has a tendency to deaden it while in their private berths and apartments. You can't imagine how different the relations are which exist between men as officers and as private individuals. Superior officers, subject to no control while on board a ship and accustomed to command inferior ones, can't help putting on airs of authority while on shore as gentlemen enjoying the same amusements.[14]

Accountable in Every Respect

A heavy responsibility it was to be a lieutenant and command a watch, but the heaviest of burdens, short of actually having a ship of one's own to command, was to be the senior or first lieutenant in a ship of war. The standards of selection were even more demanding than for attaining one's first promotion from midshipman to lieutenant. Not only must the captain be able to repose "the most unlimited confidence in the first lieutenant," even more, "the situation of first lieutenant requires a man in all respects fitted to take command of a ship in case circumstances should render it necessary."[15] Moreover, for the captain/first lieutenant relationship to achieve maximum effectiveness, another condition had to be present: their personalities had to mesh harmoniously.[16] It was the first lieutenant who, under the captain's general supervision, was responsible for managing all the details of the day-to-day routine of a ship of war, a responsibility symbolized, in part at least, by the first lieutenant's having in his care the keys to all the storerooms except the magazines. (The latter keys the captain himself kept.) Because of this broad responsibility the first lieutenant was customarily excused from standing watch unless the ship were, for one reason or another, shorthanded on lieutenants, in which case he could be found taking his turn in the rotation.[17] When all hands were called, the first lieutenant had the right to assume command and direct what was to be done; but often, especially when he had confidence in the watch officer, the first lieutenant would decline doing so and allow the watch officer to continue to give the orders. His prestige and authority were second only to the captain's; custom demanded that whenever the first lieutenant came on deck, the watch officer offer him the speaking trumpet, the symbol of authority, which the first lieutenant would then usually decline to accept.[18] After the captain, the first lieutenant was the great role model for the junior watch officers, who were admonished by the captain "always [to] be careful to carry on all kinds of duty as nearly in the manner pursued by the first lieutenant as possible, nothing contributing so much to accuracy and dispatch in performing maneuvers as uniformity in the mode."[19]

What a load of detail the first lieutenant had to oversee! When the ship was fitting for sea the captain, busy with many other concerns, gave him general instructions as to what he wished done. It was the first lieutenant who had to make certain that the stores all got on board, that the rigging was overhauled, that repairs and alterations—some essential, some perhaps the whim of the captain—were made. Then, as recruits began to arrive, the first lieutenant was expected to assign them to their watches, stations, quarters, messes, and hammock space—with, perhaps, the unwelcome sound of the captain's unsolicited advice clucking over his shoulder: "As watching the ship's company may very justly be considered the groundwork of all the rest, I have to request that you will be mindful of the advantages resulting from an equal distribution of the strength and professional experience of the men for the different watches as they are received and so stationed, as, by doing so, but few alterations will be found necessary by the time our crew is complete compared with what would be the case provided this essential was not attended to."[20]

Had one of the new recruits, imposing on the relatively inexperienced midshipman at the rendezvous, persuaded the recruiting officer to sign him on as a seaman, when his skills made him an ordinary seaman at best? The first lieutenant would observe him in action and reduce him to the appropriate rating. Whether in port or at sea the first lieutenant was responsible to the captain for the discipline of the men, the behavior of the midshipmen, and (more occasionally) the misconduct of junior officers. (Practice varied here with the personalities of particular captains and the abilities of particular first lieutenants. Some captains took a direct hand in a wide range of disciplinary and conduct matters; others preferred to tell the first lieutenant what they wanted and let him be the point of contact with malefactors.) At sea the whole business of the ship's housekeeping was in his hands: the often daily routines of cleaning decks, tiers, and storerooms; getting wet clothes up to dry; sweeping out messing places; rigging windsails to funnel air below decks; scraping tar and grease off ladders; whitewashing inside the lower decks; ventilating the magazines; coiling lines neatly; keeping the main deck clear of empty casks and useless lumber; and so on, down to the dreariest kinds of busywork. At last, toward noon, the first lieutenant could report to the captain that all was prepared for the latter's daily inspection; whereupon the captain would sweep grandly through the ship, not failing, one may be sure, to find a few things not to his satisfaction that the long-suffering first lieutenant had overlooked. Constantly pressing on his mind was the captain's directive that the first lieutenant "will be held responsible for the good order of the ship in every respect and made accountable for any deficiencies which he may neglect reporting to the captain."[21]

If all of this has created the impression that the fun went out of the young officer's life when he shed his midshipman's uniform for the responsibility that weighed far more than the lieutenant's elaborate dress coat, that impression needs correction. The proper antidote is to join *Hornet*'s second lieutenant, Charles Morris, as he writes from Charleston, South Carolina, in the earliest days of 1808 to his uncle (but peer in age), Lemuel Morris, at Boston:

> Here am I, shivering with cold, without a glass of wine to inspire me or a petticoat to warm me, while you (I hope) are seated among a dozen beauties whose enlivening conversation puts wine and even me out of your head. . . . To save you the trouble of conjecturing how I have spent my time, I beg leave

to inform you that I returned yesterday from a cruise of five days in the country. I started John Gilpin–like. My horse ran away with me. The women screamed; the men gazed; the Negroes hooted; and I hung on for about ten miles when my gentleman steed and myself both brought up in a river, which cooled us both so that we went on very well afterwards. My furious horse, however, introduced me to about a dozen fine girls, for taking it into his head that he should be well used at a house we were passing, he took the liberty of carrying me to the door, where a very polite gentleman was good enough to take his visit in good part and invite us both to stop and dine. My party soon coming up, his invitation was accepted, and in we went to partake of a bachelor's dinner as we thought. But lo! ten young ladies soon made their appearance, and Gilpin Junior and his adventures had the honor of contributing to their amusement. Dinner ended, Gilpin remounted and, with the assistance of a curb, bridle, and through the prayers of the young ladies, was fortunate enough to conquer the spirit of his Bucephalus and the next day shone to great advantage at a deer hunt.

From the deer hunt [Lieutenant Christopher] Gadsden and myself shaped our course twenty miles further to Point Pleasant, alias Quizzical Hall, the seat of a very rich planter, the father of his (Gadsden's) enamorato—and the father of her sister also, who is much the handsomest and whom in charity I was bound to entertain, that G. might have an opportunity of saying silly things to the other. I, however, took my heart away with me next day in spite of her fine black eyes, ruby lips, rosy cheeks, and inimitable graces, and returned through a fine northeast storm to town, which effectually effaced her from my imagination.[22]

14. Two Enemies

*S*HARED EXPERIENCES, common to the vast majority of the pre-1815 U.S. Navy's junior officers, are the thread that has run through the last two chapters. Two other shared experiences were encountered by only a fraction of the serving officers, but they conditioned every man's life and mindset. They were life-threatening storm at sea and combat with an enemy.

Storm

Any officer of the U.S. Navy who ever went to sea experienced storms. For most the perils these presented were not greater than those described by Chaplain A.Y. Humphreys during his last War of 1812 cruise:

[*Constitution*] stood to the northward and eastward, intending to make Madeira [and] crossing the track of the homeward-bound Brazil men. The only circumstances worth noting were a heavy gale which we encountered on the passage, which, kicking up a terrible sea, at midnight stove in the hawse plugs and deluged the gun deck. In a few moments nothing was to be heard but the swashing of a great body of water fore and aft on the gun deck; and, as my cot in the wardroom was slung to the beams of that deck (having no cabin), I was soon sensible that something novel was the matter; and I was soon confirmed in my belief by hearing the carpenter sing out [that] the ship was foundering and call upon the boatswain to turn out all hands. No water yet had found its way into the wardroom, and, though a little frightened, I concluded to remain where I was, in which I was further encouraged by Captain [Archibald] Henderson [USMC], who having been waked by the noise, ejected his head with nightcap on and eyes half-opened through the door of his stateroom and inquired what was the matter. Upon being told, he coolly observed there was no water here and then turned in, an example I speedily followed, concluding that, if he took it so easily, there was no reason why I should not. In a short time a little order was established, and, by cutting down the hammocks of the men berthed forward and jamming them in the hawseholes, further ingress to the water was denied, and egress obtained for that already shipped by manning the pumps and drawing the scupper plugs. 'Tis certain a large body of water, a weight of many tons, found its way into the ship, but I cannot subscribe to the opinion of Soundings [i.e., the carpenter] that she was settling by the head.[1]

Stout ships and good seamanship almost always kept vessels and men on the side of safety. But the sea was a violent, potent enemy; it was not unknown for U.S. warships to go down with all hands. Just how hostile the sea could be, just how much courage, desperation, luck, and superlative seamanship could be demanded, was demonstrated by the naval vessel that came closest to being lost with all hands—only to be saved by a whisker. She was the brig *Nautilus*, and had begun her existence as a merchant schooner, built on the Eastern Shore of Maryland in 1799. Purchased by the navy in May 1803, *Nautilus* was converted into a warship and filled a prominent and useful role during the latter campaigns of the Tripolitan War. In 1810 she was rerigged as a brig, a change that had compromised her previously superlative sailing qualities. Those qualities stemmed, of course, from her Chesapeake Bay schooner design. She was sharp, lay low in the water, and had so much rake to her bow and stern that her forecastle was diminutive; the captain's cabin was on a level with her spar deck, creating a poop deck above. The wheel, from which the quartermaster conned *Nautilus*, was located on the spar deck, immediately forward of the poop; directly behind the wheel was the door to the captain's cabin. Owing to her design *Nautilus* was so cramped below decks (and on deck) that, once fully weighted with guns, stores, and men, she was regarded as a comfortless vessel for winter cruising. This was especially true from the crew's perspective, only two-thirds of whom could get below at once. Not that going below in January was all that much better, for *Nautilus* was often so damp that, let freezing weather, snow, and ice appear, and several of the crew would quickly be on sick report with frostbite. *Nautilus*'s commander, Lieutenant Arthur Sinclair, was heartily sick of cruising in her under all kinds of adverse weather conditions. Add to which his armament of 14 24-pounder long guns, weighing 1,700 pounds apiece, was too heavy for a vessel of her size and had been a source of constant anxiety to Sinclair in winter cruising. "Those small vessels are very apt to be knocked down by the break of a sea, and then the great weight of metal hanging on her upper works would prevent her being saved, even by cutting away her masts; and, as for throwing guns overboard in such a time as that, when they are all under water, it cannot be done."[2] In December 1811 Sinclair was under welcome orders to sail *Nautilus* from Norfolk to Newport, Rhode Island, there to exchange her for the larger and more comfortable *Argus*.

There were other important figures besides the *Nautilus* herself among the cast of characters in the events that were about to unfold, for *Nautilus*'s voyage was to be as plagued by interpersonal tensions as it was by dangers of the sea. In December 1811 most of the crew were relatively new to the ship, having signed on in August, September, and October. Lieutenant Sinclair was one of the navy's abler young commanders of small vessels. He was also self-serving, arrogant, and insensitive to the feelings of others, and he had a history of less than excellent relations with his subordinate officers, especially his first lieutenants. This exterior persona, complemented by his tight, beautifully controlled handwriting, was a protective shell but imperfectly erected around an inner man corroded by hypersensitivity, ambition, and anxiety.

The first lieutenant, Walter Winter, rejoined *Nautilus* less than twenty-four hours before she sailed. He had served for two and a half years as one of the brig's lieutenants, but had, just a few days before, been transferred to more desirable duty in the frigate *United States*. Now he was back as an officer on loan from *United States*, to which ship he was due to return after getting *Nautilus* to Newport. Two years before Sinclair had evaluated Winter as "an extremely attentive, steady young man," but one at that time lacking the experience needed to qualify him for a first lieutenant's berth. Sinclair must also have known something about Winter's unusual past. When Walter Winter had been a novice officer in Commodore Richard V. Morris's Mediterranean squadron in 1803 he had suffered a devastating mental illness recorded by his fellow midshipman Henry Wadsworth:

> Mr. Winter, a midshipman of the Adams, from various causes which preyed on his mind, lost his senses and became a lunatic. One cause: his being arrested for neglect of duty; another—however, I cannot pretend to enumerate the causes which reduced him to his present sad situation. He will not hurt anyone— or himself. He will pay no attention to anything or answer when spoken to. He will not eat, drink, or obey any of the calls of nature for several days together— of course is much emaciated. He speaks incoherently, unconnectedly, and vehemently. He is now on board the Chesapeake and will return to his friends, who live in Maryland, provided God spares his life, which is very much doubted.

A year after the disabled midshipman's return to the United States Robert Smith heard that Winter was still not restored to mental health. Through third parties the secretary tried to persuade him to quit the navy: "The derangement of mind with which he is unfortunately afflicted entirely disqualifies him for the navy service, and, independently of this unhappy circumstance, I am induced to believe from information received from his commanding officers that he neither possesses taste nor fitness for the service. I cannot, therefore, consistently with duty, attach him to any ship; and, if he does not resign, I shall be under the painful necessity of dismissing him from the service." What happened next is not entirely clear from the surviving records. Seemingly Winter's family reported much improved mental health and urged Smith to let the midshipman demonstrate his recovery and his aptitude for seamanship by making a series of voyages as a mate in the merchant service. As evidence of his recovery, Winter presented himself in person to Smith at Washington or Baltimore. Noting that "Mr. Winter is an amiable young man, of genteel deportment and respectable descent, and I wish to restore him to the [active-duty] navy, if I can do it with propriety," Smith dispatched him on his merchant voyaging in the summer of 1804. Winter was clearly appreciative of Smith's second chance and determined to mend his mental health and deficient professional ways. From Batavia, Java, he wrote the secretary that his ship would soon sail for Calcutta,

> with which I am much pleased, as it not only affords an opportunity of seeing the continent, but gives me more time for improvement in the lunar observations and seamanship; and I flatter myself, Sir, on my return no young man who has not been longer in the service than myself will be able to show me my duty. You may rest assured, Sir, I have paid every attention since I have been on board, and I beg leave to inform you that, in my humble opinion, I have learned more of the practice of seamanship since I have been on board this ship than the whole time I was on board a public vessel. It appears to me, Sir, no midshipman on board one of our frigates can become a seaman, as I know from experience we are never allowed to take the helm, the management of which is the most essential part of seamanship. Captain [John] Mun has frequently stood hours together with me at the helm in blowing weather, doubling the Cape of Good Hope and at other times, which has learned me to

be a tolerable helmsman, and I now command the starboard watch without the captain's staying on deck, even in blowing weather, whereas before he always stayed on deck when it blew fresh.

Smith kept Winter in the merchant service, improving his seamanship and verifying his reestablished mental health, for nearly four years. From time to time the secretary would receive letters, dispatched from various ports around the world, relating Winter's adventures on the seas and brimming with anxiety to get back on active duty with the navy. By April 1808 he had so thoroughly proven himself as to earn his promotion to lieutenant; in August he was recalled to service.[3]

Two other officers completed the cast of human characters. Charles A. Budd, acting second lieutenant, has already been encountered in these pages. He was the Tripolitan War captain's clerk who grew weary of not having enough to do and persuaded his commanding officer, Charles Stewart, to make him an acting midshipman. Three years after the voyage of *Nautilus* Budd was described by Thomas Macdonough as "an intemperate man whose habits of intemperance are, I believe, so firmly rooted as to be nearly immovable. . . . He is careless or regardless of service." Something like this was clearly suspected as early as 1811–12, for Midshipman Budd was already being passed over for his lieutenant's commission. Fortunately, considering the events that were about to take place, Macdonough was to report that "his best quality is in his seamanship."[4] *Nautilus*'s acting sailing master, Midshipman Charles W. Skinner, had joined her from *United States* immediately before she sailed. He was slightly older than usual for a midshipman, twenty-two or twenty-three years of age, with extensive merchant service experience before he received his midshipman's warrant early in 1809. Skinner reported himself to Lieutenant Sinclair that December day with a high recommendation from his previous commanding officer, Stephen Decatur.[5] Thus equivocally officered, *Nautilus* sailed from Norfolk on 22 December 1811 to meet what James Beene, one of the brig's quartermasters and a veteran of twenty-six years at sea, called "the heaviest [gale] I ever was in."

By evening *Nautilus*, aided by a southwest wind, had passed outside the Virginia capes. Then the wind fell calm and the sky assumed a suspicious appearance. Sinclair decided to return inside the capes and await more favorable weather before beginning his run for Newport. "Well had it been for us had I used my judgment as it then dictated," he later reflected ruefully. When the wind did spring up again, it was from a direction that prevented a return to Hampton Roads. Monday, 23 December, found *Nautilus* running parallel with the Virginia-Maryland shore, south of the entrance to Delaware Bay, propelled by a wind from the southeast. As evening came on it was Lieutenant Winter's watch on deck. The wind began backing round to the northward and eastward, and squalls of heavy rain appeared. All signs pointed to a gale; Sinclair promptly ordered precautions taken. Down came tophamper. Guns and boats were double lashed. Shot went below deck. Hatches were secured. By seven o'clock the wind had shifted round to the north-northwest, the bearing of Delaware Bay, making any attempt to reach shelter there impossible. Sinclair ordered Winter to wear *Nautilus* to the north and east and heave to under reduced sail. At eight p.m. acting sailing master Skinner, who until that time had been forward getting all snug for the blow, came aft and relieved Winter as officer of the watch. A heavy sea was running and *Nautilus*, which, it will be remembered, had a low freeboard, was shipping great quantities of water.

Lieutenant Sinclair had come on deck about six p.m., as soon as it became apparent that *Nautilus* was in for some rough weather. By ten o'clock the storm was not getting any worse; it looked as though it would be nothing more than a routine gale. Sinclair decided to turn in and snatch some sleep, but instructed Skinner to notify him if there was any change. Be the situation better or worse, Skinner was to call Sinclair at midnight and report the state of weather. A few minutes before that appointed hour, a lightly sleeping Arthur Sinclair was awakened by the sound of orders being given to clew up the main topsail. He was just about to get up and go on deck "when I was thrown from my berth on the side of the vessel, and in an instant the cabin was filled with water. By great exertion I gained a passage on deck. But—Great God!—what a scene of horror did I witness there: the vessel laying on her beam ends; the water bursting in at every hatch; everything floating in the lee waist; a number of men washed to leeward swimming to gain the weather side; and those who were already there crying out, 'The Lord have mercy on us; we are gone!'; the storm raging with such violence as baffles all description; the hail and snow forcing too strong to be faced, from clouds of a most terrific [aspect]; and the sea making a continual breach over us; all together roaring ten times louder than thunder."

While Sinclair had been asleep Mr. Skinner's watch had proceeded more or less normally, with a heavy sea running and *Nautilus* still shipping water, but without any serious change, till about 11:30 p.m. Then the sea grew taller and the wind blew still harder, until *Nautilus* commenced rolling her lee hammock cloths under water. Skinner at once gave the order to man the main topsail clewlines and buntlines that had awakened Sinclair, whereupon *Nautilus* lurched so heavily to leeward as to bring the quarter of her launch (stowed amidships) under water. While Skinner's men were struggling to take in the topsail, Lieutenant Sinclair appeared at the cabin door. *Nautilus*'s commander immediately instructed Skinner to turn up all hands and call the officers, intending thereafter to house the lee guns and see whether that lessened the brig's heel. Even the brief time required for officers and men to begin appearing from below was enough to convince Sinclair that merely housing the guns would be too little and too late. The brig was in immediate danger of foundering; her guns must be thrown overboard. Acting lieutenant Budd was the first officer to appear on deck. Sinclair instructed him to go forward and start getting the guns over the side—a formidable task in view of the weather. Lieutenant Winter's was the second fresh face upon which Sinclair's eye alighted; he was promptly sent off to aid Mr. Budd, who surely needed all the help he could get.

Skinner, who was still officer of the watch and maneuvering *Nautilus* under Sinclair's general directions, had hardly seen Budd and Winter vanish into the darkness and spray forward, when Midshipman Richard Steuart came running aft shouting, "Hard up! Hard up!" Who gave the order to put the helm up? Skinner demanded to know. "Mr. Budd, Sir." No doubt highly irritated at having his authority as officer of the deck usurped, Skinner instructed Midshipman Steuart to go forward and tell Mr. Budd that the helm would be put up *only* on orders from Captain Sinclair. The next figure to appear out of the gloom was acting lieutenant Budd himself, who came as far aft as the mainmast and, ignoring Skinner entirely, shouted to the quartermaster, "Hard up!" To his even greater irritation Skinner saw that the quartermaster was actually beginning to obey Budd's order, and he rebuked the quartermaster sharply: *He* was officer of the deck and only *his* orders, or Captain Sinclair's *through him*, were to be obeyed.

As it happened, Budd had been correct in his assessment of what ought to be done; Sinclair was fast reaching the same decision. *Nautilus* now lay so low in the water that the heavy chop sea was constantly breaking over the vessel, knocking to leeward those who were at work forward and trying desperately to get the first gun overboard. The hatch coamings were under water. *Nautilus*, still heeled over on her beam ends, gave every appearance of foundering slowly and without ever righting herself. An attempt must be made to get before the wind. If necessary, the mainmast would have to be cut away. Fortunately, the axes were close at hand. Put the helm aweather, Mr. Skinner. Stand by to cut away the mainmast, Sinclair ordered. It worked! As *Nautilus* wore before the wind, the force of the storm on the forestaysail righted the vessel. With the goosewings of the foresail spread, the brig was able to scud before the storm, freed for the moment from her most imminent dangers.

Sinclair, standing by the wheel, scarce had time to breathe a sigh of relief when Lieutenant Winter materialized to announce that, in his opinion, the storm seemed to be slackening; *Nautilus* was not in any mortal danger. Would it not be well to belay the drastic expedient of getting the guns overboard and see how things went? Perhaps the armament could yet be saved. Sinclair was in no mood to listen to unsolicited advice, especially when he knew that it was only because the brig was running large that Winter was deceived into thinking the storm was moderating. The captain realized the guns had to go if *Nautilus* was to survive. Sinclair bothered not to conceal his anger. Go forward, Sir, and execute the order I gave you, he told Winter. I hold *myself* responsible for the ship's safety, and I shall use my *own* judgment.

The following sea, driven by the fury of the gale, was often so high that it masked the foresail from the wind, becalming *Nautilus* and causing the sea to break over her stern; Sinclair ordered the main topsail set in an effort to relieve this situation. It was now one a.m., 24 December. All of these events had taken place in the space of an hour. The rain had changed to sleet and snow. Once the main topsail was set, Winter came aft to take charge of the deck, while Skinner went forward to work with Budd in getting the guns overboard. Sinclair, who had come on deck wearing a light coat and slippers, decided to take advantage of the stabilized situation to go below, warm up, and rest—leaving, of course, the other officers on deck to face the storm. The captain found himself too uneasy to rest. He soon reappeared in the cabin doorway, where he braced himself, partly sheltered from the storm's fury, observing, directing, and from time to time climbing on a nearby carronade slide to peer over the ship's side.

Nautilus's situation had stabilized on the side of safety—but just barely. The gale continued to rage, with rain, sleet, and snow filling the air. Acting sailing master Skinner had to labor until three or four o'clock in the afternoon of the 24th before he had thirteen of the brig's fourteen cannon over the side. First the guns forward; then those aft; finally the ones amidships. The fourteenth gun was preserved against the contingency of needing to fire signals of distress. To get an enormously heavy cannon over the ship's side in a raging gale, without injury to the men doing the job, and without the gun going adrift and knocking a hole in the ship's side as it went overboard, or dropping through the deck when it was being hoisted outboard, was a measure of Charles Skinner's skill as a seaman. Even with the close-reefed topsail set, the following sea still occasionally broke over *Nautilus*. One tremendous wave—in Sinclair's eye "the height of a mountain"—came crashing down, shivered the outer boarding of her stern to atoms, and ripped all the lead off the taffrail. Strained beyond their limits, the wheel ropes and wheel rope blocks parted repeatedly and had to be secured anew. By afternoon *Nautilus* was so full of water that she "lay like a log"; had not the guns been long gone, the combined weight of cannon and water must have taken her down. Holes were cut in the lower deck to drain the water down to the bilge pumps; these, being fine equipment, kept working and finally got much of the water out of the hull. Then, just as the ropes from wheel to rudder had given way one more time and before the quartermasters could effect repairs, another following sea crashed down. When the water drained away, so did the shattered remains of *Nautilus*'s supplementary or poop deck tiller, by means of which the brig was being conned while the wheel ropes were under repair. Without a tiller the brig must broach to. The sea would break over her. *Nautilus* would capsize and go down with all hands.

Somehow a capstan bar was rigged as a tiller; the day was once more saved. But night was coming on; dangers seemed to be multiplying; each escape was narrower than the last; fatigue was growing and hope dwindling. Morale disintegrated, discipline collapsed, and all the crew except the petty officers and six or eight men—fifteen to twenty good hands at best—simply gave up, defied orders, and went below. Disgusted, but concluding that it was good riddance to get the disaffected out of the way and their weight off the deck, Sinclair secured the hatches to keep them below and continued to manage his ship with the officers and the fewer than twenty men who remained at their posts.

Now Sinclair had to face a fresh problem. Since he had gotten *Nautilus* before the wind the brig had run more than two hundred miles in a direct line for Bermuda, which now bore between three hundred and four hundred miles dead ahead. If *Nautilus* continued on her present course, the storm could well drive her ashore on Bermuda sometime the next day. The only solution was to take advantage of some momentary lull to heave the brig to; that is, to bring her head up into the wind and let her ride out the storm in that situation. The act of heaving to could be dangerous; there seemed no good alternative. Sinclair summoned his sailing master, Midshipman Skinner, to the cabin and told him of his decision. Skinner returned to the deck and directed the necessary preliminary alterations of sail—such adjustments of sail were among the responsibilities of a sailing master in a man-of-war—and then waited an hour and a half for a lull in the storm. At last it came. Skinner handed officer of the deck Walter Winter the trumpet and said, "Now is a smooth time." Winter ordered the quartermaster to put the helm down; *Nautilus*'s bow came slowly and safely up into the wind. The storm resumed its full fury soon enough, but Sinclair, who had been watching Skinner and Winter execute this critical maneuver, was relieved to see that, freed from the weight of her guns, *Nautilus* could, in this position, ride out the storm safely enough, although every part of the brig would remain soaking wet from the waves breaking over her bows and bulwarks.

Not for long was Sinclair allowed to enjoy his sense of relief. At midnight, 24/25 December, a tremendous sea struck *Nautilus*, ripping away the bowsprit and, apparently, the jibboom as well. The captain instantly ordered the fore-topmast cut away, thereby keeping the foremast from following the bowsprit overboard. That was far from the end of his problems with these broken spars. Although all the lines to the wreckage were cut, *Nautilus* drifted foul of the overboard spars. These thumped and banged at her counter viciously, creating grave fears that they would stave a hole in her planking, a hole through which the sea could rush in below decks. Lieutenant Winter, who by now had been relieved as watch officer and was directing operations forward, labored till daylight to get *Nautilus* clear of the drifting wreckage, his mood not at all improved by midshipmen arriving periodically with messages from Captain Sinclair exhorting him to hurry even faster.

Christmas day, which began so inauspiciously, actually brought the first signs that the storm was beginning to moderate. By 26 December the weather had improved sufficiently to permit Skinner to direct the rigging of a jury bowsprit and jury fore-topmast. On the 27th the wind actually shifted round to the eastward; *Nautilus* spread all the sail she could safely carry in an attempt to regain the safety of Chesapeake Bay. As he stood his watches or lay in his bunk during these first hours free of crisis and the demand for unceasing attention and instantaneous reaction, Walter Winter thought a great deal about Arthur Sinclair. Possibly the roots of his disenchantment lay as far back as 1809, when he had first served under Sinclair. Perhaps there were serious personality frictions between them. Be that as it may, the events of the last few days had completely alienated Winter from Sinclair's style of command. Not that he could fault the captain's seamanship. Sinclair had given the orders that had kept *Nautilus* safe thus far. Then, too, Winter had to admit that Sinclair had been right and he had been wrong on the question of throwing the guns overboard; had they not gone over the side, the danger of the brig's foundering would have been great indeed. Sinclair's leadership was, in Winter's opinion, another matter. It seemed to him that Sinclair had ridden out too much of the storm in his cabin, summoning key officers there to receive his orders, and leaving the actual execution of critical maneuvers to Winter and Skinner. When he did come on deck, it was to stand braced in the doorway of his cabin (which, it will be remembered, was immediately aft of the wheel) and issue his orders from there. The farthest he moved from this spot was to climb on a nearby carronade slide the better to peer over the brig's side. At no point during the storm had anyone observed Sinclair to mount the poop, the only place from which he could have seen to windward when *Nautilus* was before the wind. Neither had he once gone forward to observe conditions there at first hand. Except for a few old hands, *Nautilus*'s crew were all recently shipped men. In Winter's opinion their morale would have stayed higher, their discipline would have been stiffened, and fewer of them would have deserted their duty posts and gone below had the captain been on deck, a figure of authority, visibly exercising leadership. Was it too much to say that Arthur Sinclair was conspicuously on deck only when the weather moderated? Indeed, it seemed to Winter that Sinclair's conduct bordered on the unofficerlike. God grant he lived to rejoin *United States*, Walter Winter did not intend to make any secret of his opinion of Lieutenant Sinclair's officership.

That reunion with old shipmates was not destined to take place nearly as soon as Walter Winter and his companions hoped. The daylight hours of 27 December went as well as could be expected under the circumstances. *Nautilus* fell in with, and paused to help, a brig that had upset in the storm; the latter's master told Sinclair that he had seen other merchantmen in as bad or worse plights. Sinclair himself now began to feel extremely weak. After being awakened a few minutes before midnight on 23/24 December, Sinclair had not had even a minute's sleep until the night of 26/27 December, although he tried to maintain his strength by stretching out in his berth, the only dry spot in his entire cabin, from time to time. Nor were the other officers in any better condition. Even the caustic Lieutenant Winter had, at one point, been lying in his bunk so ill and wretched that he begged Sinclair to excuse him from performing a special assignment when it was not his watch.[6] It was the 27th at least before food or drink was served out to officer or man; everything was so saturated with water that building a fire was totally out of the question; the hatches once secured over the disaffected, no one dared open them to get at the storerooms. (When were the enlisted men who had deserted their posts and been locked below hatches on the evening of 24 December released? None of the accounts ever says.)

Whatever slender hopes of soon being snug inside the Chesapeake capes sustained these weary battlers of the storm during the 27th were that night dispelled. The wind again shifted to the northwest, rose to gale force, and lashed the long-suffering *Nautilus* with a mixture of rain, snow, and hail, weather conditions that prevailed without respite for thirteen days and drove *Nautilus* nine hundred or a thousand miles out into the Atlantic, though by keeping her larboard tacks on board and assisted by the current of the Gulf Stream, the brig was able to avoid being forced farther to the south. On 11 January the wind again shifted.[7] Now it came out of the northeast, still blowing a gale and bringing with it what Sinclair described as "more rain and hail than I ever saw." Three days of running before this wind failed to bring *Nautilus* onto soundings; then, on 14 January, the wind shifted yet again and blew with equal force from the west. Sinclair was by now determined to take advantage of any wind that would take *Nautilus* to any port in the United States. Because gaining a southern one, the captain's original intention, was an impossibility in the teeth of the westerly gale, he bore up sometime on 15 January for his original destination, Newport, Rhode Island. Twenty-four hours gave *Nautilus* her first sight of land at Montauk Point, Long Island; soon thereafter Newport Light was in plain view, and *Nautilus*'s signals brought a pilot on board. Just a few more hours and all hands would be snug in port, filling the ears of peers from other ships with tales of their adventures, eating full rations instead of half ones, and drinking all the fresh water they desired, rather than having to restrict themselves to one quart per man per day.

No, it was not to be. That close to safety, then the lowering sky unleashed yet another violent snowstorm that drove *Nautilus* back out to sea. "This lasted only twenty-four hours, but our sufferings were beyond description," Sinclair later wrote. "We never had a dry stitch of clothing of any kind. Beds, berths, and everything on board had been wet for twenty-five days with scarcely ever a fire. Many [had broken] out in raw running sores and biles from the continual wet, and now [this] was more than we could bear. I gave every encouragement and indulgence in my power to afford, and still we had much difficulty to keep [the men from] laying down and freezing to death." Perhaps only a commander as cold and as determined as Sinclair could have done it, but the next day, 17 January, *Nautilus* was once more up with Newport Light, when, "to my utter mortification, it began to snow and so thick we could not see our way. But, as the pilot thought there was a possibility of getting her safe in, I determined to risk it, and by infinite [labor] we beat her in through ice and snow, with which she was completely [covered] when we anchored." Commodore John Rodgers, who along with Secretary Paul Hamilton had long since given *Nautilus* up for lost, pulled out with his boats to meet the brig as soon as he sighted her limping into port. Rodgers and David Porter came over the side to find a skeleton whom they eventually recognized as Arthur Sinclair, a terribly frostbitten Charles W. Skinner—to whom, more than any other officer, Sinclair attributed the brig's survival—an exhausted crew, and *Nautilus* mere wreckage in every part of the vessel. Rodgers surveyed the scene and heard Sinclair's story. The commodore was a man rarely at a loss for overwrought rhetoric. In this case, however, simplicity was demanded: Yours, he told Sinclair, is one of the most miraculous escapes I have ever known.

The most amazing aspect of this closest of escapes was one that nobody mentioned at the time. *Nautilus* had not been a crack ship, with a cadre of officers experienced at working together and loyal to one another; neither had she possessed a veteran, highly trained crew. Her petty officers, praises be, were old hands; but the commissioned and warrant officers, though individually skillful mariners, were in some cases new to the ship, and interpersonal tensions were high. If such a ship's company of very flawed human beings could perform so well in extreme stress, did that not speak eloquently of the state of training and seamanship among the navy's officers on the eve of war?

Well it would have been if all hands had rallied around John Rodgers's assessment of the escape of *Nautilus* as miraculous, congratulated themselves, told a few ever-taller tales, and let it go at that. Instead there was an anticlimactic sequel. It took less than a month for word to get back to Arthur Sinclair that Lieutenant Winter was openly bad-mouthing his captain's leadership during the voyage. The latter immediately (7 February 1812) requested a court of inquiry into his own conduct. A panel composed of Isaac Hull, James Lawrence, and William M. Crane was eventually assembled, began hearing evidence on 15 September, and concluded its deliberations four days later. Close reading of the court's opinion suggests that its members were not prepared to encourage the practice of disgruntled first lieutenants bringing charges against their commanding officers. They found that "Lieutenant Walter Winter had no just cause to charge [then Lieutenant, now] Master Commandant Arthur Sinclair with unofficerlike conduct" during the passage from Norfolk to Newport, and "that the measures taken [by Sinclair] for the preservation of said vessel were necessary and proper." As significant as what the members of the court said was what they did not say. They might have expressed an opinion that Winter was censurable. They did not. They might have praised Sinclair for his skill and leadership in saving *Nautilus*. They did not. Sinclair's conduct had been correct in a narrow sense. It can scarcely have aroused enthusiasm in the minds of the court's members. Their leadership styles were each and all very different from Sinclair's. With their equivocal opinion and his own memories and assessment of his vital role in saving *Nautilus* Arthur Sinclair would have to be satisfied as best he could.

Officers of the pre-1815 navy collectively wrote thousands of manuscript pages dealing with battle: dispatches, private letters, logs, diaries, reminiscences. But all these pages, useful as they are to historians of the navy's operations, say remarkably little about the subjective experience of deadly combat, especially from the point of view of the subordinate officer.[8] The best subjective narrative that survives—though still far from telling as much about the author's emotional reactions as one would like to know—comes from the pen of a man who wrote retrospectively, but one who possessed an accurate memory and recalled the past without romanticizing it. This is the way Midshipman William Skiddy remembered *Hornet*'s March 1815 encounter with an enemy:

> Our first lieutenant (D[avid] Conner) had just landed [on Tristan da Cunha] when the signal was made to return, there being a strange sail in sight, standing down for us. We hove to and was getting dinner (it was duff day)* while she was running down. The duff was hardly swallowed when the drum beat to quarters. This required but a few minutes, and all was ready for action and every eye watching the stranger. He soon luffed to on our weather quarter about pistol shot off, hoisted the British flag, and gave us a gun. This we did not notice, waiting for him to shoot ahead more. He now gave us the first broadside, and as soon as their guns flashed ours were in operation, and in five minutes I perceived the blood running from his scuppers a stream; and, as he almost stopped firing, our little captain [James Biddle] ordered us to cease. The enemy, thinking we were disabled, renewed his fire, and of course we soon convinced him of his mistake. He then, as a last alternative, ran his bowsprit between our main- and mizzenmasts, with the intention to carry us by boarding.
>
> I was stationed with the first lieutenant in the third division on the quarterdeck (three after guns each side) and was now commanding this division, the first lieutenant having been severely wounded at the commencement and carried below. The jib halyards being shot away, the foretack was hauled down to veer the ship. The enemy was now past us [i.e., Skiddy's division], and all hands called to repel boarders. We were then hand to hand, and the enemy were soon driven back. We were now on the enemy's bows, and it required all the exertions of our captain and officers to prevent our men from boarding them. Had they gone, the enemy would have suffered very much. Their men were now (hearing the cry from us to board) running below and left their first lieutenant ([James] McDonald) alone on the forecastle. Many muskets were leveled at him, but were prevented by our officers from firing on so brave a man. He then asked our leader (the second lieutenant, [John T.] Newton) the name of the ship and was answered "U.S. Sloop Hornet," when he waved his sword and walked aft.
>
> Our ship, in shooting ahead, carried away his bowsprit, tore away all our mizzen rigging, and the enemy lay across our stern. Our captain was standing on the arms chest aft, speaking to them, when their foremast fell along the lee waist. The marines in the foretop clung, with their muskets, to the rigging as the mast fell, and, as soon as [they were] down, jumped forward, fired, and wounded our captain, the ball passing through his neck. They undertook to rake us with their bow guns, then opposite our stern. I was standing in one of

---

* One day a week, in both the U.S. and British navies, the ship's company received—in place of beef—flour, suet, and currants or raisins with which to make a duff, a stiff pudding boiled in a bag or steamed.[9]

the stern ports (being open), looking directly at them and only about twelve feet off. We were then all hands aft to prevent their boarding, and I certainly expected to see many of us fall at this fire. Had those guns been well directed, many of us must have been killed; but fortunately, at this very moment, the sea lifted our ship's stern, and the balls went under the counter in the water. Our ship now came round on the other tack, and I played my division of guns into them, raking them fore and aft. They again cried quarters, and our captain ordered us to cease.

She proved to be H.B.M. Sloop of War *Penguin*, Captain [James] Dickinson, who was killed during the action by a ball through the heart. . . . They reported fifteen men killed and twenty-eight wounded. . . . We had one killed and eleven wounded and all in the after division (my division). The poor fellow that was killed was a six-foot marine that was firing over my head, and the first I perceived was his brains on my shoes, and in turning I observed the top of his skull taken off by a ball. As he was much in the way, I shoved him through one of the ports overboard. The first lieutenant was also wounded standing by me.

In 1846, when he was sixty-three years old and halfway around the world on a three-year cruise in the ship of the line Columbus, *James Biddle wrote, "I have become heartily tired of the sea and all its anxieties and all its discomforts. I am aware that life at sea is just what it was* forty-six years ago, *when I first knew and liked it, and that the change is not in it, but in me." Here is the victor of the* Hornet-Penguin *duel when thirty-three years old, a captain, still eager for active duty and life at sea. His austere and humorless face, recorded by Charles Willson Peale in 1816, is that of an ambitious man whose persistence, abilities, and career-promoting father had taken him to the highest rank of his profession in spite of liabilities that had, in 1810, led John Rodgers to brush him off as "a genteel young man [whose] sight and hearing are both imperfect; consequently, on that account, he is not so well qualified, particularly for the first lieutenant of a ship of this magnitude [the frigate* President], *as he otherwise might be."* Independence National Historical Park Collection, Philadelphia.

I carried him out of the way of the guns and had him sent below. The most painful was the heartsickening sight (after the fight) of all those poor fellows who only a few minutes ago were well and joyful and now all mangled by different kinds of balls and splinters. Groans were heard from all quarters. We were now employed getting the prisoners on board, unbending and bending sails, repairing rigging, [and] replacing as soon as possible all damages. This called us from the dying groans of the wounded. The surgeons were all employed amputating limbs and dressing wounds. The prize [was] taken in tow, and night veiled the dismal scene. Several died during the night and were committed to the deep without any ceremony. Captain Dickinson was buried the day after with the honors of war, his own officers and mariners officiating. . . .

When our little captain was wounded a man from one of my guns pulled off his old checked shirt, tore it in strips, took hold of Captain Biddle, and wound this round his neck. He [Biddle], then holding his bandage himself, was asked by one of our officers if he thought himself much hurt, when he replied, "No, no, give it to the damned rascals!" This shot was fired, recollect, after they had once given up. After the action was all over, the doctor ([Surgeon Benjamin P.] Kissam) came to the captain (who was still at his post, holding onto his neck) and asked him if he would go down and have his wound dressed? The captain answered that, if he had got through with the rest, he believed he would go, and then we heard that the ball had passed through his neck and out through his coat collar behind.

One of our men on board the Penguin picked up a hat on the quarterdeck in which he found a man's head that had been shot off. He very deliberately pull[ed] the head out, looked at it saying, "Matey, you don't now require a hat," put it on his own head and dispatched the other overboard. I have seen him with this hat on often in New York. The sailors were also looking out for the legs amputated, that they might get some shoes and stockings, as the doctor did not take the trouble to pull them off. One very remarkable occurrence, and that was one of the English midshipmen, a young man who sat on the wardroom table, smiling and talking and joking with one of his wounded shipmates near him who had lost a leg, while the doctor amputated one of his [own] legs, without the least emotion. When it was off, "Never mind," said he, "Bond (his messmate wounded), we will soon get on sticks and have fun with the girls yet." This poor fellow was on crutches when removed on board the Tom Bowline [the U.S. squadron's storeship] with the other prisoners, took cold, and had his leg amputated a second time by their own surgeon. Poor fellow, he died. Bond I often met at St. Salvador, Brazil.

PART FOUR
To Make a Sea Officer

"Many muskets were leveled at him, but were prevented by our officers from firing on so brave a man." Midshipman Skiddy's story of the U.S. officers' response to the sight of Penguin's lieutenant left alone on his forecastle points to the existence among those officers of shared values, in this particular case respect for bravery. Equally, the adroitness of Hornet's victory over Penguin—defeating the British brig despite Hornet's first lieutenant, David Conner, being grievously wounded at the beginning of the action; her captain, James Biddle, being partly disabled during its course; and ending the battle with her twenty-one-year-old second lieutenant, John T. Newton, as the senior uninjured officer—all this suggests a high state of training and discipline among the officers. How had these shared values, these well-honed skills, been acquired?

Not by accident or inadvertence. Rather, they were the result of a conscious and sustained educational program. One could hardly overestimate the importance that the corps attached to its educational effort during the pre-1815 years. Operations aside, there may be no aspect of the U.S. Navy's early history that is more extensively documented in its surviving records. "Without officers what can be expected from a navy? The ships cannot maneuver themselves, nor will the best of soldiers answer as substitutes for seamen," Thomas Truxtun exhorted Secretary of War James McHenry as early as 1797. "If we are to have a navy, we must make officers to manage that navy."[1]

Educating officers was a task always needed, never completed. But to talk of the pre-1815 navy's educational program and of how large it bulked in the collective consciousness of the officer corps is to speak of much more than formal classroom instruction. To be sure, such instruction was a major component of the educational program; but that educational program was a broader process, one by which an entire spectrum of professional culture and values was transmitted from one generation of officers to another.[2] It extended from on-the-job training in the basics of seamanship, through the development of self-discipline, to the inculcation of ethical standards and behavior. Once this broader definition of education is perceived, one appreciates that the officer corps' educational program was going on all the time, in a rich variety of circumstances.

153

15. The Young Officer's Best Teachers

GREEMENT WAS nearly universal among the pre-1815 navy's leaders: the place to learn professional skills, values, and culture was on shipboard, and preferably in a large warship; the best transmitters of these skills, values, and culture were the experienced officers who had already internalized them.

In years of relative peace the naval leadership's concern to promote active, shipboard cruising as the way to learn to be an officer was more explicit than during wartime. When the latter condition prevailed anxiety over education took a back seat. In the years between the end of the Tripolitan War and the declaration of war against Great Britain in 1812 the leaders' preoccupation with providing realistic opportunities at sea to shape officers assumed the character of a chorus.[1] The secretaries of the navy who served between 1801 and 1812, Robert Smith and Paul Hamilton, were the civilian leaders most concerned with promoting officer formation through active duty and formal education. When the historian writes about the pre-1815 navy's program of education, the secretaries to whom one refers, and whose words one quotes, are Smith and Hamilton. Both men deserve credit for the clear vision with which they saw that such programs were essential to the navy's future and for the energy and enthusiasm they devoted to implementation. Because of the demographics of the corps, officers whose development Smith oversaw were better positioned to distinguish themselves in War of 1812 combat than those who commenced their naval careers during Hamilton's term of office. But the dark cloud that hangs over the latter part of Paul Hamilton's tenure should not obscure the effectiveness with which he worked to promote officer development, even as other aspects of his administration were beginning to turn sour.

The way to learn to be an officer was through active service; the place to perform that active service was on shipboard, especially in a large or medium-size warship engaged in active cruising.[2] The reasons for this preference were not always explicitly stated, but they are lurking just below the surface of the documents and are readily inferred. Such ships cruised to a variety of places and experienced the spectrum of possible conditions at sea; they carried a full complement of able, experienced officers to serve as teachers and role models; the discipline maintained on board was likely to be stricter and more effective. How effective was the navy's policy of teaching officership by active-duty cruises at sea? Listen to the testimony penned by Captain William Branford Shubrick as he looked back, from the perspective of the 1840s, to his earliest duty:

> From the period of my entrance upon active service (1807) until after the War of 1812 the state of the foreign relations of the country was such that no squadrons were sent abroad, but the few ships composing the navy were kept actively cruising during winter and summer, from port to port of our own coast, enforcing the embargo and nonintercourse laws, the smaller vessels occasionally crossing the ocean with dispatches. On such service . . . the ships in which I served *continuously* were employed for a period of more than eleven years, including the war. . . . There is no question . . . that such service, under the then stringent system of discipline, was the most improving to which the officers of the navy could have been subjected, the evidence of which is to be found in the results of the contests of those same ships and officers with an enemy strong in experience and in the confidence of a before-unchecked career.[3]

Where Not to Learn . . . Maybe

When the navy's leaders argued that the best possible place to learn officership was on a large or medium-size warship actively cruising at sea under an experienced commander, they also held an idea regarding the type of vessel wherein young men learned to be neither seamen nor officers. The anathematic vessel was the gunboat, and the voices raised against it formed a nearly unanimous chorus. There were many notes, of varying degrees of shrillness, in the chorus, but the line was always a variation on the objections of one mother: "On board of a gunboat, in which he has been from the time of his appointment until now, he has no opportunity to acquire a practical knowledge of his profession; he is exposed to the contagion of vicious example; gains not the advantage of discipline; forms not the valuable manners of an officer; and thus has every prospect of future service to his country blasted and destroyed. These thoughts distress and harass me."[4]

The objections to gunboats as a school for the shaping of officers, though never so fully explained as the historian might wish, can be boiled down to four. (1) The nature of the service on which gunboats were customarily employed in harbors and coastal waters prevented young men from learning seamanship, which was only to be acquired in vessels cruising the high seas. (2) Officers commanding gunboats—sometimes older midshipmen, often sailing masters— were not appropriate mentors and role models for novice officers. (3) The small number of officers assigned to each gunboat, customarily only one or two, militated against the formation of the shared routines, attitudes, ethical values, and self-discipline—in a word, the mentality—of the professional officer; such habits and outlook were best developed where many served together. (4) Gunboat service ruined potentially good officers by undermining subordination and encouraging the formation of self-destructive vices.

Abundant evidence could be cited to support every one of these contentions. Even so, the historian has to argue that gunboats may be the victims of a bad press. Generally speaking, the larger the vessel, the greater its creature comforts, the pleasantness of the duty, and the prestige it conferred. For the professional naval officer this created a built-in bias against gunboats. A few remarkable officers grew up almost exclusively in gunboats. One such was Thomas ap Catesby Jones, whose entire 1808–15 career was spent in gunboats and small craft on the New Orleans station.[5] Although he was later to claim that midshipmen "cannot learn anything on board of gunboats," it was an irrepressible teacher, Commodore Alexander Murray, who left the best recorded use of gunboats as a device for educating young officers.[6] In the middle of the Embargo of 1807–1809, Murray found himself with twenty to thirty lieutenants and midshipmen under his supervision in and around Philadelphia, experienced not a little difficulty in keeping them out of trouble's way, and saw nothing on the horizon to occupy their professional attention except some newly finished gunboats. To solve his problem Murray hit upon the scheme of fitting out Gunboats Nos. 116 and 117 under Lieutenants Bernard Henry and William Burrows, signing on ten hands per boat, giving each lieutenant four midshipmen to supervise, and sending the boats off to explore Delaware Bay. "You are herewith furnished with a book of naval regulations and also a set of signals for your government, to which you will endeavor strictly to conform to," he instructed Henry, the senior lieutenant.

> Although your command is on a small scale, yet you may derive much instruction as an officer in making yourself perfectly acquainted with most of the duties required of us *whenever you should be honored with a higher station.*
>
> 'Tis, I trust, unnecessary to point out minutely the matters contained in those regulations, *as most in point* what I now enjoin on your present cruise is to be careful in sounding all the intricate parts of the bay and river and note down in your logbook such observations as may be of moment for the guide of the next division of officers that will supersede you, and keep steadily employed in that way whenever the weather is good and endeavor to make a harbor when otherwise. The shoals about the capes you will be particularly attentive to, so that in case of an emergency you may bring a frigate into secure anchorage, as in stormy weather pilots are not always to be got; and when the weather is fine you may run out along the coast thirty or forty miles each direction, examining your chart well, to make yourself acquainted with the coast thereabouts; but I would advise you to keep a harbor in your reach every night and not suffer yourself to be caught on a lee shore, as these boats will not beat off in a stormy sea. A month or five weeks will be long enough for you to be down this trip, by which time you will be enabled to explore the greater part of the waters of the Delaware, so that, in the event of war, you may know where to take proper stations for the annoyance of any intruders.
>
> I earnestly enjoin you to preserve harmony and concord among yourselves and enforce your orders, so as to have them promptly obeyed, not with the lash of severity but by a mild and systematic deportment, so as to render this service popular among the sailors. . . .
>
> I would advise you to exercise your signals as often as possible, in order that you may acquire a quick and prompt method in the use of them, which is a very important branch of our profession.

At the end of April they were off, as Murray explained to John Rodgers, "after fish and oysters and to make the young men acquainted with all the reefs and shoals of the Delaware. . . . The intention of sending these boats down is to get the young men out of the way of expenses and bad habits and to enable them to acquire a knowledge of the bay and its contiguous coast. I send half down at a time for five weeks' cruise, and they will relieve each other alternately." Not a minute too soon was he getting them out of town, Murray added when he reported the departure of Nos. 116 and 117 to Robert Smith. Just a few nights before—primarily, Murray assured the secretary, because the young man was not more usefully employed on active duty—Lieutenant Thomas Brown had eloped with his sweetheart. "Neither of them have a cent for their support," harrumphed Murray, "and the parents not disposed to give them shelter."

History does not record whether, as they sailed down Delaware Bay, any of the lieutenants and midshipmen in Nos. 116 and 117 envied Lieutenant Brown and his bride, but they were on an assignment only a perpetual malcontent could have failed to enjoy. Not until mid-June did Bernard Henry reappear off Philadelphia and then only long enough to exchange one of his anchors. "I have put another on board and sent him down again without delay," Murray reported to Smith.

> The officers all speak in high terms of their comfortable accommodations and the satisfaction they enjoy and wish much to have the time allowed for the first division extended. But, as those who are here are equally anxious to take their turn, I should wish to be indulged with the permission to fit out another boat, which can be done without any additional expense, as all the important items in their equipment are already incurred. I propose taking out seven men from the twenty now on board the two boats below and to make up a crew out of the surplus officers and a few more marines, which can be spared from the detachment here without any inconvenience. 'Tis a great object to get these young officers out of the line of expense, and they feel the necessity of it. At the same time they are gaining some knowledge in their professional career. They live chiefly, *while on board the boats*, on the productions of the waters of the Delaware, which abounds with fish and fowl, and hope to make good pilots of them all, and, by having a third boat, they will be enabled to take a wider range.[7]

In the Tops

Great as is the mass of surviving records on the pre-1815 navy's educational program in seamanship and officership, the most vital aspect of that program remains in deepest shadow. Almost nothing is known about the actual teaching and learning experience itself, whether seen through the eyes of the teacher or those of the student. Lacking are descriptions of acquiring the basics of seamanship from experienced enlisted men and petty officers, of discovering how to behave like an officer by observing older peers or through guidance by the ship's lieutenants, of the captain's dinner table conversation as he used these social occasions to convey information to, or shape the attitudes of, his younger subordinates. Such activities were the heart of the navy's educational program for its officers, but one can judge that program's effectiveness only by its results, not by observing the process itself.

What a loss this is! Robert Smith and other secretaries set great store upon insisting that midshipmen actually go into the ships' tops alongside the seamen "and perform such other services as may contribute to their improvement in seamanship and the other branches of their profession."[8] If only one of those midshipmen had left some record that would permit the historian to follow him as he climbed the one hundred or more perilous feet to the head of the fore-topmast or inched his way out on the main yard to take in sail in adverse weather. What did he feel? What could he hear? Who helped him? Was it hard to learn what to do? What mistakes did he make? Failing the survival of records, the next best thing one can do is to turn to the writings of a fortyish U.S. Navy captain, now twenty-seven years removed from his first experiences at sea. Thomas Truxtun wrote with a vividness and an immediacy that must have drawn upon deeply etched memories when he delineated what the new midshipman would learn by being required to join the enlisted men aloft:

> If the midshipman on many occasions is obliged to mix with [the sailors], particularly in the exercise of extending or reducing the sails in the tops, he ought resolutely to guard against this contagion with which the morals of [some of] his inferiors may be infected. He should, however, avail himself of their knowledge and acquire their expertness in managing and fixing the sails and rigging, and never suffer himself to be excelled by an inferior. He will probably find a virtue in almost every private sailor which is entirely unknown to many of his officers. That virtue is emulation, which is not, indeed, mentioned amongst [the sailors'] qualities by the gentlemen of *terra firma* by whom their characters are often copiously described with very little judgment. There is hardly a common tar who is not envious of superior skill in his fellows and jealous on all occasions to be outdone in what he considers as a branch of his duty! Nor is he more afraid of the dreadful consequences of whistling in a storm than of being stigmatized with the opprobrious epithet of *lubber*. Fortified against this scandal by a thorough knowledge of his business, the sailor will sometimes sneer in private at the execution of orders which to him appear awkward, improper, or unlike a seaman. Nay, he will perhaps be malicious enough to suppress his own judgment and, by a punctual obedience to command, execute whatever is to be performed in a manner which he knows to be improper in order to expose the person commanding to disgrace and ridicule. Little skilled in the method of the schools, he considers the officer who cons his lesson by rote as very ill qualified for his station, because particular situations might render it necessary for the said officer to assist at putting his own orders in practice. An ignorance in this practical knowledge will therefore necessarily be thought an unpardonable deficiency by those who are to follow his directions. Hence, the midshipman who associates with these sailors in the tops till he has acquired a competent skill in the service of extending or reducing the sails, etc., will be often entertained with a number of scurrilous jests at the expense of his superiors. Hence also, he will learn that a timely application to those exercises can only prevent him from appearing in the same despicable point of view, which must certainly be a cruel mortification to a man of the smallest sensibility.[9]

Learning from the Merchant Service

For all the naval leadership's commitment to the frigate or sloop, the brig or schooner cruising at sea as the best school of officership and seamanship, that commitment was tempered by the recognition that, in one particular respect, its favorite school was not getting the job done. Midshipmen were making one, two, sometimes three cruises in frigates and still they were inadequate seamen. At least part of the blame for this state of affairs has to be attributed to the status tensions that were built into the structure of the navy itself: the social gulf that separated officer and seaman and the necessity of maintaining that gulf. For all of Thomas Truxtun's urgings that midshipmen get out on the yards amid the gales and the sailors' scurrilous jokes, in too many cases fear of the loss of status and authority stood between young officers and hands-on experience of seamanship in a naval vessel. George Washington Spotswood, the eccentric but far from unperceptive grandnephew of the ex-president for whom he was named, neatly fingered the source of the problem: "On board a ship of war I thought that everything was to be acquired [to become a successful officer], but after two cruises I found that it was impossible that I ever could become a seaman if I confined myself totally to a ship of war, owing to the officers not doing the manual parts, which alone can make them seamen; and, without a knowledge of seamanship, no man is fit for a commander."[10]

Robert Smith, to whom Spotswood addressed his comment, would have been the first to add a hearty *Amen*! Commencing early in Smith's tenure at the Navy Office and continuing up to the outbreak of war in 1812, the navy urged its officers who were not employed on active duty to use such time to acquire a theoretical knowledge of navigation, then to gain practical experience of navigation and seamanship in the merchant service—before the mast if need be—where no necessity for maintaining an aloof status prevented a man from getting calluses on his hands or frostbite on his face.[11] During the years from the end of the Quasi-War with France to the commencement of hostilities with Great Britain in 1812, between one-fifth and one-quarter of the navy's officers were furloughed to gain career-related experience in the merchant service.[12] In wartime things were different. The navy needed all its officers on active duty; those individuals whose service was confined entirely to the Quasi-War navy or to the War of 1812 did not have opportunities to take advantage of the furloughs-for-merchant-voyages policy. Included in these numbers are captains, masters commandant, and sailing masters who were already fully qualified as seamen. For them merchant voyaging on furlough might provide means of supplementing their incomes as officers; it was not sought as a way of learning basic seamanship, though any challenging voyage could hone the skills of the most experienced master mariner. This gross count also embraces pursers, surgeons, and other noncombatant ranks; such men did, indeed, make merchant voyages, but not for the purposes of improving their skills as seamen. Finally, just because the record shows that an officer was furloughed to make a merchant voyage is no proof that the man actually carried out his plans. Illness could intervene. A suitable situation might prove elusive.

Some insight on the nature of all this merchant voyaging and its benefits for the voyagers can be gained by examining the records of in excess of seventy-four actually completed merchant voyages undertaken by fifty-six different officers between 1802 and 1811. (For two officers the precise number of voyages made is vaguely stated in the records; hence the occasional weasel-words in the paragraphs that follow.) These are merchant service experiences for which substantive details—destination, name of the ship, length of the voyage, and other similar facts—can be determined. Only voyages performed by midshipmen or lieutenants have been included, for such are the only two ranks at which it can convincingly be argued that educational benefits were a primary purpose of the voyage. These more than seventy-four voyages are not demonstrably representative of all the merchant voyages that were undertaken by midshipmen and lieutenants of the pre-1815 navy. They are, however, those for which readily accessible records have survived.

Among the fifty-six men, forty are recorded as making one voyage, eleven as undertaking two, and a mere five as voyaging three or more times while they were lieutenants or midshipmen. If notations in the Navy Office's central personnel register are to be relied upon, four of these men made at least one additional merchant voyage for which no detailed record has been found. Granting that the precise numbers are not to be trusted too far, their general meaning is beyond doubt. The great majority of furloughed midshipmen and lieutenants made only one voyage in the merchant service; approximately one in five undertook two voyages; only a tiny minority were at sea in merchant ships three times during their careers as officers. For the typical midshipman or lieutenant, leave to make a voyage in the merchant service was a one-time experience.

Only in the case of one man can the historian be sure why this was the case. "I like not the merchant service," Lieutenant James Biddle told his friend William Bainbridge when he got home from a yearlong voyage to Canton that he described as "far from so pleasant as I could have wished. . . . I stand in need of a *cruise* [in a navy frigate] to rub off my merchant service ideas."[13] His sentiments were probably echoed by many of his single-voyage peers. Effective, brave officers, men who loved the navy, did not automatically find life in a merchantman congenial. The thoughtful and highly self-critical Lieutenant William Lewis mused on why this was so during his first and only merchant voyage, the long one to China. It was a question of personality traits:

> Money is not to be gained at once. It must be saved and picked up step by step. We [naval officers] have always had mistaken and visionary notions about acquiring it. Some fortunate mortals, born with the golden spoons in their mouths, have now and then grasped a fortune at once; but such things don't occur often. A man must drudge a little, and the devil of it is that we in the navy are almost unfitted by our habits for this drudgery. We are either indolent or, if we have industry, we don't know how to save. For my part, I am both lazy and careless.[14]

For the less than one-third of the merchant service voyagers who repeated the experience in a second or a third engagement, the first voyage must have been the positive experience that it was not for Lieutenant Biddle. Newly minted midshipman John Mercer Funck—twenty-one years old, five feet, five-and-one-half inches tall, with his dark hair, hazel eyes, and fresh complexion— found the initial excursion to sea, an eleven-month passage to India and back, so "pleasant" that he immediately sought and obtained a second furlough to renew the exotic adventure in a voyage to Smyrna and Canton.[15] To look closely at the furloughed officers who made two, three, or more voyages is to encounter the tiny minority who found the merchant service so much to their liking that they eventually left the navy to pursue the alternative career. Lieutenant Archibald K. Kearney, a veteran of eight years as an officer and two furloughs, "has been rather fortunate in the merchant service and, having made some money, considers the honor of holding the commission of lieutenant in the navy (I find) of less value than his own private concerns," grumbled John Rodgers when Kearney submitted his July 1808 resignation.[16] One or two officers prolonged their stays in the merchant service to the point that their resignations had to be extracted from them.

To what destinations did the fifty-six midshipmen and lieutenants sail in their more than seventy-four merchant voyages? Among the questions that might be asked about these voyages-on-furlough, this is the one that can be answered with the highest degree of certainty. In nearly all cases (92 percent) the voyaging officers were careful to tell the Navy Department where they had been. Approximately half of them reported voyages to Europe and the Mediterranean. There is no surprise here, for a little more than half of all U.S. commerce was with this same geographical region, and berths in so brisk a trade were relatively easy to find. Puzzling is the small number of merchant voyages—something in excess of five[17] out of more than seventy-four—that had taken ports in the Caribbean as their destination. These waters had always been a major focus of activity for the U.S. merchant marine, accounting (together with Latin America generally) for about one-third of all U.S. maritime trade. For whatever now-lost reason this part of the world held little appeal for merchant-voyaging naval officers.

While the historian could easily overemphasize the matter-of-factness with which American citizens in general, and American mariners in particular, contemplated voyages to Europe or the West Indies, there was a sense in which voyaging to these destinations was the commonplace fare of the pre-1815 merchant marine. In twenty-eight instances furloughed officers chose to embark for longer (and perhaps more dangerous) voyages to exotic destinations. All but three of the twenty-eight were bound for the region imprecisely termed the East Indies: Mauritius, India, Java, or China. They went with the particular blessing and encouragement of the Navy Office. Such a voyage was typically a year or more in length; the demands for a higher order of seamanship were great; it offered the best of all opportunities to perfect one's skills in navigation. As one midshipman put it to his parents, the "ordinary class of shipmasters" could get to Europe or the West Indies and back with but small pretensions to mathematical or navigational skill; if one wanted to learn lunar navigation thoroughly, the young mariner should undertake a voyage to India: "In that trade [the] utility [of lunar navigational methods] makes them most practiced and best understood."[18] There were more material attractions to an East India excursion as well. It was on the long-haul voyages from Java and China and nearby waters that the big profits could be made. Should the midshipman or lieutenant have, or be able to lay his hands on, enough capital to give him a financial stake in his ship's voyage to the other side of the world, chances were good he could increase his little nest egg significantly.

The elite among the navy's merchant seafarers were those who had made the voyage around the world. Midshipman James Reilly sailed from Boston, 20 December 1807, in the 600-ton 26-gun ship *Dromo*, ninety men, and got home thirty months later, having in the interim been to Peru, Mexico, California, and China and found himself "much improved as a seaman and navigator" to boot. John Yarnall of Wheeling, Virginia, circumnavigated the globe more briskly. He sailed on 16 November 1809 in the ship *Enterprize*, bound "round the world," and reported his return to Secretary Hamilton in mid-January 1812, not failing to point out that he had just completed a voyage of precisely twenty-six months and nine days. On 22 June 1812, the day after Commodore John Rodgers and his squadron had sailed from Sandy Hook hoping to overtake British ships ignorant of the U.S. declaration of war, *President* spoke an American vessel to warn of the hostilities. In her Rodgers found twenty-two-year-old

Although his home—Wheeling, Virginia, on the Ohio River—lay unusually far from salt water for a pre-1815 naval officer, John Joliffe Yarnall was, by the declaration of war in 1812, an expert seaman, his skills well honed on a twenty-six-month voyage around the world. What one might suspect from his portrait is confirmed by the memories of his shipmates: Yarnall was more adept in facing storm or battle than in meeting an officer's social obligations at a dinner party or a ball. This superlative image by Netherlands artist Charles Delin must have been painted in the summer of 1814 when John Adams, *the ship to which Lieutenant Yarnall was then attached, spent two months in Dutch waters. The lieutenant's career, so full of promise for distinction, was cut short when he was lost in* Epervier *in 1815.* Israel Sack, Inc., New York.

Midshipman William B. Hall, furloughed for merchant experience two years earlier, only now returning from a voyage that had taken him to India and the Northwest Coast, and 160 days at sea. If there was a war, Midshipman Hall intended to participate. Within minutes he had said goodbye to old shipmates; Hall and his baggage were on their way to *President*.[19]

If the historian can readily discover where officers went on their furloughs, those same officers could be frustratingly evasive regarding the capacities in which they went there. For four out of every seven merchant voyages undertaken, no mention is made of the shipboard station in which the furloughed officer served. Only one-tenth of all the merchant voyages are reported as having been made as masters of vessels. This is as would be expected. Most of those being furloughed were relatively inexperienced at sea and needed to strengthen their skills; prudent owners would scarcely entrust valuable ships and cargoes to such hands. More common was the second- or third-in-command experience; approximately one furloughed officer in five reported that he had sailed as a mate. At the other end of the scale, in only one out of every seven voyages undertaken did the officer own up to having actually been before the mast, even though this was the station that Robert Smith regarded as the most useful one for learning basic seamanship.[20] Because the facts with which the historian has to work are so scanty, one may run a risk in speculation; but there is in this evidence a suggestion that for the majority of the officers furloughed to the merchant service, the experience was not the egalitarian one of berthing, messing, and hauling shoulder to shoulder with the working seafarers who made up the crews of merchantman and warship alike. Some young officers—including a few who would later be excellent older officers—did relish the full democratic experience; for most, elite preferences prevailed. If the merchant service was to be a hands-on experience of seamanship, the majority of the furloughed officers preferred to be able to retreat to the mate's snug cubbyhole at watch's end.

Misadventures must be counted among the educational aspects of merchant voyaging. Perhaps these were the experiences of a William Peters or a Joseph L. Biggs, both midshipmen, both shipwrecked on the coast of England during separate merchant ventures, and both obliged (or taking the opportunity) to linger in England until a U.S. warship called at a British port and provided a free passage home. William C. Beard obtained a furlough to make a voyage to Europe and secured a berth, apparently as a mate, in a vessel bound for that destination, only to have the owners change the voyage to Cartagena. Upon the ship's rather unexpected arrival at the latter place, Beard's master or his supercargo purchased a schooner, gave the command to young Beard, and sent him off to Santiago de Cuba. There, "finding the schooner was [charter]ed for a voyage in which I could not enter"—perhaps a slaving voyage? Beard does not tell—he resigned his command and secured a berth home in the schooner *Hanna*. Beard's stock of problems was not yet exhausted, for *Hanna* was wrecked off Bird Rock in the Crooked Island Passage at one o'clock in the morning on 14 August 1809; both ship and cargo, in which Beard seemingly had a financial interest, were totally lost. Three weeks later he was still slowly making his way home. Other misadventures befalling furloughed merchant voyagers were the all too direct result of the worldwide war. Fitz Henry Babbit sailed from Boston on 15 November 1810, bound for Marseilles, only to have his ship captured by the British sloop of war *Blossom* off Cape San Sebastián on the Catalonian coast and sent into Gibraltar. There both vessel and cargo were condemned for violation of the British orders in council. Midshipman St. Clair Elliott, furloughed and making a voyage to Europe, had the bad luck to be impressed on board a British sloop of war, there to remain twenty-nine unwilling months before he was able to extricate himself and get back to the United States early in 1813.[21]

Whether he warmed to the experience with John M. Funck or could hardly wait for it to be over with James Biddle, a merchant voyage made the furloughed officer a better seaman. William Parker Adams reported his return from a voyage in the brig *Venus* to the Mediterranean, England, "and several other parts of Europe" with the comment that he had well fulfilled the secretary of the navy's intention in granting him a furlough, for "I can justly say that the hands of no man on board were oftener immersed in the tar bucket than my own." A more reflective Henry Stearns Newcomb elaborated the educational benefits he perceived in his recent merchant experience. "In charge of a watch, under a continual press of sail, and obliged to assist in, as well as attend to, the various duties of the ship, whatever relates to *mere seamanship* becomes comparatively familiar."[22] As on many another question in the nurture of a young navy, Robert Smith had known best.

16. Setting the Norm

WHAT HABITS, what attitudes, what characteristics did the pre-1815 U.S. Navy seek to develop in its novice officers through education, training, socialization? As one listens for the answer, a single voice will be heard more frequently and more clearly than all others. It is that of Thomas Truxtun.

A man of remarkably powerful ego, Truxtun had, from the day of his 1794 selection as the fifth among the navy's original six captains, been consumed with a self-appointed mission as the primary educator and shaper of the officer corps that was about to be formed. In the same year that he was named captain he published "A Short Account of the Several General Duties of Officers of Ships of War, from an Admiral down to the Most Inferior Officer."[1] Thereafter, till his resignation in 1802, neither Truxtun's pen nor his tongue tired of lecturing his superiors, his peers, and especially his subordinates on what it took to be a naval officer. When he wrapped himself in the mantle of the navy's great teacher, Truxtun's total experience as a naval officer was zero. At sixteen he had spent a few months as an impressed seaman in the British 64-gun ship *Prudent* in 1771. Those few months constituted Truxtun's sole direct experience of naval life. Unlike his seniors as captains—John Barry, Samuel Nicholson, Silas Talbot, and Richard Dale—Truxtun never held a commission in the Continental navy; his highly active participation in the Revolution had been entirely as a privateersman. Although Truxtun had read history as well as the French and British writers on naval professional matters, one has the impression that, more than being a reader and a student of the ideas of others, Truxtun had spent extended periods alone, thinking about what it meant to be a naval commander. Perhaps his ideas had coalesced on his long, lonely merchant voyages to China and India.

Wherever his views had been shaped, Truxtun's appointment as captain unleashed a tornado of physical energy that made him the premier battle leader of the Quasi-War with France; equally, it opened the gates for a torrent of written and spoken words as he sought to fulfill what one suspects he saw as his single-handed mission to build an officer corps. There is no reason to think that the ideas Truxtun expressed were his alone. He was simply more articulate than most of the navy's officer-leaders in delineating the normative role and

*For a man who had so big a role in shaping the new U.S. Navy and its traditions,
there are surprisingly few portraits of Thomas Truxtun—and those few are disappointing.
The most commonly seen image, Bass Otis's 1817 oil, is that of a decaying veteran, not
the navy's dynamic, mid-forties leader of 1794–1802. Perhaps the one best capturing at
least some of the force of personality that glows so radiantly in the commodore's writings
is a profile by C.B.J. Fevret de Saint-Mémin. Still, mystery lingers about this portrait.
Why has Truxtun, the self-declared professional leader of the Quasi-War navy, posed out
of uniform? One could sooner imagine him posing for Saint-Mémin in the nude.* National
Portrait Gallery, Washington, D.C.

behavior of the sea officer. Following Truxtun's resignation his ideas lived on
in the deeds, the words, and the attitudes of younger men who had served as
his principal subordinates in *Constellation* and *President*, notably his first lieutenants John Rodgers and Isaac Chauncey, both of whom would be placed in
positions to mold large segments of the pre-1815 corps. Truxtun's shaping
influence is not a matter of speculation. In the summer of 1805, by which time
he had risen to the rank of master commandant, Chauncey could tell his old
commander, "I am indebted to you, my dear Sir, for the rudiments and, in
fact, nearly all the knowledge that I possess of naval science and am proud at
all times to copy after so great a master; but am fearful it will be but a faint
resemblance of the original."[2]

Early in the Quasi-War, while Truxtun was still commanding the frigate
Constellation, Midshipman Thomas Robinson, Jr., who may have received a mild
reprimand from Truxtun, wrote him to say that he stood in need of advice on
how to be a better officer. It was a request that Truxtun was eager to oblige:

United States Ship Constellation, 18 April 1799

Dear Sir:

I have received your letter dated yesterday and observe therefrom your
determination to attend to order, benefit by example, and endeavor to make a
sea officer.

A sea officer, Sir, is a great character, a man of a dignified mind and of
independent principles; and none can ever arrive to deserve the name, even
with those qualifications, unless from time, practice, and wonderful attention
he has made himself thoroughly acquainted with the minutiae of the science of
naval affairs, for his duty can never be performed by proxy. That a seaman
will make a soldier in the field immediately those European powers who have
made the experiment admit, but a soldier or other citizen cannot make a seaman
but from long experience and actual service.

It is painful to see the difficulty every day proves of initiating some men, taken out of the merchant service, to become officers; and this difficulty arises in general from an education of equality and from their never having calculated in the outset of life on being placed so as to feel the honor and sacred trust reposed in such as mount the quarterdeck of a man-of-war, there to assert and defend the rights, privileges, and dignity of their nation. Time, however, will correct our situation in this respect, but our reliance must always be on young men of principle, good education, high sense of honor, manly deportment, prudence, and of respectable connections; such as will never imbibe the false notions and caprice of the vulgar and disappointed, but such as will learn to think and act correctly; study at all convenient opportunities every part of their business; be particular in all their actions and conduct; let nothing appertaining to the character of the various grades from an admiral down escape them; be minute in their deportment; thirst after honor and glory; be concise in their actions and in every step they take; study consequences and consider well what they are about to say before they utter a word; despise everything low and unmanly; keep choice company, always looking up; detest gambling and improper drinking or excesses of any kind; act with humanity whenever clothed with particular power; be vigilant in subordination in executing orders, obeying every superior, and of keeping up the established etiquette of the service; and, finally, to deserve the true character of an officer and gentleman by watchfulness and candor on all occasions. To such, Sir, I shall never be unmindful during my stay in the service; while, at the same time, those of every other description shall forever go unnoticed by me.

You are now, Sir, in full possession of my determination. Go on, then, and study well your business. I will cheerfully aid you with my best advice and instruction at all times and [shall] be happy in seeing you promoted to high honors in due time. And I desire that you may be assured that, whenever I hold out the hand of friendship, it is never withdrawn unless the subject proves, in my estimation, unworthy of further notice, and then I never hesitate. But, as I am sure, from your disposition and general behavior hitherto, that this will never be the case with you, I have only to say that I wish you success and am pleased with your determination to cut a figure in the catalog of your country's naval characters and am, with regard,

Thomas Truxtun[3]

That letter summed up almost everything that had been or was to be said about the goals of the navy's program of education, training, and socialization, although the words may appear antique, the meaning somewhat obscure. Qualities that the navy sought to develop in its officers may be summed up under five headings. The word *develop* has been chosen deliberately, for a clear theme in all of the navy's writing about its educational program is that this program merely cultivated attributes and aptitudes that were innate. As the leaders of that day would have put it, no amount of education could make a sea officer of someone whom Nature had never intended for that calling.

No senior officer or secretary of the navy ever listed in priority order the habits that the navy's educational program sought to develop. But there can be little doubt, if such a list had been made, which habit would have stood first: *obedience to orders and attention to duty.* "Every citizen in private life is his own master, but when he enters into the navy or army he is no longer so, for he must submit to strict subordination," Truxtun scolded an officer who had given him far greater headaches than had the promising Mr. Robinson. "If you have supposed that orders may be unattended to in our naval service and that a democratic system is to govern on board our ships, I must inform you that the reverse is, and must be, the case." Not only must officers be obedient and attentive to the instructions of their superiors in order to function properly in their defined roles, their example of obedience and deference to superiors was a lesson that silently taught the enlisted man "the most ready obedience" to all those who were placed above him. An ingrained habit of obedience was the cement that held the social order of the ship together under whatever strains—battle, deprivation, disease, life-threatening storm—might be placed upon it. But this habit was never intended to be a license for arbitrary tyranny. "It must be your constant study to obey the legitimate commands of all your superior officers," Truxtun once told a group of midshipmen. Neither Truxtun nor anyone else defined or explained *legitimate commands*. That was a prudential decision, left to be worked out by the one commanded. He had to discover his own perceptions of that which it was not right to command him to do, the risks of refusing to obey, and the weight that the prevailing deference ethos and authoritarian command structure threw onto the side of obedience against lonely refusal.[4]

If many held that obedience to orders and attention to duty were the premier habit that a naval education sought to develop, that habit disputed pride of place with a cluster of related attitudes characterized by the words *activity, industriousness, zeal,* and *ambition*. If these habits were being defined in the latter part of the twentieth century, they might be named hard work, initiative, and ambition. "In naval life no man can look forward to become conspicuous by rapid promotion or otherwise unless, by his unremitting attention to duty and from a regular deportment, he can signalize himself from the slothful and inactive," Truxtun admonished. "Let every officer say, I prefer the attention I owe the infant marine of my country to every indulgence and pleasure." For those who wished to be among the select few who would achieve the highest eminence in their profession, zeal in the naval service must become a passion. Chance played an unforeseeable role in advancing some careers and thwarting others; but the officer who was consumed by zeal was the one most likely to seize the opportunities chance put in his way.

Ambition was a positive attribute, a personal asset to be welcomed in those men in whom it existed and one to be reinforced. Captain Alexander Murray articulated best the high importance attached to ambition when he admonished the twenty-two midshipmen under his charge in *Insurgente* in the summer of 1799: "Those who do not show an ambition to excel and an ardent desire of promotion need not expect my patronage; and I beg you will not suppose that you are placed in your present line merely as drones and idle spectators, but as gentlemen sent forward to be the bulwark and able defenders of your country. You have a noble field to range in for glory and reputation. If [many of] you do not . . . soon get into distinguished rank, it must be your own fault; for, without a spur of ambition towards eminence, you had better have stayed at home."[5]

Obedience to orders, industriousness, ambition. By themselves such qualities were not enough to make the good sea officer. They must be informed and directed by practical and theoretical knowledge acquired through the habit of *professional studiousness*. As usual, it was Truxtun who came directly to the point: "If a man does not acquire in his profession that knowledge that is necessary for the faithful and complete discharge of his duty, particularly in public life, having opportunity, I consider him guilty of a heinous crime indeed."

Following the passage, quoted earlier, in which Truxtun exhorted the young gentlemen to learn their seamanship in the tops alongside the most case-hardened of old salts, he continued:

> The most effectual method to excite [the midshipman's] application to those studies is, perhaps, by looking round the navy to observe the characters of individuals. By this inquiry he will probably discover that the officer who is eminently skilled in the sciences will command universal respect and approbation, and that whoever is satisfied with the despicable ambition of shining the hero of an assembly will be the object of universal contempt. The attention of the former will be engaged in those studies which are highly useful to himself in particular and to the service in general. The employment of the latter is to acquire those superficial accomplishments that unbend the mind from every useful science, emasculate the judgment, and render the hero infinitely more dextrous at falling into his station in the dance than in the line of battle. . . . If the dunces who are [the studious midshipman's] officers or messmates are rattling the dice, roaring bad verses, hissing on the flute, or scraping discord from the fiddle, his attention to more noble studies will sweeten the hours of relaxation. He should recollect that no example from fools ought to influence his conduct or seduce him from that laudable ambition which his honor and advantage are equally concerned to pursue.[6]

If professional studiousness was primarily an intellectual habit, the fourth characteristic that naval education sought to cultivate in an officer was both social and ethical: the *behavior of a gentleman*. "The correct habits, as well as the honorable and manly feelings of a gentleman, are essentials in the character of an officer of the Navy of the United States," Robert Smith wrote in 1805, succinctly summing up the goal sought by this facet of the navy's effort at character formation.[7] *Behavior of a gentleman* was a broad umbrella, embracing ethical conduct, internalized discipline, avoidance of indulgence or self-destructive excess, courteous and harmonious relationships with one's peers, manners, personal cleanliness, neatness in one's belongings and surroundings, refined personal interests, and the habit of associating with, and emulating, those who were one's social equals or—better yet—those of superior social standing.[8] It was a demanding list of ideals for any human being to pursue. Small wonder, then, that many among the navy's officers found this standard of conduct difficult to achieve in all respects, all of the time, or that the senior officers had to spend so much time and energy dealing with backsliders and underachievers. Probably no two members of the naval leadership would have defined *behavior of a gentleman* in exactly the same way. It was an amorphous and an internalized code of conduct, acquired as much by observation as by admonition or by reading and study. Much of its force derived from the officer's perception of the social stratum to which he thought he belonged or that he aspired to achieve. To survive as an officer one had to acquire a working sense of whether particular conduct would be considered appropriate for the gentleman, but the concept possessed an elastic quality that would render futile any attempt to reduce it to a precise set of rules for behavior.

Closely related to, and almost a subcategory of, the behavior of a gentleman was the fifth habit naval education sought to instill in novice officers: *proper conduct to inferiors*. The relationship between the navy's officers and its enlisted men is such an important subject that it will be examined later in its own chapter. Enumeration of those habits of command that the navy sought to develop in its officers may be deferred until the psychological frontier between officer and subordinate is explored.

Some things are missing here. Almost nothing was written concerning certain other characteristics that one might expect the navy's educational process would seek to foster in its officers. *Bravery* or *courage* are never mentioned, nor is it hard to surmise why. Courage was an innate quality; either a man had it or he lacked it or something in between. No amount of training would make a brave man of a coward. Lacking true courage, the best one could hope was that the habit of obedience to orders would serve as a functional substitute. Neither was anything said about developing *sound judgment, prudence* or *discretion*, and the habit of *consistent, firm,* and *resolute demeanor,* certainly all essential qualities in an officer. Truxtun made brief mention of these characteristics, but neither he nor any other senior leader of the navy elaborated on them. Perhaps they judged that the first cluster were innate, if present at all, and the second best learned by observing one's superiors in action.

Going by the Book

In the making of sea officers for the young U.S. Navy there was one teacher, held in high regard at the time, the importance of which might not immediately occur to the historian absorbed in a search for role models, classroom instruction, and merchant voyages for practical experience. This teacher was the written rule of behavior, embodied in the navy's laws and regulations.

Here the historian walks on marshy ground. Because a law or a set of regulations was on the books, it does not necessarily follow that men acted in the matter specified therein. Regulations and directives can be filed and ignored. The founders of an organization may draw up an elaborate code, but the organization may never become big enough or vital enough to make the code a living reality. Only the foolhardy historian assumes that things really were the way the rules said they ought to be. For the pre-1815 navy these dangers are not great, because the rules were a living part of the organization. Secretaries of the navy distributed them to senior officers for further dissemination among their subordinates. Senior officers asked the secretary for still more copies when they found junior officers who professed ignorance of the code. Those among the ship's company who would not or could not read heard the laws and regulations read to them at Sunday musters.[9] Not everyone knew the codes as well as he should; many failed to observe them. But the codes of conduct were an integral part of the life of the navy. No organization so large could function solely on oral tradition passed from senior mentor to junior initiate. A written standard helped to establish a reasonable uniformity of practice on board the navy's individual combat units scattered about the surface of the ocean, thereby insuring that the navy functioned as a unified organization rather than an agglomeration of individualistic little fiefs. Equally vital, such written codes provided an objective standard against which to measure actual conduct.

Written rules of behavior came in several varieties. It is important to understand the distinctions among them. The primary and most important rules were those that had the force of national law because they had been passed by Congress and approved by the president. For almost the entire portion of the navy's history with which this book is concerned, that cornerstone law was "An Act for the Better Government of the Navy of the United States," signed by President John Adams on 23 April 1800.[10] This lengthy and elaborate code—when printed in pamphlet form for distribution to the navy it ran to sixteen closely printed pages—sought to achieve eight objects: (1) Enjoin good example and moral behavior on officers and seamen. (2) Prescribe norms of conduct in battle and in relation to an enemy. (3) Impose certain administrative responsibilities on the commanding officer, such as the proper maintenance of muster rolls. (4) Define, and prescribe the punishment for, a list of offenses ranging from mutiny and murder, through fraud, embezzlement, theft, and desertion, to quarreling, sleeping on watch, and misconduct on shore. (5) Delineate the commanding officer's authority to punish his subordinates. (6) State rules to govern the operations of the navy's justice system. (7) Specify the distribution of prize money. (8) Provide a pension fund for officers and seamen.

Consideration of the law's provisions for the governance of enlisted men, for prize money, and for pensions may be deferred to later chapters. These matters aside, what did "An Act for the Better Government of the Navy," which the ship's company heard read month in and month out at Sunday muster, teach about the business of being an officer?[11] In its first three articles the law enjoined the officer to act ethically, told him to set an example by his behavior, and affirmed the responsibility of those placed high to maintain their lawful authority over those subordinate to them.

> The commanders of all ships and vessels of war belonging to the navy are strictly enjoined and required to show in themselves a good example of virtue, honor, patriotism, and subordination, and be vigilant in inspecting the conduct of all such as are placed under their command, and to guard against and suppress all dissolute and immoral practices, and to correct all such as are guilty of them according to the usage of the sea service.

This was immediately followed by an article adjuring all commanders of vessels that carried chaplains to have divine service performed twice a day and a sermon preached on Sunday. Easy enough to shrug this article off as a quaint survivor from an earlier period, imposed by law but ignored in practice. True it is that the officer or enlisted man of the pre-1815 navy who was devoutly religious was the exception rather than the rule. Logbook after logbook demonstrates that one weekly divine service on Sunday (if that many) was considered ample attention to religion. The chaplain, who was but rarely a clergyman and even more rarely religious, was far too busy serving as secretary to the captain and schoolmaster to the midshipmen to be much concerned with devotion or liturgy. Even with all this granted, the roughest, most profane, most obscene, most blasphemous old sea dog would have agreed with the most intellectual and skeptical of officers that there was a Deity or Divine Being, be he ever so remote and coldly rational. This Deity stood at the summit of Nature's hierarchy, of which the navy's hierarchy was but one constituent element. Affirmation of that divinely established hierarchy rising from lowest to higher to highest was the ultimate philosophical and theological basis of the navy's authority structure. Making worship of Almighty God the second article of the navy's basic law was no mere survival from the past; it was a reminder of who it was that ultimately sanctioned all the rules that followed.

Those rules continued with an encompassing definition of ethically reprehensible conduct in an officer: "Any officer or other person in the navy who shall be guilty of oppression, cruelty, fraud, profane swearing, drunkenness, or any other scandalous conduct tending to the destruction of good morals shall, if an officer, be cashiered or suffer such other punishment as a court martial shall adjudge." In its later sections the "Act for the Better Government of the Navy" returned to ethical conduct, forbidding such acts as mutiny, quarreling, desertion, murder, sleeping on watch, or theft, and specifying the punishment of those who broke the law; these were primarily offenses of which enlisted men were apt to be accused. The two forms of unethical conduct that an officer was likely to be in a position to commit were specifically forbidden. Both involved the use of one's official position for private gain: (1) fraud through the falsification of official records and embezzlement of the public property; and (2) use of one's vessel for the transportation of merchandise for private profit. Sanctions specified for those convicted of such behavior left no question of the seriousness with which it was viewed. Enumeration of forbidden acts ended with a reaffirmation of centrality of hierarchy, authority, and order: "Every person in the navy shall use his utmost exertions to detect, apprehend, and bring to punishment all offenders and shall, at all times, aid and assist all persons appointed for this purpose, on pain of such punishment as a court martial shall adjudge."

Only after the officer's responsibility to act ethically, provide good example, and uphold authority and order had been clearly established did the law enunciate his responsibility as a fighting man, and then in negative terms:

> Every commander or other officer who shall, upon signal for battle or on the probability of an engagement, neglect to clear his ship for action or shall not use his utmost exertions to bring his ship to battle or shall fail to encourage, in his own person, his inferior officers and men to fight courageously, such offender shall suffer death or such other punishment as a court martial shall adjudge; or any officer neglecting, on sight of any vessel or vessels of an enemy, to clear his ship for action shall suffer such punishment as a court martial shall adjudge; and, if any person in the navy shall treacherously yield or pusillanimously cry for quarters, he shall suffer death, on conviction thereof by a general court martial. . . .
>
> Every officer or private who shall, through cowardice, negligence, or disaffection, in time of action withdraw from or keep out of battle, or shall not do his utmost to take or destroy every vessel which it is his duty to encounter, or shall not do his utmost endeavor to afford relief to ships belonging to the United States, every such offender shall, on conviction thereof by a general court martial, suffer death or such other punishment as the said court shall adjudge.

In his capacity as a fighter, the officer's responsibilities, insofar as they were defined by law, were to prepare his ship for battle; to seek encounter with the enemy vigorously; to behave courageously himself and to inspire courage in his subordinates; and to aid other U.S. vessels to whatever extent was in his power. If this list by no means exhausts the roster of qualities one might expect the combat sea officer to possess, the officer had to look elsewhere than the "Act for the Better Government of the Navy" to find an enumeration of those

qualities. With this definition of the officer's responsibilities as fighter, the law
reverts to the realm of ethical behavior, prohibiting the pillage of prizes or the
maltreatment of prisoners.

As for the officer's role and responsibility as a seaman, the law was quite
succinct, devoting one article to this topic: "If any officer or other person in
the navy shall, through intention, negligence, or any other fault, suffer any
vessel of the navy to be stranded or run upon rocks or shoals or hazarded, he
shall suffer such punishment as a court martial shall adjudge." Finally, the law
imposed certain parental responsibilities on the officer, particularly the commanding officer: maintenance of accurate personnel records in his muster rolls;
regular inspection of the ship's provisions and oversight of their preservation;
assurance that the sick and the disabled had appropriate care; and determination
that no frauds were committed against either the enlisted men or the United
States when the ship was paid off.

What, then, was the role of "An Act for the Better Government of the
Navy" as a teacher of what it meant to be an officer? At the most obvious level
its message was one of prohibition. It said what an officer should not do and
what would happen to him if he disobeyed. Behavior that was expected of an
officer was defined mainly by inference from behavior that was prohibited. If
cowardice was reprehensible, then bravery must be desirable. The law also
conveyed a more subtle message. An officer was one who led by example, who
maintained the highest ethical standards, who manifested courage in the face
of danger, who implicitly obeyed his lawful superiors, and who maintained, in
turn, his authority over those placed under his command.

To function effectively an officer needed more than these general and, at
least at one level, largely negative norms. For guidance he could turn to the
second great class of written rules of behavior: administrative regulations issued
by the secretary of the navy. Apprehending what the administrative regulations
taught about officership is more complicated than is the case with statutory
law. The complication arises because there were two successive, and radically
different, sets of administrative regulations in force during the navy's pre-1815
history. The second, and the one that was in use the longer, was the *Naval
Regulations, Issued by Command of the President of the United States of America*. These
were promulgated early in 1802 by Secretary of the Navy Robert Smith and
remained the basic administrative code until 1818, when they were replaced
with a much more elaborate set of *Rules, Regulations, and Instructions* drawn up
by the Board of Navy Commissioners.

The *Naval Regulations* of 1802 took the form of a list of duties enjoined
upon each grade of officer, beginning with the squadron commodore and
descending to the ship's cook; these were followed by some general regulations
covering provisions, slops, logbooks and journals, courts martial, and convoys.
This code focused on the administrative responsibilities of each grade of officer;
it said practically nothing about what might be called his higher duties:
leadership, protection of commerce, diplomacy, or battle. The bias is clearly
seen in the opening section, "Of the Duties of a Commander in Chief, or
Commander of a Squadron." Its seventeen numbered paragraphs instructed
him to communicate fully up and down the chain of command; to inspect his
ships and crews frequently and to be familiar with their sailing qualities; to
execute his sailing orders promptly; to exercise his ships in squadron maneuvers.
They defined his authority to suspend subordinates, and they forbade him to

have any financial interest in the purchase of stores abroad or to put his subordinate captains to unusual expenses for entertainment in foreign ports. A newly appointed squadron commodore who turned to the *Naval Regulations* for guidance as to what was expected of him would have discovered that they said nothing about his responsibility to formulate strategy, conduct diplomacy, or even lead his squadron into battle.

As for the prescribed duties of a ship's captain, though there were more of them—fifty-six articles in all—these were still administrative rules: know one's ship; be accountable for its stores; maintain accurate personnel records; be responsible for the vessel's physical security and integrity; carefully control the use of liquor; do not carry women to sea; inventory and seal the personal belongings of any officer who dies. A few articles provided some guidance on operational expectations. When ordered to cruise a captain is expected to remain at sea for the period specified and is not to go into port except from necessity. Officers and men are to be assigned their battle stations before the ship sails and are to be regularly drilled with their weapons. The ship must always be ready for an immediate engagement with the enemy; nothing may be stowed or be adrift on deck that will hamper the management of the guns. As for battle itself, this is mentioned only once and then to forbid the captain to lead the boarders; he must stay with his ship, "whose preservation must be the chief object of his care."

What the *Naval Regulations* of 1802 do convey, as paragraph of instructions builds upon paragraph of injunction, is an all-pervasive sense that to be an officer is to be responsible, a message that is summed up in the fifty-third paragraph of the duties of a captain or commander: "He is responsible for the whole conduct and good government of the ship and for the due execution of all regulations which concern the several duties of the officers and company of the ship, who are to obey him in all things which he shall direct them for the service of the United States."

Going by a Different Book

So spoke the *Naval Regulations* of 1802 on what it meant to be an officer. Because those rules were in force for the last twelve years with which this book is concerned, the historian assumes that their influence was pervasive. The *Naval Regulations* had, however, been preceded by another set of instructions, the *Marine Rules and Regulations*, issued early in 1798 while the nation's navy was still under the administrative control of the War Department. The *Marine Rules* may have been in force for four years only, but they were the widely distributed regulations under which the navy fought the Quasi-War with France and with which it commenced the Tripolitan War. They governed when most of the navy's pre-1815 leaders began their professional careers; as the first set of regulations those young officers encountered, they were likely to have made a strong impression. If one listened attentively, the *Marine Rules* of 1798 spoke with a different voice from that of the *Naval Regulations* of 1802 respecting what it meant to be an officer.

The latter were not a simple revision of the 1798 *Rules*. Though here and there salvaged pieces of the old *Marine Rules and Regulations* could be found in the *Naval Regulations*, the 1802 document was really a new structure, with a different philosophy. No evidence survives as to why the old *Marine Rules* were essentially discarded and replaced in 1802. One can only speculate: the new code was much shorter; some provisions of the *Marine Rules* had been incorporated in the "Act for the Better Government of the Navy"; others were apparently deemed more appropriate to ships' internal regulations. Both the *Marine Rules* of 1798 and the *Naval Regulations* of 1802 drew heavily on the British *Regulations and Instructions Relating to His Majesty's Service at Sea*, but the spirit of the two U.S. codes is so different as almost to belie their shared source. It would be wrong to think of either set as simply the product of a copy of the British *Regulations and Instructions*, scissors, paste, and a printing press. The American compilers of both editions were eclectic in the sections of the British regulations they chose to borrow or exclude; the U.S. progeny was far slimmer than its British parent; the sections of the document were radically rearranged; a fair amount of rewriting took place; original material was added. In short, although the U.S. administrative regulations clearly descended from the British *Regulations and Instructions*, they were so thoroughly reworked in the process that they became a conscious and well-digested iteration of ideal American practice.[12]

Although a captain's administrative responsibilities are not slighted in the 1798 *Marine Rules and Regulations*, his operational obligations receive far more coverage than they would in 1802. He will not linger unnecessarily in port, but will sail promptly to execute his orders. Coming into or going out of port, during stormy weather, when meeting an enemy in action, "and generally on all important occasions," the captain personally will assume operational control of his ship. He will study carefully the sailing properties of his ship, the better to command her; and he will personally supervise the ship's navigation, keep appropriate journals himself, require the watch officers to report to him regularly, and inspect the logbook to insure that it is correctly maintained. Preparations to meet the enemy must be an ongoing activity; the captain "will exercise the men at the cannon as often as possible and at proper times with a sham action to accustom his crew to repair to their posts with vivacity and understandingly. The officers of the several divisions of the crew will be present at these exercises in their uniform and with their arms as in a day of action." Finally, the *Marine Rules* of 1798 were careful to define the naval officer's ultimate and proper mission as the defender of the mercantile republic:

> The president enjoins it upon him to protect the lawful commerce of the citizens of the United States upon all occasions where it can be done agreeably to treaties, the laws of the United States, and laws of nations, to render secure their navigation and prevent, as much as in his power, wrong or injury being done to it without exacting from the merchant, under any pretext whatever, any compensation therefor or retribution for his crew.

The most striking feature of the *Marine Rules and Regulations* is the message of the officer's paternal responsibility toward his subordinates, a spirit notable for its absence from the *Naval Regulations* of 1802. To be sure the message of authority, deference, and obedience is plainly present in the *Marine Rules*. The captain "will pay attention to and maintain the strictest subordination among the officers and among the people of the crew." "He will be ready, on the first appearance of mutiny, to use the most vigorous means to suppress it and to bring the ringleaders to punishment." Still, the overriding theme is at least as much (if not more) the responsibility of him who is placed high for the welfare of those put under his authority as it is the duty of subordinates to obey and the harsh fate that awaits those who refuse obedience. The captain begins by familiarizing himself with his ship's company as individuals:

> [He] will endeavor, during the entering of the crew, to know the men and will cause an account to be rendered to him by the entering and other officers of those who show the most zeal and intelligence and, immediately after the general review and inspection of the crew, will, in presence of some one of the commissioned officers, interrogate each man upon the number of campaigns or voyages which he may have made, upon the engagements in which he has been present, upon the posts which he occupied in these engagements, whether in maneuvering or at the batteries, and will neglect no means to ascertain what post each is fittest for, after which he will proceed to the formation of the quarter bill.

This exploration of each seaman's abilities and previous experience comes immediately after the captain's review, "man by man," of the entire crew to determine that each enlisted man has a proper supply of clothing with which to commence the projected voyage. The spirit of watchful, paternalistic responsibility continues through the *Marine Rules'* twenty-six "Regulations respecting the order and cleanliness to be maintained on board of ships or vessels of war of the United States," reminding officers generally in the eighteenth paragraph, "Care is to be taken to prevent any of the crew who have been wet during their watch from lying down previous to their having put on dry clothes. And the officers of watches and divisions will be responsible that it shall not be permitted." Eighteen "Regulations respecting the discipline of the crews of the ships or vessels of the United States" make the divisional officers responsible not only for "the police and discipline," that is, the behavior, of the enlisted men of their divisions, but also charge the divisional officers to see that their men have adequate amounts of clothing and keep it mended, to make certain that they are neglecting neither cleanliness nor personal hygiene, and to keep a watchful eye on the health of their subordinates.

While the officers, because of their higher stations, have far greater privileges than the seamen, one of the captain's responsibilities is to see that those privileges are not abused or exceeded. The captain is the protector of the seaman's rights:

> He will take care in cutting up the beef that choice pieces be never purposely selected for the officers from that which is cut up for the ship's company, and that choice pieces of salt meat be never taken for the officers out of the tub or vessel from which it may be served to the ship's company. . . . He shall take care that the officers do not select casks of the best wine or spirits for their own use from those intended for the ship's company nor exchange any wine or spirits of their own for that which has been sent on board for the use of the ship.

The historian can have a healthy skepticism about how easy this paragraph was to enforce; one can even suspect it of being more honored in the breach than in the observance; but the ideal of officership defined by the *Marine Rules* is clear and unambiguous.

Differences between the spirit of the *Marine Rules and Regulations* of 1798 and the *Naval Regulations* of 1802 are perhaps best captured by what each code has to say about the captain's responsibility if his ship goes aground and cannot be saved:

In case of the shipwreck of his vessel on any coast, by rocks or any other accident, his first care will be to prevent disorder and save as much of the effects as possible of the United States. He will encourage the people of his crew and will make them pass successively to land and will be the last to quit the vessel.

In case of shipwreck or other disaster, whereby the ship may perish, the officers and men are to stay with the remains as long as possible and save all they can.

The captain's concern has, at least so far as the regulations are concerned, shifted from one of setting an example, maintaining discipline, preserving the lives of his crew, *and* saving the public property, to an exclusive responsibility for salvaging the remains of ship and stores.

To persons familiar with the responsibilities of leadership the 1798 *Marine Rules and Regulations* would appear to be the superior code, at least insofar as the earlier code enunciates a norm of officership largely missing from the 1802 *Naval Regulations*. Because no detailed record of the adoption of the 1802 *Naval Regulations* appears to have survived, the reasons behind this radical alteration in the navy's administrative code cannot now be discovered. Is it reading too much into the change to see the new regulations, with their de-emphasis on the officer's responsibility for the well-being of his subordinates, as a reaction to the democratic and egalitarian ferment of the times? A withdrawal to a more distant and a less personal relationship with enlisted subordinates? No less mysterious are the relative roles of the two codes in influencing the attitudes of the navy's leaders toward officership. A man who began his career as a midshipman during the Quasi-War with France and who had, by the end of the War of 1812, risen to captain or master commandant would have been well exposed to the *Marine Rules* of 1798 during the first three or four years of his professional life and to the *Naval Regulations* of 1802 for the next thirteen. It is now impossible to sort out the relative influence each might have had; this must have been conditioned by such factors as having assimilated the 1798 code at the most impressionable stage of his career, or finding one code more congenial to his personal temperament and philosophical outlook than the other.

If a clear standard of what it meant to be an officer emerged from the codes of behavior, it was just such: an ideal, a norm. That the constant repetition of the ideal had a positive teaching role in forming the corps' philosophy of officership is not to be doubted. Still, there was much about being an officer — perhaps the most important things of all—that one could never learn from written codes of behavior, no matter how many times one heard them read aloud. The most potent teacher of what it meant to be a leader was the senior officer himself as example and model.

17. Mentors and Challenges

ENTION THE TERM *role model* to someone familiar with the history of the U.S. Navy and the names that spring to mind are likely to be Thomas Truxtun, Edward Preble, Stephen Decatur, John Rodgers, William Bainbridge, James Lawrence, Thomas Macdonough, and others who were the navy's leaders. They stand tall because they were combat commanders, men who won famous victories. Here these well-known officers will be asked to take seats at the side of stage, while others—whose names are without instant recognition value—have their moments in the historical limelight. Good reasons exist for asking the big names to be inconspicuous at this point. Each of them has been the subject of at least one biography, volumes in which attention has been lavished on how influential the man was with younger officers who served as his subordinates. Without denigrating the great names, historians are permitted to wonder if their influence has not been exaggerated at the expense of now-forgotten captains who may have done as much as these famous men or more to mold and inspire younger subordinates.[1] As models the historian may select for a closer look two men who appear frequently enough in this volume, but who are scarcely well-known figures, even to naval historians.

No Idle Drone

Easy enough to dismiss Alexander Murray as an old fuddy-duddy. That was the way many of his contemporaries pictured him. About 1806 Robert Smith concluded that he would not again give Murray an active command at sea and relegated him to shore duties. Smith's decision to put Murray on the beach was the culmination of a growing disenchantment that seems to have had its roots in what Smith perceived as the deficiencies of Murray's ships in point of cleanliness and discipline, with the latter deficiency seemingly aggravated, in Smith's eyes, by complaints from Murray's subordinates that he would not allow them to flog the enlisted men. "Reports have been in circulation that I am considered too old, infirm, and unpopular among the officers to be employed again. They are as malicious as they are ill-founded," Murray lamented in the summer of 1807 as he gradually came to realize that Smith was not going to give him anything more challenging to do than command the Philadelphia naval station, an assignment whose duties were not exactly onerous. The month he penned that lament Murray turned fifty-three. In absolute terms he was not an old man; he was to live another fourteen years during which both his life and his letters display ample reserves of energy and enthusiasm. In July 1807 the median age of the navy's twenty-two captains and masters commandant was between thirty-four and thirty-five years. Eager to run the navy, and, in fact, monopolizing much of the actual power, these younger men were not disposed to look impartially at the contributions Murray (the third oldest man of the twenty-two) had made and still could make. In their eyes he was a relic of the Revolutionary War era, a man who ought to be put out of the way on a high, back shelf; one who could be dismissed, in John Rodgers's condescending (and historically inaccurate) formulation, as "an amiable old gentleman, [but one who] has not been regularly bred to the profession of a seaman; his pretensions, therefore, as a *navy* officer are of a very limited description."

Whatever threads of reality may have been woven into this collective view of Alexander Murray, the general impression conveyed was unfair to the living officer and to the historical figure. Even as his younger colleagues were caricaturing him as a superannuated veteran, he has just been seen making imaginative use of his gunboats to train idle midshipmen. His preaching probably became tiresome, but that does not mean that Murray's subordinates failed to internalize the skills, the habits, and the values he taught. Whether as a captain afloat before 1806 or in his shore commands thereafter, Murray's primary role was that of a teacher. In providing opportunities for hands-on training, urging the necessity for constant self-improvement and industriousness, or insisting on the highest standards of behavior, he was extolling traits that he judged had aided him in his own and—as he saw it—not the easiest of lives.

Alexander Murray never entertained any doubts that his rightful place was among the elite, whether on the score of birth, of financial achievement, or of patriotism. His father, William Murray, was a prosperous physician in Chestertown, Maryland. Unfortunately, as his son put it, Dr. Murray, "having ever lived in a style to meet his income [and] possessing the most liberal hospitality," had the misfortune to die when Alexander was thirteen years old, leaving Alexander's mother, once the estate was settled, to contemplate a life of genteel poverty. Vigorous counteraction was demanded. Of Alexander's living siblings, his two older brothers were about to launch themselves on successful careers as doctors, but his four elder sisters were all unmarried. Neither at age thirteen nor at any later time in his life was financial insecurity a prospect with appeal for Alexander Murray. He and his mother soon decided that he would discontinue formal schooling and turn his attention to a calling wherein he could begin to make good money after a brief apprenticeship: the sea.

Young Murray was shrewd or lucky in his choices of tutors; the two captains with whom he sailed both became prominent officers in the Continental navy. Murray began his career under Lambert Wickes, a native son of Kent County and his first cousin. After two years of repeated European voyages with Wickes, Murray switched mentors to become second mate to first cousin Samuel Nicholson, also from Kent County. Two voyages later, Murray, by now eighteen years old, was ready to take command of a vessel on his own; but after one

Alexander Murray in a Quasi-War-era miniature by James Peale. A man in his early forties, at the peak of his vigor, his star rising in the naval skies. Observe, though, the half-hooded eyes and the hint of contempt in the line of the mouth. Secure in his sense of superiority, a status snob, and one who kept a barrier of psychological distance between himself and his civilian superiors as well as his professional peers. Powdered hair and dapper uniform remind that Murray preferred to dress in the best of fashion, "as far as my finances would extend." Metropolitan Museum of Art, New York.

voyage to Lisbon and another to London as master, the tensions leading up to the Revolution curtailed opportunities in the merchant trade. No matter. "Enthusiasm filled the breast of every American for liberty," he recalled. Turning his thoughts landward, Murray was appointed second lieutenant in Smallwood's Maryland Regiment on 14 January 1776, rising to first lieutenant in August and captain in December of the same year. While Murray was making his way up the promotion ladder his regiment had been bearing the brunt of some of the bitterest fighting of Washington's campaign in New York and New Jersey. One reminder of the battles Lieutenant Murray never lost. While he was serving with a battery that was attempting to prevent the British fleet from ascending the North River, several pieces of artillery burst and damaged his hearing so seriously that he was partially deaf for the balance of his life.

A year of land campaigning had undermined Murray's health. After a long period of recuperation, he resigned his army commission in June 1777 and returned to his old home, the sea. During the next four years Murray commanded the privateers *General Mercer, Saratoga, Columbus,* and *Revenge,* captured a number of British privateers and merchantmen, and was himself twice taken. At last, on 20 July 1781, the lieutenant's commission in the Continental navy that Murray had long sought was awarded. He immediately volunteered for service in the frigate *Trumbull* under Captain James Nicholson (Samuel's brother and another of Murray's first cousins), only to be wounded and taken prisoner when *Trumbull* was captured by the British frigate *Iris* after a hard-fought engagement. By this time there were more Continental naval officers than there were duty assignments for them in that shattered force; Murray once more turned his energies to privateering by assuming command of the brig *Prosperity*. In her he fought off a larger and more heavily armed privateer in a desperate running engagement, participated in the Spanish expedition to capture New Providence, and came home with a headful of plans for making a major career change.

"I have not been an idle drone from the earliest period of my life to the present day," Murray later claimed. Indeed he had not. He was now twenty-seven years old; in addition to helping his mother and his four unmarried sisters financially, he had amassed enough capital to plan a life of semileisure: "I thought it high time to rest from my laborious pursuits for the more substantial happiness in private life . . . [and] to retire from the bustle and strife I had gone through." On 18 June 1782 he married Mary Miller of Philadelphia, "and flattered myself that I should never be obligated to leave the retired life I wished to live in." Then reality intruded. A substantial part of Murray's capital was invested in his former command, the brig *Prosperity*, now sailing under another captain. Murray's lucky ship had turned decidedly unlucky; she was driven ashore off Cape Henry by a British frigate, a total loss covered by not a shilling of insurance. This hard financial blow coincided with Murray's recall to active duty as first lieutenant of the frigate *Alliance* in the closing moments of the Revolutionary War; he remained attached to her—she was the last vessel of the Continental navy—until October 1784 when he resigned his commission. Murray had fought, as he liked to point out, in thirteen battles by land and by sea during the war for independence.

For the next ten years Alexander Murray, still no idle drone, directed all his energies to rebuilding his financial security. He was so successful in his efforts that when a new federal navy was established in 1794, he could afford to be an early applicant for the command of one of the six projected frigates. In the end he had to wait for the expansion of the navy during the early days of the Quasi-War with France before he actually held the coveted captain's commission in his hand. Command of the converted merchantman *Montezuma* was followed by cruises in *Insurgente* and *Constellation* during the hostilities with France. If attention-capturing victories over enemy ships eluded Murray in this war, his abilities as a teacher were highly regarded by Secretary Stoddert, who packed his ships with newly minted midshipmen in need of guidance and experience and who described Murray as "a man of good temper, good sense, honor, and bravery, with whom [the midshipmen] will be happy and from whom they will receive instruction." Soon after Robert Smith took his seat behind the secretary's table, Murray's star began to decline. Apart from Smith's not secret opinion that "Murray's ship had always appeared to his discredit in point of discipline and cleanliness," he was (in Smith's eyes) deaf, inactive, and insufficiently enthusiastic about the possibility of inflicting a military defeat on Tripoli during his Mediterranean cruise in *Constellation* in 1802–1803. Neither was Murray's standing with Smith and his Republican successors helped by the commodore's staunch adherence to the Federalist party and its policies, a preference he took no pains to conceal. This proved to be a heavy liability when William Jones became secretary, for both men knew each other well—from the opposite sides of the Philadelphia political fence. Once beached at Philadelphia in command of the navy yard and nearby waters, Murray remained

Naval officer as old curmudgeon: Alexander Murray by Rembrandt Peale. Still betraying the look of visceral superiority discovered in his Quasi-War miniature and poised, perhaps, to lecture a younger subordinate perceived to be in need of guidance and correction. But for all of that, not an unkindly face. Murray was one captain who refused to use "the lash of severity" to maintain discipline, preferring "a mild and systematic deportment . . . to render this service popular among the sailors." Private collection.

there for the balance of his career, dying as the navy's senior officer in October 1821.

In success or in disappointment Murray always had a clear view of who he was, where he had been, and how he had gotten there:

> I set out in the world under too many disadvantages with regard to education to make the improvements that I might have done, and my profession being of a laborious nature put it out of my power to profit by speculations in talents. . . . To be very circumspect in the choice of the company you keep and always endeavor to associate with your superiors in point of talents, quality, fortune, and principle [rather] than with those of an inferior cast . . . was a maxim early impressed upon my mind which I never deviated from and found the greatest benefit resulting therefrom; for be assured the better company you keep, the fewer expenses you will be involved in. I ever made it a rule with me, whenever I arrived in a foreign country and was so situated as to be able to frequent the shore, always to inquire for the finest accommodations and to dress in the best—though not the gaudy—fashions of the place as far as my finances would extend; and always found it good policy in so doing; first, as more to my satisfaction and, secondly, for improvement as well as for economy. But I strenuously avoided every species of gambling or night broils, except in some unavoidable cases. . . . I ever kept caution for my guide, not wishing to affect singularity in any respect and governed myself by the dictates of honor and prudential acts. In the whole course of my life I never failed having some object in view and seldom passed an idle hour, for if I was in company I strove to profit by it and constantly strove to make myself a serviceable member of society. . . . What I pride myself in above all others—though fighting seems to have been my profession—[is that] I never had a private quarrel or enmity of any serious moment with any individual in all my life, taking care to keep my passions and frailties under strict government, never putting it in the power of

anyone to offend me, and taking care never to give offense, by which conduct I have been enabled to live in peace in all my private pursuits.[2]

Old Cork

No subordinate is known ever to have described Captain Hugh George Campbell—nicknamed Old Cork because of the Irish origins of his family—as an old fuddy-duddy. Those who disliked him were content merely to hate his guts. Thus, in 1805, Midshipman (and acting lieutenant) Oliver Hazard Perry wrote to inform a friend that he was no longer to be found on board Campbell's ship, *Constellation*:

> You will, at the head of my letter, see that I am on board the Nautilus. This was owing to a small difference with Old Cork on account of some improper orders he gave, which I did not choose to obey. Away he posts directly to the commodore [John Rodgers] and prevails on him to order me first lieutenant here. I also waited on him. I expressed my dislike of Captain Campbell's underhanded conduct. He agreed with me in my opinion and said in a very short time he would better my situation. Since then he has offered to make me first of the Syren or take me on board of his own ship.

Surely this cannot be the same Hugh G. Campbell to whom Perry, by then a captain and the hero of the battle of Lake Erie, wrote eight years later?

> My dear and much respected Sir: Among all my friends who have offered me their congratulations on my good fortune, none has given me more pleasure than your kind and flattering letter. If I have any respectability in the service as an officer, you, my dear Sir, are entitled to a great share of the credit. It was to your friendly and frequent admonitions that I obtained a standing with my brother officers. I shall never cease to recollect with gratitude how much I am indebted to you, not only for kindness shown me when sick and at all other times, but for examples of activity which I never witnessed on board any other ship than yours. I have uniformly declared that, if you had an active command, you would show us all how to dash, and I regret most sincerely that your country is deprived by your ill health of that activity which would reflect so much honor on the service.

Of course it is the same Hugh G. Campbell. What had happened during those eight years was that the Oliver Hazard Perrys of the navy had become older and wiser. They had an enhanced appreciation of an Old Cork and of what he had to endure as he struggled to turn inexperienced young adults, undisciplined and resistant to authority, into mature and responsible officers.[3] It had not been easy, but Campbell was a man equal to the task.

Unlike Alexander Murray, Hugh George Campbell was not particularly given to autobiography or to introspection. Little is known about his early life or his motivating drives.[4] Born in South Carolina in 1760, Campbell served as a volunteer on board the schooner *Defence*, the first warship commissioned by South Carolina in 1775. Thereafter he disappears from the currently known historical record until June 1791, when he was appointed first mate of the revenue cutter *South Carolina*, which was followed in due course by promotion to master in the revenue cutter service in July 1798. During these years, or perhaps earlier, Campbell sustained an injury to one of his legs. The exact nature of his handicap is not known, but the injured leg became progressively debilitating; coping with this liability was to shape the later years of Campbell's career. About the time that Campbell was beginning his revenue cutter service he struck up a friendship with a merchant captain from Pennsylvania, a man of his own age, who made Charleston, South Carolina, his base of operations between 1790 and 1793. The merchant captain's name was William Jones. Twenty years later he would be secretary of the navy.[5]

From the revenue cutter service Campbell made the transition to the navy in the summer of 1799 at the rank of master commandant, commanded *Eagle* and *General Greene* during the Quasi-War with France, and was commissioned captain, 16 October 1800. Though Campbell was pessimistic about his chances of surviving the reduction of the navy in 1801, he turned out to be one of the nine captains retained in service. It was an outcome that seems to have owed something to the influence of Congressman William Jones with the incoming Republican administration, as well as to Campbell's own merits. The Tripolitan War heated up almost immediately thereafter and Campbell saw service—even if fame as a battle commander eluded him—as a subordinate captain in the second and fourth Mediterranean squadrons, ending his second tour in those waters as squadron commodore. With the recall of the Mediterranean squadron in 1807 in the wake of the *Chesapeake-Leopard* incident Campbell's active service at sea came to an end. The injured leg, always a problem, had become increasingly incapacitating for strenuous sea duty, but Campbell was far from ready to be put on the shelf. With the cordial approval of the Navy Department he went into a self-imposed, warm-climate exile: first as the commander of the entire southern station with headquarters at Charleston; then, when the station was divided early in 1812, as commander of naval forces in Georgia, hoisting his pennant at St. Marys.

When Campbell arrived on the southern station, where a number of younger men had been stationed for some time without the supervision of an authority figure, he found matters far from his liking:

> The conduct and appearance of our young officers generally that I have seen to the southward of Norfolk call loud for correction, a misfortune that the service must experience until an officer is placed at their head to advise and correct them in a friendly and officerlike manner, giving them an idea of discipline, etiquette, and propriety of dress, and not permit them to deviate from either; and I may add the want of common manners and decency in some of them—habits they must in some measure have contracted since entering the service in consequence of so many of them being in outports, without some person to keep them under that control so essential for young officers to be kept.
>
> As respects dress, I have frequently observed not more than three in full uniform coats cut and trimmed alike, which has frequently attracted the eye of foreign officers abroad and made us appear more like officers in different services than as officers of our navy should appear. . . .
>
> I calculated on having difficulty and trouble with them, which has far exceeded my expectations. The fact is they have been so little under control for several years that to be commanded and told of their faults is a temporary death to some of them . . . which confirms the opinion I have long entertained of many of our young officers that have been placed in command previous to their being acquainted with their duty to a commander or senior officer.[6]

Campbell's comments to the secretary of the navy were not just brave, self-serving words. His manner of dealing with refractory subordinates was brisk and to the point. While he commanded *Constellation* in the Mediterranean, Campbell had been called upon to preside at the court martial of two problem officers from *John Adams*, Surgeon's Mate Isaac Kipp and Midshipman John B. Cheshire, who had engaged in a physical and highly public brawl on shipboard. Kipp was dismissed for his role, but Cheshire got off with a public reprimand. Campbell, although presiding officer, apparently did not agree with the court's sentence in Cheshire's case; when the latter, after intermediate service in *Nautilus*, transferred to Campbell's ship and reported to his new commanding officer, Campbell summoned his first lieutenant into the cabin as a witness and said, "Mr. Cheshire, you have been once tried by a court martial. Now, Sir, for the first little fault you are guilty of I will arrest you and break you. You shall [thereafter] not remain on board of this ship but go to America in a merchant vessel." Commented Cheshire later: "It was at that time I would have given everything I possessed to be again on board of the Nautilus, but she was out of my reach, standing out of the Bay of Gibraltar." Even knowing that a sword hung over his head was not enough to cause Cheshire to shape up as an officer. Indeed, Campbell had probably already, and correctly, assessed him as one who never would. The captain eventually had to recommend dismissal: "Mr. Cheshire has repeatedly exposed himself by frequent fits of intoxication and neglect of duty, and as frequently have I confined him for trial, which he has yet evaded in consequence of his appearing penitent and assuring me in the most positive manner that I should never again have cause of complaint against him. In fact, neither arguments or persuasion is capable of correcting his manner sufficient to qualify him for an officer, and sorry I am to say that his conduct since under my command has been replete with error." Robert Smith readily concurred with Campbell's recommendation; young Cheshire was out of the navy.[7]

Saving Valuable Characters from Ruin—Sometimes

Well it was that the navy's leaders had an abiding vision of the ideal of what it meant to be a sea officer. Lacking that vision, the daily encounter with the raw human material in the form of John B. Cheshires and the like would have been profoundly discouraging. Adolescents and young adults, full of energy, full of themselves, brave, adventurous, headstrong, resistant to all authority, immature, deficient in self-discipline—such was the human clay from which responsible officers were to be molded. It was enough to make a commanding officer gray before his time.

Assigning midshipmen to vessels of war was largely a blind process. Untried, the young men were mostly just names to the civilian officials making the duty assignments. Sometimes the luck of the draw would put a majority of high achievers—future successful officers—in one ship. More often what the captain got was a mixed bag. Occasionally even the best of captains drew a full complement of losers. Fate dealt Captain Samuel Barron, who commanded the frigate *Philadelphia* on the Mediterranean station in 1801–1802, an assortment of talents, but one in which the bad apples seemed to have a secure majority, at least as the captain saw it. Admittedly Samuel Barron was no Hugh G. Campbell, striking terror into the hearts of wayward subordinates. He was a competent captain, but inclined to be too lenient and forgiving in his discipline, then suddenly changing course and trying to make everything taut all at once, before relapsing into Mr. Nice Captain again. Neither were *Philadelphia*'s lieutenants disposed to compensate for the captain by filling the role of sundowners.

In August 1801 Barron noticed that although his standing orders called for two midshipmen to be on the quarterdeck in each watch and others to be at different stations, he would often go on deck and find nary a midshipman in sight. Other times his eye might fall on a little knot of them collected somewhere, resolutely ignoring any and all directions from the quarterdeck. On the morning that Barron's simmering concern came to a boil he had instructed acting lieutenant Abner Woodruff to get the midshipmen to their duty posts. Woodruff complied and Barron went below. Six minutes later he came back onto the quarterdeck to find it bereft of officer and man, save for the lieutenant of the watch and a quartermaster at the helm! Highly distressed, Barron fired off a stiff order to the first lieutenant, John Cassin, telling him to correct the situation forthwith.

It just would not stay fixed. By March 1802 Barron was fulminating that the midshipmen had seemingly concluded that "any conduct, however improper for an officer," would be forgiven and the offender given yet another chance. "To prevent your examples totally destroying the order and regulations of this ship" Barron rattled threats of arrest and court martial and promulgated a set of detailed rules for watch officers. None of this did the job either; so in late July 1802, Barron dispatched a general order to his lieutenants to remind them of their responsibilities for discipline. He recorded, in the process, a picture of how *Philadelphia*'s young gentlemen were passing their days at sea:

> I have great cause to complain of the conduct of the midshipmen of this ship (with some exceptions). They are young men totally regardless of any order they receive and pay no kind of attention to their duty, answer no purpose on board but to create noise and confusion, and set an ill example to the people, who I'm loath to punish for conduct which officers use with impunity. I shall no longer submit to it. . . .
>
> It has already been ordered that officers of the watch are not to engage in any conversation on deck but what relates to their duty and not to appear without side arms. Both those orders have been disregarded. On the contrary, they are generally in the group or riding on the gunwale, at the gangway, lolling on the binnacle or capstan or on the guns of the quarterdeck, but more generally around a table on the gun deck, making use of such language as any decent sailor would be ashamed of. They absolutely keep the ship in an uproar; the boys and others imitate their example; and no greater scene of disorder and confusion can possibly exist than at times does on board this ship.

Whether Samuel Barron finally got his discipline problem resolved is unknown, because the surviving fragments of *Philadelphia*'s order book break off at this point in the story.[8] But even a much stricter captain than Samuel Barron, commanding a more achievement-oriented group of midshipmen, could have his headaches with his youthful subordinates. At 6:30 on the morning of 14 March 1802, as the frigate *Boston* was getting under way from Syracuse, Sicily, Captain Daniel McNeill—an officer as noted for his eccentricity as for the strictness of his discipline—observed a dearth of midshipmen at their duty posts and sent a master's mate below to discover how many were still in their hammocks, for all hands were supposed to be on deck. On learning that ten of his midshipmen, including several young men who would later be distinguished officers of the navy, were still abed, McNeill ordered them to report to his cabin forthwith. In trooped the midshipmen to confront an angry McNeill. A little lamely they tried to explain that they had just come off watch, or were too sick to go on deck, etc., etc. McNeill was having none of it: "He, in a haughty manner, pointed to the ladder leading into our berth and said 'Go!' and, as we were going, he stood heaping curses upon us," reported Melancthon T. Woolsey, one of the offending midshipmen, in his diary. "We went very contentedly to our berths and, like the philosopher that was kicked by an ass, resolved to take it from whence it came."

The midshipmen had scarcely reached their quarters before a marine officer appeared with McNeill's written order arresting the ten, suspending them from duty, and confining them to their berths. A few hours later, when the captain supposed that the ten young men were soberly contemplating their predicament, what should come to his ears but the sound of merry singing in the steerage, where the miscreants were spending their enforced leisure around an open bottle of wine! This was not exactly the mood of penitence that McNeill had in mind, and he ordered the steward to serve the ten no more wine for the duration of their arrest, a perfectly rational disciplinary measure that the aroused midshipmen chose to label "this unprecedented action, [which] shows the malicious disposition of our captain."

Midshipman Ralph Izard, Jr., no beauty himself, included a tiny sketch of his Boston *commanding officer, Daniel McNeill, in one of his letters home and added, "He is, without exception, the ugliest man in the face I have ever seen. His face is something of this shape, and his nose inclines exactly over the left corner of his mouth." Caricature? Perhaps, but this is the only unquestionably authentic likeness of the eccentric captain.* Izard Family Papers, Library of Congress, Washington, D.C.

This navy needed more than heroes. John Cassin neither won famous ship-to-ship victories nor uttered immortal words. He was exactly as C.B.J. Fevret de Saint-Mémin portrayed him: rather older than his peers (Cassin was approaching fifty when he posed in 1806, and he had only just attained the rank of master commandant); an experienced and capable seaman; a reliable officer. From 1803 till his death nearly two decades later the Navy Office posted Cassin to a succession of critical shore assignments wherein the secretaries knew they could depend on his tested skills as manager and as commander of trying subordinates. National Portrait Gallery, Washington, D.C.

McNeill was as tough as they came. He had the upper hand; he had only to wait the midshipmen out. On the day following their arrest three of the young gentlemen capitulated and wrote a letter to McNeill apologizing for their error and asking to be restored to duty. The captain accepted the apology and granted the request. Stubbornly the remaining seven decided to hold out for what they conceived to be the principle at issue. McNeill contended that only the presence of a midshipman's name on the surgeon's official sick list justified his not reporting for duty. Such a regulation was far from unique with McNeill among the navy's commanding officers, but the midshipmen elected to take the high ground of elite status and argued that the rule was "not only unprecedented but very unbecoming the commander of a frigate." One may be sure that the fifty-three-year-old McNeill thought that he was a better judge of appropriate conduct in a frigate's commander than a bunch of boys; he kept the midshipmen lingering in the discomforts of arrest—"we had nothing to live upon but salt beef and pork, beans, rice, bread, and stinking water, ours as well as the purser's store of tea and coffee being exhausted and we deprived of our ration of wine," lamented one of the seven—until the first of April. Then, after the seven had suffered nineteen days under arrest, McNeill at last restored them to duty, but under stringent watch rules, "which," complained the same midshipman, "makes our duty much harder than that of the foremast hands."[9]

Not only did the captain have to labor to instill self-discipline and a sense of duty in his less than entirely malleable novices, the steerage itself was a powder magazine of adolescent emotions, likely to explode at the smallest spark of interpersonal friction as these young men worked out the experience of living in constricted physical spaces with not always congenial peers. One day in late February 1813 Captain John Cassin, in search perhaps of a toddy to take winter's chill out of his bones, stepped into a Norfolk tavern where a piece of paper pinned to the wall caught his eye:

Notice
I Hereby certify that William L Rodgers (Midshipman on board the U.S. Frigate Constellation) is destitute of truth, honour and Courage.
Norfolk Virg.   A PHILLIPS
26th Feby 1813

Cassin took the offending paper from the wall and sent it to *Constellation*'s captain, Charles Stewart, who promptly called Midshipmen Phillips and Rogers (for Phillips had added insult to defamation by misspelling the latter's name) on the carpet. The origin of this tempest so briskly brewing in *Constellation*'s teapot was, Stewart learned, that Midshipman Phillips, finding a pile of Rogers's clothes deposited on his trunk, had moved them to the steerage dining table. When Rogers discovered the garments there he flew into a rage, asserting that the table was greasy and his clothing now soiled. Phillips tried to apologize, saying that he did not know the table was greasy. The more Phillips tried to explain, the more verbal abuse Rogers heaped on him, ending with a threat to "chastise" Phillips if it ever happened again. There was just so much that Phillips would take; when both had shore leave in Norfolk, Phillips challenged Rogers to a duel. This challenge Rogers refused, claiming (at least to Captain Stewart) that he had declined the field of honor because *Constellation*'s internal regulations forbade dueling. Hearing Rogers's refusal, Midshipman Phillips marched off to the tavern and posted the notice that had caught Captain Cassin's eye. Stewart gave the two midshipmen a stiff lecture, insisted that they apologize to each other, and explained that he now considered the matter closed.

He was wrong. As soon as Rogers could get on shore he sent a challenge to Phillips and then posted an announcement of his own in the local watering hole:

Norfolk, Tuesday Afternoon
I regret extremely My Necessity to reduce to infamy Any Man, but a duty which honor imposes, & Justice Sanctions, compels me to give publicity to the following Notice
Mr. Philips Midshipman on board the U.S. Frigate Constellation having publicly Charged Me as devoid of truth & honor, neither of which Charges he has Ability to prove just, & having refused to render Me, the satisfaction I had a right to demand & expect have No other Alternative but to publish him to the world as A *Liar* & a *Coward*.
His having ungenerously held me up to public view without Advertising Me of his intention, discovers a heart, devoid of every principle which Constitutes the Gentleman [and] Man of honour.
WILLIAM L. ROGERS

Now Rogers had really incurred Stewart's wrath, for his original claim that he had refused to fight Phillips out of respect for Stewart's rules looked like pure hypocrisy. Asserting that Rogers was "so disgraceful as an officer, so contemptuous of the rules of the service, and so disrespectful to me as his commander" that, unless stern action were taken, "it will be impracticable to keep up the order and discipline necessary in the service," Stewart referred the whole business to Secretary Jones for a decision. The latter promptly sent a letter dismissing Rogers from the navy, mainly to put the fear of authority in his heart. As soon as Rogers apologized to Stewart, which he did, Jones was ready to reinstate him in his rank, but Rogers decided, for reasons now unknown, to accept a commission as second lieutenant in the army instead.[10]

Protagonists in these emotional eruptions that made the steerage resemble a battleground as much as it did shared living quarters were by no means all misfit officers. Young men with excellent potential found themselves called on the carpet before the captain nearly as often as the bad actors who were headed for inevitable dismissal. It was the captain's job to be shrewd enough to distinguish one sort of midshipman from the other. Captain Charles Gordon transferred Midshipman Samuel W. Downing to the Norfolk navy yard in March 1814 and considered it good riddance: "His restless unhappy disposition has kept him always dissatisfied with the ship and totally indifferent to his duty; constantly complaining that the officers were all prejudiced against him and wished to injure him. Our accommodations were crowded with midshipmen; he was disagreeable among his companions and totally useless to the ship." If Gordon's letter were all the information the historian possessed about Midshipman Downing, one would expect to find his naval service coming to a speedy and abrupt halt with a resignation or a dismissal. Instead, to look up Samuel Downing in the navy's register of officers is to find him promoted to lieutenant in 1817, to commander in 1837, and to captain ten years later. What had happened? At the navy yard young Downing came under the supervision of Captain John Cassin, who had known him at an earlier stage of life and who perceived different qualities: "I do consider him a smart, intelligent young man and fear from his intelligence he has been made the butt, of which I presume has been the cause of his leaving the ship."[11]

What it took to turn borderline cases into good officers was an older mentor who cared about shaping young careers and who possessed the skills to do the job. William Bainbridge explained how this might happen in a letter concerning Lieutenant Thomas A. Beatty, an officer whose career was ultimately not salvaged. Beatty "has within him (if well directed) what constitutes a good officer," Bainbridge explained to Accountant of the Navy Thomas Turner, who was a friend of Beatty's father and who watched out for the son's interests.

> You have desired me to give you my candid opinion of him. I will do so with the frankness of friendship. He is as brave as Caesar, has an active mind, but is inattentive and negligent to himself and often so to his duty. His natural disposition is rather unfavorable to subordination, yet can be readily governed by proper and *strict* discipline. I am confident under my own immediate command that he would make an excellent officer. When he was with me in the frigate President he was a most promising lad. And he still possesses all the essential qualities he had then, but has become considerably relaxed in attention, which may have proceeded from a relaxed discipline over him. I should be sorry that the service should lose him, for I am confident he will make a good officer if well directed, and I should much fear of his turning out worse if he left the service. I wish you could get him on board some vessel where he would find a *friend* as well as a commander in the captain. By a little attention valuable characters are often saved from ruin.[12]

That is as far as it is possible to follow Captain Bainbridge into the process of aiding a young officer of equivocal promise to master counterproductive personality traits. No records survive of how, step by step, any senior officer proved himself both friend and commander to a floundering younger man and helped him salvage his career. Until such a detailed record comes to light, such an arduous, but ultimately humane, regimen will have to be left to the imagination.

Anti-hero and Role Model: A Note on Daniel McNeill

Because social history is more concerned with the typical than with the aberrant, Daniel McNeill, that most fascinating character of the pre-1815 navy, makes only brief appearances in these pages. Born in Charlestown, Massachusetts, in April 1748, McNeill was to pursue financial security, no matter how questionable the means, throughout his long life. During the Revolutionary War he commanded six privateers; of these the most notable was the *General Mifflin*, 20 guns, in which he took thirteen prizes and fought a battle with a British sloop of war. McNeill's privateering ventures were apparently financially rewarding, for before peace returned in 1783 he was himself part owner of two privateers. In the economic doldrums that followed the Revolution he turned his hand to the one line of work in which the profits seemed the most certain: the slave trade. If McNeill had ever been a man of moral scruples, he had, by this phase of his career, managed to deaden them completely. As early as 1786 records show him arriving at St. Thomas from Guinea after a voyage in which forty or fifty of his cargo of slaves had died. By 1792 McNeill had entered into a long-term business relationship with James and Thomas H. Perkins of Boston in the slave trade between Africa and the West Indies, sometimes commanding his ship, *Willing Quaker*, himself and sometimes sending her out under other masters, a business in which he continued right up to the time of his appointment as captain in the navy in the summer of 1798.[13]

Not surprisingly for one who had spent many years in so reprehensible a business, as a navy captain McNeill proved to be a man of the strictest discipline and a harsh temper, one given to sudden outbursts of violence. He was a hard drinker and, as a commanding officer, occasionally callous to the life threatening dangers to which his arbitrary methods exposed his subordinates, especially the enlisted men. A prime instance of the eccentric behavior manifested by this saltiest of old sea dogs was provided by Midshipman Melancthon T. Woolsey when he reported that the frigate *Boston* had gotten under way from Cagliari, Sardinia, "after our captain had quarreled with his second lieutenant, cursed and otherwise scandalously abused one of his midshipmen, knocked down his sailmaker (a warrant officer), and kicked his sailing master (his nephew)."[14] Nicknamed Old Thunderbolt by his terrified subordinates, McNeill was, as one midshipman reported to his mother, "very familiar at his table, but will not suffer any person to speak to him on the quarterdeck."[15]

Most of the stories about McNeill date from his command of *Boston* during the Tripolitan War, but the personality traits he manifested in the Mediterranean were already in full bloom during his Quasi-War command of *Portsmouth*, although fewer details are known. First Lieutenant Anthony Gale, USMC, reported to marine corps commandant W. W. Burrows, on 16 December 1800, "I suppose, Sir, by this date you have heard some news respecting Captain McNeill. Each of the officers and midshipmen [of *Portsmouth*] have signed a letter addressed to the secretary setting forth their grievances, and the officers wrote a particular letter requesting to be placed from under his command. Several of the midshipmen have sent letters of resignation." In spite of all this derogatory evidence, there were good officers who trained under McNeill, held him in high regard, and subsequently went on to distinguished careers in the navy. Among them the most notable was Lieutenant William Burrows of *Enterprize-Boxer* fame. Burrows began his naval service in McNeill's Quasi-War *Portsmouth* and took to the life with enthusiasm: "The crew in general speaks very highly of William. I have often heard the captain and officers say he was a smart boy and would make a complete seaman. He was continually aloft and never quit the ship all the time her rigging was overhauling," Lieutenant Gale told the young man's father. "He looked more like a boy before the mast than a midshipman." When, during the Tripolitan War, the younger Burrows had an opportunity to transfer to McNeill's ship for a second tour of duty with this strange, violent man, he did so with alacrity. Contemporaries noted that McNeill had a "great partiality" for Midshipman Burrows, whose blossoming eccentricities were on their way to becoming as famous as McNeill's.[16]

The Jefferson administration apparently intended to retain McNeill as one of the captains on the post-1801 peace establishment, but his behavior while commanding *Boston* on the Mediterranean station, 1801–1802, was so peculiar and unpredictable that his sanity came under suspicion. At Málaga, angered because some of his officers were still on shore when he decided to depart (and possibly intoxicated as well), McNeill sailed (3 January 1802) without them. Left stranded were Lieutenant William C. Jenckes and his servant, Lieutenant Edward Wyer, First Lieutenant William Amory, USMC, Nicholas Harper, *Boston*'s steward, Purser Charles Wadsworth, and two wardroom servants. Three weeks later, at Toulon, McNeill (still short all the essential officers whom he had left at Málaga) received a firm personal order from Commodore Richard Dale, who was already angered by what he had seen of McNeill's harsh and arbitrary treatment of his subordinates, to get under way immediately for Tunis. As *Boston* was raising anchor and beginning to make sail, three French visitors from shore and Commodore Dale's chaplain in *President*, Robert Thompson, stopped by McNeill's cabin to make a brief courtesy call before heading ashore. No, no, McNeill insisted, Don't leave. He poured first one bottle of wine and then another for his nervous guests, who were all the while watching Toulon getting smaller and smaller through the cabin's windows. Not until *Boston* was outside Cape Cépet would McNeill permit ship to be tacked and a gun fired for a shore boat. When none appeared, McNeill tacked again and stood out to sea, to the highly vocal distress of his involuntary passengers. From Tunis—it was now eight days later—McNeill paid passages home to Toulon in a merchantman for the three Frenchmen, who by this time were reconciled to enjoying their adventure. In Chaplain Thompson *Boston* had, by highly unorthodox methods, acquired a schoolmaster who was promptly put to work teaching the frigate's midshipmen and who remained in her till she got back to the United States in late October 1802. Meanwhile, the officers who had been left ashore at Málaga were still pursuing *Boston* around the Mediterranean. Harper, the steward, was the first to catch up, at Malta on 15 March. Purser Wadsworth and the two wardroom servants were, he reported, at Tunis. They had traveled by land from Málaga to Marseilles to Toulon to Leghorn and on to Naples without overtaking *Boston*. At Naples the trio had taken to the water, gone to Sardinia, and thence to Tunis. Two weeks later, with *Boston* still at Malta, Wadsworth and the servants finally caught up, having come over in *Gloria*, a merchantman belonging to William Eaton, the U.S. consul at Tunis. The remainder of the abandoned officers and their servant did not get back on board *Boston* till 12 and 13 May. In the meantime they had made their way from Málaga to Toulon, where they joined the frigate *President* until she fell in with the schooner *Enterprize*, which carried them as supernumeraries till she found *Boston* near Malta in May.[17]

If McNeill was not in enough trouble for all of this, at Messina he enticed a portion of a Neapolitan military band to desert and join *Boston* as musicians. The band members came on board in disguise; their instruments and possessions were spirited out to the ship at night. "This disgraceful action I think exceeds any of Captain McNeill's mean adventures since we have been within the Straits of Gibraltar," wrote Midshipman Woolsey. "The master of the band has his wife with him (who performs on the spinet), two small boys (who play the horn), and three small children, the eldest of which plays the triangle. Besides these there are two men, one of which performs on the clarinet, the other [on] the trumpet. The whole company consists of nine persons. They brought on board an excellent brass drum elegantly ornamented with the king's arms. On this instrument our second sergeant marines performs very well. We have a specimen of their performances whenever the captain sits down to his meals." Whether the presence of music facilitated smoother human relations in *Boston* during the last five months of her cruise does not appear in the historical record, but when Captain McNeill got back to Washington Accountant of the Navy Thomas Turner blew the whistle on the whole operation: musicians were not authorized on board U.S. ships of war and therefore could not be paid as such. Although six of the nine had been rated on *Boston*'s books as ordinary seamen and landsmen, they were not going to be paid under those rubrics either, ruled Mr. Turner, for they had done no duty as sailors. If the musicians were to be compensated, it would have to be out of McNeill's own pocket.[18]

To no one's surprise, except Daniel McNeill's, Robert Smith decided that the terms of the Peace Establishment Act did not permit him to keep McNeill in the navy any longer. With a few pro forma words of regret he sent Old Thunderbolt into involuntary retirement. "It hurts him amazingly, and I feel for his situation," wrote Midshipman Ralph Izard, who was on hand when McNeill got the news. "He certainly did not treat his officers as he should have done, yet I cannot help saying that he treated me more civilly than he did my co-midshipmen."[19]

It was impossible for anyone as feisty as Daniel McNeill to stay down forever. About 1805, when he was fifty-seven years old, McNeill abandoned Boston, which had been his home to that point in his life, and moved to South Carolina, where he was soon fully and energetically immersed in activities that tickled the fringes of legality and of ethical conduct. When the command of the Charleston revenue cutter came open late in 1806 he recruited his old friends Captain Thomas Tingey and Secretary of War Henry Dearborn to help him get the job, asserting, among other good reasons why he should receive a government post, that he had lost "a fortune" when the government made the slave trade illegal. Through what reasoning the administration decided to forgive and forget McNeill's earlier misadventures in *Boston* is not a part of the record, but command of the cutter he did receive; ex-midshipman Izard, now Lieutenant Izard, could soon report that "old McNeill is constantly on the go" in his cutter "and has been fortunate enough to catch one or two good prizes."[20] Daniel McNeill died in his adopted city of Charleston, at age eighty-five, on 6 May 1833.[21]

18. A School in Every Frigate

*S*HIPS AND the sea. Rules and regulations. Older mentors. If all these were busy turning green-hand midshipmen into naval officers, was there any role left for education in the narrow sense of going to school and sitting in a classroom? Yes, but it was a role that the pre-1815 navy had trouble in performing as well as it desired. It also proved to be an educational effort with a limited mission.

Waterborne Schoolmasters

FRIGATE BOSTON,
At her Anchors.

THOSE Seamen who are thoroughly experienced, as well as their Brothers, who have not had the same advantages, are invited on board the Frigate *Boston*, GEORGE LITTLE, Esq. Commander, where an opportunity is offered to men, who engage in the honorable employment of defending their country, to give full scope to their feelings. Parents that have Children, and who are anxious to put them in the honest road to fame, are informed, that a respectable School master is appointed, whose morals are considered correct, whose talents for teaching every art necessary for an American Seaman, are unquestionable. The consideration held out by Government is all that Patriotism or Prudence can desire; and those who now stand aloof will lose an opportunity of rendering their country a service, which her honor demands; and of convincing the world, that American Seamen need no protection but the law of their country proclaimed *from the Gun Deck.*

Boston Frigate's Rendezvous, North End, June 15.[1]

This prominent advertisement, which appeared in Boston newspapers in June 1799, was a clear statement of the navy's ideal: each ship with a floating classroom. When *Boston* returned from her yearlong cruise and Captain Little reported to John Adams at Quincy, the president positively glowed with pride and pleasure: "There ought to be a school on board every frigate," he announced. "Thirty persons have been taught navigation and other sciences connected with the naval service on board the *Boston*."[2] As the years went by

194

the gap between ideal and reality proved greater than the navy's leaders imagined in the idealistic early days of which *Boston*'s advertisement is a relic. What the navy wanted taught in such classrooms, and for which closely focused instruction it was quite willing to settle, was navigation and the mathematics necessary to practice it successfully.[3] Improved writing skills, increased familiarity with major works of literature, the insights of history, mastery of a foreign language—these were not customarily part of the navy's program of formal shipboard instruction. Which is not to say that they were not honored, desired, and pursued. The officer corps possessed a powerful ethos of ongoing self-improvement; its successful members worked hard at honing their prose styles, and at reading literature, history, and travelers' narratives. But these were activities one pursued on one's own or with a mentor, building on the academy education acquired before entering the navy. The service was not in the business of providing a liberal education—at least not in the classroom sense. *Boston*'s democratic promises to the contrary notwithstanding, the objects of instruction were customarily the midshipmen and master's mates only. In 1799, as in many a later day, advertising was not always to be taken at face value.

Serving as schoolmaster to a frigate's midshipmen was one of the three duties the *Naval Regulations* assigned to chaplains. Ships too small to be entitled to a chaplain could carry an officer rated as schoolmaster, but this billet was so infrequently used in the pre-1815 navy that the term *chaplain* will be employed throughout this chapter to designate the man who was charged with instructional duties. Sixty-one persons have been identified who held, at one time or another before 14 February 1815, the rank of chaplain, acting chaplain, or schoolmaster. Three of the sixty-one were actually coasting pilots, carried on their ships' rolls as acting chaplains, perhaps because they were expected to teach navigation in the hours when their piloting responsibilities made no demands on their time. Deducting the three pilots reduces the roster of chaplains in the pre-1815 navy to fifty-eight.

When these fifty-eight chaplains are examined in mass the striking feature of the group portrait is that most of them were birds of passage (Table 6). Among the fifty chaplains whose length of service in that grade can be calculated with reasonable accuracy, nearly half served a year or less in that capacity; two-thirds were gone at the end of two years. Only six chaplains out of the fifty served as such longer than four years. This latter handful of long-service chaplains were significantly more stable in their careers, showing active-duty records of between six and thirteen years. The extraordinarily transient character of a chaplain's appointment may be highlighted by comparing it with the longevity of newly appointed midshipmen, a group themselves characterized by a relatively high attrition rate (Table 45). Attrition among midshipmen reached the 50 percent mark only after four years of service; almost half of the chaplains were gone in one year. Forty-two percent of all entering midshipmen served at least five years, thereby attaining the experience threshold at which they were considered eligible for promotion to lieutenant; by the time five years had elapsed nine out of every ten chaplains were elsewhere.

A primary reason was that a substantial flock of these birds of passage were in flight to other ranks in the navy. The collective portrait of the navy's fifty-eight chaplains documents the lack of formal connection between religion and the typical naval chaplain. Among fifty-eight individuals, only three were ordained ministers (one Presbyterian, two Episcopal); a fourth (himself the son of a minister) became a clergyman after leaving the navy. Chaplains were men with career goals other than religious ones on their minds. When Gardner Thomas, who had previously served as captain's clerk to at least two different commanding officers, sought to secure a more permanent situation in the navy, he indicated that he was willing to accept a chaplain's appointment, "not, indeed, with a desire to act to the 'letter' of it—as I believe this has been rarely required," but because he could teach the principles of navigation to the younger officers and perform secretarial duties; but, Thomas went on to explain, he regarded the chaplain's berth as a mere temporary expedient till he could secure a purser's appointment.[4] Many of Gardner Thomas's peers shared his career goals. At least eleven of the fifty-eight chaplains had, like Thomas, previously held the rank of captain's clerk, a sure indication that it was primarily their secretarial skills that would be in demand in their position as chaplains. Among the fifty-eight, seventeen were successfully en route to some other rank in the navy: fourteen as pursers, two as sailing masters, and one as a midshipman. Captain's clerk to chaplain to purser was an established career path. Four chaplains who began as captain's clerks, of whom Gardner Thomas was one, succeeded in obtaining the desired purserships; an unknown number of others tried but failed to accomplish the final leg of this career journey.

If their highly transient service made chaplains atypical naval officers, they were atypical in more positive ways as well. Not surprisingly, given the roles they were expected to fill, chaplains had achieved a higher level of formal education than their shipmates bound toward the command ranks. Slightly less than one-quarter of them (at least thirteen of the fifty-eight chaplains) were either college graduates (eight men) or had attended college. Among their pupils, the navy's midshipmen, only 1 young man out of every 16 or 18 even entered college; a minuscule 1 of 150 had attained the bachelor's degree. To his role as teacher the chaplain brought the authority conferred by being older than those he was called upon to instruct, a situation that did not always obtain in the land-based academy (Table 7). The median age of chaplains when they began their service as such was twenty-six years; this made them fully nine years older than the typical midshipmen they were likely to be teaching. Although one man, newly graduated from Harvard, was only nineteen when he was appointed schoolmaster to the frigate *Boston* and another (of whom more later) was fifty-nine when he commenced his career as a naval chaplain, eight out of ten of these men were between twenty-one and thirty-four when they received their warrants. Combine this youthful profile with the brief tenure of their service, and one clearly sees that for almost all such men a chaplain's billet was but a stop along the way, not a career goal.

Though it probably had little direct effect on their teaching, chaplains were also untypical of the officer corps in their geographical roots. If the middle states dominated the command ranks, New England had its day when it came to chaplains. Of the forty American-born chaplains, more than half (twenty-two) came from New England, and only fifteen from the nation's middle seaboard, which was the heartland of its fighting officers. The historian is at a loss to explain this difference unless it be that New England was producing a surplus of well-educated individuals who were having difficulty finding appropriate employment in the land-based economy and so were available to accept naval chaplaincies.

A sailing master in chaplain's clothing. In the fall of 1812 William Bainbridge was planning an extended raid on British shipping in the southern Atlantic, with a possible incursion into the Indian or the Pacific Ocean—an intention cut short by Constitution's *encounter with* Java. *Bainbridge had never navigated these remote latitudes, so John Carlton, a fortyish Salem master mariner with extensive experience in Asian waters, was clearly a desirable addition in* Constitution. *The commodore purchased Carlton's personal set of an expensive atlas,* The Complete East-India Pilot; or, Oriental Navigator, *and appointed him the frigate's "assistant sailing master," a berth unknown to any naval regulations. In the payroll Carlton stood as chaplain. Although his Salem pastor, Dr. William Bentley, was on record that Carlton was "of good habits," it was not the chaplain's religious virtues, but his reputation as an "able navigator" that lighted up Bainbridge's eye. In 1813, when Master Commandant William M. Crane expected to be ordered on secret service in the Pacific in* John Adams, *he, too, was able to secure Carlton's coveted navigational services in the combined capacities (and pay) of chaplain and captain's clerk.* John Adams's *wartime mission was altered to one of transporting a portion of the U.S. delegation to the peace negotiations with Britain, and it was almost certainly while* John Adams *was anchored at Texel in the Netherlands during the summer of 1814 that the alert-eyed Chaplain Carlton sat for his portrait by Dutch artist Charles Delin.* Peabody Museum of Salem, Massachusetts.

Who were the human beings lurking behind those numbers? Without pretending that there existed such a person as the typical naval chaplain, three men who received their appointments primarily because of their experience (and presumed abilities) as teachers may be asked to step forward from the group portrait.

David Phineas Adams was the son of a Massachusetts farmer who was sufficiently prosperous to send his son to Harvard with the aim of preparing him for one of the learned professions. Young Adams was rather more mature than most of his classmates—he was twenty-four when he received his A.B. in 1801—which probably explains why he made his way through college with only the barest gentlemanly minimum of disciplinary infractions. The reasons for Adams's late start on a college education are unknown. It is a matter of record that he began his collegiate career with the intention of entering the ministry, but apparently changed his mind in his senior year. Like many another Harvard undergraduate, Adams had taken three-week leaves of absence during the winter vacations of 1799, 1800, and 1801 to serve brief stints as a schoolteacher; his first jobs after graduation may have been in the classroom as well. Adams tried his hand at journalism and literature late in 1803, when he became one of the founders and the first editor of *The Monthly Anthology; or, Magazine of Polite Literature*. Adams stayed at the helm of *The Monthly Anthology* through the April 1804 issue, then resigned, claiming his health had failed. Likely as not that excuse masks the real reason, which may have been as simple as the need to look out for a lucrative way of earning a living. He next turns up in 1807 in New York City, self-employed as a teacher of mathematics and navigation—one of those individuals, to be found in every port along the seaboard, to whom would-be master mariners came before they went to sea or between voyages to learn the skills necessary for advancement in their professions. If Adams's annual moves from one address to another are any indication, it was a precarious sort of genteel profession, with one's income hanging on whether or not would-be pupils came knocking at the door.

In some manner Adams learned that a chaplain's berth in the navy would provide a steady salary for performing exactly the same duties. Aided by James Lawrence, he assembled an impressive dossier of recommendations that was forwarded to Secretary Hamilton with a covering letter from Lawrence, who glowingly described Adams as "one of the best lunarians in the United States." After several months, and some prodding by Adams and his friends, Hamilton issued the coveted chaplain's warrant in May 1811. David Porter was importuning Hamilton for a schoolmaster for *Essex*'s midshipmen; the secretary responded by attaching Adams to Porter's ship in August, thus beginning a nearly three-year tour of duty that would carry Adams around Cape Horn and into the heart of the South Seas, an adventure he was to record in a series of beautifully crafted charts. By all surviving accounts David P. Adams was an able and dedicated teacher, perhaps as close to the ideal shipboard chaplain as the pre-1815 navy possessed. David Porter called him "correct, skillful, and useful," and *Essex*'s midshipmen echoed their captain's assessment. Adams liked his job and knew where his talents lay. For him a chaplain's warrant was not the first or second rung on the ladder to some better post. Still busy with his chaplain's duties, David P. Adams died on board *Peacock* en route home from the West Indies in September 1823, at forty-six the premature victim of the yellow fever then taking such a terrible toll of officers and men attached to that station.[5]

Jason Howard's career as a naval schoolmaster was typical in its brevity, but not in its termination. Born at Bridgewater, Massachusetts, in June 1773, Howard entered Harvard College with the class of 1797 and, as did David P. Adams, took advantage of college holidays to teach school. Save for tardiness in paying his fees, Howard's academic progress through Harvard seemed normal and untroubled till sometime in his senior year when he more or less drifted away from Cambridge and took up the study of law. This new career he pursued for two years, but apparently not long enough to obtain admission to the bar; neither were legal studies so all-consuming that Howard could not find ample time to contribute political essays to the press. By midsummer of 1799 he was apparently once again at loose ends and asked Hector Orr, a fellow resident of Bridgewater and surgeon-designate of the new frigate *Essex*, to recommend him for the schoolmaster's post in that ship. Orr's intercession was successful, and in January 1800 *Essex* and Jason Howard sailed for Java. Of Howard's activities and abilities as *Essex*'s schoolmaster no record survives. At 4:15 in the afternoon of 16 October 1800, in a homeward-bound *Essex*, Jason Howard, "ship's schoolmaster," age twenty-seven, died of unrecorded causes. One hour and fifteen minutes later, after the brief customary ritual, his body was committed to the ocean. A decent interval of twenty-four hours was allowed to elapse and then, once more following the established practice of the navy, the contents of Howard's two trunks—clothing, books, miscellaneous items—were sold to his shipmates for $66.55, a sum that, together with any pay due, would be transmitted, probably in the care of Hector Orr, to his next of kin at Bridgewater.[6]

David P. Adams's and Jason Howard's careers as chaplain and schoolmaster, though different, were both the careers of reasonably mainstream individuals. The post of chaplain—a roving, marginal, but genteel existence—also held the potential to attract those who deviated far from the norm, even in an officer corps that was reasonably accepting of eccentricity. The best-documented of such men was Samuel Chandler. Like Adams and Howard, Chandler was a Massachusetts native and a Harvard man. (Of the thirteen chaplains who are known to have attended college, eight were from Harvard.) There Chandler's similarity to Adams and Howard ends. For one thing, Chandler, born at Andover in November 1758, was between fifteen and twenty years their senior in age. His father, David Chandler, had rallied to the revolutionary cause at Lexington and Concord in the initial clashes of the war for independence, subsequently serving as a first lieutenant in a Massachusetts, and then in a Continental, regiment until his untimely death, apparently of smallpox, in 1776. Presumably David Chandler left his family in a reasonably secure financial position, for young Samuel was able to pursue his college education during the early years of the war, receiving his A.B. in 1779. The most notable recorded event of Chandler's college days was his participation in a riotous party late in his senior year. According to the not impartial views of the harassed Harvard officials, Chandler and seven other students "were guilty of making indecent and tumultuous noises to the dishonor and disturbance of the college," by "drinking wine to excess" in the room of one of the culprits. When a tutor ordered them to disperse they simply moved the party to another room, "where they continued the same disorderly behavior." Senior administrative officials then intervened to break up the goings-on, but the imbibing students, Chandler included, simply adjourned to a gambling house in Cambridge, an establishment strictly off-limits to students. For these offenses, "scandalous and reproachful to this society and directly subversive of good morals," Chandler lost his previously assigned place in the senior exhibition and retained his class standing only at the price of having his confession of guilt and petition for restoration read publicly in chapel while he stood in his place and behaved "with proper decorum."

Following the Harvard commencement Chandler's trail becomes a faint one. According to his own account, Chandler served as captain's clerk and possibly as chaplain and schoolmaster in one or more ships of war during the latter years of the Revolution. After this he took up a wandering existence, settling for a time in the West Indies, where he may have married and had a son. But he could never stay in one place indefinitely; by 1802 he had visited each of the United States, East and West Florida, and the West Indies. One could overemphasize Chandler's vagabond ways; he himself said that "most of my time" had been spent in New York and Philadelphia. He admitted to having been "in different occupations," but reported that he had earned his living "mostly [as a] tutor in different colleges." One place he did not spend much time was his Massachusetts home. In January 1802 it was fifteen years or longer since he had seen or even written to his mother.

The first time one can pin Chandler down to places and dates is October 1799, when he secured a chaplain's appointment from Secretary Stoddert and was assigned to the sloop *Patapsco*. Things must not have gone well in *Patapsco*, because late in the spring of 1800 Stoddert spoke of his desire "to get clear of Mr. Chandler" by telling him to present his pay account for settlement "and quit the service." Chandler somehow parried this effort and persuaded John Barry to request him as chaplain in *United States*. To the Roman Catholic Barry, Chandler, a born and bred Congregationalist, alleged, "Brought up in the Church of England, I often visit the Catholic Church and am always pleased with the devout and becoming attention observed in them. I consider the different forms of religion only so many different roads to the same final happy home." He reinforced this application with a second letter in which he claimed, with who knows what degree of truth, "Such is my partiality for the navy that, though offers have been made of a professorship in a college where I taught the mathematics and French language after graduating in the university of Cambridge [i.e., Harvard], I have declined the acceptance, ever cherishing the hope of getting reestablished in the navy."

Chandler's service as chaplain in *United States* was sufficiently satisfactory to insure his retention in the officer corps during the reduction of 1801. By the time Chandler's retention decision was made it was too late to attach him to any ship of the first squadron sent to the Mediterranean during the Tripolitan War, but the Navy Office packed him off to Norfolk to join the frigate *Chesapeake*, designated as part of the second Mediterranean squadron that would be dispatched in the spring of 1802. At Norfolk, early in that year, a letter from Samuel Chandler's long-neglected mother caught up with her wandering son. After offering as a lame excuse for not writing that he had heard, "some years past, when residing in the West Indies," that she had died of a "lingering consumption," he went on:

> You may recollect, when we were at our family habitation in Andover, how sensibly affected I was by the religious discourses delivered by the Rev. Parson French. Whatever has been my life since that time, I have now resumed the profession of a minister; and, as the morning of my life was spent in religious [services], so shall its evening be, if God spares it; and hope its meridian faults will be pardoned by him whom they have offended. The greatest consolations in this life I find are derived from a virtuous life. I am now bound to the Mediterranean against the Turks; shall visit Egypt, the place where the Israelites were once prisoners, then proceed to Jerusalem, the land of Canaan, and, if possible, go to the River Euphrates, where was situated the Garden of Eden; then return to visit my mother, if God spares my life.

Unfortunately for his travel plans, this religious charlatan was about to be unmasked. *Chesapeake*'s new commanding officer, Thomas Truxtun, arrived in Norfolk to be assailed by a cacophony of complaints by local businessmen over Chaplain Chandler's habit of running up debts and evading their payment.

Noting, for the Navy Office's benefit, that "Mr. Chandler is not a gentleman in any respect; he is known of old in this borough," Truxtun turned him out of *Chesapeake* and told the purser to pay him off. Chandler then made his way to Philadelphia, where Robert Smith confirmed, by letter, the decision that, yes, Chandler's career as a U.S. Navy chaplain was at an end. When Chandler responded that he had "flattering prospects" awaiting him in Spain but "am destitute of cash to pay my passage," Smith said he could have a free ride to Gibraltar in the frigate *Adams*. That ship's surviving muster rolls are fragmentary, so it is now impossible to know whether ex-chaplain Chandler took advantage of his free passage to Europe, there to embark on new wanderings that would eventually take him to the Holy Land and beyond. At this point he drops abruptly out of the historical record, all further trace eluding Chandler family genealogists and Harvard class historians. The latter, frustrated in their attempt to establish a death date, simply closed his file by noting: intemperate, according to Dr. Abijah Cheever, a classmate.[7]

School's Out!

John Adams's ideal—"there ought to be a school on board every frigate"— proved an extraordinarily difficult goal for the pre-1815 navy to attain. By law only frigates of 44 guns were allowed chaplains; smaller frigates were permitted to enroll schoolmasters, but at a reduced rate of pay.[8] Relatively few captains took advantage of the latter provision, and the use of the schoolmaster billet died out around 1802. At least so far as the law and the regulations ran, formal shipboard education was available only to those midshipmen fortunate enough to be attached to frigates; vessels smaller than frigates were allowed neither chaplains nor schoolmasters. As in many other matters in the pre-1815 navy, one could easily be misled by paying too much attention to the written code; chaplains turn up occasionally on the rolls of small vessels, the pragmatic response to needs and situations unforeseen when the law was written.

When the chaplain was present on shipboard, his role as teacher was often seriously compromised by a factor never mentioned in the authorizing law or in the *Naval Regulations*. Although not enumerated among the chaplain's official duties, traditional practice was to fill the chaplain's berth with someone whose primary responsibility was to serve as secretary to the captain or the squadron commodore. Unless the captain or the commodore were a Thomas Truxtun or a David Porter—that is, a leader possessed of a strong commitment to the importance of formal classroom instruction on shipboard—a captain's and especially a commodore's pressing need for assistance with the burden of administrative paperwork was likely to engross all or most of the chaplain's time, leaving little energy or enthusiasm for his role as teacher.

The commanding officer's commitment to education and study was key. When he made clear that these were a high priority, teachers could be attracted and midshipmen's motivation heightened. If the message went out from the captain, either explicitly or silently via behavior, that studious midshipmen were a lower priority, education withered. Each midshipman was a serving officer, with responsible shipboard duties, as well as an apprentice learning his profession. Except for the most self-disciplined young men, the demands of classroom and quarterdeck were often in conflict for the midshipman's time, especially given his propensity to bestow ample attention on recreation. Unless

Even though it was not taken until ten years after the end of the War of 1812, John Henri Isaac Browere's life-mask bust of David Porter captures, far better than do the pre-1815 portraits in oil, the fierce energy and penetrating mind of this dynamic leader who was both man of action and intellectual. But the eyes gleam with the inner fires that were destroying Porter's naval career even as Browere worked. New York State Historical Association, Cooperstown.

the captain was foursquare behind the educational priority, the quarterdeck won the competition with the schoolroom.

Even if the captain was an enthusiastic supporter of the every-ship-a-schoolhouse ideal, the shortage of qualified teachers was a serious inhibitor. There were simply not enough qualified applicants for chaplaincies, let alone men who were motivated to make a long-term commitment to the education of young naval officers. Recruitment was compromised by status considerations. Even though pre-1815 American society put a strong priority on the development of educated young men to do its work, schoolteaching itself was not a highly esteemed profession. All too typically it was the job a young man held during college vacations or for a few years till he got himself established in his real career. The older schoolteacher was often a downwardly mobile individual who had sunk to the level of his competence.[9] There is no evidence that the naval chaplaincy was, by and large, a job conferring higher status than that of the land-based schoolmaster. To be a commodore's secretary was to hold a post with great potential for influence and power, a state of affairs that reinforced the already ample temptations to emphasize that role in preference to the pedagogical one.

An incident during the Tripolitan War years highlights the shortage of qualified shipboard teachers. In 1804 John Rodgers, then commanding the frigate *Congress*, was told by ordinary seaman John Duffy that "he has taught the theory of navigation in the manner it is generally taught in seminaries." (One wishes one knew more of Duffy's life story!) Rodgers had no officer in *Congress* capable of providing such instruction, so, "as I am desirous that the midshipmen should become acquainted with that branch of mathematics as early as possible," he ordered Duffy assigned to the duty.[10]

School Comes Ashore

Not long before John Rodgers discovered John Duffy, thereby providing *Congress*'s midshipmen with instruction they would otherwise have been compelled to forgo or delay, Secretary of the Navy Robert Smith had decided to abandon the pursuit of John Adams's will-o'-the-wisp, a school in every ship, and move toward the more attainable goal of providing quality instruction at a centralized location.

The person Smith hit upon to provide this centralized education was Chaplain Robert Thompson. In 1802, shortly after Thompson returned to the United States from sea duty in the frigates *President* and *Boston*, Robert Smith instructed him to occupy appropriate quarters at the Washington navy yard, and to be available there to teach navigation and the other branches of mathematics. "He is a very able mathematician," commented Ralph Izard, who was also stationed in Washington, "and I intend to attend him as soon as he is settled." As Midshipman Izard's remark implies, instruction under Chaplain Thompson was voluntary, available to those midshipmen who elected to take advantage of the opportunity; but Robert Smith used all of his formidable powers of persuasion to convince his young novices to elect that option. In the summer of 1803, as Commodore Edward Preble's squadron was getting under way for the Mediterranean, Smith exhorted eleven midshipmen for whom he had been unable to find posts in the departing ships to spend the time till they could be ordered on active duty "in the pursuit of professional knowledge. . . . We have at this place an excellent mathematician retained in the pay of the department for the purpose of assisting gentlemen of the navy in the study of navigation and of all other subjects connected with it. Should you choose to come here for the benefit of his instructions, you can be placed on board of one of the ships in ordinary and you will be allowed your half-pay." The last sentence is worth noting. It explains why education under Chaplain Thompson had to be optional. Robert Smith did not judge himself authorized to offer active-duty pay and rations to the midshipmen under instruction, which markedly diminished the incentive for the less highly motivated young men to attend.

In every way except full pay Smith tried to emphasize the importance he attached to this little academy. He directed Thompson to make weekly reports of students' progress to John Cassin, commandant of the yard, which reports Cassin was to relay to Smith; he occasionally called on Thompson for personal reports on "the names of the midshipmen who are at this time receiving instruction from you at this place, the time when they severally commenced their studies under you, the days they have each attended, and your opinion of the progress they have respectively made."

Thompson continued to instruct midshipmen at the navy yard until the spring of 1804, when Commodore Samuel Barron's squadron was ordered to the Mediterranean to augment that of Edward Preble. Because almost the entire corps of the navy's midshipmen would now be on active duty in the Mediterranean, Chaplain Thompson was once more packed off on shipboard in *President*, the frigate flying Barron's pennant. Although there is little record of this phase of Thompson's career, his duties must have been almost entirely instructional, for the commodore had a second chaplain, Robert Denison, who performed the secretarial duties. Following Thompson's return to the United States in September 1805 there was a hiatus in his teaching duties that continued until mid-1806. In the interval the administration sought to interest Congress in giving the navy's centralized educational enterprise a stronger legal (and status) base by formally establishing a naval school at Washington and providing

Thompson the title of *naval mathematician* (instead of *chaplain*). Little is known about this proposal. During the first session of the Ninth Congress Robert Smith apparently attempted to persuade one of his legislative allies to introduce a bill to achieve the desired objective, but the measure sank without a trace, largely because the legislators thought it was intended to create a new office rather than merely to change the title of a man already in place.[11] In typical fashion, Robert Smith ordered Thompson, 23 July 1806, to perform the duties anyway, attaching him to the Washington navy yard "for the purpose of attending to the education of such officers of the navy as may, from time to time, apply to you for instruction in mathematics or in navigation."

Though Thompson's desire to have a formal naval academy, established in Washington with himself as its head, was frustrated, after July 1806 he was continuously involved in providing instruction to midshipmen. Occasionally Robert Smith underlined his support of Thompson by having the students examined in his presence. When *Chesapeake* sailed from Washington on her ill-fated voyage to meet *Leopard,* Thompson went as far as Hampton Roads in her so that he might continue his teaching up till the latest possible moment. After the *Chesapeake-Leopard* incident the navy was concentrated in home waters; in March 1808 Robert Smith initiated the practice of sending Chaplain Thompson to provide on-site instruction for the two largest concentrations of midshipmen, those attached to the squadrons at New York and at Norfolk. John Rodgers, commanding at New York, judged the experiment less than wholly successful: "Owing in some measure to the necessary attentions to other professional duties by some and a want of inclination in others, but few of [the midshipmen] have acquired a competent knowledge of lunar observations, finding the latitude by double altitudes, etc." Rodgers may have been hypercritical. The enterprise was sufficiently successful to justify Smith's successor, Paul Hamilton, in dispatching Thompson to make the circuit again in 1810.

Throughout his naval career Thompson saw his mission as closely focused and practical: to teach the mathematics necessary to understanding the theory on which navigation was based and navigation itself. "My experience as a public teacher of navigation in the U.S. Navy for upwards of seven years, under some of its most distinguished commanders, has enabled me to form some idea of the time sufficient for any young gentleman of common abilities to acquire a sufficient knowledge of navigation to carry a ship to any known part of the globe, which I think they may do in three months, providing they are acquainted with arithmetic. . . . I am fully of opinion that the young gentleman who cannot acquire a competent knowledge of navigation in that time is unworthy of a midshipman's warrant in the U.S. Navy."

Thompson was later to extend the optimum time desirable to acquire a good knowledge of navigation to four months, but the essential point is that his school was an academy similar to other early-nineteenth-century academies. These were characterized by a wide span of ages and abilities among the students; sporadic, short, and intense periods of attendance—often punctuated with extended interludes of work at a job—and with students arriving to begin the courses and progressing through their studies serially, rather than as a class. Of necessity such a pattern must have entailed each student, or perhaps two or three midshipmen who arrived together, working through the course of study at his own pace, with instruction in the form of a one-to-one relationship with the teacher rather than a class all attending the same lecture. What made this practical is that there was never a large number of midshipmen under Thompson's instruction at any one time. Although the lack of attendance records prevents an absolutely accurate statement of numbers, it was probably rare for Thompson to be instructing fifteen or more pupils simultaneously; for most of these years it may have been closer to ten.

As a human being Robert Thompson remains obscure and one-dimensional. Nothing has been discovered about his life or background before his appointment, in July 1800, as chaplain in Thomas Truxtun's *President*, a post for which Truxtun had recruited him largely on the basis of a strong recommendation from Colonel William Ward Burrows, the commandant of the marine corps. The only clue to Thompson's personality is that he and his messmates quarreled irresolvably during his Quasi-War duty in *President*, one of them labeling the chaplain "a sycophant and a tattler," presumably with Captain Truxtun as the recipient of these services. Even the place, the cause, and the precise date of Thompson's death, let alone his age at the time of death, are a mystery. All that is certain is that he was alive, apparently well, and teaching on board *United States* near Hampton, Virginia, on 19 September 1810; a little more than a month later Secretary Hamilton was writing Commodore Rodgers, "Mr. Thompson, late chaplain in the navy, being dead. . . ." For slightly more than ten years Robert Thompson had instructed midshipmen and lieutenants in the basics of mathematics, astronomy, and navigation. If the officers of the War of 1812 were able to—and did—"carry a ship to any known part of the globe," most likely it was Robert Thompson who had taught them how to do it.[12]

A New Schoolmaster

Paul Hamilton's search for someone qualified and willing to fill Thompson's shoes proved to be a protracted one. Not until February 1811 did the secretary learn that Andrew Hunter, former professor of mathematics and astronomy at the College of New Jersey, was interested in the job. Because of enrollment and financial problems at Princeton, Hunter's professorship had been discontinued in 1808; he was now superintending Allison Academy in Bordentown, New Jersey. A man of approximately sixty years of age, Hunter had graduated from the College of New Jersey in the class of 1772, one year after President James Madison; he had served as an army chaplain through almost the whole of the Revolutionary War, during the course of which he was ordained a Presbyterian minister. Following the war, Hunter filled two pulpits and operated two academies in New Jersey, giving him stronger credentials for both of a chaplain's officially defined duties than most of those who held the warrant in the pre-1815 navy. In the late 1790s Hunter resigned his pulpits and gave up teaching to retire to a seven-year sabbatical as a gentleman farmer near Trenton. From this retreat he was gradually drawn by increasing involvement with the business of the College of New Jersey, where he had been a trustee since 1788, an involvement that culminated in his appointment to the chair of mathematics and astronomy in 1804.[13]

Normal chaplain's pay and rations ($624 per year) were not sufficiently attractive to lure a man of Hunter's stature from his post in New Jersey, but the persistent Hamilton offered him the same incentives earlier granted Robert Thompson. The secretary would use his administrative discretion to increase the principal naval instructor's pay and rations to $1,085 per year, with the assurance that any travel expenses he incurred, if ordered from ship to ship, would be paid. Hamilton further sweetened the deal by providing quarters for Hunter and his family in Washington to the tune of $250 per year. When Andrew Hunter learned Hamilton's terms he discussed the job and the compensation with friends. Some urged him to accept; others remonstrated against a late-life career change: "Many gentlemen told me that I should have rugged employment in instructing young gentlemen who wore a sword and that perhaps would not be subject to such discipline as would be necessary. I had little apprehension or fear on that subject, having for a number of years been acquainted with military men as well as with the government of university students for a considerable length of time." With that Hunter accepted the offer and reported for duty in the national capital on 20 April 1811.

The scope of the educational program that Hunter thought appropriate for his naval academy was substantially greater than that pursued under Thompson, though the core course remained mathematics, astronomy, and their practical application. When asked by Hamilton, shortly after his arrival at Washington, for his views "on the course of instruction most useful and proper for the midshipmen or junior officers of the navy of the United States," Hunter responded:

> Those branches of science . . . which qualify and enable midshipmen or naval officers for the honorable and useful discharge of their professional duties should obtain their principal attention. And these appear to me generally to be a correct knowledge of arithmetic, geometry, trigonometry, logarithms, astronomy, navigation, geography, and the use of the globes. . . . There are other branches of science which I conceive to be of vast importance to their reputation individually as gentlemen and collectively as a corps. Among these I would class a scientific acquaintance with our own language, both in speaking and writing. For amongst all the upper grades of society, scholars as well as others, a man's proper or improper use of the vernacular tongue is a good criterion of his genteel or vulgar education, and his reception into improved company will correspond with his style; and perhaps his useful influence in behalf of the great nation to which he belongs will be lost for want of this accomplishment. To this I would add a short course of history and chronology, together with some parts of natural philosophy, particularly mechanics, hydraulics, and some selections of chemistry and electricity. The time which might be deemed necessary for relaxation from ardent studies might be employed in more extended historical reading and biographical research.

How far this ambitious plan of study was carried out under Hunter's direction is uncertain. When the first group of midshipmen were ordered to Hunter's academy, Hamilton told the chaplain that they were to be "instructed in the theory of navigation. This is the principal object of ordering these young gentlemen to join you, but it will be discretionary with you to instruct them in any other useful branch of education." Because Hunter had himself proposed the enlarged course of study, one might presume that he seized on this discretionary authority. This does not necessarily follow. First and last, upwards of one hundred midshipmen passed through Hunter's academy. The median length of attendance was around sixty to sixty-five days, with some two-thirds of the midshipmen remaining at Hunter's academy between three and eighteen weeks.[14] Intensive though the course was, one doubts that a residency of that length allowed time for more than a basic course in mathematics and its practical application, with *possibly* some remedial instruction in spoken and written rhetoric. Reinforcing this supposition is Robert Thompson's assertion that it required 84 to 112 days for students to work their way through his narrowly defined course of theoretical and applied mathematics. Moreover, the certificates that Hunter gave his pupils referred only to their having completed the "usual course of theoretical navigation." Students who stayed five weeks or less under Hunter's instruction (approximately four out of every ten who attended the academy) were primarily those who had strong backgrounds in mathematics and who possessed some knowledge of navigation. For them, study with Hunter was a brief period of testing competencies and strengthening existing skills before receiving their first assignments or returning to active duty. Almost all of Hunter's pupils were too young to attain responsible posts as lieutenants or acting lieutenants during the War of 1812; consequently, his influence on the pre-1815 officer corps was much slighter than that of the now-faceless Robert Thompson. Only in the postwar years, as the navy moved into new areas of responsibility, did Andrew Hunter's pupils come into their own.

Perhaps the best snapshots of Chaplain Hunter's naval school and of some of the day-to-day problems the instructor encountered are afforded by the reports on individual pupils that Hunter sent to the secretary of the navy.[15] Reports survive for only eighteen of the more than one hundred young men who passed through Hunter's naval academy; their representativeness as regards the full range of pupils demands some skepticism. Of the eighteen, thirteen evaluations were favorable, among which that of Midshipman Albert G. Wall, who was promoted to lieutenant in 1818 and died in service in 1825, may be taken as typical: "Midshipman Wall has gone through the usual course of theoretical navigation greatly to my satisfaction and wishes now to be attached to the Constellation. He will, however, with your approbation, continue with me till she be ready for sea. He is a modest, gentlemanly young man and is very desirous to improve his mind."

All five of Andrew Hunter's unfavorable evaluations involved students who refused to stick to their studies. "Midshipman [Robert] Hamersley reported himself to me some ten or fifteen days ago and attended one or two days in my office," Hunter reported in June 1812. "I have seen him almost every day since swaggering about in his uniform and have frequently spoken to him respecting attending his duty. He has stated to me that he had your permission to be absent, but had no written permission. He is this day, I am told, gone to Alexandria in company with Midshipman [Edward C.] Carter, who I presume has gone without permission. I am afraid these young men are not in the road to honor." Hunter's was a perceptive eye when it came to future merit. Among the five midshipmen who received unfavorable evaluations, four were soon dismissed or otherwise eased out of the corps. Unique among the five who received bad reports was Midshipman French Forrest. He and a companion in idleness (who was summarily dismissed in 1813) were described by Hunter thus: "Remarkably ignorant and inattentive; and, taking the amount of these qualities into view, I think they can promise very little to their country or their friends." In spite of such unpromising omens Forrest made it all the way to captain in the U.S. Navy before resigning to fight for the Confederacy; but along young Forrest's road to professional success there yet lay some formidable and chastening disciplinary difficulties.

Within a few months after William Jones came into office the new secretary announced that there was no authority in law for the additional salary, over and above a chaplain's base pay, that Hunter received as "mathematician" at the Washington navy yard. He shut down Hunter's academy and confined him to traditional chaplain's duties at the yard. An undercurrent of tension in the Jones-Hunter relationship suggests that the secretary may not have held the chaplain in high esteem. Having been Hamilton's appointee and one of his special favorites certainly did not enhance Hunter's standing with the new secretary, especially when Jones felt he had a mandate to clean house of Hamilton's men. The mutual lack of esteem may even have had its roots in prenaval contacts between the two. All that aside, the truth was that, with the navy fighting its biggest war to date, assigning officers to the naval school was an activity a corps of less than a thousand officers could no longer afford. Learning would have to take place on the job. This was apparent even before Hamilton left office. When, on 24 November 1812, the secretary asked Hunter for the names of some midshipmen who had completed their studies and could be ordered to active duty, he learned that the pool had just about dried up. "There are no midshipmen under my care at present who are fit for the Charleston station or, indeed, any other station at sea," Hunter replied. "They are almost all children and have made very little progress in their studies. Their want of learning and their inefficacy on board of a ship will, in my opinion, be sufficient reasons for their continuing at their present moorings."[16]

The Schoolhouse Moves North

William Jones's disbanding of Andrew Hunter's academy for midshipmen early in 1813 marked the end of the Navy Office's pre-1815 attempt to provide centralized education for its novices. It was not the end of classroom instruction for officers. In the winter of 1814–15 Commodore Isaac Chauncey, acting on his own initiative, ordered Chaplain Cheever Felch to open a "mathematical school" at Sackets Harbor, New York, for the benefit of the icebound officers of the Lake Ontario squadron. Ninety-five midshipmen and lieutenants attended the school (usually about sixty at any one time), where they were busily engaged in the study of mathematics, physics, astronomy, geography, and navigation under Felch's personal direction, while seventy-one of the squadron's boys, some of whom may really have been acting midshipmen, pursued more elementary studies under one or more of Felch's unnamed assistants. Chaplain Felch, a rather questionable character, the true dimensions of whose personality came into clear relief only in the years after the War of 1812, was inclined to complain: "My health is very poor, but I am confined here by the naval academy. . . . The charge is too much for me and there is nothing to enliven it; for, although I had every promise if I would undertake it, yet I fear nothing will be done. It is rather a hard case that I should have so much imposed on me while Mr. Sands [another chaplain], on board the Mohawk, derives the same pay and does not the least thing." Felch must have possessed skills as a teacher, however much a complainer he may have been, and his students must have been strongly motivated, for Chauncey could soon point with pride to the fact that they were making "great progress" in their professional subjects.[17] Peace and the disbanding of the Lake Ontario squadron shut down Chaplain Felch's school in the spring of 1815.

Chauncey and Felch's educational effort of 1814–15 was no isolated event, but rather a harbinger of renewed hankering among the navy's leadership and certain members of Congress for a more formal and elaborate naval academy, one that would address the aims of Andrew Hunter's ambitious, but largely unfulfilled, program to enhance the corps' professional respectability.[18] Not only was the war winding down, thus permitting the leisure for contemplating long-term professional issues, the corps was emerging from the War of 1812 with a sense of heightened reputation, status, and permanence that generated a keen desire to make itself a better, stronger institution. The story of this attempt to establish a superior professional academy is, however, part of the history of the post–War of 1812 navy. With William Jones's symbolic killing of Andrew Hunter and Cheever Felch's short encore the curtain falls on the navy's pre-1815 efforts at classroom instruction for midshipmen.

19. Learning to Be a Navy

ARLIER, NAVAL EDUCATION was called the broad process by which an entire spectrum of professional culture and values was transmitted from one generation of officers to another. To this point that process has been scrutinized in terms of how individual young men learned to be naval officers. The answers, if not always as complete as might be wished, were there to be found in the records. An education question remains that has not been asked. Where and how did the U.S. Navy learn to be a navy? The *where* part of the question is readily answered. The new nation did not have to invent what a navy did and how one functioned. The federal navy of 1794–1815 was created in a world full of mature sea forces and established naval traditions. The newborn organization could discover how to be a navy from one or more of those already in existence.

Which direction to turn for a model? The question was never even asked; the choice was predetermined. The navy of Great Britain was part and parcel of the American colonial heritage. British and American seamen shared a common language and a common cultural tradition. Independence could neither repeal nor diminish so powerful an inheritance. Culturally determined though it was, the selection of a model was also a conscious choice. "We must imitate [the British] in things which tend to the good of the service," Benjamin Stoddert wrote when the U.S. Navy had been cruising the seas for a little more than a year. Visceral acceptance of Britain's navy as the standard was reaffirmed a decade later when Lieutenant Arthur Sinclair pointed to what he and all of his peers had so deeply internalized that they rarely needed to articulate it: "The customs, too, of [the] British sea service, in cases not embraced by our laws, has usually been the criterion by which we have been guided."[1]

If *where* the U.S. Navy turned when it sought a model has long been known, the equally important question of *how* the new organization acquired and internalized British naval culture is much more difficult to answer. In spite of the hundreds of thousands of pages of records created by the pre-1815 navy, these records fail to capture this transfer of culture. It is a process that slips between the solid planks of documented history. Fragments and clues are caught, but much of the answer must be speculative and inferential.

The historian is struck by the speed with which the transfer was accomplished, by the early date at which the fledgling navy of the Quasi-War and the Tripolitan War acquired the professional polish and established methods characteristic of a far more mature organization. Five ways may be surmised in which the British naval tradition could have been acquired by the pre-1815 U.S. Navy: (1) internalization by the Continental navy of the Revolution, from which the tradition passed to the 1794 federal navy; (2) British naval officers imported to train the new American force; (3) previous experience in the British service by some of those serving in the new U.S. Navy; (4) study of British professional naval writing; and (5) observation of, and interaction with, ships and officers of the British navy. It is not a question of choosing one and excluding the other four. All five means could have made some contribution.

True it certainly is that the Continental navy and the state navies of the Revolution emulated the methods and the traditions of the British parent. But the navies of the Revolution occupied only a small corner in the consciousness of the federal navy of 1794–1815—and even less in its emotional heritage. For the navy of John Rodgers, Isaac Hull, and William Bainbridge, the naval side of the American Revolution was a past they were eager to forget. There had been little to inspire in the Continental naval experience. Most of the ships of its ambitious building program had never gotten to sea; those few that did were almost all, sooner or later, captured by the British. At no time did its vessels conduct concerted operations as a fleet or squadron. John Paul Jones, whose subsequent cult was the product of the late-nineteenth-century navy's search for an enhanced identity, was basically a British carpetbagger who spent only a short segment of his life in the United States and who fought his most famous battle with a ragtag collection of predominantly European mariners and entirely European ships. Commodore John Barry's preeminence in the federal navy of 1794 owed everything to the fact that of all the Continental captains, only he and Joshua Barney emerged from the Revolutionary War with their vessels and reputations intact. The prevailing attitude of the leaders of the federal navy toward the Continental naval experience was concisely summarized by Boston navy agent Stephen Higginson in June 1798: "Our navy in the Revolutionary War was a bad school to educate good officers in."[2] Correct Higginson appears to have been. Barry aside, of the four senior officers with significant Revolutionary War experience who had the greatest shaping influence on the new federal navy, two had been privateersmen (Thomas Truxtun and Alexander Murray), one an officer in the Massachusetts state navy (Edward Preble), and one an army officer (Silas Talbot).

Another way a young nation might go about developing a military force would be to import experienced officers from abroad and award them commissions (usually at more exalted rank than they had held at home) in its army or navy. The Russian navy of the late eighteenth century had done exactly that, recruiting numbers of British naval officers—as well as some from other nations, including the Continental navy's own John Paul Jones—to provide a cadre of experience around which its native corps could grow. A similar process has been followed by countless developing nations over the past two centuries. Such a solution was not alien to the American experience, for the Continental army of the Revolutionary War had employed this expedient, albeit with mixed results. If the U.S. Navy of 1794–1815 had elected to follow this well-traveled path, that would have been a principal route by which British naval philosophy

Thomas Truxtun's caustic (and all too memorable) evaluation of Captain Stephen Decatur, Sr., as fit for nothing higher in rank than boatswain or sailing master was excessively harsh. A notable privateersman during the Revolutionary War, then a successful master in the merchant service, the elder Decatur (here portrayed by C.B.J. Fevret de Saint-Mémin) secured his Quasi-War reputation by scoring the new federal navy's first capture of a French prize. Decatur could surely have parlayed that victorious moment into a lifetime naval career. Unfortunately, by asking to be excused from sea duty in the first campaign of the Tripolitan War he insured his inclusion on the list of captains with whose services Secretary Robert Smith and President Thomas Jefferson concluded the leaner officer corps of 1801 could afford to dispense. Decatur's decision to sidestep the Tripolitan War assignment is probably evidence that, as he approached fifty, the captain no longer felt the all-consuming passion for naval life and combat that motivated his more famous son and namesake. Private collection.

and practice were introduced into, and assimilated by, the American officer corps. The historical reality is quite otherwise. Both philosophically and practically the founders of the U.S. Navy rejected the appointment of experienced officers from abroad. "To introduce foreigners into our navy would appear to me a very dangerous policy," Thomas Truxtun had warned Secretary of War James McHenry when the first officer appointments were being considered in 1797.[3] Clearly he was not alone in his opinion. The best explanation for this rejection is that the leaders who collectively established the U.S. Navy in the 1790s were motivated both by pride in their new national identity and by a well-grounded confidence that they could build an able and a professional navy from native materials.

Those few men with experience as officers in the British navy who later joined the U.S. force were generally of two types. Some had been officers, but at a very low rank. Such a person was Thomas N. Gautier, who served as a midshipman in the British navy during the Revolutionary War, then emigrated to North Carolina after the war's end. During the Quasi-War with France he was a lieutenant in the frigate *Congress* for less than two years. Discharged in the reduction of naval force in 1801, Gautier was recalled to service in 1807 as a sailing master and given a coastal command in North Carolina for the remaining seven years of his naval career.[4] During his service in *Congress* Gautier may well have familiarized his shipmates with British naval traditions and British ways of doing things—there exists no evidence one way or the other—but he was scarcely a primary conduit for the transfer of culture. After 1801 his naval role was too marginal to be in any way influential.

The other type comprises the handful of former British officers serving in the pre-1815 navy who were genuine bad actors, men seeking to escape unsavory pasts. Such a person was John Pittman Lovell, the precise circumstances of whose entrance into the U.S. Navy are now lost. What is known is that he joined the frigate *New York*, seemingly as acting sailing master, in August 1802. There was always something a little mysterious in Lovell's story of his life and of how he came to the United States, but he was obviously a correct and an able officer, a man of some experience in the British navy. In *New York* he earned the good opinion of John Rodgers, who persuaded Robert Smith to issue Lovell (20 December 1803) a warrant as a sailing master. Thereafter Lovell held, and performed well in, a variety of responsible assignments: at the Washington navy yard, in *Adams* and *Hornet*, as commander of Gunboat No. 1. Then, in the spring of 1806, when John Rodgers was commodore of the Mediterranean squadron, he had to suffer acute embarrassment as he attempted to explain to Robert Smith the news he had just learned from a British captain, a man whose story was not to be doubted. Lovell, it seems, had been the first lieutenant of a British warship in the West Indies. One day, as the ship was about to sail, the captain sent Lovell ashore to pick up the crew's share of prize money for distribution. Lovell collected the money all right; then he put the cash and himself on board an American merchant vessel and made off to the United States before anyone could figure out what had happened. By 1806 the British authorities had discovered that Lovell was serving as an officer in the U.S. Navy and intended to demand his extradition to British authority when his precise whereabouts were determined. Robert Smith was eager to cooperate in such proceedings—"It is mortifying to me that such a man should have insinuated himself into our navy"—but Lovell had died in March, shortly before his true identity was revealed. He was now beyond the reach of earthly justice at least.[5]

Useful as he may have been as an experienced officer, it is doubtful that John Pittman Lovell brought with him any British lore that the U.S. Navy had not long since made its own. By 1802–1803 it was too professional and too polished to need that kind of instruction. A more likely conduit for the transfer of British naval culture is glimpsed by one single tantalizing reference. In a letter describing the frigate *Constitution*'s first cruise in 1798 newly fledged midshipman John Roche, Jr., wrote his father, "Our petty officers are very good men. Most of them, such as quartermasters, master's mates, gunner's [mates], master-at-arms, etc., are either English or Irish who have sustained the same berths on board British men-of-war."[6] Was this an isolated instance? Or was it repeated in U.S. Navy ship after U.S. Navy ship during the Quasi-War? The answer is unknown, but if the latter was the case, here was a large sluice down which British practice would have flowed to nourish the infant

American force. The only question is whether those higher on the social scale (commissioned officers) would have been willing to learn from their inferiors (petty officers). Did the openness and flexibility necessary for a superior to become the pupil of his subordinate exist in the stratified U.S. Navy of 1794–1815? No definite answer can be given.

This possible route for the transfer of British naval culture shades off into another potential source: American mariners who had been impressed into the British navy. It can be estimated with reasonable confidence that one out of ten or one out of fifteen U.S. naval officers had been impressed into the British service for longer or shorter periods of time. Some British naval culture must have crossed over into the U.S. Navy by this route, even though no documentary evidence exists to establish such a transfer. One note of caution: Almost all those known to have experienced impressment were either junior officers or sailing masters during the pre-1815 years.[7] The navy's leaders had begun their service careers before impressment became a truly serious problem; few of them had experienced British naval culture firsthand, but unwillingly. Their knowledge of British practice must have come by other means.

Among those means were reading and solitary or group study. An ethos of continuing professional self-education was strong in the pre-1815 navy. "Captain Perry, as you well know, is a good officer but, I do not believe, has ever paid so much attention to naval science as to qualify him for such a situation." With those words John Rodgers dismissed the pretensions of the victor of Lake Erie to serve on the newly created Board of Navy Commissioners. Five days after the grounding and capture of *Philadelphia*, when her company had scarcely gotten their bearings in their prison life, William Bainbridge instructed his first lieutenant, David Porter,

> The late unfortunate event prevents the midshipmen from receiving that information in their profession which they would otherwise have done; and, that the distressing time spent here may not be entirely loss to them, you will inform them that it is my request that immediately after breakfast they repair to their room to study navigation and read such books as we are in possession of that will improve their minds.

From a contingent of officers stationed at Portland, Maine, in the fall of 1808, Lieutenant Charles Morris reported to his uncle at Boston, "We still continue perfectly idle so far as it relates to public service, having received no orders to employ the [gun]boats in any manner. We employ most of our time in reading and in endeavoring to acquire useful general and professional knowledge."[8]

American naval officers owned, borrowed, read, and internalized the professional British naval literature.[9] Without entering on a tedious litany of titles, the historian can note a few pieces of evidence. London's monthly *Naval Chronicle*, which began publication in 1799 and which recorded the victories and the reverses of British sea power, commemorated the lives of that navy's leaders, and disseminated professional papers, circulated briskly among U.S. naval officers as well. When Lieutenant Cyrus Talbot of the brig *Richmond* lost a rudder in a gale in 1799 he turned to his copy of David Steel's *A System of Naval Tactics, Combining the Established Theory with General Practice, and Particularly with the Present Practice of the British Navy* to discover a successful method for coping with his problem under difficult conditions of wind and sea.[10] Pursers, captain's clerks, and even commanding officers found an authoritative and trustworthy guide to the voluminous intricacies of naval paperwork in the successive editions of Robert Liddel's *The Seaman's New Vade Mecum: Containing a Practical Essay on Naval Book-keeping, with the Method of Keeping the Captain's Books and Complete Instructions in the Duty of a Captain's Clerk.*[11] Whatever the situation, be it a barrel of rotten beef or a shipwreck, Liddel offered a sample form to be copied and filled in. In matters of naval justice John McArthur's *Principles and Practice of Naval and Military Courts Martial* was a familiar and oft-cited guide.[12] The Navy Department subsidized an 1805 American edition of J.J. Moore's *British Mariner's Vocabulary* by purchasing two hundred copies for distribution to newly appointed midshipmen. The grateful publisher dedicated *The Mariner's Dictionary*; *or, American Seaman's Vocabulary of Technical Terms and Sea Phrases Used in the Construction, Equipment, Management, and Military Operations of Ships and Vessels of All Descriptions*—as the "improved from an English work" re-publication was titled—to the angel who had made it possible: Secretary of the Navy Robert Smith.[13]

Important as books and periodicals were in transmitting British naval culture and helping American officers to establish a professional identity, they were not the most potent of all sources for learning. After all other factors have been tallied, personal observation—watching, asking questions, making mental or paper notes—stands out as the best and the most influential teacher. From the time the first U.S. ships of war put to sea in 1798 until the *Chesapeake* affair of 1807 triggered serious hostility between the two forces, the British and U.S. navies had cruised the same seas: the Caribbean, 1798–1801, in an informal alliance against the French; the Mediterranean, 1801–1807, in reasonably congenial cooperation. For a decade the officers of the U.S. Navy interacted, professionally and socially, with their peers from the British service. Given such continuous contact it would have been impossible for the younger American force to avoid absorbing the British naval mentality unconsciously. Add to which there was a great deal of conscious trying to learn, whether it was a Master Commandant John Smith reporting from England that "we have found the facility much greater in visiting [the British] dockyards than I could have imagined; in satisfying us they have been very attentive" or an Edward Preble acquiring from British officers Vice-Admiral Sir Roger Curtis's standing regulations for the squadron under his command at the Cape of Good Hope, the official British *Instructions for Navy Surgeons*, and Sir Home Popham's newly devised system of telegraphic signals.[14] Is it to be doubted that in these almost daily contacts, the careful observation, the admiring emulation—and in the avid study of the older navy's professional literature—one touches the fundamental means by which British naval culture became American naval culture?

PART FIVE
Confided to Their Care

20. Leaders

ISTORY CAN BE UNFAIR. Take two examples from 1814, the last year of the War of 1812. When Charles Stewart put to sea in the frigate *Constitution*, among the navy's biggest ships, only one man in fourteen among the ship's company was an officer. Descend the scale of ship size, and the proportion of officers rose. In Johnston Blakeley's command, the 22-gun sloop of war *Wasp*, one man in seven held that status.[1] Whatever the ship, wherever she was bound, her officers were always the minority. All the rest of the human beings whose names stood on her muster roll were enlisted men. They were the people who did the ship's hard, dirty, and dangerous work. They stowed the cargo. They cleaned the head. They went out on the yards in the foulest of weather. They fought the great guns in battle.

If the navy's enlisted men have been honored by novelists, too often they have been served short rations by historians. Nor will that neglect be mended in the pages that follow. Here the portrait of the enlisted man must be one-sided and distorted. It is not the picture he would have painted of himself; neither is it the full and true record that could be created by the historian whose eye is focused on the enlisted man. This book's concern is with the officer as leader and commander. It asks, How did the pre-1815 navy define the officer's leadership role? Was the officer's authority maintained chiefly by brutality, force, and fear? If yes, why was such a state of affairs tolerated in a society simmering with democratic and egalitarian ideals? Might not the real basis of authority have been a tradition of more positive leadership? One may start by asking, In what light did the officer of the pre-1815 navy see that service's enlisted man?*

---

* It will be useful to be aware of certain demographic facts regarding before-the-mast U.S. mariners in the pre-1815 years. Approximately 80 percent of all seafarers, whether merchant sailors or naval enlisted men, were sixteen through twenty-nine years of age; 15 percent were thirty or older, and less than 5 percent had not yet reached their sixteenth birthday. The single most common age bracket was 22/23. Seafaring was not a lifelong occupation. Three-quarters of all mariners served less than ten years at sea before falling victim to the seafarer's sightly higher mortality rates or beginning second careers on land. Blacks (free and slave) constituted between 15 and 20 percent of the navy's enlisted men and served in crews that were integrated, if far from free of racial prejudice and tension. Approximately half of the enlisted men serving in U.S. Navy ships were foreign nationals; more than half of them (perhaps 56 percent) were foreign born; and three-quarters of these "foreigners" were natives of the British Isles.[2]

A Drunken Sailor Is Worse Than the Devil

For his knowledge of the sea, for his skills as a mariner, for his bravery in battle, and for his physical endurance the officer had the highest respect for the experienced, capable enlisted man. There were on Lake Ontario during the War of 1812, wrote one historian who entered the navy as a midshipman just before the end of that conflict, "a large proportion of as good seamen as ever trod a ship's deck; the genuine long queues abounded there. Commodore [Isaac] Chauncey, a thorough seaman himself, had a passion for the collection about him of all the most finished specimens of the true man-of-war's-men that could be found."[3] The experienced and well-regarded commander, the man with whom a seaman had himself sailed or who was known to him through the scuttlebutt of fellow tars, could usually count on the loyalty of his enlisted men. "This place is now drained of seamen," lamented David Porter from Norfolk in the summer of 1811, "and there are three recruiting parties employed in it for different vessels whose commanders have a great advantage over me in established reputations with seamen."[4] Moreover, the officer recognized that the enlisted man had good survival instincts, a cunning necessary to protect his interests. In the spring of 1809 *Wasp*'s commander, Master Commandant Thomas Robinson, saw that the enlistments of thirty of his best men were due to expire on 10 June. *Wasp* was, at the moment, anchored at Portland, Maine, and Robinson offered the thirty shore leave, and a month's pay to take advantage of it, if they would sign up for another two years. The men turned him down cold: "They made but one objection, which was that all the lieutenants were taken from the ship who had commanded. They were perfectly satisfied with the treatment they had received [from the old lieutenants], but they could not calculate on what might follow from strange officers, and that they would be better able to tell when their times were up and [they were] discharged; [then] they could freely act."[5]

Respect the enlisted man all he might for these qualities, the officer saw him not only as a person who occupied an inferior place in the social order, but equally as a childlike—or at least adolescentlike—individual in much of his behavior. Both perceptions were well demonstrated by an incident that took place in June 1810. Commodore John Rodgers returned to the frigate *Constitution* to find that Lieutenant Charles G. Ridgely had placed thirteen of the vessel's midshipmen, including several young men who were subsequently among the navy's distinguished commanders, under arrest. The midshipmen, fearful of becoming the objects of Rodgers's notorious wrath, sought to explain how this situation had come about:

> For our hammocks, like our dress, we have considered ourselves individually responsible and that in both there was a wide line of distinction to be drawn between us and the people [i.e., the enlisted men]. Unfortunately for us, many of the hammocks were dirty in the extreme and such as a gentleman never should have slept in, nor even alongside of, without the greatest reluctance. On this account, when the people were called to scrub hammocks the midshipmen were likewise turned out. With this order we generally complied, looking on it as a punishment justly brought upon us by our negligence. . . . The next day we understood an order was issued to stow them with the people's. This step was to us entirely new. . . . We felt unwilling to suffer a punishment which . . . exposed us to vermin and disease without a respectful attempt to avert it.

Whereupon the young gentlemen had protested the order to Lieutenant Ridgely. The latter, not disposed to argue, promptly clapped the thirteen under arrest "in a manner that strongly indicated that . . . [Lieutenant Ridgely] felt himself at liberty to bestow on us treatment little better than that due to the people or different from that of children."[6] John Rodgers's eventual resolution of this particular controversy need not be pursued here. What is important is that these apprentice officers clearly recognized two social realities: that a broad and clearly delineated social gulf ("a wide line of distinction") separated officers and enlisted men, two very different kinds of persons; and that the types of punishments officers awarded the enlisted ranks were analogous to those parents enforced upon children.

In the officer's eyes the enlisted man was a creature more often motivated by emotion than by reason. No harm could come from having three ships recruiting in one port at one time, William Bainbridge explained to Secretary of the Navy William Jones, "as sailors are whimsical and often enter for one ship when they will not for another."[7] As creatures of emotion, there were many ways in which they could not be trusted. The treatment of new recruits to insure that they would not desert before reporting to their ships clearly delineates the level of such distrust. Lieutenant John Downes, who had been recruiting at Boston for the frigate *Essex*, sent Midshipman Robert M. Rose off to Norfolk in the schooner *Ann Gardner* with twenty-three new men. If *Essex* is at sea when the *Ann Gardner* arrives at Norfolk, Rose is to put his recruits temporarily on board of any U.S. naval vessel that may be in port, Downes tells him. Be there no ship in which the recruits can be placed, Rose will apply to the commanding officer of the navy yard, who will point out a secure place for them. "Should it be required for the better security of the seamen, you will request that a guard of marines from the navy yard may [be] placed over them." The marine guard was not being put in place to protect the recruits from external danger![8]

Not only was the sailor, sooner or later weary of his enlistment bargain, likely to slip over the side and try his luck in a merchant vessel or even a different U.S. Navy ship, there was also his proverbial fondness for alcohol. "When you arrive at Schenectady or Albany," Lieutenant George W. Rodgers told Sailing Master William Knight as the latter set off from Sackets Harbor with a detachment of men being transferred to *Macedonian* at New York, "be particularly careful that your men are not permitted to loiter about the town or enter into grogshops, for you know that a drunken sailor is worse than the Devil." Rodgers must have found it easier to preach than to practice; when he subsequently came to settle his own travel accounts, he explained that he had expended $35 or $40 for which he had neglected to take receipts "in the hurry and confusion incident to bringing on drunken sailors." Nor was the problem limited to over-the-road travel with the enlisted men. There was the difficulty presented by the navy's allowance of half a pint of distilled spirits per day per man in the form of grog. "It requires great attention to prevent their being continually in a state of intoxication from this great allowance of spirits," wrote Thomas Truxtun as he argued unsuccessfully for a reduction in the rum ration, "for they will, in addition to their allowance, find landsmen and boys who will privately barter their rum to them for butter, cheese, etc., or sell it."[9]

Closely related to the enlisted man's fondness for alcoholic excess was his proneness to disorder and petty violence of all kinds. Novice midshipman

*Easy to believe that when this handsome young midshipman obtained his first command
a few years after this portrait was painted by an unknown artist he was regarded by
subordinates as brave, able, and generally kind. But the miniature also hints at a darker
side to his conflicted personality, a suspicion confirmed by the memories of his contemporaries. Under the right circumstances he might fly into almost uncontrollable rage. A
man of powerful physique, he was then prone to satiate his anger in a direct and physical
manner. When one large enlisted man remonstrated against a grog-stopping punishment
in a tone of voice that was perceived as insolent, the irate lieutenant felled the far bigger
sailor with one well-aimed fist that caught its target squarely between the eyes. The passionate officer is George Washington Rodgers, the younger brother of Commodore John.*
Private collection.

Joseph E. Smith, placed in charge of Gunboat No. 6 at New York, appealed in
alarm to his squadron commodore, John Rodgers, when the boat's steward was
carried ashore to the hospital: "I have now no one that I can trust when my
duty calls me out of the vessel. If I leave her for ten minutes, when I return I
hear of some riotous disturbance. They have twice broken into the cabin and
stolen the vessel's liquor. Being young and inexperienced in the service, I am
at a loss how to remedy those difficulties, which occasion me much uneasiness."[10]
Surgeon's Mate Usher Parsons, traveling with a party of seamen through upstate
New York in the fall of 1812, recorded in his diary, "In the course of the night
our men swam across the Mohawk [River], which runs within a few rods of the
house where we put up, and returned with [an] abundance of fruit, poultry,
etc. Others in the night took from a neighbor's hog pen, contiguous to a barn
in which two persons watched, a large hog undiscovered." Two days later he
added, "The sailors continue to plunder."[11] Among a midshipman's travel
vouchers may be found his claim for reimbursement "for this sum paid Elias
Eckhart of Bedford County [Pennsylvania], for property destroyed by seamen
on their way from Philadelphia to Erie, per receipt herewith—$10."[12]

The heavy drinking, the petty theft, the minor vandalism, all of these
characterized the typical enlisted man in the officer's eye not as an essentially
evil person, but as a kind of overgrown adolescent, ready to lapse into all sorts
of misbehavior unless kept under strict discipline. Thomas Truxtun, an officer
with a sensitive appreciation of the enlisted mentality, divided a typical ship's
company into three behavior groups. The great majority of the men were well

disposed or at least neutral in their behavior. A substantial subset of that mass was always ready to participate in misbehavior and minor antisocial acts, given the proper leadership and the opportunity. Finally, there was a small element of more sinister hue: a core of troublemakers, if not hardened criminals, ill-disposed people who must constantly be controlled by fear and who must be prevented from infecting the whole ship's company, "a crew of abandoned miscreants, ripe for any mischief or villainy, [many of them] equally destitute of gratitude, shame, or justice and only deterred from the commission of any crimes by the terror of severe punishment. . . . The pernicious example of a few of the vilest in a ship of war is too often apt to poison the principles of the greatest number, especially if the reins of discipline are too much relaxed, so as to foster that idleness and dissipation which engender sloth, diseases, and an utter profligacy of manners."[13]

The Art of Governing Men

The single most potent factor in establishing and maintaining the authority of the officer was that, almost universally and instinctively, both officer and enlisted man accepted the rightness of the principle of deference. To repeat here the definition given earlier, deference was an ethos predicated on the notion that God (or Nature) had ordained a social and economic hierarchy in which some men were placed high and others low; that those who were placed higher had a right and a duty to command and to lead; that it was the duty of those placed in subordinate stations to obey their leaders and to be content in their lowly positions in life; and, finally, that the good of the whole social order depended on respecting this hierarchical social structure, for without that ordered ranking anarchy, destruction, and other unnameable evils would ensue.

Given such a philosophy, it was only natural that officers would see themselves in the role of parents and enlisted men as their children-dependents. But it would be wrong to perceive the deference ethos as only teaching the rightness of obedience by inferior to superior. Call it stewardship, call it paternalism, the deference philosophy equally emphasized a reciprocal duty: the person in authority had a heavy responsibility for those subject to him, a charge that was, in its naval setting, repeated so often and in so many ways that eventually it became instinctive. Each officer was to know every enlisted man by name, so that he could use that name whenever he had occasion to address him. Officers were expected to see that the men under their command were clean, were well fed, and had adequate clothing. They were equally responsible for the moral health of their subordinates: "Blasphemy, profaneness, gambling, and all species of obscenity and immorality are peremptorily forbid," William Bainbridge admonished in *President* in 1809, "and it is hoped that the officers of every denomination will, upon all occasions, discountenance and discourage such disorderly and despicable practices among the men." A daunting assignment indeed! But the obligation was reciprocal: for the able officer debasement and abuse should form no part of the art of leadership. "It is particularly recommended by the captain to the officers of every class to avoid swearing or using reproachful or degrading appellations to the men, it being contrary to every idea of true discipline and [the] character of an officer; besides, it must be discouraging to good men and cannot convey any information to those who are ignorant." Lieutenant William M. Crane summed up an entire philosophy of officership in one sentence when he instructed his midshipmen in *Argus*, "They will recollect that the crew are confided to their care and that no circumstance can warrant a breach of this important duty."[14]

Such passages in ships' standing orders aside, officers of the pre-1815 navy said little, in writing at least, about the practice of leadership. Almost all that they did write concerned leadership in its negative mode: the maintenance of discipline and authority. This absence of written record is perhaps understandable. "The art of governing men," as Isaac Chauncey called it, was just that: an art or skill learned by practice and counsel.[15] It was no more to be acquired by reading about it than was the skill needed to bring a ship to a safe anchorage in a winter storm. Leadership and discipline, though closely related, are not exactly the same thing. The maintenance of authority is but one component of the art of leadership. Without doubt the navy's experienced commanders gave plenty of good advice to their younger subordinates and themselves provided superior examples of the role and skills of a leader. Would that the historian could eavesdrop on some of those talks! What survives in the documents is mostly about discipline.

On one point all agreed: the foundation of discipline and authority over subordinates was the example set by the officer himself. An officer must be attentive to his duty, obedient to his superiors, correct in his conduct, and respectful to his peers. This standard of behavior internalized, he was then in a position to demand and receive "the most ready, unequivocal, and respectful compliance with his orders" from his subordinates.[16] The maintenance of authority was a continuous process; the officer could never afford to let things go slack. "Exercise your authority as commanding officer and never permit an impropriety in *officer* or man to pass unnoticed," Hugh G. Campbell counseled a young subordinate in a rare moment of self-revelation, "for discipline once lost is difficult to regain."[17]

Equally valuable were positive incentives to order and correct behavior. "The good conduct of the petty officers and seamen will receive every encouragement, and all indulgences the service admits of will be granted to those who are distinguished by their correctness," William M. Crane promulgated when he commanded the schooner *Madison* on Lake Ontario during the War of 1812. "All promotions will be made from those who are cleanly, obedient, and seamanlike in their deportment." On which subject John Rodgers made the added point that it was important for the officer to distinguish and reward such men, not only so that appropriate behavior would receive positive reinforcement, but also because thereby "the undeserving [are] to be made sensible of the vigilance of their officers and of the advantages resulting from good and respectful conduct."[18] Comparison with peers was a powerful motive force for discipline, whether it be within one ship's company or between ships. "When a number of vessels are together," said John Rodgers, "I have always found that discipline is easier preserved by the emulation which is excited between the officers and crews of the different vessels."[19] Active employment, preferably by cruising at sea, was an essential and equally positive ingredient in the maintenance of both morale and discipline: "It is much more trouble to command fifty seamen on board of a hulk [in harbor] than it is to command five hundred on board of a ship in active service," was William Bainbridge's to-the-point advice.[20]

So far little has been said about the role of punishment, and especially physical punishment, in the maintenance of discipline in the U.S. Navy. Where are irons and the lash in all this leadership and disciplinary theory? Listen to former surgeon's mate Usher Parsons describe his old Lake Erie comrade-in-arms, Lieutenant Daniel Turner:

> The prominent trait of his character as an officer was rigid discipline, obedience to superiors in rank, and strict exaction of it from his subordinates, a principle that he copied from Commodore [John] Rodgers, under whom he served some years. The crews of our ships of war were a rough and rugged class of men; many of them had served in the British navy, where punishments were severe, and they required similar treatment, to some extent, in our vessels. Some commanders, however, more than others possessed the art of governing a crew by the hope of reward and by kindness, as well as by the fear of the lash. Reared under the discipline of Rodgers, Mr. Turner was a terror to evildoers and thought more of the motive power of fear than of affection.[21]

Parsons's vignette of Daniel Turner certainly encapsulates the accepted view of how officers maintained discipline in American ships of war. But, as Dr. Parsons also reports, the U.S. Navy had another tradition of discipline that was just as strong: "the art of governing a crew by the hope of reward and by kindness." The articulate spokesman for that tradition was Thomas Truxtun, who taught that the basis of discipline and order in a ship of war was the captain's manner, his air of command, and the authoritarian but evenhanded fashion in which he dealt with his subordinates. The lash he rejected, save on

Although frequently reproduced, John Wesley Jarvis's 1814 portrait of Commodore John Rodgers escapes the status of a visual cliché because it so skillfully records the dominating—not to say domineering—force of Rodgers's personality, which made him the navy's unchallenged professional leader from 1807 until 1837. The Napoleon-like thrust of hand into coat notwithstanding, Rodgers's preeminence ran only in administrative and professional matters. As a combat commander his record was equivocal, and the officer corps looked elsewhere for inspiration when it came to war's conduct and battle. United States Naval Academy Museum, Annapolis, Maryland.

the rarest and most capital of occasions. "In doing your duty, while vigilance is required of you, civility to those under you is desired and expected," Truxtun admonished the midshipmen under his command. "Consider men in an inferior station as your fellow creatures, and when they do their duty with your cheerfulness to encourage them, always remembering that rigid discipline and good order are very different from tyranny—the one highly necessary and the other abominable and disgraceful to the character of an officer and a gentleman."[22] The officer should regard himself as

> surrounded by a crew composed of so many Arguses that every action and expression will be noticed and that the greatest caution and circumspection will be necessary for him to adopt in every part of his deportment. He should treat those under him with respect and in a manner decent and becoming an officer and a gentleman, as the only method of supporting his own dignity and joining their affections. . . . He should always remember that discipline consists in this sort of conduct and enforcing strict regulation and obedience with moderate punishment (where punishment is necessary), such as the laws of the navy authorize and none other, as to strike or lift a hand to a poor seaman or marine, on whom the maintaining of the honor of the national flag depends in the hour of trial, is ungenerous and what no officer should ever do or suffer to be done—unless on some aggravating or special occasion when immediate correction ought not to be dispensed with.
>
> During the whole war with France . . . none ever saw me strike a man, nor does the records of the Constellation produce more than one solitary instance of a man being flogged at the gangway* (though several have been seized up for misdemeanors at different times and pardoned); and during my entire command of the frigate President . . . there was not a man publicly whipt—though several were put in irons and had, at different times, their grog stopped for misbehavior or neglects of duty. I merely mention this fact to show that good order can be maintained without much whipping on shipboard; and I can assure you that the worst-disciplined ships I ever saw in our or the British navy was those renowned for severe punishment.
>
> Hence, Sir, experience and observation, in a life thus far spent at sea in all sorts of ships from a British 64 down to a small merchantman . . . has taught me to believe that a correct, uniform deportment and an observance of strict justice to the seamen in all respects, with attention to law, rules and regulations of a wholesome nature, and the checking those too fond of lifting their hands on every occasion to such as they think their inferiors, is the only true and sure system to command respect and insure proper discipline.[24]

To this point focus has been on the theory of discipline in the pre-1815 navy, but here and there a hint of evidence has suggested that there might have been a less than perfect congruence between theory and reality. One final piece of disciplinary theory provides a useful bridge to an examination of reality. Late in 1810 Midshipman Beekman V. Hoffman was hauled before a court martial for (1) striking a marine sergeant over the head with a cane several times in response to what Hoffman perceived as the sergeant's insolence, and (2) knocking to the deck and kicking a marine private who had failed to salute him properly. Though Hoffman was acquitted of the second charge on a technicality, he was found guilty of the first and sentenced to be reprimanded

---

*Elsewhere Truxtun admits that he also flogged "one or two marines," members of a corps he heartily despised and tried to have abolished, "who had behaved in such a manner that it was not to be well avoided."[23]

by Commodore Thomas Tingey. Fortunately the text of that reprimand has survived and provides a good example of the kind of counsel senior officers gave their young subordinates on matters of authority, discipline, and punishment:

> Permit me to offer you the advice of an old and experienced officer who is well aware how difficult it is to be completely master of the strict necessary discipline on shipboard without incurring among the people in some degree the character of proneness to tyranny [and] how rarely it falls to the lot of an officer to be both truly beloved and respectfully feared by those under his command. Yet, Sir, the latter is far from being so hard of attainment as [is] generally conceived; and in order to gain it, in your progress [toward] the highest ranks in our profession, be careful:
>
> 1st: Never to give your orders with petulance, violence of gross oaths, or imprecations.
>
> 2nd: Never to strike an offender yourself, it being degrading to an officer so to do, as the rules and regulations of the service point out distinctly the modes of punishment generally to be inflicted and custom has allotted by whom it shall be performed.
>
> 3rd: Never (unless in cases of extreme emergency, such as mutiny, etc.) punish an offender while anger or passion, excited by the offense, is predominant in your breast. In the cooler moments of reflection argument frequently subdues the mind of the delinquent and works reformation more often than stripes.
>
> Wishing your future conduct may be exemplary of strict discipline, aided by firmness, and tempered with moderation, I am, respectfully, Sir, your obedient servant,
>
> THOS: TINGEY
> Commandant of the
> Navy Yard Washington[25]

Sailors' Friends and Sundowners

Samuel Leech was a young English boy captured in *Macedonian* early in the War of 1812 who thereupon switched his allegiance to the United States and enlisted in his adopted country's navy on board *Syren*, Master Commandant George Parker. "My first impressions of the American service were very favorable. The treatment in the Syren was more lenient and favorable than in the Macedonian. The captain and officers were kind, while there was a total exemption from that petty tyranny exercised by the upstart midshipmen in the British service. As a necessary effect, our crew were as comfortable and as happy as men ever are in a man-of-war. . . . On board our brig [in contrast to Leech's experience of British practice] we seldom saw more than a dozen lashes inflicted at one time, and that not very often." Leech's subsequent U.S. Navy service, a peacetime cruise in the brig *Boxer*, commanded by Lieutenant John Porter, was not as happy as his *Syren* enlistment. Porter "was inclined to tyranny and severe discipline," and the subordinate officers took their cue from him. Leech, a reflective young man, thought much about the contrast between *Syren* under Parker and John Porter's *Boxer*; he asked shipmates how two such different sets of working and living conditions could exist in the same navy. Berth deck cynics replied that during a war enlisted men received better treatment than their peacetime counterparts. There might be something to that argument, Leech wrote, but the true answer was more fundamental: "I think the difference in these two brigs was owing more to the character of their respective officers than to anything else."[26]

The historian must agree with Samuel Leech that the key element in the effective handling of officer-enlisted relations was character—that is, personality or, more accurately, leadership style. These terms embraced a broad spectrum of interpersonal behavior, stretching from what every seaman would have agreed was the best to what all would have labeled the worst. Two officers who must have stood close to the spectrum's respective ends mark the range of possibilities.

Edmund Pendleton Kennedy was a native of Talbot County, Maryland, born probably in 1780. A highly independent-minded young man, Kennedy, then aged not more than fourteen, had a falling out with his family that led him to run away from home and leave his kinsmen without any news of him for several years. On 17 March 1794, one of the few dates in his life he remembered with any precision, Kennedy entered the merchant service as a foremast hand. Four years and several merchant voyages later, he was serving in a merchantman, commanded by William Flagg of Charleston, South Carolina, which traded to South America. Kennedy impressed Captain Flagg as a young man of ability; when Flagg was named one of the lieutenants of the new frigate *John Adams*, he took Kennedy along as an ordinary seaman. After Kennedy had served five or six months as captain of the foretop *John Adams*'s commander, Captain George Cross, appointed him an acting midshipman, in which capacity he finished out the Quasi-War with France. Because he had never been more than an acting midshipman, serving merely under his captain's appointment, Edmund P. Kennedy did not stand a chance of surviving the 1801 reduction in the officer corps. In common with most of his fellow officers he returned to the merchant service. By then he possessed the experience to command a mate's berth, in which capacity he sailed to different parts of the world, in various ships, until one day in the West Indies he was impressed by the British frigate *Amphion*. From her he soon thereafter made his escape, eventually reaching Philadelphia.

It was the winter of 1802–1803, and the Tripolitan War was in progress. As spring came on the brig *Syren*, 16, was fitting in that port for Mediterranean service. Two of Kennedy's old friends and age peers, Midshipmen Robert T. Spence and Joseph J. Maxwell, were attached to her. Kennedy's elite origins— "his connections are among the most respectable in the state," fellow Marylander Charles W. Goldsborough later commented—made him at least potentially eligible for officer status. Neither had he abandoned the idea of regaining his midshipman's warrant lost at the close of the Quasi-War. He talked over his aspirations with Spence and Maxwell. The authorized number of midshipmen was small; competition for appointments was intense; it was nine years since Kennedy had left home and cut himself off from his family and thereby his most accessible source of clout in his search for a warrant. Spence and Maxwell persuaded Kennedy that the best available route to a midshipman's warrant under such circumstances was to accept a vacant petty officer's berth as *Syren*'s gunner's mate. If as a gunner's mate Kennedy made a good impression on Lieutenant Charles Stewart, the latter promised to use his influence to secure Kennedy's reappointment to the officer corps. Stewart also promised to write Kennedy's alienated family to let them know that he was alive and probably on the road to a career as a naval officer.

If one knows Edmund Pendleton Kennedy only from the written record, this miniature, painted by an unknown hand while Kennedy was still a midshipman, comes as a surprise. There is a daydreamy look about the man that one would scarcely have expected in a young adult so resolutely self-reliant. But notice, on second glance, the firm set of the mouth, the flicker of inner fire in the eyes. For all his superlative leadership qualities, this was a man of hot (if usually controlled) temper and one thoroughly acculturated to the casual violence endemic to the life of a warship. On a February night in 1806, while Kennedy was serving as officer of the watch in the brig Franklin, *the marine lieutenant's servant came up from below bearing a brimming chamber pot, walked to the weather (instead of the lee) quarter, and attempted to dump the contents overboard. Alas, the wind was brisk and a portion of the chamber pot's noisome cargo flew straight into Mr. Kennedy's startled face. The acting lieutenant's response was harsh: an immediate and severe flogging, apparently administered by Kennedy himself, a chastisement he eventually found himself explaining to a far from happy Secretary of the Navy Robert Smith.* Frick Art Reference Library, New York.

In the explosion of Gunboat No. 9 in Edward Preble's 7 August 1804 attack on Tripoli, Spence and Kennedy were the heroes of the hour, attempting to fire their gun even as the wreck slid under the waves. For Kennedy the reward was Stewart's appointment of him (with Preble's concurrence) as an acting midshipman, a pro tempore designation that Stewart was readily able to persuade Robert Smith to replace with a regular midshipman's warrant when Stewart and Kennedy got home to the United States in 1805. Because of his age and his experience, Edmund P. Kennedy never actually served as a midshipman under this warrant. Robert Smith and later Paul Hamilton kept him in a succession of acting lieutenancies until the appropriate amount of time and service had elapsed and he could be formally commissioned to that rank in March 1811.

As might be expected from his nontraditional career pattern, Kennedy the officer was especially effective as a leader of enlisted men. Few other officers inspired the same degree of fanatical devotion. Just how strong a bond existed was revealed on 5 June 1813 when Kennedy, then commander of the schooner *Nonsuch* at Charleston, South Carolina, was approached by two footsore and ragged figures dressed in the remains of sailors' attire, men who proceeded to turn themselves in as deserters. Kennedy recognized them at once. Their names were Oliver Cromwell and William Davis; they had been under Kennedy's command in the cutter *Scorpion* in the Potomac earlier during the war. Without a cent of pay on their persons, the two men had deserted from *Scorpion* at Washington on 7 May and walked all the way to Charleston solely so that they might again serve under Kennedy. "They must have had a wretched time of it," Kennedy wrote in appealing to William Jones not to treat the men as deserters. "Their feet are very much swelled and blistered, and they appear very much broke down. Both of them are excellent seamen; I have always placed the utmost confidence in them. . . . To use their own expressions, 'They would expend their whole lives in the service of their country, provided they could be indulged with the privilege of serving under me.'" The normally coldhearted Jones could be impressed by that kind of officer-seaman loyalty; he readily forgave all.[27]

No enlisted man would have followed John Orde Creighton anywhere—unless it were down a dark alley to put a knife in his back. Creighton was born in the West Indies around the year 1785, a place and a date that suggest his parents may have been Loyalists who subsequently returned to New York City in time for their son to be appointed a midshipman late in the Quasi-War with France. Midshipman Creighton served in *President* during the less than a year that remained of that conflict, then saw duty in *Vixen, John Adams,* and *Constitution* during the Tripolitan War. Promoted to lieutenant in January 1807, he served as such in *Chesapeake, Vixen,* and *Wasp.* August 1810 found Creighton first lieutenant of *Argus* under James Lawrence. He stood high in the estimation of John Rodgers: "There is no officer in the service whom I would prefer to Mr. Creighton as a first lieutenant. His experience is considerable, and his ambition to do his duty cannot be excelled by any officer." Creighton's career had followed a different course from that of Edmund P. Kennedy; along its way he had developed a radically different approach to leadership. His methods were surely no secret to his shipmates, but they became a part of the public record when Samuel Miller, seaman in *Argus,* was put on trial in December 1810 on charges of disobedience of orders and mutinous conduct brought by Lieutenant Creighton. In the trial testimony, including Creighton's own, there was general agreement to the following sequence of events:

In the absence of James Lawrence, Creighton had, on 13 August 1810, gotten *Argus* under way and was working her down the East River from the New York navy yard. On the forecastle more confusion and sloppy seamanship were on view than pleased Mr. Creighton's eye; in particular, Creighton noticed that the main topgallant brace was fast. He ordered it let go; the order went unexecuted, and Creighton's ire began to rise. Boatswain's mate William Thomas was told to send Miller, the captain of the forecastle, aft to the quarterdeck. When Miller arrived Creighton asked him, apparently none too gently, why he had not let go the topgallant brace, to which Miller replied, with more than a hint of insolence in his tone, "It's not my duty, Sir."

"I'll make it your duty," snapped Creighton, as he instructed Thomas to bring a cat-of-nine-tails and ordered Miller to step to the gangway and remove his jacket. Miller balked and stood on the regulations; in no way tempering the assertiveness in his voice, he refused to be punished until Lieutenant Lawrence returned on board. By this point most of the Arguses were aware that a confrontation with the unpopular Creighton was in progress. Through body language, if by no more overt means, solidarity with Miller was manifest. One man, Michael McDermott, was bolder; he clapped Miller on the shoulder: "Well done, my boy! I glory in you, by God!"

Miller's defiance fired Creighton's rage beyond hope of self-control. He began kicking the seaman, striking him in the face with his fist, then took up a rope's end and beat him with it. His anger temporarily appeased, Creighton ordered a marine sentinel to take Miller to the berth deck, where, Creighton announced ominously, he would deal with Miller later.

Once *Argus* was safely anchored, Creighton took boatswain's mate Thomas and headed to the berth deck, where he told a seated Miller to rise and prepare for punishment. Miller did not move. Creighton repeated his order; Miller continued to ignore it. Finally, after Creighton had summoned the master-at-arms and told him to tie Miller up for punishment, using force if necessary, Miller said he would submit, and received ten lashes over his shirt. Creighton thereupon ordered Miller to return to his duty, went himself up the fore hatch, and started walking toward the quarterdeck. Miller followed him as far as the mainmast, protesting loudly, "Mr. Creighton, I cannot [or, some heard, "will not"] go to my duty until Captain Lawrence comes on board."

"Do you refuse to do your duty?" Creighton asked. Miller's response was that he would rather remain a prisoner till Lawrence came on board.

Variations on this exchange were several times repeated, each time with heightened anger on Creighton's part till all of his limited patience was exhausted. Then, as the Arguses watched in horror, Creighton started to pick up the ship's grindstone to throw at Miller. Luckily for the seaman the grindstone was too heavy for Creighton; he had to vent his rage merely by flogging Miller over the head with a rope's end, driving him forward till he got as far as the fore hatch and crying all the while, "You refuse to do your duty, do you?" Some witnesses recalled seeing Creighton strike Miller with his fist and kick him as well. Miller completed his retreat to the forecastle, where Creighton did not pursue him and where the seaman continued what the lieutenant called his "disorderly" behavior. In an attempt to force Miller into explicit refusal of an order, Creighton passed the word for *Argus*'s sails to be furled. Miller, too sly to fall for that one, went up with the other hands. The trick obviously a failure, Creighton told the boatswain to pipe belay. Down Miller came to the forecastle, where, in Creighton's eyes at least, "he still continued his disorderly manner, throwing his arms about." Lieutenant Creighton thereupon did what he should have done in the first place and ordered the master-at-arms to confine Miller in irons. With that the incident itself was over.

For Creighton the fat was still very much in the fire. John Rodgers knew that Paul Hamilton would read the trial transcript with care before approving it; he could imagine Hamilton's reaction to the testimony exposing Creighton's conduct. The best strategy to protect Creighton, of whom Rodgers still held a favorable opinion, was to attempt to beat Hamilton to the punch. When he forwarded the proceedings to Washington, Rodgers made an effort to portray the whole business as the "intemperance of momentary passion peculiar to youthful indiscretion." The commodore had correctly estimated Hamilton's reaction. Checkmarks in the margins of the trial transcript still testify to the care with which the secretary read; his response to Rodgers preserves his outrage:

The passionate and inconsistent conduct of Lieutenant Creighton has been beheld with much concern, as being disreputable to himself and of evil tendency on the public service. It is only when an officer exercises his authority within the bounds of law and reason that he is entitled to respect and obedience, and, where he overleaps these, the consequences to be expected are disgust, hatred, a disposition to desert and mutiny, not only in the minds of the immediate sufferers but also of their comrades. . . . The circumstance of an officer beating with his fists and kicking a man about the deck is, in my estimation, so out of character and horrid that, but for your intercession and Lieutenant Creighton's previous good conduct, I should feel it incumbent on me to hold him answerable before a court martial for unofficerlike conduct.

Because Rodgers had come so strongly to Creighton's defense there was little that Hamilton could do by way of disciplinary action that would not compromise working relations with his senior officer afloat. He did, however, insist that Creighton take an involuntary furlough with the hope that, "when he is restored to service, he will by reflection have acquired a greater command over himself, the only requisite (I am induced by your representation to believe) he needs to be a correct officer."[28] Although John Orde Creighton eventually became a captain and remained in the navy until his death in October 1838, Rodgers's and Hamilton's hopes that he had learned better leadership methods from the Miller incident were illusionary. Direct physical brutality remained his ultimate weapon when pushed to the wall. His relations with subordinate officers were no better than those with enlisted men.[29]

Creighton's story raises an issue that the social historian of the navy's leaders must address: What was the role of physical force in officer-enlisted relations in the pre-1815 U.S. Navy?

21. Sanctions

*P*ETER JEALOUS, a U.S. Navy seaman attached to the New Orleans station, was tried by a court martial in May 1810 on the charge of "deserting under aggravating circumstances." This was the third time Jealous had deserted and been caught—doubtless the "aggravating circumstances" of the charge—and the officers composing the court were in no mood to be merciful:

> Having duly considered the prisoner's [guilty] plea to the charge, as well as what he alleged in his defense, the court are of opinion that he is guilty of the charge and do therefore adjudge, sentence, and direct . . . that the said Peter Jealous shall receive 270 lashes with a plain cat-of-nine-tails on his bare back in the usual manner; that he be branded with a proportional letter "**D**" two inches in length on the most conspicuous part of his right cheek; that the left side of his head be shaved clean; and that he be dismissed from the service (in the most disgraceful manner usual in it) as unworthy of further service in the Navy of the United States.

When the station commander, Master Commandant David Porter, came to review and approve or mitigate the sentence, his mood was in sanguinary harmony with that of the court:

> The foregoing sentence is approved, and it is hereby directed that the senior officer off Fort St. Johns cause the number of lashes to be given in equal proportions alongside of such vessels as may be laying there, observing the usual ceremonies in such cases. When the other part of the sentence has been carried into execution, he will cause the prisoner to be towed (by the boats of the vessels) in a boat stern-foremost, under a gallows with a halter, to the shore, the drum beating the Rogue's March. The prisoner is then to be thrown out of the boat, with the halter remaining around his neck.[1]

The historian, being human and therefore attracted by the sensational, cannot fail to be pierced with horror at the ferocity with which Peter Jealous was treated. Taking this case in isolation, or perhaps noting one or two other sentences equally shocking, one must exclaim, Indeed, the pre-1815 navy was ruled by the most insensitive brutality! In fact, however, the punishments of Peter Jealous and a few others that immediately attract notice by their sensational severity are atypical. Jealous's was, so far as the record shows, the third most

233

severe flogging ever awarded in the pre-1815 navy. Branding was equally rare. The navy of 1794–1815 may perhaps have been a brutal place by later standards, but that should be established by the norm, not by extreme examples. What, then, were the realities of authority, of discipline, and of punishment in the navy's ships?[2]

A Rough and Rugged Class of Men

One begins by recognizing that a high threshold of tolerance existed for casual, day-to-day brutality and interpersonal violence. In the previously quoted words of Dr. Usher Parsons, no sadist himself, the crews of U.S. warships were perceived by their officers as "a rough and rugged class of men," accustomed to and requiring severe physical punishment for their management. Neither should this be surprising. The naval officer was philosophically committed to the principle that the ultimate defense of the nation's rights was its ability to use organized violence. It required no mental leap to pass to the position that, in the last analysis, one's ability to maintain authority over subordinates depended on the potential or actual infliction of physical violence. Consider this case, which is only a single example from among a number of fascinating ones that might be related.

On the New Orleans station in the summer of 1810 boatswain James Hutchins of Gunboat No. 16 was brought before a court martial on charges of oppression and cruelty. Prosecution and defense agreed on the facts of the case. One day during the previous November, Midshipman William Peters, the commanding officer of No. 16, had ordered Hutchins, his second-in-command, to get the gunboat under way. When Peters came up the hatchway a few minutes later Hutchins told him two men were still below eating. One of them was marine John Lewis, a notorious character: lazy, fond of feigning illness, and even fonder of drink. Show the men the way up, Peters ordered Hutchins; hands were scarce, and it was no time to be below. Peters then went back to the cabin to get his coat; he returned to the deck to discover that Hutchins had not merely started Lewis from below with a rope's end, but was actually chasing him up and down the deck, hitting him with the rope, till Lewis fell over a sweep.

"Did [Hutchins] start Lewis more severely than boatswains generally start men on board United States armed vessels?" the court asked marine corporal James A. McDonald.

"I never seen such a starting before in my life," replied McDonald.

Peters intervened and told Hutchins never again to beat a man in such a manner: a starting meant only that sluggards could be struck as they came up the hatchway. Lewis thereupon chimed in, damned Gunboat No. 16, and said that he would get clear of her even if he had to jump overboard, in response to which abuse Peters told Hutchins to flog Lewis again. After about six or eight blows had fallen upon Lewis's back, the marine again threatened to jump overboard. "Jump and be damned," said the aggravated Peters, and overboard John Lewis went. Lewis was clearly an excellent swimmer, so after Peters had let him cool his temper in the Mississippi's waters for a while, he sent No. 16's gunner and two hands in a boat to chase Lewis. Every time the boat caught up with Lewis, the marine would dive and elude his pursuers. Finally, patience at an end, the gunner watched for his chance, deftly unshipped the tiller, struck Lewis over the head, stunned him, and hauled him into the boat.

Except for the ferocity of Hutchins's starting, about the degree of which there was some difference of opinion, no one examined by the court disputed this narrative of events. Yet the court, composed of five experienced and case-hardened officers, concluded that "the charges have not been proven and that they are frivolous and unfounded." Clearly Hutchins's, Peters's, and the gunner's employment of physical violence were well within the limits of the officer corps' collective tolerance.[3]

What Sea Lawyers Heard

Before proceeding from a prevalent atmosphere of casual interpersonal violence to the evidence regarding the pre-1815 navy's use of corporal punishment it will be useful to survey briefly the law's provisions for the discipline of seamen as set out in the "Act for the Better Government of the Navy of the United States."[4]

Five types of acts could be punished by a court martial with the death penalty: (1) cowardice or disobedience in battle; (2) mutiny or attempted mutiny; (3) disobedience to an officer, striking him, or threatening him with a weapon; (4) desertion or attempted desertion; and (5) murder committed outside the territorial jurisdiction of the United States. With the exception of conviction for mutinous assembly or "attempt to make any mutinous assembly," a court martial had, in all cases, discretionary authority to award a lesser sentence than death.

Five additional classes of acts, for which the death penalty could not be inflicted, were required to be tried by courts martial and the offender, if guilty, punished at the court's discretion: (1) seditious or mutinous words; treating a superior with contempt while in the execution of his office; concealing or conniving at mutinous or seditious practices; failing to assist in the suppression of a mutiny; (2) quarreling with another person in the navy or using "provoking or reproachful words, gestures, or menaces"; (3) waste, embezzlement, or fraud in relation to public property; (4) theft in excess of $20 in value; and (5) plunder or abuse of civilians or their property. (Omitted here are a few potential offenses cited in the law with which, as far as the records show, no enlisted man was charged in the pre-1815 navy.) These offenses were not subject to capital punishment; neither could a court martial impose a sentence in excess of one hundred lashes for any one crime.

Finally, the captain was authorized to confine in irons or to flog, "not exceeding twelve lashes," enlisted men guilty of (1) "oppression, cruelty, fraud, profane swearing, drunkenness, or any other scandalous conduct tending to the destruction of good morals"; (2) sleeping on watch, negligence in the performance of assigned duty, or leaving one's station before being properly relieved; and (3) theft not in excess of $20. If the captain judged that the offense required a stiffer penalty than confinement in irons or twelve lashes, he was to have the offender tried by a court martial.

In addition to this hierarchy of offenses and punishments, the "Act for the Better Government of the Navy" had several important general provisions respecting discipline:

No commanding officer was permitted, on his own authority, to inflict a punishment on an enlisted man in excess of twelve lashes with a cat-of-nine-tails.

On the other hand the captain was presented with a large loophole in the form of article 32, which provided that "all crimes committed by persons belonging to the navy, which are not specified in the foregoing articles, shall be punished according to the laws and customs in such cases at sea."

When the commanding officer was temporarily absent from his ship, no subordinate officer was to inflict any punishment other than confinement in irons. For such confinements the subordinate was to account to the captain on his return.

Within the territorial waters of the United States a court martial could be convened only with the prior approval of the secretary of the navy; on foreign stations the squadron commander's authorization was mandatory.

Any death sentence imposed by a court martial required the concurrence of two-thirds of the members, and it could not be carried into execution within U.S. territory until it was personally approved by the president of the United States. On foreign stations a death sentence required the squadron commander's confirmation.

Sentences other than death required only a simple majority of the court's members and could be executed on the approval of the squadron commander.

Instant Justice

The lowest grade of corporal punishment, and the most common, was one that the law in no way recognized except in that clause about punishment "according to the laws and customs in such cases at sea." This was flogging with a simple rope's end, ordered by a subordinate officer—customarily the first lieutenant—and inflicted immediately upon the commission of an alleged offense.* A story told by former carpenter's mate Samuel Holbrook shows how the practice functioned.

One morning during a gale in the North Atlantic it happened that the watch officer in *Firefly* was newly commissioned lieutenant John Paul Zantzinger. Holbrook and a buddy, seaman Tom Burns, were sitting, one on the forward pivot gun, the other just below him, when Zantzinger, who was fat and not well respected by the crew, came huffing and puffing up to the gun. The lieutenant had noticed that the staysail, supposedly snug in its netting, was working loose.

"Go up and secure that staysail," he ordered Burns, who promptly went up and did the job in what he thought was an adequate manner.

Perhaps thirty minutes later the bulky lieutenant again hove in view of the pivot gun; his eye detected a small corner of the staysail once more working loose.

"You, Burns, you —— scoundrel, didn't I send you up to stop that sail?"
"Yes, Sir."

---

* Not here considered are minor immediate punishments such as grog stoppages or being made to ride the spanker boom for three hours as a sanction for falling asleep on watch. For purposes of historical research detailed records of such punishments are almost wholly lacking. Besides, these were not *corporal* punishments in the sense that a flogging or a confinement in irons was.

"Well, come here."

Whereupon Zantzinger summoned a boatswain's mate, ordered Burns to remove his jacket, and proceeded to have the mate lay a dozen lashes with a rope's end across Burns's back, covered only by a shirt.

"Now," said Zantzinger, "go up and see if you can stow that sail in a proper manner."

Burns scrambled up the rigging, but made the mistake of saying, primarily to himself, as he went, "I thought I did my best before."

Alas, Lieutenant Zantzinger heard him: "What's that you say? Grumbling again, are you? Come down here!" The boatswain's mate was instructed to lay another dozen on Burns, who then had to go up and make yet one more attempt to secure the problem sail. When Burns came back down Holbrook could see that his buddy's back was a mass of blood and that the man was weeping.[5]

Apart from long-standing naval custom, the only sanction for such on-the-spot punishment was to be found in the various sets of ships' internal regulations, some of which laid out specific norms and conditions. In *Argus* in 1811 William M. Crane decreed, "No person is to be put in irons whilst I am on board but by my directions. No officer on board the vessel, excepting the first lieutenant, is permitted to punish a man. For trifling offenses [the first lieutenant] may chastise him with a piece of nine-thread ratline, but he is never to exceed one dozen." Not all captains had stipulations about on-the-spot punishment in their internal regulations; certain of them, more restrictive than most, limited the lashes to six. Some, as did Crane, reserved the infliction of instant discipline to the first lieutenant; others permitted any officer commanding a watch to exercise this prerogative.[6] The latter was clearly the practice in *Firefly*, because Zantzinger was the most junior lieutenant in the vessel. In at least some ships of the pre-1815 navy, no officer was allowed to exercise this form of punishment. Lieutenant Charles Gordon lamented (August 1805) that he had just been assigned to serve as first lieutenant in the frigate *Adams* under Commodore Alexander Murray: "A first lieutenant is generally disagreeably situated with Murray in consequence of his easy disposition. He will not allow his officers to chastise the men."[7]

Instant, on-the-spot chastisement was the most common form of discipline practiced in the pre-1815 navy, but it is impossible to measure the practice in any way. It was so much a part of everyday life on shipboard that it went everywhere unrecorded, save for the reminiscences of enlisted men and an occasional, passing mention in a court martial transcript. Regarding other, more noteworthy but less common, forms of corporal punishment it is possible to offer some estimates, of greater or lesser accuracy, for their frequency and severity. Concerning these better-known forms of punishment it must always be recollected that they represented the upper, smaller portion of a pyramid, the broad base of which was the infliction of swift and on-the-spot corporal punishment for what it pleased the captain to call petty offenses.

In Irons

The lowest grade of punishment recognized by law in the U.S. Navy was the captain's right to confine a man—almost always in irons, though sometimes simply under a sentry's charge. Here was a punishment regarding the practice of which there should be ample documentation for analysis. In every well-regulated ship the master-at-arms was expected, each and every day, to give the captain a morning report of prisoners in confinement, specifying for each man so secured (1) his name; (2) his rating; (3) at what officer's instance the captain had ordered his confinement; (4) the date since which he had been confined; and (5) the offense for which he had been secured. Strange to report, this class of document, potentially so valuable for the navy's social history, has all but entirely vanished from the record. One rummages through officers' papers in a vain search for groups of master-at-arms morning reports. Most were probably long ago discarded as routine records of no historical importance. At present only one collection of these reports is known to exist: those for the frigate *Constitution*, under the command of Edward Preble, during the months January through June 1804.[8] One hesitates to argue that half a year's records from one ship—and that ship commanded by a captain notorious as one of the navy's sterner disciplinarians—can be taken for typical of an entire navy. Still, because these are the only reasonably complete run of master-at-arms morning reports extant, it is useful to record what they reveal.

At least thirteen enlisted men were confined as prisoners for disciplinary reasons during the period covered by *Constitution*'s morning reports. One has to say "at least" because there are gaps in the file of reports; it is possible other enlisted men were confined for brief periods of time. Preble's well-established reputation as a sundowner is confirmed when one discovers that eight of the thirteen men had been incarcerated by the commodore's direct order, while only five men found themselves in irons at the instigation of one of the ship's lieutenants. Whether or not one of *Constitution*'s enlisted men found himself enjoying master-at-arms John Burchard's dubious hospitality bore no relationship to his experience or inexperience at sea. Burchard's prisoners were a cross-section of the ship's hands: two quartermasters, four seamen, four ordinary seamen, two boys, and the frigate's cook. There was more discernible pattern to the offenses for which the thirteen found themselves in irons. Six were there for alcohol-related offenses, including cook James Brumade, who was charged with drunkenness and with purchasing liquor; three were in confinement for desertion or attempted desertion; three for neglect of duty; and one (and he one of the two boys) for theft. For six of the thirteen prisoners confinement was their only punishment; upon release they returned directly to duty. Seven of those confined discovered that a period in irons was only a prelude to a more severe punishment: flogging. Preble certainly had his own good and sufficient reasons why some men got off with simple confinement while others had to endure a flogging, but existing records do not enable the historian to recover any particular pattern for this aspect of his disciplinary practice. In spite of his notoriety as a harsh disciplinarian, Preble seems to have made relatively light use of confinement as a means of correction. During the half-year in question there were 342 enlisted men and petty officers serving in *Constitution*, of whom only some 3.8 percent were at any time placed in confinement for disciplinary infractions. Neither, save in certain rare and exceptional cases, was Preble a commander who put a mariner in irons and threw away the key. Among the twelve seamen the precise lengths of whose confinements are known, the shortest period of incarceration was one day and the longest twenty.[9] Preble's median confinement in irons, thirteen days, was a good indicator of his attitude: seamen were too scarce and too valuable to keep locked up. Better to punish a man, by flogging if need be, and get him back on duty.

How typical of the navy was Preble's use of confinement? A single comparison is possible (Table 8). The log of the brig *Hornet* for eight months (October 1809–May 1810) of the period that she was commanded by Lieutenant Theodore Hunt appears to be unusually faithful about recording confinements and releases from confinement.[10] The risk of being confined was greater in Hunt's *Hornet* than in Preble's *Constitution*: nineteen different enlisted men from *Hornet*'s crew found themselves so restrained at one time or another. One man, seaman Joseph Dickson, was so quarrelsome and ill-tempered that he had to be confined three times for fighting; quartermaster James Anderson was almost as pugnacious, for he found himself detained twice in the eight-month period. (Preble's *Constitution*, by contrast, had no repeat offenders.) Even though the confinement record for *Hornet* covers eight months to *Constitution*'s six, that difference does not account for *Hornet*'s larger number of confinements, because the number of enlisted men available to be punished in *Hornet* (168) was half that in *Constitution* (342). Whereas only 3.8 percent of Preble's men were placed in confinement, 11.3 percent of Hunt's shared that fate. If Preble confined fewer men than did Hunt, the latter's confinements were much less severe. The maximum and minimum confinements of each captain were about the same, but there the similarity ended. Preble's average (mean) sentence was

This might have been a famous face. The rank and experience peer of Jacob Jones and James Lawrence, possessor of a distinguished record as a junior officer, Master Commandant Theodore Hunt resigned his commission under somewhat murky circumstances just thirteen months before the declaration of the War of 1812. Did he misread the navy's future? Did he throw away a thirteen-year career in a fit of oversensitivity to whispered criticism of his conduct as Hornet's *commanding officer? Was the lure of potentially greater financial security as a civilian merchant too strong to be resisted? Whatever the answer, behind Hunt's handsome profile, as recorded by C.B.J. Fevret de Saint-Mémin, there lurked a fatal flaw that robbed him of the highest distinction in any of his endeavors. Following a postresignation voyage to China for John Jacob Astor, Hunt left the sea and moved to Saint Louis, where the merchant's financial success eluded him. A federal job as recorder of land titles kept the wolf from Hunt's door until Andrew Jackson became president and replaced him with one of the president's political allies. Shortly thereafter Hunt suffered a stroke, then gradually declined to quiet and peaceful death, sitting in his favorite armchair, in the last days of 1831.* National Portrait Gallery, Washington, D.C.

approximately twelve days. Hunt's was half that. Even more revealing, Hunt's median confinement (four days) was less than one-third as long as Preble's. Further accentuating the severity of Preble's discipline is the fact that about half the men he confined were also flogged, while only one in four of Hunt's prisoners came under the lash. Altogether the comparison is suggestive of certain differences in disciplinary philosophy. Preble punished more selectively but more severely. If the infrequency with which punishment has to be inflicted and a low number of repeat offenders are evidence of an effective system of discipline, then it appears that Preble's stricter methods were better at controlling undesirable behavior than Hunt's more lenient measures. Both had to deal with the chronic problems of alcohol abuse and desertion, but Hunt was especially concerned about, and severe with, those who quarreled and fought, offenses that Preble may have regarded as more appropriate for the instant justice of a rope's end applied by a boatswain's mate.

The Lash

Carpenter's mate (and later carpenter) Samuel Holbrook witnessed many a flogging during his seven years in the navy, but no other made such an impression on him as a pair he saw in the winter of 1814–15, while David Porter's flying squadron was being assembled at New York. Porter himself was temporarily absent, which made Lieutenant Wolcott Chauncey the senior officer present. "And he was a Tartar, sure enough," recalled Holbrook.

> Two young men, who, I believe, were mechanics' apprentices, had shipped for the squadron and had been at the navy yard but a few days when, probably feeling a little homesick, [they] took French leave one evening and went over to the city. On the following morning they were missed at muster and their absence reported to Captain Chauncey, who immediately sent a midshipman to find them. They were both found together, having met with some of their companions, and who had all been on a frolic. These young men were brought on board an old bomb ketch [*Vesuvius*] and confined with double irons two days; and on the morning of the third, at nine o'clock, all hands were called alongside the ketch to witness punishment. . . .
>
> Here were about three hundred men, boys, and marines assembled round the old hulk to see these two young men nearly flayed alive for going over to New York without leave. When all had assembled, the two prisoners were brought from their place of confinement, apparently more dead than alive. The first was stripped and seized up. . . . Captain Chauncey, standing on a slight elevation and with a stentorian voice, thus addressed the crowd:
>
> *"Men! What the law allows you, you shall have. But, by the eternal ———, if any one of you disobeys that law, I'll cut your backbone out."*
>
> "Go on with him, boatswain's mate, and do your duty or, by ———, you shall take his place."
>
> The shrieks of the youngster were dreadful, calling upon God and all the holy angels to save him. After the first dozen another boatswain's mate took the cat; and, when he [the prisoner] had received two dozen, he fainted and hung by his wrists. The punishment was suspended for a few moments until he had revived sufficiently to stand on his feet. He then took four dozen more, making six in all; and, when taken down, he could not stand.
>
> The other received seven dozen. He fainted, however, before he had received the first [dozen] and received the greater portion of his punishment

in that state. The flesh was fairly hanging in strips upon both backs; it was really a sickening sight.[11]

As it happens Samuel Holbrook's is the only fully detailed description of a flogging in the pre-1815 U.S. Navy, although flogging practice on board the U.S. schooner *Carolina* was also scrutinized at a court of inquiry in 1814.[12] Because descriptions of floggings in the U.S. Navy either are taken from memoirs and works concerning the post-1815 navy or are extrapolated from British practice, it is appropriate here to note exactly what these two contemporary sources tell about the execution of this severe punishment in the navy of 1794–1815.[13]

The malefactor or malefactors were almost always confined in irons overnight or for a few days. Not only did this allow the captain time for reflection and deliberation, thus avoiding the poor leadership of punishing while in the heat of anger, such suspense reinforced the psychological impact of the flogging. Often captains kept offenders in irons until there were several men to be punished at once. No one ever bothered to record the reasons for this practice, but it is not hard to surmise that they were a blend of administrative convenience and the desire to make punishment a more fear-inspiring occasion by combining several chastisements. When an appropriate opportunity offered, the captain ordered the entire ship's company assembled to witness punishment, for such public flogging had two purposes. It demonstrated to the offender that he could not violate the rules with impunity and gave him good reason not to repeat his crime. Equally, these solemn inflictions were cautionary examples of the captain's authority and the reward in store for the transgressor of that authority. Floggings were customarily awarded at the ship's gangway, with both officers and men standing bareheaded throughout. The precise sequence of American naval practice is obscure, but it appears that the offender was usually stripped of his shirt and his hands tied to the hammock nettings or rail above his head. At this point, having milked the maximum psychological advantage from the situation, the captain might pardon the greatly relieved offender and return him to duty. More typically he announced the offense or offenses of which the man was guilty, read the section or sections of the "Act for the Better Government of the Navy" under which the offenses fell, announced the number of lashes to be inflicted, and ordered "Boatswain's mate: Do your duty." Then, with his full strength, one of the boatswain's mates would lay the cat-of-nine-tails across the transgressor's back . . . One . . . Two . . . Three . . . Four, the master-at-arms counting aloud as the lashes fell. At the end of each twelve lashes the boatswain's mate administering the flogging was relieved by another to insure that the force of the blows was not diminished as the punishment progressed.

Occasionally flogging took on an explicitly prurient tone. In the British navy men were sometimes flogged on the bare buttocks while tied over a gun.[14] Was this practice copied by the U.S. service? One might never have known for certain and gone on assuming that logbook entries stating that So-and-So, seaman, received so many lashes always referred to floggings inflicted on the bare back, were it not for the log of the U.S. schooner *Sylph* on Lake Ontario during the War of 1812. Therein it stands recorded that, on 29 January 1814, Henry Briggs, coxswain, and Arnold Hill, boy, each received thirty lashes "on the backside" for desertion.[15] Was this a unique and eccentric use of this punishment in the U.S. Navy? *Sylph's* commanding officer, Master Commandant Melancthon T. Woolsey, was too junior an officer to have introduced a novel form of punishment unsanctioned by his seniors and especially by his commodore, Isaac Chauncey. Odds are that this especially embarrassing and even sadistic punishment was reserved for occasional use on particularly heinous offenders; established it is that in the pre-1815 navy the lash sometimes fell elsewhere than on the bare back.

The Logbooks Speak

Samuel Holbrook was an accurate autobiographer, apparently basing his memoir, *Threescore Years*, on journals supplemented by a keen memory. There is little reason to question the reliability of his description of Wolcott Chauncey's flogging of the two teenage boys, but what made the event stand out in Holbrook's memory was the extraordinary savagery of Chauncey in inflicting the discipline. Neither is there any reason to doubt the obscure reference in a court martial transcript to Lieutenant Louis Alexis's having a marine flogged, then keeping him standing on deck, shirtless, for three hours on a winter's day so that every half-hour he could be "pickled" by a bucket of brine sloshed over his back.[16] Here again the historian faces the danger of being lured astray by the single dramatic, but perhaps extreme, example. Is there a more reliable way to establish a sense of the role and the dimensions of flogging in the pre-1815 navy?

The answer is yes. A number of ship's logs from the period scrupulously record details of punishments inflicted in those vessels.[17] Most ships' logbooks from the pre-1815 navy have long since vanished. Among those that survive it is clear that, in some instances, captains preferred not to have the details of their disciplinary practices on the official record. Consequently, many a surviving log is barren of all references to punishment or simply records that So-and-So, seaman, was punished without providing any useful details. Other captains, and by no means always the most lenient, wanted the record to report faithfully what they had done. For all of these reasons no one can prove that the surviving logbook information on flogging as practiced in certain ships by particular captains is typical of the pre-1815 navy as a whole, but the picture is remarkably consistent and includes a number of the navy's most important commanders and role models (Tables 9 and 10).

Figure 4 takes all the cases of flogging of naval enlisted men recorded in the logs in which the number of lashes administered is reported and summarizes these punishments. It provides a bird's-eye—or, if one prefers, a masthead—view of flogging practice across the navy. The most immediate observation is the frequency with which the twelve-lash punishment was awarded. It accounts for just over half of the recorded instances of flogging. Indeed, punishments of twelve or fewer lashes constitute nearly two-thirds of the recorded floggings, while almost nine out of every ten floggings were of fewer than twenty-five lashes. Floggings in excess of twenty-nine lashes occur in less than 13 percent of the recorded cases; and floggings on the order of those Samuel Holbrook alleges Wolcott Chauncey inflicted on the two teenagers, seventy-two and eighty-four lashes respectively, would be among a minuscule proportion of extreme punishments recorded in the logbooks; indeed, they would be the third and

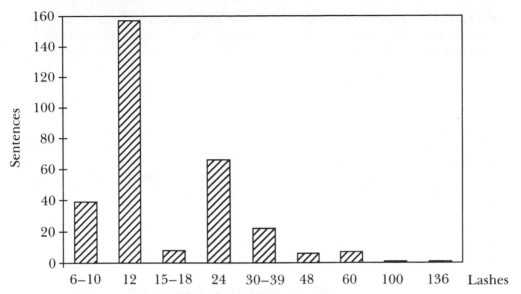

*Figure 4 Floggings on the Captain's Authority: Lashes Awarded per Sentence, All Cases
Cumulated (N = 307)*

fourth most severe floggings by a captain's authority on record if they had
been found in one of the logbooks.

This is, as stated, a masthead view of navy-wide flogging. If one comes a
little closer and examines the practices of selected individual captains (Table
10), differences begin to come into focus. Dissimilarities are most evident if
one runs one's finger across the line for maximum number of lashes given one
man. The range of possibilities extends from Silas Talbot's unexceptionable 12
to Isaac Chauncey's 136 awarded in *John Adams*. But to focus attention here
would be to fall again into the trap of judging from extreme examples. For the
same reason one should be wary of the line for mean number of lashes given;
this measure is too easily distorted by one or two extraordinarily severe
punishments to give a true picture of typical flogging practice. It is in the
median lash sentences and the most commonly awarded lash sentences that the
similarities and the differences among the captains can be most accurately
detected. There one sees the dominance of two favorite punishments: twelve
lashes and twenty-four lashes. Indeed, with the exception of William Bainbridge,
the eight captains consistently sort themselves into two groups. One set (James
Biddle, David Porter, Silas Talbot, and Melancthon T. Woolsey) regularly favors
twelve lashes; a second, more severe, group (Isaac Chauncey, William M. Crane,
John H. Dent, and Edward Preble) depends upon the twenty-four-lash flogging.

Two additional points about the pre-1815 navy's punishment of what it
considered undesirable behavior may be extracted from this forbidding mass
of figures. Admitting that any flogging, even one of six lashes, was a painful
and degrading experience, the odds that any particular seaman would have to
endure this ultimate sanction were not high. In the seven cases in which it is
possible to calculate the portion of the ship's company who were flogged one
or more times, this number is found to range from a low of approximately one
man in thirty-six under William M. Crane to a high of one man in eight in
David Porter's *Enterprize* and Melancthon T. Woolsey's *Sylph*. Edward Preble

and Isaac Chauncey seem to have been remarkably consistent in punishing one man in ten. The numbers, then, bear out the subjective observation of contemporary writers as diverse as Thomas Truxtun and Samuel Holbrook: only a small number of men in any ship of war were real disciplinary problems—troublemakers, if you will—and likely to experience the lash.

Equally interesting are the differences between the number of floggings awarded and the number of individual enlisted men who were flogged. The importance of these figures is more clearly perceived when they are restated as they have been in Table 11. This shows the number of men in each ship who received two or more floggings and the percentage that these repeat offenders constituted among the number of men flogged in that ship. The captains—with the equivocal exception of Isaac Chauncey's command of *John Adams*—again divide themselves into two groups. William M. Crane, Edward Preble, and Isaac Chauncey (in *Hornet*) found it necessary to flog few men more than once. In the ships commanded by Silas Talbot, David Porter, James Biddle, and Melancthon T. Woolsey approximately three or four out of any ten men

The face of a great organizer. Intelligent, direct, and piercing eyes; firm mouth; resolute chin. Isaac Chauncey, here portrayed by John Wesley Jarvis, was a man of formidable drive and administrative skill, one who developed on wartime Lake Ontario the largest fleet, the biggest ships, and the most elaborate support organization of the pre-1815 navy. The same personality that made Chauncey a failsafe administrator was a handicap to him as a strategist and combat commander: he lacked the gambler's instinct that almost certainly would have gained decisive victories over his equally cautious War of 1812 opponent, Sir James Lucas Yeo. Not surprisingly, it is as administrator and disciplinarian that Chauncey is met in these pages. Art Commission of the City of New York.

flogged would be repeat offenders. Woolsey appears to have had the worst problems in this regard. In his case sixteen men were flogged only once; six underwent this severe punishment twice; three experienced the cat-of-nine-tails three times; and a final three were lashed an astounding total of four times, a figure unequaled by any other ship whose punishment record survives.

The most arresting feature of the table is discovered when the two right-hand columns are compared. Those captains whose floggings most often conformed to the legal maximum of twelve lashes experienced the most frequent problems with repeat offenders, but those captains who flogged first offenders severely—favoring twenty-four-lash and even thirty-six-lash sentences—had far fewer problems with repeated misconduct. This, it will be noted, parallels the relationship between the severity of initial punishment and the number of disciplinary problems that was discovered when Edward Preble's and Theodore Hunt's records on confinement in irons were compared.

There is a way in which the figures on the captains in Table 10 are misleading. At first blush it appears that Edward Preble, with his forty-five floggings, punished more often than any other captain. To pause and analyze is to see that in *Constitution* Preble had three times as many enlisted men and petty officers as did Isaac Chauncey in *John Adams*; further, the record of Preble's punishments covers some thirteen months, while Chauncey's in *John Adams* is for approximately four months. The lines of Table 10 that are distorted by these disparities are the total number of floggings awarded and total lashes administered. One can get a much truer picture of the relative reliance of these captains on flogging as a form of discipline if one adjusts the figures to see what might have happened if each ship's punishment record had been equal in duration and if each captain had commanded the same number of petty officers and enlisted men.[18] If these hypothetical conditions could ever have existed, the captains in question would probably have awarded this many floggings to the enlisted men and petty officers under their commands:

Isaac Chauncey	*John Adams*	51
Melancthon T. Woolsey	*Sylph*	46
Isaac Chauncey	*Hornet*	37
David Porter	*Enterprize*	21
John H. Dent	*Hornet*	18
James Biddle	*Hornet*	17
Edward Preble	*Constitution*	15
William Bainbridge	*President*	7
William M. Crane	*Argus/Nautilus*	5

When the numbers are presented in this manner Isaac Chauncey and Melancthon T. Woolsey stand out as the captains most prone to use flogging to enforce discipline; Porter, Dent, Biddle, and Preble are seen as moderate to steady employers of flogging; Bainbridge and Crane resorted to flogging only as an infrequent cautionary example.

Some words of warning are in order about these figures. More than the means, medians, and modes of Table 10 these numbers would have been affected if the sailing masters who kept the logs were less than compulsive about recording every flogging. Except in the case of Biddle's *Hornet*, no way exists of verifying the completeness of any log, though in that one case the log's accuracy and completeness are fully vindicated.[19] It also needs to be kept in mind that this is only a numerical attempt to provide some sort of uniformity among records so diverse that they are difficult to compare. It does not necessarily follow that if Isaac Chauncey had had twice as many men in *John Adams*, he would have awarded twice as many floggings. To assume so would be to ignore the unpredictability of any particular collection of enlisted men whom chance and historical forces might throw together as a ship's company. The figures just given offer clear proof of the variability of ship's companies in this regard. When one equalizes Isaac Chauncey's punishment records for his successive cruises in *John Adams* and *Hornet* it is to find him punishing more frequently in the former than in the latter ship.

One is certainly entitled to ask, Are these nine captains truly representative of punishment practice throughout the navy? By definition a Thomas Truxtun or an Alexander Murray, men opposed in principle to the use of flogging, are not here. For at least one key figure of the pre-1815 navy, John Rodgers, no record of his shipboard punishment practice has thus far been found. The men here spotlighted are simply those captains whose punishment-recording logbooks have survived. Does the loss of other logs conceal some notorious sadist of the stripe of Wolcott Chauncey? There is no way to prove how representative of the navy as a whole these surviving punishment records may be. But when one looks at the names at the heads of the columns and sees there many of the navy's key leaders and role models, it is to feel a high degree of confidence that one is viewing a reliable cross-section of flogging on the captain's authority as practiced in the pre-1815 U.S. Navy.

What of the statutory provision that forbade a captain to flog a man in excess of twelve lashes without the sentence of a court martial? In nearly four out of ten floggings that limitation was circumvented or simply ignored. Some captains creatively subdivided a single incident into several charges. A seaman

Master Commandant John H. Dent as seen by C.B.J. Fevret de Saint-Mémin around 1809. His sundowner philosophy of discipline may betray a fundamentally flawed inner man, ill concealed by the callous, haughty persona he presented to the world. John Rodgers said Dent lacked stability of character. For certain Dent earned the contempt of his naval peers by his seeming maneuvers to avoid sea duty during the War of 1812. The shore command he retained throughout that conflict was his last active service, although he remained on the navy's roll of officers until his death at his South Carolina plantation in 1823. National Portrait Gallery, Washington, D.C.

stole some whiskey, got drunk, could not function properly on his watch, and mouthed off to the officer who had to cope with him. If the captain were so minded, this one case could be divided into four charges each bearing the maximum lawful penalty—theft (12 lashes), drunkenness (12 lashes), neglect of duty (12 lashes), insolence to a superior officer (12 lashes)—and a total of forty-eight lashes inflicted without violating the letter, if not the spirit, of the law. Edward Preble was the most faithful practitioner of this form of legalism. Other captains simply ignored the limitation. When Secretary of the Navy William Jones questioned John H. Dent on his practice of ordering punishments of three dozen and five dozen lashes on the Charleston station during the War of 1812, the veteran captain appealed to tradition as his authority. When there existed a need for serious and exemplary punishment, when a court martial could not be convened for a long time, and when the services of the prisoners were needed,

> it is well known that commanding officers of ships and stations have taken upon themselves to extend the punishment beyond what is specified in the Rules for the Government of the Navy and was sanctioned [in so doing] by your predecessors. It is also well known to every officer of the navy that one dozen lashes will make little impression on the minds of men not possessed of feeling or principle. There are many such who would at any time receive that punishment [in exchange] for an allowance of grog. Indeed, I have known such.[20]

John H. Dent practiced what he preached. In *Hornet* during 1806–1807 the smallest number of lashes he awarded was twelve, and nearly three-fourths (71.9 percent) of his recorded floggings exceeded that number.

Before the Court

There is another side to discipline. As important as the means used to enforce discipline are the reasons why enlisted men were punished. The logbooks scrutinized for flogging practices may also be sifted for the offenses with which the captains charged the seamen whom they punished, whether by flogging, by confinement in irons, or (in a few cases) by some alternative punishment. These fall into six broad categories: (1) alcohol-related misconduct, principally intoxication; (2) theft; (3) negligence in the performance of one's duty; (4) fighting; (5) desertion and absence-without-leave; and (6) disrespect to, or defiance of, authority. Although much that is historically interesting could be recovered by investigating these six categories in detail, the first four are more immediately appropriate to a history of the pre-1815 enlisted man than to the story of the officer. The last two are another matter. They will be explored not in connection with the punishments the captain inflicted on his own authority and recorded in the ship's log, but as part and parcel of disciplinary machinery of great formality and awesome power: the court martial.

In examining the enforcement of discipline by courts martial the historian is on firmer statistical ground than in looking at flogging on the captain's authority. Transcripts of all courts martial were supposed to be forwarded to the secretary of the navy for review. Proceedings against 128 enlisted men and petty officers (but excluding master's mates) who were tried and convicted between 1799 and 1815 have been found.[21] With the exception of the year

1805, trial transcripts for enlisted men are sparse before the winter of 1808–1809, but from that time forward the records appear to be reasonably complete and to offer a reliable picture of discipline by court martial (Table 12).[22]

What is most immediately apparent from analysis of this mass of court martial proceedings is that the pre-1815 navy reserved the solemnity of formal trial proceedings almost exclusively for two offenses that it considered especially subversive of discipline: desertion, which accounted for three-quarters of all convictions, and mutiny/sedition, with the latter providing about one-fifth of court martial convictions. Prosecutions for murder or attempted murder were rare occurrences in the early navy. In part this was because naval courts martial had authority to try murder charges only when the crime occurred outside U.S. territorial waters; other murders were remanded to the civil courts. One may further surmise that only a shipboard murder committed in the heat of passion or under the influence of alcohol was apt to be detected; premeditated murder was too easily concealed as an accident or a battle death. The single conviction for cowardice arose out of the search for scapegoats for *Chesapeake*'s 1813 defeat by the British frigate *Shannon*.

Why was it desertion that accounted for nearly three-quarters of all court martial convictions? Desertion was a most serious problem for the pre-1815 navy. During Edward Preble's command of *Constitution* in 1803–1804 one enlisted man or petty officer in ten (9.3 percent) terminated his relationship with the frigate by desertion. While Isaac Chauncey and John H. Dent commanded *Hornet* in 1805–1809 the desertion rate for petty officers and enlisted men was 12.8 percent.[23] Clearly, keeping ships manned and seamen on the job was a major anxiety for captains. But why? The idea that those who got away were the lucky ones who were able to escape hellish conditions in U.S. ships of war can readily be rejected. Save for slaves enlisted in the navy by masters who thereafter collected their wages, every man who served in a U.S. warship was there by his own choice, however influenced that choice may have been by alcohol. There was no draft, no impressment. The only form of coercion that may have been present would have been the absence of better opportunities because of one's social origins, one's economic options, or one's personal weaknesses, such as excessive fondness for distilled spirits. The escape-from-hell-afloat supposition may be further discredited by the fact that some deserters left the U.S. Navy for the British service—where conditions were no better and perhaps worse—while others would desert from one U.S. Navy ship only to enlist in a different U.S. Navy ship under a changed name.

Reading the seamen's autobiographies and their defenses when tried for desertion by courts martial suggests the answer to the question, Why was it desertion that accounted for nearly three-quarters of all court martial convictions? Although U.S. warship crews were highly disciplined and efficient—their safety at sea and their success in battle depended on it—individual members of these crews were neither automatons nor slaves in the service of the state. The seaman's philosophy was one of live for the day. Desertion was a way of asserting his value and independence as an individual human being, of expressing resentment at conditions he found oppressive, of ridding himself of officers with whom he was at odds, or of merely relieving boredom through change. Liquor could provide the trigger or the resolution to act on any of these motives. Of the hundreds of men who deserted from U.S. Navy ships between 1798 and 1815 only a small fraction were ever caught and punished.

Although six men were punished in Preble's *Constitution* in 1803–1804 for desertion or absence-without-leave, thirty-three deserted without being caught. Given such odds, it is understandable why courts martial treated desertion so seriously. Deterrence through fear of severe punishment was the only real hope of controlling the problem.[24]

Punishments Sadistic?

Only behavior that the navy regarded as the most damning kind of misconduct found its way before courts martial. One would expect the punishments handed down by courts to be correspondingly more severe. Were they?

The first and most obvious attribute of court martial punishments was the courts' preference for flogging as the premier punishment for enlisted men and petty officers. Of the 128 men convicted by courts martial, 1799–1815, flogging was the whole or a part of the punishment for 111 (86.7 percent). If the number of enlisted men and petty officers sentenced to be flogged but whose floggings were remitted on clemency recommendations be added, then an overwhelming 120 (93.8 percent) of those found guilty were condemned to receive this severe infliction. Here, if anywhere, is where the historian will find cruel and even sadistic punishments. Does one?

Not surprisingly, given the gravity of offenses referred to courts martial and the greater solemnity of the proceedings, flogging sentences of the courts were more severe than those awarded by the captains on their own authority (Table 13). Both the median and the most commonly awarded number of lashes assigned by those captains whose punishment records have survived was twelve; but the median number of lashes given the seaman unlucky enough to find himself convicted in court martial proceedings was seventy-two, while the most commonly awarded sentence was one hundred. Even more awesome in retrospect is the maximum court martial sentence of 320 lashes! The figures in Table 13 are, by themselves, somewhat misleading; a more revealing profile of flogging sentences awarded by courts martial is provided by Figure 5. For purposes of comparison floggings awarded by captains on their own authority (from Figure 4) are also shown. Two spikes, taller than the others, immediately call attention to the most popular court martial sentences: fifty lashes (fourteen cases) and one hundred lashes (twenty-eight). A closer look reveals equally interesting features. About one-third of all executed sentences were for thirty-nine or fewer lashes; nearly half of the sentences for sixty-four or fewer. Only in 17 out of 111 cases (15.3 percent) were court martial sentences in excess of one hundred lashes actually inflicted.

For all practical purposes two offenses, desertion and mutiny/sedition, were the ones courts martial spent almost the whole of their time judging. When it came to handing down sentences, the two charges received markedly different treatment from the courts (Table 14). Although mutiny/sedition accounted for only 17.7 percent of the convictions as between the two offenses, the convicted mutineers were awarded 28.2 percent of the lashes. The maximum sentences for desertion (270 lashes) and mutiny/sedition (320 lashes) may not look that different, but the minimum inflicted flogging for desertion was a mere six lashes, while the smallest flogging awarded for mutiny/sedition was a far more serious seventy lashes. If one looks at either the mean or the median sentence,

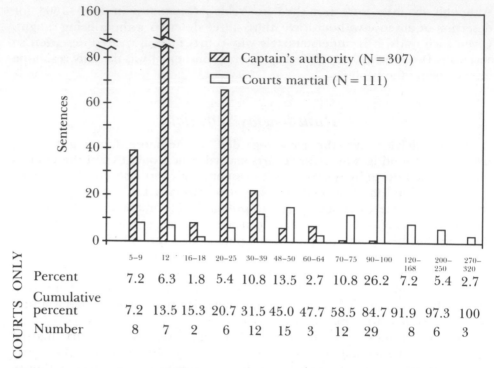

		5–9	12	16–18	20–25	30–39	48–50	60–64	70–75	90–100	120–168	200–250	270–320
COURTS ONLY	Percent	7.2	6.3	1.8	5.4	10.8	13.5	2.7	10.8	26.2	7.2	5.4	2.7
	Cumulative percent	7.2	13.5	15.3	20.7	31.5	45.0	47.7	58.5	84.7	91.9	97.3	100
	Number	8	7	2	6	12	15	3	12	29	8	6	3

Figure 5 Lash Sentences Awarded by Courts Martial Compared with Sentences on the Captain's Authority

the story is the same: mutiny/sedition is punished twice as severely as desertion. Only in the most common sentence, one hundred lashes, do the two offenses look alike. Desertion may have been the most frequent misconduct that courts martial considered, but there can be no doubt that, in the eyes of the navy's officers who made up those courts, mutiny/sedition was far and away the more serious crime. The exception to this general rule are sixteen of the seventeen punishments in excess of one hundred lashes.[25] Given the perceived gravity of mutiny/sedition one would expect that a majority of these severest sentences would be for this offense; but, in fact, ten of them are for desertion, only five for mutiny/sedition, and one for a combination of both offenses.

If flogging was the premier punishment awarded by courts martial, it was far from being the only one. Slightly more than one-quarter of the men flogged (30 out of 111) received some additional form of punishment and sometimes a combination of additional punishments. The most frequently awarded supplementary penalty was the forfeiture of pay, followed by reduction in rank, serving of additional time in the navy, and dismissal from the navy. Four men were sentenced to wear some kind of label as a mark of shame and of warning, a case in point being seaman Thomas Trask of *Constitution*, who was sentenced in October 1814 to receive thirty lashes with the cat-of-nine-tails and to wear on his back for the term of thirty days "a label containing, in legible characters, the word DESERTER."[26] Four of the six dismissals were ignominious ones, similar in character if not necessarily in severity to that of Peter Jealous described at the beginning of the chapter. Among these four ignominious dismissals are to be found the only two cases of branding awarded as a part of a sentence by a court martial in the pre-1815 navy.

In addition to the 111 men who were actually flogged by sentence of a court martial, 9 received flogging sentences but saw those sentences remitted because of a clemency recommendation. When seaman Samuel Miller of *Wasp* was tried for desertion in December 1809 he pleaded guilty and threw himself on the mercy of the court. That body responded with a sentence of fifty lashes with the cat-of-nine-tails, remarking that this was "the mildest punishment that they could possibly inflict for such an offense," but recommended him to Commodore John Rodgers as an appropriate subject for clemency because, immediately after Miller's guilty plea,

> Lieutenant John Trippe, a member of the court, voluntarily rose and made oath "that the prisoner, Samuel Miller, had been with him in the Enterprize for seven months, during which time he had behaved in an orderly manner; that he belonged to a boat where he had repeated opportunities of effecting his escape, and that he had never even made the attempt; [and] that the prisoner had never behaved in a manner to deserve or receive corporal punishment, and that he had never been even reprimanded."

Rodgers accepted the clemency recommendation and remitted Miller's fifty lashes.[27] Among the nine men sentenced to be flogged but granted clemency, five received no additional or alternative punishment; the other four each received one substitute infliction: a reduction in rank; the loss of pay; dismissal; and, in the case of Samuel Miller, a requirement that he witness the punishment of a shipmate who received the full one hundred lashes for desertion. Why were such a small portion of all flogging sentences remitted on clemency recommendations? Only enlisted-man cases that were regarded as serious offenses in which guilt was blatant, and in response to which there existed a desire to set the example of public trial and punishment, were taken as far as courts martial. Such a court involved a goodly amount of bureaucratic maneuvering before it could be convened, including, in U.S. waters, the prior consent of the secretary of the navy. Dubious and clemency-prone cases were more easily handled by the captain acting on his own authority.

Beyond the 120 convicted men accounted for thus far, 4 additional men received sentences that did not include lashes in any form, inflicted or remitted. These individuals received punishments that included one, or a combination, of the following: public reprimand, loss of pay, serving additional time, hard labor chained to a cannon ball, or already served pretrial confinement. A court martial sentence that did not incorporate flogging in some form played but a tiny role in the American tradition of naval discipline.

The quick mental calculator will have realized that 4 of the 128 men sentenced by courts martial have not yet been mentioned. A reason may have been suspected: these are the men condemned to death. In fact, the number of death sentences was actually six, but two men so condemned on mutiny/ sedition charges in *Congress* in 1800 had their punishments reduced to one hundred lashes each, loss of pay, and dismissal; they are included in the 111 executed floggings described above. Another court martial death sentence, one that was clearly disproportionate to the crime, was overturned by Secretary of the Navy William Jones because the court was convened without his prior approval.[28] That leaves a total of three death sentences that were actually executed between 1799 and 1815. What of the five crimes, including both desertion and mutiny/sedition, for which the "Act for the Better Government of the Navy" authorized the death penalty?

Truth is that looking exclusively at the law governing the navy gives an altogether more fierce and bloodthirsty view of naval discipline than if one goes the next step and examines actual practice. Whatever the law might authorize, the navy's officers awarded the death penalty only with the greatest reluctance. In practice, the officer corps did not feel a necessity to maintain discipline at the price of men hanging at the yardarm; but those same officers would have supported the retention of the death sentence authorizations in the law. Potential death sentences were held to possess strong deterrent value as ultimate sanctions that could be invoked in extreme necessity. The dire language of the law resonated, too, with a long tradition of naval justice inherited from the British role model; the pedagogical and conservative roles of tradition were not to be ignored. Divergence between possible punishments and actual sanctions imposed in the navy was only a reflection of a parallel divergence in civil society's criminal law and practice. In England the number of offenses defined by law as carrying the death penalty quadrupled during the eighteenth century; but during the same period, when so many more crimes were in theory punishable by death, the actual number of executions remained stationary or declined. In the early nineteenth century U.S. juries appear to have been measurably more reluctant to convict those guilty of certain crimes that carried a mandatory death sentence than when other punishments for the same crimes replaced the death sentence.[29] In this respect the navy's attitudes reflected those of the society that had created it. The possibility of inflicting a death sentence was seen as a potent force for maintaining discipline and order; but part of its potency came from the rarity of its application. Both officer and man knew the death sentence authority was there, ready to be used. On extraordinary occasions it actually was awarded, thereby demonstrating that capital punishment was still a real sanction. But to read only the law and to conclude from such reading that executions were a common occurrence in the pre-1815 navy would be grotesquely to misunderstand the real navy of that time.

The three death sentences actually carried out come at the opposite ends of the navy's pre-1815 history. In October 1799 seaman George Galligher of *Eagle* was sentenced to be hung at the fore yardarm of his ship for the murder of a shipmate, John Buckley. The two men had quarreled while Galligher was under the influence of alcohol—and with tragic results.[30] While it cannot be absolutely proved that Galligher was executed, because no muster roll survives for his ship, he almost certainly was. The fate Galligher suffered is the one he would have met in the civil courts for the same crime.[31]

Not until late in the War of 1812 did a court martial again see the need to execute a death sentence on a naval enlisted man. By that point in the war desertion had become a serious and rapidly growing problem on the Great Lakes; the navy felt itself driven to invoke the ultimate sanction. On the Lake Erie station in June 1814 seaman Henry Davidson found himself facing a court martial on a whole battery of charges: drunkenness, mutiny, theft, and desertion. Davidson was a serious disciplinary problem, but it was the final charge that sealed his sentence: "to be hung by the neck until dead . . . taking in consideration his former bad conduct and frequent desertions."[32] When seaman Robert

Elixson of *Superior* was tried for desertion in November 1814 on Lake Ontario the members of the court, in directing that Elixson be shot to death, were even more explicit than those at Erie regarding the reasons that compelled them to depart from the navy's long tradition of noncapital sentences:

> Having taken into their serious consideration the profligate repetition of the prisoner's offenses . . . the dangerous frequency of this offense, and the alarming consequences attending it to the naval service of our country, [the court] have reluctantly resolved to exert the power delegated to them by law and to endeavor, by one terrible example, to endeavor to deter others from thus withdrawing their services from the state in this season of national peril.[33]

Once the navy had demonstrated that it really would use its legal authority, did the death penalty prove an effective deterrent? It is impossible to say. The war ended too soon thereafter, and too many other factors then came into play, to enable the historian to measure a decline in desertions, if one there would have been. Is it reading too much into the court's words—"to endeavor to deter"—to say that these men invoked the ultimate sanction with a certain sense of futility? Did they suspect that the death sentence was a punishment most effective when left unused?

Death Sentences by Another Name?

Or were the officers really that reluctant to impose the death sentence? Some historians have asserted that flogging sentences involving 150, 200, 250, 300, or more lashes imposed by courts martial were really death sentences in disguise; they argue that the condemned man could never survive such a flogging.[34] Were men like John Baptiste—for desertion sentenced to receive two hundred lashes on his bare back with the cat-of-nine-tails, after which he was to have the left side of his head and one eyebrow shaved bare, be drummed out of the Boston navy yard and dismissed from the service of the United States—really being condemned to death?[35] To answer this question the subsequent fates of forty-five men sentenced by courts martial to receive one hundred or more lashes (and whose sentences were not remitted or reduced below one hundred lashes because of a clemency recommendation) were sought through the navy's surviving records on its enlisted men: its pay- and muster rolls. Although eight of the forty-five men could not be traced because the appropriate rolls have not been preserved, the fates of the thirty-seven men who can be so traced may safely be presumed to be representative of the entire forty-five who endured one hundred or more lashes.

Six men among the thirty-seven (16.2 percent), including Peter Jealous, were expelled from the navy in disgrace immediately after their flogging sentences were executed. There is no way to determine if they subsequently died as a result of the floggings. The historian notes, however, that Jealous had survived earlier floggings of 210 and 200 lashes to come back for more, so there is reason to think he probably survived 270 lashes just as well. Four seamen (10.8 percent) responded to their floggings in excess of one hundred lashes by deserting at the first opportunity and succeeded in making good their escapes. This small number is an interesting one. Given the ease of desertion and the low probability of getting caught, one would expect enlisted men to respond to severe punishment by deserting, as did these four. Or rather, one would expect it unless enlisted men in general, and punished men in particular, accepted the basic soundness of the navy's system of corporal punishment. The correctness of this supposition is supported by the fact that of the thirty-seven men who received one hundred or more lashes, nearly two-thirds (twenty-four or 64.9 percent) not only survived these intense punishments but continued to serve until the expiration of their enlistments or for as long as their careers may be followed in the muster rolls. Seaman Edward Jones of *President* received three hundred lashes on 8 November 1811 for mutinous and seditious conduct, the second most severe sentence ever inflicted by a pre-1815 court martial. Did it kill him? By no means. Did he take the first opportunity to escape from his ship? Not at all. Nearly two years later, Edward Jones was still present on active duty in *President*.[36]

That leaves exactly three instances in which a severe flogging sentence may have caused death or disability. On 25 November 1808 Thomas B. Bennett received two hundred lashes in *Argus* under a mutiny/sedition charge. The following 27 April he was discharged as "unfit for duty." Maimed for life, poor bastard, one thinks. Then the historian notes that the "unfit for duty" notation follows many discharges in this roll and is not so certain that a proven relationship exists between the flogging and the unfitness.[37] One of the two John Wilsons serving in *United States* was discharged in June 1812 to the hospital at Norfolk, Virginia. Is he the same John Wilson who had received the previous September one hundred lashes for desertion?[38] If he is and has been incapacitated, is it likely Captain Stephen Decatur would have waited nine months to conclude he was too injured to recover and be useful on shipboard? Improbable. Finally, there is the case of Anthony Merritt, also of *United States*, flogged one hundred lashes for desertion on 16 September 1811, transferred to *Wasp* the day following, and dead 10 February next.[39] A lingering death from the lash? Maybe. But Merritt might just as likely have fallen overboard and drowned or come down with a sudden fever. Only *Wasp*'s log may have recorded the cause of death, but it does not survive for this period.

In short, as far as the pre-1815 U.S. Navy is in question, there is no positive evidence that a single one of the sentences of one hundred or more lashes was a de facto death sentence. Perhaps one or more of these forty-five men did later die as a result of his ordeal—the mind has difficulty imagining an Edward Jones absorbing three hundred lashes and surviving—but there exists no evidence on which to base such an assertion.

22. The *Hermione* Phobia

MUTINY AND SEDITION, sinister words that resonate ominously in the mind, have been repeated many times in recent pages. Courts martial almost always tried men for one of two offenses, but they punished men far more severely when they were found guilty of mutiny/sedition charges than when the offense was desertion. What did those two words—*mutiny* and *sedition*—signify?

Both officer and enlisted man agreed on the idea that the words conjured. It was a phantasm that transfixed the imagination: the British frigate *Hermione* on the night 21/22 September 1797, when her crew, goaded to the breaking point by the sadism of her captain, brutally hacked to death with cutlasses and tomahawks and/or threw overboard to drown, the captain, three lieutenants, the lieutenant of marines, a midshipman, the purser, the surgeon, the boatswain, and the captain's clerk. The mutineers then sailed off to the Spanish Main in *Hermione*. Thirty-three of them were later apprehended or gave themselves up, of whom twenty-four were hanged; but more than one hundred other Hermiones simply faded from sight, never to be traced.[1] Given what is known about the ethnic origins of "American" mariners it is virtually certain that some former *Hermione* crew members, with changed names and silent prayers no one would recognize them, found their way into U.S. warships and were serving there during the pre-1815 years.

Certain, too, it is that the *Hermione* mutiny—swift, brutal, bloody, vengeful—and not the much more famous British mutinies at Spithead and Nore in 1797 captured the imagination of both quarterdeck and lower deck in the U.S. Navy. When the word *mutiny* was used, the image released, genielike, was of that ultimate revolt: murder of the officers and seizure of the ship. In *Essex* on 10 May 1800 an intoxicated William Ash, forecastle man, harangued the crew of the frigate and urged them to fall on the officers and serve them "as we did on board the *Hermione* and serve them right." No actual mutiny occurred and Ash quickly found himself clapped in irons, a situation in which he was still lingering 110 days later, when he wrote Captain Edward Preble begging for release, blaming his troubles entirely on alcohol, and telling his obdurate commanding officer, "I call Almighty God to witness that my heart is entirely innocent of what my lips uttered."[2]

Whether Preble released William Ash or kept him in irons till the end of *Essex*'s voyage in November is not known. If he suffered nothing more than a couple of hundred days in irons, Ash could count himself lucky. More serious was to be the fate of Robert Quinn, a seaman in *President* in 1804 who was discovered as the author of this letter addressed to Commodore Samuel Barron:

> The horrid usage that has been carried on in this ship of late by the principal officers is enough to turn every man's heart to wickedness. We are kept on deck from three o'clock in the morning till eight at night. There is no regulations in any one thing. We have been on deck for several days without one bit of victuals and durst not look for it. We cannot wash a single article for fear of being cut in two. You expect everything done at a word. There is no allowance made for our friging day and night. But the time will come when you will drive all thoughts of fear out of our minds. Tyranny is the beginning of all mischief and generally is attended with bad doings at the latter end. Any commander or captain that had the least feeling or thought would not suffer this horrid usage. It is almost impossible for us to live. The President is arrived to such a pitch as to exceed the Hermione. Some of our friends in America and other parts shall know of this shortly and in time we hope to get redress. Death is always superior to slavery.

> We remain Your
> UNHAPPY SLAVES

This was too direct a challenge to be tolerated. Even though Quinn pleaded guilty and put himself at the mercy of the court when brought to trial, his judges responded with the harshest noncapital sentence on record in the pre-1815 navy:

> To have his head and eyebrows shaved, branded in the forehead with the word MUTINY, to receive 320 lashes equally apportioned alongside of the different ships of the squadron, during which time he shall wear a white cap with the label MUTINY in large capital letters inscribed on its front, and to be drummed on shore under a gallows in a boat towed stern-foremost by a boat from each ship in the squadron as unworthy of serving under the flag of the United States.

Purser John Darby witnessed the simultaneous punishments of Quinn and John Kirkpatrick, the latter sentenced to 150 lashes for desertion:

> They were both stripped with a sheet thrown over their backs. Each of them had a white cap on, the words MUTINY wrote on one and the words the REWARD OF DESERTION wrote on the other. They were both tied in a boat called a launch, under a gallows which was erected for the purpose, and towed from ship to ship with five armed boats [to receive an] equal number of stripes alongside of each ship, [there] being five in the squadron now laying in Hampton Road. They both received their proportion alongside of the President [sixty-four lashes for Quinn; thirty for Kirkpatrick] and were towed by a boat from each ship alongside the Congress, where the mutineer, after receiving twelve stripes, fainted; he was then put into a boat and carried on board of the President to receive the balance of his punishment as soon as he was able to bear it. The deserter, being a strong Irishman, he was able to stand the whole of his punishment and was taken from ship to ship until he received the whole. Our ship [*John Adams*] was the last that he came to, and I think a more distressful sight I never experienced. . . . It is, to be sure, most cruel punishment, but the very existence of the navy require[s] it.[3]

Purser Darby forces the historian to face the central question, How did the officers, a minority of any ship's company, maintain their psychological ascendancy over a majority who outnumbered them so heavily? Was it only physical brutality, and the fear of it, that kept mariners from rising *Hermione*-style on their overbearing officers and throwing them into the sea? Surely there is something here or the *Hermione* fantasy would not have been such a pervasive one with officer and man. Arguing in favor of Darby's perception is the navy's use of a spectrum of physical coercion to enforce its code of behavior, ranging from casual brutality, through formal floggings, to rare death sentences. Arguing against Darby is the fact that service in the U.S. Navy was voluntary; sailors had other employment opportunities if they chose to use them. Equally telling is the argument that, because the organization worked, because internal order was maintained, and because missions were fulfilled—in short, because the navy did function effectively in the pre-1815 years—the vast majority of its officers and seamen must willingly have accepted their mutual roles and supported the system of hierarchy and discipline as it then existed.

Potent fetish though the *Hermione* incident was in the minds of officer and enlisted man, there was no *Hermione*-style mutiny in the U.S. Navy of 1794–1815. William Ash and Robert Quinn were not ringleaders in plots of bloody revenge, but single individuals acting as they did for reasons now beyond the hope of recovery. Still, the pre-1815 officer could hardly be expected to view those incidents from the Olympian perspective of two hundred years of U.S. naval history. For him the real *Hermione* mutiny was an event of the recent past. Its repetition, with him as a victim, was a genuine fear. Perhaps a Robert Quinn was a symptom of tensions heated almost to the flash point. Could one afford to take that risk? No, better one man should suffer punishment of exemplary brutality.

In point of fact, of all the times the words *mutiny* and *sedition* were applied to events in the pre-1815 navy, only one incident even faintly resembled the classic, *Hermione*-style mutiny, and little is known about that one incident. Almost all of the surviving facts are contained in a newspaper story datelined New York, 12 April 1800:

> The sloop of war Portsmouth, now in the stream, was, on the night of Thursday last [10 April], discovered to be on fire, which was extinguished without any injury. It was at the time supposed to have caught accidentally, but the conduct of the crew the following day excited strong suspicions in the minds of the officers, which led to an investigation; from which it appeared that measures had been concerted by part of the crew to mutinize after the ship had put to sea and to carry her into a French port. The principal ringleaders and a number of their accomplices were last evening secured and put under a guard on Governor's Island.

Portsmouth was commanded by the notorious and eccentric Daniel McNeill, whose own account of the business has not survived. From the one other source, a letter by Secretary of the Navy Benjamin Stoddert, it is known that McNeill believed seventeen men to be actively involved in the plot; that Stoddert told McNeill not to delay *Portsmouth*'s departure for France in order to hold a court martial; and that he instructed McNeill to leave the mutineers behind in jail as well as enough witnesses to try them. There the story abruptly ends.[4] Were the mutineers ever tried? No record of such a court martial survives. Did McNeill sail, but fail to leave his witnesses behind? It would have been entirely in character. Did the mutiny, on calmer investigation, prove the product of a mind too excited and too suspicious? The last is perhaps no farfetched outcome, for paranoia about mutiny may well have infected parts of the officer corps in the spring and summer of 1800. About four months later Lieutenant Richard Somers reported, "I had the pleasure of accompanying the commodore [John Barry] to New Castle, [Delaware], last week concerning some mutineers on board the Delaware, sloop of war. When, on examining, [Commodore Barry] found no proof against them, he then ordered them out of irons who had been confined for six weeks. The poor fellows, on their being released and seeing the commodore, gave him three cheers."[5]

Leaving aside such melodramatic, and perhaps specious, mutiny charges, what does the historical record show about the reality of mutiny/sedition in the pre-1815 U.S. Navy? Most of the men so charged were simply disruptive, defiant individuals whose conduct could not be allowed to go unpunished and order be maintained.[6] More interesting, and historically more important, are those incidents that illuminate the fundamentals of the officer–enlisted man relationship. Sailors who manned the navy's ships were not galley slaves. They were mariners by choice and had enlisted freely, if not always soberly. Given sufficient provocation, determination, and luck, they could desert, if they chose to run the rather low risk of subsequent capture. The strictest of discipline was the rule in the navy's ships, but this was the product of the dangers of life at the mercy of the sea, of the essential nature of a warship's role, and of the seafarer's live-for-the-day mentality rather than any conception of the seaman as a kind of conscript/prisoner, kept on duty by the lash and the gun. In that little wooden-walled world made up of officers and enlisted men each had certain tradition-defined roles to play and tradition-defined rules by which to play those roles. That there must be officers, subordination, regulations, obedience, and punishment the seaman—a visceral conservative—accepted at enlistment. Up to a point. When the officer tried to enlarge the traditional scope of his authority, when he attempted to abridge or abrogate in some degree the unspoken contract between the navy and the enlisted man, then was when the sailor balked and the words *mutiny* and *sedition* were heard on the officer's lips.

An incident from one of the frigate *Constitution*'s War of 1812 cruises under Charles Stewart well captures the enlisted man's sense of implied contract between officer and sailor, of his voluntary adhesion to the ship, and of the tenuous dependence of the officer's authority upon the enlisted man's voluntary assent to that authority. On 9 January 1814 Stewart mustered his crew and told them that it was desirable to extend the cruise on which they were embarked as long as possible; to accomplish this it would be necessary to reduce the allowance of each mess by one or two rations of bread and whiskey, although beef and pork would be served at full allowance. "To this proposal none seemed to assent," Stewart wrote in his journal. Presumably the crew murmured discontentedly or were silent and sullen looking, conveying through body language their lack of enthusiasm. Because *Constitution* had sailed from Boston only on the first of the month, the news that the men were so soon to be put on reduced rations must have come as a distinct and unwelcome surprise. The first lieutenant, Henry Ballard, thereupon suggested to his captain that the latter might get more enthusiastic cooperation if he reminded the men that they would be paid in cash for their undrawn rations. Stewart made the suggested announcement, "but the crew remained silent." Confronted with a crisis of command, Stewart contented himself with calling the roll of the ship's

Thomas Sully's 1817 bust portrait of Charles Stewart was the basis of the medal issued to commemorate the captain's capture of Cyane *and* Levant *in the last days of the War of 1812. Are the bright, alert eyes searching the horizon for enemy warships or for opportunities for profit through prize and freight? With Stewart, it might have been either.* United States Naval Academy Museum, Annapolis, Maryland.

company and dismissed the men. *Constitution* finished her cruise, returning to Boston in April without further commander-crew confrontation, but her captain had been reminded that his was not an authority without limits.[7]

An earlier, and quite typical, "mutiny" incident that involved the disputed frontier of authority and consent between officer and enlisted man had taken place in *Constitution* in June 1807, at which time the frigate had been stationed in the Mediterranean. *Constitution*'s crew were already restless because many two-year enlistments had expired, but the men whose time was up would not be discharged till the ship got home to the United States. Of the relief frigate, *Chesapeake*, there was as yet no definite news. On the evening of 8 June *Constitution* was anchored in Syracuse harbor. Her commander, Hugh G. Campbell, had gone ashore, leaving the first lieutenant, Charles Ludlow, in charge. Between five and six o'clock Ludlow gave the crew permission to go overboard to swim, but with the customary injunction to stick close by the frigate. A few minutes later he came on deck to discover two of the men farther from the ship than he allowed and seemingly swimming toward a nearby British frigate. Admonishing the officer of the deck, Lieutenant William Burrows, that he was not paying attention to what was happening on his watch, Ludlow told him to get the men back to the frigate. Burrows went forward to summon the men—they were swimming away from the frigate's bow—but he had to shout several times before he could make himself heard or obeyed. When at length he got the two alleged delinquents on board, Burrows ordered them forward on the forecastle and told them to pull off their jackets preparatory to receiving a flogging with a rope's end for disobedience of orders. (Visitors from shore were on the quarterdeck at the time, else the men would have been punished there, as was customary.)

The next thing Lieutenant Ludlow heard was the noise of men rushing toward the forecastle and three cheers being given. Then he saw Burrows, standing on one of the guns, surrounded by a crowd of angry sailors. Ludlow waded in to rescue Burrows, dispersing the knot of men in the process, and learned that John Smith, one of the swimmers, had responded to Burrows's order to strip for punishment by declining to remove his jacket and by refusing to stand and receive a whipping. Either before or just after Smith's refusal, John Hughland had stepped out of the gathering crowd of enlisted men and told Smith that he was a damned fool if he pulled off his jacket; then, turning to Burrows, he had asserted that Smith "should not be flogged." Simultaneously boatswain's mate George Prince, instructed to flog Smith, had thrown down his rope's end and refused to administer punishment. An angry crowd of men was continuing to collect, their mood exacerbated because Burrows had responded to Smith's refusal of punishment by aiming at him a lethal blow with a handspike, a blow avoided only through Smith's agility. The gathering crowd were cheering their assertive shipmates, and boatswain's mate William Pinkney had seized a crowbar in response to Burrows's wielding of his handspike.

Ludlow had walked into an ugly situation, but by now *Constitution*'s marine guard were under arms and Ludlow soon had Smith, Hughland, Prince, and Pinkney secured in irons. All was still far from well or even under control. Moments later Ludlow heard the crew vent their displeasure at his action by giving three cheers. Immediately he armed himself and all his officers and sent a boat, manned by a trusty crew, off in search of Commodore Campbell. While the officers were arming, the crew gave another three cheers. Taking up a general cry of "On the forecastle! On the forecastle!" they started rushing there as fast as possible. With admirable presence of mind, Ludlow ordered the drummer to beat to quarters, which had the tonic effect of silencing the men and restoring discipline. As the crew went to their accustomed posts one man, James Thompson, could be seen pulling another away from his quarters and shouting, "On the forecastle!" Thompson quickly joined the four enlisted men already in irons, and all five were secured just outside the cabin door under the watchful eye of two sentinels. Calm at last restored, Ludlow called the roll, ordered the drummer to beat the retreat, and told the men to get their hammocks and bed down for the night. When the starboard watch was set at eight p.m. all was peaceful, though officers and marines remained under arms.

A few minutes later Hugh G. Campbell's boat pulled alongside; within seconds the crippled captain appeared in the gangway. One glance took in the marines and the officers under arms. "Follow me to my cabin," he told Ludlow, then he stumped off muttering, "I fear me there is some misconduct among the officers as well as among the crew." Exactly how Campbell acted to restore discipline is not clear from the record. Several matters had heated officer-enlisted relations to the boiling point. From the sailors' perspective they were being unjustly detained in the navy after their enlistments had expired, a situation calculated to put them in an ugly mood. Then there was Ludlow's and Burrows's overreaction. The swimmers had been heading not for the British frigate but to a buoy ahead of the ship. They had been delayed in responding to Burrows's shouted orders because the sound of water in their ears had drowned out his first commands. The punishment was, in the eyes of the shipmates, not only unjust, but the latest and worst evidence of what they saw as Ludlow's and Burrows's excessive reliance on the lash at small provocation. Finally, there was the issue of flogging men whose enlistments had expired, always a tender point with sea lawyers among the navy's enlisted men. Although Campbell almost certainly made it clear to his junior officers that they could have handled the situation far better had they been as skillful as he at command, the captain nevertheless reported the incident to the secretary of the navy when *Constitution* at last got home in October 1807; in doing so, Campbell recommended court martial for the five principal offenders, whom he had, until that time, kept in "close confinement" because their "conduct has been of so atrocious a nature." Robert Smith demurred at the idea of trying, half a year after the alleged offense had taken place, men whose enlistments had expired; they were let off with a simple discharge—word the five men must have received with great joy.[8]

After close scrutiny of the rather petty events labeled mutiny and sedition in the pre-1815 U.S. Navy, it is necessary to remind oneself that these were the offenses most severely punished by courts martial. Authority, deference, and obedience were so integral to the idea of a military force that the officer corps could, and often did, bring its harshest sanctions to bear on those who challenged that structure, even though, to later eyes, the specific incident and the administered punishment may seem grossly disproportionate. Officer and enlisted man were consenting parties to a mutual relationship that had been evolving for centuries. Essential to the effective functioning of that relationship was the officer's sense of responsibility for the welfare of his subordinates. So long as this sense of responsibility existed in appropriate measure, officer and man lived and worked in an adequate degree of harmony for the organization to function effectively. But, for some officers authority and discipline outweighed and obscured responsibility to subordinates. Then the officer-enlisted relationship went sour. The new ethos of liberty, of man's individual worth and of his freedom, provided an appealing alternative to the philosophy of deference, most especially on those occasions when the latter was perverted to an attitude of all authority and no responsibility.

Hermione's mutiny was a beacon example of violent revolt in the name of that new philosophy of man. A fantasy can be a safety valve that prevents an actual explosion. The *Hermione* fantasy served that safety valve role, as did hundreds of little acts, be they the cases of indiscipline, insolence, and rebellion that found their way into the pages of the court martial transcripts or the anonymous shot rolled along the deck at the unwary teenage midshipman with his grand and overbearing airs. In no ship of the U.S. Navy did the officer-seaman relationship deteriorate so far as to touch off a *Hermione*-style mutiny. But surely some enlisted men thought, "If things get bad enough I could do it"; and some officers certainly feared, "Do conditions appear so bad to the men that they will do it?" Both officer and enlisted man of the pre-1815 navy lived and worked with the bloody phantasm of the *Hermione* close to the surface of the collective memory.

Did the Punishment Fit the Time?

The navy of 1794–1815 operated in turbulent and contradictory social currents set in motion by deep changes in society's collective mindset. Since the sixteenth century and perhaps longer most European and American men and women had accepted the necessity of harsh, even brutal, corporal punishment as essential for maintaining the greater good of a stable social order. In the last decade of the eighteenth century and the first decade of the nineteenth other ideas were on the wind: the dignity and worth of the individual person might be paramount to the collective needs of social order; men were seen as equal before the law; no person had a natural or a God-given right to use or exploit another human being. Such philosophical persuasions had their political expressions in the American and French Revolutions. Mariners had found congenial, and had sailed for several centuries under, the older philosophy of deference with its emphasis on the collective good, hierarchy, subordination, implicit obedience, and the corporal sanctions to protect these deeply held beliefs. But the navy could not remain immune to the force of changing attitudes. Long-unchallenged beliefs and practices, corporal punishment among them, were being called into question in the name of the new philosophy of man.

In 1800–1801 one John Rea, who does not appear to have been a professional mariner, made a cruise as an ordinary seaman in the U.S. ship *George Washington* under Captain William Bainbridge. About a year later, in 1802, Rea published a twenty-four-page pamphlet, *A Letter to William Bainbridge Esqr., Formerly Commander of the United States Ship George Washington, Relative to Some Transactions on Board Said Ship during a Voyage to Algiers, Constantinople, &c.* Rea's is a savage, and seemingly more or less accurate, exposé of the young Captain Bainbridge's despotic brutality during the voyage. One paragraph will have to serve as an inadequate sample of the pamphlet:

> Would it be believed, was I to mention the case of J. *Robinson*, whom you put hands and feet in irons, for *intoxication*, and whose *scull* you afterwards, for *a little impertinent language, fractured with your sword*, bringing him to the deck— whom you then took out of irons, streaming with blood, seized up at the gangway and gave *thirty* lashes with the cat on the bare back! "Have you no compassion on a poor buggar, after splitting his scull, to whip him so?" said he, looking over his shoulder at you. "No," replied your *honor*, "I have no compassion on such a d——d rascal." "Then whip away, and be buggar'd," said he—"I'd rather *die* than *live*." He was however put in irons, as before, and kept in confinement at least six weeks; though part of the time, through rage, vexation and pain, labouring under such strong convulsions that four men were obliged to keep watch with, and were scarcely able to hold, him!![9]

Rea's is an attack on one captain and certain of his subordinates, not on the practice of corporal punishment as such, but he frames the attack in terms of the new view of human freedom and dignity: "The news of your arrival in the *land of freedom*, once more, affords me greater satisfaction than any other of a recent date," Rea begins his pamphlet:

> It has been my determination, since we made the Rock of Gibraltar [on our outward passage to the Mediterranean], if I should ever be so fortunate as to set my feet *at liberty*, on my native shore, to do myself the *honor* of addressing you in public. . . . *You* was then invested with power, which in the hands of a man as destitute of reason and humanity, as you, was truly dreadful: and *I* divested of every privilege of a freeman—even the privilege of vindicating my own innocence. But . . . we are now on a level—on the main deck of America, where "all men are equally free." *You* are divested of your tyrannical power;

and *I* am invested with the liberty of speaking, and writing.... Being very young when the American Revolution commenced, the principles which gave rise to it, are ingrafted in my nature; and I am, to this day, what is vulgarly called a *Democrat*.[10]

Contrasting views of human nature and freedom set the philosophical stage on which were acted out many of the incidents that would lead to charges of mutiny and sedition. They also prepared the way for the ultimately successful antiflogging movement that would divide the navy in the years before the Civil War. Therein, too, lie the roots of a problem for the historian. The historian not only knows the more recent history—what happened to naval flogging after 1815—but also is steeped in the humanistic sensibility that produced the change. Compounding the problem, the sources of information on naval corporal punishment that lie closest at hand were products of, or heavily influenced by, the campaign to abolish that corporal punishment. The historian is in peril. One runs the risk of subtly or explicitly measuring the past by the moral or social standards of the present, customarily to the denigration of past actors, and almost always with an implicit, and perhaps unconcious, assumption of human progress.

If the historian wishes to see some portion of the past not as better or worse, but as different, then the years 1794–1815 offer an excellent point at which to examine corporal punishment in the U.S. Navy. The surviving records, though far from as extensive as one might wish, permit quantitative measurements in which one can have reasonable confidence. While there was already debate on the efficacy and appropriateness of corporal punishment in the pre-1815 years, that debate had not become polarized and emotional, as it was to be in the middle years of the nineteenth century.

Leaving aside the casual, day-to-day presence of the whack over the back or the buttocks with a rope's end or a rattan, a presence that cannot be measured from surviving records, only a small proportion of the men serving in the U.S. Navy at any given time experienced corporal punishment. In the two ships, *Constitution* and *Hornet*, for which confinement records have survived, less than 12 percent of the men were subject to this, the mildest of formal punishments. On board *Constitution*, a ship with a reputation for stern discipline under the tough Edward Preble, fewer than four men in one hundred found themselves confined in irons. Moving up the scale of severity to flogging on the captain's authority, the highest portion of men in a ship's company so punished was 13.3 percent, the lowest 2.7 percent. One man in ten is a reasonable approximation of navy-wide practice.

For the minority of enlisted men who did suffer a formal flogging at some point in their careers the severity of the experience was by no means as sensational as the anecdotal and polemical literature of the nineteenth century might lead the reader to suppose. In the case of flogging on the captain's authority, almost 88 percent of all men flogged received twenty-four lashes or fewer; floggings of twelve or fewer lashes were, in fact, inflicted in something more than six out of ten cases. Roughly 85 percent of court martial sentences were for one hundred lashes or fewer; about one-third of the sentences involved not more than thirty-nine lashes. When the historian focuses on punishments of 100 or 150 or 200 or 300 lashes and fails to put them in a comparative perspective, the result is to draw attention to a real, but relatively minor, aspect of naval discipline and to distort, to exaggerate, and to sensationalize the practice.

None of this is to argue that a flogging of even twelve lashes was anything but a painful ordeal. If it had not been so, the captain or the court martial would not have ordered it. None can question the objective fear inspired by the prospect of a severe flogging. In July 1809 seaman David Kennedy deserted from the frigate *President* and William Bainbridge sent two midshipmen, John Packett and George W. Hamersley, in pursuit of him. The midshipmen overtook an intoxicated Kennedy about thirteen miles outside of Baltimore, and, as Packett later related, "in putting him in the stage [to return to *President*] he drew his knife upon us, and we had a great deal of difficulty to get it from him; at length succeeded and put him in the stage with the assistance of several others. He was very obstinate and said he would rather die than to be flogged through the fleet."[11]

Most immediately, flogging was a punishment directed at that small minority of any ship's company whose behavior could not be made to correspond to essential norms of conduct by any other means. Above and beyond individual behavior modification, flogging had a cautionary purpose. It was theater, a kind of seagoing morality play, and neither the captain nor the court martial was subtle in pointing out the lesson that it taught. Sentences of one hundred lashes apiece, to be inflicted in twenty-five-lash segments alongside *General Pike*, *Madison*, *Sylph*, and *Oneida*, were awarded in January 1814 to quarter gunner Samuel Lolly for disobedience of orders and disrespectful and abusive language to a superior officer, and to ordinary seaman Thomas Johnson for desertion. William M. Crane, senior officer on the Lake Ontario station in the absence of Commodore Isaac Chauncey, approved the sentence and ordered its execution "not without hopes that the example placed before the crews of the squadron may be attended with a beneficial effect. The magnitude of their crimes would warrant a much more severe punishment; and the lenity of the court on this occasion it is hoped will make a proper impression."[12]

Brutal? Perhaps by some twentieth-century standards, but any person inclined to condemn life in an eighteenth-century warship as brutal would do well to reread a detailed account of the trench warfare on the Western Front in World War I or of the Pacific Islands campaigns of World War II before rushing to judgment. One needs to remember that the men in question, whether officers or seamen, were not clergymen in their studies, lawyers in their offices, merchants in their countinghouses, or scholars amid their books. They were men of action: tough, highly physical, live-for-the-day-and-live-hard people, who inhabited an environment that rendered human violence pallid in comparison with the violence of nature, and one where disease was a sudden, silent, potent, and often mortal enemy. To those who lived in such a world, punishment that was painful, harsh, and quickly executed was neither alien nor inappropriate.

Corporal punishment continued to be used by the world's navies in general and by the U.S. Navy in particular because it was practical and effective. Practical, because certain forms of misconduct demanded severe punishment to discourage their repetition; but keeping any number of men in confinement on shipboard for a length of time posed difficulties. These could be avoided by a short confinement and a flogging. The transgressor was thereafter returned to duty, unless he were one of that small percentage of scofflaws so hopeless of reform that discharge at the next port was the only remedy. Moreover, like it or not, the only data thus far discovered indicate that enforcement of discipline by corporal punishment *did* deter undesirable behavior (Table 11). One could correctly argue that these data are limited. More punishment records would be welcome. But, thus far, nothing has been discovered to invalidate the conclusion drawn from the existing numbers: corporal punishment was used because it was a proven and an effective means of controlling undesirable behavior.

Indeed, the infrequency with which the captains and the courts martial had to employ flogging may be seen as evidence of its effectiveness as a deterrent. Speaking of a Louisiana plantation whereon the great majority of the slaves were whipped at least once, one historian points out,

> The frequency with which a punishment is administered is a poor measure of its effectiveness in curbing errant behavior. Presumably, it is the *fear* of eventual punishment, not the ex post administration of punishment, which motivates or deters behavior. But there is no obvious correlation between the number of times an individual is punished and his fear of being punished. A slave need never have felt the lash to know the consequences of disobedience. Indeed, the execution of a punishment is an indication of the failure of the punitive system. *A successful system of physical discipline would experience few lapses of behavior and exhibit a low incidence of actual punishments.* A high incidence might simply indicate that the prescribed punishment was not a strong deterrent.[13]

To which analysis the historian of naval corporal punishment can only say, Amen.

Although corporal punishment was widely accepted within the navy's officer corps, such acceptance was by no means universal. Thomas Truxtun was its most eloquent and convincing opponent, but even he did not entirely abjure the use of flogging. Probably few of Truxtun's fellow captains felt themselves able to equal the commodore's feat of maintaining authority by the sheer force of his personality, a formidable asset of which ample documentary testimony survives and vibrates with life to this day. The idea that flogging might be abandoned as a means of maintaining discipline was not unknown to pre-1815 military men. Corporal punishment had been abolished in the French army— during the Revolution, significantly—and the Prussian army partly abandoned the practice in the course of the Napoleonic Wars. In the British Parliament there was substantial but largely unsuccessful opposition to flogging, more especially as it was practiced in the army. Just before the War of 1812 Congress forbade the use of whipping punishments for members of the militia ordered into actual service with the U.S. Army. Although the prohibition technically protected only former militiamen, the army as a whole observed it. This hardly amounted to an abolition of corporal punishment or a new spirit of humaneness in discipline, for in practice the army simply substituted cobbing—paddling with a board or strap—for flogging with a whip. Flogging formally returned to the U.S. Army's panoply of sanctions in 1833 as a punishment for desertion when ordered by a general court martial and was not entirely abolished in the land forces till August 1861.[14]

All of these abolition movements focused on the land forces. Flogging in the sea services did not come in for serious scrutiny, perhaps because it (unlike army flogging) was largely out of sight from the public eye, perhaps because of a generally accepted notion that the ship, a lonely object at sea, possibly hundreds of miles from the nearest assistance, required this severe sanction to support authority and sustain order. The navy's civilian leadership was certainly aware of the emerging opposition to flogging. In 1814 tough-minded William Jones, himself a former merchant captain, argued to William Bainbridge,

> As to the improvement of discipline by corporal punishment, the best examples of discipline in the universe are to be found where corporal punishment is unknown. It may brutalize, but cannot reform; and its adoption in the service of a mild and humane people would display a strange dereliction of principle when the most enlightened and able officers, even in the British service, where the practice has had the sanction of ages in its support, protest in the most solemn manner against its continuance.[15]

Jones's words struck no responsive chord, either in the mind of William Bainbridge or in that of the navy's officer corps in general. Left to itself, the pre-1815 officer corps would never have abandoned corporal punishment.

Officer and seaman were consenting parties in a relationship that had been evolving for centuries, one with its own philosophy, responsibilities, rules, and rituals. It was a relationship in which both parties accepted the essential rightness of hierarchy and the sometimes distasteful propriety of rough, corporal discipline to maintain that hierarchy. The evidence suggests that, on balance, pre-1815 enlisted men supported corporal punishment as a means of discipline in about the same degree as did their officers. Some totally rejected it; most saw it as a painful necessity. Basic acceptance of corporal punishment by the enlisted force is reflected both in the reality that the navy was able to keep its ships voluntarily manned in an economy that was often a seller's market for the services of seafarers, and in incidents such as that recorded in the journal of the brig *Nautilus* for 26 June 1812: "This day John Bray was tried by the crew for desertion and was sentenced to run the gauntlet five times, which punishment he received."

One should probably hear with skepticism the notion either that enlisted men who were flogged were marginal members of a ship's company or that the man who had been severely flogged became a secretive, degraded, sullen individual, all self-respect destroyed. There is no intrinsic reason why a flogging should lower a mariner's status in the eyes of his peers. It might have the opposite effect, serving to validate his superior status as a tough man who could take a tough punishment.[16] One piece of evidence may be cited. Among the ten handpicked enlisted volunteers who participated in Richard Somers's heroic, highly dangerous—and, in fact, fatal—attempt to blow up the Tripolitan shipping with the infernal *Intrepid*, on the evening of 3 September 1804, were two sailors who had experienced corporal punishments by Edward Preble's order: William Harrison, flogged twelve lashes for neglect of duty three months earlier, and Hugh McCormick, punished with twelve lashes for a similar offense in October 1803 and confined in irons from 21 October till 9 December 1803 for attempting to desert.

Few comments survive in the record to tell how pre-1815 enlisted men felt who actually experienced formal floggings. Given what is known about the sailor's attitudes, there were certainly those who shrugged off corporal punishment as a price to be paid for getting caught breaking the rules of the elaborate and well-understood ritual that constituted the officer-enlisted relationship, just as there were surely those of the get-it-over-with school of thought who preferred the briefer pain of a flogging to an extended period in confinement. To read the writings of the enlisted men themselves is to learn that there is no inconsistency in the picture of a man who would run the risk of punishment to enjoy forbidden pleasure, and who could still be a fine seaman or a heroic fighter.

For longer than anyone knew or could discover corporal punishment, the application of direct and often brutal physical force, had been an important means by which the maritime world maintained internal order. In 1794–1815 it still was. Even in a later navy, long after flogging had been forcibly retired, rough, highly physical justice lived on as a means by which naval seafarers policed themselves.[17]

PART SIX
Competing for Honor

Ambition. The motivation to achieve. A desire to stand higher than certain of one's fellow human beings. Name or describe such a driving force as one wishes, it played a key role in the lives of the navy's officers of 1794–1815. This inward fire burned especially bright in those relatively few officers who sought fame through heroic deeds. Its more common manifestation was the desire for advancement in rank, advancement that brought public acknowledgment of one's achievements. A successful naval career could provide financial security, but wealth only occasionally. Once an officer was fairly launched in his career, his search for the psychic rewards of rank became the primary incentive to accomplishment.

All military organizations demand some kind of hierarchical command structure. These command structures may be less or more elaborate, but the theory of command dictates that they be pyramid-shape: the few in number command the more numerous, who in turn command the many. The higher one climbs on the pyramid, the smaller the number of posts available to be filled.[1] Advancement to a higher place on the pyramid is measurable, public evidence of superior status, ability, or achievement. For purposes of examining matters of rank in the U.S. Navy of 1794–1815 the image of a pyramid is not the most appropriate one; better to think of a ladder much narrower at the top than at the bottom. Throughout the pre-1815 years this ladder had only four rungs: midshipman, lieutenant, master commandant, and captain. Advancement up the ladder was essentially a competitive process. Among the young men who survived the weeding out as midshipmen the motivation to achieve, to climb to the higher rungs of the ladder and receive this public recognition of worth, was strong. A history of the pre-1815 officer corps that failed to examine the desire to climb and the competition among the climbers would be seriously incomplete.

Surgeons, surgeon's mates, and pursers sought other goals in their naval careers than the public recognition conferred by upward progress through the ranks. But there was one category of officers for whom promotion—or, to speak more accurately, the denial of its possibility—caused keen distress. These were the navy's sailing masters. By 1815 they constituted nearly one-fifth of the officers on active duty. The desire of at least some among them to step onto the promotion ladder at the lieutenant rung is a special part of the story of rank and promotion in the pre-1815 navy.

The Shape of the Ladder

Although more than twenty-nine hundred individuals served as officers in the U.S. Navy before 14 February 1815, the focus of attention here will be one man in ten among *them: the 306 who entered the navy at one rank (midshipman, sailing master, lieutenant, or master commandant) and were promoted to a higher rank or ranks before 1 June 1815 (Table 15).*[2]

So far as numbers were concerned, and, consequently, the amount of time and attention the Navy Office devoted to the matter, three-quarters of the promotions were from the midshipman or sailing master ranks to lieutenancies. Lieutenant was the single most crucial rung on the ladder, the one that primarily concerned the vast majority of serving officers of the pre-1815 navy. Forty-six young men who had entered the navy as midshipmen by April 1804 advanced to the navy's second highest rank, master commandant, by June 1815. A smaller cadre, twenty-one individuals, traversed the entire rank structure from midshipman to captain between the Quasi-War with France and the approximate end of the War of 1812. Here is clear testimony of the opportunities for advancement in a young organization, one that was almost continually involved in active warfare or near-warfare conditions and the abilities of whose members were constantly being tested through arduous active duty or actual combat.

Thirteen officers who entered the navy at the rank of lieutenant because of previous experience at sea and one man who transferred from the revenue cutter establishment at the rank of master commandant also advanced to captain by the end of the War of 1812.

Why is the hint of a smile tickling at the corners of this man's mouth? Perhaps it is because he can count himself among the twenty-one able and fortunate men who traversed the navy's entire rank structure, from midshipman to captain, between the Quasi-War with France and June of 1815. Many a year would pass before the officer corps would again experience so happy a climate of rapid upward mobility. The sitter is Charles Goodwin Ridgely. He is in his mid-thirties. On the other side of the easel: portraitist John Wesley Jarvis. Private collection and the Naval Historical Center, Washington, D.C.

Although this group was small in absolute numbers, it embraced many of the men who were the navy's key combat and administrative leaders through the War of 1812 and (in some cases) for many years thereafter: William Bainbridge, James Barron, Hugh G. Campbell, Isaac Chauncey, Isaac Hull, Edward Preble, John Rodgers, John Shaw, John Smith, and Charles Stewart.

23. Discovering Merit

*I*F THE STORY of promotion in the U.S. Navy of 1794–1815 is not to dissolve into a bewildering swirl of ambitions, self-seeking, contention, and hurt feelings, one needs to understand the issue of principle that spawned this gale of emotion. From the earliest days of the pre-1815 navy the story of promotion threads its way along one disputed question: How large a role should merit play in selecting those promoted?

There exist two theoretical models that a military organization may follow in choosing those who are to rise to the next highest grade. Either the authorities charged to select officers for promotion—in the case of the pre-1815 navy, its civilian leadership—may pick those individuals they judge the most capable of performing at a higher level of responsibility, or they may allow the rule of seniority to operate mechanically: those with the longest periods of service at a lower rank are those who advance when there are vacancies at the next higher rank. The argument supporting choice-by-merit is apparent. Although the method is far from infallible, it offers the strongest likelihood that those men with the greatest abilities will be available to fill the most demanding posts. Less obvious, but equally real, is the case for the seniority system. The criterion that it employs is clear and readily measured. It can nurture the inner harmony and morale of an organization by removing a cause of competition, jealousy, and injured feelings. Promotion-by-seniority obviates the abuse (or the suspicion of it) to which the merit system is prone: favoritism. Persons of average ability, who make up the mass of any organization, almost always feel more comfortable with, and less threatened by, the seniority system than its alternative. In reality, neither of these pure models for promotion—merit vs. seniority—can be entirely practical for a military organization. Save perhaps under the supremely demanding conditions of wartime, no leadership, in selecting officers for promotion, could afford to ignore entirely the criteria of experience and the relative length of that experience in favor of pure native ability; the risk of failure would be too high and the organization would soon be in turmoil. Likewise, any system, however rigidly committed to promotion-by-seniority, must have ways of bypassing those who are incapable of rising to a higher level of command and responsibility.

Which Shall Prevail?

Respecting the pre-1815 navy it is a fair generalization to say that the civilian leadership, with some quiet support from key leaders of the officer corps, was the primary force for merit-based promotion. The officers themselves were, by and large, mind and emotions, committed to promotion by seniority.

During the Quasi-War years, when the corps grew from a mere handful of officers in the early months of 1798 to approximately seven hundred individuals in July of 1800, promotion policy was a mixed bag, although Secretary of the Navy Stoddert laid down a number of principles that he attempted to keep from disappearing beneath the waves as he worked to get the navy afloat and fighting. As late as August 1800 Stoddert was reserving the right to appoint men directly to the rank of lieutenant as new ships were put in commission. In reality, however, this practice, common in the earlier years of the Quasi-War, was by then dead. Of the 102 men who received direct appointments as lieutenants in the Quasi-War navy, 94 were commissioned before December 1799. Whenever midshipmen qualified by sufficient experience were available, the secretary preferred to promote his lieutenants from among them. He steadily maintained that young men who entered the service as midshipmen had a stronger commitment to a naval career than did the experienced merchant masters appointed as lieutenants. The latter, Stoddert thought, often would make a cruise or two and then, already weary of a naval life, return to the merchant service.* But, he was careful to specify, midshipmen should always be selected for promotion on the basis of merit, "without regard to dates of their warrants."[1]

In the matter of promotions, as in so much else that concerns the professionalization of the navy's officer corps, it was Robert Smith, with his longer term of office and presiding, as he did, over a smaller and relatively more stable body, who enunciated principles and regularized practices that would govern advancement in the navy at least through the War of 1812. Smith's philosophy: Promotions from midshipman would be made on the basis of merit and experience, but in cases of young men with equal merit and experience the most senior in terms of their original appointments would be the first promoted. This policy was repeatedly stated, in letter after letter, throughout Smith's term of office, but never more lucidly than when he wrote Midshipman Daniel Todd Patterson at the end of May 1803: "When promotions are making we shall be guided in the selection more by the service and qualifications of gentlemen than by the date of their warrants. Where qualifications are equal, we shall respect the time of service as well as the seniority of

---

* Stoddert's opinion is only partially supported by the record. Of the 102 men who received direct appointments as lieutenants in the navy during the Quasi-War with France, 85 (83.3 percent) served three and a half years or less. But, among the eighty-five, at least forty-five served until the end of the Quasi-War, at which point the postwar reduction in force terminated their naval careers willingly or otherwise. Only thirteen men who were appointed lieutenants directly from civilian life during the Quasi-War had naval careers that exceeded seven years in length; however, the thirteen included Edward Preble (9.4 years service), William Bainbridge (35.0 years), John Rodgers (40.4 years), Isaac Chauncey (40.7 years), Isaac Hull (45.0 years), James Barron (53.2 years), and Charles Stewart (71.7 years). In expressing his opinion Stoddert seems to have been operating more on impression than on hard data.

appointment; but, in cases of inequality in merit, the most meritorious gentlemen will be preferred."[2] When Robert Smith passed over a senior midshipman in favor of a junior, it was a signal either that the neglected young man had better modify his behavior if he expected promotion—"Mr. [William P.] Smith has been unfortunate in not having acquired as much experience as some of his junior brother officers, and this is attributable entirely to himself, as he failed to embrace the opportunity afforded him in the year 1802 of acquiring professional knowledge"[3]—or that his resignation would be acceptable and perhaps wise.

Robert Smith wrote often about his principles in selecting men for promotion from midshipman to lieutenant. He was silent on his rules for promotion above the rank of lieutenant. There were areas of administration wherein Smith was prone to keep his own counsel, never reducing to writing his reasons for particular decisions. Access to the navy's highly restricted upper ranks was one of them. His principles in these matters must be entirely inferred from his practice, a subject to be taken up in the next chapter. Paul Hamilton wrote nothing of significance respecting promotion policy during his three and a half years in office. His successor, William Jones, reaffirmed Smith's principle of the primacy of merit in the selection of lieutenants: "If you have conceived the idea of *rank* among *midshipmen,* you are mistaken," Jones told one allegedly aggrieved young man. "No such principle ever has prevailed nor ought to prevail. They are all novitiates, and the rule is to promote them according to their several merits, acquirements, and services."[4] By then this particular principle was so well established that Jones was compelled to spend little effort defending it, in contrast to Robert Smith's frequent and necessary restatements. However, Jones took the policy one step farther and applied it vigorously in selecting those lieutenants who would be advanced to master commandant. Jones judged he had an especially strong reason to be highly selective at this particular step: "Naval promotions above the rank of lieutenants become immensely important. The honor of the nation is as completely involved in the command of a sloop of war as in that of a frigate. The commander is *in chief* and without control, everything depending upon his skill, judgment, and prowess. . . . The promotion from lieutenants to masters commandant is a most important step indeed—a distinct and important command requiring the highest degree of professional knowledge and experience."

For Jones seniority as the basis for claim to promotion was especially unpalatable: "If seniority of date was the absolute rule, the task would be very simple and less irksome to the secretary; but it never has been—*it never ought to be*—except where merit and knowledge are equal in the candidates. . . . I pray [seniority] may never become the absolute rule; for I should, from thence, date the decline of our infant naval Hercules, unless, as in some other countries, the executive could promote an indefinite number to get at an officer of distinguished merit and talents." The Navy Office must reserve the right to pick at will from the roll of lieutenants those men most likely to be capable of, and to distinguish themselves in, the responsibility of commanding a ship. Reservation of this right was grounded in Jones's view of the human condition:

> Were [promotion] otherwise [than on the basis of merit], genius, valor, talent, and skill would be leveled to the dull equality of the humblest pretensions; and, instead of those brilliant feats which adorn our annals, every commonplace automaton who performed the ordinary acts of duty with sufficient prudence

to avoid court martials would rise, by the mere lapse of time and the casualties of mortality, to the highest honors of his profession. . . . The inherent inequality of man demonstrates the absurdity of indiscriminate claims to this vital trust [command at sea]. Again, gallant and distinguished actions have an indubitable claim to precedence, even where the merits of officers may, in other respects, be equal. Were it not so, the best stimulus to noble deeds would be destroyed. But others are equally brave and pant only for the opportunity. True. But it is the use of opportunity that develops the real character of an officer, and equity must yield the palm to him whom hard-earned victory crowns.

It was, as William Jones was the first to admit, easy for the secretary of the navy to assert the primacy of merit in the selection of officers for promotion. Far more difficult was the task of discovering the most meritorious among those clamoring for it.[5]

Testing Spawns Testiness

Who were the officers most qualified for promotion? Why not give the candidates a test to find out? Robert Smith had the same idea after he had been in office about a year. "Midshipmen and sailing masters," he decreed in a general order of 18 August 1802, "before they obtain commissions of lieutenancy, will hereafter be duly examined by a board of two or more captains of the navy specially constituted from time to time by this department in each and every case." He charged the first such examining board "by the strictest examination and inquiry [to] satisfy yourselves with respect to [the candidate's] knowledge and skill as a seaman and also with respect to his habits and principles as a man of honor."[6]

For about two and a half years Smith's examination system worked well. Between August 1802 and March 1803 nine midshipmen went before boards, passed the tests, and received their commissions.[7] If there was serious opposition to the examination system, the record of those objections has failed to survive. Then it became a casualty of the Tripolitan War. Both the Edward Preble and the Samuel Barron/John Rodgers squadrons, with their large numbers of ships, had needed far more lieutenants than held commissions or were allowed by law. Legal limitations or no, lieutenants there had to be, if the war was to be fought. Robert Smith appointed some midshipmen as acting lieutenants; Preble and Barron appointed more. All of these young men hastened to acquire lieutenants' uniforms, moved to better shipboard quarters, dined in the wardroom, and commanded their former midshipman peers. When it became possible to commission these men formally as lieutenants, Robert Smith sent their commissions to Barron with instructions to let the candidates know that the commodore had the coveted documents, which would be issued as soon as they presented themselves to an examining board and passed the qualifying test. The commissions all bore the same nominal date (18 May 1804); seniority was to be established by numbers to be assigned on the basis of perceived merit; other qualifications being equal, relative standing as midshipman was to be respected. In mid-November 1804 Barron appointed his examining board and at least thirteen midshipmen were notified that the board was ready to hear them. Five appeared. Sybrant Van Schaick "answered perfectly to the satisfaction of the board" and presumably left the room in confident expectation of soon receiving his permanent commission. John Trippe, his heroic conduct in the battles off Tripoli the previous summer notwithstanding, received only a laconic "will do" rating from the board; Christopher Gadsden was evaluated "will not do at present"; Joseph J. Maxwell "will not do exactly." Both were told to try again in six months. Samuel Blodget fared a little better. He "will do in preference to some others," but was instructed to wait three months, then take the examination again.

Where were the other eight would-be lieutenants? Perhaps word was out that the board, under the chairmanship of John Rodgers, was being tough. Samuel Barron reiterated Robert Smith's order: no examination, no commission. Still, as far as the record shows, all the other candidates fought shy of the examining board. Midshipman and acting lieutenant John M. Gardner explained to Rodgers that he had secured Samuel Barron's permission to postpone his examination until after he returned to the United States: "I hope the gentlemen who compose the court [i.e., the examining board] will not attribute my declining to appear before them for examination to any other cause than my own feelings. I have acted as lieutenant upwards of two years. If I should not be so fortunate as to pass the board and still hold the same rank on board the President, I never could reconcile it to my feelings to appear on her decks as an officer."

Surely Gardner spoke for all his fellow acting lieutenants. To appear before the board and fail rendered one's status ambiguous at best. In the worst case it might compel one to revert, Cinderella-like, to humble midshipman. Better to procrastinate, to sidestep the examination, and to see what the future might bring. What happened next is not entirely clear in the surviving records. Apparently there were too many acting lieutenants, appointed by too many authorities, too sensitive about their enhanced but threatened status, and too easily able to circumvent the examination. Neither examining board nor squadron commodore was willing to assume the invidious task of deciding an order of merit and seniority under such circumstances. Samuel Barron was too ill—and too lenient when well—to pursue the matter vigorously and firmly with his difficult young subordinates. By the time John Rodgers assumed command of the squadron in May 1805 the relative seniority situation was so hopelessly muddled that he passed the buck back to Robert Smith: such lieutenant-aspirants as presented themselves for examination would be heard; if qualified, they would be certified to the department as such; but any determination of relative rank would have to be made after the ships and officers returned to the United States. Even then the candidates might, if the secretary so decreed, have to submit to reexamination to determine their relative pretensions to rank.[8]

Though no one may have recognized it at the time, Rodgers's decision was the last gasp of the examination-before-promotion policy. Robert Smith apparently concluded that there was small hope of persuading proud young men who had been serving and strutting as acting lieutenants for two or three years to take a test to prove that they were qualified to do what they had been doing. The whole vexed question was allowed to slumber uneasily, with ships heavily or entirely staffed by acting lieutenants, until the winter of 1806–1807. By then Congress had increased the number of authorized lieutenants to seventy-two. Following considerable investigation of the times at which midshipmen had been appointed acting lieutenants in the successive Mediterranean squadrons, Smith proceeded to issue sixty-one lieutenant's commissions dated between

January and March 1807, with relative standing based on the information he had collected.[9]

In the aftermath of Smith's abortive experiment, no examinations were held to determine worthiness for promotion until several years after the end of the War of 1812. Faced with the decision of which men to promote, Secretaries Smith, Hamilton, Jones, and Crowninshield each and all depended on precisely the same method Benjamin Stoddert had employed.

Eyewitnesses of Their Conduct

When Stoddert recommended John Mullowny to President John Adams for promotion to captain in May 1799 he required few words to do the job: "Lieutenant Mullowny, of the frigate *United States*, has been a lieutenant ever since the 9th March 1798 and is very strongly recommended by Captain Barry as a good seaman. Everybody speaks of him as a brave man."[10] The rationale was a simple one: Mullowny, the second eldest lieutenant in the navy, had been serving in *United States* for more than a year as the second lieutenant to Commodore John Barry, the navy's senior officer and its most prestigious figure, who "very strongly recommended" him for promotion. The president readily agreed. (The navy's and the frigate *United States*'s senior lieutenant was in disciplinary hot water and was not considered for this promotion, which otherwise would have been his.)

Although it had probably wrenched him to see it go astern, Robert Smith's examination-before-promotion policy had been only a secondary tool in determining the men best qualified for advancement. When it became a liability, he could afford to let it drop without seriously compromising the quality of the officer corps. For Smith, as for Stoddert and every other secretary, it was what a junior man's commanding officer said about him that carried the most weight when it came time to pick for advancement. "In judging of the qualifications of gentlemen in the navy [for promotion]," Smith himself admitted at a time when the examination policy was still in force, "we are guided by the reports of their commanding officers, who, being eyewitnesses of their conduct, can, in most respects, form a more correct opinion of their merits than we can."[11]

The surviving files of the Navy Department bristle with letters from commanding officers recommending subordinates for higher ranks. Picking a single letter to represent them all is no enviable responsibility, but one written by Master Commandant James Biddle to Secretary William Jones about a month and a half after the death of James Lawrence in the *Chesapeake-Shannon* battle of June 1813 is perhaps as good an example as can be offered of the words, the facts, and the reasoning on which secretaries of the navy based their decisions:

> I take the liberty of recommending to your notice acting lieutenant [David] Conner of this ship [*Hornet*] as an active and meritorious officer. On my joining this ship the late Captain Lawrence spoke to me in terms of high approbation of Lieutenant Conner's deportment during the whole period of his being with him; and, since my being in command here, his conduct has been such as to give me entire satisfaction. To Commodore Bainbridge, with whom he served as a midshipman, Mr. Conner's merits are well known. In 1811 Mr. Conner was promoted to be [acting] sailing master of this ship and continued to perform the duties of that station until September last, when he was appointed an acting

lieutenant by Commodore Bainbridge. Under these circumstances, and knowing it to have been the intention of the late Captain Lawrence to have interested himself in this promotion, I have taken the liberty to address you in his behalf. I feel much reluctance in taking upon myself to address you on such a subject; but my reluctance has been overcome by the recollection that the N[avy] Department, for the most part, can know the merits of the junior officers only from the reports of their commanders.[12]

Biddle not only throws the weight of his own prestige behind Midshipman Conner's promotion, he conjures up the specters of the dead James Lawrence and the very much alive William Bainbridge to put every ounce of available clout into the endorsement. It was an effective letter, and well timed. If there had been any question in the mind of Secretary Jones whether Conner was ready for inclusion in the long list of lieutenant nominations that President Madison sent to the Senate on 23 July 1813, Biddle's letter certainly removed them. David Conner was soon in possession of his lieutenant's parchment.

As best one can judge from the historical record, the system of depending on commanding officers' enthusiastic endorsements, such as the one Biddle gave Conner, got the job done. The navy's combat performance in three wars

The future probably never looked brighter to David Conner than it did when John Wesley Jarvis painted the lieutenant in his mid-twenties. A badly wounded hero of the Hornet-Penguin *battle of 1815, now nearly fully recovered and about to embark on an extended cruise to the Pacific as* Ontario's *first lieutenant, Conner confronted his responsibilities bright-eyed, handsome, tested and proven, self-confident but approachable.* Frick Art Reference Library, New York.

is the strong supporting evidence that the method picked good men. So too is the fact that among the 306 men promoted from one rank to another before 1 June 1815, only 12 (3.9 percent) were dismissed or forced to resign during that same period. But the practice suffered from two serious weaknesses.

First, the system was to some degree haphazard. It depended on a commanding officer spontaneously remembering to report on the merits of this or that valued subordinate—and many commanders were highly conscientious about this responsibility—or on the aspiring officer asking his superior for such a letter, as David Conner probably did. Fitness reports, that is, the systematic collection of information on the abilities, qualifications, and performance of all officers, were not an ongoing practice in the pre-1815 navy. Such reports were collected in 1801 and 1809, at the time of the reductions of the corps, as a means of determining which officers to retain in the service; but the closest the Navy Office came to requiring the periodic completion of such documents was under Robert Smith, who often asked commanding officers returning from cruises to submit evaluations of the officers under their command. In this vein, Alexander Murray, just back from patrolling the southern coast in *Adams*, furnished Smith with brief but eloquent notes on each of his recent subordinates:

> Lieut. [Charles] Gordon, an excellent officer
> Lieut. [Jacob] Jones, a good officer but unaccommodating
> Doctr. [James M.] Taylor, an excellent surgeon
> Doctr. [Robert Smith] Kearney, his mate, worthless and indolent
> Mr. [Isaac] Garretson, purser of the first rate
> [Midshipman] Edward Nicholson, well disposed but dull and inactive
> [Midshipman Alfred] Hazard, a smart young officer
> [Midshipman William L.] Travis, middling
> [Midshipman George R.] Rice, unfit for naval service

And so on through a list of sixteen other names.[13] Such evaluations were brief and to the point, but they gave Robert Smith all the information he needed to determine who were the promising officers.

Smith's system, incomplete as it was, lapsed during the tenure of Paul Hamilton, who depended on oral evaluations and individual endorsements in letters of recommendation rather than on comprehensive attempts at information gathering. By the time William Jones had been in office half a year he realized that the selection of the right men for promotion had hung, to far too great a degree, on the information that the secretary of the navy "may chance to acquire of the relative merits and qualifications of the officers." The paper records of the department were of precious little help, because such recommendations and evaluations as might exist were usually buried in the mass of retrospective correspondence that no responsible administrator could ever find the time to sift.[14] To remedy this situation Jones drafted a proposal that would have required the commander of a naval station in the United States in July of each year, and a ship's commanding officer at the termination of each cruise, to submit a fitness report on the officers serving under him, stating (1) date of warrant, acting appointment, or commission; (2) age; (3) physical and mental capabilities; (4) knowledge of writing, grammar, arithmetic, mathematics, and nautical astronomy; (5) actual naval service and other nautical experience; and (6) "moral and general character in all the essential requisites of an accomplished officer." These reports were to be compiled in a register that would be a principal source of information when it came time to select men for promotion. Jones's idea never got beyond the draft stage. Presumably he decided that the middle of a war was no time to attempt to institute a new personnel procedure and deferred the promulgation of his general order till after the conclusion of hostilities. By the time peace came, Secretary Jones was out of office.[15]

The second serious defect from which a system of depending on endorsements from commanding officers suffered was that some recommending officers had more clout than others. The subordinate, try though he and his parents might to get him placed under a particularly well-regarded commander, was really at the mercy of the Navy Office as to whether he was ordered to a ship wherein he could earn powerful backing. It is impossible to read the surviving records for the pre-1815 navy without concluding that there were some senior officers who stood in especially high regard with the secretaries and who, consequently, had excellent track records at securing promotions for their able subordinates. When an Edward Preble, a John Rodgers, a William Bainbridge, a Stephen Decatur, or an Isaac Hull threw his full support behind an officer, advancement came promptly. Let the recommendation be from a commanding officer who did not enjoy the full measure of the secretary's confidence—say, Alexander Murray during Robert Smith's tenure of office or Oliver Perry during William Jones's[16]—and promotion could be discouragingly slow.

But *slow* is a vague and a highly subjective measure of time. It is the perception of the impatient one who waits. High time to seek more concrete dimensions of the promotion experience in the pre-1815 naval officer corps.

24. Impatient Youth

EVERY SECRETARY OF the navy spent an inordinate part of his term of office reading letters exhorting him to promote Midshipman So-and-So who, in the writer's eyes, was badly overdue for advancement to lieutenant. The larger the officer corps grew, the more incessant the clamor: from the officers themselves, from their parents, from the parents' political cronies. "The *excessive* impatience of youthful ambition must be checked," declared William Jones late in 1813, his own patience at an end.[1]

If the surviving letters are to be believed, the aspirants, their parents, and their friends were rarely prepared to be realistic about time and experience when the object of desire was a commission at the next higher grade. Sixteen-year-old Ralph Izard, a midshipman for less than two years with but limited experience at sea in that period, could, in all seriousness, write his mother from Boston in August 1801 as he prepared for what he expected to be a one-year cruise to Europe and the Mediterranean, "After our return from the Mediterranean we are informed that those young officers who behave themselves in such a manner as to merit [a] recommendation and certificate of their proper behavior from the captain and officers may make themselves sure of lieutenancies; and I shall be very proud if I (when I return home) can have the honor of wearing a *swab* upon my shoulder."[2] Young Mr. Izard would have to wait until 1807 before he held that coveted lieutenant's commission in his hand.

Illusions of the unrealistically swift fulfillment of ambitions were by no means the exclusive prerogative of naive midshipmen. David Conner, who just a few pages ago was delighted to secure his promotion to lieutenant in late July 1813, had, by early October of the same year, bigger game in view. "We have [in *Hornet*] a crew of as fine fellows as ever stepped a ship's deck," he told his sister Rachel.

> Captain Biddle, of whom you may have heard, as he hauled down the Frolic's flag for her, commands us, and your dear brother is first LIEUTENANT!!! Mr. [John T.] Shubrick, who was first lieutenant, has been so ill that he went on shore and finally left the ship. It's a higher rank than I expected. However, promotion now will be very rapid, and I don't despair of obtaining a command by the end of eighteen months, should I keep my head clear that long.[3]

Even with the impetus provided by his heroic role in the *Hornet-Penguin* battle, David Conner was not to receive his first independent command until 1821, and the postwar slowdown in promotions would prolong his climb to the next rung on the ladder, the rank of master commandant, for eleven years and eight months.

How Swift the Climb?

Among the pre-1815 secretaries of the navy Robert Smith was the most articulate and insistent in expressing the minimum experience a midshipman should possess before promotion to a lieutenant's berth was appropriate. "I have learned since I have been in the Navy Department that it requires many years to make a navy officer," he told President Jefferson late in 1805. "Although most of the officers introduced into the navy since the year 1800 have been constantly at sea, yet not one of them is qualified for the station of a lieutenant on board a man-of-war." The reason was not far to seek. "The duties of a lieutenant are arduous and require a degree of professional knowledge which is not generally acquired by less than four or five years of actual service," explained Smith as he fended off importunities to promote a midshipman with two and a half years of service. "A lieutenant having the charge of a watch is often entrusted with the entire command of the vessel—hence the absolute necessity of his being an experienced seaman." Even as he was clearing his desk at the end of his tenure as secretary, Robert Smith was still fighting to maintain his standards. When Jefferson gently twisted his arm to promote to lieutenant a midshipman of less than two years' standing, Smith balked: "He cannot possibly have acquired in this short time that knowledge of seamanship which would justify the placing him in a situation where a public vessel, with the lives of all on board, might depend upon his skill as a seaman."[4]

The navy's surviving paper record is completely silent on other questions: How long should a lieutenant serve before he became a master commandant? Or a master commandant before promotion to captain? What of minimum age requirements for each rank? Even if the paper record were not silent regarding normative expectations, the historian would still want to know how much congruence existed between official desire and daily reality in the pre-1815 navy. What was the true relationship between age and rank? How long did men actually serve in rank between promotions? To what degree did merit prevail over seniority in promotions?

Age

Chronological age was rarely a direct factor in the promotion decision. Apart from the handicap that the Navy Office had only a general sense of how old many of its officers were, quality and length of service were the primary determinators of eligibility. A man's age when he attained a particular rung of the ladder was heavily determined by the age at which he entered the corps (Chapter 6) and by the Navy Office's success in maintaining its minimum service requirements at the next lower rank. Even so, it is still helpful to have an idea of how old an officer was likely to be when he mounted a particular rung on the ladder (Tables 16, 17, and 18).

Viewing the pre-1815 navy as a whole, the typical midshipman (the median man) was twenty-two years old when he received his lieutenant's commission.[5] If he was eventually promoted to master commandant, he gained that rank at twenty-nine, and he was thirty-two if he was one of the select company who ran the entire course from midshipman to captain between the Quasi-War with France and the end of the War of 1812. Occasionally new lieutenants were as young as sixteen or as old as thirty-five; one man made master commandant at twenty-two; another (Stephen Decatur, as it happens) was a captain at twenty-five, at which benchmark many of his age peers considered themselves lucky to have their lieutenant's parchments in hand.

Knowing that there was an occasional youngster or oldster attaining promotion can be a red herring. The real question is whether most promotions occurred in a particular clump of ages. With midshipmen-turned-lieutenants (Figure 6) the prime years were twenty through twenty-four. More than two-thirds (67.2 percent) gained their coveted promotions then. Nearly nine out of every ten new lieutenants (84.6 percent) were between nineteen and twenty-six years of age. Although the smaller numbers of men promoted to master commandant and captain do not lend themselves to visual presentation, still there is a distinct age window associated with each rank. Nearly three-quarters (72.9 percent) of lieutenants-turned-masters-commandant were between twenty-seven and thirty-two years of age; three-quarters (74.2 percent) of the captains attained the navy's highest rank somewhere along the ten-year time line between ages twenty-eight and thirty-seven, with the greatest concentrations (41.9 percent) in the years from thirty through thirty-three.

It may be helpful to think of the median age at which each rank was attained (lieutenant at twenty-two, master commandant at twenty-nine, and captain at thirty-two) as the crest of a wave. These ranks are not waves that are marching along, distinct and equidistant; rather, they are overtaking one

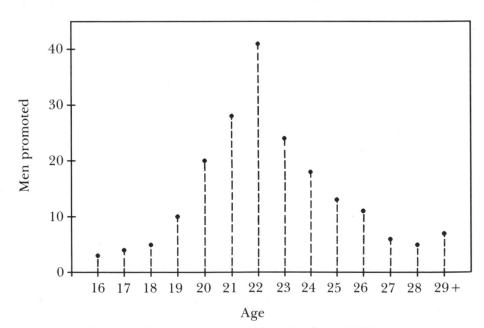

Figure 6 Lieutenants: Age at Promotion from Midshipman

another and merging, most particularly at the upper ranks. At age nineteen approximately one-third of the midshipmen are just beginning or have not yet begun their careers in the navy. By that same age, one lieutenant in ten (11.2 percent) will have his commission in hand. At the master commandant and captain ranks, the successive waves, while still distinguishable, have virtually merged, for there was little clear-cut distinction between the ages at which men might expect to become masters commandant and the ages at which they might anticipate captaincies. By age thirty nearly half (45.2 percent) of the captains have attained the navy's ultimate goal; but at that same age more than one-third (37.5 percent) of the future masters commandant are still waiting for promotion from lieutenant. If one man aged twenty is beginning his career as a midshipman while another of the same age is now a commissioned lieutenant, if a senior lieutenant's age peer is already one—and, in some few cases, two—rungs ahead of him on the promotion ladder, the basis has been laid for intense professional jealousy and anxiety.

For lieutenants (Table 16) active warfare meant gaining the lieutenant's commission a year or two younger than in more normal times. During the Quasi-War with France the median age of new lieutenants was twenty-one; during the War of 1812 it stood at twenty-two. In between, especially during the cold war of 1807–12 with Great Britain, in a navy only partially mobilized, the median age for promotion rose to twenty-three and a half. The Tripolitan War years, 1802–1807, when one would expect the median age of new lieutenants to drop because of active hostilities, are an anomaly: the typical new lieutenant is twenty-two years old. This, of course, reflects the examine-or-not-to-examine dilemma, narrated in the last chapter, which held up all lieutenant commissions between March 1803 and January 1807. If normal commissioning had occurred in these years, the typical age would have dropped to twenty-one and, perhaps, lower.

Because so little is known about the ages of the Quasi-War's relative handful of masters commandant, there are only two groups of men of this rank to compare: those promoted May 1804–July 1812 and those promoted March 1813–March 1815 (Table 17). Contrary to the situation that obtained with the lieutenants, masters commandant who obtained their promotions during the War of 1812 were, on the average, slightly older than those promoted during the Tripolitan War and the interwar years.[6] The reason is not far to seek. The War of 1812's thirty newly promoted masters commandant were almost exclusively men who had entered the navy as midshipmen during the Quasi-War with France, men who had become highly experienced and senior lieutenants during the Tripolitan War and the years of American-British tension; men who had been waiting impatiently for places to open up for them at the next rung on the ladder. They included some of the navy's soon to be famous commanders—James Biddle, Johnston Blakeley, Thomas Macdonough, Daniel T. Patterson, Oliver Hazard Perry, Lewis Warrington—thirty-year-olds consumed with anxiety that the War of 1812 might be over before they could get to sea in command of their own ships. The earlier group of masters commandant, the men promoted between 1804 and 1812, had been more of a mixed bag. It included the likes of John Cassin and Jacob Jones (masters commandant at ages forty-seven and forty-two respectively) who had begun their naval careers rather late in life; other men—Isaac Hull, Charles Stewart, John Shaw, Isaac Chauncey—with substantial merchant service experience before they joined the navy; and still others—David Porter, James Lawrence, John H. Dent (at twenty-two the youngest master commandant)—most of whose formative career experiences had been received in the navy. Had the War of 1812 continued for another two or three years, there certainly would have been a measurable drop in the typical age of masters commandant.

With newly promoted captains the age picture at different periods between 1798 and 1815 is the reverse of that for masters commandant (Table 18). Captains were getting younger as the navy matured from the Quasi-War through the Tripolitan War to the War of 1812. Of necessity, the lieutenants and masters commandant promoted to captain during the Quasi-War with France had to be men with extensive experience at sea prior to their naval appointments. Under such conditions, their typically higher age is no surprise. Similarly, a majority of the captains promoted between 1804 and the summer of 1812—Isaac Hull (33), Charles Stewart (27), John Shaw (34), John Smith (30), Isaac Chauncey (34), and John Cassin (54)—entered the navy with sufficient experience in responsible posts in the merchant service to justify bringing them on board at the entry rank of lieutenant; they, too, would, on average, be somewhat older when they attained the ladder's topmost rung.

However, the pattern is not simply one of the typical captain getting younger all the time; it is more complex. At the same time that most new

Olivio Sozzi's 1805 watercolor-on-ivory miniature of Stephen Decatur, Jr., is clearly a product of the romantic movement; but, far more than better-known portraits of the subject, it reminds the viewer that, at age twenty-five, Decatur was the most youthful person to attain captain, even in the pre-1815 young man's navy. The uniqueness of Decatur's age should not, however, be exaggerated; others were but a year or two behind him. **United States Naval Academy Museum, Annapolis, Maryland.**

captains were reaching that rank at a younger age, it was also becoming increasingly difficult for exceptional men to become captains in their mid-twenties. During the Quasi-War both John Rodgers and William Bainbridge had gained the top rung at twenty-six. Stephen Decatur made captain at twenty-five and Charles Stewart at twenty-seven during or in the immediate aftermath of the Tripolitan War. But the War of 1812's youngest captains—Charles Morris, Daniel T. Patterson, and Oliver Hazard Perry—were all comparative oldsters at twenty-eight before they reached the top. The earlier years had been less structured; opportunity for rapid advancement was more open for persons with unusual abilities and the good fortune to be in the right place at the right time. As the navy became more established and professionalized, training up its own leaders from the ranks of the officer corps, it became more and more unlikely that a young man would find himself in a position of responsibility that enabled him to gain the high degree of distinction that could bring a captaincy at twenty-five or twenty-six or twenty-seven.

Experience

The more structured and professionalized the navy became, the more potency did length and quality of experience acquire in determining when a man was going to be promoted. Of the two factors, length of service is the more easily measured (Table 19). A typical midshipman entering the pre-1815 navy could expect to serve between five and six years at that rank before he received his lieutenant's commission. An additional period of roughly six and a half years of experience was necessary before he might advance to master commandant; when he attained that rank he would be perhaps twelve and a half to thirteen and a half years into his naval career. For the officer who traversed the entire course from midshipman to captain by June 1815, the master commandant's commission was a rung on the ladder where he paused only briefly—a little less than two years—before climbing. Then, finally, he was at the topmost rung: captain, fourteen and a half years after he first received a warrant and walked the deck of a U.S. warship. For the twenty-one men who made that swift passage it must indeed have been a heady experience of success.

How well did U.S. Navy practice adhere to Robert Smith's criterion of four to five years' actual service before promotion from midshipman to lieutenant? The record (Figure 7) commands respect. Nearly nine out of every ten (86.5 percent) new lieutenants possessed at least four years of active-duty experience; two-thirds (64.5 percent) had a full five years or more to their credit. Indeed, the track record is actually better than that, because twenty-five out of the thirty-five midshipmen promoted to lieutenant with less than four full years of experience actually gained that promotion during the Quasi-War with France, when the navy was not old enough to possess any midshipmen who had served four years in rank. If these twenty-five are dropped out, the result shows a Navy Department highly consistent with its stated policies: nearly every midshipman promoted to lieutenant (95.7 percent) displayed a minimum of four years on his service record.

Indeed, during both the Tripolitan War years and the cold war period of August 1807–May 1812 young men were typically trained and tested for approximately six and a half years as midshipmen before they were commis-

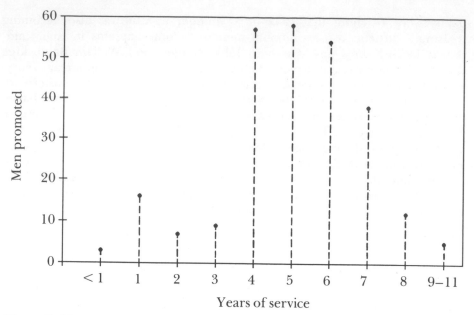

Figure 7 Lieutenants: Years of Service Completed When Promoted from Midshipman

sioned (Table 20). During the War of 1812 this typical probationary period dropped to something just over five years; then, fifty-six men received the lieutenant's parchment in less than five years, while a lucky eight had it handed to them with less than four years' wear on their midshipman uniforms. Robert Smith had said it took four to five years to train a good lieutenant. Were these rapidly promoted young men of the War of 1812 really up to their jobs? Perhaps not.

"I lament to say, Sir, that I fear promotion has been too rapid lately for the good of the service," John Rodgers commented to William Jones as early in the war as October 1813.[7] "I agree," replied Jones defensively, responding at length to Rodgers's offhand comment; but, he went on to explain, the expansion of the navy to meet wartime conditions left him no acceptable alternative. Naval forces on Lakes Ontario and Erie alone demanded as many officers and men as were needed to man five 44-gun frigates, and more new ships were under construction on the seaboard. The alternative to the promotion of relatively inexperienced midshipmen was to go outside the existing corps of officers and bring in experienced master mariners as lieutenants, as had been done with mixed results during the Quasi-War with France. It was an option the corps was prepared neither to welcome nor to accept. "If it is true that promotions have been too rapid of late," concluded Jones, "it is a good argument for suspending further promotions."[8]

Brave words, but in fact Mr. Jones had no realistic choice other than to continue promoting less than fully trained midshipmen to lieutenant. Some of these fast advancers compiled admirable records. Predictably, others turned out in a fashion similar to two young men who found themselves under Thomas Macdonough's command at the battle of Lake Champlain in September 1814. Concerning the age of Nathaniel Lawrence Montgomery there is conflicting evidence. The most reliable indicates that he was only twelve when he received his midshipman's warrant in January 1811. He cannot have been older than fourteen when he lost an arm in *President*'s running fight with *Belvidera* in 1812. Two years later, Montgomery, now sixteen at best, participated in the battle of Lake Champlain and was again wounded. The pair of serious combat wounds facilitated Montgomery's promotion to lieutenant on 9 December 1814, at which date he was possibly still sixteen, though he may just have turned seventeen. In either case, he had been a midshipman a mere three years and ten months. That Montgomery had "behaved well" in the battle of Lake Champlain, Macdonough was the first to admit, but "his merits, as to knowledge of his profession, hardly entitle him to a lieutenant's commission."

About Lieutenant Walter Noel Monteath, Macdonough had even less good to say. Appointed midshipman in September 1811 at the age of seventeen, Monteath made lieutenant the same date as Montgomery (9 December 1814), but with even less experience: three years and three months, all of it on the inland waters of Lake Champlain. Macdonough was appalled:

> Monteath was promoted without deserving it, and as it would appear from his date of [his midshipman's] warrant. He was [when] with me an intemperate young man; that habit appeared to be confirmed in him. He is a very smart, intelligent young man [who] would make a good officer, were he to leave off drinking. He is nothing of a seaman. He, however, has many good and promising qualities, though they appear to be choked by that bad one, drinking, of which I think he might be broken.[9]

Few among the handful of still-famous combat commanders of the pre-1815 navy left historical records so reticent about themselves as human beings as did Thomas Macdonough, the victor of Lake Champlain. A man of intense religious conviction and active Christian practice, Macdonough (here captured by an unknown miniaturist) may have seen himself as one possessing greater strength of character than many of his peers and subordinates. Rare indeed was the senior officer who could be as unflinchingly honest— or was it censorious?—when it came to evaluating a subordinate. Memorable and typical was his description of Lieutenant Francis J. Mitchell of Virginia as "the most profane man in the service"—surely no small achievement in itself! "He is no seaman; neither do I consider him a man of courage, speaking from what I was eyewitness to on Lake Champlain. I think he does the service more disgrace than honor." Still, Macdonough could be a powerful friend to a troubled young subordinate, provided the counseled one was prepared to emulate the older man's intense commitment to self-discipline. Private collection.

What might eventually have been the professional fate of either of these too green lieutenants will never be known. Both died relatively young, and both still lieutenants—Monteath in 1819 and Montgomery in 1824.

How long men served as lieutenants and as masters commandant before ascending to the next higher rungs of the ladder was driven more by available places becoming vacant and by the need for additional officers at these command grades, coupled with the willingness or unwillingness of Congress to authorize the positions, than by any ideal length of service. Still, some patterns are discernible.

Among the fifty-eight lieutenants promoted to master commandant (Tables 21 and 22), two-thirds had served more than five but less than eight years as lieutenants, with the largest number clumped at seven years' service. Looked at from another perspective, eight out of ten had gained five or more years of experience as lieutenants before they were allowed to assume the far more responsible post of master commandant. There was a definite tendency for the new masters commandant created during the War of 1812 to have longer service as lieutenants than those promoted in earlier years, just the reverse of the case with the newly created lieutenants. This reflected the situation that the navy entered the War of 1812 with a corps of highly experienced lieutenants who had been growing up with it since the Quasi-War with France, men who were ready for more responsible posts when wartime conditions and the navy's victories at sea stimulated expansion of the two top echelons of the corps.

Length of service as master commandant before promotion to captain (Table 23 and 24) was even more governed by circumstance than was the step from lieutenant to master commandant. Among the nineteen masters commandant who served less than three years at that grade before rising to captain, fourteen made captain in War of 1812 promotions. Special note should be taken that the shortest period of service from midshipman to captain in the pre-1815 navy, approximately six years (Table 19), is deceptive. This is the very special case of Stephen Decatur, promoted from lieutenant to captain as a reward for the destruction of the frigate *Philadelphia* in the harbor of Tripoli. Of the remaining twenty men who traversed the course from midshipman to captain by February 1815, none did it in less than thirteen years and three months, while seventeen had required fourteen or fifteen years for the entire passage. The underexperienced, underqualified captain was not to be found in the navy that fought the War of 1812.

That, indeed, is the essential message of all these numbers. The pre-1815 navy had been fortunate. Promotion had not been so slow that good men, with a small number of exceptions, became discouraged and quit. Neither, save *perhaps* for some War of 1812 lieutenants, had it been so rapid that inexperienced, inappropriate, or unqualified men had been placed in positions they were unable to fill competently. As the historian searches for an explanation of the high level of professionalism and achievement in the navy's pre-1815 officer corps, this strong record of adequate experience before promotion must certainly be accounted a major factor.

Merit

Assessing the roles of age and experience in determining when a man was promoted is essentially a question of making some obvious, albeit tedious, measurements. But what of merit? Is there a way to discover whether the Navy Department's oft-stated position—that, other factors being equal, merit would always take precedence over seniority in determining who would be promoted—was only a pious platitude? Or was it a cherished principle, rigorously followed? This might seem a historical judgment so subjective as to be beyond measurement. In fact, a satisfactory answer to this fundamental question can be discovered. Although the evidence is too bulky to be presented here, the conclusions drawn from the evidence may be summarized.[10]

Forty-six men who entered the officer corps as lieutenants (9) and midshipmen (37) between March 1798 and April 1804 were still alive and on active duty on 1 May 1815, by which date all had advanced to captain or master commandant. One sees here a tiny minority of the navy's pre-1815 officers. Employing the commonly accepted criterion of military achievement, rank attained, these forty-six men are the navy's highest achievers and most successful officers. One may assume that these are the corps' most competitive and capable officers. If discriminations of merit can be uncovered among them, it is reasonable to assert that the same criteria were applied to promotions among the larger mass of officers. The forty-six can be listed in the order of seniority in which they stood at the time of joining the corps—that is, by their official date of appointment—and in the order of seniority in which they stood on 1 May 1815. If promotion by seniority had been the primary criterion, the order of the names in the two lists should be identical or closely similar. Instead, the sequence in the May 1815 list is scrambled almost out of recognition. Thomas Macdonough has gained thirteen places on his peers at appointment; Jesse D. Elliott, eleven; Jacob Jones, seven. Some losses of relative position have been even more spectacular: Louis Alexis and Michael B. Carroll have both dropped twenty-six positions; Robert Henley has lost fifteen.

Was the new order of 1815 truly the result of using merit as the basis for selection for promotion? Or might favoritism and outside influence have been at work? At least seven of the twelve men who advanced most rapidly—Thomas Macdonough, Lewis Warrington, Jesse D. Elliott, Charles Morris, Stephen Decatur, James Biddle, and Jacob Jones—are officers whose names would be recognized by anyone with even a casual knowledge of American naval history as outstanding battle commanders who owed their promotions to those achievements. Charles Gordon was widely regarded as an exceptionally able officer before grievous dueling wounds in the aftermath of the *Chesapeake-Leopard* affair left him a semi-invalid. John Downes, though his name may not draw instant recognition, was David Porter's able senior subordinate during *Essex*'s Pacific Ocean adventures during the War of 1812; he owed his faster than usual advancement partly to that role and partly to uniformly superior evaluations from his commanding officers.[11]

The primacy of merit in the promotion process can be brought into even sharper focus by comparing the relative standings of the same forty-six officers at two points between their initial appointment and 1815: 1 July 1804 and 1 May 1810. At the height of the Tripolitan War, although most changes in rank order had been relatively modest one-, two-, three-, or four-place adjustments of position, scrambling of the sequence was already under way. Men who had entered the Quasi-War navy as more or less equal lieutenants and midshipmen had, in reality, been highly unequal in their prenaval experience and acquired skills. As a consequence, and largely through the discrimination of Benjamin

Stoddert, a good deal of shaking out and realignment has taken place. Six men have gained positions, in some cases rather dramatically, at the expense of sixteen officers who have lost positions, if in no instance very seriously. In the earliest list of eleven lieutenant nominations sent to the Senate for confirmation the names of John Rodgers, James Barron, Charles Stewart, and Isaac Hull stood in that order. Six years and four months later Rodgers and Barron have been captains since 1799, Stewart and Hull are but newly minted masters commandant, and William Bainbridge, not even appointed lieutenant till five months after the other four, has overtaken all but John Rodgers in the seniority race. Two Quasi-War midshipmen—Charles Gordon and Jacob Jones—have been discovered to possess much more experience at sea than their peers and have rapidly gained their lieutenant's commissions. Stephen Decatur has had a similar experience to Gordon and Jones, winning his lieutenant's commission on 21 May 1799. There the similarity stops; it is Decatur's special promotion to captain as a reward for the destruction of the frigate *Philadelphia* that has moved him ahead of nine of his seniors.

By 1 May 1810 the effects of this Quasi-War shaking out have been absorbed and, with some minor adjustments of one, two, or three relative positions because of Tripolitan War service, the order of seniority bears a reasonable resemblance to that of 1 July 1804. Isaac Chauncey and John Shaw have reversed the seniority they held as masters commandant—over the shrill protests of Captain Shaw to be sure.[12] The Henley brothers' relative merits are beginning to be discovered. Robert, the younger, was the first to become a midshipman, at the age of sixteen; eighteen-year-old John Dandridge was not appointed till six months later. Among the forty-six men whose promotions are here traced, Robert originally outranked John by eight positions; by May 1810 John has caught up with Robert, in part because Robert has slid five places in standing relative to his original peers, while John has gained two. By 1815 John will have moved two places ahead of Robert, but Robert will have lost fifteen relative positions on his peers since appointment.* The 1810 list is a reflection of Robert Smith's approach to the merit-vs.-seniority issue. Save for the Decatur promotion, Smith had been fairly conservative in his adjustments of relative seniority. One relative ranking here, a couple there; nothing that would cause excessive dissatisfaction in the ranks. He himself had said it. If merit were equal between two men, he would respect seniority.

It was William Jones who was brutal in his enforcement of the primacy of merit over seniority. He elected to draw the line at the rank of master commandant. The fifteen lieutenants whom Jones selected for master commandant in July 1813 were nominated to the Senate in a rearranged seniority

---

* Robert Henley's long slide in relative standing was at least partly attributable to his not having been on active duty at sea since 1805, at which time he had been second lieutenant of *Constitution*. Under plea of weakened health he occupied a shore and coastal billet at Norfolk before and during the early part of the War of 1812; but there was more to Robert Henley's loss of standing than simple ill health. Captain John Cassin, shortly after assuming command at Norfolk and clearly choosing his words with care, suggested to Paul Hamilton that "Mr. H. perhaps would suit better elsewhere. I would prefer a more active officer." He was transferred to Lake Champlain under Thomas Macdonough in time to salvage his career by playing a conspicuous and aggressive role as second-in-command at the battle of Lake Champlain, 11 September 1814. "He behaved like a brave man" that day, Macdonough acknowledged, "though his vessel was badly managed. . . . I look upon him to be very deficient in seamanship, and in the equipment of a vessel of war he is a stranger; his disposition I take to be malicious."[13]

sequence that the secretary judged to reflect the relative merits of the nominees. Neither did Jones hesitate to jump or entirely pass over eight, ten, fourteen, or even twenty-two senior lieutenants in picking and rank-ordering his new masters commandant. Some of the restructuring of seniority reflected conspicuous or heroic roles in battle: James Biddle had been first lieutenant in the *Wasp-Frolic* battle; William Henry Allen held the same post when *United States* captured *Macedonian*; Jesse Duncan Elliott was promoted over twenty-two senior lieutenants for his capture of *Caledonia* and *Detroit* on the Niagara frontier. Most other adjustments of men up or down on the list of masters commandant— or their omission from the nomination—reflected Jones's perception of relative merit as he gleaned it from their senior officers and their service records and his responsibility, as he saw it, to pass by lieutenants, however senior, whom he did not judge worthy of the supreme confidence that the master commandant's commission demanded.

So radical, if courageous, a measure unleashed a wholly predictable firestorm of protest from those who lost seniority and an even hotter one from those entirely passed over. This outcry had two consequences: it forced Jones to explain his reasons at length—a great benefit to historians—and it made it all but impossible for him to repeat the act. Those who felt aggrieved by the July 1813 list stampeded to complain to their senators; when the time came, late in his term of office, for Jones to send forward six more names for promotion to master commandant he elected to pass over for a second time only two of the senior lieutenants whom he had passed over in July 1813. Even then the Senate held up approval of one of the promotions for nearly a month as an indication of its displeasure at the secretary's disregard of seniority.

So much numbers can tell. However, human beings were experiencing the exhilaration of accelerated promotion or the pain of its denial. It is time to turn to their story.

25. Promotion Blues

EDWARD O'BRIEN FROM Cumberland, Maryland, had been a midshipman since 31 October 1799, but had seen rather less active duty than many of his peers when, in the spring of 1804, he was ordered to join Samuel Barron's squadron fitting out for the Mediterranean at the Washington navy yard. Early in May Midshipman O'Brien decided he had a grievance, one that he proceeded to explain to Commodore Barron:

> From some recent promotions of officers (younger in service than myself) I am compelled, if I pay any respect to my feelings, to resign unless I am also promoted. I feel conscious of my inability to discharge the duties of a lieutenant in the manner I conceive they *ought* to be performed; nevertheless, without incurring the imputation of vanity, I think I may aver that I am as adequate to the task as some of these officers are. It was, and still continues to be, my wish to leave the U.S. a midshipman, but any attention to my own sensations now renders the completion thereof impossible. I wish to have your permission to go to the Navy Office today—make known my intentions to the secretary either to be promoted or to resign.

If Barron counseled O'Brien to remove the large chip from his shoulder before presenting himself to Robert Smith, the advice fell on deaf ears. The face-to-face interview can hardly have been pleasant or rewarding for either the midshipman or the secretary of the navy, because four days later young O'Brien was handed a terse note from Robert Smith: "As we have no longer occasion for your services in the Navy of the United States, I have directed your name to be stricken from the roll of navy officers."[1]

Although relatively few such appeals ended with a discourteous and obstinate officer's career suffering involuntary termination, the navy's archives bulge with letters requesting, pleading for, or demanding promotion; with self-serving narratives of services rendered; with missives from relatives, friends, and political allies exhorting the promotion of Officer So-and-So; and with laments and cries of outrage when someone else was advanced and the writer not. Given the Navy Department's commitment to merit as the basis for promotion, it could hardly have been otherwise.

Among the twelve officers in Chapter 24 who had made the greatest gains in rank and seniority over their appointment peers by May 1815, five men—James Biddle, Stephen Decatur, Jesse D. Elliott, Thomas Macdonough, and Charles Morris—owed all or part of that rapid rise to the navy's and the nation's identification of them as heroes. They had been either commanding officers at spectacular and welcome naval victories (Decatur, Elliott, and Macdonough) or first lieutenants in such contests (Biddle and Morris). But for the hand of fate, the latter category would have been even larger. Two of the lieutenants who advanced the farthest ahead of their peers in William Jones's July 1813 selection of masters commandant—William Henry Allen and George Parker—owed that distinction to having been first lieutenants at, respectively, *United States*'s capture of *Macedonian* and *Constitution*'s defeat of *Java*. By 1815 both men were dead, and they do not appear in the final tally of rapid advancers.

Promotion by merit was never confined exclusively to men who won or helped to win conspicuous victories, but the navy did see promotion based on heroic deeds as the consummate form of recognition-for-merit. The historian needs to clarify what was meant by the term *heroic deeds*. In the cases of commanding officers and/or their first lieutenants what was being rewarded was not only conspicuous bravery—though a Stephen Decatur's personal example at the capture of *Philadelphia* or a James Biddle leading *Wasp*'s boarders into *Frolic* was certainly that—but highly noteworthy acts that promoted the national interest. It was a navy's willingness and ability to fight and to win that gave it credibility as an instrument of national policy. When Thomas Macdonough was advanced to captain as a reward for his victory in the battle of Lake Champlain, the nation honored him because the successful outcome of that bloody naval conflict had halted a British invasion of the United States at a particularly dark hour during the War of 1812. William Henry Allen was promoted for his role as second-in-command to Stephen Decatur in the latter's capture of *Macedonian* not because he acted more bravely than any other subordinate officer in the ship—though he certainly bore more responsibility—but because the victory at sea, as with others in the opening months of the War of 1812, had served the national interest in a spectacular way by establishing that U.S. naval vessels could defeat their British counterparts. Allen's reward was in a certain sense symbolic. In promoting this one man the navy saw him as the representative of, and model for, other officers in the ship and in the navy.

The principle of rewarding those who advanced the national interest by significant combat achievements began with the new navy's first major victory at sea, *Constellation*'s 1799 capture of *Insurgente*. The U.S. ship's first lieutenant, John Rodgers, was promptly promoted to captain (the intermediate grade of master commandant was not then in existence), but the extraordinary nature of his advancement was muted because Rodgers was the navy's second most senior lieutenant and poised for early advancement in any case. Rewarding spectacular service with extraordinary promotion was more starkly apparent the next time the navy had occasion to call it into play. When Lieutenant Stephen Decatur led the risky expedition that destroyed the captured frigate *Philadelphia* in 1804 he turned a bitter defeat into a victory that could be a

*If Lieutenant Andrew Sterett looks a little miffed in this portrait by C.B.J. Fevret de
Saint-Mémin, perhaps he has just learned that junior lieutenant Stephen Decatur has
been promoted captain over his head as a reward for the destruction of the frigate* Philadelphia *in Tripoli harbor. Sterett, victor of the first ship-to-ship engagement of the
Tripolitan War, had to settle for a personal letter of commendation from President Jefferson
as the tangible evidence of his exploit. Unable to come to terms with wounded feelings,
Sterett resigned from the navy in June 1805. Neither did Sterett find extended satisfaction
in resuming his former civilian career in the merchant service; he died, a year and a half
later, at Lima, Peru.* National Portrait Gallery, Washington, D.C.

source of national pride and self-congratulation. Robert Smith was determined
that Decatur's reward would be correspondingly spectacular and exemplary:
he was promoted to captain over the heads of seven senior lieutenants. (The
rank of master commandant had not yet been reestablished.)

Although there seems to have been the inevitable grumbling about Decatur's
extraordinary advancement, only one of the seven men who had formerly
outranked him resigned in protest. Lieutenant Andrew Sterett held out for the
absolute and inviolable principle of seniority as title to promotion: "It is
impossible to be reconciled to the promotion of a junior officer over me, nor
is it compatible with correct principles of honor to serve under him." Robert
Smith defended the supremacy of merit vigorously:

> The president made this promotion to testify the high sense he entertained
> of the brilliant act achieved by Mr. Decatur that other officers in the navy
> might, by the prospect of such honorable reward, be stimulated to deeds of
> equal valor. At the time the promotion was made it was confidently believed
> that this principle would be clearly understood by the officers of the navy and
> would be very acceptable to them. It was thought it would gratify the ambition
> of the aspiring officer. . . . The very same principle might ultimately raise you
> to the highest and most honorable command in the navy in preference to
> gentlemen senior to you in original appointment.

He would be sorry to lose so valuable an officer as Sterett, Smith concluded,
but he would rather accept the former's resignation "than give up a principle
believed essential to the good of the service, reflecting on no one in particular,
because forming the law for all, and holding out to all equally the means of
obtaining its benefits."[2]

By 1805, then, two practices were firmly established by precedent. A combat
victory promoting the national interest would insure for the commanding

officer, if he was not already a captain, immediate promotion to the next higher grade. In cases wherein a commanding officer was already a captain, his first lieutenant could expect the exemplary promotion. When Oliver Hazard Perry, the victor of Lake Erie, suggested that he would be willing to have his commissioning as captain delayed rather than leapfrog the one master commandant senior to him, William Jones's notes for a reply went straight to the point: "Say that no one can doubt of the policy or justice of special promotions for signal service. The practice is perfectly established in the naval service of the U.S., and without it [a] stimulus to noble deeds would be withheld."[3]

How thoroughly these principles were fixed in place before the War of 1812 has been obscured by the furor that broke out in the early months of that conflict over Charles Morris's promotion for his role as first lieutenant in the battle between *Constitution* and *Guerriere*. In one of the unhappier examples of his shortfall in administrative skills, Paul Hamilton chose to advance Lieutenant Morris not to junior master commandant but to junior captain, thereby leapfrogging not only seven lieutenants but eight masters commandant. Exactly what motivated Hamilton's extraordinary decision is not certain. Perhaps his judgment was overpowered by his euphoria from Hull's spectacular victory over a British ship. In harking back to the Rodgers and Decatur precedents Hamilton may have overlooked the fact that no masters commandant had, in either case, existed to be overleaped. Suffice it to say that the masters commandant over whom Morris had been promoted, as well as some of the lieutenants, did not share the extent of Hamilton's ecstasy over the *Constitution-Guerriere* battle. The storm broke round his head with speed and with fury.

Several of the aggrieved picked up their pens to protest directly to Hamilton. Not content to stop there, they enlisted senior captains thought to have special places in the secretary's confidence in support of their complaint. Although much ink was expended, many sheets of paper filled, and several allegedly mortally wounded egos paraded, the arguments advanced may be briefly summarized:

1. Promotion of Lieutenant Morris to the rank of junior master commandant over the heads of his senior lieutenants would have been reward enough. The cases of Lieutenants Rodgers and Decatur did not constitute precedents because the rank of master commandant did not exist when either man was promoted.

2. Although he was seriously wounded during the battle, Morris had done no more than was his duty in the engagement. His conduct had been exemplary, but a number of the navy's senior lieutenants could have been expected to do just as well, if good fortune had placed them in Lieutenant Morris's shoes that afternoon. "Had the Guerriere been taken by boarding and Lieutenant Morris have headed the boarders, or had Captain Hull been unfortunately killed or [been] wounded so severely as to have obliged him to leave the deck, and Lieutenant Morris have fought the ship afterwards and the result been as glorious as it has terminated," then and only then would the lieutenant-to-captain promotion have been justified. So argued Daniel T. Patterson, one of Morris's old seniors as lieutenant who now saw the junior man leave him far in his wake.

3. The promotion of one subordinate officer in a victorious ship, when all the officers had behaved "with signal but equal brilliance," was detrimental, if not destructive, to morale among the unpromoted officers. "It is a tacit reflection

upon the conduct of those officers who are overlooked," charged James Lawrence.

4. Once passed over at the step from master commandant to captain, an officer's relative seniority could never be regained, no matter how great a deed he might perform, because captain was the navy's highest rank.

5. The promotion of Morris was a particularly flagrant injury to Master Commandant James Lawrence. He had been Stephen Decatur's first lieutenant in the expedition that destroyed *Philadelphia*. Decatur had been rewarded by extraordinary promotion, but Lawrence had derived no advantage in rank from his role in that famous exploit.

6. Many of those passed over by Morris would resign because of this affront to them. The promotion of Morris over his head was "in fact," argued Charles Ludlow, "a declaration to the public that I was incompetent to discharge the duties of a situation to which I was entitled by my rank. And how, Sir, I would respectfully ask, have I deserved this stigma on my character?" Unless Ludlow were restored to his previous seniority by being promoted ahead of Morris, resignation was the only means of vindicating his injured honor.

So far as the record shows, Paul Hamilton never explained or defended the Morris promotion. By the time it had been made public and the storm of protest had broken, Hamilton was neck-deep in the other difficulties that led to his resignation as secretary of the navy at the end of 1812. That left the Morris promotion in the pile of problems that William Jones inherited, because although the session of Congress had begun on 2 November 1812, the Morris nomination had not yet been sent up to the Senate for confirmation. Jones had a red-hot potato on his hands; he and President Madison procrastinated till almost the end of the session trying to decide how to deal with it. Because the Morris promotion had been publicly announced in Washington's quasi-official *National Intelligencer* and a recess commission sent to Morris, the administration could hardly back down and withdraw the promotion; neither was the prospect of several of the navy's ablest masters commandant threatening to resign and backed by the likes of John Rodgers and William Bainbridge a bluff Jones and Madison were eager to call.

Apparently it had been Hamilton's intention to place Morris immediately after Samuel Evans in the seniority ranking of the navy's captains. In the list that was finally submitted to the Senate for confirmation on 24 February 1813—a week before the session was due to end!—the names of Masters Commandant Charles Gordon, Jacob Jones (victor in the *Wasp-Frolic* battle), and James Lawrence (belated recognition of his role in the *Philadelphia* exploit, for his capture of *Peacock* was as yet unknown) were inserted ahead of Charles Morris. Such an announcement still left four other masters commandant (one had died in early January) passed over. Even with this modification the controversial Morris nomination was not exactly welcomed by the Senate. That body had already received petitions from Masters Commandant Lawrence and Ludlow opposing confirmation of Morris, and it kept the latter's nomination tied up in committee until the very last day of the session. Then Morris finally won the Senate's advice and consent, but at the price of an accompanying resolution: "In the opinion of the Senate, it would hereafter be inexpedient to advance an officer more than one grade by the same nomination; and the departure from the practice in the case of Captain Morris ought not to be considered as an imputation on the merit or services of any other officer."

The practical consequences of this controversy were that William Jones had managed to maintain the principle of "special promotions for signal service," but the firestorm, and especially the grudging Senate confirmation, insured that future special promotions would be to the next higher grade only. Charles Morris would remain a solitary case. As for the brandished threats of resignation, only one was actually carried out. Charles Ludlow, whose career commitment to the navy had of late years been an ambiguous one, seized the occasion to retire to the life of a country gentleman. Others grumbled, but they stayed on board.[4]

The major exploits that led to, and the controversies surrounding, extraordinary promotions for men such as Stephen Decatur and Charles Morris capture the attention of historians and obscure the operation of hero promotions at lower ranks. Among such less conspicuous achievers was Francis Hoyt Gregory. A native of Norwalk, Connecticut, Gregory was nineteen years old when he received his midshipman's warrant in February 1809. By then he already considered himself an old salt, a man with "several years" of experience in the merchant service and just escaped from British impressment. After the briefest of service with John Rodgers's squadron based at New York, Midshipman Gregory was ordered to New Orleans, where his previous experience at sea made him a valuable acquisition on a station chronically short of officers. When yellow fever broke out in the ketch *Vesuvius*, the vessel to which Gregory was attached, all the other officers and many of the crew were incapacitated. Gregory remained healthy and for three months found himself the de facto commander and virtually the sole officer of the ketch. It was August 1809; he had been a midshipman for barely six months.

For Francis H. Gregory this was only the first of a long chain of adventures along Louisiana's fever-ridden coast and in the bayous, adventures that remained clearly etched in memory three decades later: capturing would-be slave runners; chasing French privateers off the coast; battling the Barataria pirates and recapturing their prizes. Almost all this time Gregory had been the commander of a gunboat, operating with only the general supervision of his station commander, and developing habits of independence, discretion, and initiative. When he was transferred to Lake Ontario early in the War of 1812 Isaac Chauncey recognized in Gregory a valuable man and an experienced officer, appointed him acting lieutenant, and attached him to his own ship.

Three battle experiences—Kingston (November 1812), York (April 1813), and Fort George (May 1813)—only served to increase Chauncey's good opinion. But in August 1813, four and a half years after he had received his midshipman's warrant and four years since he had borne sole responsibility for the fever-stricken *Vesuvius*, Francis H. Gregory was still a midshipman. In earlier years this would not have been unusual, but the wartime acceleration of promotion was under way and thirty-one midshipmen who had entered the navy with or after Francis Gregory, including some of his messmates in *General Pike*'s wardroom, were commissioned as lieutenants in July 1813. When the parchments reached *General Pike* from Washington, the newly commissioned held a party to celebrate. Wine flowed freely, tongues wagged, alcohol stimulated irritability. The new lieutenants made—or appeared to make—invidious comparisons between themselves and those, like Gregory, who had not been selected. Awash in wine and condescension, it was easy for Gregory to believe that he had been gratuitously neglected in the promotion, that resignation was the only honorable recourse. Pushing aside the dishes and glasses that littered the wardroom table, he wrote an angry letter of resignation, then sealed and posted it.

Time brought sobriety, better judgment, and remorse. In his alcoholic anger Gregory had not even bothered to keep a copy of the letter. He could not recall exactly what he had said, but he had an ugly suspicion that he had violated the frontiers of decorum and propriety. What was worse, he wanted his warrant back and to remain in the navy. What to do? He consulted Isaac Chauncey, who went to work on his behalf. If William Jones would accept Gregory's apology, let him withdraw the offensive resignation, and forget that it had been written, "I would," wrote Chauncey, "be willing to pledge myself for his future good conduct, and whenever you may think him worthy of a commission, he will, I know, prove himself worthy of it. . . . He is brave, honorable, and intelligent, and possesses all the requisites to make a most valuable officer and, in my estimation, would be a real loss to the service." Jones's response was graciousness itself: the incident would in no way prejudice future promotion. All well and good, but Gregory was still no more than an acting lieutenant. Oral and written attempts by Chauncey to change his status had met with no success by June 1814, when Gregory was ordered on special service.

Chauncey was aware that Kingston was supplied by brigades of boats that came up the St. Lawrence River. Perhaps one or more of these brigades could be surprised and captured or destroyed. It was a job for which Francis Gregory's Louisiana experience had prepared him well, and Chauncey sent him off with three gigs to hide among the Thousand Islands and await his chance. Once there, Francis Gregory realized it was going to be a much tougher assignment than Chauncey had imagined in the comfort and security of *Superior*'s cabin. Not only did the British have a gunboat stationed every six miles between Prescott and Kingston, these were linked by lookouts and telegraphs on each of the high islands. Difficult as it would be to catch supply boats out of sight of their protectors, it was only a matter of time before the presence of the U.S. boats was detected. Sure enough, on the morning of the fourth day, they were caught. There was a British gunboat, mounting an 18-pounder and manned by Royal Marines, close aboard Gregory's hiding place. A decision had to be made instantly. Gregory's party manned their gigs, sped through the water, overpowered the gunboat, and carried her by boarding. Barely taking the time to discover that his prize was named *Black Snake*, Gregory manned her and was making his escape up the St. Lawrence when he found himself pursued by a large gunboat propelled by forty sweeps and mounting two large guns. There was no getting away with the smaller, slower *Black Snake*. Only the swift gigs could escape. Gregory reluctantly scuttled *Black Snake* and watched her sink quickly into the river's deep waters before he and his men slipped away from the enemy through shallow channels where pursuit was impossible.

Chauncey related the entire exploit to Secretary Jones, reminding him that Mr. Gregory, despite five and half years of service in the navy, still did not have his lieutenant's commission. With this Jones finally capitulated: "The gallantry of our navy has become proverbial," he replied to Chauncey, "and though its deeds are among the familiar objects of the day, their luster still attracts the public eye and admiration with unbounded pleasure. Whether the theater be the deck of a 44 or the sheets of a gig, the same dauntless spirit and thirst of glory are equally displayed. The achievement of Lieutenant Gregory is the precursor of a fair renown when time shall have matured his professional career." A lieutenant's commission was enclosed.[5]

Did They Get a Little Help from Their Friends?

William Lewis of Spotsylvania County, Virginia, had been a midshipman less than three years when, in June 1805, Edward Preble appointed him acting lieutenant and put him in command of the bomb ketch *Vengeance* for a voyage from Boston to the Mediterranean. When *Vengeance* reached her destination Commodore John Rodgers confirmed Lewis's pro tempore advancement by making him acting third lieutenant of the brig *Argus*. Lewis was proud of his accomplishment when he wrote home:

> But still, it would be of very great benefit to me, by placing me beyond all doubt, if some of my friends would exert a little interest with the department to obtain and send me a written appointment [as acting lieutenant] from the secretary. It has been, and is, my determination to rise in the service as much from my own exertions as possible. But, although the secretary [Robert Smith] holds out a principle of merit as the only title to promotion, yet I begin to find that a great many get on through the means of influential friends at home, and I don't see the impropriety of taking advantage of the same assistance, provided I can obtain it.[6]

What is one to make of Lewis's assertion? Was Robert Smith talking promotion-by-merit-alone, but actually handing out advancement on the basis of influence? Or was Lewis simply manifesting the human tendency to assume that, if someone else seems to be getting ahead more quickly, dark and devious forces, not superior merit, must be at work?

The latter appears the better answer. Yes, political and family power could get a young man an appointment in the navy. Thereafter it was primarily his abilities, character, efforts, and (sometimes) professional good luck that determined whether he remained in the navy and how far and how quickly he advanced within it. The records of the pre-1815 navy abound with examples of attempts by parents and family members to advance the naval careers of loved ones, but the same records may be searched from end to end without producing a single convincing example of an officer being promoted out of turn or undeservedly because of family or political clout. What such a search does reveal is the successive secretaries spending a substantial amount of time and effort explaining that they were *not* going to succumb to such campaigns and defending the principle of promotion based on merit and service. The story of one secretary of the navy's attempt to defend the pass single-handedly may be picked from among many. Appropriately enough, in view of Midshipman Lewis's charge, it is a tale of Robert Smith alone against the advancing swarm.

Events began with the arrival on Smith's desk of a letter, dated 25 March 1802, from former Quasi-War naval captain Christopher Raymond Perry, a staunch and vocal member of the Republican party, then enduring with such dignity as he could muster his enforced retirement to civilian life at the hands of his own political comrades. Perry's letter regarded his son Oliver Hazard, a sixteen-year-old midshipman holding a warrant dated 7 April 1799; its burden

*Midshipman Oliver Hazard
Perry* (left). *Not yet the self-as-
sured hero of the battle of Lake
Erie portrayed by John Wesley Jarvis* (opposite), *but a promising
young man with a most political
parent anxious to promote a son's
career. Father Christopher Raymond Perry reckoned without Robert Smith's firm grip on principle.
The talented miniaturist is now
identified as Edward Greene Malbone.* Museum of Fine Arts,
Boston; Detroit Institute of
Arts.

was a lament that two midshipmen with warrants of dates similar to Oliver's—
George Washington Tew (21 February 1799) and Joshua Blake (6 April 1799)
had long since been promoted to lieutenant (1 April and 4 July 1800 respectively)
while neglected son Oliver was still a midshipman. Naturally enough, Perry the
father conveniently overlooked the fact that both Tew and Blake were much
older—Tew about twenty-four and Blake approximately twenty-one at the time
of promotion—and possessed strong prenaval experience at sea, assets that
Oliver lacked. Smith tried to be reassuring when he replied to C.R. Perry, but
one senses that his patience was being put to the test:

> With respect to the appointment of Mr. George W. Tew and Mr. Blake,
> not having been in office then I cannot say what considerations influenced their
> promotion, but I presume they merited it. With respect to your son I can only
> say that he has been mentioned to me in very handsome terms and that I feel
> every disposition to promote him as early as I shall be enabled with propriety
> to do so. The meritorious midshipmen must rise agreeably to their rank. This
> is a principle which I shall invariably adhere to.

On the same day that Smith signed, franked, and mailed his letter to the
elder Perry, James Nicholson, captain in the Continental navy, Republican
collector of customs at New York, and father-in-law of Treasury Secretary
Albert Gallatin, sat down at his desk—obviously at the request of political crony
C.R. Perry—to reinforce the father's request. Smith patiently dispatched to
Nicholson a copy of his earlier letter, from which he trusted Nicholson would
perceive that Oliver's promotion "now is impracticable, inasmuch as it would
break in upon a rule which I conceive it indispensably necessary to adhere to

in all cases of promotion." Smith may have hoped that would end the matter, but, two weeks after his letter to Nicholson, along came one from Thomas Tillinghast, member of Congress from Rhode Island, extolling the merits of Oliver Hazard Perry. Once more Smith's pen scratched across the paper: "There are other young gentlemen in the navy, represented to be of equal merit, who are senior in appointment to Mr. Perry; and I have laid it down as a rule never, unless on some extraordinary occasion, to reverse the order of antecedent relations among the officers of the navy. A contrary principle would, I am convinced, be productive of great evils."

There, at last, the matter slumbered for a year, when, at the behest of C.R. Perry, Christopher Ellery, Republican senator from Rhode Island, reawakened it with yet another pro–O.H. Perry letter to Smith. The latter stuck to his guns: "To promote Mr. Perry in preference to his brother officers of superior rank and equal merit would be degrading them. Mr. Perry's character stands very fair, and he will be promoted as soon as he can be with justice to other officers." Ellery was not to be put off so easily; within the month he passed on to Smith yet another letter from C.R. Perry exhorting Oliver's immediate promotion. To this Smith felt compelled to reply directly to the father in self-defense: "To promote your son to a lieutenancy at this time is impossible. . . . I am not ignorant of his merit and will not be inattentive to his interest whenever he shall come in competition with his brother officers on fair and honorable grounds."

Maybe that letter finally silenced Christopher Raymond Perry on the subject of his son's promotion. Perhaps there were further efforts that have not survived or come to light. Whichever was the case, Robert Smith held firm. Oliver Hazard Perry had to wait till April 1807 to receive his commission along with the rest of his peers in age and service.[7]

This Inactive, Forlorn Station

"Officers serving [here] are exposed to hazard[s] far beyond those of battle without having that evil compensated by any chance of exerting or signalizing themselves in the service of their country. Almost every other station affords opportunity for enterprise and ambition to the officers; but *here* they are cut off ingloriously by pestilence and disease." The unenviable duty assignment was New Orleans; the writer was Master Commandant Daniel Todd Patterson, lamenting what he saw as the Navy Department's cruel policy of keeping him attached to what he had earlier labeled "this inactive, forlorn station."[8]

The perception for which Daniel T. Patterson served as eloquent spokesman was one widely shared by those officers ordered to the Gulf Coast. To be sent there was to be given a duty assignment wherein the risks of fatal disease ran high, but one where the odds of a lingering professional death were even greater. The station was remote from Washington; officers felt they were ordered there and forgotten. Far worse, the nature of the duty—combating smugglers, illegal slave traders, fringe-of-the-law privateers, and outright pirates by means of gunboats and other shallow-draft vessels—gave officers attached to the New Orleans station, they said, neither opportunities for the dramatic accomplishments that insured promotion nor chances for the professional growth that could assure better assignments.

Lending credence to these perceptions were some measurable facts. Among the forty-six officers whose relative seniority records were traced in Chapter 24, the two who lost the largest number of positions over the course of their pre-1815 careers—twenty-six in both cases—were Louis Alexis and Michael B. Carroll, men who spent long stretches of their careers on the New Orleans station. Several of the senior lieutenants who fared the worst in William Jones's July 1813 selection of masters commandant could point to a common denominator: extended service at New Orleans. Alexis, Carroll, and Daniel S. Dexter were long-service lieutenants; Carroll, indeed, was the navy's most senior lieutenant. All were totally passed over in the selection of new masters commandant. Daniel T. Patterson, although he made the list of nominees, had the mortification to see thirteen men who had been junior to him as lieutenants given seniority as masters commandant. Neither did William Jones conceal that their long appointments to New Orleans had damaged their chances for promotion. When the protests began to roll in, Jones became testily defensive, but kept a firm grip on his knack for no-sugar-coating messages: "It is not my fault if they [the officers passed over for master commandant] have been confined for some years almost exclusively to gunboat service and have seen little else since their last promotion [to lieutenant]. The question is, Are they now qualified to command a ship of war? Or does not the interest of the service require that they should previously serve as senior lieutenants on board some of the frigates or as lieutenants commanding some of the smaller vessels?"[9]

If Daniel T. Patterson could have read that letter he would have been beside himself. True, he had been attached to the New Orleans station almost continuously since 1806, but he had hardly been passively acquiescent in the assignment. As early as 7 February 1811 he asked to be reassigned to some post in which he would have a better chance at combat distinction when the anticipated war with Great Britain came. Yes, Paul Hamilton replied, as soon as Commodore John Shaw, the station commander, judges he can dispense with your services, he may order you to Washington for reassignment. Daniel T. Patterson lived a century and a half too early to know the phrase *Catch-22*, which is all the more unfortunate because he needed the concept to illuminate the situation in which Hamilton had placed him. He could leave the station as soon as Shaw gave him permission, but Patterson knew that Shaw, chronically short on capable officers, would never voluntarily order him away. His commanding officer would seize one excuse after another to hang onto so valuable an asset as Lieutenant Patterson.

Why should John Shaw be sympathetic? He wanted to be out on the Atlantic, commanding a frigate in single combat with the enemy as were his peers Decatur, Hull, and Stewart. He, too, was stuck on the Gulf Coast. "We are all caught here at the commencement of a war," he told Lieutenant Daniel S. Dexter when the latter asked permission to return east and seek a better command. "I regret myself it has been the case, as I can not see what honor or profit can be gained on this station. I have long since requested my recall from this station. The government has refused to comply."[10]

Each of these three men—Shaw, Dexter, and Patterson—pursued his own course. (Regarding the responses of Carroll and Alexis the record is more or less silent.) Shaw badgered the Navy Office for a command at sea until he was ordered to Washington and then given the frigate *United States*, hopelessly blockaded at New London for the duration of the war. Dexter, deeply hurt at being passed over for master commandant, appealed to members of the Louisiana congressional delegation, especially Senator James Brown and Representative Thomas B. Robertson, for help. He also wrote, but was apparently persuaded not to present, a memorial to the Senate, advocating a strict rule of promotion by seniority (except for hero promotions) and asking to be advanced to his proper seniority as a master commandant.[11] Dexter eventually received his coveted promotion to master commandant, but not until 20 December 1814 and without recapturing the year and a half's seniority he had lost to the masters commandant of July 1813. A year before his promotion Dexter was ordered away from the New Orleans station. If he thought a new assignment meant better chances for distinction, he was sorely disappointed. Fame, that most elusive of pursued objects, continued to evade him; he died, 10 October 1818, commander of the Lake Erie naval station, a post arguably more obscure than New Orleans.

For the historian, who knows how events turned out, the story of these men and their efforts to leave New Orleans in pursuit of fame and promotion is heavy with irony. Daniel T. Patterson, promoted to the command of the New Orleans station on Shaw's departure, apparently concluded that being Number One, even in Louisiana, provided adequate ego gratification and tapered off his campaign for transfer. As everyone knows, the battles that John Shaw and Daniel Dexter had impatiently sought elsewhere came to New Orleans in the conflict's final weeks, and Daniel Todd Patterson shared with Andrew Jackson hero's honors for the War of 1812's last, memorable victory.

When the smoke of battle cleared, literally and figuratively, assignment to New Orleans had proved no more detrimental to one's career than many another duty post, whatever the subjective impression may have been. For all his anguish in the interim, Daniel T. Patterson attained the rank of captain with the loss of only one relative seniority position in a race that had lasted fifteen and a half years. Louis Alexis and Michael B. Carroll had been big losers—if promotion to master commandant a year and a half after one's peers can really be called losing—and that largely because of long service at New Orleans. But Daniel S. Dexter, in spite of anguish as articulate as that of Daniel T. Patterson, made master commandant with exactly the relative standing he would have had if everyone had been promoted by seniority alone. What befell Daniel Todd Patterson restates one of the oldest, most shopworn—but no less true—rules of the military experience: no amount of career planning can begin to substitute for having war's unpredictable fortunes drop the opportunity to win a famous victory on one's doorstep, even on an "inactive and unwholesome station."[12]

26. Mortification's Berth

IDSHIPMEN, LIEUTENANTS, and masters commandant jostling one another on the ladder of ranks as they climbed toward captain are far from the whole story of the search for achievement and its rewards in the pre-1815 navy. The four-rung ladder was the classic vision of how a professional naval organization perpetuated itself. The novice began on the midshipman rung. Unpromising young men were eliminated there. The residue, a minority, received their basic training and socialization at this rank, then, thoroughly tested for fitness, climbed to the lieutenant rung. The lieutenant expanded and perfected the skills that could lead to his selection as commanding officer of one of the navy's small cruisers and a master commandant's commission. Having proved himself as the independent commander of a small cruiser, the master commandant knew it was only a matter of time before he was told to ascend to the navy's most responsible rank: captain.

This theoretical ladder of rank and promotion was simple, clean, and readily understood, but it was not a wholly accurate representation of the way things worked in the pre-1815 U.S. Navy. Theory's classic four-rung ladder contained no provision for a group of officers who, by the War of 1812, constituted about one-fifth of the corps. These were the sailing masters. That there would ever be so many of them the navy's founders, back in the days of Benjamin Stoddert and Thomas Truxtun, had never imagined. Sailing masters represented pragmatic reality's subversion of classic theory. Many of them were eager to gain a foothold on the promotion ladder at its second rung, the rank of lieutenant; some were succeeding, in spite of the almost frantic efforts of those on the first rung, the midshipmen, to pull them off.

When the navy established the rank, the role of a sailing master was clearly defined. According to the *Naval Regulations* of 1802 a sailing master was a ship's officer who was charged with navigating her under the direction of the captain, supervised the keeping of her log, oversaw receipt and inspection of provisions and stores and the stowage of the hold, kept the ship in her best sailing trim, and was held accountable for the ship's charts, navigational books, and instruments. There was but one sailing master in a ship; he was assisted in his duties by a number of petty officers called master's mates. In theory, and sometimes in the actual practice of the pre-1815 navy, master's mates were hired in the same fashion as were other petty officers; that is, they signed on for the cruise when the ship was recruiting her crew. Under normal practice, however, the navy preferred to assign experienced midshipmen to this mate's role, the better to prepare them in practical seamanship for subsequent appointments as acting lieutenants. The sailing master was not on the promotion ladder; he was subject to the orders of the ship's lieutenants, but was socially their equal in the ship's dining and sleeping arrangements, eating as they did in the wardroom and berthing in one of the tiny staterooms adjacent to it.

Of sailing masters in this classic sense the navy needed only as many as it had ships in commission, plus a few extras to allow for furloughs and to fill certain shore billets at navy yards. Until after the *Chesapeake-Leopard* incident of June 1807 sailing masters as a proportion of the officer corps remained constant at approximately one man in twenty. At the height of the Quasi-War with France (July 1800) there were a mere twenty-nine masters on the navy's roll of nearly seven hundred officers; during the Tripolitan War the navy operated with a cadre of fourteen to sixteen masters. It was only in 1807–1809 that the number of sailing masters began to increase so markedly as to alter the proportion, and consequently the visibility and the importance, of this rank in the corps as a whole, a trend that intensified during the War of 1812 until sailing masters on active duty numbered some two hundred, and roughly one officer in five held that rank (Table 1).

The primary reason for this explosion in the use of sailing masters was the growth in the navy's gunboat-size units in the years between the *Chesapeake-Leopard* affair and the Treaty of Ghent. Despite the seemingly ineradicable myth that the gunboat represented a craven retreat from the real role of a navy by the allegedly pacifistic and impractical President Jefferson, in point of fact the world in which the post-*Leopard* U.S. Navy operated and the roles assigned to it demanded the existence of small, shallow-draft units as a major component in the force. All the frigates and sloops of war in the world would have been of little value as patrol vessels on the Mississippi and the Louisiana coast, where the navy's quarry were pirates, slave traders, and smugglers who relied on their ability to elude pursuit among the bayous and the Spanish moss. The same held true for the sea islands of South Carolina or the notoriously porous American-Spanish frontier near St. Marys, Georgia.

To assign such coastal gunboat commands to midshipmen was objectionable and impractical for two reasons, which reasons were simply the opposite sides of the same coin. Because gunboats often had to operate independently for extended periods, they demanded commanders of maturity, seamanship, and sound discretion. There were not enough experienced midshipmen available. Young men placed in these commands often went bad quickly, took heavily to drink, or otherwise became discipline problems, which is another way of saying that the immature could not be trusted with posts out of the sight of senior authority figures. Nor should they have been.

To meet this need for commanders for its rapidly growing flotilla of small coastal craft, the navy took the old rank of sailing master and largely changed its purpose. Sailing masters now became mature, experienced seafarers recruited directly into that rank to command the navy's gunboat-size units. Both the nature of the duty they performed and the fact that the rank of sailing master was not on the promotion ladder made the masters a distinct (and perhaps isolated) corps within the navy. The navy's need for sailing masters in the classic sense for its sloops, schooners, brigs, and frigates continued concurrently with the need for gunboat-commanding masters. Both wore the same uniform, both carried the same warrants, and all were called masters. In fact, the classic sailing master, especially for the big frigates, had always been a hard man to find. The nature of the duties demanded that he be a kind of Thirty-second Degree Sea Dog; mariners that skillful could find more profitable employment in the merchant marine. It was generally recognized, both by commanders afloat and at the Navy Office, that the vast majority of the men appointed sailing masters in 1807 and later were not qualified to serve as sailing masters in the big ships.[1] Responding to this acute shortage of qualified sailing masters for its brigs, sloops, and schooners, the navy often preferred to assign its most experienced and skillful midshipmen as acting sailing masters, with this billet constituting the immediate prelude to a lieutenant's commission.

Although the growth of the gunboat force is rightly perceived as the principal factor driving the expansion of the corps of masters, there was a secondary motivation now almost lost to sight. Throughout the Tripolitan War, and even more so during the initial buildup of the gunboat force, Robert Smith was always aware that the navy's system of selecting young men as midshipmen and training them for a minimum of five years was a frustratingly slow process that was not producing an adequate number of mature, trained, and experienced lieutenants fast enough. Recall of discharged Quasi-War lieutenants—a practice that was the subject of a brief experiment—raised explosively divisive questions about the relative seniority of the recalled Quasi-War veterans as against men who had never been out of service. Commissioning experienced mariners as lieutenants from civilian life, as had been done in the earlier part of the Quasi-War, would not only arouse the indignation of every midshipman who longed for his lieutenant's commission but, as the Quasi-War experience and a brief Tripolitan War flirtation with the practice had shown, it ran a high risk of saddling the navy with problem officers who then had to be eased or shoved out.

Smith's solution was to use the sailing master corps as a second avenue of access, equal to that of midshipman, from which lieutenants could be selected for commissioning. He apparently saw the sailing master route as appropriate for young adults, older than the typical midshipman and with greater experience at sea, who could be commissioned more quickly than the young men recruited as midshipmen. Apart from providing a source of mature, well-trained men for potential lieutenant berths, the plan had two other advantages. Because masters served under warrants, rather than commissions, the navy was easily rid of them if they proved unfit timber for lieutenants. Equally important, they, like newly promoted midshipmen, would enter the lieutenants' roster at the bottom; troubling questions of seniority would not arise as had happened during the recall of discharged Quasi-War lieutenants. Ever since Smith's earliest months in office use of the sailing master track as a second avenue of recruitment for lieutenants had been settled policy, though the small number of men involved had perhaps obscured the secretary's intent. His general order of 18 August 1802, the one that announced his policy of examinations as a prerequisite for promotion, began, "Midshipmen *and sailing masters*, before they obtain commissions of lieutenancy . . . "—words that clearly implied equality of access for the navy's masters.[2] Such a policy was wholly consistent with Smith's insistence that merit was the true basis of promotion. In formalizing the process Smith knew that he was not proposing a radical innovation. Access to lieutenant commissions for masters was already part of the U.S. naval tradition: thirteen Quasi-War lieutenants had begun their naval careers as sailing masters or master's mates.

The Capable Mariner

Would the sailing master's warrant continue to be a means of recruiting for possible lieutenancies able men who were too old or too experienced for midshipman berths? Before following the pre-1815 navy through its erratic response to that question, it will be well to pause and look at the men who became the navy's masters, to determine if and in what ways they differed from the men it recruited as its midshipmen.

All in all 505 sailing masters have been identified who received appointments between 24 July 1797 and 6 February 1815. The words *have been identified* are key here. Among officer billets, sailing master was the one most prone to be filled through acting appointments made by station, squadron, and ship commanders. Because only a portion of the pre-1815 navy's muster rolls survive, it is impossible to tally every man who held a sailing master's appointment. The number 505 simply reports those who have been found. Neither should one imagine the 505 spread evenly over the first eighteen years of the navy's history (Table 25). Two-thirds of all the sailing masters who served in the pre-1815 navy received their appointments during the War of 1812. The growth in the sailing master rank mirrors the years of the navy's most intensive use of its gunboat-size units for coastal and harbor defense, 1807–15; eight out of ten masters received their appointments during these same years. Because the great majority of the navy's sailing masters are crowded into one brief period, no attempt will be made, as was done with the midshipmen, to determine if and how the composition of the corps of masters changed over the years. The number of pre-1807 masters is just too small and too little is known about them as people to make valid comparisons with the War of 1812 masters possible.

The clear and striking difference between midshipmen and sailing masters was age (Table 26). A typical newly appointed sailing master (the median man) was twelve years older than the comparable new-fledged midshipman. The heart of the corps of newly appointed midshipmen was made up of young men aged fifteen to nineteen; that same central core of entering sailing masters ranged between twenty-four and thirty-six years of age. This last point provides an important clue. Whereas a dramatic picture (Figure 3) could be drawn to illustrate that more than half of all new midshipmen were fifteen to eighteen years of age and that nine out of ten new midshipmen fell somewhere between thirteen and twenty-two, no such striking illustration can be drawn for the ages of new sailing masters. The latter are spread out fairly evenly across the years from twenty to thirty-six. About all that can be said by way of generalization is that half the new sailing masters were men in their twenties; one-third were men in their thirties; one man in ten was in his forties; and one man in twenty was fifty or older. Only two rare individuals managed to obtain a master's appointment at nineteen (Table 27). Age difference alone goes a long way toward explaining the hostility between the midshipmen and the masters when both were competing for the same prize.

In geographical roots, too, the two corps were different, though less so than in their ages (Table 28 and Figure 8). New England supplied one-quarter of all the navy's sailing masters; New York, New Jersey, Pennsylvania, and Delaware more than one-third. The proportion of masters hailing from either of these geographical areas exceeded the corresponding proportion of midshipmen by several percentage points. South of the Mason-Dixon line the situation was reversed. One-third of all midshipmen called Maryland, Virginia, or the District of Columbia home; only a quarter of the masters did so. Approximately one master in ten hailed from the Deep South, which region supplied roughly the same proportion of the navy's midshipmen. Practically no masters came from the western states and territories, though this assessment might change if the historian could learn more about the geographical origins of sailing masters appointed on the New Orleans station.

The distribution of places that sailing masters called home reflects two more basic realities about the navy's masters. First, an absolute prerequisite for securing a sailing master's warrant was that the applicant must have established himself as a professional mariner, either through service in the navy or (more commonly) by gaining a master's or a mate's berth in the merchant service. The prenaval careers of the navy's sailing masters were universally those of men who followed the sea. A second underlying reality followed from the first. Among the 371 naval sailing masters who can be traced to a particular city, town, village, or county, two-thirds came from one of six cities: Philadelphia (74), New York (52), Baltimore (41), Boston (26), Charleston (25), and Norfolk/Portsmouth, Virginia (22). These were the centers of U.S. maritime commerce and it was in these places—or in smaller ports such as Marblehead, Wilmington (North Carolina), or Newport (Rhode Island)—that professional mariners, wherever they may have been born, had to live if they were to pursue their profession.

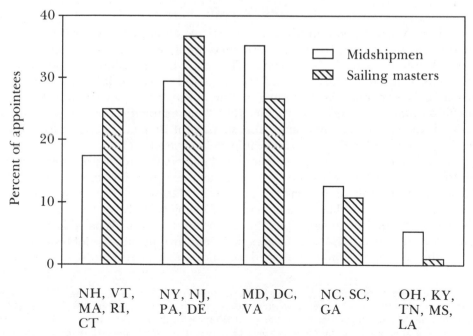

Figure 8 Midshipmen and Sailing Masters: Geographical Origins

That the navy's sailing masters were mature adults, already established in a calling, explains why so little can be discovered about their parents. Unlike midshipmen, sailing masters were appointed on their own merits as master mariners; parental status was hardly ever mentioned in applications and recommendations. Consequently, parent information has been found for only about one sailing master in ten. This is hardly men enough to draw any valid inferences about the corps of sailing masters as a whole. However, those few parents of sailing masters who have been identified appear to belong to the same layers of the social pyramid as do the parents of midshipmen discussed in Chapter 7. If sailing masters did come from the same social ranks as midshipmen, just that much more fuel would have been added to the anxieties the masters felt because of their inferior status within the navy.

More than one-fifth of all sailing masters held some other naval rank before accepting a master's warrant. Forty-six had earlier served as midshipmen or lieutenants, positions on the promotion ladder that they had lost either through resignation or through the discharge of surplus Quasi-War officers. Because such men could not be restored to the navy with their old seniority, sailing master warrants were the only option if they wanted to go to war again, as many of them did during the 1812 conflict. Invidious comparison of new status with old and keen desires to regain lost rung-holds on the promotion ladder burned especially hot in such men. Fourteen of the sailing masters had occupied that same rank at some earlier point in their lives; they were returning to a familiar status and to well-understood duties. More significant are the forty-three masters who had previously held the berth of master's mate.* Here was a well-trodden career path: one gained experience in the master's duties as his mate; when an opening occurred for a master one moved up.

Status Pangs

There was one point on which every articulate man who ever held a sailing master's warrant agreed: the rank provided ample exposure for frequent and painful wounds to one's self-esteem. "The many mortifications incident to the situation of master loudly demand that I should aspire to [a] more dignified situation," complained *Essex*'s sailing master, John Glover Cowell, on the eve of his ship's famous cruise to the Pacific.[3] The "many mortifications" were at once so well known to contemporaries and so painful that no sailing master ever listed them all in detail. They can readily be surmised.

Lieutenants, bearers of commissions and eligible for still further promotion, all too often flaunted what they perceived as their superior status, if they did not actually rub the sailing master's nose in it. Masters, mere warrant officers, were junior to in the chain of command, and subject to the orders of, not only the commissioned lieutenants but the acting ones as well. What made all this especially galling was that the masters had their own brand of snobbism. Older than the lieutenants and possessed of more experience at sea, they saw

---

* The figure 43 certainly undercounts in a serious way those men among the navy's 505 sailing masters who had previously served as master's mates. A true number could be discovered only by searching all the pay- and muster rolls of the pre-1815 navy for the names of future sailing masters then serving as mates. Scouring the rolls would be a huge and a terrifying task. Even so, it would not produce a truly correct answer: too many of the rolls have been lost.

Few portraits of pre-1815 sailing masters, painted while they held that rank, exist. Perhaps this splendid image of Marblehead's John Glover Cowell is the only one. If so, it may offer a clue to certain saltier-than-thou affectations employed by masters to assert themselves. Note the gold earring in Cowell's left lobe and the telltale ribbon revealing that his hair is braided in a queue. Cowell's desire to escape "the many mortifications" of sailing master status through promotion to lieutenant would surely have been gratified, in consequence of his key role in David Porter's Pacific Ocean adventure, had he not been mortally wounded in Essex's *February 1814 battle with* Phoebe *and* Cherub. *Cowell was then twenty-eight years old.* Marblehead Historical Society.

themselves as the better seamen, all too frequently called upon to save the lieutenants from the results of the latter's inferior skills. "I fear the Honorable Secretary will think it impertinent in me in Giving my oppinion unasked," Nathaniel Haraden, perhaps the navy's quintessential sailing master, once wrote. "But I hope he will not. I am an old Seaman my Self and have Experenced heavy gales in Every a class of Vessels from a Cod Smak to a ship of the line."[4] Most of the navy's masters would have been proud to stand on Haraden's self-description, but no sailing master ever articulated the expert seaman's contempt for the lieutenant better than Quasi-War sailing master Robert Monroe Harrison of Virginia:

> In fact I made myself a perfect slave in the ship [*Constellation*] . . . not idly looking on, but doing more labor than any man belonging to the vessel while others have enjoyed themselves contented below [and] have had as much thought of them and more than me who did the duty of the ship; there is men that are lieutenants in that same vessel who, upon my sacred honor, can scarce write their names, cannot take the sun for their lives, and, what is more, never will know; for they think they are lieutenants and that's sufficient; [that] there is no need to learn any of the duty attached to their lieutenancy; men who think of nothing but grog.[5]

There existed a second factor that made the sailing master's berth a bed of "many mortifications." Not only could they be ordered about by the youngest and (in the masters' eyes) greenest of lieutenants, but swinging onto the promotion ladder at the lieutenant rung had turned out to be a difficult feat. "Because I felt myself qualified, [I] applied for a master's warrant in preference to a midshipman's, believing that a master was certainly as eligible to advancement as that officer who is evidently junior in point of grade," lamented thirty-six-year-old Jonathan D. Ferris. "But in this I have too many demonstrations of my error; and, indeed, it's almost proverbial 'that a master never rises except by the mere effect of *Chance*, great god.' I cannot reflect on my situation but with the deepest regret and, even at this period, would prefer receiving a midshipman's warrant to that of holding a master's, subject to capricious fortune."[6]

There was one sailing master who, more than all the others, refused to remain silent on what he perceived as the indignities of the rank, and who, in fact, seems to have taken a perverse delight in stripping off his psychic shirt to parade his wounds. His name was James Trant and he was a well-known character in the navy in his day. To begin with he was something of an anomaly in that he was one of the older officers on true active duty in the U.S. Navy, for he had been born in Ireland, probably in 1763. Indeed, he must have been a man with an amazing physical constitution. The sea was for the young. Its rigors wore men out at an early age. By their thirties or early forties almost all seafarers, be they officers or enlisted men, were ready to pursue less demanding careers ashore. Trant was nearly forty-nine when the War of 1812 began, apparently in excellent health, full of vigor, and feistier than many a younger man.

Exactly when James Trant left his native Ireland and decided to build a life for himself in America is not known, but he can be traced back at least as far as 1779, when he sailed with Captain Silas Talbot in *Argo*, a vessel that was technically under the Continental army rather than the navy. The one piece of baggage that history knows Trant brought with him from the Emerald Isle was an abiding hatred for England, Englishmen, and all things English, though what personal experiences fired the hatred will probably never be known. After the Revolution James Trant disappears from the readily accessible historical record, but it is safe to assume that he commanded merchantmen, probably out of the port of New York. It is also safe to assume that Trant's career in the merchant service was less than fully satisfying, because he began applying for a sailing master's appointment in the new federal navy in the earliest days of the Quasi-War naval expansion. "I prefer the publick Service to Sail in" was his terse explanation. Although Trant made a strenuous effort to get a berth under his old Revolutionary War captain, Silas Talbot—"would much Rather Serve under you than any other"—it was to his fellow New Yorker, Captain Richard V. Morris, that Trant owed his appointment as sailing master of the *Adams* when that frigate went afloat in 1799. It was *Adams* to which Mr. Trant remained assigned until the end of March 1802, when he resigned his warrant rather than serve under "inexperienced officers"—the commissioned lieutenants—and the frigate's new commander, Edward Preble, whom Trant described as "Cross pevish and ill tempered Surley and proude."

It was a strange characterization, because Trant was not himself known for a sunny disposition. *Adams* was not big enough for two men with such volatile tempers. By 1802, when James Trant was thirty-eight, his personality had assumed the contours that it would present to the world for the balance of his life. James Fenimore Cooper, who may himself have known Trant, and who absolutely knew many naval officers who had, recorded some glimpses of that personality. "Few persons have given rise to more traditions in the service than Mr. Trant. His eccentricities were as conspicuous as his nautical peculiarities and his gallantry. His whole life was passed in or about ships, and his prejudices and habits were as thoroughly naval as those of Pipes himself. . . . He was usually supposed to be a man of obdurate feelings and of a cruel disposition, but he was not without some of the finest traits of human nature. A volume might be written of his eccentricities and opinions." Naval history is the poorer—and naval historians the sadder—that Cooper failed to pursue that last-mentioned opportunity! An enlisted man who served under Trant during the War of 1812 recalled him as "a singularly brave patriot who deserves the notice of every well-wisher of his country. His only fault was that he was incautiously brave—he knew no fear and feared no danger." Another sailor recalled him as "one of the oddities of the service, and a man with whom the blow often came as soon as the word"; he went on to make it clear that fear was more than outbalanced by fond amusement at Trant's eccentricities and by respect for his courage.

This is getting well ahead of the story, which left Trant in March 1802, his warrant turned in and himself on the beach. Return to civilian life was brief; for, as he later explained, "I allways prefered the Publick Service and never liked to come cap in Hand to a Merchant for his Employ." He decided to swallow his pride in the spring of 1804 and applied to Robert Smith for reinstatement as a sailing master, a request he apparently had no difficulty in persuading Smith to honor. When he joined his ship, the frigate *Essex*, at Washington, Trant called on Smith at the Navy Office and asked if he, a master, was eligible for promotion to lieutenant. Smith assured him he was, but at the time Trant did not pursue the matter, perhaps because, like others among his peers, he balked at the idea of going before an examining board.

After Mediterranean service in *Essex* and a furlough to pursue a merchant voyage, Trant was ordered, December 1807, to the New York navy yard under Captain Isaac Chauncey, thereby beginning Trant's long association with that senior officer "with whom," as one enlisted man succinctly put it, "he was a great pet." It was about this time that the rank of sailing master began to be too confining, for Trant was now beginning to see midshipmen who had started their careers as his green subordinates giving him orders as newly fledged lieutenants. He asked Robert Smith to promote him. He asked Paul Hamilton. He asked William Jones. All of them ignored his appeals, probably judging sailing master to be the rank for which James Trant was best qualified.

It galled him badly. Late in 1811 Sailing Master Trant found himself, by Chauncey's order, in temporary command of the ketch *Vesuvius* at the New York yard. Midshipman George Washington Storer and a companion, both attached to the ketch, decided to take the day off without bothering to seek permission. When they reappeared, well after dark, they were confronted by an irate Trant who demanded to know the reason for their gross neglect of duty. One can presume that the midshipmen had been drinking; Storer replied, as Chauncey later explained to Paul Hamilton, "in language highly improper" and then, adding insult to injury, "disputed the right of Mr. Trant to question him on that subject, contended for rank with Mr. Trant, as midshipmen were entitled to promotion and sailing masters not, and much language to that effect, all tending to insubordination and the subversion of discipline." That was more than Trant's temper could bear. Instead of arresting Storer on the spot, Trant—as Chauncey decorously explained—"entered into a discussion of the subject in dispute and language passed between them highly disreputable to officers of any grade." Mr. Trant had developed a colorful vocabulary during his nearly four decades at sea!

Chauncey resolved this particular disciplinary problem without bringing either Storer or Trant before a court martial, but when war came and Chauncey carried Trant off to serve with him on Lake Ontario, sailing master status still rankled in the latter's mind. Not only were former midshipmen now his seniors, but sailing masters appointed far more recently than Trant were making the crossover to lieutenant. Following the battles at York and Fort George in 1813 Chauncey volunteered that he was planning to recommend Trant for promotion, but nothing ever seemed to come of it. Perhaps Chauncey was angry because Trant and his command, the schooner *Julia*, were captured by the British squadron on the night of 10/11 August that same summer. For his part Trant even managed to weave his sailing master's status into the explanation of *Julia*'s capture! *Growler*'s crossing *Julia*'s stern and tacking to the southward, he later explained, "Induced me to Follow her, as She was Commanded by a Lieut. [David Deacon], my Superior Officer, [and] I as A Sailing Master. As it was the Greatest Cause of our being taken, Perhaps I am to Blame"—presumably for trusting a less experienced lieutenant—"as it Carryed us Right into the Center of the Enemy." He was not done yet. Trant ended his narrative with an offer to return to Lake Ontario, now that he had been exchanged, but could not resist adding, "Have only to Say that I do not Admire the Mode of Promoting so many young Midshipmen over me while I continue as only a Sailing Master these fifteen years past."

James Trant did finally obtain his coveted lieutenant's commission, though not until March 1817. Cooper calls it "an honor that appeared to console him for all his hardships and dangers." One is certain that it did. James Trant enjoyed being *Lieutenant* Trant for three and a half years. When he died, 11 September 1820, at the age of fifty-seven, the story was that a pair of pistols was found stowed under his pillow the better to keep doctors away.[7]

Equal Access to Promotion?

Robert Smith's vision of the sailing master rank as an alternative route by which experienced mariners could be recruited as naval lieutenants flourished during the middle years of his secretaryship. Although he never abandoned his position that sailing masters *could* be promoted to lieutenant, by the close of his term in office he had shifted his ground somewhat and restricted the openness of access: "The situation of masters in our service differs from that of masters in the British navy in this material respect, that they are in some measure in the line of promotion; that is, if a master shall be found to possess distinguished merit, he may, consistently with the rules of the department, be promoted to a lieutenancy and thence in regular succession to the higher stations."[8] The door may not have been as wide open as it had appeared to be two or three years earlier, but the important point was that it definitely stood ajar.

Paul Hamilton slammed it shut and locked it. No more sailing masters were going to be promoted, Smith's successor announced:

> There are in the service a number of the most promising young midshipmen, who entered the navy, at an age when professions are usually chosen, with the determination to make it their sole profession, and of whom the most favorable reports have uniformly been made by their commanding officers. Many of these young men have been years in the service and have acquired a degree of professional knowledge which would justify their immediate promotion, if they could be promoted consistently with the limitations of existing laws. To introduce a stranger, however respectable, however meritorious, over the heads of young men under these circumstances would be mischievous in its tendency and obviously unjust. These young gentlemen have claims that cannot be disregarded.[9]

When William Jones succeeded Hamilton, he rattled the door to make sure it was still locked. Stephen Decatur attempted to have John D. Sloat, a Quasi-War midshipman since returned to the navy as sailing master, transferred to the promotion track as a lieutenant, but Jones responded with an emphatic no: "The many claims of merit and standing similar to Mr. Sloat's, interfering as they do with the just claims of midshipmen for promotion, have produced a regulation which excludes the claim of Mr. Sloat to promotion."[10] Less than six months later, the door was once more unlocked and standing ajar. Under certain circumstances, Jones then found himself explaining, masters could be promoted to lieutenant: "Sailing masters in the navy are not in the regular line of promotion, either in this or any other service. Neither are they absolutely excluded. Their promotion depends on particular merit and circumstances."[11]

What was going on here? Why all these changes of course? The fact was that Robert Smith's program of granting sailing masters equal access to the lieutenant rung on the promotion ladder was bound to ignite opposition. The number of lieutenancies was severely limited; for every sailing master who secured one of them, there sprang up one or more agitated senior midshipmen who felt the dire deed had been done at his expense. The midshipmen's arguments were self-serving and often couched in terms calculated to exacerbate the sailing masters' sensitive feelings of inferior status[12]; but still the younger men's sense of grievance and acute unhappiness was a reality no secretary of the navy could afford wholly to ignore. Both the Navy Office and the senior officers who supported the commissioning of individual masters were pulled by two strong, if opposed, needs: on the one hand, to provide a rewarding goal for the midshipmen in whom the navy had such a substantial training investment and who had made a long-term career commitment; on the other, to recruit to the corps men too old and too experienced to enter as midshipmen who yet promised to make able and badly needed promotion-track officers. Problems spawned by the existence of the nonpromotion sailing master rank were ones that the pre-1815 navy never resolved, at least at the level of theory and policy, coping pragmatically and erratically with these conflicting demands and needs instead. Lieutenants continued to lord it over the masters. Sailing masters still felt deeply wounded by what they perceived as their inferior status; transfer to the promotion track remained the keen desire of many. Those who won the object of their desires were hotly resented by the midshipmen. But the fact was that some masters did make it onto the promotion ladder at the rung marked lieutenant. Who were they and how did they get there?

Swinging onto the Ladder

Henry Henry from Baltimore, Maryland, was probably born in 1789. In the mid-1790s his father, Hugh Henry, was a high-stakes flour dealer and wholesale grocer, but—perhaps through lack of caution—he lost most of his fortune, leaving his widow to cope as best she could with genteel poverty and son Henry to make his own way in the world. Fortunately, Henry Henry's educational assets, including a year at Georgetown College in 1803–1804, were excellent. This good preparation enabled him to secure, early in 1806, a position as a clerk, and thus an apprentice businessman, in the countinghouse of Baltimore merchant Luke Tiernan. There Henry Henry was beginning to build a good career for himself when the Embargo of 1807 struck. With shipping at a standstill, Mr. Tiernan had no need of countinghouse clerks; he did, however, need to reduce expenses. Young Mr. Henry was out of work. Conditions that had compelled Luke Tiernan to let him go prevailed everywhere along the seaboard; no use for Henry Henry to go looking for a job similar to the one he had just held. Instead, he took his savings and set off on a yearlong tour through the Western Country, a kind of vagabond existence appealing to a young man just turned eighteen.

Countinghouse jobs there were to be had in the West, if Henry Henry had wanted to settle there; but somewhere along the line he had caught a bad case of sea fever. The end of September 1808 found him back in Baltimore applying for a midshipman's warrant in the navy. Henry's letter of application was impressive; he had strong support from Luke Tiernan, navy agent John Stricker, and other Baltimoreans to whom their fellow townsman Robert Smith was likely to listen; and Henry reinforced the paper file with a personal call on the secretary. The upshot was that Smith endorsed Henry's application "Particular notice," which was tantamount to saying that an early appointment was assured. Then Smith began to have second thoughts that he was candid enough to share with the applicant. The problem was Henry Henry's age: nineteen. Smith's experience with novice midshipmen of similar years had been far from happy. They found it hard to fit in and accept naval discipline; soon they grew weary or proved to be real behavior problems; in a few months they were gone. Henry tried to reassure Smith that he was not like the others: "It was always my desire to go to sea. . . . I have been on board of the gunboats of this station and have got acquainted with a great many officers of this station, who have informed me in what manner I am to conduct myself when in service." Apparently Smith had been burned too many times. He could not overcome his reluctance, and Henry's warrant as a midshipman never materialized.

Disappointed, Henry Henry turned his attention to the reviving merchant marine of 1809 and soon rose to the post of mate, working out of Baltimore in that city's fast-sailing schooners. By 1812 he had changed his residence to Norfolk, where he seems to have found employment chances even better. His old dream of a naval career was far from dead; the June 1812 declaration of war signaled opportunity. Mustering potent support in both Norfolk and Baltimore, Henry applied for a sailing master's warrant and received it promptly, 6 July 1812. Henry spent the entire war on the Norfolk station, either commanding a gunboat or supervising the flotilla's recruiting efforts—a skill at which he seems to have been especially adept—there and in North Carolina. Twice he saw action: in a gunboat attack on the British frigate *Narcissus* and in the defense of Craney Island. As the war drew to an end, and the prospect of peace, discharge, and a return to the merchant service loomed, Henry Henry launched a strenuous effort to secure a permanent naval career through transfer to the promotion track as an acting lieutenant in the flying squadron being organized at New York, a post for which, he pointed out, his experience as a mate in swift Baltimore schooners made him especially appropriate. Thanks to strong support from Captains John Cassin and Joseph Tarbell he succeeded, gaining an appointment as acting lieutenant dated 17 March 1815. Although Wolcott Chauncey, his new commanding officer in *Torch*, evaluated him merely as "appears to be a good seaman, but wants experience as an officer," Henry Henry was at last set on his long-desired course as a career naval officer. He served in the Mediterranean till early 1817 and later that year received his commission as a lieutenant. Thereafter, in the post-1815 slowdown of promotions, Henry Henry had to wait twenty years for advancement to commander, but when he died at York, Pennsylvania, in July 1857 he had been a captain for more than ten years.[13]

Men like Henry Henry were a highly select cadre. Five hundred and five sailing masters have been identified who received appointments between 24 July 1797 and 6 February 1815. A mere forty-three of them—fewer than one master in ten—ever achieved promotion to lieutenant. Moreover, there were clearly defined moments in the navy's history when access to the promotion ladder was a reality, moments of opportunity separated by long years when no masters made the crossover. The earliest opportunity came during the Quasi-War with France. Between 1798 and 1800 thirteen sailing masters (including two master's mates) were promoted to lieutenant. The officer corps was new, expanding rapidly, and the idea of a rigid ladder of recruitment and promotion was not so firmly established as it was to be in the smaller, more professional officer corps that came into being with the Peace Establishment Act of 1801. As far as the long-term effect on the navy was concerned, these Quasi-War masters-turned-lieutenant were birds of passage; for one reason or another none of the thirteen was still on active duty in the Tripolitan War navy.

Although Robert Smith was the secretary of the navy most positive in his policy toward the admission of sailing masters to lieutenancies, his term of office was actually a time of only moderate opportunity. Five sailing masters were promoted to lieutenant—four in 1807, one in 1809—but four of the five were midshipmen who had been made sailing masters en route to lieutenancies. Only one of the new lieutenants, Nathaniel Haraden, had entered the navy as a master. In part, this apparent lack of access to promotion for masters during Smith's secretaryship was owing to forces beyond his control; several masters who seemed assured of promotion either died or resigned before they could be commissioned. Five masters recruited by Smith with the understanding that lieutenancies were open to them did, under later secretaries, gain the promotion ladder.

Paul Hamilton declared himself determined to deny promotion to sailing masters. He was as good as his word. From the time Robert Smith left office in March 1809 till the summer of 1813 no sailing masters were promoted to lieutenant, though toward the end of Hamilton's term in office he had so far

Secure at last on the promotion ladder, Lieutenant John Percival could afford to have Ethan Allen Greenwood paint this 1817 portrait with its prominently positioned epaulet proclaiming the subject's commissioned status. But what of the eyes? Do they betray an anxiety the former sailing master must have known in his five-and-a-half-year effort to regain the promotable status he once held as a Quasi-War midshipman, then lost in the 1801 reduction of the officer corps? Soon the vulnerability would be hidden under the new personality Percival was creating for himself: Mad Jack or Crazy Jack, memorably sketched in Nathaniel Hawthorne's American Notebooks *and the terror of New England missionaries struggling to indoctrinate the residents of the Hawaiian Islands with a Christian vision of sexual morality.* United States Naval Academy Museum, Annapolis, Maryland.

crumbled under pressure as to appoint a tiny number of masters as acting lieutenants. By the time Hamilton weakened, wartime conditions prevailed. It was the War of 1812's voracious demand for experienced lieutenants that created the next moment of opportunity. Fourteen masters were commissioned as lieutenants during the war, three in 1813 and eleven in 1814. William Jones set out trying to deny lieutenancies to masters in favor of midshipmen; by his second year in office reality had inundated theory.

Between 1798 and 1814 thirty-two sailing masters were promoted to lieutenant. In 1815, perhaps in part because of a petition of protest to the Senate by ninety-nine midshipmen, no masters gained the promotion ladder. Then came the final moment of opportunity for sailing masters who had entered the navy before or during the War of 1812: 1816 and 1817 saw ten more of them, including James Trant and Henry Henry, swing onto the ladder. One pre-1815 master remained to make the crossover. In 1832, Jonathan Ferris, the man who had bitterly lamented the fate that gave him a master's instead of a midshipman's warrant, persuaded his fellow veteran of the battle of New Orleans, now President of the United States Andrew Jackson, to issue the long-desired reward.[14]

Did the forty-three masters who eventually became lieutenants differ from the larger mass of masters of whom they were a privileged subgroup? Yes, in some ways. Rather surprisingly, previous service in the U.S. Navy appears to have conferred little advantage in gaining lieutenant status. Among the twenty-four sailing masters appointed to that rank between February 1809 and January 1814 who later made lieutenant, only five had earlier experience in the Quasi-War navy: three as midshipmen, one as a master's mate, and one as a captain's clerk. Under the rubric of age the small group of masters who gained the promotion track and the larger group from which they came do not appear too different—at first glance. The typical master (the median man) entered the navy at twenty-nine; the typical master who became a lieutenant also received his warrant at twenty-nine. But on a second, closer look there are differences. Among all masters the average (mean) age on joining the navy was 31.2 years and masters entered the service as late in life as 64. With the masters who were able to make the transfer to the promotion track the average age at which they joined the navy was twenty-eight, and none was older than thirty-seven when warranted. In tallying the age at appointment for all masters the third quartile falls at age thirty-six; with the masters who became lieutenants it falls at thirty-one years. Reduced to its starkest terms the message of the numbers is this: sailing masters' chances of gaining the promotion ladder were greatly diminished if they were older than thirty-one or thirty-two when they received their warrants; those who joined the navy in their mid- to late twenties had the best chance of all.

Ages at which the lucky sailing masters gained their promotions to lieutenant ran all the way from twenty-three to fifty-five, but the spread is deceptive. In this, as in all other respects, it was still a younger man's navy. Nine out of every ten of the sailing masters who gained lieutenancies were in their twenties or thirties when they swung onto the promotion ladder. More than half of those promoted were between twenty-seven and thirty-two when they made lieutenant, with the typical (median) age for promotion standing at thirty-one. Once a sailing master had reached age forty it became extremely difficult, though not utterly impossible, for him to cross over to the promotion track.

Although pre-1815 sailing masters who eventually gained lieutenant's commissions served as masters as briefly as Robert Monroe Harrison's three months or as long as Jonathan D. Ferris's twenty-three years before achieving the coveted promotion, typical times in purgatory were at the short end of the scale. Almost exactly half of the masters served less than two years under their warrants before receiving their commissions as lieutenants.[15] Three-quarters held their master's appointments less than four years before promotion. Only three masters—Nathaniel Haraden, James Trant, and Jonathan D. Ferris—had to wait more than six years before transferring to the promotion track. It was decidedly to a master's advantage to make the effort to attain the promotion track early in his naval career. After four or five years did most masters give up the attempt as hopeless and resign themselves to careers at that grade? Or did the Navy Office operate on an undeclared perception that after four, five, or six years of service the masters who had not succeeded in making the crossover were not really lieutenant material? There is probably truth in both guesses.

More certain is the direct relationship between the period at which a master joined the navy and the speed with which he became a lieutenant. That half of the group who made lieutenant in less than two years were appointed either during the Quasi-War with France or during the War of 1812; two-thirds of them were Quasi-War masters. Ten masters who served more than two, but less than four, years before swinging onto the promotion ladder were all of them War of 1812 appointees. Sailing masters who had accepted their warrants in the period between the two wars typically endured a wait of four to almost six years before opportunity smiled. All this confirms a trend already glimpsed: the Quasi-War and the War of 1812, with their rapid expansions of the officer corps and their voracious need for experienced, able lieutenants, were the great years of opportunity for those masters eager to gain the promotion ladder and the higher status it conferred. This is but one more instance of a well-understood generalization: wars almost always weaken rigid hierarchies and provide the conditions for social mobility—in both directions.

Once a sailing master had swung onto the lieutenant's rung of the ladder, what were his chances of climbing higher? Under certain conditions surprisingly good, considering that they were men who had started their careers with a handicap. Among the forty-three masters who made it onto the lieutenant rung, fifteen subsequently gained promotion to master commandant (later called commander); eleven of the fifteen went all the way to captain. This opportunity was not equally accessible to all. Thirteen of the fifteen former sailing masters who made master commandant and ten of the eleven who made captain were from among the twenty-four masters-turned-lieutenant who received their warrants between February 1809 and January 1814, an indication perhaps that the War of 1812 had created a greater equality of opportunity for masters-turned-lieutenant and a more accepting atmosphere that permitted these favored few full integration into the postwar promotion track. Age, or rather the lack of it, was a definite asset, too. No master who was older than thirty-two when he received his warrant advanced beyond the lieutenant's rung.

What of Jonathan Ferris's cry of anguish that it was only by the operations of chance—the good fortune to participate conspicuously in a naval victory— that a master gained a lieutenancy? Records of the forty-three pre-1815 masters-turned-lieutenant give but qualified support to Ferris's assertion. Leaving aside Ferris's own late-in-the-day recognition for his role in the battle of New Orleans, seven only among the forty-three could trace their promotions more or less directly to their roles in U.S. naval victories or victory-surrogates: two to *United States*'s capture of *Macedonian*; two to the battle of Lake Erie; one each to *Peacock*'s capture of *Epervier* and to Macdonough's victory on Lake Champlain; and one to *Essex*'s heroic defense against *Phoebe* and *Cherub*. Grievous wounds sustained in War of 1812 combats clearly played a role in two additional promotions. There is no gainsaying that for these nine masters the fortunes of war had provided powerful thrust to their quest for lieutenant status. However, a far more common denominator may be detected among the masters who gained promotion to lieutenant: each of them was highly anxious to gain the lieutenant's rung of the ladder; to that quest he was able to bring not only his own abilities, but powerful support as well. Here is a classic example of how things worked:

It will be remembered that when, in February 1813, Stephen Decatur asked that Sailing Master John D. Sloat be transferred to the promotion track, William Jones had shot back a prompt no. Within two months Jones was compelled to reverse himself and appoint Mr. Sloat an acting lieutenant, a step that virtually guaranteed his commissioning the July following. What Jones had failed to take into account was how difficult it was to say no to the likes of a Stephen Decatur. The captor of the *Macedonian*, not a little taken aback that Jones would have the effrontery to turn down a request he had pressed with all his clout, conferred with Sloat. The two of them decided that the next step was for Sloat to state his case in writing directly to the secretary. He was to explain that he had been appointed midshipman during the Quasi-War with France; that he had served in *President* under Thomas Truxtun; that he had been discharged under the Peace Establishment of 1801 only because he had been on shore at sick quarters when *President* sailed for the Mediterranean on the outbreak of the Tripolitan War; that he had pursued a career as a captain in the merchant service until the early weeks of 1812; that his old shipmate from *President* days, Commodore Isaac Chauncey, had then persuaded him to apply for a sailing master's warrant; and that he and Chauncey had met in person with Paul Hamilton, who had assured them both that if war was declared on Great Britain—and there was every reason to suppose that it would be—Sloat would immediately be appointed lieutenant.

Sloat waited about a month for Jones to reply, whereupon, no acting lieutenant's appointment having appeared in the mail, Decatur gave him permission to make the trip to Washington and appeal to William Jones in person. Sloat apparently bore with him a second letter of support from Decatur; for certain he carried one from William Henry Allen, newly promoted to the command of *Argus* as a reward for his role as *United States*'s first lieutenant in the capture of *Macedonian*. Allen sang Sloat's praises and said that *he* would be delighted to have Mr. Sloat in *Argus* as one of his lieutenants. Enough was enough; Jones capitulated and sent Sloat back to *United States* with an acting lieutenant's warrant in his pocket, the secretary covering his 180-degree modification of course as gracefully as he could by explaining to Decatur that it was done "in consequence of the high recommendation you have given Mr. Sloat and in consideration of the circumstances by which he lost his rank [as midshipman]."[16] Sailing Master Sloat's story delineates the combination of native ability, determination, and powerful support required if a sailing master was to gain the lieutenant's rung on the ladder of rank. His quest, its methods, and the persistence demanded were by no means unique. They were common to every sailing master who sought lieutenant status and fought to attain it.

PART SEVEN
Money and the Officer

William Winder, the first accountant of the navy, did not long remain in office. Neither did his contributions while there begin to rival those of his successor, Thomas Turner. But when, in his earliest days on the job, Winder referred to money as "the nerve and soul of enterprises," without which they must fail, he was stating a root reality too often ignored by historians of the U.S. Navy.[1] Except when dramatically large sums of prize money are mentioned, to judge from most histories and biographies that take the early-nineteenth-century navy as their subject, one might mistake that organization's officers for members of a religious order who had taken vows of poverty, their basic earthly needs mysteriously met in the spirit of the scriptural lilies of the field.

This is exactly the opposite of the way things really were in the pre-1815 navy. As with members of the middle classes in many another time, the navy's officers were keenly concerned with making and spending money. One has only to recollect that the staff of the office of the accountant of the navy was roughly twice as large as that of the secretary's office to affirm, in unison with William Winder, that, yes, money was the "nerve and soul" of the navy and of its operations. One of the more accessible motivations that can be discovered for men's choice of careers as naval officers in the United States of 1794– 1815 was that government appointments were a secure source of steady and comfortable, if not luxurious, income. These were among the handful of jobs in the pre-1815 United States that paid a fixed salary, month after month, relatively free from the dangers of sudden unemployment and impoverishment to which the wild roller coaster of the American maritime economy in the Napoleonic era could and did expose men who cast their fortunes in the private sector. Financial incentives and perils are an important thread in the history of the pre-1815 navy. To ignore them is to miss a key part of the story.

27. Cash Rewards of Service

EVERY OFFICER IN the U.S. Navy of 1794–1815 drew a salary. At first encounter, figuring out how much a particular man was paid may seem forbiddingly complex (Table 29). Actually, however, calculation of a naval officer's annual cash compensation is a relatively simple matter. From the appointment of the first officers below the rank of captain at the outbreak of the Quasi-War with France through the War of 1812 officers' basic salaries remained those outlined in the "Act Providing a Naval Armament" of 1 July 1797, supplemented by an act of 25 February 1799. The latter specified two different rates of pay for captains, depending on the size of the vessel commanded, and provided pay for certain ranks—masters commandant and lieutenants commanding small vessels—not anticipated in the 1797 legislation.[1] These basic salaries were always stated as so many dollars per month and so many rations per day. The meaning of the first is obvious; the second requires explanation.

The navy provided one basic food ration per day for each officer and man on active duty, from the captain down to the greenest boy, and it expected him to draw that ration and eat it.[2] Officers, however, were entitled to varying numbers of extra rations per day depending on their rank. Whatever its origins in the past of military organizations, by 1797 the practice of extra rations was a simple recognition of one aspect of the naval hierarchy: the higher one climbed in that hierarchy the (relatively) better one might expect to eat and the more the officer, be he the captain or a member of the wardroom mess—or even of the midshipmen's mess—was expected to entertain.[3] While all officers might, and some occasionally did, draw these extra rations in kind, the customary expectation was that the extra rations would be converted to cash at a fixed rate as a compensation for the cost of purchasing private sea stores: food and liquor.

Base salaries remained constant through 1815. What fluctuated was the value at which the extra rations were converted to cash. During the Quasi-War with France the conversion rate was set at 28 cents per ration per day; on 1 May 1801 it was cut to 20 cents and then increased to 25 cents effective 1 January 1814.[4] The reduction in the value of the ration in 1801 meant that the typical lieutenant took an annual pay cut of 8.5 percent; the captain, at the top of the scale, lost 10.6 percent of his previous annual compensation. When the value of the ration was increased in 1814 the lieutenant received, in effect, a 5.8 percent pay raise. The captain's increase was 7.4 percent.

Two other special situations could affect an officer's annual cash compensation.

Throughout the Quasi-War with France, except in those cases in which there was a specific stipulation to the contrary between the Navy Department and an officer, all officers, whether on active duty or not, drew their full compensation in salary and ration money.[5] Because almost the entire officer corps was on active duty, this particular wrinkle in the law had not posed serious practical problems. When, at the close of the Quasi-War, the Navy Department and Congress worked together to draw up the Peace Establishment Act (3 March 1801) the resulting legislation contained the provision that officers not "under orders for actual service . . . shall be entitled to receive no more than half their monthly pay."[6] A hasty reading of the law might suggest that this meant that an officer not on active duty took a 50 percent pay cut. Actually, it was worse than that. What the law meant was that the officer not on active duty drew half of his salary and *no rations*.[7] Consequently, a lieutenant who elected to stay ashore or whose services were for a period not needed took, after May 1801 and before January 1814, a 61.5 percent cut from his active-duty income, while a captain in the same situation had his income reduced by 64.8 percent. Half-pay was seen not as a sum of money adequate to an officer's support while awaiting orders, but as a kind of retainer, giving the government the right to call him to active duty when he was needed. Unless he had an ample private income, a man not on active duty was expected to be supporting himself by supplemental employment in the merchant marine.

As 1813 turned into 1814 it became increasingly apparent that the navy was experiencing severe difficulties in maintaining its squadron on Lake Ontario at full strength. The squadron's officers confronted a cost of living on the lakes frontier that had increased nearly 100 percent since the declaration of war, a situation that—along with other factors—fueled a steady stream of requests for transfer to duty elsewhere. As for recruiting enlisted men, the dim prospects for prize money on the lakes, contrasted with the glittering hopes on the oceans, especially in privateers, was a woeful disincentive. Officer and enlisted man were alike appalled by the upstate New York climate and the station's reputation for sickliness. To combat these negative factors Congress authorized the Navy Department (18 April 1814) to add as much as 25 percent to the base pay of officers and enlisted men "engaged in any service the hardships or disadvantages of which shall, in [the president's] judgment, render such an addition necessary." The 25 percent hardship pay was immediately granted to all those serving on the northern lakes.[8] The net effect of the addition for hardship pay coming on top of the almost simultaneous increase in the cash value of the ration was that a typical lieutenant serving on Lake Erie or Lake Ontario in 1814 received an across-the-board increase of 25 percent in his total cash compensation, as did his captain. This hardship pay provision remained in force until 22 February 1817, at which time it was repealed and base salaries returned to their long-established levels for all officers, though the ration continued to have the higher cash conversion value of 25 cents.[9]

In addition to his cash compensation the officer on active duty had a major fringe benefit: servants. This benefit could take one of two forms. If an officer regularly employed a free man as a servant or if he owned a slave who served as such he could have that individual entered on the ship's rolls as a member of the crew—seaman, ordinary seaman, boy, whatever was appropriate—but employ him as his shipboard servant. The slave's pay customarily went to the owner; the free man's pay stayed in his own pocket. An officer who did not have a servant from civilian life was permitted to select a man from the crew for that purpose. The reasons behind this practice are not far to seek. In the hierarchical world of the eighteenth and nineteenth centuries it would be inconceivable that those occupying the positions of leadership would be expected to tote their own baggage, prepare their own meals and serve themselves, wash their own dishes and glassware, or do their own laundry. Moreover, this was a time when the employment of household servants extended much farther down the social and economic scale than is now commonly realized. Service was a major form of employment; the use of servants was by no means the prerogative and status symbol of the elite. Although the practices just described were followed in every ship in the navy and were common knowledge, the historian searches the navy's regulations in vain for a single mention of servants, which officers were entitled to them, and how many an officer might expect to support from the public payroll. The practice was based entirely on tradition and custom, with the British navy as the obligatory role model.[10] How many servants could an officer expect to have? This was dictated by custom as interpreted by an individual commanding officer. Officers on the social level of lieutenants— that is, the denizens of the wardroom—were certainly allowed one or two apiece; the captain would have needed at least two and perhaps more; the midshipmen collectively were probably allowed one or two, but they could hardly have expected to be allocated individual servants, save for the rare young man who might own a personal slave. Because taking care of an officer's needs was often not enough to occupy a servant's full time, custom also decreed that the servants would perform some regular shipboard duties as well; they were certainly assigned battle stations when the crew went to quarters.

This practice conferred an additional economic benefit on slave-owning officers. If an officer was not on active duty and he had no useful role for a slave in his shore-based situation, the officer could enlist his experienced mariner-slave in the navy at an appropriate rating and receive the slave's wages as income. What portion of the navy's officers were in a position to benefit from this practice is impossible to say, but enough cases survive in the records to suggest that the unrecorded instances were probably more numerous than heretofore suspected.[11]

Making Ends Meet

Dollars. The word has appeared repeatedly in the pages since the beginning of the chapter. It is both a dangerous and an elusive concept. Dangerous because the purchasing power of the U.S. dollar has changed so radically in nearly two centuries that salaries and compensation in the pre-1815 navy seem almost incomprehensibly small. Too easy to slip unawares into a feeling that the naval officer's cash compensation from government was miserly or to fall into a quaintness-of-past-times nostalgia that inhibits an understanding of that former reality. Neither is it an adequate antidote to say that *y* pre-1815 dollars is equal to *x* 1990 dollars, increase Lieutenant So-and-So's pay and rations by the appropriate multiple, and translate the result into a late-twentieth-century standard of living. Therein lies the elusiveness, for what a pre-1815 officer needed to purchase with his money differed in many ways from what his 1990 counterpart must buy. The earlier world was a different world. Except for the 20-cent-a-month deduction for the marine hospital fund, no taxes were assessed against the pre-1815 officer's pay. All of it went directly into his pocket. On the other hand, the middle-class man of that day had an ongoing expense that he considered essential, but that his latter-day counterpart would regard as a luxury: full-time servants. The problem of understanding the real value of the pre-1815 dollar is compounded because once a person passes the subsistence level, how much money one *needs* to live becomes a highly subjective concept. Living quarters entirely acceptable to Family A may be deemed cramped and a little down-at-the-heels by Family B, even though the two families may have similar incomes.

No officer's detailed records of what it cost him to live for a month or a year have been found. Neither do the archives contain a discussion, with specifics, of what an officer expected as his standard of living. But, if the latter point was never directly addressed, the answer lurks just below the surface of the documentary record with hints of its shape now and again breaking the water. The officer, because he was an officer, expected to be *respectable*, that is, at least middle-class in his status. He wanted to dress well, and to have an appropriate number of servants (slave or free). Marriage was a common expectation, and when he married the officer wished to be able to pay for his children's education and to help them get started in life. His home, if typically far from opulent, suggested modest financial competence, station attained, and discreet good taste. Even if the officer did not come from the wealthiest stratum of the elite, he could anticipate, in the course of his professional career, that he would be the guest of, or entertain on shipboard, the civilian leadership of his own country or high officials of foreign nations. Equally, he expected to be able to entertain his professional peers with a degree of elegance. Not only did the officer have to meet all these current expenses, he expected to accumulate savings, whether to meet extraordinary events or as a means of support in declining years. How many *dollars* did it take to cover these expectations in the United States of 1794–1815?

One can begin by noting a few comparisons. The secretary of the navy drew a salary of $4,500 per year. As with many another cabinet official in years since, the secretaries tended to complain that the money really was not adequate to support the style of life they were expected to maintain, a claim that should perhaps be treated with a certain skepticism. Salary for the chief clerk of the Navy Department was $2,045, a figure on which Charles W. Goldsborough managed to sustain a two-story house, the main part of which measured forty-four by twenty feet, containing two rooms and a hall on the ground floor, four bedrooms on the second, and a finished attic. Behind the main portion of the house, and presumably extending at a right angle to it (though it may have been entirely detached), was a wing that contained storeroom, office, library, bathhouse, vegetable cellar, and home dairy. Two-story porches ran along the back of the main structure and around the subsidiary building. The grounds were enhanced by a large vegetable garden, fruit trees, and a grape arbor. All in all the quarters were sufficiently elegant that, with a small enlargement, Secretary William Jones was happy to rent them ("the rooms are rather small but will be large enough to entertain genteelly") when the temporarily unemployed Goldsborough had to give up the house in favor of more frugal shelter.[12] Subordinate clerks in the offices of the secretary of the navy and the accountant of the navy (except for the rank novices) earned approximately $1,000 to $1,300 per year, of which sum the typical clerk spent, in 1812–13, $100 for house rent, $48 for each female servant, $96 for each male servant, and $20 per child for education.[13]

It is further possible to appreciate a sense of the purchasing power of so-and-so many dollars for the naval officer of 1794–1815 by listening attentively to his subjective comments on the adequacy or inadequacy of pay and rations for support. At the bottom of the pay scale the midshipman's $228 a year, plus one ration per day, was considered adequate to support him when he was at sea.[14] The midshipman was a young apprentice. It was universally expected that he would neither marry nor be married at that rank. His only expenses were uniform, supplementary food and wine for the mess, and entertainment in port. Some thrifty souls were occasionally able to send money home to a widowed mother; others certainly received financial assistance from parents. However, considering what is known about the midshipmen's social origins, it would be a mistake to exaggerate the number of U.S. Navy midshipmen with significant private income over and above their pay. If midshipmen ran short of money on an active-duty cruise, it was attributable to youthful inexperience in money management, most often taking the form of a mess living beyond its means. When midshipmen were attached to shore stations $228 a year plus one ration a day was a sum on which it was extremely challenging to exist.[15]

When the midshipman advanced to acting lieutenant ($624 a year, 1801–13) or acting sailing master ($552 in the same period) he thought he had come into a fortune. "Since my last [letter I] have been promoted to [acting] sailing master," crowed Midshipman David Conner. "My situation is considerably better. My pay now amounts to $52 per month. With this I can live very handsomely."[16] Let it be noted that Conner was both a bachelor and on active duty. Still, a useful benchmark is here established, and it is confirmed by other sources: in the United States of 1812 a single man could live very comfortably on $624 a year. Not to be overlooked is the word *single*. Wiser and older heads undoubtedly cautioned lieutenants to wait at least until they were masters commandant or (preferably) captains before they considered marriage. But it was a subject on which younger men were not necessarily prepared to be coldly rational. Those who decided not to wait, but married as lieutenants, found it a test to live on $624 a year. "It is well known to you that a lieutenant's pay, in supporting himself and family, requires the greatest economy," lamented Nathaniel Haraden to Paul Hamilton in 1809. Some simply could not master that degree of frugality. Captain Isaac Hull (himself unmarried at the time) reluctantly approved Lieutenant Stephen Cassin's request for a furlough to make an East India voyage: "His conduct has been that of a correct, good officer, and I should be sorry to have him leave the ship. Yet, knowing as I do that he has a growing family which depend on him for support, and having no other means than his pay as a lieutenant, which is scarcely sufficient to support himself with the strictest economy . . . I am induced to aid him in his application." Cassin had, Hull explained, been maintaining his wife and children

*Unlike the commonly seen portraits of the older man, this miniature of James Barron,
painted during his self-imposed exile in Denmark, still radiates the warm human qualities
that helped to make him one of the navy's highly respected captains until the* Chesapeake-
Leopard *incident of 1807 inflicted a mortal wound on his professional reputation. James
Barron had carried within himself the seeds of his own downfall. A man of repeatedly
proven bravery in the face of danger, he was also prey to a deep pessimism that could
reduce him to inaction at critical junctures when an ambiguous situation demanded moral
rather than physical courage.* Private collection.

with the aid of a subsidy from his father, Washington navy yard second-in-
command John Cassin.[17]

Even at the master commandant's annual compensation of $1,008 (1801–
13) supporting a family was problematic. Thomas Robinson, fearing that his
command, *Wasp*, was about to be ordered abroad, asked to be relieved: "The
pay and emoluments of a master commandant are by no means adequate to
the support of a *family* on shore and such a table as the commander of the U.S.
Ship Wasp *must* always keep, together with the numerous expenses attending
the latter, particularly on a foreign station."[18] Only when the rank of captain
was reached—and especially the higher annual compensation accruing to the
senior captains ($1,906 in 1799–1801; $1,704 in 1801–13; $1,830 after January
1814)—did the complaints about inability to support one's family almost wholly
cease. From this a second benchmark can be established: for the married officer
with a family, comfortable middle-class existence was possible at a threshold
falling somewhere between $1,300 and $1,700 per year.

If a captain could support himself and family on his active-duty pay and
rations, most assuredly he could not do so on his half-pay of either $600 or
$450 per year. Not only was his pay cut in half, but he also lost all of his cash
compensation for rations: $576 and $432 respectively in the 1801–13 years. In

other words, half-pay was a euphemism, because the cut in actual income was more like two-thirds. Robert Smith excelled at ignoring officers he felt had let him down. Samuel Barron was such an officer. Chronic liver disease and a disappointing performance as Mediterranean commodore in 1804–1805 had been bad enough, but then had come the *Chesapeake* disgrace under his brother, James. That was more than enough of the Barrons for Mr. Smith! In the summer of 1807 the secretary beached Commodore Samuel at his home in Hampton, Virginia, and proceeded to ignore him for the balance of his term of office. There Barron remained at $600 a year when, about twelve months into Paul Hamilton's tenure, William Bainbridge came calling. "I have this day visited Commodore Samuel Barron of our navy," a troubled Bainbridge hastened to write Hamilton. "After seeing the rigid economy with which he is necessitated to live—so different from what he was ever before compelled to do—and believing that his reduced funds is owing to many years' services to his country," Bainbridge urged that Barron be given the command of the Norfolk navy yard, an active-duty post that would restore him to full pay and rations, as well as give him free quarters in the yard. Later that year Hamilton assigned Samuel Barron to the desired post.[19]

The half-pay-and-no-rations issue affected far more men than Samuel Barron. It stuck in the craw of the corps. Alexander Murray, ever the master of colorful prose, best articulated the anxiety:

> The rank we hold while in actual service unavoidably leads us to keep up a style of expense that requires the whole of our pay to entitle us to proper notice while abroad and to support the respectability of the navy, our acquaintance being—or ought to be—among the first class of society wherever we go. . . . What, then, is to become of our families in the intervals on the present half-pay regulations? Few of us have independent estates, and the circle of our acquaintance in the private walks of life ought to be respectable. Is it, then, consistent with the dignity of the U. States, thus flourishing in its commerce and rendered in a measure secure by our little navy, that their officers should be compelled either to seclude themselves from the eyes of the world or fly to the *dernier resort* of accepting menial commands in the private sea service— when to be obtained—and to expose themselves to the view of foreign nations vending their wares where they had held high and distinguished commands? For my own part I never was ashamed of an honest occupation, but I should feel for the dignity of my country upon such an occasion.

If captains, the navy's best-paid officers, were living so close to the edge that a year or two on half-pay brought to Alexander Murray's vivid imagination visions of senior officers compromising the dignity of the United States by "retailing bunches of onions, etc., etc., from droghers in ports where we had [previously] held high commands," no wonder the typical officer's fantasies dwelt so often and so lovingly on certain perfectly legal ways he could solve his financial problems while fulfilling his duty to his country.[20]

28. Big Money

*F*RUGALITY AND THE SLOW, steady accumulation of capital are not always easy habits to acquire and practice. The big payoff that substantially alters one's economic fortunes for the better holds perennial fascination. Apart from out-and-out dishonesty, of which only slight evidence exists among pre-1815 naval officers, there were two ways these men dreamed of fulfilling that fantasy: freight and prize money.

Banking by Ship

Freight had a peculiar meaning that requires explanation. It did not imply that an officer was loading a U.S. warship with goods for private speculation. Rather, suppose that an American merchant had a substantial amount of hard money—gold or silver—in a foreign port and wanted to get it back to the United States. He could try to send it home in a merchant ship. Even if the merchantman survived all the natural hazards of the sea, there was the very real danger that she might fall prize to one of the warring powers—and the money with her. Or he could send it home in a warship, which was infinitely safer, especially as long as the United States remained neutral in the Napoleonic conflict. The naval captain would have to take charge of the money, protect it, and deliver it safely. For his trouble and risk he was entitled to charge a percentage; this was called freight. Because of its high potential for abuse, the practice was closely watched by the Navy Department.

So far as the records show, commanding officers were the only ones who could claim the privilege of carrying freight in a warship. Money potentially to be earned by this means became a significant fringe benefit of attaining command status. The secretary of the navy's prior permission was not required for a captain to carry freight. This was specified in a rather backhanded fashion by article 23 of the "Act for the Better Government of the Navy," which stipulated that a captain could not, without the express permission of the Navy Department, receive any "goods or merchandise" into a public ship, "except gold, silver, or jewels." The latter three, by clear implication, could be carried without such permission; for, when ships were on distant stations it would have been impossible to obtain such permission in a timely fashion. The Navy Department did impose two restrictions: First, the cash had to belong to U.S. citizens; the danger of involving the U.S. Navy in unneutral activities through protecting the cash of one warring party against the attacks of another must be scrupulously avoided. Second, the captain could charge 0.5 percent freight on the first $10,000 of a particular individual's money and 0.25 percent on the balance. If the money shipper volunteered to give the captain more, that was the shipper's prerogative; but, if the captain demanded more, the shipper could appeal to the Navy Department and have the charge reduced to the permitted maximum.

Here was a situation in which a little circumspect cheating was a real temptation. If a captain brought $50,000 from Havana to Philadelphia for Messrs. John Doe & Son he could legally charge $150 for his trouble: the equivalent of a month and a half's salary, a nice addition to income, but assuredly no fortune. The real money was to be had just beyond the fringes of the regulations. Making foreign liquid assets look like the cash of U.S. citizens was certainly not beyond the ingenuity of merchants and naval captains. The greater the dangers to money in transit, so much higher the temptation to charge more than was officially allowed. Because these were always private transactions between merchants and captains, there is no way for the historian to know how great a traffic there may have been or how much extra income captains earned. Unless somebody squealed. At least two telling incidents survive in the records. During the latter part of the Quasi-War with France Captain Henry Geddes agreed with the Havana agent of Messrs. James De Wolfe & Brothers of Bristol, Rhode Island, to bring $30,000 to the United States in *Patapsco* in return for an agreed-upon freight of 1 percent, or $300. When Geddes got home, however, he insisted on receiving 2 percent ($600) before he would release the money. In this particular instance James De Wolfe & Brothers complained loudly to acting secretary of the navy Samuel Smith, who made Geddes refund the extra $300. The money Geddes was allowed to keep was still the equivalent of four months of his base pay as captain of a 20-gun ship, a nice windfall for relatively little extra work.

The real dimensions of the possible profits from freight are even more clearly delineated in an incident from 1811. In November of that year James Lawrence was preparing to sail for Europe in *Hornet*. These were years when few U.S. warships left North American waters; this relatively rare opportunity to get cash across the wartime Atlantic in almost total safety was not overlooked by alert merchants—nor, it must be added, by James Lawrence. How actively Master Commandant Lawrence solicited the business is not clear, but by the end of the month he was expecting to receive on board *Hornet* between $180,000 and $200,000 in Spanish gold. Apparently Lawrence had some qualms about whether he should ask the secretary of the navy's permission to carry the cash, so he consulted John Rodgers, Stephen Decatur, and Isaac Chauncey, all of whom pointed to the wording of article 23 of the "Act for the Better Government of the Navy" and assured him that it had been the practice (of which they presumably spoke from personal experience) from the earliest days of the navy for captains to carry money, and to charge freight for so doing, without bothering to seek permission. Rodgers could see not "the smallest impropriety" in carrying the money and was certain Secretary Hamilton would "feel a pleasure" in giving his approval to the plan, if Lawrence had time to consult him. Besides which, Lawrence argued to himself, Samuel Evans had recently asked permission to transport specie to Europe in *Chesapeake* and had been told yes. Why trouble Mr. Hamilton with having to make the same decision all over again? One final rationalization: There would not be time to receive permission before *Hornet* was supposed to sail.

Meanwhile, word of what was afoot had reached the ears of Hamilton and, more significantly, President Madison. On 29 November Lawrence received a letter from the secretary: "It having been intimated that application would be made to you to convey in the Hornet specie abroad on private account, I have it in charge from the president of the United States to inform you that such conveyance is wholly inadmissable; any such application, therefore, is to be rejected; and should you have received any specie on private account, it is immediately to be relanded." Master Commandant Lawrence was now in the highly embarrassing position of being required to tell all of the merchants who had sent their cash on board *Hornet* that they would have to take it back to the bank. He covered his embarrassment as best he could by explaining that freight "has been a privilege allowed the commanders of our public vessels since the establishment of our navy," and that his unpleasant experience was "the first instance wherein a commander has been debarred the privilege of carrying specie." There was more than just embarrassment involved. The merchants had been required to pay the banks a premium of 4 percent to obtain gold. When they returned the gold to the bankers it would be credited to them only at par value, a loss, in the case of one firm, of $6,000. The principals of that particular firm were planning to shake their heads and absorb the penalty, but others, less able to afford graciousness and generosity, were threatening to bill James Lawrence for their loss.

Whether compensation for the merchants' losses was ever actually extracted from Lawrence's pocket is not on record. Had not Madison and Hamilton squelched the deal, it would have been a highly profitable venture for the

C.B.J. Fevret de Saint-Mémin's image of James Lawrence manifests less of the cockiness and excessive self-assurance that were to bring him fame through his February 1813 capture of Peacock, *then bitter defeat and death four months later in combat with* Shannon, *than do the hero's later portraits. Perhaps the subdued and inward-looking quality of the Saint-Mémin engraving reflects Lawrence's receipt of word that Secretary of the Navy Paul Hamilton was squelching the acquisitive master commandant's potentially lucrative plan to turn* Hornet *into a floating bank.* National Portrait Gallery, Washington, D.C.

master commandant. Isaac Chauncey, a man not given to hyperbole when it came to money, claimed that Lawrence expected to earn between $8,000 and $10,000 in commissions. Assuming that the lower figure is the more realistic one and that the specie going out in *Hornet* was $180,000, it is then possible to calculate that Lawrence planned to charge 4 to 4.5 percent in commissions, a measure of the risk of transporting cash across the ocean in 1811. If the $8,000 figure for total commission is correct, James Lawrence would have earned for his trouble a sum equal to eight times his annual pay and rations as a master commandant! It is unlikely that the transportation of cash by captains of the pre-1815 navy was halted by Lawrence's big disappointment, though one may be sure that commanding officers thereafter did it as inconspicuously as possible to avoid attracting unwelcome attention from Washington. Opportunities for profit through freight were so excellent that it is difficult to imagine many captains resisting them. The pity is that the historian cannot find more evidence of these lucrative deals.[1]

Pocketing the Spoils of War

A senior officer intent on improving his financial situation through legitimate activity was probably well advised to concentrate on quietly seeking freight commissions, rewarding if undramatic. But money decisions are often made on other grounds than purely rational self-interest. Another way in which an officer might gain a large cash windfall is far better known and better documented: prize money from the capture of enemy ships, public and private. There is no question that the dream of substantial cash windfalls in wartime was a major motivator for every man from the captain down to the greenest landsman. The historian needs to deromanticize prize money, to ask, How much was there to be made from prizes? Who got the most? Who the least? What were the odds of getting any?

Unlike freight, the rules governing prize money were both elaborate and widely known. They were part of the navy's basic legislation, the "Act for the Better Government of the Navy of the United States" of 23 April 1800. These provisions were somewhat complicated, but they need to be understood if the stakes at issue are to be fully appreciated. The single most important rule was a distinction made between (1) prizes "of equal or superior force to the vessel or vessels making the capture" and (2) prizes "of inferior force" to the vessel or vessels making the capture. In the former case every penny of the net proceeds from the sale of the prize and her cargo became the property of the captors. If the prize were "of inferior force," then only half of the net proceeds went to the captors; the other half accrued to the U.S. government to be added to the principal of a fund for the payment of naval pensions. Because the law did not define how superior or inferior force was measured, both motivation and grounds existed for maneuver and litigation between the captors and the United States in those cases in which the differences between the combatants were slight. It was in the clear and present self-interest of the captors to make the prize appear at least equal, if not a little superior; the government had just as powerful an interest in demonstrating the superior strength of its warship.

The possibility of litigation over a few dubious cases aside, that rule was relatively straightforward and readily understood. Thereafter things became more complicated. The captors' share of the net proceeds of the prize and her cargo was divided into twentieths, which twentieths became the basis on which the cash was actually distributed. Although the law and naval officers of the time always spoke of prize shares in terms of twentieths, these figures will be more easily comprehended if they are converted into increments of 5 percent. Right off the top of the captors' share, whether the half or the whole of the net proceeds, the captain of the ship making the capture received 15 percent; *but*, if the capturing ship were part of a squadron, the squadron commodore received one-third of the captain's 15 percent. Put another way, the squadron commodore, no matter how remote from, or how involved in, the combat he might have been, took 5 percent of the captors' share of every prize captured by any vessel of his squadron. The remaining 85 percent of the net proceeds was then allocated as follows:

10 percent divided among the ship's lieutenants, captain of marines, and sailing master

10 percent divided among the chaplain, the marine lieutenants, the surgeon, the purser, the boatswain, the gunner, the carpenter, and the master's mates

17.5 percent divided among the midshipmen, the surgeon's mates, the captain's clerk, the schoolmaster, the boatswain's mates, the gunner's mates, the carpenter's mates, the purser's steward, the sailmaker, the master-at-arms, the armorer, the cockswains, and the cooper

12.5 percent divided among the remaining petty officers (e.g., quartermasters and quarter gunners), the sailmaker's mates, and noncommissioned marines above the rank of private

the remaining 35 percent divided among the ship's seamen, ordinary seamen, boys, and marines

One final provision complicated the law even further. If other U.S. naval ships were "in sight" when a ship or ships made a capture, all naval vessels in sight shared in the prize(s) "according to the number of men and guns on board each ship in sight." The possibilities for acrimony and litigation—let alone astounding feats of distance vision—created by this provision may be left to the imagination.[2]

How did this formula for distributing prize money work out in real life? Several statements of actual distributions of prize money can be found (Table 30). Unfortunately for the cause of discovering the typical, all of these statements are from the War of 1812 or the subsequent Algerian War; none has been recovered from the Quasi-War years. There were significant differences in the amounts of prize money earned in each of these two conflicts (Table 31). The largest single award of prize money to the captors of enemy ships during the War of 1812 (Macdonough's Lake Champlain victory) was nearly four times as great as the largest Quasi-War award (*Constellation* vs. *Insurgente*); the total amount of prize money earned during the War of 1812 was almost seven times as great as that earned during the French conflict, clear evidence that Britain's maritime hegemony made her a far more tempting and lucrative enemy for those with ambitions in the prize money lottery. The typical (median) 1812 prize was three times as valuable as the comparable prize made in the earlier French war. Not only is Table 30 distorted by its exclusive reliance on War of 1812 and Algerian War prize money, but, with the exception of *Torch*, each of the prize money awards shown would fall in the top quarter of all prize money awards made during the War of 1812. In short, *Torch* aside, this is prize money at its best for the U.S. Navy of 1794–1815.

If one wanted to be rich, by far and away the best battle in which to have fought was Perry's victory at Lake Erie.[3] The man with the biggest reward was someone who was not even present: Perry's superior officer, Commodore Isaac Chauncey, who took his 5 percent off the top of the $255,000 award, netting himself $12,750, the equivalent of seven and a half times his annual base pay and rations. Oliver Hazard Perry and Jesse D. Elliott each pocketed $7,140, almost exactly the equivalent of seven years of their pay and rations as masters commandant. A lieutenant or sailing master in command of a vessel made nearly $2,300, very roughly four times his yearly pay and rations under normal circumstances. The lowest-paid officer—the $228-a-year midshipman—made three and a half times that amount in prize money.

Lake Erie prize money, let it be repeated, was prize money at its most spectacular. It was far indeed from being the norm. More useful in that regard is *Torch*'s $3,744 share of the Algerian prize money. This sum is close enough to the War of 1812's median prize money award ($2,908) to give a fair idea of how the ship's company of a typical small cruiser in that conflict might have fared. *Torch*'s commanding officer, Wolcott Chauncey, was handed $374, 43 percent of what he would earn that year in pay and rations. Chauncey's lieutenants pocketed $125, 19 percent of annual compensation; his midshipmen received $55 or 24 percent of annual salary. Before leaving the subject of the distribution of *Torch*'s prize money one may recall that the median Quasi-War prize netted its captors $1,049—very roughly one-third of the War of 1812's median prize. By dividing each *Torch* share by three one can draw an approximate idea of how a counterpart in a small Quasi-War cruiser may have fared from a typical capture.

The historian is now ready to state some conclusions about prize money. One has long been known: the higher an officer's rank the more, both absolutely and relatively, he was likely to make in prize money. What the figures also suggest is that for most officers the idea of prize money as the road to wealth was a chimera, as it has been a will-o'-the-wisp for subsequent historians. Throughout these paragraphs the standard of comparison has been a year's active-duty pay and rations. It would almost certainly require a lump-sum payment of prize money equal to, or a multiple of, one year's pay and rations to enable the prudent officer to make the kind of investments that would either insure financial independence or provide a marked difference in financial status. Lump sums less than a year's salary would have been welcome, if only to clear old debts or to make some modest purchases; but, save for the most penurious and the shrewdest of investors, such a payment would not have put one on the road to financial independence. Applying this year's-pay-and-rations standard, the only officers in Table 30 who came out significantly ahead in the prize money sweepstakes were (1) all participants in the battle of Lake Erie; (2) Commodores Isaac Chauncey and Stephen Decatur; and (3) the following captains, with the figure after each name representing the multiple of annual compensation that prize money represented: Master Commandant Jacob Jones of *Wasp*, 3.7×; John Rodgers, captor of *Falcon*, 1.5×; Charles Stewart's share of *Levant*, 1.9×.

The role that prize money could play in a lucky officer's life is nowhere better illustrated than with Pliny Hayes, Jr., a medical student from Connecticut.

Perhaps Hayes had run out of money to continue his medical education; maybe he wanted to enhance his classroom learning with some actual work experience; it may have been nothing more than a desire to participate in the war. Whatever his motive, Hayes secured an acting surgeon's mate's berth in *Hornet*, Master Commandant James Lawrence, in the early months of the War of 1812. Then, to Hayes's chagrin, *Hornet*'s new surgeon, Charles Cotton, appeared and announced that he had his own candidate, one Micajah Hawkes, for the mate's job. Angry and hurt, Hayes was preparing to go ashore when Lawrence intervened and pleaded with him to make the cruise in the capacity of captain's clerk, to which Hayes agreed.

> As we had rough weather at first, I was miserably seasick for several days, after which I was attacked with a dyspepsia which lasted till we arrived in St. Salvador, seven weeks from the time we left Boston. I was so sick as to be incapacitated from business the whole time and so emaciated that some of the officers prognosticated my death before we should return. The vast quantities of the most excellent fruits and fresh provisions which we obtained at St. Salvador, together with a little wine which I purchased, had an almost instantaneous effect in restoring my health, and from that time I gained astonishingly in health and strength. After the battle with the Peacock I had an opportunity of being present at the performance of (I think) seven amputations of the leg and arm, five of them performed by Cotton and two by the English surgeon, and all of them on British subjects. I also assisted in dressing the wounds during our return.

Pliny Hayes, Jr., quit the navy (4 April 1813) after *Hornet* reached New York, but he now had $850 in prize money in his pocket, approximately two years' pay and rations for a surgeon's mate, or three years' for a captain's clerk—enough, with frugality, to enable him to finish medical school, which he did, earning his M.D. at Harvard in 1815.[4]

There may be an Achilles' heel in the argument just made that there were few real winners in the prize money lottery. The Algerian exception aside, each of the cases (Table 30) is a single capture. Over the course of an entire war or even an entire cruise, might not an individual participate in several prizes and might not these successive prize shares add up to a truly significant sum? This question can be tested by looking at the prize money experience of all officers commanding ships during the Quasi-War with France.[5] Commanding officers were, after squadron commodores, potentially the biggest winners in the prize money lottery; the fate of subordinates may be extrapolated from the experience of their seniors. First and last, fifty-five men commanded naval vessels for shorter or longer periods during the Quasi-War. Of these fifty-five, twenty-three (41.8 percent) captured no prizes at all; thirty-two (58.2 percent) captured only one prize or no prizes; and three-quarters (76.5 percent) captured three or fewer prizes. Indeed, just seven commanding officers (12.7 percent) captured five or more French armed vessels during the entire Quasi-War with France. The commanding officers in question, and the number of French armed prizes captured, were Hugh G. Campbell (10), George Little (8), Richard V. Morris (7), William Maley (6), John Shaw (6), Stephen Decatur, Sr. (5), and Benjamin Hillar (5). If the standard of success in the Quasi-War be defined as the number of enemy vessels captured, these seven men were the war's most valuable officers, although some of the names are obscure, even to naval historians. Seen in this light, one understands why Campbell and Morris emerged from the Quasi-War with enhanced reputations that, in Morris's case, failed to survive the Tripolitan War.

Were these same seven men the war's big prize money winners? If so, how much did they earn? Among the thirty-two Quasi-War commanding officers who earned prize money from the capture of French armed vessels, nineteen (59.4 percent) earned less than $300; another four (12.5 percent) made between $320 and $500 in wartime prize money. The median gain among commanding officers was $266: approximately three months' pay for a master commandant. While all of these commanding officers were surely glad to pocket any money they could, sums of such magnitudes could hardly have made an appreciable difference in their general financial standing.[6]

Nine commanding officers—16.4 percent of all Quasi-War commanding officers, 28.1 percent of those earning some prize money during the war— gained more than $500 from this source (Table 32). Five (or perhaps four[7]) of the nine earned a windfall approximately equal to half a year's pay, possibly a nice little nest egg to be cultivated, but certainly not wealth by any stretch of the imagination. Four men earned substantial sums of money from enemy prizes during the Quasi-War: Thomas Truxtun, George Little, John Shaw, and Hugh G. Campbell. Shaw and Campbell made their money the hard way, through the assiduous pursuit of many small prizes. Although Shaw earned the equivalent of less than two years' pay and Campbell the equivalent of only one, later subjective comments by their contemporaries suggest that both men were shrewd investors who made the most of their windfalls. If neither was truly wealthy, both were highly secure. Two men became rich—or, more accurately, richer—George Little and Thomas Truxtun. In Truxtun's case $8,028 came from his capture of the French frigate *Insurgente*. Little earned $1,034 from the French naval corvette *Berceau*, but did even better—$2,696— by his capture of the rich prize *Deux Anges*.

Were these four rich or comfortable captains just happy men on whom a capricious Fortune smiled? Maybe. But, in looking at the evidence, it is hard not to conclude that wealth in the Quasi-War came to men of unusual abilities who assiduously sought it. Some captains pursued fame and seemed relatively indifferent to prize money. Edward Preble would be an example. Hugh G. Campbell courted economic security, unconcerned about posthumous fame; he found what he sought and is all but forgotten today. Thomas Truxtun pursued both fame and fortune with extraordinary abilities and great assiduity; but Truxtun's spectacular example must not be permitted to mislead. For the vast majority of Quasi-War commanding officers significant financial gain from the capture of French armed vessels was not to be. A few—very few—grew rich; most made little or nothing.

There is a way in which Table 32 misleads. The total-prize-money-earned column simply shows the commanding officer's 10 percent of all prizes. If the ship's commander were also the squadron commodore, or if the ship were operating independently, then an additional 5 percent went into the captain's pocket. No attempt has been made to add the 5 percent, when appropriate, to the 10 percent. It would be most difficult to ascertain which prizes summarized in Table 32 were eligible for a 10 percent captain's share and which 15 percent. Precise dates of some captures are not known; certain captains were highly ingenious about avoiding their commodores and the payment of their commodores' shares. Division of prize money between a commodore and his subordinates was a private matter; the Navy Department played no role and kept no records. Only if the historian possessed the commodores' prize accounts, which do not now exist, could one be sure of how to assess this 5 percent.

Calculating Thomas Truxtun's full Quasi-War earnings well illustrates the difficulty of navigating without an officer's records of his prize money. Truxtun was always a squadron commodore, never a subordinate; consequently, his total earnings from French armed vessels captured by his own ship were actually $13,158 or nearly seven times his annual pay and rations. But Truxtun's acquisition of wealth did not stop there. As squadron commodore he was entitled to 5 percent of every prize taken by any ship of his squadron. Although Truxtun's correspondence with his prize agent, Charles Biddle, survives, Biddle's detailed accounts of the prize money he received, as Truxtun's agent, from the commodore's subordinates do not. This lack puts beyond reach any accurate estimate of Truxtun's income from this potentially lucrative source. One is especially cautious about such estimates, because several of Truxtun's subordinates were creative and persistent in figuring out ways to procrastinate on, or altogether avoid, paying him his 5 percent. More than three years after the fighting had stopped, Truxtun was still trying to collect his share of two prizes taken by Hugh G. Campbell, but finally threw up his hands: "Contending with such people and the trouble of a lawsuit, perhaps, is not worth my while." Not that Truxtun was a sissy when it came to rounding up his prize money, even if the equally acquisitive Campbell finally wore him down. Truxtun had Biddle hound recalcitrant subordinates and their prize agents. The commodore personally pocketed the shares of *Constellation*'s *Insurgente* prize money that belonged to men who had deserted or died since the battle, though he certainly would have had to cough up if legally qualified heirs came looking. Although prize agents usually charged a commission of 5 percent for their time, trouble, and risk in handling such business, in Charles Biddle's case Truxtun insisted on a kickback to himself of half the net commissions on all prize business he sent Biddle's way; with respect to *Insurgente* alone this meant another $2,113 in Truxtun's pocket.[8] It was not just as a combat leader and molder of professional subordinates that Thomas Truxtun excelled!

The impact of being a squadron commodore on a captain's prize money earnings is more clearly seen in the War of 1812, a conflict in which commodores' income from captures of enemy armed vessels by ships under their command can be estimated with reasonable accuracy. Again a warning: These figures cannot be regarded as absolutely precise. In no case has a commodore's personal record of his earnings, the only fully reliable source, been found. Some squadrons may have operated under agreements to share equally in all prizes made by any constituent ship. As in the Quasi-War, certain subordinate commanders struggled to avoid paying the commodore his 5 percent. In the days and weeks immediately preceding James Lawrence's fatal meeting with *Chesapeake* a fair share of that captain's energy was expended in attempting to resist William Bainbridge's claim for a commodore's share of *Hornet*'s prize money earned subsequent to the date when Bainbridge's battle-damaged *Constitution* parted company with Lawrence's *Hornet* and shaped her course for Boston.[9]

Eight War of 1812 commanding officers earned more than $10,000 in prize money from the capture of British ships (Table 33). Of the eight, five were also squadron commodores. Stephen Decatur, at the head of the list with prize earnings in excess of $30,000, was something of an anomaly. Almost all of his money came from a single source: the government's highly generous response to his success in not only capturing *Macedonian*, but in bringing her into port, the first captured British frigate to be added to the rolls of a proud U.S. Navy. (Decatur's $30,099 in prize money here discussed does not include his earnings in the Algerian War of 1815.) Thomas Macdonough, the second man on the list, owed his prize money to a single event, the September 1814 battle on Lake Champlain, but the size of his reward was a reflection of his position as squadron commodore; Macdonough's senior subordinate, Robert Henley, earned only $5,698 for his role on that eventful day. John Rodgers and Isaac Chauncey won no memorable sea battles during the War of 1812. If fame eluded them in combat, neither had cause to quibble with the war's financial rewards. Rodgers earned in excess of $11,000 from prizes made by his own ship, *President*, as well as another $8,000 and more through prizes made by other ships of his squadron. He stands immediately below Decatur and Macdonough as the third most successful prize money earner of 1812–15. Chauncey's case is, as mentioned earlier, the most striking example of a commodore's advantageous post. Although Chauncey made some respectable gains from ships captured by his own vessel or by his squadron on Lake Ontario, his greatest windfall came from a battle in which he played only a remote supervisory role: Perry's 1813 victory on Lake Erie, which earned Chauncey $12,750. William Bainbridge garnered fame (and a relatively modest $7,500) from his capture of *Java*, but it was *Hornet*'s prize taking while she was part of Bainbridge's squadron that put him above the $10,000 mark in cash gains. Then consider three men who were not squadron commodores. Charles Stewart's nearly $15,000 in prize money derived from the capture of a mixture of British naval vessels (*Cyane* and *Levant*) and rich merchantmen. Lewis Warrington made his stake in a single capture: the British naval brig *Epervier* and her cargo of $118,000 in cash. Finally, one must not fail to note the presence on the select roll of eight of Samuel Evans, a name now known only to specialists in the history of the nineteenth-century navy. Evans won no famous victories in the War of 1812. In *Chesapeake* (before he turned her over to James Lawrence) Evans went after only merchant ship prizes, and he had the good luck to find them.

What was the final balance sheet on the financial rewards of being a commodore in the War of 1812? It was no sure road to riches: Stephen Decatur gleaned a mere $99 from his commodore's role. Even the acquisitive Hugh G. Campbell could wring little more than $2,000 in prize money out of his potentially profitable command in Georgia and Florida waters. Samuel Evans, Charles Stewart, and Lewis Warrington proved that an officer could be a big winner in the prize money lottery without being a commodore. All that admitted, the squadron commodores were still the officers best positioned to find war's financial rewards. William Bainbridge, Isaac Chauncey, Thomas Macdonough, and John Rodgers had every reason to smile contentedly as their carriages drove past the bank.

Rescuing the Fellow Citizen

So far this is only half the story on prize money. There was another side to financial gain from war for the pre-1815 navy: salvage, the recapture of ships of one's own country before they had been legally condemned by the enemy nation.

Money arising from salvage was distributed among the ship's company according to the same formula as prize money, but the sums available to be so distributed are much harder to estimate than is the case with prize money. Neither the Navy Department nor the Commissioners of the Navy Pension Fund had any financial stake in salvage money; consequently, they kept no records. Salvage was entirely a matter between the recaptors of the vessel and/ or cargo and the former owners, who were required by law to pay a certain portion of the vessel's and/or the cargo's value to the salvors.[10] Should the former owners and the recaptors not be able to agree on the value of the property saved, the dispute might have to be turned over to arbitrators or (more rarely) to the courts. Save in the exceptional case of the recapture of a former U.S. warship, the Navy Department had no role in the transaction.

The upshot of all this was that the historian is left with only a few shards of evidence from which to reconstruct the story of money arising from salvage. Still, some estimates may be attempted. Hugh G. Campbell of *Eagle* has already been acknowledged as one of the most successful commanding officers of the Quasi-War, his ten captures of French armed vessels netting him $1,139 in prize money. In addition to these ten French armed vessels, Campbell's *Eagle* also recaptured twelve other ships from which she earned salvage. There exists no evidence respecting the value of any of Campbell's recaptures; however, if a recapture were at least as lucrative as the typical French armed vessel that fell prey to *Eagle*, then Campbell may be imagined as earning another $1,367 from salvage, to make his total Quasi-War earnings from prize *and* salvage approximately $2,500, or the equivalent of two years and three months of his pay and rations.[11]

Insights into salvage earnings gained from Campbell's record can be extended through a comprehensive list of captures and recaptures made by the squadron under the command of Richard V. Morris during the eight months of October 1799 through May 1800.[12] The eleven ships under Morris's command captured a total of seventeen French armed ships, but recaptured thirty-one American ships—almost twice as many. In the capturing of French armed vessels Morris's ship, the frigate *Adams*, was the most active member of his squadron, bagging seven of the seventeen prizes, with his other ten ships capturing one, two, or none. In the case of salvage the same imbalance reappears. Four ships do the lion's share of the work: *Adams* (10 recaptures), *Pickering* (6), *John Adams* (5), and *Insurgente* (4). The seven French armed vessels captured by *Adams* put $578 directly into his pocket, because as squadron commodore his share was 15 percent, not 10. This was hardly fabulous wealth, a reflection of the fact that many of the prizes were vessels whose sale produced sums such as $218, $235, or $553 to be divided among *Adams*'s ship's company. Beyond his $578, Morris earned $652 through his 5 percent share in the French armed ships captured by other vessels in his squadron. This made his total income from French armed ships captured by himself or his subordinates $1,230, something less than one year's pay and rations for the captain of the 28-gun *Adams*. If the historian conservatively assumes that Morris did no better with his ten cases of salvage than with his seven armed vessel prizes, his direct earnings would have been $826. To this one would still have to add his 5 percent of the money earned by ships of his squadron from salvage of the other twenty-one vessels. Thus, the whole amount earned by Richard V. Morris from prize and salvage, October 1799–May 1800, might have been as follows:

Captain's and commodore's share, seven French armed vessels at 15 percent	$578
Commodore's share, ten French armed vessels taken by subordinates at 5 percent	652
Captain's and commodore's share, ten vessels salvaged at 15 percent	826
Commodore's share, twenty-one vessels salvaged by subordinates at 5 percent	<u>1,369</u>
	$3,425

When conservatively guessed salvage is taken into the picture, Richard V. Morris had, in eight months, probably earned two and a half times his annual pay and rations from prize and salvage combined.

The lack of better figures on Quasi-War earnings from salvage frustrates the historian. Insufficient data exist to permit even a reliable estimate for the typical case of salvage. Extrapolating from the records of Hugh G. Campbell in *Eagle* and the Richard V. Morris squadron, it is certainly safe to speculate that, if all French armed vessels captured during the Quasi-War earned their captors a total of $239,125, salvage may well have earned equally as much or perhaps half-again as much: hypothetically $350,000, of which sum $52,500 would have gone into the pockets of captains and commodores. Unless and until better records become available, the question will have to rest with that best guess.

29. Money Men

*M*ONEY WAS, in one degree or another, the concern of every officer. For one class of officers it was their primary responsibility. They were the navy's pursers.

Three heavy responsibilities rested on a purser's shoulders: (1) paying the officers and men of the ship (or station) to which he was attached and maintaining the detailed records to enable him to perform this function; (2) storing and issuing the ship's provisions to all messes; (3) selling clothing and small articles, called slops, to the ship's company. To these three responsibilities the captain might add a fourth: paying the ship's miscellaneous bills incurred during a cruise in places where there was no U.S. navy agent; this, however, was not always the purser's job, as some captains preferred to assume the responsibility themselves.

To fulfill his duties a purser requisitioned, with the commanding officer's approval, large sums of cash. Thereafter it would be the purser's responsibility to account to the Navy Department for every penny he so received. A successful purser needed to be accurate, systematic, and hardworking, and to possess a compulsive fondness for detail, for the paperwork burden of the job was staggering. Simply to meet his payroll function the purser was required to maintain a number of records:

1. A general muster book showing, for each man in the ship's company, his name, his rank, date of entry and date and place of appearance on board (as well, eventually, as the date, place, and reason of his departure from the ship), whether he was present, or officially excused from, each of the ship's weekly musters, and the date to which he had last been paid.

2. A register, which repeated all the information from the muster roll but added more data concerning compensation: advances on account of pay, deductions for allotments paid directly to dependents on shore, summary charges for slops issued, and penalties—for example, loss of pay for days absent without leave.

3. A payroll, made up at the time a ship's company was paid off, which displayed a man's rank, the time for which he was being paid, his rate of pay, and all debits for allotments, slops, and so on. This had to be supplemented by

a receipt roll in which the man's signature or mark, as well as the signature of an officer witness, proved that the man had actually received his pay.

4. A slop account documenting the types and quantities issued to any member of the ship's company.

5. A provision account showing the rations drawn or undrawn by each man. Here would be credited the officers' undrawn extra rations. Although each enlisted man was expected to draw a full ration, if the ship ran short of any articles and the company had to be put on reduced allowance, the shortfall was compensated in cash at the end of the pay period.

6. A monthly muster book, which summarized the information in the general muster book and the register and which was to be forwarded to the Navy Office as an interim personnel record pending the purser's submission of his complete pay- and muster rolls for a cruise, although in practice the rule of monthly submissions by pursers was as much honored in its breach as in its observance.

When one adds to the multiplicity of these parallel records the realization that, with discharges and enlistments, a purser's rolls might contain anywhere from a few hundred to well upward of a thousand names by the end of the cruise, that thousands upon thousands of calculations had to be made by hand, and that all these records would be checked against one another for accuracy at the office of the accountant of the navy, the paperwork burden on a purser becomes truly mind-boggling.[1]

Actually, the preceding paragraph is guilty of oversimplification, both in describing the amount of finicky detail required for each record and by failing to mention a whole universe of subsidiary records that were just as necessary. Was a barrel of beef found unfit for use and thrown overboard? Three officers, other than the purser, had to draw up and sign a document to that effect. If a man died during the voyage and the purser paid his wages to the next of kin, he had to make certain he received and kept on file proof that the person who received the dead man's pay was legally entitled to it. Fail to get and keep such proof, and the illegal payment would be debited to the purser by the accountant. Being a navy purser was no bed of roses.* When the navy had been sailing and fighting for a little more than a year Benjamin Stoddert said, "The purser

---

* One conscientious and able purser actually suffered a mental breakdown while trying to cope with this overwhelming mass of detail. James Reid Wilson, one of the most highly regarded and industrious pursers in the navy, was attached to the gunboat flotilla at New York harbor during the War of 1812, a post in which he had single-handedly to keep financial track of more than twenty-three hundred men on the station rolls, as well as a thousand more passing through en route to other stations. By August 1813 Wilson was beginning to crack and appealed to Thomas Turner to support him in his appeal to William Jones to order another purser to relieve him: "I beg you will use your influence in having me superseded on this station in order that I may be able to ease my mind and thereby save my life by having a spare time to prepare my heavy accounts for a settlement, the necessity of which preys so heavily on my mind and spirits as to deprive me of my regular sleep. I must, therefore, request your aid in having me relieved, else I certainly shall not be fit for anything a month hence." Relief did not come soon, and when it came it was too late. By the spring of 1814 James R. Wilson was confined to City Hospital at New York, hopelessly insane, a condition in which he remained until he died on 17 August 1819. This historian does not say that the demands of his position were the root cause of Wilson's insanity, but they certainly appear to have been either a contributing or an immediate cause. As early as November 1812 Isaac Hull had said half-jokingly, but all too prophetically, of Wilson, "I should not be astonished to find him very soon a *mad*man from the trouble and vexation he has with the gunboats." When Purser Wilson's accounts were settled in 1815 there was a positive balance in his favor of $7,888.79, so solvency should not have been the cause of his anxiety.[2]

ought to be a good accountant and a man of integrity."[3] Those things he certainly had to be, but he had to be a good deal more as well. What manner of individuals became the navy's pursers?

The People behind the Ledgers

For one thing they were a small corps. Between March 1798 and July 1814 some 123 individuals received appointments as pursers; fifty-two of these began their purser careers during the Quasi-War with France; twenty-three were appointed during the secretaryship of Robert Smith and thirty men by Paul Hamilton; the War of 1812 resulted in a mere eighteen new pursers being introduced into the navy, in part a reflection of the recall of pursers who had been laid off in earlier reductions of the corps.[4]

Pursers were relatively mature men when they received their appointments (Table 34). Three-quarters of them were between twenty-one and thirty years of age. The typical (median) age of the newly appointed purser was twenty-seven, about five years older than the typical new lieutenant and about two years younger than the typical newly fledged master commandant or sailing master. As with the lieutenant, the master commandant, or the sailing master, the purser was expected to be an individual capable of assuming grave responsibilities, in the purser's case very large sums of money. Too much should not be made of the one seventy-seven-year-old purser. This was an extreme aberration. During the Quasi-War with France Captain Christopher Raymond Perry was able to secure the purser's post in his ship, the *General Greene*, for his venerable and needy relative Jabez Champlin, without the Navy Office becoming aware of just how mature Purser Champlin was. Among the fifty-three pursers of known age, only four were over forty. For money men, as for all others, the sea had no place for the middle-aged and the elderly.

When it comes to the geographical roots of the 123 pursers, the various parts of the union were far from equal (Table 35). Across the entire 1798–1815 period the New England states supplied about one-quarter of all pursers, with New York, New Jersey, Pennsylvania, and Delaware providing an equal number. The Deep South was home to about one purser in twenty, and the western states and territories supplied even fewer. As with midshipmen, so even more pronouncedly with pursers: the geographical area most immediately contiguous to the national capital was the most fertile source of such officers. Nearly half of all pursers claimed Maryland, Virginia, and the District of Columbia as home. The reason for this regional imbalance must be assumed to be the same as was surmised for midshipmen: the closer a man lived to the national capital, the stronger his sense of identification with the national government and with its navy as a career choice. Because (as will shortly be discovered) most purser recruits already had experience in maritime-related careers when they gained their appointments, one is not surprised that nearly all new pursers listed port towns and cities as their places of residence. Among the twelve pursers from Massachusetts whose residences can be positively established, nine were from Boston, and one each from Gloucester, Marblehead, and Newburyport. In Maryland (18 pursers with known residences), Annapolis (4), Baltimore (7), Easton (2), Port Tobacco (2), and Cambridge, Chestertown, and Elkton (1 each) monopolize the list of hometowns.

Thirty-six pursers—slightly less than one-third of the entire 123—held

A prudent purser. There is no hint in C.B.J. Fevret de Saint-Mémin's representation of Samuel Hambleton that the thirtyish Marylander was a faithful friend, a compulsive and unfailingly interesting letter writer, or a knowledgeable aficionado of the horse. What the émigré French portraitist did record in his chalk drawing is the unsmiling determination of a man intent on achieving lifetime financial security. Burned in an early business venture, Hambleton was soon thereafter able to secure an examining clerk's position in the office of Accountant of the Navy Thomas Turner, the post he still held when he sat for Saint-Mémin. Superb performance under Turner was his ticket to the potential rewards of a pursership. The secret of Hambleton's success? He was a meticulous and thrifty individual, with an eye for turning a profit and a willingness to take moderate risks when an opportunity offered. By the middle of 1815 the fixed-purpose man had built a net worth equal to nearly sixty times his annual pay and rations as a purser. When not on active duty, Hambleton lived in frugal and sedate elegance as a salt-tinged gentleman farmer whose property stretched along the waters of Chesapeake Bay. Financial security, no matter how much of it one possessed, could never be taken for granted or abused. Constant vigilance in monitoring and enhancing one's assets was essential. Private collection.

appointments as captain's clerks, chaplains, purser's stewards, acting pursers, clerks in the Navy Office, or navy yard clerks before attaining purserships. To these thirty-six should perhaps be added the five pursers who had held a midshipman's (and, in one case, a lieutenant's) appointment before switching career tracks; including these five raises the proportion of pursers with previous naval experience to exactly one-third of the entire cohort of pursers. In light of the Navy Department's expressed preference for appointing pursers from among men who had gained experience and documented their abilities in one or more of the specified roles, this is a surprisingly low number. Indeed, it is inexplicable unless these sources did not provide an adequate supply of purser applicants—or the recommenders of the two-thirds of all pursers who secured appointments without previous naval experience were so persistent and so importunate as to carry the day. Either supposition can be only that: a guess.

The historian finds precious little evidence as to why and how secretaries of the navy made their choices of pursers from among the applicants. The consequences of selecting so many men who lacked established records as naval money managers were serious. Of those consequences, more shortly.

Earlier naval service aside, information on previous careers is sketchier than one might wish. Eight men had been merchant captains or supercargoes; seven had been clerks in stores, merchant's countinghouses, or banks; another six had been in business either for themselves or as partners. With the latter six, failure of the business in question was the immediate occasion for seeking a pursership—not, one might think, the most auspicious of qualifications. Five pursers were attorneys in their civilian days. The presence of the five ex-attorneys among the ranks of the pursers signals another way in which these naval money men were distinctive: the quality of their formal educations. Twelve pursers (one man in ten) had completed a college education. This was not, to be sure, as impressive a record as the chaplains' 1 man in 4 with some collegiate education, but clearly different from the midshipman ranks wherein 1 man in every 16 or 18 had even entered college, and only 1 among 150 had graduated. All of these facts add up to mark a naval pursership as a career to which a man gravitated only after gaining experience in several other jobs.

If pursers' educational achievements distinguished them from the midshipmen, the parents of the two groups look remarkably alike. Both came from the same layers of the social pyramid. The numbers of purser-parents identified are so small that warning flags must be hoisted immediately. Forty-six names of parents have been discovered (37.4 percent of all pursers); parental status or occupation is known for thirty-three pursers (26.8 percent). View such small numbers with extreme caution, but then observe that one purser-parent in five held a federal appointment of some kind; one in three was (or had) engaged in some kind of business; one in six was a farmer or planter; one in eight was a master in the merchant service; a similar proportion pursued one of the learned professions (attorney, physician, clergyman). The sole way in which the parents of pursers appear different from the parents of midshipmen is that only one purser-parent can be identified as a master craftsman.

Did pursers, like midshipmen, have relatives in the navy? For the money men the pattern was the same, only more intense. The key relationship was, once again, that of the brother or the brother-in-law. Twenty pursers had one, two, or three brothers in the navy, but, as with the midshipmen, two brothers (the purser and one other man) was the most common constellation (thirteen instances). In addition to the twenty men with brothers, five pursers could count anywhere from one to four brothers-in-law among the navy's officers. The significance of both of these bonds is the same as that discovered among the midshipmen: once a brother or a brother-in-law held an officer's appointment, he was advantageously placed to leverage his siblings by blood or marriage into the corps if they had a strong desire to join. Lieutenant Charles Ludlow certainly helped brother Robert attain a purser's warrant in 1809. Once Captain John Rodgers set his mind to the task it was only a matter of time before brother-in-law Henry Denison was named a purser. When it was a question of relatives, the midshipmen and pursers diverged in one significant way: only three pursers had fathers or fathers-in-law who were officers, though with Captain Thomas Tingey and his son-in-law Tunis Craven, as well as with Samuel Nicholson and his daughter Ann's husband, John Rose Greene, it was clearly the father-in-law who was instrumental in securing the purser's appointment for the younger man.

Money Men

ই⚫

355

Profiteers?

As far as the law was concerned sailing masters, chaplains, and pursers all received the same cash compensation for a year's active duty: $581 through the Quasi-War with France, $552 from 1801 through 1813, and $570 thereafter. There the similarity ended. Modest amounts of prize money aside, the sailing master and the chaplain had to get along on pay and rations. For the purser these were only part of his compensation, and not the part that made a purser's appointment so desirable. Next to the commanding officer, with his access to substantial supplemental income from freight and prize money, the ship's purser was the officer who stood to make the most from his profession. He was the man who ran the company store for a captive clientele.

One of a purser's major responsibilities was to sell certain merchandise, lumped under the generic name slops, to officers and enlisted men. It was a sale in which no cash changed hands, because the price of the slops was deducted from any pay due when it came time to pay off a ship's company or to discharge a man or an officer. Slops fell into three broad categories:

1. Basic clothing, which in a typical frigate might include blue jackets, blue trousers, flannel shirts, flannel drawers, duck trousers, cotton stockings, wool stockings, shoes, hats, madras and black silk handkerchiefs. With both officer and enlisted man, the purchase of appropriate clothing was an individual's responsibility; the navy did not issue uniforms to either group. In the case of the enlisted ranks at least part of the reason must have been the perception that if garments were issued free of charge, it would be even more difficult than it already was to keep the men from bartering their clothing, particularly to obtain liquor.

2. More or less essential small equipment, such as razors, combs, brushes, soap, needles, thread, tin pots, spoons, and knives.

3. Nonessential extras, such as food to supplement the basic ration. In this category would fall supplies of sugar, tea, tobacco, mustard, pepper, and chocolate, as well as fine shirts, fancy vests, and ribbon.[5]

Such a system of supplying enlisted men, who, save for rare shore leaves, had little or no opportunity during a two-year enlistment to shop elsewhere than with the purser, was open to at least two potential abuses. Either the purser might issue more slops than a man really needed in order to enhance the purser's cash flow; or he might charge an excessive profit to his captive clientele. There was no shortage of accusations that both abuses flourished.

Against the first the enlisted man's only real defense was the ship's commanding officer, his sense of responsibility toward the crew, and the urgency with which he communicated this sense of responsibility to his subordinate officers. The *Naval Regulations* of 1802 provided only limited protection for the enlisted man. They specified that the purser could not issue slops in excess of half the pay actually accrued and that slops were to be issued in the presence of an officer, appointed by the captain, which officer was also to serve as a witness to the receipt of the slops. Some, and perhaps most, captains elected to buttress these somewhat flabby provisions by building additional protections for the enlisted men into their ships' internal regulations. In *President* John Rodgers decreed, "All sorts of slops and clothing must be issued only on a special order from me, as well as such other articles in the Purser's Department . . . except tobacco, tea, and sugar, respecting which I shall give such directions as circumstances from time to time may render necessary." William M. Crane in his wartime regulations on Lake Ontario was, if possible, even more restrictive and protective: "The purser is forbidden to furnish any supplies of clothing or stores to the crew without my written order, which will be given, provided the division officer deems them necessary for their comfort. All requisitions by the crew for clothing or small stores are to be made out in writing and, if approved, signed by the division officer and presented to me."[6] Because only a few examples of ship's regulations survive from the pre-1815 years, it is impossible to assess with certainty how prevalent such protective restrictions were.

They were certainly not universal. A particularly vocal critic of pursers' practices, and a man with ample experience from which to recognize an abuse when he encountered it, was Alexander Murray. In May 1809 Murray wrote Accountant Thomas Turner in a state of high dudgeon:

> I beg leave to trouble you respecting a letter I have received from *Captain* [Charles] *Gordon* respecting a Negro man of mine who was about eighteen months on board the frigate Chesapeake and entered as a seaman. When I put him on board he was well clad and no month's advance received, with orders not to advance him anything without Captain Gordon's orders. His name stands on the books *Peter Cook* and was drafted from the Chesapeake to the Syren and gone out with *Gordon*, who tells me with great surprise that the purser has left

Could an astute viewer guess this officer's rank from his face alone? Is the mouth tight? Are the brown eyes those of a man more taking than giving? Certainly there is cool appraisal in the steady gaze. Gilbert Stuart is the artist, and this is his splendid oil-on-canvas image of Purser James Moore Halsey as a man in his mid-twenties. University of Arizona Museum of Art, Tucson.

only a balance of $11 in his favor. . . . It appears to me that there must be some mistake in this business . . . for under the pursers' regulations they are not authorized to issue slops or advances without an order from the captain and never to exceed more than half their pay, and this fellow . . . ought not to have been suffered to run up to such an enormous expense.

When a sympathetic Thomas Turner replied, "I fear the privileges that have been allowed the pursers are very much abused and call aloud for corrections"— and Turner, if anyone, was in a position to know, because he settled the pursers' accounts—Murray fired a second broadside:

> As you seem to coincide in opinion with me that there is something radically wrong in the pursers' privileges, I must again intrude with my ideas, as I cannot acquiesce in the conduct pursued by them—not warranted by the regulations adopted for their guide, but by too many precedents of their own adoption— to the disadvantage of the poor ignorant sailor[s], willing to take anything upon their discharge, however trifling, after a long cruise, and which has been the occasion of rendering the service very unpopular among them, who make no scruple in saying they are defrauded by their pursers.[7]

Murray's was certainly no lone voice in making such charges. Hugh G. Campbell sounded a similar note when he complained that pursers "have too long been allowed by many commanders to consider slops as a private perquisite of their own, which has certainly enabled them to make considerable sums of money at the expense of the poor sailors who, at the end of a two years' cruise, have been discharged with little more than the price of a suit of clothes, a procedure that discourages the seaman from readily shipping again and materially tends to injure the service."[8] Was it true that, in defiance of regulations, a major portion of the sailor's monthly wage was going not into the enlisted man's pocket, but into the purser's through the medium of slop purchases?

For at least one ship of the pre-1815 navy it is possible to answer that question with a high degree of accuracy and to gain, in the process, a glimpse of how pursers could get around Navy Office regulations and congressional scrutiny. Purser Robert W. Goldsborough's slops issue book in the brig *Argus* for the period 20 March–26 June 1805 survives in the archives, as does the brig's payroll of the entire cruise.[9] From the payroll an end-of-cruise pay statement, as it would have been drawn up by Purser Goldsborough, can be constructed for, say, seaman James Savage, who enlisted on 16 August 1803 at Boston and who was turned over to the frigate *Congress*, 19 August 1805, for a passage home at the end of his two-year enlistment:

Gross pay due @ $10 per month	$241.00
Less:	
Advances by *Argus*'s previous purser, Timothy Winn, including cash advance at enlistment	123.26
Purchase of slops from R.W. Goldsborough	1.05
Cash advanced by R.W. Goldsborough	58.88
Marine hospital fund deduction	4.82
Net pay due James Savage	$ 52.99

Because Purser Winn's *Argus* records (Goldsborough had replaced him as purser on 11 November 1804) no longer exist, there is no way now to discover the components of Winn's $123.26 deduction from Savage's pay. However, had an inquisitive congressman examined *Argus*'s payroll, he would have assumed that James Savage had, during Goldsborough's tenure as purser, been exercising great restraint in his purchases of slops—a mere $1.05 worth—but had been receiving frequent advances on his pay as it came due, cash that he presumably spent during shore leaves or still had in his possession. Goldsborough's issue book reveals the real story. During the three months and seven days between 20 March and 26 June of 1805 alone, James Savage had purchased $35.15 worth of slops. How had Goldsborough concealed these purchases in his payroll? When, in mid-April, seaman Savage purchased two pounds of tobacco, the purser had him sign a receipt that read:

> Received from Robt. W. Goldsborough sixty
> Cents on Account of Pay
> April 18th 1805
>
> JAMES C SAVAGE

This transaction, and all of Savage's other purchases of slops, except the stalking horse $1.05, appear in Purser Goldsborough's payroll not in the column headed "Advances . . . Slops," but in the column headed "Advances . . . Money."

The actual buying habits of Savage and his shipmates can be summarized (Table 36). During the three months and seven days covered by Purser Goldsborough's issue book, Savage and his thirty-seven peers rated as seamen typically earned $32.33 in wages (only two seamen earned at the higher $12-a-month rate). Three of Savage's mates were able to resist the lure of Goldsborough's slops to the degree that they spent either nothing or small sums—44 cents or $1. At the other end of the scale, eight seamen, including Savage himself, spent two-thirds or more of the pay they earned on slops. At $35.15 Savage was, in fact, the biggest spender among the seamen and committed himself for slops that exceeded his earnings in the same period by $2.82. The typical (median) seaman in *Argus* spent more than one-third of his earnings on slops. As for the other enlisted ranks in *Argus*, the buying habits of the ordinary seamen closely parallel those of their more capable shipmates, the seamen, but were trimmed back proportionally to correspond to their lower pay rates ($25.87 at best). The boys (typically earning $19.40 during the three months and seven days in question) surrendered a higher share of their pay to Goldsborough for slops, as might be expected from the conjunction of a lower wage and a desire to emulate older shipmates in dress and behavior. *Argus*'s elite men, the petty officers, with their typical earnings of $58.20, fared the best when it came to keeping their pay for themselves, a reflection both of far higher monthly wages and presumably greater opportunities to buy elsewhere during shore leaves.

Purser Goldsborough was skimming his third of the crew's earnings through slop sales at a time when the pursers were keenly aware that congressional investigation of their practices was gaining steam, and he was collecting it in a ship whose commanding officer, Isaac Hull, was more than usually concerned for the welfare of his enlisted men. If this was Purser Goldsborough's practice under such restrictive conditions, what, the historian wonders, went on at other times, in different ships, under less humane captains? Alexander Murray's and Hugh G. Campbell's cries of outrage were not the eccentric fulminations of a couple of old cranks! Their concern, and that of other captains who spoke out in criticism of the pursers, is one more example of deference's other face: stewardship. What did it matter, the pursers might have said, if the enlisted man chooses to spend a major part of his pay on fancy shore-leave clothes, tobacco, sugar, or tea? It was the enlisted man's money to spend, was it not? Not so, the captains would have replied. It is our responsibility as officers to protect the enlisted man alike from his own worst instincts and from the abuses of men in positions to take advantage of those worst instincts.

The truth about the other abuse of which pursers were often accused is more difficult to ferret out. This concerned the purser's margin of profit: the difference between the cost of slops to him and the prices he charged his customers for those goods. It is a subject with a convoluted history, but some attempt must be made to unravel the strands.

At the navy's beginnings during the Quasi-War with France, at least as far as basic clothing articles were concerned, the Navy Department adopted a policy of having its agents at the various ports where ships were fitting out purchase slops and turn them over to the pursers.[10] The purser was to distribute the slops to the ship's company as needed and charge the men's pay accounts at a 10 (or sometimes a 12) percent markup on the price the navy agent had paid for them. The margin was not a profit that went into the purser's pocket, but was intended to compensate the government for the inevitable loss and damage that stores of slops sustained at sea. In short, the government purchased the slop clothing and issued it to enlisted men at a markup to cover losses; for his disbursement role the purser's compensation was his pay and rations—nothing more. Benjamin Stoddert said it repeatedly: the government's issue of slop clothing "is meant as a humane regulation to preserve the sailors from suffering and to prevent imposition on the part of the pursers."

There the stiff regulations stopped. When it came to what were deemed nonessential or luxury items, be they sugar, tea, chocolate, tobacco, tin pots, jackknives, or chest locks, the Quasi-War Navy Office contented itself with admonishing the pursers, "There are smaller [articles] which may be supplied [to the enlisted men] by yourself, but it is expected that you will be contented with a moderate profit so as to give the crew no cause of complaint." Clearly this was a toothless adjuration unless the ship's captain stepped in, as did John Barry and Thomas Truxtun, and insisted on setting the prices the purser could charge.[11] Moreover, it was one thing to set policies and another to enforce them in every case. Stoddert was constantly having to fight off pursers who wanted to purchase the slop clothing themselves rather than having it supplied by navy agents, or who pleaded that *their* slop transactions were special cases that ought to be exempt from the general regulations.[12]

Shortly after Robert Smith came into office he decided to modify the Quasi-War rules respecting the distribution of slop clothing. Slops would continue to be purchased by the government and turned over to the pursers, who were authorized to mark them up 10 percent when issuing them to crew members. The markup, though called a profit, was actually a commission on sales that went directly into the purser's pocket on a no-questions-asked basis to compensate him for his "risk and responsibility." The "risk" in question was any loss, such as secret pilferage, that the purser could not document; losses through damage that could be established by hard evidence were credited to the purser's account over and beyond his 10 percent commission. Although the policy as enunciated by Smith was officially a change, in fact it merely confirmed a practice that earlier secretaries had been approving on a case-by-case basis. If a purser had to account for all the slop clothing he received, but could only be credited for the losses he could prove, then many would actually lose money on the distribution business because of undocumentable losses that were all but wholly unavoidable.[13]

What happened next is not entirely clear. The regulations on slops were never popular with the pursers. They would have liked nothing better than to be allowed to purchase their own slops, mark them up to what they thought their captive customers and the commanding officer would bear, and pocket the difference. As Benjamin Stoddert had discovered, the rules were difficult to enforce in the face of all sorts of special pleading by a long line of pursers, each arguing that, in *his* case, an exception to the rules was clearly justified. Finally, a congressional committee appears to have been poking into the whole issue of pursers' profits during the session of 1803–1804. All of these circumstances led Smith to try a different tack with the pursers of the squadron that sailed for the Mediterranean in the spring of 1804. Each purser was advanced so many dollars to purchase his own slops. Before he sailed from the United States the purser was to submit a complete accounting, establishing the prices he had paid for each article. During the cruise the purser would take a specific receipt for every article issued, which articles were to be doled out only with the commanding officer's explicit approval. While the squadron was abroad Robert Smith would examine the evidence of prices paid and set the commission or profit to be allowed. The final cash settlement with the pursers would be calculated by having each of them exhibit his detailed receipts for issues to the accountant of the navy for audit. All of the relevant documentation was to be submitted to Congress during the next session.

The attempt was a notable failure. Only under threat of removal from their ships, with their lucrative posts turned over to others, could the pursers be persuaded to account for the money advanced them. Squadron commodore Samuel Barron did little or nothing to enforce the regulations. Instead of the percentage of markup being determined by the Navy Office, Barron, his successor John Rodgers, and their subordinate commanding officers had, in fact, set their own prices at which slops could be sold—prices that were fixed for each item, rather than cost-plus, so as to leave ample room for quality cutting by profit-eager pursers. The pursers, more or less unsupervised, deliberately kept poor records, which made an audit of their sales all but impossible. In the end no accounting could be, or at least none was, made to Congress. With the return of the ships of the Barron-Rodgers squadron from the Mediterranean, the size of the U.S. naval forces on active duty dwindled rapidly, making the question of slop profits less immediately pressing. Discouraged by this experience, Robert Smith made no further major effort to supervise pursers' sales, contenting himself with letting some pursers purchase their own slops, making others take those furnished by the department, and allowing commissions of 20 percent except at New Orleans, where high, undocumentable losses led him to approve 25 percent.[14]

There the matter of purser profits rested until the early days of Paul Hamilton's term of office, when Alexander Murray's letters complaining about purser abuses in general and the plight of Peter Cook in particular came before the sympathetic eyes of Accountant of the Navy Thomas Turner. Apparently

Turner, who had ample documentary evidence on which to decide whether or not pursers were making excessive money at the expense of enlisted men, had only been waiting for a sympathetic secretary and an excuse to complain. He carried Murray's antipurser fulminations to Hamilton's office and added his own oral variations to the theme Murray had intoned. Would you be willing to put all this on paper? Hamilton inquired. He certainly would! Turner replied, went back to his own office, wrote up his recommendations, and dispatched them to Hamilton the same day.

After some subsequent negotiations with Commodore John Rodgers that modified and clarified the Turner-Hamilton plan, the Navy Office issued on 6 June and 27 July 1809 a new set of regulations on purser profits, regulations the essential features of which were as follows:

1. Slops were to be purchased by navy agents and supplied to the pursers, whose operations would henceforward be subject to a strict scrutiny and accounting by the office of the accountant of the navy.

2. Clothing was to be issued at a commission of 5 percent. This commission was to cover unavoidable wastage and was intended to result in no profit to the pursers.

3. Coffee, tea, sugar, and tobacco were labeled luxuries; on these pursers were allowed to charge a 50 percent markup.

4. Toilet articles, utensils, knives, ribbon, needles and thread, mustard, and chocolate became "articles of second necessity"; these the pursers were permitted to mark up 25 percent.

5. Because the food items among the luxuries and articles of second necessity were, on shipboard, subject to substantial undocumentable wastage—by small-scale pilfering, for example—pursers were allowed an additional no-questions-asked 5 percent on these items in ships of 20 or more guns and 10 percent in smaller vessels.

Although the ultimate sanction in enforcing such regulations was the accountant's authority to settle a purser's accounts, the first line of enforcement remained the commanding officer's individual sense of responsibility for the welfare of the men under his command in protecting them from a purser's cupidity.* With one exception, the regulations instituted by Hamilton in 1809 appear to have continued to operate reasonably well through the War of 1812 years, in part, one thinks, because Thomas Turner remained at the helm in the accountant's office throughout that period, not to mention the presence of Hamilton's successor, William Jones, who would have been only too delighted to lower the boom on any purser misdeeds. Some variation from the 25 and 50 percent rules seems to have been allowed, depending on the station to which

---

* This role is well illustrated in a 16 March 1822 deposition of Captain James Biddle respecting charges of corruption made against Purser William P. Zantzinger of *Hornet*: "While in New London [in 1814] I examined the accounts of Mr. Zantzinger and found he had charged a higher commission upon his issues to the men than was allowed by the Navy Regulations. I pointed it out to him and made him correct it. He assured me it was a mistake. Afterwards, while at sea in 1815, I again examined his accounts and, perceiving he had again committed the same offense, I placed him under arrest. On my return to the United States after the peace I consented to take off the arrest upon his refunding to the men and acknowledging his guilt. But, with a view to prevent his ever saying I had arrested him without cause or had taken off his arrest from inability to substantiate the charge, I required of him to acknowledge his guilt in [the] presence of some of the officers, and which he accordingly did on the Hornet's quarterdeck."[15]

the purser was attached and the risks involved. But the 5 percent rule on clothing suffered an early demise. This was, all soon agreed, too low to cover unavoidable losses and was adjusted upward to 12.5 or 15 percent, contingent upon the hazards to which a particular purser's stores were subject.[16] As two experienced pursers once graphically explained, "In a long cruise a large quantity of the clothing will be eaten by rats and mice, some rotten by being wet from leaks or injured by being spotted with tar water, and we have always found it impossible to prevent considerable loss from stealth, owing to the clothing's being so often overhauled."[17]

Before leaving the subject of slops the historian needs to translate these regulations—or the lack of them—into actual dollars in purser pockets (Table 37). Two informal estimates exist. In response to Hamilton's proposed regulations of 1809, John Rodgers attempted to calculate what a purser's profits on luxuries and articles of second necessity might have been before and after the regulations went into effect. Rodgers took as the basis of his before–June 1809 retail prices "the rates heretofore customary." His estimate of the quantity of each article issued to an average enlisted man in a given year was based on his experience as a ship commander over the previous decade. Rodgers excluded from his calculations "handkerchiefs, fine shoes, and hats, and other articles of clothing which heretofore have not been considered as, or included under the head of, slops." Before Hamilton's regulations, according to Rodgers's calculations, a purser stood to make $42.86 from each petty officer, seaman, or marine in a typical ship. With four hundred captive customers, the purser of a large frigate might earn a gross profit of $17,144 per year. From this had to be deducted the purser's loss by spoilage, pilferage, and like problems, which Rodgers guessed at 5 percent of profits, to make the purser's annual net profit on the sale of luxuries and articles of second necessity $16,287, or thirty times his annual pay and rations! If Rodgers knew what he was talking about—and he was certainly in a position to have accurate data—then there existed ample grounds to accuse the pursers of profiteering at the expense of the enlisted men. Under the 1809 regulations, and again reducing gross profits by 5 percent to cover wastage, Rodgers made the purser's annual net profit from luxuries and articles of second necessity $5,176 in a four-hundred-man frigate, or something just short of ten times the purser's annual pay and rations.

Paul Hamilton's estimate of a purser's profits, made in 1812, was far more conservative. He calculated the gross profit at $5.30 per man, but deducted 80 cents (approximately 15 percent) for wastage, making the net profit per man $4.50 or $1,800 per year for four hundred men, from which he additionally deducted $300 per year for the supplemental pay that the purser had to give his steward to get and keep a reliable man. All in all, Hamilton estimated the net profit at $1,500 per year, less than three times a purser's annual pay and rations.[18]

Why do Hamilton's and Rodgers's estimates of purser profits diverge so widely? Not, it would appear, because they missed the mark when they estimated the typical purser's costs. Rodgers's and Hamilton's estimated wholesale prices for slops may be compared with the detailed and accurate records kept by Purser James R. Wilson regarding the actual amounts he paid for slops over a four-year period (Table 38). On some items Rodgers and Hamilton may overestimate the costs; on others they may be a little low; but, generally, reality confirms their estimates. The point on which Rodgers and Hamilton diverge is the quantities issued to the typical enlisted man in one year. Did he use twenty-six pounds of tobacco, as Rodgers thought, or Hamilton's ten pounds? Ten pounds of tea—or four? Because Hamilton's estimate was prepared for a hostile congressional committee that was poking into purser profits, the secretary had powerful motivation to report the lowest reasonable figure he could conjure. Surely John Rodgers must have had ample direct experience of how much sugar and tobacco sailors used, but he may have harbored an antipurser animus that tempted him to inflate the figures. Who was right? The only way to know for certain would be to examine several pursers' issue books for luxuries and articles of second necessity and calculate the quantities sold per man in a one-year period. This historian has failed to find any purser issue books that include these articles. Until such come to light, one is free to make a choice of Paul Hamilton's estimate or John Rodgers's. The truth may lie somewhere in between—in this historian's opinion, probably nearer Rodgers's end of the scale.

The slop regulations of 1809, for all their improvement over earlier practice, did not totally dispel a visceral national hostility to the idea of one group of officers profiting, in whatever degree, from the basic human needs of the navy's enlisted men. Before the War of 1812 threw a merciful, if temporary, veil of gunsmoke over the pursers and their profits by diverting attention to more pressing concerns, the money men had an ordeal to endure. Its denouement occurred only weeks before war was declared. The arena of their torment was the halls of Congress.

30. Poisoning the Rats

WHETHER ONE HOLDS Congressman John Randolph to have been a mentally unbalanced individual unfortunately set in a place of power or a man of principle at odds with the trend of his times, there is no disputing that he was an eloquent and a dangerous opponent. One of his favorite targets was the U.S. Navy. Although Randolph's overriding motivation was a general hostility to standing military and naval establishments, a strong, if minor, theme in his continuing criticism of these establishments was their financial operations, which he scrutinized microscopically to discover ammunition to further his general cause.

On 24 May 1809 Randolph rose in the House of Representatives to move,

> That a committee be appointed to inquire and report whether monies drawn from the treasury since the 3d of March 1801 have been faithfully applied to the objects for which they were appropriated and whether the same have been regularly accounted for; and to report, likewise, whether any further arrangements are necessary to promote economy, enforce adherence to legislative restrictions, and secure the accountability of persons entrusted with public money.

In the version finally passed by the House (31 May 1809) the latter clause of the resolution (everything after the semicolon) was struck, but the committee's investigative role was preserved and a seven-member panel, which came to be known as the Committee of Investigation, was appointed with Randolph as its chair. The eccentric-looking congressman from Virginia was a man happier in the role of critic and scourge of officeholders than as a constructive member of the party in power. Throughout its history—it faded out of existence with the coming of the War of 1812—the Committee of Investigation was primarily a fishing expedition in search of evidence that Randolph and his allies hoped to use to embarrass President Madison, Treasury Secretary Gallatin, and former secretary of the navy Robert Smith. So far as is known Randolph had no particular animosity toward Paul Hamilton when the committee was called into existence, but the South Carolinian came to have ample reason to repent its creation.

Randolph went right to work, firing off to Gallatin (3 June 1809) a list of nine questions regarding expenditures on a variety of objects ranging from foreign intercourse to the President's House. The committee was putting a lot of lines in the water, and it is well beyond the scope of this book to examine all the fish they brought up. Navy yards, for example, were a convenient, vulnerable, and frequent object of hostile congressional scrutiny; there could almost always be found disgruntled former or current employees willing to point out the best spots to drop a line. Only four among the many subjects canvassed by the Committee of Investigation at Randolph's instance are of concern here: (1) the nature and amount of extra allowances made to officers of the navy "beyond the compensation allowed by law"; (2) the manner in which advances were made to pursers; (3) principles on which their accounts were settled; and (4) "the nature of their emoluments other than the pay allowed them by law"—meaning, of course, the profits from slops.

The extra allowances made to officers in addition to pay were eventually listed in excruciating detail by Thomas Turner and proved to be unexceptionable reimbursements for travel and living expenses ashore while engaged in official duties.[1] Nothing worth pursuing here, the committee soon concluded and moved on in search for more fecund fishing grounds. It found them in the questions of (1) whether the pursers were able to, and in fact were being compelled to, account for the money they had been advanced for official purposes and (2) profits on slops.

Not that it was easy to get the fish to the surface. In his 7 June 1809 reply to Randolph's questions Paul Hamilton correctly pointed out that it was going to take a long time to compile all the data the committee wanted. He forwarded some papers with his letter of 7 June and another batch from Thomas Turner ten days later. On the question of the effectiveness of measures to hold pursers accountable Hamilton stuck to generalities:

> Advances are made to pursers on account of the pay of officers and seamen by warrants drawn on the treasurer [of the United States] and, sometimes, by navy agents. These advances are, of course, charged to the pursers and they account for them in an ultimate settlement of their accounts. Monies thus advanced are applied by the pursers, under the direction of their commanding officers, to the making [of] occasional advances to officers and men and to finally paying off crews when discharged from the service. In the settlement of their accounts they must exhibit a satisfactory voucher for every expenditure.

When it came to slop profits Hamilton was even more slippery:

> The emoluments of the pursers "other than the pay allowed them by law" arise from a percentage, fixed by this department, upon slops, the property of the government under their charge and delivered to the seamen under the direction of the commanding officer; and from a percentage upon certain small articles (such as needles, thread, tobacco, jackknives, etc.) fixed by the commanding officer of the vessel. These percentages are charged not to the government, but to the individual receiving the slops, etc., and are considered as reasonable remunerations to the pursers for the responsibility, risk, and trouble thus imposed upon them. Slops thus delivered are considered as so much pay to the persons to whom they are delivered, and the amount is deducted from the sum they would otherwise be entitled to on being discharged from the service.

John Randolph was not about to be diverted from his purposes of exposure and embarrassment by bromides like these; when his committee came to make an interim report on the next to the last day of the short session (22 May–28 June 1809) he fustigated Hamilton publicly:

> It will be perceived that the respective communications from the War and Navy Departments are of an unsatisfactory nature, differing in character from those required by the committee. A representation to this effect has been made to the heads of those departments, respectively, and they have been notified that the information sought by the committee is essential to the prosecution of the inquiry with which the committee have been charged by the House of Representatives.

In the small volume of printed documents that accompanied the committee's interim report, Hamilton's responses in particular were singled out for embellishment with caustic editorial comments obviously from the pen of chairman Randolph: "This paper is unsatisfactory. . . ." "THIS is not such a statement as the committee have required. . . ." "This paper is defective. . . ." Of the six documents submitted by Hamilton, only one was labeled "SATISFACTORY."

During the second session of the Eleventh Congress (27 November 1809 to 1 May 1810) chairmanship of the Committee of Investigation passed to Daniel Sheffey of Virginia, and Randolph's antinavy venom was concentrated on a resolution he had introduced calling for the reduction of the military and naval establishments. Sheffey lacked Randolph's killer instinct; although his prodding compelled Hamilton to produce a number of papers called for by Randolph at the May–June session, but which there had not then been time to compile, and to elaborate others that Randolph had rejected as unsatisfactory, the committee produced no report on its investigation during the second session and lapsed into total inactivity during the third (3 December 1810 to 3 March 1811).

Early in the first session of the Twelfth Congress (4 November 1811 to 6 July 1812) the Committee of Investigation was restored to full life and snappy vigor when Randolph moved (13 November 1811) that it be empowered to "inquire and report whether monies drawn from the treasury since the 3d of March 1801 have been faithfully expended on the objects for which they were appropriated and whether the same have been regularly accounted for." Defending his resolution five days later, Randolph relieved his pent-up malicious eloquence on the hapless and evasive Hamilton:

> To show how different the information received was from that asked for, Mr. R. proposed to read a short letter [Hamilton's of 17 June 1809]. The object of the committee was to know in what way the pursers of the navy received their money and what was the amount of their emoluments. . . . We inquired, said he, what were their emoluments, other than those allowed by law? Answer: "They arise from a certain percentage upon *slops* detailed to the seamen. . . ." It was scarcely possible to have given a more evasive answer. We asked, What were their emoluments? They answer, "A certain percentage fixed by the department"; but what that percent was the committee was left to find out by instinct. It had been understood that large sums of money were advanced to these pursers, who laid it out in slops, which they retailed to the seamen at an advance, in some instances, of 20 percent! This was a fact, Mr. R. said, which ought to be looked into. It was essential to the reputation of the government, essential to its honor, indispensable to the fair fame of those who administer

Long-service purser John H. Carr joined the navy in that capacity in 1800 and resigned three decades later. The human being behind the name eludes the historian until one day late in 1814 when his commanding officer, Captain John H. Dent, appeals for Carr's removal from the Charleston, South Carolina, station. "Daily complaints" against the purser have become so loud that Dent will not be able to enlist "one man more" as long as Carr remains on duty. "The general complaint is the want of attention on the part of the purser to the wants and accounts of the men, with a disposition not to accommodate them in any respect." C.B.J. Fevret de Saint-Mémin's chalk portrait captured the unaccommodating Mr. Carr sometime around 1810. Library Company of Burlington, New Jersey; National Portrait Gallery photograph.

the finances of the United States, that abuses such as these should be probed to the quick to show to the world that if we cannot govern the great beasts, the mammoths of the forest, we can at least poison the *rats.*

While Randolph's auditors may have been left intentionally confused as to the precise identity of the mammoths of the forest—President Madison? Secretary Gallatin? Secretary Hamilton?—all knew who the rats selected for poisoning were: the navy's pursers. The Committee of Investigation was unanimously reestablished, and Randolph once more appointed its chair.

He went to work with enthusiasm. On 27 November 1811 Randolph appeared at the Navy Office where, to Hamilton's and Chief Clerk Charles W. Goldsborough's consternation, he began asking a series of questions that turned up what might charitably be called sloppy administrative practice—or, more harshly, downright abuse of office—in the enforcement of the legal provision requiring pursers to post bond. The most damning discovery was that Purser Robert W. Goldsborough, brother of Charles and dead since the previous April, did not have a valid bond on file. Leaving no room for evasiveness this time, Randolph fired off (29 November 1811) a list of questions he wanted Hamilton to answer with detailed specifics:

> Pursers: Their emoluments as fixed by [the Navy] Department at various times and the amount.
> Requisitions for SLOPS: How made and complied with?
> With what description of articles, other than necessaries, are the pursers allowed to supply the navy? Are these purchased with public money? How are the profits of the pursers on these articles regulated? What check upon false bills of cost? Do not the principal profits of the pursers . . . arise out of this branch of their business?

Have monies (and to what amount) been at any time and how long left in the hands of pursers?

Last, he wanted to know the balances, as yet unaccounted for, standing against the names of individual pursers. For two months Hamilton made no move to respond to Randolph's questions. Perhaps he hoped this whole issue would go away. In early January the Committee of Investigation called Thomas Turner to testify on a number of money matters, an experience that Turner appears to have survived intact because of his competence and his ability to give precise answers. Finally, 5 February 1812 having arrived but no responses having been forthcoming from Paul Hamilton to Randolph's questions of 29 November, the chairman pointedly reminded the secretary that the committee was waiting—and with dwindling patience.

That broke the logjam. The clerks in the secretary's and the accountant's offices were put to work; a series of reports began flowing toward Capitol Hill. Fortunately, Alexander Murray's complaints about purser abuses, coming just at the time that Congressman Randolph was beginning to show an intense interest in the scope of their profits, had stimulated the Navy Department to clean up its own act on this matter in the summer of 1809. Hamilton (heavily aided by Thomas H. Gilliss of the accountant's office) was able to produce a report that seems to have mollified, but not silenced, criticism on the question of profits from sale of slops.

Less satisfactory was the report on pursers' outstanding balances. Of the twenty-nine pursers listed, nine had unsettled balances in excess of $30,000 standing against their names, the largest being the nearly $133,000 charged to the late and aforementioned Robert W. Goldsborough, the man without a valid bond. In the case of Goldsborough and several others the report included notes to the effect that the accounts were currently being examined and adjusted; when this process was complete it appeared that the money would all be accounted for. If the Committee of Investigation suspected that, in some cases, this was more a pious hope than an accounting reality, they were on the right track. When Goldsborough's accounts were finally closed, some time later, it appeared that he had received approximately $10,000 for which there was no offsetting record of expenditures. His case was far from singular, but the problem of purser debt may be deferred for a few pages. Even as Hamilton's reports began to roll in, the Committee of Investigation was fading from the scene as an active threat to the pursers. In part, it was being overtaken by events. War with England loomed as a distinct possibility and an alternative focus for public interest. In the end Randolph's committee made no report. No one seemed to care really, for by then the focus of congressional interest in pursers had shifted to the Senate. There it reached a resolution of sorts.[2]

A new purser was to be appointed to the lucrative post at the Washington navy yard, and Senator William Branch Giles of Virginia had a candidate in mind for the job. Giles called on Paul Hamilton to reinforce his candidate's application, stating "that he had never asked anything of the government for himself and very seldom for his friends, and that he should feel himself personally obliged by the appointment" of his man. Hamilton pleasantly promised to "pay attention" to Giles's candidate when the appointment was made, and the senator doubtless left the Navy Office with a sense of mission accomplished. His euphoria evaporated soon thereafter when a rumor began to circulate that the coveted post was about to be given to Lewis Deblois, a fifty-one-year-old Washington businessman. Back to the Navy Office rode Giles to confront Hamilton with the Deblois rumor. The secretary was evasive—not a good sign—but did promise that "he would take occasion to converse with [Giles] again on the subject" before the appointment was made.

The promised conversation never occurred, but Deblois's appointment was announced. Now the fat was really in the fire. Someone tipped Giles off to an old newspaper war that established pretty conclusively that back in the days of the Adams administration, when Deblois had been working for Washington navy agent William Marbury, he had been guilty of hiring workmen at one rate, billing his reimbursement at a much higher rate, and pocketing the profits. For his efforts Deblois had been dismissed by Marbury. Giles may also have questioned Deblois's financial stability and consequent suitability as a purser, for Deblois was to go bankrupt in 1814 and his dubious solvency must have been apparent to the financially shrewd at an earlier date. In any event Senator Giles had plenty of evidence of Deblois's inappropriateness for the job; he proceeded to spread it before the president, members of the cabinet, and his fellow senators. When confronted by the outraged Giles, Hamilton defended himself by making the astounding claim that Deblois's "appointment had been made without his consent"! Over at the White House President Madison insisted *he* had had nothing to do with the appointment. The finger of suspicion pointed strongly in the direction of Mrs. Dolly Payne Todd Madison as the decisive influence behind the Deblois appointment, a role she stoutly, if unconvincingly, denied.

Deblois was in office—apparently without anyone having put him there—and Paul Hamilton had made a skillful and inveterate enemy. On 6 March 1812, as a bill to appropriate funds for the repair of certain naval vessels was making its not untroubled way through the Senate, Giles or someone acting on his behalf moved to amend the bill by adding a section that would make pursers commissioned officers whose appointments would require the advice and consent of the Senate and voiding all previous purser appointments, if not nominated and confirmed anew, as of 1 May 1812. The amendment was accepted without recorded opposition, and the bill became law on 30 March 1812.

It did not come as a surprise to Paul Hamilton. Giles's pique may have been the immediate occasion, but the work of the Committee of Investigation had raised so much uneasiness about pursers' operations and profits that some kind of congressional regulation was almost inevitable. On 23 January 1812, in the course of a long and acrimonious debate over the role and size of the nation's navy, the House of Representatives had passed a resolution calling on the secretary of the navy to lay before them "a statement of the names, rank, pay, and rations of the commissioned officers and midshipmen belonging to the Navy of the United States." Although the careful reader might note that the resolution did not ask for data on warrant officers (to which class pursers belonged), Hamilton, administering yet another self-inflicted wound, supplied them anyway, "presuming that the House wished full information upon the subject." The House made the list available to the Senate committee that was considering the bill to strengthen the navy, and this committee, toward the middle or end of February, called Secretary Hamilton to testify before it. He did not make a good showing.

How many pursers does the navy need? asked one senator.

"About thirteen," replied Hamilton. Purser Samuel Hambleton, sitting in the audience, shook his head in disbelief at the secretary's ignorance. Sixteen or eighteen were on active duty even as he spoke.

If that is the case, asked another senator, referring to Hamilton's ill-advised list of warrant officers—which showed thirty-eight pursers, of whom fourteen were on half-pay—why has it been necessary to appoint so many unnecessary pursers?

"I have been much pressed to make appointments," Hamilton answered.

Now a senator moved in for the kill: Is there not a Mr. Deblois in service, and how is he employed?

Hamilton walked into the trap: "Yes. Purser of the [Washington] navy yard."

Then why, Sir, does his name not appear on the list just sent to the House of Representatives?

"It must have been accidentally omitted," was Hamilton's lame reply. Fortunately for Hamilton the senators had not discovered that three other serving pursers had also been omitted from the list, making the total roll of pursers forty-two rather than the reported thirty-eight.

When informed that the committee proposed to add the section requiring Senate approval of purser appointments, Hamilton could only reply that "it would be very agreeable to him."

The Senate was not yet done with Hamilton or the pursers. On 24 February 1812 Hamilton was called on to supply "the date of the last settlement, the amount of bonds given and of public money unaccounted for in the hands of pursers [currently on the roll] respectively; and of the several balances outstanding or public monies unaccounted for by former pursers who are not now in the service of the United States." The requested information was not supplied by the office of the accountant till 16 April, but the Senate committee almost certainly had access to the earlier version (lacking the dates of most recent settlement) given to the Committee of Investigation.

While the accountant's list was being prepared, the law requiring Senate approval of purser commissions was signed on 30 March. The question then became, Which pursers among the forty-two were now to be nominated for new commissions? At this point the record goes blank until 13 April, when President Madison's secretary, Edward Coles, arrived at the Senate Chamber with a message nominating twenty-six pursers for reappointment. Why twenty-six? The historian cannot be sure. The Senate committee were equally puzzled. They invited Hamilton to tell them, in person or by letter, "What number of vessels of war now are, and will speedily be put, in commission? And for what objects the additional pursers are wanted? And under what law they are to be appointed?" Hamilton apparently elected to defend the number in person, so one cannot be certain why he settled on twenty-six. About this time the list of unsettled purser balances reached the Senate committee. This showed the same disturbingly large balances as had the list sent to the House; it added the disquieting information that in at least six cases (including the suspicious Robert W. Goldsborough one) the most recent settlements of accounts were as long ago as 1805 to 1808. Although it was widely assumed that Lewis Deblois, one among the twenty-six nominated, would not survive a Senate confirmation vote, and that it would go hard with pursers with large unsettled balances, in fact all twenty-six names cleared the Senate. For the war's duration, pursers evaporated as a serious political issue. Of the sixteen serving pursers not nominated on 13 April 1812, seven were eventually reappointed to fill the wartime navy's need for more money men. The issue of purser debt and accountability, briefly examined and then ignored amid the demands of a shooting war, bubbled and rumbled just below the surface. It would explode during the postwar years.[3]

31. The Perils of Accountability

*D*EBT. TO UNDERSTAND the problem this could pose for the navy's officers, one needs to understand how the pre-1815 U.S. Navy paid its bills.

There was, of course, no central computer sitting somewhere in Washington churning out checks to compensate contractors who built ships, merchants who sold slop clothing, pilots who took ships to sea, officers in need of salaries, or widows waiting for pensions. Rather, the navy relied on a system of placing large sums of money in the hands of several different classes of disbursing officials, men who were responsible for paying the navy's creditors. Navy agents, political appointees and almost always men already in business as merchants, were the navy's primary dispensers of money. Each major U.S. port where the navy's ships were stationed or where they were likely to call had its navy agent, as did the principal ports on foreign duty stations. The agents were expected to order and deliver supplies for individual ships, to pay for their necessary repairs, and to dispense the monthly pay allotments that naval seafarers might have assigned to mothers, wives, or children. Pursers, too, were given large blocks of cash to pay a ship's officers and men, to purchase slops before a voyage, or perhaps to secure supplementary provisions in places where no regular navy agent was established. A captain or a squadron commander needed cash on hand to pay for things as mundane as pilotage into a distant port or as exotic as a bribe to a foreign official. Even the lieutenant or midshipman sent to recruit in an outport was handed a fistful of cash to pay for the rendezvous, for the music, for the liquor, and for advances to the recruits.

In each of these cases, from the hundreds of thousands of dollars placed with navy agents down to the few hundred dollars handed the recruiting lieutenant, the agent or the officer requisitioned so much money and, when he received it, gave the government a receipt for the amount, stating that he was accountable for its expenditure. That is to say, he either had to prove that the money had been entirely spent for legitimate official purposes, or he had to repay any part of the advance not so expended. With the purser or the recruiting officer, the requisition for cash required the captain's or the commodore's approval, a control that acted (or was supposed to act) as a check to insure that no more money was requisitioned than was needed for legitimate purposes.[1] In the cases of commanding officers and navy agents the secretary of the navy had to accept their word that they needed so much money and say either yes or no. He possessed no means, apart from the presumed integrity of the requisitioner, of verifying that the money really was required for the navy's business and was not being applied to the requisitioner's private cash needs. Especially with the navy agents, who were also private merchants, the temptation to use the ability to requisition government funds as a source of interest-free capital to shore up shaky businesses was too obvious to be ignored or (in many cases) resisted.[2]

A day of reckoning did come. In the language of the time, the officer or disbursing agent was "held accountable" for the money he had received or the stores that had been placed under his care. To exonerate himself of this accountability he had to produce acceptable documentary evidence that the money or goods had been legitimately applied to naval purposes. If he could prove that he was entitled to more money than he had received in advances, then the government owed him and, this fact once established, he was promptly paid. But if, as was all too commonly the case, the officer or agent could not prove that the entire cash advance had been spent on the navy's business, then he owed the U.S. government the unaccounted-for balance and *he* had to pay up.

Determining whether the government's money had been properly expended was the primary responsibility of Accountant of the Navy Thomas Turner and his staff of clerks. They fulfilled this charge with rigor, integrity, and pickiness that make a twentieth-century Internal Revenue Service or General Accounting Office auditor seem downright permissive. The accountant of the navy's decisions were subject to review by the comptroller of the treasury and were sometimes modified or reversed in his office, but the vast bulk of approval or rejection work was done at the accountant's level of authority.[3]

Good accountants are, by nature, orderly, systematic people, and they are inclined to think that the world would be a better place if everyone followed their sterling example. "It is really wonderful that the officers in the navy should be so extremely inattentive and commit so many blunders" in their financial record keeping, Thomas Turner moaned early in his term of office. "The system laid down for them is plain and simple and requires nothing but a little attention to enable them to exhibit all their returns correct—and, by doing it, they would prevent much trouble and labor in the adjustment of accounts at this office that we have to encounter from their incorrectness."[4] Turner would have been willing to reaffirm that sentiment at any time till his death in office in March 1816.

The primary principle of the system was that any vouchers offered as proof of an expenditure must be "fair, explicit, and unequivocal, and containing the best evidence the nature of the case will admit of" and "stated in such a manner as to enable the comptrolling officers to judge of the propriety."[5] To take a mundane but real example, when Melancthon T. Woolsey paid Solomon Wilton $6 he had to be careful to take a receipt for the money which read exactly thus:

Received Sackets Harbour [N.Y.] May 21st 1811 of Lieut. Commdt. M.T. Woolsey six dollars for making a suit of sails for the Launch belonging to the U.S. Brig Oneida

$6

Witness
ABBEY VAUGHAN

his
SOLOMON X WILTON
mark[6]

For this amount to be credited to him in the settlement of his accounts Lieutenant Woolsey had to remember to follow a number of fussy rules: (1) the place and date had to appear on the receipt; (2) the words "Received . . . of Lieut. Commdt. M.T. Woolsey six dollars" had to be written out in full (no numerals); assuming Mr. Wilton had been literate he could not simply have scribbled his name or "paid" across the face of his bill; (3) the purpose for which money was disbursed had to be specified; and (4) because Solomon Wilton was not a literate man, Woolsey had to have a witness to his mark; neither could Abbey Vaughan simply have signed for Wilton, unless there had been attached to the receipt Wilton's written authorization for Vaughan to receive the money for him.

If Woolsey had omitted, say, to get Vaughan's witness to Wilton's mark, the accountant would probably have credited him with the $6 if Woolsey had been prepared to certify upon oath, and subject to the penalties of perjury, that he had actually paid Wilton the money.[7] The rub was, of course, that Lieutenant Woolsey, the senior officer on Lake Ontario, had to be this structured and compulsive not just in one transaction with Solomon Wilton, but in hundreds or thousands of cash transactions while he held that command and had, at least part of the time, more critical concerns on his mind, such as fighting the War of 1812. It was one thing for accountants to pick apart imperfect receipts in a hot Washington office; it was quite another to get acceptable ones from a pilot anxious to get ashore before a storm broke or a stage driver impatient to be on the road.

The pre-1815 navy had few Edward Prebles, the captain who was a great ship commander and combat leader, but simultaneously exhibited a positive enthusiasm for figures, neatness, accuracy, and compulsive record keeping. Typical, perhaps, was the captain who was more skillful and more at ease in clawing off a lee shore in nasty weather or facing down a mutinous seaman than in keeping the best and most complete financial records. For such a captain getting credit for all the money he had spent could be an arduous process. The final settlement of Christopher Raymond Perry, a man not particularly noteworthy for his ability to follow any rules, shows well the kinds of problems an officer could encounter in getting his accounts adjusted. In March 1804, nearly three years after Perry had ceased to be a captain in the navy, Thomas Turner wrote Senator Christopher Ellery, who was acting as Perry's intermediary with the accountant's office, to report that the ex-captain was still debited with $1,341.15 in receipts and charges that the accountant could not admit to his credit for a variety of reasons.

Item: Lieutenant George Washington Tew's travel expenses to and from Boston on navy business. Perry had reimbursed Tew $59.50, but produced travel receipts in support totaling only $47.16. Result: A debit of $12.34 to Captain Perry.

Item: Perry had paid Thomas Tew $12.30 for apprehending one R. Coulson, a deserter from *General Greene,* but had neglected to have Purser Jabez Champlin deduct the sum from Coulson's pay. Result: Captain Perry had to pay the $12.30, unless he could prove he had told Champlin to make the deduction and the purser had been negligent, in which case the $12.30 would be charged to Mr. Champlin.

Item: An undocumented claim by Captain Perry that he had purchased old cannon as extra ballast for *General Greene* for $567. Turner's rejection: "If it was necessary to have more ballast for the ship, it should certainly have been purchased on the best and most economical terms and vouchers produced for it." Result: Claim for $567 in reimbursement suspended for further information.

Item: Small charges amounting to $7.99, receipted by the sellers in the name of Lieutenant Robert Palmer, but now appearing in Perry's accounts with no evidence that Perry had reimbursed Palmer. Result: Suspended until Perry produced Palmer's receipt proving Perry had paid him.

Item: A claim of $215.60 for subsisting two French officers and their servants on board *General Greene* in the West Indies. Turner's comment: "This cannot be a charge to this department. If they were taken on board by direction of the [U.S.] consul, application, I presume, should be made to the Department of State" for reimbursement. Result: Claim rejected by the Navy Department.

And so on for three closely written pages, the figures adding up as rejection was piled on suspension. But there was good news of a sort. When the accountant's office had started its latest round of work on Perry's accounts he had been in the hole to the tune of nearly $3,000. Since then $79 had been found in Purser Champlin's accounts that should be credited to Perry; he still had $1,269.93 in uncollected pay and rations coming to him; and $1,052.37 in claims and vouchers, suspended at an earlier stage of the accounting process, had since been admitted to his credit. Now Captain Perry owed the Navy Department only $551.23![8]

Debt and the Officer

In 1830, just as it had done annually since 1809, Congress published to the world a list of "Balances remaining on the books of the Fourth Auditor of the Treasury, due from individuals for more than three years prior to the 30th September 1830."[9] There, among the names of some six hundred present and former naval officers the curious could find enrolled the famous (Captain James Lawrence, with an unsettled balance of $11,275.85) and the obscure (Midshipman Julius Humphreys, with $429.29); enormous debts (Purser Thomas Shields's $98,471.30) and tiny ones (Midshipman Henry P. Casey's $3.98). Although it was now more than fifteen years since the end of the War of 1812, any curious reader with a moderate knowledge of the navy's history or an analytical eye for the list itself would quickly have realized that many of the men whose names appeared on this roll of dishonor had ceased to be members of the officer corps as long ago as the Quasi-War with France or had, like Master Commandant Richard Somers, a debtor for $413.31, been dead almost that long.

What did this annual listing of some six hundred officer-debtors mean? Were these men deadbeats who had welshed on their obligations? Were they individuals in such perilous financial circumstances that they were unable to pay bills they earnestly desired to honor? Or were they simply unethical individuals—crooks—who had embezzled the public money? Truth to tell, there were some who fell into each of these categories. But to take all the naval officers whose names appear on the annual list of persons with unsettled balances on the books of the navy's accounting officers and label them defaulters to the public would be grossly to misrepresent the situation through oversimplification.

To understand the varieties of debt and indebtedness as they impinged upon the lives or the estates of naval officers, the historian does not need to examine all the hundreds of cases of officers with unsettled balances whose names appear on the annual list issued by the accounting authorities. A subset of the officer corps, its pursers, may stand representative for the whole. There was no shape that debt could take among the corps at large, no process for its recovery that was attempted, no crime so gross, no bankruptcy however poignant, that cannot be found among the pursers. By the nature of their jobs as the navy's uniformed money men, the pursers are the most appropriate group to scrutinize to understand the problems of debt and the officer.[10]

Forty-five warranted or commissioned pursers and four acting pursers who had joined the navy's officer corps before February 1815 were in debt to the government by the end of the War of 1812. *In debt to the government* means, in

For a century and a quarter no one could answer the questions, Who is this unidentified man who sat for C.B.J. Fevret de Saint-Mémin? What is the unfamiliar uniform that he wears? A recently discovered solution to the puzzle: the sitter is John Green, who posed in the purser's uniform as prescribed by the regulations of 1802. Mystery surrounding the image is appropriate, for historians have been unable to discover the cause of the collapse of Purser Green's professional competence. In the months after Green was detached from the brig Hornet *in 1811 Accountant Thomas Turner and Secretary Paul Hamilton repeatedly instructed him to produce his accounts and settle them. When the purser was finally threatened into compliance, the reason for procrastination became apparent. His records were a mess; some simply did not exist. Principal Clerk Thomas H. Gilliss of the accountant's office spent uncounted man-hours in 1813 and 1814 unraveling this chaos, heroically reconstructing Green's statement from his ledgers, his checkbooks, a mass of loose papers, and the voluntary testimony of a variety of individuals that, Yes, they had received so-and-so much money from Mr. Green. Medals were not given to accounting officers for service above and beyond. Thomas Handy Gilliss may have thought he deserved one for rescuing John Green from a debtor's fate.* National Portrait Gallery, Washington, D.C.

this context, that when the purser came to settle his accounts he was unable to demonstrate that he had expended all of the money he had requisitioned on legitimate naval business; that he owed the unaccounted-for money to the government; and that he was expected to repay it, but either could not or would not do so. To be counted here among the forty-nine purser-debtors, this situation must have persisted for at least three years—though most debts remained unsettled much, much longer—and the greater part of the indebtedness must have been incurred by the end of the War of 1812, even though, in the massive accounting backlog that developed in the wake of the War of 1812, the actual negative balance may not have been uncovered until several years after the guns stopped firing. These forty-nine pursers and acting pursers owed the government a nominal total of $437,387.10. The forty-five warranted or commissioned pursers who wound up owing the government money added up to a little more than one-third of all the pursers who served in the navy from the onset of the Quasi-War with France through the War of 1812. To rush from this simple statement and say that one purser out of three in the pre-1815 navy was a deadbeat, a cheater, or a defaulter would be a great injustice. It would also obscure much about life in the navy and the risks of a purser's job. Debt came in many varieties.

Nine of the forty-nine debts arose as a result of chargebacks. That is, after Purser A had apparently settled with the accountant's office and established that he had expended all the money he had received on legitimate naval business, departing the officer corps with all obligations seemingly met, a subsequent settlement of Purser B's or Captain C's accounts turned up receipts with which Purser A should have been debited in his settlement, but had not been. Onto the accountant's books these sums went as a negative balance against Purser A.

The amounts involved were usually small. Of the $437,387.10 nominally owed by pursers, only $2,725.09 came from chargebacks; $1,591.07 was a chargeback to one man. The Navy Department expended little effort in trying to collect these small balances, and years might go by before the former purser knew that he was being annually proclaimed to Congress and the world as a public debtor. In 1819 Thomas Johnston, who resigned as a purser late in 1806, had gained and lost a fortune as a Baltimore merchant in the interim, and was then making ends meet on a clerk's salary in the office of the quartermaster general, was outraged to learn that the government was dunning him for a $9 chargeback balance. Far from owing the United States money, Johnston retorted, *he* had a claim for $200 for supplementary pay from serving as judge advocate at courts martial, which claim had not yet been honored. By his reckoning the United States owed Thomas Johnston $191.[11]

Whichever party wound up with the positive balance in the ultimate settlement of that particular disagreement, in Thomas Johnston's case, as with most of the chargeback balances, the United States was eventually able to collect or otherwise liquidate the debt. Only $580.66 in chargeback debts went unresolved, in most cases because the purser had died several years before anyone tried to collect the money; whatever estate he may have possessed was long since dispersed. Such was the case with former purser James Tootell, dead since September 1809, who was carried on the list of public debtors each year until 1841 because of an after-the-settlement discovery that he had overpaid certain enlisted men to the tune of $34.50. Unless some interested party could find evidence that the United States owed James Tootell an equal or a larger sum of money, there existed no legal means, short of an act of Congress, to absolve the debt on the government books.[12]

Eliminating the nine individuals whose indebtedness arose from after-the-settlement chargebacks, there remain forty pre-1815 pursers and acting pursers who among them owed the United States a nominal $434,662.01. Of these forty men, fourteen, with a combined nominal debt of $225,088.70, had died without having a chance to adjust their accounts with the examining clerks in the accountant's office, a circumstance that had a definite bearing on their presence among the debtors. It was one matter for a purser to settle his accounts in person with the office of the accountant of the navy. If receipts were missing the purser could try to collect them. Transactions that, on the paper record, appeared questionable to the accountant might well be approved if the purser were there to explain them in person and perhaps muster the support of his commanding officer. Undocumented credits would sometimes be accepted on the strength of a purser's oath. If a purser and an examining clerk really worked at it, it was often possible to turn an unpromising mass of papers, with an odor of deficit hovering about them, into a settlement that balanced or perhaps left the purser a few hundred dollars to the good. It was quite another matter for one of the accounting clerks to sort through a dead purser's books and papers. Whether slow or sudden, the purser's death itself almost certainly meant that he left his records incomplete and often in some disorder. Knowledge of supporting papers he had intended to assemble and of any half-completed transactions to his benefit died with him. A dead purser could make no oral or written explanations to the accountant of the navy. Neither could he take any oaths. When a purser died with significant unsettled accounts, the odds were good that, do what the accounting clerks might toward reconstructing a final statement from his surviving papers, the late purser's account would wind up showing a negative balance.

Joshua Brackett Langdon, a native of Portsmouth, New Hampshire, is a good case of what happened when death caught a purser with his financial affairs in disarray. Twenty-four years old when he was appointed a purser late in 1809, Langdon had attended Phillips Exeter Academy and then tried his hand at business in Boston, with little financial success, in the difficult economic environment of the Embargo years, a situation that left him significantly in debt to his brother-in-law and perhaps to others as well. Langdon still held one superlative asset: his aunt was married to Secretary of War William Eustis. The latter put his shoulder to the wheel and secured nephew Joshua a purser's warrant. Langdon now had a good job and, given a little luck, the prospect of being able to recoup his finances. Fortune failed to smile. Langdon's first duty assignment was the brig *Vixen*, Lieutenant John Trippe, en route to the New Orleans station in the summer of 1810. Unhappily for Langdon, *Vixen* put into Havana where the novice purser contracted yellow fever and died on 3 July, after two days' illness. When the accountant's office finally adjusted Langdon's accounts, he was $1,347.30 into the red ink.

How could a purser who had just barely begun his career owe so much money? As with all pursers at the beginning of a cruise, the Navy Department had advanced him a healthy sum of money. Part of this money was used to pay officers and enlisted men; it could be more or less accounted for through the ship's rolls. Other money purchased officially sanctioned slops for resale to

Vixen's ship's company. The goods inventoried as remaining on hand the day of Mr. Langdon's death, when added to the quantities charged his shipmates in his slop records, should, with the customary allowances for wastage, have added up to account for that money. But, even making all possible allowances, Langdon's books did not balance. When Purser Langdon's sea chest was opened not a dollar was to be found in it, only a small amount of clothing and some sketchy financial records. As far as anyone could discover, Joshua B. Langdon had died completely insolvent. How, then, to account for the nearly fourteen hundred missing dollars?

Several things may have happened; all of them probably did in one degree or another. Langdon was not the only man stricken by yellow fever. Six days after Langdon's death, *Vixen*'s commanding officer, Tripolitan War hero John Trippe, also died of yellow fever. In the confusion attending the more or less simultaneous deaths of purser and commanding officer, records were probably not well kept. The situation offered an almost ideal opportunity for pilfering of official slops, especially if Langdon's steward was less than scrupulously honest. Moreover, Langdon had surely used part of his advance to purchase slops not on the official list, which slops he carried at his own risk. Using a government advance for this purpose was a common, if not strictly proper, practice and one that was winked at by the Navy Office. In common with all of his purser peers Langdon expected to be able to repay the unofficial shelf-stocking loan from his profits. Because such private stores would never have appeared in Purser Langdon's official slop records, any on hand at the time of his death would not have been credited to his account—if any could have been found, for these "luxury" articles were a highly tempting target for pilferage. Although by the strictest standards of government ethics it was highly improper, it seems almost certain that Langdon, a young man with numerous small debts, employed some of the money to pay off private scores, figuring to recoup the self-loan in pay and rations by cruise's end. Finally, even though there was no cash in Langdon's chest when his fellow officers inventoried its contents after his death, can one be sure there was no money therein as he lay dying or in the few moments after his death? Did the steward or some other interested party have the key? Historians will never be certain why the late Purser Langdon wound up owing the United States $1,347.30, but this scenario, perhaps aided and abetted by poor record keeping, seems a likely one. Langdon was a young, unmarried man who owned nothing beyond his wardrobe. To him it could have mattered little whether he died solvent or insolvent.[13]

Four of the purser-debtors who died with unsettled accounts were in a quite special category. Among them they "owed" $51,638.87. Each of the four had gone down with a ship—*Epervier, Insurgente, Pickering*, or *Wasp*. Vessel, ship's company, purser, stores, slops, and financial records vanished without a trace into the depths of the sea. Because each of these ships had disappeared in midcruise, its purser became technically a debtor to the United States: he had received cash advances with which he was charged, but his accounts would not have been settled or his expenditures fully credited until the end of the cruise. Unless some interested relative could persuade Congress to pass a private act absolving the debt (as, in fact, one did) there was no way for the accounting system to liquidate this negative balance. Forty years after their ships had gone down in the hurricane of September 1800 Pursers Clark Wheelock of *Pickering* and Samuel John Cox of *Insurgente* still appeared in the annual published list of debtors to the United States for the sums of $9,923.46 and $10,373.09 respectively.

If, after identifying the nine pursers or acting pursers who were labeled debtors to government because of chargebacks to them that were discovered after their accounts had been settled, and after identifying the larger group of fourteen purser-debtors who died without having an opportunity to settle their accounts in person, the historian asks these two groups to step, please, to one side; then the twenty-six pursers or acting pursers who remain in formation can be identified as the hardcore debtors to government. These were men who were alive and present at the settlements of their accounts, but who were either unwilling or unable to pay the balances due from them. Collectively they owed the United States a nominal debt of $209,573.31.

If one steps a little closer, it is to discover that these twenty-six do not all look alike. Even hardcore debtors came in several varieties. Six of the purser-debtors found themselves publicly pilloried as such because of long-standing disputes over whether certain amounts should be credited to them or because of prolonged procrastination in paying up on balances they owed and were perfectly capable of reimbursing. In the former category was Purser Robert Ludlow, member of a family prominent in the pre-1815 navy, who died in 1826 without ever having paid the $1,749.76 the United States claimed he owed. Ludlow's response was a counterclaim that the so-called debt came about because, owing to the national government's weakened financial posture during the latter part of the War of 1812, he had been debited at face value with money remitted to him in the form of treasury notes, but had been compelled to convert the notes to cash at a heavy discount. Ludlow's plight was far from unique among the navy's officers, but the only legal way an officer could be credited with such losses in the settlement of his accounts was a private act of Congress for his relief.[14] Although a number of officers followed this route successfully, Ludlow either disdained or neglected to try. The treasury accounting officers, sympathetic to the justice of Ludlow's claim, but unable to grant a credit without congressional authorization, never made any serious attempt to collect the money before Ludlow's death and only a halfhearted and ineffective one thereafter.[15]

The determined and creative procrastinator could stave off paying for many years. Purser John Darby tendered his resignation on 22 November 1805 in a huff because he disliked the duty station to which he had been ordered. He was told by Robert Smith that his resignation would be accepted once he had settled his accounts, which at that moment showed a substantial balance against him. For the next decade and a half Darby, from his home in Richmond County, Virginia, kept up a sporadic correspondence with the naval accounting officers over whether he owed the government $473.74, as the accountant claimed, or whether certain disputed items should be passed to his credit. The ex-purser used every stalling tactic he could devise: demanding copies of voluminous papers from the treasury files, threatening a direct appeal to President Madison. He might have succeeded in stalling indefinitely had not the United States obtained a judgment against him in federal district court in December 1818. This turn of events finally forced Darby to request a stay of execution and to make the trip to Washington to seek, by direct negotiation with the accounting officers, some final resolution of this long-unsettled business. Darby's procrastination had worked to his advantage. The treasury was now more malleable on the disputed amounts than it had been when they were first challenged, a new mood possibly prompted by the fact that most of Darby's detailed accounts and vouchers had been burned in the destruction of the treasury offices by the British in 1814. The negotiation ended with the accounting officers deciding that the United States owed John Darby $138.13, which sum was paid him on 3 March 1820. Perhaps encouraged by this success, Darby decided that the government also owed him his full pay and rations from the date of his tendered resignation (22 November 1805) until his account was finally closed nearly fifteen years later, on the grounds that Robert Smith had told him that his resignation would not be accepted till his accounts were settled! Attorney General William Wirt advised the Navy Department that he could imagine no legal basis for rewarding someone financially for fifteen years of procrastination; if Darby thought he had a case, he could appeal to Congress.[16] At that response, Mr. Darby threw in the towel and disappeared, to trouble the federal authorities no more.

The majority of the hardcore debtors to government—fifteen of the twenty-six pursers and acting pursers who were alive at the settlement of their accounts and who were unwilling to pay the balances they owed—were simply men who were insolvent and utterly unable to settle up. Such pursers often chose to blame external misfortunes for their plight, but in all the cases that can be reconstructed their financial debacles can be superficially ascribed to lack of training in a purser's duties but more profoundly to the absence of the natural abilities or the personality traits necessary for a successful pursership. That the navy enrolled so many pursers fundamentally incompetent to their duties is perhaps no surprise. Unlike its intensive and successful on-the-job indoctrination for midshipmen and lieutenants, the navy paid little attention to basic training for pursers. As with surgeons and surgeon's mates, pursers were expected to join the navy with their basic professional education already acquired.

True, the navy did have a sort of in-house apprentice program: slightly fewer than one-third of all pursers had previously held positions as captain's clerks, chaplains, purser's stewards, acting pursers, navy yard clerks, or clerks in the Navy Office. Because all of these jobs provided a greater or lesser opportunity to learn a purser's duties, the navy preferred to recruit such men for its purserships. Desirable as this recruitment route might be, the Navy Office was unable or unwilling to adhere to it. Eighty-seven of 123 warranted pursers were given jobs that might involve the handling of up to hundreds of thousands of dollars on the recommendation of trusted informants, but without any in-service track record on which to base a judgment of possible performance in these responsible roles. (Among the more than one-third of the navy's pursers with previous experience as clerks or chaplains or in similar berths, only three were discovered to be incompetent to a purser's duties or became insolvent.) Moreover, the evidence suggests that a navy pursership was often a tempting alternative career for a man who had been less than successful in the world of private business. Purser Joshua B. Langdon is an excellent case in point. Unfortunately for such individuals, the qualities required for success as a purser were essentially those required for survival in the world of private business: hard work, thrift, caution, accuracy, attention to detail, and an eye for opportunities to make money or maximize profits.

Robert Lewis may well have been a nice, likable young man. Once he found his niche as a bank clerk and stayed there, he survived. Unfortunately, this

Philadelphian was neither bright, strong of character, nor especially effectual. His father had died shortly before the outbreak of hostilities in the Quasi-War with France, but not before he had made young Robert a partner in his business, a business that was already heavily in debt. This ill-advised move had the effect of rendering the son legally responsible for debts he could otherwise have walked away from on his father's death. It was a stunning financial blow and one from which he never recovered. In some manner now lost to history Robert Lewis secured an appointment as purser of *Ganges* when that ship was added to the navy in 1798. *Ganges*, the navy's first ship to get to sea, served the nation throughout the Quasi-War with France. Purser Lewis's naval career was markedly shorter. By late 1799 Lewis was on the beach at Philadelphia; the settlement of his accounts was the sole formality lacking to sever his connection with the navy. He had proved incompetent to his duties, and such records as he had kept were chaotic. One of the first pursers appointed, Lewis had labored under a handicap, because no official instructions had yet been issued respecting how a purser ought to keep his records. Several pursers worked with this disadvantage, but only Lewis and one other man failed to come up with a homegrown system that could be accepted and settled by the accountant's office. Lack of native ability may not have been Purser Lewis's only problem. Heavy drinking, triggered by his involvement in his father's debts and a deeply confirmed habit by 1806, may already have been present in 1798–99. Based on the records that Lewis sent to the Navy Office he was $4,047.44 in debt.

Between 1800 and 1806 two secretaries of the navy and Accountant Turner tried every form of threat or cajolery they could devise to persuade Lewis to come to Washington and attempt to close out his pursership. Nothing worked. Lewis refused to budge out of Philadelphia and his job at the bank. Philadelphia navy agent George Harrison, a frequent emissary to Lewis, assured Thomas Turner that ex-purser Lewis had almost certainly not embezzled the unaccounted-for money: "He has, through ignorance and incapacity, neglected to take regular vouchers. . . . I [do not] believe, from the confused state of his accounts as purser, that he will ever be able to settle them. . . . I presume [they] are so irregular that he knows not how to take them up." Why, pleaded Turner, doesn't Lewis bundle up what records he has and bring them on to Washington? Almost certainly the clerks can salvage enough from them to reduce the balance. Still Robert Lewis refused to cooperate, so the treasury played its last card: suit in federal district court. It was an empty gesture. The United States obtained a judgment against the former purser, but he had not a single asset that could be seized to satisfy the judgment. Lewis lived hand-to-mouth on his salary at the bank. When the record of his case was closed in 1829—though his name and the $4,047.44 were still carried on the list of public debtors a few years more—it was with the note, "Dead. Insolvent many years."[17]

Although forty-nine pursers and acting pursers were, for one reason or another, debtors to the government, in only three of those cases did the accounting officers uncover what they regarded as unethical behavior or dishonesty, let alone outright embezzlement. True, there were occasional complaints against this or that purser for price gouging or excessive deductions or holding up pay, but by and large the navy's pursers seem to have been a relatively honest group of men.[18] If they were inclined to cut an occasional ethical corner to their financial advantage, it rarely took the form of fundamental dishonesty. From the government's perspective there was far greater danger from the incompetence and consequent insolvency of its pursers than there ever was from fraud or embezzlement. That said, the truly dishonest purser did occasionally turn up in the ranks of the corps.

The ethical ambience of the Georgia station, where the United States faced Spanish Florida across the tidal St. Marys River, was incisively captured by the station's commodore, Hugh G. Campbell. At Amelia, on the Spanish side of the frontier, on 11 November 1814, Campbell counted more than fifty square-rigged vessels flying Swedish, Russian, and Spanish colors, two-thirds of which he estimated were really British property. The attraction of Amelia was its proximity to the U.S. border. Along this porous boundary Campbell and his gunboats attempted to prevent illegal trade, "in which the inhabitants of this frontier are ready and willing to participate. . . . Depravity in man I have seen through[out] life, but Amelia and [St. Marys] are examples I never before witnessed. The fact is villainy being the principal requisite to effect the purposes of traders to Amelia has rendered the assistance of a considerable proportion of this community essentially necessary."[19] To this congenial climate the Navy Department unsuspectingly ordered, early in the War of 1812, newly minted purser Nathaniel W. Rothwell.

The full scope of Purser Rothwell's quasi-legal and plainly illegal dealings will surely never be known. He did, however, make one big mistake: he procrastinated on paying a master's mate, Charles Snell, who had spent two years serving as Rothwell's steward. Angered at his inability to collect his pay and prize money, Snell blew the whistle on his old boss in a letter to the secretary of the navy: "I can assure you that I have been forced to go in the dark of the night to smuggle bales of cloth [for] the purser from Amelia to St. Marys [and] several other transactions that has been committed on this station that I can, if requested, bring sufficient proof concerning it." When questioned by Chief Clerk Benjamin Homans, officers who had been attached to the station confirmed Snell's story of Rothwell's smuggling activities and of his procrastination and refusal to pay out money he was required to disburse. There was even a suggestion that he was speculating in prize goods captured by U.S. vessels by purchasing them himself as a private individual, although he was prize agent for the station, a blatant conflict of interest.

After Homans's questioning, the sequence of events grows obscure. Apparently the complaints against Purser Rothwell became so numerous that Campbell arrested him and ordered him to New York, there to await court martial. No court ever sat on Rothwell, though why this is so remains unknown. Seemingly the arrest was lifted, and Rothwell was ordered to Washington to settle his accounts covering the more than $250,000 in government funds that had passed through his hands. The purser's idea of presenting his statement to the accountant's office was to dump a mass of disorganized loose papers—including, as it happened, his personal correspondence, which still remains in the accountant's archives—on the clerks and expect them to make sense out of chaos. Rothwell stayed in Washington a short time, achieved some progress in putting his papers in order, ran up against gaps in his records that rationalized procrastination, applied (9 September 1815) for a furlough of four weeks, and thereupon disappears from the navy's records so completely that, although it is known that he died, probably in late January or early February 1818, not even the precise date of his death is on file. This left the overworked accounting clerks to try to reconstruct his transactions and draw a balance, which they finally had time to do in 1823. The late Purser Rothwell was found to owe the United States $23,771.68; his estate was long since declared insolvent. Where had the money gone? No one could ever say. The evidence suggests that Mr. Rothwell was a careless wheeler-dealer who probably spent the money in speculation and high living. If any substantial part of the missing cash was still in existence, so far as the U.S. Navy was concerned Mr. Rothwell had carried the secret of its whereabouts to his grave.[20]

Getting the Money Back

With forty-nine pursers and acting pursers owing their government an aggregate nominal debt of $437,387.10, what means did the United States possess to recover its money? Did it eventually have to be written off as bad debt?

For the first decade of the navy's existence the treasury's only formal recourse against a defaulting or a recalcitrant purser was a suit in federal court. In spite of this apparent shortage of coercive means for settlement and collection, during that decade—a period that included both the Quasi-War with France and the Tripolitan War—the problem of delinquent purser debt was minimal. Seventeen former pursers had failed to account for $37,900.16, from which total one should deduct the $20,296.55 in unaccounted funds attributed to the pursers lost in *Pickering* and *Insurgente*. Of the remaining $17,603.61, the incompetent and hard-drinking bank clerk Robert Lewis was charged with $4,047.44, while the largest single delinquency was John Lyon's $8,273.95. Lyon, a compulsive gambler, was deeply overdrawn before his habits came to light and he was dropped from the roll of pursers. His was a sad and hopeless case—the money forever gone so far as the United States was concerned, because Lyon, like Lewis, remained utterly insolvent till the day of his death.[21]

With the possible exception of the Lyon business, the navy of 1798–1808 could hardly be said to have had a serious problem with delinquent pursers. Indeed, the smallness of the problem stands in a clearer light when one realizes that between 1798 and 1808 the navy had expended $5.9 million for pay and subsistence under sometimes chaotic wartime conditions. Most of this money would have passed through the hands of pursers, as would a now-indeterminate portion of the navy's expenditures under other heads of appropriation. Yet only $17,603.61 (excluding the money lost with *Pickering* and *Insurgente*) remained unaccounted for. This impressive record must be attributed to the vigorous efforts of Thomas Turner and his staff, who worked hard at running delinquent pursers to the ground and squeezing the money or the documents out of them. In one or two cases wherein the purser himself was a lost cause, a more solvent relative was persuaded to cover the loss under threat of publicly exposing the family as harboring a deadbeat in its bosom.

Effective as had been Turner's means of coercing settlements, Congress, at the session of 1808–1809, decided to strengthen his hand still further by adding a weapon to the settlement-and-collection arsenal. By an act of 3 March 1809 that dealt with a variety of accounting matters, Congress directed that "every purser of the navy shall give bond, with one or more sufficient sureties, in such sums as the president of the United States may direct, for the faithful discharge of the trust reposed in him." The act of 30 March 1812, which made pursers commissioned officers, modified the bonding provision by setting the penalty at $10,000 and requiring that there be "two or more sufficient sureties." In requiring the posting of surety bonds, Congress was not singling out naval pursers for special evidence of distrust. Similar bonds had previously been required for certain classes of federal officials who received large sums of public money; the act of 3 March 1809 merely extended this requirement to pursers of the navy and paymasters of the army.[22]

This law was not without its weaknesses. In 1809 and 1812 the $10,000 penalty on the bond seemed adequate protection for the government's money. No default to date had exceeded that sum by a significant amount: the John Lyon gambling loss, for example, would have been fully recovered had a bonding provision been in effect during Mr. Lyon's tenure as a purser. With the coming of the War of 1812 the sums of money in default from individual pursers shot up. A $10,000 bond was grotesquely inadequate to protect the United States against the misdeeds of a Nathaniel Rothwell, in default by $23,771.68. Equally problematic, the law did not require that the penalty of the bond be put in escrow, secured by mortgages, or otherwise insured. All that was needed was that the purser find two or more men who would sign a legal document binding "ourselves, and each of us, our and each of our heirs, executors and administrators, in the whole and for the whole, jointly and severally" for the sum of $10,000, on the condition that the bond would be void if the purser in question "shall regularly account, when thereunto required, for all public monies received by him from time to time, and for all public property committed to his care, with such person or persons, officer or officers of the government of the United States, as shall be duly authorized to settle and adjust his accounts, and shall moreover pay over, as he may be directed, any sum or sums that may be found due to the United States, upon such settlement or settlements, and shall also faithfully discharge, in every respect, the trust reposed in him."

Neither were the signers—the sureties—absolutely required to prove that they could pay the penalty if demanded. Often they were men of sufficient prominence, credit, and apparent fortune that the secretary of the navy would accept the bond on the basis of his knowledge of their reputations. In other cases a kind of independent verification was established, as when Elias Glenn, the U.S. district attorney for Maryland, certified that Robert T. Spence, one of the sureties for his brother, Purser Groeme K. Spence, "is perfectly good and sufficient security for the amount of the penalty of the bond."[23] The effectiveness of the bonding protection depended in large measure on the secretary of the navy, on his firmness and persistence in enforcing it, and on the degree to which he was prepared to refuse to accept bonds if he was unconvinced of the ability of the sureties to meet their obligations. In the case of Paul Hamilton, under whom many of the pre-1815 pursers were bonded, one can well question the strength of this commitment. To his chagrin William Jones discovered in May 1814 that ten pursers, including some of the most senior and most respected in the navy, had never taken out the new bonds absolutely required by the act of 30 March 1812, even though that law specifically directed that the bond had to be executed before the purser entered upon the duties of his office.[24]

So long as the surety was a man of probity and fortune, and so long as that fortune remained intact amid the financial vicissitudes of the early nineteenth century, the bonding system worked reasonably well. When the accounts of

Commodore Samuel Nicholson's son-in-law, Purser John Rose Greene, who died in August 1812, were finally closed in May 1815, Greene was found to owe the government $7,356.51. Because there was no estate from which the debt could be recovered, Accountant Thomas Turner asked Boston navy agent Amos Binney to notify Greene's surety, Benjamin Weld, that he would have to cover the debt. Turner may have sensed that Mr. Weld was going to procrastinate, because he added, "If the amount is not shortly paid, the bond must be put in suit." The following October Weld settled up.[25]

Doubtless Benjamin Weld, a thrifty Yankee, was deeply pained to part with his money, but at least he was able to pay. In all too many cases—at least seven and possibly more—the bonding provision proved to be a foundation laid on financial sand. What happened when the United States tried to collect the $1,781.11 debt owed by one of the less than competent pursers left out in the reduction of April 1812 fully illustrates the problem. "John Davis of Philadelphia, formerly a purser in the navy, is in debt to the United States," Thomas Turner wrote Philadelphia navy agent George Harrison on 31 May 1814. "It appears by his bond that a man by the name of William Brown is his security, but his residence is not stated. Will you be pleased to make inquiry and ascertain, if you can, if such a man lives in Philadelphia and, if he does, what is his situation and circumstances?" Harrison's prompt reply of 2 June was not encouraging:

> It will be impossible to come at *the* William Brown, security for Purser Davis, without asking each William if he is the man. There is a William B. I suspect to be the man, but it is not worth the trouble to ascertain it, as neither him nor Davis could clear off their whiskey tavern scores, and they are nearly burnt out. Davis was once a man of fortune and of excellent reputation. The loss of the former has caused the forfeiture of the latter, and he is an object of commiseration. He had not strength of mind to bear up against adversity that has been the fate of many an honest man. . . . By sending me the signature of Mr. B. it is possible I may ascertain the man through the bank.

Turner promptly dispatched Davis's original bond to Harrison, who reported the results on 12 June:

> I have found the witnesses to the bond of Davis and Brown, but their memories are treacherous and they cannot recall the transaction; but even this much they would not commit themselves to say until they had had a consultation. Their signatures was then acknowledged, but they added they "must have been called in accidentally." The truth is they perfectly know for whom they signed as witnesses, but they are nearly of a stamp, and it is my opinion that the balance unaccounted for by Davis can never be recovered. From the information I have taken I have no doubt that the security is William Brown, distiller, but I question if you could by incarceration squeeze the costs of a suit out of him. The secretary, [if] he recollects him, will confirm this to you.

As advised, Turner passed Harrison's letter along to Philadelphian William Jones, who returned it with the note, "I know the surety, William Brown, distiller of spirits, by the too free use of which he has destroyed himself and rendered hopeless his responsibility." Jones's identification was confirmed by a simultaneous letter from Harrison, returning the bond: "The security of Mr. Davis is the man I supposed: *William Brown, distiller.* Davis took the advantage of the act of insolvency a short time since, and I am informed Brown lives on his wife's property." Not one dollar of the debt was ever recovered.[26]

Ultimately, the effectiveness of the bonding requirement depended on a more basic power, the ability of the United States to sue an accountable public official (or his sureties, if he was bonded) in federal court for any debt owed to the United States and, in the event of a favorable judgment, to seize property or to imprison the debtor to force payment of the debt.[27] The weakness of this provision was that it assumed the debtor had property to seize in execution of the court's judgment, whereas the estates of most dead purser-debtors were hopelessly insolvent. Live purser-debtors, Robert Lewis for one, had absolutely no property to seize and were living hand-to-mouth on the salaries from their jobs, if they had them. As for the imprisonment provision, if a man had no property and was just getting by on what he earned, putting him in jail was not going to help in collecting the debt. This was so sufficiently obvious at the time that only two insolvent pursers were imprisoned for their inability to pay court judgments; both were quickly released once their utter lack of assets had been verified. Finally, as the accounting system bogged down in the mass of unsettled War of 1812 transactions, ten or twenty years might pass between the time a bond was taken out and the suit against the sureties was tried in federal court. By that time the sureties themselves were often dead or insolvent or both—or gone without a trace.

Given these formidable weaknesses, the record on recovery of debts owed by pursers through the federal courts was not an impressive one. Suits against pre-1815 purser-debtors or their sureties were undertaken in eighteen instances. Two of the suits were not pressed to a final resolution, in both cases because there did not appear to be anything to gain by further investment of effort. In ten of the suits the United States obtained a verdict entirely in its favor, but under only three of the ten favorable verdicts was the government able to collect the debt. With the remaining seven cases the United States had to be satisfied by an empty victory in court: the pursers and/or their sureties were found to be hopelessly insolvent. In six cases juries brought in verdicts that wholly or partially absolved the purser or the sureties from the debt.

Peter Trezevant of Charleston, South Carolina, had been appointed purser of the frigate *John Adams* early in the Quasi-War with France. He owed his job primarily to the fact that he was the brother-in-law of the frigate's captain, George Cross. Whether Purser Trezevant was the victim of beginning his duties while there existed no printed instructions for pursers, as a consequence of which he made costly errors, or whether he was a man of only average competence who had secured a purser's post after unsuccessful ventures in private business—or some combination of both—is no longer clear. When the accountant's office finally finished adjusting his accounts (Trezevant himself was discharged at the end of the Quasi-War) he owed the United States $1,874.89. The greatest part of this sum arose from overpayments to officers and seamen of *John Adams* to the tune of $1,552.23, though how these overpayments occurred does not appear in the record. After several administrative attempts to collect the debt had failed, suit was instituted against Trezevant in 1807. By various maneuvers, chiefly vague suggestions that he was entitled to this or that credit that the accountant had not admitted, Trezevant—now existing solely on his salary as discount clerk of the South Carolina Bank—was able to stall a trial until 15 December 1819, on which date he finally had to face a jury.

He was probably not wholly displeased with the outcome. The jury concluded that Trezevant had indeed produced proof that he had paid $50.40 for sheeting linen that had been disallowed by the accounting office; that he was not liable for an $80.70 deduction from pay for the marine hospital fund that he had failed to make when so august a figure as Commodore Hugh G. Campbell testified that notice of the required deduction had not been given to Trezevant; and that he was not liable for a $437.47 overpayment to one of *John Adams*'s lieutenants, because the overpayment had actually been made by the navy agent and unwittingly carried over by Trezevant to his payroll. Result: The district court ruled that Peter Trezevant owed the United States only $1,306.32.

Should the United States appeal this partially adverse decision? Thomas Parker, the district attorney for South Carolina, advised against it:

> Under all [the] circumstances, it is better for the case to be closed than to be continued open. Our juries of late have been much disposed to support the verdicts of each other and have given some remarkable instances of such disposition; besides which, they generally lean to the defendant, and I would not be at all surprised if another jury should acquit him *altogether*. Besides which, where are the United States to get payment even for the sum found [in their favor]? The defendant has no means with which I am acquainted tangible by an execution. He lives by his daily labor. If his body is not taken, he will never pay; and if it is, he most probably cannot pay. And to imprison him for life under the third section [of the] act [of] 6th June 1798 . . . would be a harsh punishment for what might, in truth, only have proceeded from an error in judgment.

There the matter might have ended, with Trezevant declaring himself insolvent and unable to pay the $1,306.32 judgment. But he was now anxious to clear his name, and in January 1824 he petitioned Congress, claiming that he had found additional evidence, including books and papers, that could not be admitted as proof by the government's strict accounting rules or by the rules of evidence in force in the federal courts, but that would exonerate his debt if Congress were to pass a private act directing the accounting officers to settle on equitable principles. Trezevant's petition was referred by Congress to the fourth auditor of the treasury, who examined the ex-purser's newly produced evidence during the winter of 1824–25. By this time the federal accounting officers were highly motivated to close out the old debts on the basis of any plausible evidence that could be produced, and Trezevant's papers were apparently sufficiently convincing to enable the fourth auditor to liquidate the remaining balance and close the account on 28 February 1825.

Unlike that of so many of the purser-debtors, Peter Trezevant's story has a happy ending. Late in 1826 or perhaps early in 1827, the fifty-eight-year-old bank clerk and his wife, Elizabeth (Farquhar) Trezevant, learned that she was one of the seven heirs to the £1.5 million fortune of her British uncle, John Farquhar. Remarking that "he had been poor all his life, but that thereafter he expected to live on turbot," Peter Trezevant, accompanied by Elizabeth and their younger children, said a none too fond farewell to Charleston and sailed for England, where he reveled in the sedate pleasures of financial security, turbot and all, until his death at Brighton in 1854 at the age of eighty-five.[28]

Peter Trezevant was neither the first nor the only purser to think of the expedient of turning to Congress for help in lifting the burden of debt off his back. This route was likely to be taken whenever a purser or his sureties thought a plausible case could be made (or concocted) that circumstances justified congressional intervention, by means of a private act, to suspend the traditional accounting rules. Although the appeal to the national legislature was often attempted, Congress was notoriously reluctant to pass this kind of legislation. Many petitions were presented; few private bills were enacted. Among the forty-nine purser-debtors and their sureties from the pre-1815 navy, only two pursers and two sureties obtained the prayed-for congressional relief.

Edwin T. Satterwhite of Williamsboro, North Carolina, had studied law briefly and worked as a clerk and bookkeeper to a merchant in Williamsboro before deciding, early in 1809, when he was eighteen or nineteen years old, that he wanted to try a midshipman's life. His recommendations contained a possibly ominous note: "He is a young man of very good talents, but has been dissipated. This, I am informed, he has not only quitted, but declares that he never will do like again." For his first two years in the navy Satterwhite was on his good behavior and earned his commanding officer's "warmest approbation" and recommendation for "integrity and firmness." At the end of those two years as a midshipman, Satterwhite decided (for reasons not on the record) that he wanted to become a purser, and produced—among other documents supporting his appointment—his old Williamsboro employer's assurance, "Of bookkeeping he had a considerable knowledge and in other respects was a good accountant. He was remarkable in his writing and calculations for expedition and correctness. In short, of the many young men who have lived with me, he, as an accountant, has been excelled by none and but very few have I found equal to him." Because Satterwhite had powerful congressional support, Paul Hamilton was easily persuaded to accede to a change of rank. Those same good friends in Congress meant that Satterwhite was virtually assured of being one of the pursers who would survive the April 1812 reduction in the number of pursers, as indeed he was.

Satterwhite was purser of the brig *Vixen* when she was captured by *Southampton* on 22 November 1812. *Vixen* surrendered late in the day; Sir James Yeo, *Southampton*'s captain, ordered *Vixen*'s officers to his ship and promised to have their belongings, among them Satterwhite's books and papers, transferred the next day. Satterwhite, it must be added, made no special effort to take his records with him. The weather turned foul, preventing the removal of anything from *Vixen*, and five days later both ships were wrecked on Conception Island. All of Satterwhite's papers, save for a fragment of a receipt book, were lost.

Capture and shipwreck might be exciting adventures, but Thomas Turner and the new secretary of the navy, William Jones, had to figure out how to pay the repatriated Vixens and settle Purser Satterwhite's accounts with his records vanished. This would not necessarily have been all that difficult—if Satterwhite had been doing his job. It was against just such a contingency that the standing instructions to pursers required them to send monthly muster books to the Navy Office from which, if necessary, a payroll could be reconstructed. From the day he had joined *Vixen* in March 1811 till the day she was lost, E.T. Satterwhite had sent in not one such monthly book. Equally bad, he had taken with him in *Vixen* all of his records for his previous duty assignment in *Hornet*; these, too, were totally destroyed. Worst of all, Paul Hamilton had been allowing Satterwhite to perform his duties without renewing his bond as required by the act of 30 March 1812. Attorney General Richard Rush was reasonably certain that the old bond was no longer valid. Its sureties could escape paying up for Satterwhite.

As Thomas Turner summed up the situation, Satterwhite had received as purser of *Hornet* $3,479.47 (including an $80 advance on pay); as purser of *Vixen* before her loss, $19,064.91; and as *Vixen*'s purser since that time, $6,263.25. For the first two sums he possessed not a scrap of documentation to account for the money; for the $6,263.25 his only record was scathingly described by Turner: "The evidence offered by him for the payments alleged to be made to the crew of the vessel after their capture is a book of accounts signed by the crew . . . and in almost every instance the figures have evidently been erased and altered." Against these debits there stood documented credits of only $501.66, making the total apparent balance against Satterwhite $28,305.97. Jones and Turner did not hide their doubts that, even with his lost records in hand, Satterwhite would have been able to account for all the money. The erased book of accounts looked suspiciously like fraud. His situation was so hopelessly bad that one suspects Satterwhite had been dysfunctional for much of his service as purser because of renewed drinking.

Mr. Satterwhite looked like a sure candidate for the published list of public debtors. Such a conclusion reckoned without his powerful friends in Congress, especially Representative Nathaniel Macon and Senator James Turner. First Satterwhite obtained a private law (22 July 1813) that instructed the accountant of the navy to assume that Satterwhite's accounts were balanced and settled as of the day *Vixen* sailed on her last cruise, thus exonerating him of $18,643.25 in debits. (Credits in Satterwhite's favor for $421.66 had apparently been discovered since Turner's earlier statement of Satterwhite's account.) A second private act (31 March 1814) required the accountant to settle Satterwhite's *Hornet* accounts "upon principles of equity and justice." This essentially whitewashed another $3,399.47 in debits, because, as William Jones disgustedly remarked, "it is impossible for me to determine whether such settlement will accord with the principles of equity and justice, as the defalcation in his accounts rests upon the alleged loss of all his vouchers by the shipwreck of the U.S. Brig Vixen after her capture." In Jones's opinion the two private acts had been obtained to cover up the fact that Satterwhite could not account for much of the money he had drawn as purser for *Hornet* and *Vixen*. Those private acts still left Satterwhite owing $5,841.59, against which he had some small credits coming for pay and rations. At this point Satterwhite's congressional friends must have intervened directly with Secretary Jones or Accountant Turner and persuaded one or both of those officials to accept the altered book of accounts to which Turner had objected so scathingly. Three months after Turner's reservations had been put on the record, $5,722.20 of these questionable charges were admitted to Satterwhite's credit. Although he was off the hook as a potential debtor, Purser Satterwhite was never again given an active duty assignment; when he was finally eased out of the corps in 1817, Edwin T. Satterwhite was in the black on the navy's books by $201.67.[29]

What was the final balance sheet on the government's attempt to collect from its purser-debtors? The forty-nine pursers and acting pursers who became debtors to the government between 1798 and 1815 accumulated a total nominal debt of $437,387.10. From this total one should certainly deduct the $51,638.87 accruing from the four pursers lost with their ships; this could be called a debt only in a technical accounting sense. Such a deduction would leave a balance of \$385,748.23 as the true nominal debt owed by the pre-1815 pursers. Of that sum, using all the means at its disposal—settlements and administrative adjustments of accounts, suits in federal court, payments by sureties—the treasury was able to recover or settle \$155,961.40, leaving \$229,786.83 eventually to be written off as bad debt. In other words, of every \$10 outstanding in purser debt, the United States was able to recover approximately \$4 and had to write off \$6. From one perspective this was not an impressive record, especially when the historian discovers that \$212,183.22 of this bad debt had accumulated since the institution of the surety bond system in 1809. The primary reason for this poor recovery record was the tremendous accounting backlog that afflicted the Navy Department and, to a greater or less degree, every other federal department in the wake of the War of 1812. By the time the United States figured out how much a particular purser or ex-purser owed and made an attempt at recovery, it was often ten, fifteen, or twenty years after the fact. Purser and sureties were all too often dead, bankrupt, or vanished. Thomas Turner's death in March 1816 almost surely had an adverse effect on settlements and collections. Perhaps not even Turner could have coped successfully with the flood of War of 1812 accounts. Certain it is that none of the rapid succession of people who sat in his chair in the years immediately following 1816 had Turner's passion for keeping business up to date or his success in settling with, and collecting from, recalcitrant pursers.

From another perspective, however, the navy's accounting record may not have been all that bad, especially if one takes as a yardstick the total amount of money that passed through purser hands. There exist no records that would enable the historian to calculate precisely how much money pursers received (and for which they were accountable) between 1798 and 1815, but total expenditures for pay and subsistence alone (most of which category of expenditure passed through the pursers) were approximately \$15.8 million. With this as a point of reference the historian might conservatively estimate that the navy's pre-1815 pursers had been required to account for at least \$18 million. Of this total only \$229,786.83—1.3 percent—had not been proved to have been spent for legitimate naval purposes. Given the conditions under which the pursers of 1798–1815 performed their duties, it was a not unimpressive achievement.

PART EIGHT
Pathology of a Profession

On the evening of 14 February 1815, when official news of the Treaty of Ghent ending the War of 1812 reached Washington, Secretary of the Navy Benjamin W. Crowninshield presided over the largest corps of naval officers the United States had ever assembled: more than eleven hundred men (Table 1). But behind the active-duty officers stood an even larger corps of ghosts: the 1,788 men whose names had appeared on the rolls at one time or another in the years since 1794, and who were no longer there on that February night in 1815. What had become of them?

Some among them had disappeared without a trace. William Jasper was a highly regarded midshipman who obtained a furlough from the frigate Constitution in March 1811 to make a voyage in the merchant service. On 23 November following he wrote Secretary of the Navy Paul Hamilton from Savannah, Georgia, to announce his arrival from Liverpool in the ship Mary. The Navy Office promptly responded with an order for Midshipman Jasper to report for active duty on the Wilmington, North Carolina, station. Jasper neither acknowledged the order nor reported to Thomas N. Gautier, commanding officer at Wilmington. He simply vanished. Nearly two and a half years later his father, Robert Jasper of Culpeper County, Virginia, wrote Secretary of the Navy William Jones: "Not having heard from [my son] for the last three or four years, did believe him dead, but having lately observed his name in a list of the present naval officers, am flattered with a hope that he still lives. Believing that you know whether he is alive and still in the navy, I am induced by a father's affection for his son to beg the favor of you to inform me if he lives, and how I may direct to him." Jones had to dash Robert Jasper's rekindled hopes by reporting that the Navy Office had no positive knowledge that Midshipman Jasper was alive. Because his death had not been officially reported to the department, his name was being continued on the register until the fact could be determined one way or the other. That was all anyone ever learned about what had become of William Jasper.[1]

Most men who disappear from the navy's records and cannot be traced did not have stories as dramatic and mysterious as that of William Jasper. Without doubt the great majority of the men who vanish from the rolls (approximately one in fourteen of those who left the navy before February 1815) are to be explained by deficiencies in the surviving records. Long since destroyed pay- and muster rolls would show some of these disappearing officers being discharged and others dying on active duty. A letter from a commanding officer reporting the death of a subordinate was sometimes sent downstairs to the accountant of the navy's office to establish the terminal date for the settlement of his pay with his legal *representatives. Such letters were filed with the other records of that last settlement and subsequently destroyed by fire, either when the British burned the public buildings at Washington in August 1814 or in the great Treasury Department fire of 1833. Other disappearing officers, angry at some turn of events or radically unhappy with naval life, simply walked away with their commissions or warrants and never bothered to report again for active duty. A handful of problem officers whom it was inconvenient or politically awkward to dismiss or court martial departed the navy on furloughs granted with the unspoken understanding that the furloughed officer would never again report for active duty or draw pay.[2] Over and above the one former officer in fourteen who disappears from the navy's records with no formal resolution of his fate or status, another one out of every twelve or thirteen is simply a name, a date of entry, and a date of discharge in the rolls. All were alive when they terminated their service; beyond that they are names without faces. Almost all such had been serving on appointments that were at the pleasure of the ship or the station commander.*

Even after eliminating the disappearing men and the names-only men, history is still able to say how almost 85 percent of the navy's officers who were no longer on the rolls on 14 February 1815 had ended their naval careers (Table 39). To each of 1,517 men one of four reasons can be assigned for his separation from the corps:

> *he had died*
>
> *he had been discharged in a reduction in the size of the navy*
>
> *he had resigned*
>
> *he had been dismissed*

Few ways of examining the officer corps that came to professional maturity in the War of 1812 tell as much about that corps as the stories of men's departures from it.

32. The President of Terrors

BOUT TEN O'CLOCK [this morning] *Death*, that President of Terrors, took from us our surgeon, Doctor John Goddard. He had for some time been complaining of a slight fever and debility. Not ten minutes before his eyes were closed in death he went up on the forecastle to take the fresh air, when he fainted. After he came to he was led aft on the quarterdeck and laid on the arms chest under the awning, where we were all witnesses to this unexpected and melancholy event. Doctor Goddard left behind him a wife and three small children and also an old tender mother to lament his loss. He served his country as surgeon two cruises in this ship before the present [cruise] and was in the action with the Berceau. . . . About eleven o'clock his body was committed to the deep, with the forms usual on such occasions, at the entrance of [the] Straits of Messina and at the foot of Mount Aetna.[1]

Midshipman Melancthon T. Woolsey describes an event that must have made even the most lighthearted and convivial man more reflective than usual: *Boston*'s stunned officers standing about the frigate's arms chest on a July morning in 1802, witnesses to the unexpected death of a shipmate. Reflective, because it was a voluntary willingness to die, if need be, for what was seen as the greater good of one's country and one's fellow citizens, and because it was the ability to lead others by that example, that gave the officer corps its credibility as a fighting force. Not that the typical officer of the pre-1815 navy was in love with death or with the idea of death. He saw dying for one's country as a worthy end to life. It gave meaning and a higher purpose to the incomprehensible, but universal, phenomenon of death. Such a death palliated the grief of those left behind, helping them to come to terms with this traumatic event. The bereaved would be sustained, too, by the knowledge that the deceased officer had lived and died with integrity. All men must die; better, therefore, to leave the world with the esteem of one's fellows. Even if a man's life was considered a failure or marred by behavior that deviated too far from the norms of his brother officers, such a life could be wholly redeemed through death for his country.[2]

What was the likelihood that a man would meet death as a member of the officer corps? Was the phrase *to die for one's country* only a rote formula? Or was death always an impending reality? At least 331 serving officers are known to have met their deaths between 12 September 1797, when yellow fever claimed the life of Sailing Master John Lockwood in the frigate *United States*, and 14 February 1815, the day on which official news of the Treaty of Ghent, ending the War of 1812, reached Washington (Table 40). These 331 men are almost exactly one-fifth of the 1,660 officers about whom it can be definitely learned whether they were alive or dead at the time they left the navy.

Enemy Action

When an officer used the phrase *to die for one's country* its usual meaning for him was what he called *glorious death*: death in battle with the enemy. It was the death of popular, elegant Lieutenant Archibald Hamilton, son of Secretary of the Navy Paul Hamilton, killed by a grapeshot in *President*'s 15 January 1815 encounter with *Endymion*, and who fell even as he shouted to the men of his division his favorite exhortation to battle or party: "Carry on, boys! Carry on!"[3] But, as every officer who gave the subject any thought must have realized, heroic death was a rare occurrence in the pre-1815 navy. Among the 1,660 officers whose naval service ended in a known manner before 14 February 1815, only forty-eight can be positively identified as having been killed in battle or to have died of wounds sustained in action with the enemy. If one adds to the forty-eight two officers still alive on 14 February 1815—Kirvin Waters, who did not die of the mortal wound sustained in the 5 September 1813 *Enterprize-Boxer* battle until 26 September 1815, and Midshipman Richard S. Dale, wounded in the *President-Endymion* encounter of 15 January 1815, but not dying a prisoner of war at Bermuda until 22 or 23 February—the total number of officers known to have died as a result of enemy action in the Quasi-War with France, the Tripolitan War, and the War of 1812 amounted to no more than fifty, less than 2 percent of the 2,902 men who had enrolled in the officer corps by the end of the War of 1812.

The comparative rarity of death by enemy action is even more striking if one examines when those deaths occurred. The Quasi-War with France, in which there were three major frigate actions (*Constellation-Insurgente*, *Constellation-Vengeance*, *Boston-Berceau*), plus more than one hundred small-ship encounters, saw only two officers die as a result of enemy action. One of them was the only purser killed in battle between 1798 and 1815: Samuel Young, mortally wounded while serving as a quarterdeck volunteer during *Boston*'s engagement with *Berceau*. Enemy action took six officer lives during the Tripolitan War, all in Edward Preble's August–September 1804 attacks on the city and its shipping. When the officer corps entered the War of 1812, it had been cruising the seas for fourteen years, had fought two wars successfully, and had lost only eight of its number to the enemy. With the declaration of war against Great Britain in June 1812, death in action with the enemy became more common: thirty-nine of the forty-eight officers dying as a result of combat before 14 February 1815 were killed during the War of 1812.[4] Even so, death in battle was hardly an everyday occurrence. Many well-known and hard-fought single-ship actions—*Constitution-Guerriere* or *Wasp-Frolic*, for example—cost no officer lives. Indeed, the single-ship and fleet actions during the War of 1812 that resulted in clear victories for the U.S. units claimed in all only eleven officer lives.

Taking the whole span of the navy's combat history from the Quasi-War's *Constellation-Insurgente* battle of February 1799 to *President*'s January 1815 encounter with *Endymion,* over half of the officer deaths from enemy action occurred in just six conflicts.[5] Of these six the meeting between *Chesapeake* and *Shannon,* lasting only fifteen minutes, stands out as the costliest single slaughter of officers in the navy's pre-1815 history, the price paid for Lawrence's overconfidence and the British desire to avenge a reputation tarnished in earlier encounters with U.S. warships. When one realizes how costly *Chesapeake*'s defeat was, it becomes easier to understand the corps' attempt to rationalize the blow by seeking scapegoats for a deserved defeat, by turning Lawrence into a martyr, or by claiming that some mysterious "Jonah ship" curse hovered over *Chesapeake.* Preble's campaign had been nearly as costly in lives as *Chesapeake*'s defeat—the two together accounted for more than one-quarter of all officer deaths in battle between 1799 and 1815—but Preble's efforts could be correctly viewed as a valiant struggle against preponderant odds and a moral victory. Only a great amount of self-deception could turn the dying Lawrence's "Don't give up the ship" into a rallying cry for future battles.

If death in battle was a relatively rare occurrence in the pre-1815 navy, it was not because that navy ever shirked a fight. Despite movie-induced mental images of cannon spewing roundshot, grape, and canister at point-blank range, of great oak splinters flying through the air, of flames bursting up through the hatches, of yards and rigging raining down on the heads of hapless men stationed on the spar deck, and of boarders literally armed to the teeth with razor-sharp cutlasses, the typical War of 1812 naval battle was not an extraordinarily lethal place to be. *Constitution*'s defeat of *Java* on 29 December 1812 may be chosen as an example, because it was neither a walkover victory for the U.S. ship nor a conflict of sadistic ferocity, but a hard-fought battle, involving both maneuver and gunnery, which lasted two hours or longer. Out of a ship's company of 436, the U.S. frigate lost 9 men killed outright and 5 more (including an officer) who died as a result of their wounds before 15 February 1813, to make a total of 14 dead: 3.2 percent of the ship's company. In addition, four of the wounded required the amputation of limbs, and the seven men (including Captain William Bainbridge) described as "dangerously" or "severely" wounded in the official records probably embraced some who would be totally or partially disabled from those wounds. These eleven seriously wounded make up another 2.5 percent of *Constitution*'s complement. Finally, an additional eleven men (including one midshipman) are described as "slightly" wounded; to whom must be added, according to the ship's surgeon, a "few more" so slightly wounded as not "to require particular notice." The slightly wounded may be estimated at not more than 3.9 percent of the ship's roll, making the whole spectrum of casualties, from dead and dying to the badly bruised, not more than 10 percent of the vulnerable by the most generous conjecture.[6]

One must not allow the distance of time or the comparative rarity of death in battle to obscure the fact that it was not a picturesque event taking place in quaint costumes, but as terrifying, ugly, and horrible in the era of the sailing ship as it has been at any time in history. To gain a sense of the reality one has only to reread Midshipman Henry Gilliam's picture of *Guerriere* after her defeat by *Constitution* on 19 August 1812—"pieces of skulls, brains, legs, arms, and blood lay in every direction, and the groans of the wounded were enough almost to make me curse the war"—or Robert T. Spence's description of the aftermath of the explosion of Gunboat No. 9 off Tripoli: "The only part [of the boat] remaining was that on which the gun stood. . . . Around me lay arms, legs, and trunks of bodies, in the most mutilated state. . . . I saw [Lieutenant James R. Caldwell] after he came down, without arms or legs, his face so mutilated that I could not discriminate a feature. By his dress only I recognized him. He was not dead, although he sank instantly."[7]

Lost at Sea

There was another way in which an officer might meet death in the line of duty, one for which the odds were about a third again as great as for death in battle. But for those who met death in this matter there would be neither monuments erected, mottoes coined, nor ballads printed. They were the officers who went down with their ships.

An often overlooked aspect of life and death in the pre-1815 navy is that a substantial number of its vessels sank with all or part of their companies. Four vanished without a trace. The brig *Pickering* and the frigate *Insurgente* sailed from U.S. ports in August 1800 neither to be seen nor heard from again; both were presumptive victims of the hurricane season. Gunboat No. 7 departed New York on 20 June 1805 but never reached her Mediterranean destination. *Wasp*, the most famous disappearance in the navy's early history, was in the full heat of a successful war cruise when she met the Swedish brig *Adonis* on 9 October 1814. Two officers from the late U.S. frigate *Essex*, passengers in *Adonis*, elected to transfer to *Wasp*, which then sailed away from *Adonis*, over the horizon, and out of history. Among them, these four ships that simply disappeared account for forty-eight of the sixty-seven officers who went down with their vessels. To those forty-eight may be added three officers who vanished in merchant vessels: men such as Midshipman William Dawson, placed in charge of *United States*'s prize, the British schooner *Adeline*, by Stephen Decatur on 16 August 1812, dispatched in her to a U.S. port, but never seen or heard from after that August day.[8]

In the cases of the remaining sixteen officers who went down with their ships, how the vessels were lost is known. Typical, perhaps, was the story of Gunboat No. 46, commanded by Lieutenant Samuel G. Blodget, which attempted to tack close in with the south point of Conanicut Island, near Newport, Rhode Island, under adverse weather conditions (29 September 1812), missed stays, and went broadside to the shore, where the sea broke over her, washing officer and man alike overboard. Though the station commander, Oliver Hazard Perry, avoided any explicit criticism of his late friend, Perry's report makes it plain that Blodget's poor judgment and equally weak seamanship were at least partly responsible for the disaster. The long line of former commanding officers who had complained bitterly of Blodget's inadequacies as a subordinate and pleaded for his removal from their ships or stations would probably have breathed a collective sigh of relief when they heard he had been washed overboard and his body never found, had not eight good men (out of a ship's company of eighteen) shared his fate.[9]

One of the heaviest losses of young lives, and certainly the most needless, was that of the five midshipmen who went down in Gunboat No. 2. This unarmed veteran gunboat was employed by Commodore Hugh G. Campbell to carry men and supplies among the three stations of his southern coastal

*"I am a young man of no fortune and have only to depend on my own industry,"
Midshipman James R. Caldwell wrote when peace and a reduction in the navy appeared
certain in the closing months of the Quasi-War with France, "circumstances which make
it necessary for me to turn my mind on some mode of providing for myself." Anxiety about
the future, while not to be avoided, was doubly unnecessary. Promoted lieutenant in November 1800, Caldwell was one of the thirty-six officers of that rank selected for retention
in the Jeffersonian navy. Less than four years later he was killed in the explosion of Gunboat
No. 9 during Edward Preble's 7 August 1804 attack on Tripoli. Caldwell's chalk portrait
by C.B.J. Fevret de Saint-Mémin was probably taken in 1800, for the anxious young
officer is pictured in the midshipman's uniform as prescribed before August 1802.* United
States Naval Academy Museum, Annapolis, Maryland.

command: Wilmington, Charleston, and St. Marys. On 29 September 1811 she
sailed from Charleston with supplies and extra seamen for the St. Marys station.
Probably because he regarded it as a good opportunity for a training cruise,
Campbell had placed a larger than usual complement of midshipmen in her.
The only survivor of No. 2 was one John Tice, a seaman found clinging to a
spar at sea by a schooner from Rhode Island, and he did not know why events
had gone the way they did. The wind had been fair for St. Marys when No. 2
sailed from Charleston; it should have required only two days to make the
passage. Perhaps the five midshipmen, once away from Campbell's strict but
effective discipline of junior officers, decided to turn the passage into something
of a lark. Not until 4 October, a full five days after leaving Charleston, did
they make Cumberland Island and hoist the signal for a pilot. None appeared.
The weather looked ugly, the sea was running high, and night was coming on.
No. 2 stood off shore. The next morning, 5 October, the wind had increased
to a heavy gale from the N.N.E., compelling No. 2 to heave to under a trysail.
At eleven a.m. the gale became even more furious and the trysail was hastily
taken in—only minutes before the sea broke over the boat and hove her on
her beam ends. Cool heads and good seamanship might yet have saved the
day, but the members of the crew who were below succumbed to panic and
forced open No. 2's hatches as she lay on her beam ends. The sea rushed in.
No. 2 filled instantly and sank like a rock, carrying with her to their deaths all
save seaman John Tice.[10]

Accidental Death

After totaling up the roll of officers lost with their ships, the historian still does not have the full story of those whom the sea swallowed. One must also look at nineteen men whose names stand recorded under the rubric accidental death. Among those nineteen one finds fourteen-year-old Midshipman William C. Hall—the robust orphan from Queen Annes County, Maryland, in Chapter 11 whose aunt was anxious for him to get an early start on a naval career— killed by a fall from *Constellation*'s mizzen topmast in March 1814.[11] There also to be found are the names of Commodore Richard V. Morris's secretary and his clerk, who died as a result of severe burns sustained in the explosion in the gunner's storeroom on board the frigate *New York*, 25 April 1803. All the rest died by drowning.

At least half of the drownings involved small boats, and the death of Midshipman Gustavus Douglass may represent them all. The gunboat under Douglass's command was ascending the Mississippi from New Orleans to Natchez, and had proceeded a few miles on her way, when the vessel's business compelled her commander to return to New Orleans in a small boat on 5 March 1810. As Midshipman Douglass was working his way back upriver to his command, a flaw of wind upset the small boat. Douglass, who was presumably seated farthest aft in the stern sheets and who could not swim, was swept away by the current and drowned before any of the small craft on the river could reach him with assistance. The boat's crew—seated, of course, farther forward— managed to save themselves, one man by swimming ashore, the others by clinging to the boat. The body of Gustavus Douglass, carried off by the Mississippi's powerful currents, was never found.[12]

An additional five of the sixteen drownings were officers who fell overboard from large ships and could not be saved. That such accidents were not the product of inexperience at sea may be seen by the case of twenty-three-year-old Midshipman William P. Smith. Midshipman Smith, son of the late Dr. William Pitt Smith, former health officer of the port of New York and former member of the state legislature, had been sent to college at Princeton. Finding the idea of a life at sea more appealing than books and lectures, Smith quit college without his family's knowledge and entered the merchant service. About the year 1807, while his ship was lying in the port of London, young Smith was impressed into the British navy and hustled off to India. After five years' service in those waters, his ship returned to England late in 1812, where Smith learned of the hostilities between Great Britain and the United States. He at once refused to serve longer in the Royal Navy and insisted on surrendering as a prisoner of war. Promises were tried. Threats were made. His prize money was forfeited. Still Smith demanded that he be treated as a prisoner of war. The British authorities finally gave up and confined him to the prison hulk *Glory* at Chatham. Smith's family now learned of his whereabouts and commenced exerting their political muscle to secure his early parole, which was effected after he had been enjoying *Glory*'s hospitality for some eight months. Arriving at New York early in September 1813, Smith was anxious to "help to repay to the British the many courtesies I had received from their hands." A midshipman's warrant was at last obtained on 17 March 1814, and Smith was ordered on to Lake Ontario. There, on 18 September following, the schooner

Conquest, in which Midshipman Smith was serving, was struck by a severe gale and William P. Smith swept or knocked overboard to his death.[13]

If the 16 officers who died by drowning are added to the 67 known to have gone down with their ships, the historian discovers that 83 of the 247 men the causes of whose deaths are known, one-third of the whole, went to watery graves. For the pre-1815 naval officer the great occupational hazard was the sea itself.

Fatal Duels

But the sea, that most real and present danger in any officer's life, has been overshadowed in the minds of most naval historians by death in more dramatic guise: the duel.

Looking at death by dueling solely in terms of objective statistics, it is difficult to see why the custom should be the subject of such perennial interest, for its importance has certainly been exaggerated. Dueling pistols fired in anger claimed the lives of exactly eighteen naval officers before 14 February 1815, approximately 1 percent of the total number of officers who left the navy before that date. One can be virtually certain that the number eighteen does represent all the deaths by duel in the corps before February 1815. The dramatic nature of the event insured that the fact and the cause of death would invariably find a place in the records.

Why has such a statistically insignificant manifestation of death stood so tall in the historian's field of vision? There is the violent and dramatic nature of the event itself, which has certainly been enhanced by the notorious Stephen Decatur–James Barron duel of 1820. Then, too, the duel is a strange custom from the past. Ships still go down at sea. Enemy fire still claims its victims. Men do not fight formal duels as a means of settling interpersonal hostilities. The absence of any reliable statistics on the early navy has left historians free to follow their subjective impressions about the prevalence of dueling, which has led to such gross distortions as one writer claiming that "almost as many officers died in duels as in combat" with the enemy during the first half of the nineteenth century; another says it was two-thirds as many![14] Above all, the duel has caught the attention of historians because it has seemed to them, as it did to many of the officers' contemporaries, a senseless and wasteful loss of human life. "I can't omit one piece of disagreeable information," Captain James Barron wrote his brother from Malta in the early days of 1803, "namely the situation of Mr. [Henry] Vandyke, who is now laying momently expecting death to his relief from a most horrid wound which he received in a duel from Mr. [William S.] Osborne, lieutenant of marines. Two days will end his voyage through this life, and all for the preference in a simple game of billiards."[15]

In spite of the misleading impression created by the Barron-Decatur duel, the practice of dueling was all but entirely confined to the younger members of the officer corps. Among the eighteen officers killed in duels before February 1815, twelve were midshipmen, four were lieutenants, one was a surgeon, and one a surgeon's mate. (The pattern remains the same if one includes in the calculations the eleven survivors of fatal duels among naval officers: eight were midshipmen, one a lieutenant, one a surgeon's mate, and one a sailing master.) Although the ages of only six of the eighteen duel victims are known, it may be assumed from their ranks and what is known of the age structure of the navy at the time that all were in their late teens or early twenties. Almost certainly none was older than the one surgeon-victim, Dr. Starling Archer, or than Lieutenant Henry Vandyke, both twenty-four years old when dueling pistols terminated their lives and their careers.

These two facts, rank and age, tell much that the historian needs to know to understand the phenomenon of dueling. One is dealing with men whose defined role was as fighters who must have the courage to face death, and with *young* men still in the process of establishing personal identities. The psycho-dynamics of the challenge-and-duel situation were similar in almost all cases. A group of active adolescents or postadolescents were crowded together in the confines of a ship. It was boring peacetime duty. Or, worse yet, it was wartime, but circumstances had prevented the ship from active cruising or meeting the enemy. Tensions mounted. A minor incident ignited the situation. Harsh words were exchanged—perhaps blows—then came the formal challenge. For one psychological reason or another apology and reconciliation were impossible. The challenger and especially the one challenged were now left in this situation: if either of them refused to fight, then he would be labeled a coward and suffer stigmatization, if not social ostracization, from his messmates. Unless superiors got wind of the affair and intervened with their authority to halt it, or unless messmates acted to calm the excited pair, they were now irreversibly headed for the dueling ground. No nineteen-year-old midshipman, one who had never established his bravery through combat, could in that society have his courage challenged and still remain a member in good standing of his peer group. "I at present am unable to acquaint you of the origin of the quarrel of these two young men," wrote John Rodgers of one fatal duel. "But, from the information I have been able to collect . . . it was something of a very trivial nature. Indeed, it would appear that they went out rather from motives of bravado than anything else, and after getting on the ground were ashamed to return without fighting."[16] By contrast sailing masters are totally absent from the list of duel fatalities and almost entirely absent from the roster of duel participants. Nor does the historian have to seek far for a reason. Masters were older than the midshipmen and the junior lieutenants. As with the captains and masters commandant, also conspicuous by their absence from the list of duel fatalities, sailing masters were usually secure enough in their identities not to need to fight duels to maintain status or self-respect.*

In the minds of many who lived in 1800 dueling was a reprehensible practice, out of sympathy with the rational and enlightened spirit that men like to think was the hallmark of the times. There was ample public disapproval of the custom. When Lieutenant Allen McKenzie, USN, was killed in a duel with First Lieutenant Anthony Gale, USMC, in November 1799, the Presbyterian clergyman who delivered the graveside address noted in condemnation, "We are called to surround the grave of a soldier who has fallen by the arm of a

---

* There were exceptions: Charles Gordon, a master commandant, fought two duels with civilians in 1807 and was grievously wounded in a third in January 1810. Lieutenants Jacob Jones (aged thirty-nine) and James T. Leonard (about twenty-nine) fought at a distance of only nine feet in March 1807. Leonard was seriously wounded, but recovered completely. John Rush, a thirty-year-old sailing master, killed Lieutenant Benjamin Turner in an October 1807 duel. As subsequent events established, Rush was the victim of a severe emotional disturbance and was eventually institutionalized as hopelessly insane. The concern here is with the general pattern, not with the occasional deviation from that pattern.

brother soldier, the victim of mistaken honor, slain in the prime of life. . . . Here let all who are directed by false honor behold its effects. Those closen eyes shall no more open on the light of day. Human things shall no longer engage his attention. He has taken a solemn departure from this world, and dark and dismal are the shades of night that descend upon his tomb. To his Judge he has gone to answer."[17]

But any impressionable young midshipman hearing such a rationalistic condemnation of dueling would have to balance that impression against the potent example of two highly respected role models: the serving vice-president of the United States (Aaron Burr) fighting a fatal duel with the former secretary of the treasury (Alexander Hamilton). In fact, dueling survived among the junior officers because the senior officers, as a group, were ambivalent toward it. Captain Arthur Sinclair could condone a particular duel as "one of those imperious cases, which frequently occurs among military men, where life must be hazarded to save what's far more valuable, his reputation." So far as is known, Sinclair never fought a duel himself; but apparently the possibility of resorting to the field of honor was an arrow he wanted to have in his quiver. John Rodgers, who often threatened to fight duels—and who just as many times backed off from actually so doing—put himself on both sides of the issue by seeking to "discourage a practice so much at variance with morality and the common law of our country," but said the particular fatal duel in question was "a misfortune for which there was no honorable remedy."[18]

Dueling's outspoken opponent among the senior officers was Alexander Murray, who shocked his subordinates in *Constellation* by refusing to attend the funeral after Captain James McKnight, USMC, was killed in a duel with Lieutenant R.H.L. Lawson, USN, but even more by proposing to engrave on McKnight's tombstone that he had fallen a victim to a false idea of honor. That same death encouraged Murray to go farther and become, as far as surviving records show, the first senior officer to urge that dueling be made a court martial offense, with sanctions up to and including dismissal from service for officers who participated.[19] From the Navy Department's point of view, here was the real obstacle to curtailing the practice: it was not explicitly forbidden by the basic disciplinary code, the "Act for the Better Government of the Navy" of 23 April 1800. (Dueling was forbidden by law in the U.S. Army, but the prohibition was not enforced.) Because no secretary of the navy formally proposed amending the law, all must have judged that sufficient congressional support for such a change did not exist. Indeed, when influential Congressman Joseph H. Nicholson's relation, Midshipman William R. Nicholson, was killed in a duel with Midshipman F.C. de Krafft, Congressman Nicholson himself requested that de Krafft be in no way punished: "However reprehensible the practice of dueling may be, yet the wisest legislators and the most able magistrates have, for some hundred years, in vain endeavored to check it. It is one of those evils which is consequent upon society and most frequently proceeds from the noblest feeling of the heart. Before it can be stopped, the state of society itself must change; and till then, human laws and human punishments will be vain."[20]

In the absence of any positive legislation prohibiting dueling among officers of the navy, both Secretary Robert Smith and Secretary Paul Hamilton—the latter called dueling "no test of bravery, but rather the offspring of frivolous or morose dispositions"[21]—considered trying to bring court martial prosecutions under the article of the "Act for the Better Government of the Navy" that prohibited "any other scandalous conduct, tending to the destruction of good morals," or another article that forbade one person in the navy to quarrel with another or to use "provoking or reproachful words, gestures, or menaces." No case was ever brought to trial, presumably because both the secretaries and the senior station commanders ultimately judged that such a prosecution would be stretching those clauses of the law farther than they were ever intended to be expanded. Even more significantly, they doubted that a court martial composed of fellow officers would convict the accused or award him any substantial punishment. William Jones and James Madison went so far as summarily to dismiss one midshipman, John T. Ritchie, who was a second in a duel in which both of the principals were killed. However, on his last day in office Jones relented and restored Ritchie's warrant, perhaps under pressure from the midshipman's influential friends, who may have argued that the punishment was excessive in light of the navy's previous practice in such affairs.[22]

Actual administrative sanctions awarded to duelists were relatively mild, as might be expected from the attitudes of senior officers. The survivor (or survivors) and the seconds were usually arrested and suspended from duty for a period, then released with a verbal reprimand. As an additional mark of displeasure, the offenders—especially if they were old thorns in the commander's flesh—were often transferred to less desirable duty or sent on extended furlough. Given existing laws and regulations, Alexander Murray went about as far as a commanding officer could in the wake of the already-mentioned McKnight-Lawson duel. He arrested Lieutenant Lawson for murder, confined him to his cabin under guard (arrested officers were normally allowed to exercise on the gun deck and make use of the wardroom), and kept him there, in spite of all Lawson's pleading, until *Constellation* returned to the United States five months later and the case could be turned over to Robert Smith. "You ought to know the laws of our own country, which doth not admit of bail or of granting furlough to persons laboring under the serious charges for which you are now under arrest," responded Murray to Lawson's appeal for greater freedom—probably not without a degree of delighted sadism as he thought of Lawson penned up in his tiny cabin.[23]

However much ink secretaries of the navy and older officers might expend deploring the practice of dueling, however caustic might be the oral reprimands station and ship commanders administered to subordinates who participated in duels, neither the senior officers of the navy as a body nor national opinion as expressed through Congress regarded the total abolition of the duel as a high priority. The majority of opinion setters apparently judged that the duel fell into an area of personal freedom not to be abridged by positive legislation. Or else they held that it was a practice to which they themselves hoped never to resort, but which it was just as well to hold in reserve as a kind of ultimate sanction in case their sense of self-worth were too directly assailed. The custom lingered on after the end of the War of 1812 to claim its occasional victims, men famous and men obscure.

Suicide

Another death, as dramatic as the duel and equally shocking, was an extremely rare occurrence. Suicide claimed the lives of six serving officers, thus accounting for 2.4 percent of all officer deaths whose cause can be determined, or less than one-half of 1 percent of all who left the officer corps before 14 February 1815.

Beyond noting that suicide *may* have been slightly more frequent among naval officers than among their counterparts in civilian life, there is little that can be said about these six suicides by way of generally applicable analysis, if for no other reason than because the numbers involved are so small.[24] Four of the six gave no recognized sign of emotional disturbance or of impending self-destruction before the fatal act, nor did they leave any explanation. One suicide—that of Midshipman Robert Stewart, an experienced and highly capable officer then on furlough and in command of an Indiaman—was clearly the product of physical illness. In a state of delirium induced by a high fever, Stewart threw himself overboard and drowned in the Tigris River. Only in the case of one other suicide—that of Lieutenant John Davis—do the records inform that "his mind has been in a deranged state for some weeks past[;] he has for a long time past been in the habit of drinking to excess[;] he died much involved in debt."[25]

More insight into the dynamics of suicide in the early navy is to be gained from a case not included in the six. This man, Purser Humphrey Magrath, is not here counted as a suicide because he had severed his connection with the navy shortly before his death. His story is particularly informative because an unmistakable emotional breakdown had occurred well in advance of the suicide attempt, and with ultimately tragic consequences. In retrospect at least, emotional instability had been evident in his behavior for some years before the denouement. A native of Charleston, South Carolina, Magrath began his naval career as a midshipman in 1799. For reasons now unknown, he requested transfer out of the promotion track and became a sailing master in 1803, but discovered within a year that "my feelings will not at all accord with that calling," presumably because of the notorious status inequities that galled many another master. Magrath temporarily laid aside naval service in 1806 by accepting a one-year furlough to serve as second-in-command of the Charleston revenue cutter. Later, in 1810, he sought to leave the navy permanently by soliciting the command of the revenue cutter *Gallatin*. In between, Magrath had returned to the promotion track in the navy with a lieutenant's commission dated 3 February 1809. This commission he abandoned two years later when he sought and obtained an appointment as a purser. All the while the financial anxieties of supporting his mother and sisters were preying on his mind.

Psychic unraveling began to accelerate for Humphrey Magrath in the spring of 1814, at which time he was purser of the Lake Erie station. He was no longer able to cope with the stress-laden duties of that dispersed station, and his records were growing more and more disorganized. Worst of all, it was his misfortune to be placed under a commanding officer especially insensitive to the art of leadership: Arthur Sinclair. Magrath's emotional disturbance was manifesting itself most obviously in uncontrollable outbursts of temper. After them he was quick enough to apologize, but they were difficult for a proud man like Captain Sinclair to endure. Sinclair recognized that Magrath was suffering from mental illness and had already requested that another purser be sent to the station. But when, in one of his outbursts of anger, Magrath submitted his resignation to Sinclair on 27 May 1814, the latter—apparently without reflecting on how the loss of a fifteen-year naval career might affect a man suffering from severe mental illness—accepted the resignation. In forwarding Magrath's commission to the Navy Office, Sinclair did urge Secretary Jones to call Magrath to Washington to settle his accounts, reprimand him, and then reinstate his purser's commission. "It may prove a useful lesson to him. He is a good-hearted, unfortunate fellow, and I feel pity for him." But none of this could Sinclair bring himself to tell Magrath, who—his professional career, as far as he knew, at an end—remained at Erie, Pennsylvania, trying to pull his accounts together for settlement and deteriorating psychologically from one day to the next. Finally he lost all touch with reality. Magrath's friends searched his room for weapons so that he could harm neither himself nor others. He was too cunning for them. On 11 July he produced a dirk from its secret location and attempted to stab Purser Samuel Hambleton, who fought Magrath off until others could arrive and secure him in his room. There, about eleven o'clock that night, Humphrey Magrath took out a carefully hidden pistol, put the muzzle in his mouth, and pulled the trigger. "I have not seen his body, although it is in the next room," wrote Hambleton. "It is said to be a most shocking sight: the top of his head is blown off, and his brains are scattered all over the walls and ceiling."[26]

Natural Causes

The final category of death in the U.S. Navy—death by natural causes—is the largest, embracing 89 men, or more than one-third of those 247 individuals the nature of whose deaths are known (Table 40). In fact, it was probably much larger. Eighty-four deaths have been assigned to the category cause of death unknown, because the fact of death is definitely confirmed, but how it occurred is not a matter of record. However, it is unlikely that those eighty-four unknown-cause deaths embraced any instances of entire ships lost, any deaths by enemy action, or any deaths in duels. Such deaths were too noteworthy not to be specifically mentioned in the records. Assuming, then, that accidental death, suicide, and death by natural causes are present in about the same proportions as in the group whose causes of death are known, the eighty-four unknown-cause deaths might break down approximately as four suicides, fourteen accidental deaths, and sixty-six deaths from natural causes. If these numbers were added to the cases wherein the cause of death is definitely known, the sources of death among the pre-1815 officer corps would look not as they do in Table 40, but as they have been recalculated for Table 41.

Although death by natural causes accounted, in all likelihood, for nearly half of the deaths in the officer corps, there is less definite, satisfying information about these natural causes than about any of the other forms of death. Records are deficient or totally lacking. Symptoms are vaguely described. Imprecise, catchall names are applied to diseases. What can be discovered about the eighty-nine cases in which it can be positively determined that men died of natural causes? One point on which definite information exists is where the deaths took place. Fourteen officers died at home, in almost all instances at the end of a lengthy illness. The remaining seventy-five died either away from their homes or while on active duty. When one looks at where those seventy-five men were stationed when they died, a striking pattern can be observed.

Deaths at sea (excluding West Indian waters) claimed twelve officer lives from natural causes during seventeen years of active cruising. With these should perhaps be grouped the six men who died on the Mediterranean station during the Barbary Wars, making an average of about one death a year on the high seas. The Great Lakes stations were not popular duty with the officers of the early navy, in part because they were regarded as unhealthy: subject to long, cold winters and fever-ridden summers. Despite this bad reputation, only seven officers can be positively identified as having died from natural causes on the Lake Erie and Lake Ontario stations. All seven deaths occurred during the three years of the War of 1812, intensifying both their real and their psychological impact. When one turns one's attention to the chain of active naval stations that ran from Boston to New Orleans, all may, at first glance, seem about equally healthy or unhealthy. Nine officers may die at New Orleans; but seven die at Norfolk, five at New York, and six on the South Carolina–Georgia station. However, if one draws an imaginary line just to the north of Hampton Roads, Virginia, and examines the deaths from natural causes on either side of that imaginary line, a different pattern emerges. New York has its five officer deaths, but Philadelphia has only two, and one apiece occur at Washington, Baltimore, and Boston. Even if one includes the seven deaths on Lakes Erie and Ontario, the total north of the imaginary line is still only seventeen, in contrast to forty officers dying south of it.

Within the area below the imaginary line the environment most hostile to officer health was the West Indies. These waters claimed eighteen lives, although the figure is somewhat distorted by the fact that nine of the eighteen deaths occurred in one ship, *Warren*, in the summer of 1800. But *Warren*'s disastrous cruise was only the most dramatic and tragic example of a more general

A hero's life could be so brief. This handsome lieutenant commandant was not older than twenty-four when he sat for C.B.J. Fevret de Saint-Mémin. John Trippe had been a national hero since he was nineteen. That summer, during Edward Preble's 3 August 1804 attack on Tripoli, Trippe and ten companions boarded and captured an enemy gunboat manned by thirty-six well-armed and exceptionally hostile Tripolitans. The year after Saint-Mémin took his likeness, John Trippe was dead of yellow fever. Fortunately, he died before he learned that Secretary of the Navy Paul Hamilton had denounced him for what was arguably the most courageous act of his life. On 24 June 1810, near Stirrup Key, the British brig Moselle, *20, fired twice at Trippe's more lightly armed* Vixen, *one shot striking the vessel. Although cleared and ready for action, Trippe elected to accept the British commander's written apology for the incident, rather than blasting away in defense of what the hypersensitive secretary perceived as grievously wounded national honor. Trippe, displaying wiser judgment than the civilian twice his age, knew that the truly brave man does not need to parade machismo.* National Portrait Gallery, Washington, D.C.

condition. The great majority of the officer corps came from that portion of the United States lying north and west of the imaginary line, and their bodies were but poorly prepared to encounter the new and unfamiliar health threats they met in West Indian waters and in the coastal South. This point is further confirmed by the fact that of the forty officers who died from natural causes south of the imaginary line, only two were natives of that area. This desire to flee what was correctly perceived as a health-threatening environment manifested itself in a steady stream of letters to the Navy Office from officers assigned to southern stations, letters pleading with varying degrees of urgency for other duty.

When the historian turns from the geography of illness to illness itself the information at hand is less—and less reliable. In twenty-six of the eighty-nine cases of death by natural causes no record has been found of the nature of the terminal illness; another five are simply described as lingering illnesses; and four are called consumption, a word that normally referred to the disease now known as tuberculosis, although it was occasionally applied to other wasting illnesses.

Five of the deaths by natural causes were those of veteran senior officers. If four of the five "veterans" were scarcely more than middle-aged, all were worn out from hard, though memorable, lives at sea: Samuel Barron (45 years old), John Barry (58), Samuel Nicholson (68), David Porter, Sr. (54), and Edward Preble (46). In Barry's case as early as 1801, during his last command afloat, a senior subordinate had remarked that "great cordiality prevail[s] amongst the officers, except the commodore, who from old age and the accumulations of infirmities is at times extremely fractious, and the language he makes use of at these times on the quarterdeck is, in my opinion, highly improper, particularly when directed to his officers, and in any other person would not be borne." In late August 1803, a close relation reported that the old commodore "is now thought to be on his last tack. He said to me this day that he was nearly done, which I fear is too true."[27] He died less than a month later.

Pulmonary illnesses brought eight officers to their graves, and in six of the eight cases the symptoms described appear to be those of tuberculosis. Two deaths by pneumonia complete the toll of eight. This relatively low number of deaths is almost certainly deceptive. Pulmonary disease, and especially tuberculosis, was a greater health hazard to the officer than that small number would suggest.[28] But the slow, wasting nature of the disease meant that the afflicted officer more often than not made it home on furlough to die. In the case of these deaths at home, it is usually only the fact of death and not the specific disease, or even a hint of its symptoms, that is to be found in the surviving records.

From all that has been said thus far of fatal illness it will come as no surprise that the most frequently identified death from natural causes was that produced by fever. Its course was swift; men died at their duty posts, and the cause of death became part of the official record. Fevers were the characteristic diseases of the geographical area extending south from Hampton Roads that proved so fatal to officers of more northern origins. In all, thirty-seven of the eighty-nine deaths from natural causes were attributed to fevers; twenty-eight of these deaths by fever took place south of the imaginary line demarking the danger zone for most officers; and twenty-four of the thirty-seven were specifically identified as yellow fever.

In looking at the geography of illness or the statistics of death it is too easy and too comforting to lose sight of the human reality. To understand what a fatal illness meant to an individual officer no case is better than that of Dr. Thomas Gates McAllister of Fort Hunter, Pennsylvania, who was appointed a surgeon's mate early in 1805, and who spent the next two years cruising the Mediterranean in *John Adams, Constitution*, and *Enterprize*. At the end of July 1807 *Enterprize* arrived at the Washington navy yard carrying a desperately ill Dr. McAllister, a man so sick that he could not even write his family in Pennsylvania to tell them that he was ill or where he was. Only by accident, and almost a month later, did his father, Archibald McAllister, discover that the son was apparently dying at Washington. Thomas's brother was immediately dispatched to the capital to bring Thomas home—with what effort the story does not tell—and the best medical men Archibald McAllister could find were set to work on the case. For a while Thomas appeared to be getting better and was even strong enough to climb the stairs to his room on the second floor. Then, one day in the middle of October 1807, as Dr. McAllister was ascending the stairs, he began coughing violently, a blood vessel ruptured, and before the hemorrhaging could be arrested he had lost what appeared to his alarmed parent to be three and a half quarts of blood. "Since the bleeding he has never been up," wrote Archibald McAllister to Robert Smith in February 1808, "and so extremely ill that we dare not leave him, night nor day, five minutes at a time. God only knows whether he will recover."

Surprisingly, improvement did take place, and by July 1808 Dr. McAllister was at last strong enough to attempt his own letter to the secretary of the navy: "It is with pleasure I inform you of an amendment of my health, which enables me to sit up part of the day and, with the assistance of an armed chair with casters, to enjoy the air at the door and in the garden." He talked optimistically about going to the sulfur springs in Adams County for further recovery. Whether the doctor made the trip to the springs or not, it was a fresh relapse, not further recovery, that lay ahead. On 23 January 1809, McAllister's father reported that "he continues extremely ill. His limbs are so contracted that he is drawn as it were in a lump. If ever he should recover, I am afraid he will be without the use of his limbs: his knee joints are out of place, also his ankles. You would think it impossible for [a] human being to have life and have so little flesh as he has." Within a month Dr. Thomas McAllister was dead. He was twenty-four years old.[29]

33. Shrinking the Corps

*D*EATH WAS THE most dramatic way officers left the pre-1815 U.S. Navy, but a greater number of men departed in a manner that will never capture the attention of the sensation seeker. They are the officers discharged in systematic reductions of the size of the corps. Under this rubric stand 336 men, approximately one-fifth of all the officers who left the navy permanently before 14 February 1815 (Table 39). All were excess officers whose services the nation no longer needed.

There were four such reductions in the size of the officer corps between the midpoint of the Quasi-War with France and the end of the War of 1812. Three of the four involved numbers of officers so small as to be historically unimportant, though they were surely traumatic for the individuals who suddenly had to find different ways of earning their livings. At least seven Quasi-War revenue cutter officers, serving temporarily under the operational control of the secretary of the navy, terminated their connection with the navy when their cutters were returned to Treasury Department jurisdiction or were taken permanently into the navy between May and August 1799. So far as is known, these seven were not put out of work. They simply transferred back to the payroll of the Treasury Department. As has been related in an earlier chapter, eight pursers were discharged (and not subsequently reappointed as War of 1812 purser or chaplain berths came open) when Senate confirmation of such appointments was mandated by law and the number of serving pursers was reduced in April 1812.

A third minor reduction of the officer corps took place early in 1813. In response to the predictable public demand for comprehensive protection against wartime British raids, Secretary of the Navy Paul Hamilton ordered all existing gunboats on active duty in 1812—usually under the command of sailing masters recruited from the merchant service—and distributed them as widely as possible along the coastline. Soon after William Jones assumed the helm at the Navy Office he concluded that he had at his disposal neither the manpower nor the financial resources to maintain this large gunboat force on active duty. A drastic reduction ensued, with the forty-eight boats Jones proposed to keep in service being concentrated at a few strategically critical locations: "They are now scattered about in every creek and corner" throughout the union, he claimed, "as receptacles of idleness and objects of waste and extravagance, without utility." With all boats other than the forty-eight taken out of service, many of the sailing masters recruited from the merchant marine at the beginning of the war were no longer needed. Announcing that there was "a vast excess of sailing masters in the service, and among them are many very worthless," Jones instructed the station commanders to select the best masters to command the boats retained on duty and to discharge all the rest. Those it was desirable to keep in the officer corps he characterized as the "brave, capable men and friends to government [i.e., members of the Republican party]; not merely those who want employ[ment] most, but those who are fittest for service."[1] For neither the first nor the last time during his term of office, Secretary Jones's rhetoric had outrun reality. By the time this cut in the officer corps had sorted itself out—including callbacks to active service of masters who, it turned out, really *were* needed—the reduction through discharge in the "vast excess" of sailing masters appears to have numbered twenty individuals. Perhaps it was a few more; the records are occasionally incomplete or ambiguous.

These three small reductions aside, the pre-1815 U.S. Navy experienced only one major loss of officers through discharge. It embraced 298 of the 336 officers who can be identified as having left the navy in reductions of force, and it arose out of the Peace Establishment Act of 3 March 1801. The Quasi-War with France had compelled the United States to build a naval force that, over a three-year period, encompassed forty-nine ships and galleys and an officer corps that, at the height of Quasi-War operations in July 1800, numbered nearly seven hundred men. Hostilities at an end, it was neither necessary nor desirable to retain this navy in its existing configuration. Many of the ships were converted merchantmen, scarcely appropriate for a standing naval force. The officer corps, developed with rapidity and drawn almost entirely from the merchant marine, was heavily civilianized. Many of its members were too old and too set in their ways ever to acquire the mentality and habits of professional naval officers. Some were patently undesirable. One has only to read the pages of court martial transcripts accumulated during the years of the Quasi-War navy and then turn to similar courts martial for the War of 1812 years to realize that in the earlier of these two wars the historian is, in large measure, studying a crowd of citizens in uniform. Whichever political party had won the election of 1800 would have faced the necessity of disposing of undesirable vessels, of reducing the number of seamen employed, and of reorganizing the officer corps. What the Republican victory in that election did was to make the reorganization more draconian than it might have been had the Federalists retained control of Congress and the presidency.

The Peace Establishment Act of 1801 directed the president to retain in the navy 9 captains, 36 lieutenants, and 150 midshipmen, and "authorized" him to "discharge all the other officers in the navy service of the United States." The number of surgeons, surgeon's mates, pursers, sailing masters, and chaplains to be employed in the smaller peacetime navy was left subject to the discretion of the president and to budget limitations. Omission of any masters commandant from the list of officers to be retained was likely the result of end-of-session legislate-in-haste carelessness. Both Federalist and Republican secretaries of the navy agreed on the necessity of such a rank. It was reinstituted in 1804 by executive action, without bothering to consult Congress.

There has been a goodly amount of hand wringing over the Peace Establishment Act by naval historians influenced by the seapower theories of Alfred T. Mahan and his disciples. These writers see the act of 1801 as a turning away by the United States from its Quasi-War commitment to build a navy that would command the respect of other seafaring nations. A wiser perspective views the Peace Establishment Act as the true foundation of the fully professional officer corps that the United States developed between 1801 and 1812. At the height of the Quasi-War with France the United States had approximately seven hundred naval officers in service. In 1801 it was offered the opportunity to select, on the basis of their actual performance, the 240 or 250 best of those officers to form the core of the permanent, professional force.* Fortunately for the navy, the task of carrying out the congressionally mandated reduction fell to a man who fully appreciated the opportunity and its importance. Between Benjamin Stoddert's resignation as secretary of the navy (31 March 1801) and Robert Smith's assumption of office (27 July)

---

* A cadre sorely in need of beneficial pruning were the Quasi-War's direct appointments as lieutenants. A classic example of these bad apples is provided by Henry Seton, son of William Seton, the first cashier of the Bank of New York. On 1 February 1799 Benjamin Stoddert wrote to Alexander Hamilton, who was in a position to provide a frank answer, to inquire: "Mr. Henry Seton, son of the late William Seton, a very respectable man, wants to be made a lieutenant in the navy. A story was some time ago in circulation to the disadvantage of this young gentleman which I hope was unfounded. Will you be so good as to let me know his character, if it be a good one? If otherwise, you need not trouble yourself to answer this letter." Five days later, and without having allowed himself enough time to determine whether or not Hamilton was going to reply, Stoddert picked up his pen to address the general a second time and a little sheepishly: "I wrote you some days ago respecting Mr. Henry Seton. I ought to have waited long enough for an answer, but his appointment was so much pressed, he was so well recommended, I was so well satisfied [that] a story which I had heard was without foundation, and a lieutenant being instantly wanted, he is appointed. I wish he may turn out well."

The pressure to which he was being subjected should have been a red flag to so experienced an administrator as Benjamin Stoddert. From *Maryland*, off Surinam, Captain John Rodgers wrote Stoddert the following November: "The conduct of Lieutenant Henry Seton has been generally—with justice I may say continually—so basely infamous since he has served on board this ship that at last I conceived it my particular duty to arrest and suspend him from any further command on board *of this ship* until your pleasure or the sentence of a court martial should be known. . . . He is an intolerable drunkard and has been guilty of innumerable other unpardonable misdemeanors such as would tend to disorganize the best-regulated ship in the world in a very little time, provided he was acting in as important a station as he was acting in on board of this ship. It is possible, owing to delicate feeling for himself and friends, that I continued him in the command his commission entitled him to longer than I ought to have done, cordially wishing for a reformation." Rodgers went on to relate how, one night in late October, he had approached, under cover of darkness, what he suspected to be a French privateer anchored in shoal water. Having run within long gunshot of his prey, Rodgers dared go no farther at night because of the treacherous waters. About eleven p.m. the captain went below, leaving orders to be called "precisely at three in the morning," so that he might close the privateer by the first light of dawn. "Having layed down with my clothes on, I did not sleep much. I got up and found by my watch it was past three o'clock, the hour at which I was to have been called, when I immediately went on deck and there found Lieutenant Seton asleep on the companion and was informed by the officer next to him in rank, then on deck, that he had slept full three hours of that watch on one of the seats in the head; and, on the following night, he was so beastly intoxicated that he could not be got on deck by any means."[2]

Even in the face of such damning evidence of inadequacy, Seton's friends were still able to protect him. He was given two other appointments afloat and remained a lieutenant until May 1801, when the Jefferson administration, having no old political ties to Seton's late father and his father's friends to restrain them, dropped the tippling lieutenant in the reduction mandated by the Peace Establishment Act.

Secretary of War Henry Dearborn served as titular acting secretary of the navy, but the duties of the office were largely performed by Representative Samuel Smith of Maryland. On Samuel Smith rested the primary responsibility for making the retention or discharge decisions. He decided to use three principles in determining which men would be kept: (1) merit; (2) past services to the nation; and (3) equity to individual states. In addition, two rules were applied mechanically. First, no officers serving on acting appointments, which appointments had not been confirmed by the Navy Office, were retained on the Peace Establishment. Those affected by the application of this rule were principally acting midshipmen appointed by the commanding officers of the various ships of war. Second, a now-unknown number of noncitizens had been granted officer appointments in the Quasi-War navy, so that advantage might be derived from their experience gained in other navies. As far as these individuals could be identified, they were systematically excluded from the limited number of Peace Establishment appointments.

Every commanding officer was asked to determine which of his subordinates wished to leave the officer corps from personal motives—to command merchantmen, from dislike of the navy, or whatever—and which wanted to be considered for retention on the Peace Establishment. For each of the latter the commanding officer was asked to submit an evaluation, specifically made for the purpose of determining the "most promising" officers. It was these evaluations that became the primary basis for the retention/discharge decisions made by Samuel Smith, heavily assisted by Principal Clerk Abishai Thomas. When the whole selection process was complete at least 298 officers had left the navy permanently.[3]

The 1801 reduction, though arduous because carried out with thoroughness and care, did not pose any insuperable administrative problems. A few highly promising young officers were lost to the navy because they had been given ad hoc appointments as acting lieutenants by squadron commanders. Such men could not be retained among the thirty-six authorized lieutenants in preference to equally able men who held lieutenant's commissions confirmed by the Senate. If they wished to stay on, these unlucky ones must go back on the roster of midshipmen and await regular and early promotion. Some found it too degrading to serve again as midshipmen where they had so recently strutted as lieutenants and elected discharge. Their excessive pride is lamentable for, as things turned out, natural attrition among the lieutenants would have brought speedy commissions. Misreading of the future was an additional motivation for these shortsighted decisions by the able to leave the navy instead of displaying a little patience. They assumed the U.S. Navy was about to enter a period of neglect and degradation at the hands of the incoming Republican administration. What was, in fact, dawning for the officer corps was an era of opportunity, one of intense professional development and relatively rapid promotion.

Reducing the captains to the statutory nine proved to be the thorniest administrative problem. All agreed that the captains whom it was desirable to retain numbered several more than that number. The final cut would involve invidious distinctions. Two of the nine potential posts were occupied by the navy's senior officers, John Barry and Samuel Nicholson. Neither would probably hoist his broad pennant at sea again, nor could their shore duties be too arduous; but no one could seriously contemplate turning these two veteran

captains, men who had commanded frigates of the Continental navy, onto the streets. With some difficulty the list of captains whom it was desirable to retain could be cut to fourteen or perhaps fifteen names; but further cuts would be too traumatic or too crippling to the available supply of highly qualified commanding officers. Samuel Smith and Henry Dearborn gave some thought to asking Congress to expand the statutory number of captains to eleven. But, whatever its rhetorical commitment to the supremacy of the legislative will, the Jefferson presidency practiced administrative discretion as boldly as almost any in American history. In the end, rather than make further cuts in the number of captains or go back to Congress for a modification of the Peace Establishment, it allowed time and events—in the form of three resignations, one death, and one case of highly eccentric behavior that demanded a discreet retirement under the face-saving cloak of the Peace Establishment—to do the final cutting. It was not until the death of Commodore John Barry on 13 September 1803 that the number of captains was at last reduced to the nine mandated by the act of March 1801.

Because the officer corps as it stood on 3 March 1801 had been appointed in its entirety by a Federalist administration and was now to be cut by a Republican one, the charge that politics influenced the selection of those to be retained was bound to be rattled, both by the excluded officers and by latter-day historians. Samuel Smith resented such accusations. "Permit me here to remark that you are mistaken when you suppose that the politics of the party will be the criterion by which the selection of officers will be made," he told one who leveled the charge. "Merit and services and a due proportion for each state will be a better criterion. They will govern this department; and this rule cannot fail to meet your entire approbation and that of every good American."[4] Samuel Smith seems to have been true to his word. "In this department," he told a Federalist congressman—apparently drawing a distinction with the army, over the political affiliation of whose officers there was keen concern in the new administration—"I have attended much to character, nothing to the political caste of the gentlemen." A squadron of three frigates and one schooner was to sail for the Mediterranean in ten days. Its commanders: Commodore Richard Dale, Captains Samuel Barron and William Bainbridge, and Lieutenant Andrew Sterett. "All good *Feds* and, what I esteem more, excellent officers."[5]

This historian finds no reason to dissent from Samuel Smith's self-assessment. No evidence exists that partisan politics influenced the choices made. Silas Talbot had been a Federalist member of Congress. He was among those selected for retention, but decided instead to resign late in the summer of 1801. Everyone knew that Captain James Sever was an avid and vocal Federalist, so it was easy enough to attribute his exclusion to party affiliation. Doubtful it is that, given the difficult choices to be made, any secretary of the navy, of either political persuasion, would have elected to retain Sever in preference to a single captain who was kept on board, for Sever was too poor a leader of men. His distant, haughty manner speedily alienated him from most of the officers who served as his subordinates. The captain once declared that "he would not be plagued with any officers he did not like, and, if he could not get rid of [a disliked officer] any other way, he would make his situation so irksome as to force him to commit himself," thus giving Sever an excuse to arrest the unwanted man and dispose of him by judicial proceedings.[6] Even as the captains to be retained were being selected, Sever's *Congress* was ending her Quasi-War service with a series of acrimonious courts martial of subordinates, courts martial requested by Sever on charges sufficiently minor that more skillful commanders of men would certainly have found other means of dealing with them. The courts were held at the Washington navy yard, practically on the front steps of the Navy Office, which did nothing to reduce Sever's visibility at a time when Samuel Smith was looking for captains' names to cut from his list.

On the other hand, at least three captains positively identified as Jeffersonian Republicans—Daniel McNeill, John Mullowny, and Christopher Raymond Perry—were discharged under the Peace Establishment Act. None of the three had unblemished records, and the veil of party affiliation was decidedly not drawn to hide the blemishes. McNeill was not discharged until October 1802, by which time his eccentric behavior during his Mediterranean cruise in *Boston* had called his mental health into serious question. Mullowny was under a cloud because of extreme brutality to a seaman; and enough other accusations against him, including charges of personal corruption, had reached the secretary's desk to make his retention out of the question by any objective standard.* An

---

* Mullowny's version of the alleged brutality incident appears in his journal on board *Montezuma*, 4 August 1799: "At half past two p.m. got under way, the crew apparently determined not to proceed on the cruise. At seven p.m. Daniel Hawthorn was heard to make use of insulting and mutinous language. I called him aft and, proceeding to chastise him, he resisted and attempted to seize me, which he in fact did—at the same time calling for assistance to put his infamous designs into execution. He was, however, quickly secured in irons." Hawthorn's account of the incident is rather different: "I am really afraid the treatment I received from Captain Mullowny I shall never get the better of," he told Benjamin Stoddert a year and a half later. "My skull is much hurt, and I fear I shall lose my sight. The blows I received from him were disgraceful to humanity. They forced the blood from mouth, eyes, ears, and nose. I expect he has had a check from you, as I understand he acts better. I sincerely wish for my brother tars he may see his folly." Stoddert seems to have thought there was more than a grain of truth in Hawthorn's version—"it was represented to me that for some misconduct the captain had ordered Hawthorn to kiss the deck before his feet; the man thought it a degradation to which he was not bound to submit"—but, because of a legal technicality, it was not possible to have the incident investigated by a court martial, and the facts of the case cannot now be uncovered.[7]

extended court of inquiry into Perry's conduct while commander of *General Greene* had cleared the captain of various charges pointing to lax standards of personal ethics, if not to the blatant use of a U.S. ship of war for his personal profit, but had found him chargeable with excessive procrastination in executing the orders of his squadron commander, Silas Talbot, and with failure or inability to maintain proper discipline among the unusually rowdy midshipmen in his vessel. Perry had thereupon been suspended for three months without pay.[8] When captains with unblemished records were being let go, it was not to be expected that one as compromised as Christopher Raymond Perry would be kept on.

It would be hard to overestimate the contribution that this draconian housecleaning made in preparing the officer corps for the intense professional development of the next decade. Much remained to be done by Robert Smith to build the navy that went to war in June 1812, but the task would have been severely inhibited if the civilianized Quasi-War navy had not first taken the strong medicine of the Peace Establishment Act of 1801. Fine results were not foreordained. Samuel Smith held firm to his conviction that "character" must be the basis of selecting those to be retained. Had "political caste" played a larger role in the choices, the high degree of competence and the apolitical professionalism that characterized the navy of the next fifteen years might have been severely compromised. Brief as was his tenure in the Navy Office, Samuel Smith should receive full credit for the contribution he made to the navy's future in those few, if intense, months.

Disabled in Their Country's Service

As that long file of 336 men discharged from the navy in reductions of the officer corps marches past, one must not fail to notice a handful of men who can scarcely hobble by the reviewing stand or who seem to be experiencing great pain in so doing. They are the officer pensioners, and they number only twelve. Not even all of the twelve can technically be counted as having been discharged in reductions in the size of the officer corps. Two of them resigned their appointments, and three others were still officially on the roll of officers on 14 February 1815. What these twelve men have in common is this: while serving as an officer in the navy, each had sustained some disability so serious that the U.S. government felt a moral obligation to compensate him for his partial or total inability to earn a living in civilian life. They are considered here because, whether they resigned or were discharged, whether they were still technically on the roll of officers on 14 February 1815 or not, their disabilities were serious enough to remove them from the navy's corps of active-duty officers.[9]

The law under which these twelve men received their pensions, "An Act for the Better Government of the Navy of the United States," of 23 April 1800, devoted but few words to the subject. It simply provided that any officer (or enlisted man) "disabled in the line of his duty" was entitled to receive for life, "or during his disability," a sum not exceeding one-half of his monthly pay. (In 1816 the commissioners who administered the navy's pension fund were given discretionary authority to increase pensions to an amount not exceeding the monthly pay of the disabled pensioner.) Although the law did not explicitly state such a rule, up to, through, and for some years after the War of 1812 the act was almost always interpreted by the Navy Office as granting benefits only to those individuals whose disabilities were serious enough to prevent their remaining on the roll of naval officers. To accept a pension was to accept de facto and permanent discharge from the corps. So long as pensions could not exceed one-half of monthly pay, this stringency in benefits provided ample motivation for partially disabled men to attempt to remain on the register as serving officers, however incapable they may have been of performing any significant duty. For this reason, or perhaps for some other reason now unknown, relatively few officers sought to take advantage of the pension provision in the pre-1815 years. Their small number does permit some of these pensioners to step out of line as they file past so that the historian may take a closer look at them as individuals.

There is Midshipman Enoch Brown, "a smart young man, but rather wild," who lost the use of his left hand when he and a number of his fellow midshipmen from the frigate *Insurgente* allegedly went to the rescue of a number of *Insurgente*'s enlisted men who were involved in a street brawl at Fells Point, Baltimore, in July 1800. It never was clear that the sailors needed any help, or that the midshipmen had not rushed to their aid principally out of the love of a good fight. Be that as it may, Midshipman Brown had every reason for gratitude for his injury; because of his physical condition, Brown had to be left on the beach when *Insurgente* sailed in August 1800, never to be heard from again.[10]

Sailing Master James F. Goelet catches the eye principally because he is the much older brother-in-law of James Lawrence and was probably responsible for getting young James his midshipman's appointment. By 1800, after a year and a half of service, Goelet was under a heavy cloud because Secretary Stoddert had discovered his serious drinking problem, which, the secretary declared, "always amounts to a disqualification of any kind of confidence in the public service." Goelet, with obvious sincerity, assured Stoddert that he wanted to reform. The latter agreed to give him one more chance and made him sailing master of the frigate *New York*. Whether Goelet would have defeated his addiction must remain forever unknown. In July 1800, while climbing down into *New York*'s bread room, Goelet fell through a hatchway and broke his leg. The certificates of disability subsequently filed to justify a pension are just vague enough in their wording to suggest that Goelet may have been less than sober when he fell. Whether he incurred it drunk or sober, the broken leg left Goelet so badly crippled that *New York* had to sail without him, and there were enough questions about his fitness to rule him out for retention on the Peace Establishment in 1801. Not long after his discharge Goelet's troubles multiplied: he suffered a stroke that cost him his speech and the use of some limbs. In 1805 friends and family rallied round to secure him a $20-per-month pension, on which he and Sarah (Lawrence) Goelet managed to eke out an existence of genteel poverty at Perth Amboy, New Jersey, until his death in November 1809.[11]

Captain's Clerk Isaac Baldwin's health was utterly destroyed by the exposure he suffered following the wreck of the schooner *Revenge* on Watch Hill Reef in January 1811. Exposure triggered an illness marked by a "violent cough, rheumatic pains, and vomiting of blood." Wrote Baldwin in applying for a pension nearly five years later: "I regret that I cannot appear before you personally, the injury having been accompanied with visible marks that speak more forcibly than words, and which I must carry to my grave. . . . My sufferings have been witnessed by hundreds in [New York] City, but they never can be described." In an attempt to help Baldwin recover his health in a milder climate, Oliver H. Perry, his old commanding officer, gave him a sinecure appointment as captain's clerk in the frigate *Java* on the Mediterranean station. His pension application was still pending in Washington when Isaac Baldwin died off Algiers on 12 April 1816.[12]

An explosion in the gunner's storeroom on board the frigate *New York* in April 1803 left Surgeon Nathaniel Weems with an umbilical hernia, the loss of part of one ear, and a right arm so contracted and withered as to be practically useless.[13] Sailing Master Nicholas O'Connor was thrown from his horse while reconnoitering British movements at Lynnhaven Bay on 1 December 1814 and became thereby an invalid for the rest of his life.[14] A British rocket seriously injured Midshipman Richard Suter at the battle of Bladensburg in 1814; he was still drawing a small monthly pension when he died in 1848.[15] Sailing Master James Rogers had the fingers of his right hand damaged beyond repair in the battle between *President* and *Endymion*.[16] Of these and similar cases is the line of officer pensioners who march past composed. Some of them—James Rogers or Enoch Brown or Richard Suter—continued to pursue other careers while supplementing their incomes with the frugal pensions. But for men such as Isaac Baldwin, or Nicholas O'Connor, or even James Goelet naval service had brought with it risks that destroyed health and made useful, productive lives forever out of the question. Barely adequate though they might be, monthly pensions were an absolute and an imperative need.

34. Departure Voluntary—and Otherwise

ESIGNATION. AT FIRST glance that seems to be the big story of men's departures from the pre-1815 officer corps. Twice as many officers resigned as died in service; twice as many resigned as were discharged in reductions in the size of the corps; and three times as many resigned as were dismissed for misconduct (Table 39).

But, when these resignations are examined more carefully, what appears to be fact proves sadly misleading. In more than two-fifths (42.9 percent) of the recorded resignations the reason for that apparently voluntary departure is unknown. Among the other three-fifths of the resignations, the only information about motivation is all too frequently the officer's own statement. But motives expressed in letters of resignation are often not the actual reasons for the act; in some instances the writer may be self-deceived. Then, too, the business of categorizing reasons for resigning is imprecise at best. In death a man is clearly a casualty of enemy action, or the victim of a duel, or lost with his ship. In a resignation many causes may interact and cumulate: inability to live on one's pay; dislike of the climate where one is stationed; the slowness of promotion; friction with a commanding officer. Which one triggers the actual decision to leave the navy? Or are all only manifestations of a hidden, deeper reason? Consequently, no table will be here provided attributing so many resignations to this cause and so many to that one, all broken down into neat percentages. To do so would be to create an illusion of precision about a subject that cannot but be either fuzzy or slippery. Apparent or stated reasons for resigning will be discussed as approximate fractions of those departing the corps, and always with the warning that it is a subject on which hard figures must always prove more or less illusory.

The necessary first step in investigating the 352 officer resignations for which the reasons can be known or inferred is to exclude one group of "resignations" that do not really belong in that category. These are the eighty-eight officers who had the good sense to resign in order to avoid court martial or administrative dismissal. Such resignations to avoid dismissal account for one quarter of all known-cause resignations. Assuming, conservatively, that the same proportion holds among the 264 unknown-cause resignations, the historian may deduce another 66 resignations to avoid dismissal, bringing the total for that category to 154.* These 154 may be removed from the resignation category altogether and added to the dismissal category to give a more realistic analysis of departure from the officer corps (Table 42). True resignations now account for three men out of every ten who left the pre-1815 officer corps. Resignation remains the premier way in which men left the navy, but not by so wide a margin as appeared on first analysis.

Approximately one man in nine stated motives for resigning so varied and personally idiosyncratic as to elude easy classification. Among them are the only two officers who cited discouragement over the future of the navy as their sole reason for quitting. However, five men who gave other primary reasons for resignation instanced the navy's dubious future as a reinforcing motivation. Talented Lieutenant Jaqueline B. Harvie referred to the death of his brother and sister in the disastrous Richmond, Virginia, theater fire of December 1811 and the necessity of assuming responsibility for two orphan nephews when he resigned on 23 April 1812. He revealed what was perhaps a more basic motivation when he added, "The navy question has undergone a more ample discussion this session of Congress than ever before, and it is evident from the turn it has taken that the majority of the people are decidedly opposed to it. The preparations for war are carried on so slowly and with so much indifference that I am convinced that the administration does not intend to declare it. Under these considerations, I am induced to resign my commission in the navy."[1] What a cruelly mistaken reading of the future! Lieutenant Harvie lost faith less than two months before the declaration of war in June 1812. It can never be known in how many other cases deep misgivings about the navy's prospects were the unexpressed motivation for resignation; but the fact is that among the 264 officers who gave a reason for resigning, only 7 expressed such misgivings as a primary or secondary motivation for getting out. Because the officer corps as a body, like Lieutenant Harvie as an individual, perceived the congressional attitude toward the navy as fluctuating between indifferent and hostile, one can only take the tiny number of resignations attributable to that reason as evidence of high morale within the officer corps as well as a strong spirit of group solidarity that steeled the corps against difficulties and discouragements.

Leaving aside the one man in nine who resigned for highly individual motives, the reasons assigned by the other departing officers fall into one of five broad categories: (1) dissatisfaction with or disputes over rank or status; (2) ill health; (3) dislike for or a sense of being unsuited to naval service or a sea life; (4) family responsibilities or family pressure to give up a naval career; and (5) the desire to pursue some other vocation.

Anxieties about rank and promotion, as well as status tensions between the promotion and nonpromotion tracks, were sensitive and serious issues throughout the first twenty-one years of the navy's existence. Whether it was a Joshua Barney declining one of the first six captain's commissions because Silas Talbot was ranked ahead of him, or a Master Commandant Charles Ludlow quitting

---

* This is almost certainly still too low. One cannot spend much time working with the subject of resignations from the officer corps without exciting a strong suspicion that a substantial number of the remaining 198 "reason unknown" resignees were probably getting out before they were asked to leave. However, sixty-six is the total number that the data in hand will support; it is better to err on the side of conservatism.

when Lieutenant Charles Morris was promoted captain over his head, or a midshipman of two years' experience angered because a messmate had been selected for acting lieutenant, resignation in protest was one way to treat the psychic wounds these anxieties inflicted. Among the resigning officers, one man in nine was choosing this solution, usually making certain to lay on the secretary's desk ample documentation of aggravation and alienation.

Pleading poor health is a hoary face-saving device for getting out of an organization when one is in trouble from some entirely different cause. For this reason, ill health must necessarily be the most suspect category of motives for resignation. Certainly some of the ill-health resignations—roughly one-fifth of the total resignations for which a reason was assigned—do look suspicious. To counterbalance this skepticism, one can recall the health hazards that resulted in nearly half of all deaths in the officer corps being attributable to natural causes. Remembering that fact, the historian is inclined to conclude that the majority of these ill-health resignations probably were just that: departures because of sickness. The descriptions of the illnesses are usually too imprecise to make a closer analysis possible: "my constitution is not sufficiently strong to withstand the many hardships of a maritime life"; "too bad a state of health to do duty"; "for twelve months past I have not seen one well day"; "a severe relapse of my former disease has again seized me"; "my constitution, originally feeble, has been essentially impaired by the fatigues and irregular mode of living inseparable from the service and is now daily exhibiting indications of a progressing decline."[2] In the minority of the ill-health resignations in which the nature of the illnesses is specified, the illnesses appear to be of the same types that led to death from natural causes among the officer corps.

One vague category of ill health is unique to the resignations and does not appear among the natural causes of death: inability of the body to adjust to life at sea. This was a complaint restricted to novice midshipmen making their first trial at a maritime occupation, and it was cited by at least nine of them in submitting their resignations. Some may simply have been adolescents who gave up without giving naval life a fair try. That was certainly the case with Midshipman John Seton Vining, son of the late John Vining, congressman and senator from Delaware in the 1790s. Young Vining, whose mother was dead as well, had been raised by an overindulgent aunt "in too tender a manner" and was prepared in neither body nor mind for the hardships of life at sea. When winter cruising in *Argus* during his first year in the navy precipitated a bout of serious illness, he sent his resignation on to Washington. While Midshipman Vining was waiting to hear of its acceptance, *Argus* made a run to the southward, where warmer weather restored Vining's health and longer service at sea began to toughen his body. He decided he liked the navy much better than he had at first thought and asked his commanding officer, Jacob Jones, to help him withdraw the resignation. Jones tried, reciting the story of growing up with the overindulgent aunt and adding his own evaluation of Vining as "a young man of very correct principles and conduct, and whose mental and personal activity is such as may enable him to become a distinguished officer." But Paul Hamilton held that inability to stick to a decision was not a desirable characteristic in an officer. He let Vining's resignation stand.[3]

Young men like Vining, whose bodies experienced extraordinary difficulties adjusting to life at sea and who submitted resignations on grounds of ill health, provide a useful bridge to the third category of resignations: the one man in fourteen who left the navy because he judged himself unsuited to it or to a sea life. It is possible that some or many of these resignations should be blended with those of the young men whose bodies could not adjust to shipboard life and who resigned pleading health considerations. But here health was not mentioned; the motive for resignation was expressed as a generalized statement that the resigning officer and the navy had found themselves badly mismatched. Commanding officers clearly encouraged a number of these mismatch resignations. Occasionally they would express an opinion that the resigning officer had entered the corps at too advanced an age to make a complete and successful adjustment to life in the navy; but generally it is the statement of the individual's own self-discovery of his unsuitability for naval life that survives, sometimes so vaguely worded as to suggest that this formula actually conceals resignation to avoid dismissal. In the absence of any explicit evidence of the latter, such resignations must be taken at their face value, but with a wish that more of the resigning officers had detailed the ways in which they found naval life not to their liking.

In a tiny minority of these letters of resignation a better historical record does exist. One from Surgeon's Mate Theodore C. Van Wyck of New York was lengthy, complaining of other men, including a medical school classmate, appointed surgeon over his head, but the first sentence said it all: "My observation has enabled me to discover that I am a burden to the service, and, while I am aware of the fact, I should be criminal in the highest degree did I not remove that burden." This time the commanding officer's letter that transmitted the resignation was explicit about the burden Van Wyck posed. "In my opinion, he has mistaken his profession," wrote John Rodgers:

> That he will ever be qualified to do the duties of surgeon of a man-of-war I much question. There are certain indications about some men's persons and faces which explain the profession that nature intended them for and that cannot be mistaken; and, in allusion to Mr. Van Wyck, I can only say that even if he was genteelly dressed, and you were to meet him in a blacksmith's shop among a dozen blacksmiths, you would find it difficult to decide which was the doctor. . . . Indeed, I have hardly ever looked at Mr. Van Wyck without reflecting on the deplorable condition in which I should consider myself should I ever be under the necessity of permitting him to amputate a leg for me.[4]

Officers who cited family responsibilities or family pressure as the cause of their leaving the navy—approximately one-fifth of all those who stated a reason for resigning—actually represent a spectrum of domestic situations that could terminate an officer's career. Bands within the spectrum are sufficiently distinct so that each may be assigned a label: marriage; illness or old age of parents or members of one's family; death of one or both parents; parental pressure on a son to leave the navy.

"Captain Sinclair . . . is now out, but will be in for the winter in about three weeks," wrote Sally (Kennon) Sinclair, the bride of Lieutenant Arthur Sinclair, in November 1810:

> Indeed, it is now time for them to let him stay at home a little while; for since last May he has not, I am confident, spent three weeks at home. If he has been with me three, it is, as the Negroes say, the outside. I almost wish the Nautilus did not sail as fast as she does, for it is on that account, I am told, that

they keep him out so constantly. If ever you are placed in a similar situation, you will find it not the most pleasant of all things in this life to be one-half of the time that is allotted you separated from your husband. That is, if you love him. Now if, on the contrary, you do not care "no sight" for him . . . it would be vastly pleasant to be your own mistress ten months out of the twelve. But if, on the contrary, like me, you loved him most ardently and were still separated, no situation on earth can be more distressing. He is now cruising off the coast of North Carolina, which is, I am told by tars, the most dangerous on our coast. He has just returned from that place and was very near being lost. God knows what can induce the department to send him there again, so soon after his being so nearly lost. They have their reasons, I suppose.[5]

To marry a man whose profession was the sea was to embark upon family life under conditions of stress unknown to lawyers, farmers, merchants, or clergymen and their wives. Some officers of promise decided they preferred living at home with their spouses to roaming the oceans and coastal waters. Many a wife or fiancée wanted no part of a marriage that involved functioning as the de facto head of household for long periods of time. Eight men cited actual or impending marriage as the occasion of their resignations. The most famous of them was Midshipman James Cooper, whose bride persuaded him to elect the life of a gentleman farmer in preference to that of a naval officer, a decision that eventually led to a career as one of the nineteenth century's most distinguished men of letters under a name by which he is more widely recognized: James Fenimore Cooper. Although the officers who resigned to marry or to stay at home were often rated highly by their superiors in fitness reports, one suspects that their career commitment to the navy and to a sea life was weak. So far as can now be determined, of those who resigned to marry none ever applied to resume his naval career.

The three remaining bands within this spectrum of family responsibilities as causes of departure from the officer corps emanate, in some way or other, from the parent-child relationship. Nine officers pointed to the old age or illness of a parent or other family member as the reason for handing in their commissions or warrants. To resign while his country was in the midst of war with Great Britain was not to the liking of Joseph Smith, a midshipman from Queen Annes County, Maryland, but an obligation to mortally ill family members came first: "My parents being in a very infirm state of health and not expecting to survive the same, it is their fond wish and desire that I, being the only son, should stay with them and transact their business; and I think it a duty incumbent on me, as a son, to comply with their request."[6]

Reasons such as Midshipman Smith's shade off into the family-responsibility reason most frequently cited by officers as impelling them to leave the navy: the death of one or both parents or parent-surrogates. Such a death could terminate a naval career in many ways. It might mean the end of the subsidy from home that had enabled the midshipman to make ends meet on his pay. If a father's estate were large, or heavily encumbered with debt, or in dispute, its settlement might run on for years, precluding a career in which the son might at any time be ordered to some station distant from the county seat and the attorneys. Much more rarely a parent's death meant the inheritance of so much property that staying home, managing it, and living in comfort off the income had more charms than a life at sea. "My father has deceased since I have been in the service and has left me a good real estate," wrote George

Coggeshall, Jr., another midshipman who left the navy midway through the War of 1812, "and it is my mother's earnest request that I should stay at home and take care of the property."[7] But in the more typical resignation, it was not a question of mother and son living in thrifty ease on the income derived from the prudent management of an adequate estate. Far more often, the father's death left the mother dependent on the son for support; he then dropped out of the officer corps to seek some other calling that promised greater income to meet enlarged responsibilities.

In other family-responsibility resignations parental illness or parental death was not at issue. The parent simply wanted the child out of the navy. Although the Navy Office required a parent's approval before it would issue a midshipman's warrant, the archives reveal instances in which this approval, though granted, was extracted amid severe misgivings. Sometimes such anxieties would not down, even after the son was launched on his career as an officer; then the pressure began to build for the son to give up a sea life and return home. One such story is well documented and is probably not too different, in its essence, from all the rest.

William Dabney Strother Taylor was the older brother of Zachary Taylor. His father, Colonel Richard Taylor of Louisville, Kentucky, had arranged for William to be educated as an attorney. Just when Colonel Taylor thought that his son was about to commence practice, William informed his father "that he was so averse to the profession that he could not think of following it"; rather, he had a strong desire to enter the navy as a midshipman. William D.S. Taylor was twenty-four years old, past what Robert Smith considered the most desirable age for starting a sea career. Young Mr. Taylor was also, however, the second cousin of Secretary of State James Madison, so Smith politely ignored any doubts he may have harbored and, in October 1806, issued the midshipman's warrant Madison had requested for his cousin. William D.S. Taylor thereupon made his way back to Louisville where, on his arrival late in December 1806 or early in January 1807, "I found my parents involved in the deepest distress by the death of one of my brothers, from whose talents and acquirements they had formed the most sanguine expectations. They immediately demanded my resignation as the test of filial obedience, and I should have been doubly a ruffian had I not complied with the request of parents whose only foible is an over degree of tenderness for their children. Their objections originated from the detached situation of that line of business from this Western Country; and that, from the irritable state of their minds in consequence of the death of [my] much lamented brother, they would have fancied a shipwreck in every gale of wind." William Taylor obediently resigned his midshipman's warrant. At once he and his father set about trying to secure him an army commission in its place. The sequel was a lesson in the eternal futility of parents attempting to direct their children's lives so as to spare themselves worry and distress. In less than two months after his resignation from the navy William D.S. Taylor had his commission as a second lieutenant in the army; a year and a half later he was dead—at Fort Pickering, Tennessee, in the heart of the safe Western Country.[8]

Midshipman Taylor's story is one more instance of the difficulty of analyzing a process as mercurial as the resignation decision by subdividing motives into neat, self-contained compartments. His resignation has been categorized as one induced by parental pressure; but it is only because so much is known about his reasons for quitting that Taylor is placed with that group of resignees. If the record were less ample, he probably would have been counted with the largest group of all: the approximately three out of every ten resigning officers who left the navy to pursue different careers. Three-quarters of these seventy-seven individuals departed to pursue lives that capitalized on the experience they had acquired in the navy. Nineteen exploited navy-gained skills in the merchant marine. Twenty left to accept or seek commissions in the army. Another twelve accepted or sought similar commissions in the marine corps. Two men quit to become officers of revenue cutters. Four surgeons or surgeon's mates elected to pursue private practice ashore.

Although the army was a popular alternative career with many officers who resigned from the navy, almost nothing survives in the records to explain the motives of those who actually made that choice. Midshipman Philip D. Spencer merely indicated that he has "conceived a disgust to the sea service and wishes very much a lieutenancy in the army."[9] More insight on men's decisions to move from the navy's officer corps to that of the army is provided by a naval lieutenant who considered making the change, but decided to remain afloat. Charles Morris felt his ambitions frustrated when the Navy Office ignored his application for the command of a small cruiser and continued his assignment as first lieutenant of the frigate *Constitution*, a post in which he must always be in the substantial shadow cast by his commanding officer, Captain Isaac Hull. Only through success in an independent command, thought Morris, could he hope to earn early promotion to master commandant. When, on the declaration of war in 1812, Secretary Hamilton ordered him out on yet another cruise in *Constitution*, Morris obeyed—but he also applied to be appointed a lieutenant colonel of artillery in the expanding wartime army. Because *Constitution*'s August capture of *Guerriere* resulted in Morris's immediate (if controversial) promotion to captain, his army ambitions were ultimately rendered moot. The motives that drove an experienced and highly regarded lieutenant to contemplate a radical career change were certainly those that made the army attractive to others who did abandon the navy for the land service: frustration at the slowness of promotion in the navy; expectation of greater opportunity in the larger army officer corps; commissioned rank immediately on entering the army as a junior lieutenant, in contrast to the extended apprentice status of a naval midshipman.[10]

There is a sense in which leaving a naval officership for one in the marine corps should not be considered a resignation. Both forces were part of the naval rather than the army establishment; both were subject to the direction of the secretary of the navy. However, in the minds of those officers of the navy electing to pursue marine corps commissions, the decision represented a distinct career choice, and legally speaking the crossover did involve the resignation of a naval warrant or commission. As with those men who chose to transfer their career hopes to the army, the surviving record of motivations is scanty. They must have been closely related to the motives—immediate commissioned status, swifter promotions—that impelled other men to seek army commissions. This supposition is reinforced by the discovery that the would-be career changers often sought army and marine corps commissions simultaneously. One motive that impelled men from the navy toward the army officer corps definitely cannot have been the lure in the case of the marine corps; as the smallest of the nation's three military forces, the marine corps could not offer the greater opportunities endemic to a larger organization.

The most revealing statement of motivation for switching to the marine corps was that of a man who did not make the change. For Frederick Baury, the son of a French officer of West Indian origins who had served in the United States during the Revolutionary War and who afterwards became an American citizen and settled in Middletown, Connecticut, the appeal of the marine corps was the immediate commission: "It is twelve months since I have made a trial of a seaman's life, and I find that it does not agree with me. The hope of promotion is so long deferred that the most ambitious and useful period of my life, that on which my future fame and support must depend, will be spent in my very subordinate capacity. I am now nineteen, and promotion rarely takes place before six years. I shall, therefore, at any rate, have attained my twenty-fourth year before my prospects can alter for the better."[11] Even granting the shorter life expectancies of naval officers in the pre-1815 years, one can still imagine the smile of amusement with which graybeard Paul Hamilton (aged forty-seven) read Baury's assertion that his future life was all but foreclosed at nineteen! Hamilton merely noted "at present no appointments are making in the marine corps" on the letter, and the application ended there. Baury, still ranked midshipman, disappeared along with *Wasp* and all her ship's company somewhere in the South Atlantic in October 1814.

If the record of the reasons men chose to resign from the navy to become army or marine corps officers is sparse, that of the motivation of those who quit to pursue careers in the merchant marine is ample. It is also invariably the same: anticipated economic advantage in private enterprise. No one expressed the pressures toward the life of a merchant captain better than did Master Commandant Thomas Robinson, Jr., in a July 1809 letter that set the stage for his resignation six months later:

> I find it is impossible for me to do justice to my family and my own feelings in the command I am honored with [*Wasp*] under my present circumstances. While there was a prospect of war with England, the anticipation of *again* participating in some honorable service for my country made every burden light, and I was willing to drain from my *scanty* purse. But, Sir, that stimulus has ceased, and it will be some time ere we know the decision of France. The pay and emoluments of a master commandant are by no means adequate to the support of a *family* on shore and such a table as the commander of the U.S. Sloop Wasp *must* always keep, together with the numerous expenses attending the latter, particularly on a foreign station. Under those circumstances . . . necessity and common prudence forces me to request relief from my present command. . . . I have but two alternatives: either to effect this or run deeply in debt to the department for my necessary support. The latter I cannot think [of]. . . . The Wasp will be a proper plaything for some of our young officers, who are fighting for such a command. It has no charms for me unless in war. I should be mortified to be obliged to give up the service, but I cannot leave my family to a very scanty subsistence and myself flourishing away in a foreign country as commander of a sloop of war.[12]

If naval officers abandoned the security—and the stringencies—of a fixed salary for what they perceived as the greater income of private business, they had no guarantee that the change insured economic success. Merchant service during the years of the Napoleonic Wars was a high-risk enterprise. If some men became wealthy, far more suffered severe financial setbacks or total economic ruin. Did one know more of the life histories of the nineteen officers who resigned to pursue merchant service opportunities, their stories might be found to resemble that of Peter Leonard. A protégé of Edward Preble's, Leonard had served as the commodore's secretary during Preble's 1803–1804 Mediterranean command with the rank of captain's clerk and (later) chaplain. Because captain's clerk to chaplain to purser was a normal career path, Leonard had only to wait patiently until time and Preble's influence brought him a pursership and relative economic security. Leonard, however, chose to resign his chaplain's warrant in March 1805, alleging that ill health made it impossible for him to perform the duties of his post. Leonard's ill-health resignation is one more piece of evidence how suspect all letters of resignation must be as indicators of motivation. Almost immediately he was off in search of private fortune in the merchant service. A year and a half and a financially disastrous voyage later he came home, crestfallen and wiser: "My desires and wishes are humble," he told Preble in September 1806, "a continued series of calamities and disappointments having reduced them to moderation and reason." Now the prospect of a purser's snug berth looked far more attractive than it had eighteen months earlier. Leonard asked Preble to try to help him secure one: "To buoy myself up with the hopes of procuring an eligible or permanent situation, without such assistance as you can afford, would be as vain and absurd as if I expected to have found the Philosopher's Stone." Preble tried: "I have the highest opinion of Mr. Leonard's integrity, stability, and of his talents and qualifications for a purser," he wrote Robert Smith. The secretary rejected Leonard's application; his reasons are not known, but given the success Preble usually experienced in securing appointments for his protégés, it is likely that Leonard's having abandoned one warrant on a specious pretext motivated Smith's decision not to award him a second. With more than a few misgivings, Peter Leonard once again turned his attention to a merchant service, which looked less golden than it had in March 1805.[13]

Even after all the cautions and all the correctives have been applied to the nominal figures, resignation remains the most common way officers ended their careers in the pre-1815 navy. That nearly one-third of the departing naval officers left through resignation says something vital about the organization. The U.S. Navy was not, for the vast majority of those who enrolled therein, a lifetime vocation. True, there was a small cadre of officers who chose to make such a commitment. For the more typical young adult of 1802 or of 1813, being a naval officer was an honorable and rewarding career that a man pursued for a while in his twenties and maybe in his early thirties. Then he was young and vigorous; traveling the world and encountering all sorts of hardships was full of appeal. Some young adults did not fit in any better as naval officers than they had elsewhere in society, and the corps soon expelled them. Death touched other officers while they were relatively young men and still on active duty. But the most common experience of all was to serve as an officer for a briefer or a longer period, then leave the sea behind to spend one's middle years pursuing an entirely different life ashore. Sea and navy alike demanded the energies of young adults. When an officer could no longer meet these high demands with enthusiasm, he resigned.

35. Exit the Unwanted

*A*NY ORGANIZATION NEEDS a means to remove from its ranks certain of its members: those who are inadequate to the duties assigned them; persons whose uncorrectable behavior departs so far from the spectrum of conduct expected as to handicap the organization in performing its assigned functions or to create an intolerable degree of turmoil within its ranks; individuals who grossly violate the ethical norms of the organization or of the larger society that it serves. Let an organization lack the means of expelling such members, let it fail to use the means at its command, in either case it will eventually become ineffective in the execution of its assigned responsibilities; its morale will corrode from within.

For the U.S. Navy of 1794–1815 dismissal was the means by which the harmful or the counterproductive members were removed from the registers. If this definition of the role of dismissal is correct, then the pre-1815 navy was an organization with a keen concern for its internal health and its external effectiveness; it possessed the resolution to maintain those assets. Among the 1,517 officers for whom the nature of their severance from the navy can be determined, 322 can be positively identified as having been dismissed or persuaded to resign under fear of dismissal. However, in the earlier discussion of resignation, this historian estimated that at least sixty-six of the unknown-cause resignations were ones to avoid dismissal. If these 66 were added to the 322, the result would be to bring the true number of dismissals up to one-quarter of all attrition from the officer corps (Table 42). Be that as it may, for the balance of this chapter and for the two that follow, the focus will be only on the 322 officers who can be positively identified as having left the navy involuntarily. Sources for such an examination are bewilderingly abundant; reasons for dismissal are known in 255 of the 322 recorded expulsions.

The vast majority of these dismissals were achieved by administrative action alone. With the 88 officers who "resigned" but are included among the 322 dismissals, either their commanding officers, or the secretary of the navy, or their own good judgment persuaded them that the course of wisdom lay in quitting rather than running the risk of court martial or outright dismissal. If voluntary resignation from the corps could not be secured, or if the misconduct

430

of an individual seemed to warrant a stronger example being set, the secretary of the navy possessed the right, acting on behalf of the president, to dismiss an officer without formal judicial proceedings. This right had been established as early as January 1799 and was never seriously challenged in the pre-1815 years. "As a general principle, it is better to dismiss unworthy warrant officers than to impair the dignity and importance of courts martial by the too frequent use of those respectable tribunals on worthless occasions."[1] Such was William Jones's philosophy of administrative power. All three of his predecessors would have agreed, and they would have added the words *or commissioned* just before the word *officers*. Officers holding acting appointments from ship or station commanders were always liable to have their appointments revoked by those from whose hands they received them without judicial proceedings and even without the secretary of the navy being consulted.

"I think in all cases the president has a right to dismiss an officer, because he holds his commission on them terms," Commodore Richard Dale wrote in the fall of 1800. "But at the same time I think it more prudent, when it can be done, to hold court martials on officers when they commit faults that require it, [as it] has a much greater effect on the rest of the officers. It gives them an opportunity of knowing what the officer was broke or punished for, [and] it impresses on their minds [that], if they are guilty of the like faults or behave improperly, they will be brought to a court martial and punished according to the crime they have committed."[2] Neither the secretaries of the navy nor the great majority of the senior officers shared Dale's opinion. Despite such a convincing rationale for using formal judicial proceedings as the basis for dismissing officers, only 27 out of the 322 dismissed officers departed the navy as a consequence of formal courts of inquiry or courts martial. An additional four were dismissed by secretaries of the navy after formal court proceedings either had failed to establish guilt or had awarded a lesser punishment.

Examination of the twenty-seven dismissals resulting from court proceedings reveals that in only four cases were the offenses for which these officers were dismissed different in kind or in gravity from offenses for which other officers suffered administrative dismissal. Why were judicial proceedings so little used? The personalities and preferences of the different squadron and station commanders certainly were a factor. Some liked formal judicial proceedings, doubtless for the reasons enunciated by Richard Dale; others preferred the speed and simplicity of administrative action. Remote stations—St. Marys, Georgia, where the large flotilla of gunboats under Hugh G. Campbell were entirely commanded by midshipmen and sailing masters, would be a good example—never possessed enough commissioned officers to form a legal court martial; neither could the defendant, the prosecutor, and the witnesses all be transported to another station for a trial. At such places dismissal and coercive resignation were the only options. Additionally, there was no way the pre-1815 navy could have coped with judicial proceedings for 322 officers: the small corps of commissioned officers would have had to spend all its time sitting on courts martial and courts of inquiry. Administrative efficiency made a more summary method of discipline imperative.

Perhaps most important of all, both secretaries of the navy and commanding officers preferred administrative dismissals and coercive resignations because they were certain and final. From reading the court martial transcripts the historian draws the distinct impression that, unless the person on trial were a

Although he carried a midshipman's warrant, experience as captain of a prewar merchantman earned twenty-five-year-old William Richards Graham an acting appointment as a sailing master and immediate command of a gunboat on the Norfolk station when he joined the officer corps in June 1812. Within a year some character traits not mentioned in his glowing letters of recommendation had surfaced. Graham was pugnacious and physical, qualities not overlooked by the miniaturist, who may be Philippe Peticolas. He "is either fighting on shore at fisticuffs or wrangling with his brother officers," complained Captain John Cassin in June 1813. Neither had Cassin forgotten an earlier incident in which the irritable Graham had stabbed a fellow sailing master with a dirk during a quarrel. Then he had escaped a court martial with an apology and a warning; this time there would be no leniency: Graham was out of the navy. He drowned off Cape Charles on 23 October 1819. Phillips, Fine Art Auctioneers and Appraisers, New York.

notorious offender who had rendered himself generally obnoxious to the group, the peers who composed such courts were reluctant to award the ultimate sanction of dismissal. A commanding officer might go to great effort to bring a seriously deviant member of the corps before a court martial, only to have the court award some sentence such as a verbal reprimand, a punishment that would still leave the corps encumbered with the offending man. In the spring of 1809 John Rodgers requested the secretary of the navy to order a court martial on Sailing Master Joshua Maddox on the grounds that Maddox "is intemperate in his habits and by no means qualified to the rank of a sailing master in the service. Indeed, his example for some time past has rendered him dangerous to the morals of the inexperienced young officers on this station. . . . His general demeanor is such as to render him very exceptionable to the post he now fills, his intemperate habits having completely destroyed the activity, care, and arrangement so very necessary to the first officer of a vessel of war." Yet, when the court martial convened, although no one disputed that Mr. Maddox was a drinking man, neither could it be proved by any of the witnesses that Maddox had been drunk on duty or ever been rendered incapable of performing that duty by reason of overindulgence. The court concluded, "The charge has not been substantiated." Unconvinced, acting secretary of the navy Charles W. Goldsborough dismissed Maddox anyway.[3]

Because midshipmen were the chief class of apprentice officers—the rank at which young men tested the corps and were tested by it—this rank, in absolute numbers, tallies to more than half of all dismissals (Table 43). But if the screening process for promotion from midshipman to a higher rank was this rigorous, why were thirty-one lieutenants dismissed? That number accounts for nearly one dismissal in ten from the ranks of the corps. Closer analysis of the thirty-one shows that eighteen of them were dismissed between 1798 and 1801, that is, during the rapid expansion of the officer corps in the Quasi-War with France, and that twenty-five out of the thirty-one were dismissed between 1798 and 1805. Twenty of the twenty-five entered the navy directly as lieutenants without passing through the apprenticeship of a midshipman's or a sailing master's appointment and had not been subject to the winnowing process that those ranks provided. If dismissed lieutenants who joined the navy directly in that capacity are excluded from consideration, only eleven lieutenants who had attained that rank by way of promotion were expelled between December 1798 and February 1815, an excellent indicator that the navy's process of screening candidates for promotion to lieutenant, and by that route to the higher ranks, was both a rigorous and a practical means of picking those qualified to function effectively and harmoniously as members of the organization.

Sailing masters amounted to nearly one-quarter of all the officers dismissed from the pre-1815 navy. As with the men who received direct appointments as lieutenants during the Quasi-War, sailing masters were recruited from the civilian merchant marine, and they were, typically, older. Habits, good or bad, had been formed and fixed. There was, besides, a natural tendency for men who were less successful members of the merchant marine to seek an alternative career in the navy in greater numbers than those who possessed the qualities that insured success in the commercial service. For all these reasons the corps of sailing masters embraced a high proportion of men who were markedly unsuited for careers as naval officers and who had to be expeditiously restored to civilian status.

What kinds of behavior triggered the decision to dismiss? Three classes of members were identified at the beginning of this chapter that any organization needs to remove from its ranks if it is to remain healthy. In fact, the pre-1815 naval officer corps had few members who fell into the third category: those guilty of serious criminal behavior. Most officers who became subjects for dismissal did so either because they were inadequate to the role they were expected to fill or because their general behavior was so disruptive in a variety of ways that they constituted a liability to the navy. As often as not, several components of deviant behavior can be seen in the same dismissed man.

Here is an unsurpassed example of the latter kind of behavior: "I now beg leave to inform you that the conduct of Mr. Hugh Steel (midshipman) has been so notorious and unofficerlike as to oblige me to order his arrest," Hugh G. Campbell reported from Charleston in February 1811.

> He has long been in the habit of frequenting the lowest description of brothels in this place, taking for his associates the common prostitutes and

sailors, and this in open day to the disgrace of himself and the service. On the 7th instant on board [Gunboat] No. 3, two of the men disputed. In the absence of Mr. [William] Sinclair, Mr. Steel desired them to fight it out. Mr. [John] Chew, midshipman, forbid it and ordered the offender in irons. Mr. Steel ordered him out—without effect. Such, Sir, has been the conduct of Mr. Steel, who stands charged with inebriation, ungentlemanly and unofficerlike conduct.[4]

As with Midshipman Steel, so with the great majority of men who were dismissed from the navy's officer corps. It was not the single misdeed that brought dismissal, but a spectrum of unacceptable behavior that the corps was no longer willing to tolerate. Consequently, the historian simply cannot classify dismissal-inducing behavior as so many cases of alcohol abuse, so many cases of desertion, and this many more cases of fraud, embezzlement, and theft, add them together to get the total number of men dismissed, calculate the percentages, and present the results in a table. It would all be very neat, but human behavior is not that readily broken down into discrete packages for convenient handling. Analysis of components of behavior that led to dismissal will here be explored in an orderly manner, but it is hoped that the ambiguity and complexity of each individual case will be expressed as well.

Crossing the Status Frontier

Even more than the nation it served, the navy of 1794–1815 was a hierarchical and a deferential society. Any action that called into question the essential rightness of these ranked orders and the implicit obedience that subordinate owed to superior was enormously threatening. This was especially true of the gulf that separated officers from enlisted men. The officer who crossed that frontier at the social level did so at his peril.

In all but two of the less than a dozen dismissals in which the crossing of status lines was involved, the offense is associated with other components of behavior unacceptable to the officer corps. Midshipman Thomas Colter is charged with "associating with the common soldiers while on shore in a state of extreme intoxication," as well as sundry other offenses. Accusations of intoxication and disobedience of orders are mingled with the charge that "those persons he has made choice of as associates are young men of extreme dissipated habits and generally of the lower class" and laid against Midshipman James A. Miller. Midshipman John Kreps disappears for six days and is finally found at a house in the suburbs of Charleston, South Carolina, "at cards with a number of very low characters." When a court martial investigates the charge that Midshipman John W.B. Thompson has been drinking and fraternizing with the crew of Gunboat No. 58, it also considers charges of disobedience of orders, intoxication, and cruel and oppressive behavior to a marine. Not only is Midshipman Thomas Riddle charged with disobedience of orders, treating his superior officer with contempt, and mutiny; he is also reported to be guilty of "dancing and drinking with sailors in low houses."[5]

Of the two instances in which the crossing of status lines was the principal offense, the first was routine: Midshipman Edward Atwood of the frigate *Adams* smuggled rum to a pair of enlisted men confined on charges of desertion. Atwood admitted his guilt to a court martial in May 1801 and was promptly dismissed.[6] The other case deserves a closer look. Late in June 1805 a thirty-nine-year-old seaman named Starbuck, who had previously served as a quartermaster with John Barry in *United States*, died on board the frigate *John Adams* on the Mediterranean station. Two facts about Starbuck were not in dispute. First, he was dead. Second, about four weeks before his death he had twice been severely flogged with a rope's end at the order of an angry Lieutenant Archibald K. Kearney, who had told John Dixon, the boatswain's mate giving the actual flogging, "Lay on, or I'll cut your damned guts out." That the flogging had been a vindictive and brutal one no one denied. What was in dispute was the cause of Starbuck's death. To some of his mates who visited him as he lay in his hammock Starbuck said that he was dying of an illness of three or four years' standing, apparently aggravated by a local fever; that he had been sick even before he signed on; but that need had driven him to work. To others he said the flogging was the cause of his dying. Perhaps he knew he would die anyway and saw a chance to be revenged on Lieutenant Kearney in death. In any case Starbuck found a sympathetic ear in a novice midshipman from New York, William Reed, Jr., who, apparently outraged at the brutality he had observed on his first naval cruise, vowed to bring Lieutenant Kearney to justice for Starbuck's death. Older and more prudent heads, such as Dr. Archibald McAllister, told Reed that they, too, recognized the problem of excessive physical punishments by the ship's lieutenants but advised, "You had better let the thing alone." Heeding no counsel, Midshipman Reed persisted in his plan and sent at least two letters to Commodore John Rodgers denouncing Kearney for an "unparalleled piece of cruelty—especially in one of our ships that are so celebrated for their clemency and protection." However, it was not Lieutenant Kearney who found himself facing serious consequences, but rather Midshipman Reed, when the latter was arrested, charged with "writing a malicious and false letter to the commodore," brought before a court martial, found guilty, and sentenced to be dismissed from the navy.[7]

The court transcript provides practically no insight into Reed's motives— Was he an idealistic and disillusioned youth? A troublemaker out to get an authority figure? and little evidence whether he had failed to fit in as a midshipman in other ways. Certain it is that he had egregiously threatened the navy's established structure of deference and control by taking up the cause of an enlisted man against his superior. In each of the cases in which charges of violating the line of status demarcation were advanced to justify an officer's dismissal, the charge was brought against a midshipman. These must have been novices who found themselves ill at ease with the exercise of authority over other men; sensitive adolescents who could not reconcile the democratic ideology—if not the reality—of Jeffersonian America with the rigid stratification of the naval society and the distance that the navy demanded must separate officer and enlisted man.

Cruel and Wanton Punishments

At its most primitive level the existence of this ranked naval society depended at least partially on force, whether it was the casual blows of the boatswain and his mates or the ritualized violence of a formal flogging. For that reason, the handful of officer dismissals in which brutality, oppression, and the abuse of power were at issue deserve special analysis. The striking feature of the dismissals involving such conduct is their tiny number: no more than seven at most. Why were these seven individuals singled out for dismissal?

One of the seven, Lieutenant John Latimer, made the mistake of striking a midshipman, William Giddings. Because midshipmen were, by definition, young gentlemen, any kind of corporal punishment or physical brutality was forbidden by law. When Midshipman Giddings demanded to be treated as the law directed and threatened to report Latimer to his superiors, Latimer swore that Giddings's warrant had no more value than a drumhead. "Do you suppose that piece of newspaper can make you a gentleman?" he taunted, and threatened to knock Giddings overboard if the midshipman did not stop asserting his rights. Lieutenant Latimer stands as an excellent example of the kind of unsuitable individual who had entered the navy on direct appointment as a lieutenant during the Quasi-War with France, a man who had to be removed by one means or another. On 11 May 1801 a court martial sentenced him to dismissal, a punishment readily confirmed by President Jefferson.[8]

Latimer and Andrew McCombe, another Quasi-War lieutenant dismissed on a similar charge, had made the mistake of striking officers.[9] Sailing Master Nathaniel Jennings went out of the navy summarily in 1812 under a complaint most appropriately defined as abuse of power. Aggravated when a civilian in a passing market sloop threw a potato into his gunboat, Jennings "took a loaded musket from the sentinel and took deliberate aim, with intent to *kill*," reported Isaac Chauncey, "and he has the hardihood at this moment to say that he regretted that he had not killed one of them."[10] Two other dismissals involving brutality were those of midshipmen, young men whose conduct made them such clearly unpromising officer material that "cruel and oppressive behavior" was only one among many charges brought against them. With these five dismissals examined and set to one side, that leaves only two officers who were dismissed on the exclusive grounds of brutality to enlisted men: Sailing Master Batran G. Hipkins (1812) and Midshipman John Chew (1814).

Hipkins was charged with "a cruel and wanton manner in punishing his crew, by beating them himself with sticks, etc., instead of the mode authorized by law, when deserving, which course of proceeding has entirely rendered his vessel unserviceable from the frequent desertion of his crew. An example of this cruelty is the situation of the master's mate of that vessel, now under the surgeon's care from a blow given him by the commander with a large stick." Hipkins had been called on the carpet for such behavior more than once by his commanding officer, Hugh G. Campbell, and this time Old Cork's patience was finally exhausted. Even in the Hipkins case it was as much the fact that he was depleting a scarce resource—manpower—as the brutality itself that sent him on his way out of the navy.[11]

John Chew was a midshipman of three and a half years' standing, from Anne Arundel County, Maryland, whose turn it was to command the guard boat attached to the brig *Jefferson* at Sackets Harbor on the evening of 28 June 1814. In the boat that night was a seaman named John Harris who had just come off four weeks on *Jefferson*'s sick list, was slightly tipsy, and did not pull his oar as well as the other men in the boat's crew. Seeing this, Chew struck Harris once—and possibly as many as three times—with the back of his hand:

"You damned son-of-a-bitch, why don't you pull?"

Harris answered that he was pulling as well as he could. He had been sick for four weeks; he did not like being struck for no reason; and he would certainly report Chew to *Jefferson*'s commanding officer, Charles G. Ridgely.

"You damned son-of-a-bitch, I'll give you something to report me for," snarled Chew, who snatched up a cutlass and struck Harris three times with the weapon in the scabbard, then drew the blade and gave Harris an additional dozen blows with scabbard and cutlass alternately. Chew brought the point of the cutlass up to Harris's chest: "You damned French son-of-a-bitch, were it not for the law, I'd run you through the body and throw you overboard. Nothing but the law saves you." His rage still not satisfied by all this violence, Chew soon thereafter ordered the boat to pull inshore, picked up a piece of rope about the size of nine-thread ratline, laid it together, knotted it, and wrapped the end around his hand. Pull off your jacket, Chew told Harris. "What for?" asked the seaman. "You'll report me, will you?" said Chew, punctuating his words with a blow from the knotted rope. "You'll report me to the captain, will you?" Then, when Harris's jacket was off, Chew proceeded to give him thirty blows as hard as he could lay them on, until, as Master Commandant Ridgely later testified, "the back of Harris was as badly beaten as if he had received six dozen with a cat. I have seen six dozen inflicted with less effect."

John Chew had crossed the line into a pathological sadism that even the officer corps' strong stomach could not tolerate. The Marylander was sentenced to dismissal by a court martial. Even in this case there was more behind the dismissal than a single incident of extreme brutality to one enlisted man. Said one of *Jefferson*'s lieutenants of Chew: "I have no opportunity on board a ship to know to what extent of cruelty he might go, for there he is restrained; but I should say he is exceeding irritable and in his general conduct toward the men rude and overbearing in the extreme." Another lieutenant testified to the repeated complaints about Chew, who must have been one of the oldest midshipmen in *Jefferson*, bullying and physically abusing his younger mess-mates.[12]

Because of the diminutive number of dismissals of officers for cruel and oppressive behavior to enlisted men, compared with the numerous well-documented cases of such behavior, the historian is compelled to conclude that this was a type of conduct that the corps was willing either to overlook or to moderate as best it could by such means as informal counsel from senior officers and private reprimands. A reason is not difficult to surmise. The navy's fragile social order, dependent on the deference and the obedience of the many to the few, had for its ultimate sanction harsh physical punishment and brute force. The corps certainly recognized, as it had in the case of Sailing Master Hipkins, that wanton brutality in punishment was excessive behavior that tended to "create an antipathy to naval service," and was, consequently, counterproductive.[13] Equally clearly, the corps was unwilling to allow many prosecutions for such behavior, lest such prosecutions undermine the basis of its own authority.

A Puritanical Navy?

Granted the proverbial promiscuity of those who follow the sea, it is surprising to find officers dismissed for sexual misconduct. But there they stand on the record: at least five dismissals involving such behavior. In only two of the dismissals, however, can sexual misbehavior definitely be proved to have been the primary factor in the dismissal.

The extent of homosexual relations and behavior in the pre-1815 U.S. Navy as well as in the Royal Navy of the same era has been the source of considerable speculation.[14] Such speculation has rested on two grounds: the mass of officers and men were cut off from the possibility of heterosexual relations for long periods of time; and homosexual relations were regarded with extreme abhorrence by the judicial systems of the two navies. Leaving all speculation aside, in the case of the officer corps of the U.S. Navy there is only a single piece of indisputable historical evidence. So far as the record shows, of all the men who left the officer corps unwillingly only one was being disciplined for sodomitic activity. In March 1812 Midshipman John R. Sherwood and Sailing Master Lewis B. Page reported to Stephen Decatur that, as instructed by him, they had examined

> Thomas Williams and Daniel Tylor relative to the attempt of sodomy committed on them by Midshipman William Cutter, when it appeared that Midshipman Cutter made the attempt on Thomas Williams (boy) sometime in the month of November [1811] while on shore, but did not succeed. Daniel Tylor (a Negro boy) stated that sometime in the month of September last that Midshipman Cutter made the attempt on him early in the night in the cabin of [Gunboat No.] 68 and after some time positively succeeded.

Decatur forwarded the Sherwood and Page report to Secretary of the Navy Hamilton with the brief comment that it was "a paper relative to a crime of too detestable a nature to name, committed by Midshipman William Cutter. It appears from all accounts that this monster, as would be expected, is in all respects dishonorable." "Take Midshipman William Cutter's warrant from him," Hamilton replied. "Inform him that his name has been stricken from the roll of navy officers. He does not deserve a trial. His offense is of such a character that I wish not to disgrace the files of the department with a record of it."[15]

One might argue, as does historian Arthur Gilbert, that homosexual activities were widely practiced by naval officers, but that, by common understanding, the convention was to wrap such activity in total silence. Or, the argument might be made that among the resignations and dismissals the causes of which are unknown or are vaguely worded, some were for sodomitic activity. To the first proposition, the reply must be that the outrage expressed by Decatur and Hamilton in the Cutter case—or that shown by Edward Preble in 1803 when Moorish prisoner-of-war officers attempted to sodomize some of *Constitution*'s boys—was too extreme for this form of behavior to have been common or tolerated.[16] As for the second argument, this historian can only respond that in the course of reading all the sources for the history of the pre-1815 navy, sources ranging from the driest of official reports to erotically explicit love letters and together numbering uncounted thousands of pages, this is the sole fully reliable reference, explicit or veiled, to homosexual activity by an officer.*

---

* The only other evidence of homosexual behavior by an officer is suspect—or at least equivocal. On the New Orleans station in November 1813 Philip Philibert, a troublesome acting midshipman against whom Lieutenant Thomas ap Catesby Jones had recently taken disciplinary action, accused Jones of committing an act of sodomy with the cook of Gunboat No. 156 during the night of 28 July. Philibert was arrested; his alleged witnesses were summoned before Lieutenant Louis Alexis on 9 November, whereupon and under oath they all denied any knowledge of the act of sodomy. Philibert was kept under arrest until June 1815, but was restored to duty long enough to take part in the battle of New Orleans and to earn a commendation for his battle conduct from Master Commandant Daniel T. Patterson. Victory secured, Philibert was returned to confinement,

Given the evidence, the only supportable verdict is that homosexual activity by members of the U.S. Navy officer corps, 1794–1815, was almost totally nonexistent.

Heterosexual behavior? It seems as though almost everyone was participating. Documentation is reasonably ample, if one digs into the records. The only surprise is that the occasional officer did find himself facing disciplinary action because of such conduct. In fact, in all the years between 1794 and 1815 only one officer was dismissed solely for heterosexual behavior. The man who holds this dubious distinction was Sailing Master Nathaniel W. Craft, whose story is worth telling in some detail. It begins with a July 1808 letter from John Rodgers to Robert Smith:

> Enclosed is a letter from Sailing Master N.W. Craft, commanding Gunboat No. 47, offering his resignation, which proceeds from a reprimand he received from me for conduct I was compelled to notice, and which in its nature was not only (I conceive) derogatory to the character of a gentleman, but insulting to every sense of delicacy as well as disgraceful even to human nature, and such as—if not discountenanced by the force of severe example—would no doubt be productive of similar acts of low, contemptible dissipation in the young officers on this station, particularly those who are unacquainted with the world and not aware of the disgrace attached to the indulgence of such contemptible, odious habits. The charge I have to allege against Mr. Craft is his having kept a common prostitute on board the gunboat he commands in a manner not only to insure contempt to himself from every individual under his immediate command, but so public as to reach my ears through several citizens.
>
> I am ready to make every reasonable allowance for the capricious follies of human nature; but, putting morality out of the question, there is a certain delicacy which every man of genteel standing in life, whether he be an officer or citizen, is bound by the strongest ties of honor to observe. I am, therefore, compelled by a sense of duty and decorum, however I may dislike the subject, to say that the conduct of Mr. Craft cannot be passed over in silence, more particularly as he appears to be as entirely insensible to everything like self-

---

from whence in mid-April he repeated the accusation of homosexual behavior by Jones—now a badly wounded hero of the New Orleans campaign—to the secretary of the navy. This time Philibert produced sworn depositions by four enlisted men, James Rowlée, Charles Fordham, James Nowlan, and Henry Jackson, recounting in specific and realistic detail homosexual encounters between themselves and Lieutenant Jones. Rowlée claimed that he was alone on board No. 156 with Jones one day in July 1813 when the latter ordered him to go into the powder magazine to overhaul the cylinders. A few moments later Jones followed him there and "immediately took hold of the deponent and attempted to unbutton his pantaloons, but he escaped and went on deck." Jones then ordered Rowlée to the berth deck to take an account of the shot. "Jones pursued him to the berth deck and made another attempt to unbutton his pantaloons. Finding he could not succeed, he unbuttoned his own and ordered the deponent to 'rub him off,' which he refused to do but was told, if he did not, he should receive five dozen lashes. He, the deponent, in consequence of his threats, was obliged to comply and became an instrument of gratifying his unnatural propensities." James Nowlan claimed that Jones forced him "to commit an unnatural crime" (apparently fellatio) at gunpoint on Ship Island in September 1814, as well as two other times when no gun was used to threaten. Secretary of the Navy Benjamin W. Crowninshield, having "duly considered the accusation made by acting midshipman Philip Philibert against Lieutenant Thomas ap Catesby Jones . . . and the evidence produced in support of said accusation, decides that it is malicious and vindictive and destitute of any proof upon which a court martial or any other tribunal could condemn the said Lieutenant Jones; the secretary therefore directs that [Daniel T. Patterson] dismiss acting midshipman Philip Philibert from the U.S. service." Philibert, meanwhile, under the guise of a few days' leave to recruit his health, had departed New Orleans, never to return.[17]

reproach as he is ignorant of the evil consequences which naturally result from bad example.

Smith responded with a private, off-the-record letter to Rodgers:

> The sentiments expressed in your favor . . . cannot but command the approbation of every man who has any pretensions to the character of a gentleman. No man of such low, vulgar dispositions as N.W. Craft has manifested is worthy of a commission of any kind in the Navy of the U. States. And never, with my knowledge and approbation, will any such low fellows be in it. Enclosed you have my official acceptance of his resignation. This is done under an apprehension that, if arrested, he probably could not be broke by the sentence of a court martial. It would be well, if practicable, to make an example of this man by the sentence of a court martial. But, being on the spot and knowing all the circumstances, you can best judge whether the letter accepting his resignation ought to be delivered to him or whether he has committed an offense for which he ought to be arrested. I submit the whole to your discretion, and I will be satisfied with whatever course you may take.

This provoked an equally interesting reply from Commodore Rodgers:

> The lieutenants at present on this station being generally very young . . . I was apprehensive that I should not be able to form a competent court *in such a case as that of Craft's*, it being a subject more proper for the investigation of men of years, of steady habits, and of matured minds than for the more youthful and less considerate; and, under this impression, Sir, I have been induced to prefer the mode you authorized to rid the service of so contemptible a fellow, by accepting his resignation.[18]

What is the historian to make of all this? Was the pre-1815 officer corps really so puritanical? Were such standards of behavior expected and enforced? Scarcely! What makes the Craft incident stand out is that Smith's and Rodgers's reactions to it and the sanction imposed seem incongruent with the reality and the frequent toleration of such behavior. Excellent evidence of this divergence is seen in Rodgers's fear that the young officers of the station, if sitting on Craft in court martial, would not have awarded any significant punishment— certainly not dismissal. True, there were two other cases in which heterosexual misconduct was a factor in an officer's dismissal from the navy, but it was far from the primary cause. Midshipman William Mallam Brooks was a young man whose conduct Hugh G. Campbell had found "frequently reprehensible" during the two and a half years he had been under his command at Charleston and St. Marys, and which behavior Campbell's "frequent admonitions and friendly advice" had not been able to modify for long. "At a time when I thought he was on board his vessel, to my astonishment he was found in a brothel of the lowest order, about the hour of four in the morning, where he had drawn his dirk on a black woman and stabbed her in the body—fortunately not mortal."[19] Sexual misconduct may have been an aggravating circumstance in Midshipman Brooks's subsequent dismissal. But the root cause of it? No. True, also, that a New Orleans station court martial in November–December 1809 found Lieutenant John B. Nicholson guilty of living with a prostitute on board his gunboat and taking her with him on a voyage in violation of the regulation that forbade a ship's commanding officer to carry any woman to sea in his ship without the permission of the Navy Department or of the squadron commodore. A close reading of the court martial transcript suggests that it was Nicholson's other behavior—maliciously harassing Purser Samuel Hambleton and accusing him of fraud in payroll transactions—that produced the court's sentence of dismissal.[20] One strong reason for supposing that the sexual misconduct alone would not have provoked Lieutenant Nicholson's dismissal was that when, only six months later, Midshipmen Thomas C. Magruder and William Peters were tried by courts martial on the same station for living with prostitutes on board their respective commands, the two were merely sentenced to receive reprimands from the president of the court in the presence of their peers.[21]

What light does all this shed on the prevailing standards of sexual morality in the officer corps? Only a confusing one, it is feared. The point that most requires explanation is that the Craft administrative dismissal and the Nicholson, Magruder, and Peters courts martial all took place in the two years between July 1808 and June 1810. There were no known disciplinary actions on the grounds of sexual misconduct before July 1808, and only one between June 1810 and February 1815. In December 1813 Master Commandant James T. Leonard was court martialed for, among other offenses, living openly with his mistress, a Mrs. Williamson of New York City, on the Sackets Harbor station during the winter and spring of 1812–13. The evidence is contradictory whether Mrs. Williamson was a member of the world's oldest profession or whether she

Would you want to be this officer's squadron commodore? Samuel L. Waldo's portrait of James T. Leonard captured the supercilious attitude—or is it a mocking sneer?—that roiled Isaac Chauncey's conventional soul until Leonard's sexual escapades at Sackets Harbor provided the commodore with an excuse for unburdening himself of the by-then unwelcome master commandant. United States Naval Academy Museum, Annapolis, Maryland.

was a married woman who had fallen into an affair with Captain Leonard during her husband's extended absence from the country. Leonard claimed the latter. The Leonard court martial is difficult to assess because of several ambiguous issues involved. Was it living with Mrs. Williamson or was it allowing her to pass as Mrs. Leonard in the social circle at Sackets Harbor that was the more grievous offense? Certain it is that there was a serious personality clash between Leonard and Commodore Isaac Chauncey, and that this conflict had as one of its chief friction points Chauncey's desire to get Mrs. Williamson out of Sackets Harbor on the grounds that "Captain Leonard's conduct in this particular was doing the officers and service an injury." Possibly none of this would have come to any formal disciplinary action had not Leonard's dalliance with Mrs. Williamson ashore led him to negligence in his responsibilities afloat— to sleep not in his ship as directed by Chauncey, but snug-abed with Mrs. Williamson, culminating in the near loss of *Madison* from high winds and drifting ice on the night of 12/13 April 1813, while Leonard was not on board. For his misdeeds the court sentenced Leonard to a public reprimand by the secretary of the navy and suspension for a term of one year.[22] (Leonard's career never recovered. After the War of 1812 he was placed in command of the Whitehall, Vermont, naval station, where his duties consisted of watching the Lake Champlain squadron quietly rot at its moorings and presiding over a handful of misfit officers who, for one reason or another, had to be retained on active duty, but in a place where they could do no real harm to the navy.)

Could one argue that there was a sudden departure from the previously high norms of sexual conduct by some officers about 1808–10, and that the corps moved to reassert its traditional discipline? Improbable. In his defense before his court martial Peters contended that the practice of officers cohabiting with women on board their commands, within U.S. waters, had been winked at until his prosecution, although he gave no clue as to how widespread the practice was or for how long it had been prevalent.[23] There is ample documentation to establish that the navy of 1798–1807 was noteworthy neither for its chastity nor for its continence. If the sudden appearance of these disciplinary actions around 1808 indicated a change in the values of American society toward a more puritanical morality, why were there no additional prosecutions, save for the ambiguous case of Captain Leonard, between mid-1810 and the end of the War of 1812?

No definite answer can be given. In this historian's opinion a wide range of heterosexual activity existed in the pre-1815 navy, and much unconventional behavior was overlooked, tolerated, or even personally savored by the typical commanding officer. The disciplinary prosecutions just described probably occurred when the exceptionally blatant practice of such unconventional behavior came into collision with a commanding officer possessing stricter than usual standards of sexual morality and who was actually prepared to enforce the *Naval Regulations'* prohibitions in these matters. Even then one suspects that the senior officer may have had it in for the subordinate on other, less prosecutable grounds. When all is said and done, there remains no question that in the years immediately surrounding the War of 1812 the values of American society were undergoing some kind of deep change, and that the 1808–10 prosecutions of Craft, Nicholson, Peters, and Magruder are symptoms of that change. It is impossible for this historian to imagine formal disciplinary prosecutions for sexual behavior taking place in the more permissive and ebullient atmosphere of navy and nation during the John Adams or early Thomas Jefferson presidencies.

Exit the Unwanted

ॐ

443

Misconduct More Common

To scrutinize violation of status distinctions or brutality/oppression or sexual misconduct is to examine three components of dismissal-provoking behavior that, however much they say about the pre-1815 navy, appear in but a small proportion of all dismissals. Three additional components of behavior can be identified among the 322 dismissed officers, components that are found with much greater frequency and that bring the historian closer to understanding why men failed to make for themselves successful careers in the corps: desertion, fraud-embezzlement-theft, and alcohol abuse. Of the first but little need be said. The second demands slightly more attention. Alcohol abuse, *the* premier factor in ruined or aborted naval careers, requires close inspection.

Over the Hill

Desertion, an element in at least twenty-six of the dismissals the reasons for which are known, comprehends two related but distinct types of deviant behavior: true desertion in which the officer simply walked away from his duty, never to return, and single or (more usually) repeated absences-without-leave, often combined with other kinds of behavior that wore out the patience of a commanding officer. Each type of misconduct accounts for about half of the twenty-six cases. As with other behavior categories, the horizon between the two kinds of desertion is so indistinct as to prohibit any absolutely precise classification.

The aspect of dismissals for desertion and absence-without-leave that most immediately catches one's attention is that these are offenses overwhelmingly associated with the ranks of midshipman and captain's clerk. Of the twenty-six dismissals in which desertion or absence-without-leave was a factor, twenty-one involved young men who held one of those two ranks. Manifestations of adolescent behavior? A look at the individual cases confirms the suspicion. A midshipman who was guilty of repeated absences-without-leave was usually not trying—at least consciously—to exit the officer corps. Typically, he was the young man who had so much difficulty conforming to naval discipline that he was in trouble in a whole spectrum of ways. Already-mentioned Midshipman James A. Miller, attached to the Charleston station in 1808, may stand for them all. He overstayed shore leave or disappeared without leave on three different occasions. During one of these disappearances another officer reported, "I saw him in the street. The moment he observed me he behaved so much unlike an officer as to run from me." These were far from Miller's only offenses, for his commanding officer could also accuse him of "disobedience of orders; a selection of associates of the most inferior grade; and intoxication."[24]

Instances of out-and-out desertion almost always involved unhappy or misfit midshipmen or captain's clerks who elected to resign with their feet, rather than select some more acceptable way of severing themselves from the navy. Few did it as spectacularly as Midshipman Josiah Shaw of the frigate *John Adams*, then lying in Baltimore harbor. Shaw began by informing his captain in mid-September 1809 that he had recruited two or three seamen for the frigate, and received from the captain $100 to pay the men the usual advance for signing up. The $100 in pocket, Shaw then made the rounds of Baltimore merchants, purchasing to the tune of about $200 from those who would give him credit. Finally, he stopped by a livery stable, said that he had a dinner invitation a few miles out in the country, hired a horse for the ostensible purpose of going there, and headed up the road toward Frederick, Maryland— pausing only long enough somewhere en route to deposit a letter of resignation in the post office—never to be seen again. Shaw's captain, Samuel Evans, sent another officer in pursuit of the disappearing midshipman, but it took twenty-four hours to determine the direction in which Shaw had fled; after pursuing him nearly twenty-eight miles up the road, the huntsman abandoned the chase as hopeless: Shaw had too great a lead ever to be overtaken.[25]

What sort of life awaited young fugitives from the navy? Not promising, if one can extrapolate from the one runaway whose postdesertion career can be tracked for a few months. Midshipman Pearson Shute, of New Bern, North Carolina, absconded from Gunboat No. 146 in October 1812 and entered on board the privateer *Snapdragon*; was turned out of her at some European port as a drunkard; made his way to Lisbon; and from thence skulked home to North Carolina in a merchant ship. As he came ashore his former commanding officer was waiting for him with an offer: resign or be arrested and court martialed. A wise Pearson Shute chose the former and vanishes from the records.[26]

Other People's Property, Other People's Money

The flight of Midshipman Josiah Shaw has already introduced the second component of behavior that led to a substantial number of dismissals: fraud, embezzlement, and theft. It was the sole cause, or a contributing cause, in at least twenty-nine of the dismissals the reasons for which are known, making it the second most common component of dismissal-provoking behavior. Fraud, embezzlement, and theft were, as was desertion, behavior associated preeminently with midshipmen. Of the twenty-nine dismissals in which these crimes were a factor, twenty-one of the dismissed officers were midshipmen, three were sailing masters, and two were chaplains; a surgeon, a surgeon's mate, and a lieutenant account for the balance.

Those lurid terms—*fraud, embezzlement,* and *theft*—cast a dramatic glow on a type of behavior that was, in the vast majority of the cases, prosaic and monotonously similar: the purchase, on credit derived from one's status as an officer in the U.S. Navy, of goods or services for which the officer either had no intention of paying or subsequently found himself unable to pay. Isaac Hull reported from Boston in the spring of 1810 regarding Surgeon's Mate Joseph Trevett that "soon after the Chesapeake was laid up in ordinary and the doctor furloughed . . . he took a house in Charlestown near the ship at a high rent and furnished it on a credit; which credit he obtained by telling the man that owned the house that he was surgeon of the ship and that his pay would be adequate to all his expenses. This story he had told to his baker, butcher, etc., indeed to every person that he wished a credit from, and has, in some instances, taken up goods on credit and sold them immediately at auction for cash to pay his first creditors who were pushing him hard for cash. The moment I discovered this species of swindling I sent for him and gave him his choice: either to send me his warrant immediately to be forwarded to the department or take his chance of a court martial." To Hull's relief Trevett chose resignation, for the captain feared the doctor "would make his escape, taking his warrant with him; and, by having it, practice the same manner of swindling in whatever place he might visit, by making people believe he was still in the service by producing his warrant as proof."[27] Nor was Hull's fear by any means unrealistic: six years after Midshipman Philip Moses had been dismissed for fraudulently obtaining money to which he was not entitled, Moses was still roaming the hinterland surrounding New York City, running up inn bills on the strength of his old warrant, which he had managed to retain, and absconding without paying them.[28]

Story could be added to story. The historian could tell of Midshipman Jesse V. Lewis of Virginia, who managed in 1800 and 1801 to collect varying sums of money from three different navy agents in New England ports on the basis of his plausible appearance, his claim that he was related to Secretary of State John Marshall, and his sad story of illness and wanting to get home to Virginia. Armed with a single statement of his account from the purser of his last duty assignment, Lewis extracted money from each of the agents successively until his deceptions caught up with him and he found himself snugly lodged in the Boston jail.[29] Though the details might vary, the stories would be in essence repetitive. More interesting is the question, Why was this type of behavior the second most common of all those likely to be cited as an occasion for dismissal?

The sums involved were relatively small: a gold watch worth $24; a uniform coat of "superfine blue cloth" priced at $37; a month's lodging at a boarding-house. What one is seeing here is certainly not the age-old human fascination with the one big bonanza that could make a man financially independent for life—or at least for several years. These small-time frauds and embezzlements were the crimes of a society in which even high-status members of its middle class were chronically short of cash. They are most especially the crimes toward which members of the midshipmen's mess would be tempted, because pay at that rank was inadequate to cover the style of dress, of dining, and of entertainment to which its members usually aspired. Pressure from peers could create debts far beyond a midshipman's ability to cover. Temptation to defraud can only have been increased by realization that transfer to a duty station in a distant part of the nation would make it difficult, if not impossible, for the defrauded creditor ever to catch up with the absconding debtor.[30]

Three dismissals were for fraud of an entirely different sort: the use of falsified credentials to secure appointments in the navy. Nathaniel Ruggles Smith of Roxbury, Massachusetts, was a Dartmouth graduate, class of 1808, who may have studied divinity for a while, but who had never been ordained. Smith—or perhaps it was someone claiming to be Smith—appeared at Paul Hamilton's office on the morning of 11 September 1811, introduced himself as the Reverend Nathaniel R. Smith, and presented Hamilton with a sealed letter addressed to President James Madison. Smith explained that the letter recommended him for appointment as a chaplain in the navy; that he had been waiting three weeks to deliver it personally to the president; but that Madison was absent at his country home in Orange County, Virginia, and that it was uncertain when he would return to Washington. Hamilton sensed that Smith was uneasy about waiting longer for the president to return, although that uneasiness failed to arouse his suspicions, and he allowed Smith to pressure him into opening the letter on the grounds that it related solely to the chaplain's appointment. A glance confirmed that Smith was correct as to the letter's message, but Hamilton was immediately seized with a paroxysm of guilt for having violated etiquette by opening a letter addressed to the president. Guilt at once translated itself into a letter of abject apology, but one that also ended, "I have assured Mr. Smith of the success of his application, for he appears to be an interesting man; and we need men of his description as chaplains in our navy, of which grade of officers we now have only three." Waiting not for a reply from the president, Hamilton the next day appointed Smith chaplain of the frigate *Congress*, then escorted him to the Washington navy yard and introduced him all around in a highly flattering manner. Chaplain Smith's tenure was less than one month. On 9 October the scales were struck from Hamilton's eyes when he learned—how is unknown, perhaps from President Madison himself—that Smith's glowing letter of recommendation was a forgery prepared by none other than Nathaniel R. Smith.

This debacle, one of the earliest evidences of that earnest gullibility as an administrator that would contribute to Hamilton's dismissal from office fifteen months later, apparently did no irreparable harm to Smith's career. For a number of years he worked his way gradually westward, teaching school and writing incessantly for local newspapers, until he again surfaced at Pittsburgh in 1823. He stayed there till 1840, still teaching, writing unpublished plays, editing one newspaper and publishing another, and issuing a speller and grammar, *The First Productive Spelling Book* (1834), designed for teaching English to foreigners. In 1840 Nathaniel Smith resumed his westward wanderings, which finally came to an end on the banks of the Des Moines River in Farmington, Iowa, where he was known as *Professor* Smith, and where he died on 15 September 1859.[31]

36. Foremost of Crimes

$\mathcal{B}$RUTALITY AND THE oppression of subordinates. Crossing the frontiers of status demarcation. Sexual misconduct. Desertion. Fraud, embezzlement, and theft. Any of these could abort an officer's career. They shrink away almost to insignificance in the light of the one component of deviant behavior that contributed to three times as many dismissals as either desertion or fraud-embezzlement-theft, and that precipitated more than ten times as many dismissals as brutality and oppression. It was a type of deviant behavior both widespread and openly practiced. At the same time it was the object of the corps' strongest taboo. It was, of course, alcohol abuse.

Among the dismissals the causes of which are known, slightly more than one-third involved alcohol abuse as the primary or, in a few cases, the secondary factor. Unlike desertion and fraud-embezzlement-theft, alcohol abuse was not the near-exclusive domain of that novice officer, the midshipman. The ranks of those men dismissed for alcohol abuse closely parallel the ranks of men dismissed for all causes (Table 44). No charge of alcohol abuse contributed to the dismissal of an officer occupying one of the two top grades; the proportion of lieutenants dismissed for alcohol abuse was less than that rank's share of the officer corps. The historian can only view these facts as evidence that the rigorous selection system at the top of the promotion ladder effectively excluded men with such self-destructive tendencies. This supposition is reinforced by the discovery that, so far as the record shows, only one man who had attained the rank of captain by 1815, Joseph Bainbridge, was denied responsible commands in his later career because of suspected alcoholism.[1] Sailing masters were among the most-dismissed officers for alcohol abuse for the same reasons that they were prominent in the ranks of those dismissed for all causes: they were older and they were untested when they entered the navy from civilian life. The master mariner whose bottle was his too constant companion would be one of the last to be hired by merchant owners when commands were scarce, and one of the first to turn to the navy's sailing master berth as an alternative means of earning a living. The absence of captain's clerks from the list of alcohol abusers should not be taken as an indication that these young men were more sober than their midshipman messmates, who make up more than half of those dismissed for alcohol abuse. The bibulous clerk was simply discharged by his captain without any reason for that discharge being reported to the Navy Office.

Who, typically, were these alcohol abusers?

Surgeon's Mate William Steel of *Wasp* was a 1792 graduate of Dickinson College from Carlisle, Pennsylvania. Steel's captain transmitted the doctor's August 1808 resignation with a report that "he was found intoxicated in my cabin during my absence on shore. He got so in company with one of my servants. It is a practice he has long been addicted to, and did (not long since) in a fit of insanity commit violence to himself by stabbing his body with a knife in several places."

Purser Abraham Cordrey's habit of alcohol dependence has "lately grown upon him to that degree that he could not go on shore upon business without getting drunk and making himself a subject of ridicule to everyone who saw him. I have," wrote Lieutenant Nathaniel Fanning, commander of Gunboat No. 1, in August 1805, "taken several occasions to talk to him privately on the score of his getting so often intoxicated. At one time particularly (I believe about a fortnight ago) I then told him that, if he did not reform, I should certainly report him to you without delay. He at the time appeared penitent, and promised reformation, and even shed tears. Nay, so far has he acted to the contrary that he was even detected a few days ago hiding a junk bottle of rum (such as is dealt out to the people) by one of his brother officers in the room which they occupy."

Sailing Master John Allen was attached to the Mediterranean squadron and his command lying at Gibraltar when, reported Hugh G. Campbell, "between nine and ten o'clock on the night preceding his arrest, I called on board the Ranger—not without strong suspicion of his improper conduct—where I found Mr. Allen in his bed, dressed in full uniform, and in such a state of intoxication that he neither knew me, nor recollected where to have seen me, nor could he be persuaded to rise from his bed."

Lieutenant John Rowe, of Portland, Maine, described by Edward Preble in happier times as a "promising young man" and "a very brave officer," had, by the summer of 1808, "been extremely intemperate for a long time past, indeed, even so much so as to produce insanity. Consequently," wrote John Rodgers, "I can no longer entrust him with the command of a gunboat. The vile habit of drinking to excess has been growing on this young man, I understand, for these four or five years past. . . . [He] is certainly a fitter subject for an insane hospital than for the situation he at present occupies."

"Wednesday evening, at the theater, I heard a loud, violent, and abusive altercation between two men, in one of whom I recognized [Midshipman Robert] Hill of the Revenge and the other proclaimed himself the acting boatswain of the Syren. Oaths and threats of personal chastisement were mutually abusive," reported Midshipman Henry S. Newcomb to John Rodgers in the fall of 1809. "From this disgraceful scene I forcibly led [Hill] amid a multitude of people who had flocked from the boxes to witness it. I soon after left the theater, and on my return I cannot express my astonishment at seeing Mr. Hill in a full dress coat in the lobby, half sitting, half lying, in open view of all coming from the boxes, sound asleep and stupidly drunk." In urging the acceptance of Hill's resignation Rodgers added of Hill that, "although not more than twenty or twenty-one years of age, he has been reported to me, by those acquainted with his habits, as being a confirmed sot, past all hopes of reformation."

William B. Maxwell, a newly appointed midshipman from Savannah, Georgia, "running on in the most extravagant manner and apparently the object of ridicule," was "the first object that presented itself to my view" when his commanding officer, Midshipman Jesse Wilkinson, stepped into Charleston's Merchants' Hotel on the evening of 8 May 1809. Called on the carpet by Wilkinson the next morning, Maxwell showed no signs of penitence. "I care not for you. I am as good a man as you are; and, by God, Sir, if you'll waive the authority which you now hold over me, I'll fight you. I love drink, and without it I am unhappy. I will, therefore, seek that relief whenever I think proper."[2]

Was habitual overindulgence in alcohol an offense so heinous that its discovery automatically disqualified the offender for membership in the officer corps and led to his immediate expulsion? Did the navy dismiss three times as many officers for alcohol abuse as for any other form of deviant behavior because the extreme seriousness of the offense made it one neither to be overlooked nor condoned? Taking the naval leadership's official statements at face value, one might certainly suppose such was the case. In the eyes of Benjamin Stoddert "drunkenness amounts to a disqualification for an office of responsibility [or] any kind of confidence in the public service." A decade later Paul Hamilton said, "Drunkenness is the foremost of crimes in an officer on board ship. It cannot be too severely punished when habitual, and it is difficult to tolerate it when only casual." In a War of 1812 court martial that found the accused guilty of frequent intoxication "the court would pointedly express its abhorrence of a vice destructive of morals, ruinous to the individual, and disgraceful to the public service, and sentences the prisoner to be cashiered with a perpetual incapacity to serve in the Navy of the United States."[3] In reality, the inflamed rhetoric reveals the pervasiveness and the intractability of the problem, for the overwhelming weight of evidence demonstrates that both occasional and habitual alcohol abuse were widespread, if not epidemic, in the navy; that the hegemony of alcohol-abuse dismissals over dismissals for other forms of misconduct measured the real prevalence of this one form of deviant behavior; and that official condemnations of the practice by secretaries of the navy and senior officers evince genuine alarm at the omnipresence of alcohol abuse.

Consequently, there is every reason to think that the eighty-eight dismissals in which alcohol abuse was a factor hardly define the limits of overindulgence in a corps of more than twenty-nine hundred officers. There is no way to measure quantitatively the extent of the alcohol abuse that did not lead to dismissal; but the evidence, though only suggestive, carries strong conviction. Lieutenant John Pettigrew is passed over for promotion to master commandant because he "has been represented as intemperate," but remains a member of the corps until his death by drowning in the oversetting of the schooner *Quaker* in March 1820. Sailing Master John Carson is "apt when on shore to drink more than [is] of service to him" and to disappear for days at a time, but is sober and "an excellent seaman" when on duty. Lieutenant Augustus Conkling, commanding officer of *Tigress* at Perry's victory on Lake Erie, is later remembered by a comrade as "an elegant officer in appearance, but too convivial even for the navy." He does not resign until 1820. At the 1800 court martial of Dr.

John Brewster's 1796 oil portrait of forty-year-old Isaac Collins makes the Quasi-War lieutenant appear stern and resolute. In reality, he was a man hiding a secret: alcohol addiction. This Revolutionary War veteran of land and sea service may have sought his 1799 naval commission because rumors of his problem were making it difficult for him to obtain commands in the merchant service; for certain he was entangled in significant financial difficulties to which the addiction may have contributed. Lieutenant Collins was attached to Constitution, *where several of his wardroom messmates, including the first lieutenant, Isaac Hull, were conscious of his problem; but they sheltered Captain Silas Talbot from the knowledge out of fear of Collins's formidable temper.*

His naval career destroyed itself at a state dinner in Haiti in July 1800. Talbot had barely sat down when "Lieutenant Collins began to expose [his already intoxicated con-

Amos Windship, which court found the medical man not guilty of the charge of being a confirmed drunkard, a witness is asked, "Did you ever see Doctor Windship disguised with liquor?" "I never did see him so much so, but that he was capable of doing his duty," is the reply. "He is a man who drinks, and can bear, a large quantity of liquor." When Dr. Windship attempts to defend himself by asking another witness on cross-examination, "Did I make a practice of drinking more than other officers?" he hears the witness respond, "Yes, Doctor Windship, I presume you did drink more."[4]

Fears of the navy's leaders were justified. Alcohol abuse was corroding the corps. Even if that body's essential effectiveness had not been absolutely compromised by this abuse, drink was exacting a heavy toll, both in attrition and in loss of reliability among serving officers. Why? And, why alcohol? Apart from occasionally attributing the downfall of this or that particular officer to the bad example of others, so far as this historian is aware, no secretary of the navy or senior officer ever offered his opinion as to why alcohol abuse was the most serious disciplinary problem of the pre-1815 officer corps. Consequently, one is forced back upon speculation, based on what is known about conditions in the navy and in American society.[5]

First of all, there were simply a lot of intoxicants in the normal naval environment. Until the beginning of the nineteenth century, no one seriously questioned that they ought to be there. Every person in the navy was entitled by law to receive a half-pint of distilled spirits, usually rye whiskey, day in and *dition] by much foolish and rude conversation and kept constantly filling his tumbler with wine and water and very soon began to drink whole tumblers of clear wine, keeping the wine bottle in [one] hand and the tumbler in the other; and he once fell partly out of his seat and would have tumbled on the floor if the adjutant general to the commander-in-chief had not took hold of him and prevented his fall.*" The captain attempted to have two of Constitution's officers ease Collins out of the room, but the fully intoxicated lieutenant refused and began behaving in an even more embarrassing manner. Talbot, "*mortified beyond description,*" told a senior lieutenant and Constitution's captain of marines to get Collins back on board ship as soon as the dinner broke up, but this proved an impossible assignment. "*After they got him into the street,*" said Talbot later, "*he could not walk without tumbling into the gutters, as he did frequently; that he frequently called Lieutenant Hamilton 'a damned Scotch bugger' and threatened to put his dirk into Captain Carmick . . . ; that he ran into the houses as he came along the street and abused the ladies and gentlemen and damaging their goods, demanding, at the same time, some brandy.*" Carmick and Hamilton finally maneuvered Collins as far as a sailors' coffeehouse, where they abandoned him. He spent the entire next day drinking slings at a tavern, literally fell into Constitution's shore boat that evening, then dropped off into alcohol-induced slumber in his berth in full uniform, but started in on grog the morning after and kept at it till well past dark. Before dawn of the fourth day Collins was vomiting and convulsed by stomach cramps, but the day after that he was sober enough to attempt an apology to Captain Talbot, blaming the whole problem on his failure to eat breakfast the day of the state dinner.

 Collins's was truly a pitiful case. Talbot gave him a choice of resigning his commission or being placed under arrest. The lieutenant chose arrest, probably thinking that he could persuade Talbot to withdraw it later. Whatever chance this ploy had of success was destroyed when, three days after his apology, Collins was once more so intoxicated he could not rise from his berth. Realizing finally that resignation was the only way to avoid a public court martial, Collins turned in his commission. Massachusetts Historical Society, Boston.

day out as part of his official ration; in 1806, when the authorized naval establishment was about sixteen hundred men, the navy dispensed about forty-five thousand gallons of spirits annually.[6] Before Edward Preble sailed for the Mediterranean in the summer of 1803, with Consul General Tobias Lear as his cabin guest, he laid in a half-pipe and six demijohns of ordinary madeira, twenty dozen bottles of high-quality madeira, ten dozen bottles of old port, four cases of claret, two barrels of strong beer, six hogsheads of London porter, eight gallons of old cognac, two cases of geneva, a case of cherry brandy, and ten dozen bottles of cider, as well as smaller quantities of more esoteric liquors for cabin hospitality stores. Preble's total liquor bill came to $793.50—roughly the annual compensation of a lieutenant commanding one of the small ships in his squadron—but he was almost certainly able to obtain reimbursement from the government as part of the contingent expenses of his command.[7]

 In wardroom and steerage, which took the captain's wine list as a model to be emulated as far as thinner purses and lack of ability to pass the bill along to the government permitted, the liquor supply had a very practical purpose. More often than not, it was the best part of the meal and made the rest bearable. Every officer was expected to draw at least one ration per day from the purser's stores. Even if the steward picked out the better-quality stores for the officers, what they got was still the basic weekly diet served out to the enlisted men: three and a half pounds of beef, three pounds of pork, one pound of flour, half a pound of suet, ninety-eight ounces of bread, six ounces of cheese, two ounces of butter, a pint of peas, a pint of rice, half a pint of molasses, half a pint of vinegar—plus, of course, the three and a half pints of rye whiskey.[8] To be sure, the members of the officers' messes used part of their pay and such personal income as they may have had to lay in ample supplies of private stores to supplement or replace the official ration. Even so, after four or five weeks at sea the best public or private stores got old, rancid, moldy, rotten, or merely monotonous. The supply of live animals with which the officers began the voyage ran out. It was only when a ship was in port or had recently left port that mealtime could be anticipated as any kind of culinary treat. One anticipation could relieve this dreary prospect: uncorking a bottle of good wine. The ship's bread might be indistinguishable from a five-pound shot. The beef might prove rotten, stinking, and unfit for human consumption when the cask was broached. But it was just about impossible to spoil a bottle of madeira. It stood heat. It stood cold. It stood jiggling about in a steward's locker for weeks on end. When the mess waiter pulled the cork, it tasted just as good as an officer thought it should. Maybe even better.

Then, too, life in a frigate or a brig on the high seas or in a gunboat patrolling coastal waters involved a heavy component of physical discomfort. One was hot. One was cold. One could be wet. If one was not actually wet, one got out of damp blankets to put on clammy clothes. All hands, with the possible exception of the captain, had too little personal space. The ship pitched and rolled. Add to these the terrible pressure of responsibility. A mistake by the watch officer could earn him a severe dressing down and relief from duty by the captain. Or it could send him and all his shipmates to eternity. Severe stress existed side by side with the waiting, the sameness, the boredom that are eternally a part of military life. To every one of these conditions alcohol and fellowship with one's messmates were sure palliatives.

When one's companions were all drinking, it was the easier to cross the line from relaxation to intoxication. That there existed a strong element of adolescent peer pressure toward overindulgence is not to be doubted. "Spirituous liquors I scarcely ever drink," Midshipman Charles G. Ridgely told his squadron commodore after too many wines and cordials had reduced him to an admitted state of complete inebriety, "have been intoxicated but seldom during my life, and then being in a party of young men where I was necessitated."[9] Exacerbating this peer pressure was the unavoidable practice of mixing in the midshipmen's mess fifteen- and sixteen-year-olds, and some younger, with midshipmen in their early twenties. "He unfortunately drinks hard," said Stephen Decatur of one notoriously bibulous midshipman whom he wished out of *Chesapeake*, "and I fear, should he be continued on board this ship, his example will be injurious to the younger midshipmen."[10]

If there were reasons peculiar to the naval service that made it a hothouse for the potential alcoholic, let it also be noted that the officer corps was experiencing alcohol abuse as its most threatening disciplinary problem at a time when an epidemic of excessive consumption was sweeping through American society. Between 1790 and 1830 Americans drank more alcoholic beverages than at any other time in their history. During the 140 years from 1845 until 1985, the annual per capita consumption of alcohol for each person aged fifteen or older in the population fluctuated between 1.5 and 2.8 gallons. With this may be contrasted the corresponding figures for the years in which the U.S. Navy's officer corps came into being:

Year	Gallons of alcohol
1795	6.2
1800	6.6
1805	6.8
1810	7.1
1815	6.8

Obviously, not every person ingested his or her six or seven gallons. Rather, the most thorough scholar on the subject has estimated that half of the adult males—one-eighth of the country's total population—were drinking two-thirds of all the hard liquor (distilled spirits) that was being consumed in the United States. This national orgy of overindulgence had several roots. Surplus grain crops, most easily transported and sold as whiskey, made liquor cheap and abundant. It was during these years that Secretary of the Navy Robert Smith switched from imported rum to native rye whiskey as the alcohol component in the navy's grog ration, thereby insuring that the beverage would be dubbed Bob Smith by the sailors.[11] By contrast, water fit to drink was not always easy to come by, on land or at sea, while many of the monotonous, fried foods Americans ate were far more palatable when washed down with cider, wine, or whiskey. Most persons regarded the consumption of alcohol as making a positive contribution to health. Patronizing infant U.S. distilleries was a laudable (and pleasurable) act of patriotic nationalism, one that promoted the young republic's economic self-sufficiency. Perhaps most important, both the superficial and the deep changes that took place throughout U.S. society in the years on either side of 1815 appear to have been producing a high level of anxiety among affected Americans, anxieties that they attempted to manage through the relief afforded by alcohol.

Alcohol addiction, once formed in an officer, was unbreakable, at least so long as the officer remained in the navy. There is not a single known case of a pre-1815 officer who was able to dispel the habit permanently *once it had become firmly established*. William Sim, the hard-drinking midshipman whom Stephen Decatur wanted out of *Chesapeake* before he corrupted his messmates, eventually appeared on the New Orleans station, where David Porter noted that he was on his good behavior and predicted, in the summer of 1808, "I have no doubt of being able not only to reform him, but to render him a deserving officer." The optimism proved unjustified, and fifteen months later Porter found himself recommending the midshipman's dismissal from the service with the note, "The late conduct of Mr. Sim has been beyond bearing. . . . Since he has been under my command I have used every means in my power to reclaim him; but, finding my exertions fruitless, I now give up all hope of making him an officer." Once returned to civilian life in Prince Georges County, Maryland, Sim apparently had no difficulty staying away from the bottle, so much so that, two years after his December 1809 dismissal, Sim's congressman, Joseph Kent, urged his reinstatement as midshipman: "The deportment of Mr. Sim, so far as it has come within my knowledge or that of my neighbors, has been correct and gentlemanly and calculated to invalidate any charge of intemperance or irregularity that may have been made against him at the Navy Department." Paul Hamilton consented to Sim's reappointment in December 1811. For six months or a year all went well enough. The midshipman's conduct, reported an observer from the Norfolk station to Accountant Thomas Turner, an old friend of the Sim family, "had been as correct as that which could be expected from young men governed by so *loose* a discipline as the best that is practicable on board so small vessels of war as gunboats. At *best* it can be but a bad *school* for young men, [for] nothing short of the discipline of a frigate can promise success to the exertions of a young man in his attempt to acquire naval knowledge effectually." If this hedging report stirred any uneasiness in Turner's mind, that uneasiness was fully justified eighteen months later when Sim's commanding officer enclosed the midshipman's resignation to the secretary of the navy with the note, "If brought to trial, [he] would have been broken for repeated drunkenness and neglect of duty; and permit me to say he is a disgrace to the service. I have repeatedly given him good advice, but all to no effect."[12] This time there would be no reappointment for William Sim.

Only a single example of the advice older officers gave their younger subordinates with drinking problems appears to have survived. Late in 1814 Thomas Macdonough learned that Midshipman John T. Drury had become deeply depressed and was drinking heavily to combat his melancholia. "Now let me advise you in the most earnest and strong manner to refrain from such a mode of quieting or alleviating your feelings," wrote Macdonough in a long letter. "Your own good sense will, I trust and sincerely hope, point out the fallacy of such a remedy. It will be momentary, and returning to the same thing again [will] be the sure and natural consequence, which will ultimately terminate in destruction and misery to yourself and be to your family an everlasting sting of bitter pain and regret. No, my dear Sir, you would do extremely wrong even to indulge at all in this deceiving and destroying substitute to exterminate any affection of the mind. Believe me, it leads to ruin, certain ruin." Macdonough urged Drury to turn instead to the inner strength he would find in sincere religious faith to combat his tendency to brood upon a past event about which he could now do nothing.[13] The strong religious tone in this letter of admonition was surely atypical of the advice usually given, for Macdonough possessed intense spiritual convictions not shared by most of his fellow captains, whose commitments to religion were typically formal and perfunctory.

Whether, over the long time span, Macdonough's intervention and advice would have been effective in diverting Midshipman Drury from the road to alcohol addiction can never be known: he disappeared at sea in the brig *Epervier* late the following summer. If Drury had been saved, it would only have been because his overindulgence was of recent origin and not yet serious. With those for whom the dependence was of longer duration and the habit more deeply imbedded, hopes of effective reform were contingent on the victim's practice of future self-control. The medical or the psychological ability to reach the root causes of the victim's inner drive toward alcoholic relief and to provide appropriate support was lacking. Hope for cure or change was almost always illusory.

John Shattuck was thirteen years old when appointed a midshipman late in 1799, established a highly favorable reputation with his early commanding officers, and was in due course promoted to lieutenant early in 1807. March 1809 found him commanding one of two gunboats stationed in the waters around Passamaquoddy, Maine, when acting secretary of the navy Charles W. Goldsborough received a private letter, apparently from Boston navy agent Francis Johonnot, asserting that Shattuck "is perpetually in a state of intoxica-

When Rembrandt Peale painted national naval hero Jacob Jones during the War of 1812, the artist's image of the victor in the Wasp-Frolic *battle captured perfectly Commodore Alexander Murray's five-word 1806 fitness report on the then-lieutenant Jones: "a good officer but unaccommodating." Hidden to Murray's eye as well as to Peale's was another side of Jacob Jones: the former physician who worked to rescue subordinates from alcohol addiction. If only history could tell more about Jones's methods and his successes! The one officer from this period known to have overcome a recent habit of alcohol abuse started his reformation under Jones. William Knight, a veteran sailing master, was put on the beach from* President *by William Bainbridge in November 1809 because excessive drinking had completely destroyed the latter's confidence in him. Jones then took him in the smaller* Argus *as master. By the following April the sympathetic master commandant could report of Knight, "He has certainly been addicted to drinking to excess, but," he added significantly, "it has not been for any length of time; therefore, I hope he has got free of the vice." So far as is known, Knight experienced no further problems with alcohol during a naval career that continued until his death, aged fifty-nine, in July 1834.* New-York Historical Society.

tion, insomuch that he keeps [to] his bed for a fortnight from inability to get up." Goldsborough asked John Rodgers to investigate and eventually learned, from the remote reaches of Maine, that it was all too true; in fact, the twenty-two-year-old Shattuck's addiction was so serious that he was suffering from delirium tremens.

The new secretary, Paul Hamilton, was ready to dismiss Shattuck forthwith and even had a letter of dismissal prepared; but several influential Bostonians persuaded him to give Shattuck a furlough to make a merchant voyage, during which the lieutenant was to demonstrate his determination to reform. In convincing Hamilton to adopt this plan Shattuck's friends argued that the lieutenant's father was dead; that he had entered the navy quite young; that he had been almost constantly at sea and away from the protection and guidance of older relatives; and, of course, that the habit of indulging to the point of inebriation had been formed when drinking "with his young friends." Sometime in early summer 1809 John Shattuck set off on his merchant voyage to Mediterranean waters, solemnly pledging his relatives "that it shall never be possible to repeat the charges against him." There cannot be a doubt that Lieutenant Shattuck sincerely wanted to give up the bottle, or that friends and relatives were willing to do anything in their power to help him; but it required a more effective program of support and treatment than was available in the United States of 1809 to bring alcohol addiction under control and return the victim to a productive life. Exhortations to avoid ruin, a determination to use one's willpower, and a voyage in a merchant ship where monotony and liquor were both available in abundance surely would not do the job. Undoubtedly some few persons of heroic inner resources could and did extricate themselves from the entanglements of alcohol addiction by intense self-discipline. No such hero is known among the pre-1815 navy's alcoholics; John Shattuck was not the exception. He returned in February 1810 from his merchant voyage as addicted as he had left the previous summer, and his relatives sadly advised Paul Hamilton that the latter had better reactivate Shattuck's dismissal. They did not yet wholly despair of reforming him, though it would be not as a naval officer, but in a less "conspicuous situation," one "where he could not be known."[14]

What sort of fate awaited a young man such as Shattuck with a confirmed alcohol addiction? Not a pretty one, if the story of Samuel Naylor is a true indication. One of the first dozen lieutenants appointed in the Quasi-War naval expansion in May 1798, Naylor served in *Ganges* till 3 December of that same year. Then he resigned, but left no explanation on the surviving record. The brevity of Naylor's service and the precipitateness of his departure raise the suspicion that an alcohol dependency had come to light and that Naylor had decided resignation was to be preferred over dismissal. Nine and a half years later the unidentified body of a derelict was found in or near Baltimore and hastily interred in that city's potter's field. Only later did the authorities discover that the mystery corpse was that of Samuel Naylor, "formerly a lieutenant in the U.S. Navy," and arrange to have the remains moved to the English Episcopal burying ground, so that Naylor might at least in death regain the status he had forfeited to alcohol in life.[15]

Alcohol abuse of seemingly epidemic dynamics in the officer corps. Universal inability either to arrest or to cure the disease once it took a firm hold on its victim. No wonder there was deep alarm among the naval leadership, alarm reflected in the rhetoric with which the leadership denounced alcohol excess. Such fears must certainly have been heightened by the realization that the rot of alcohol addiction affected not just the navy but the whole of American society. Many midshipmen and sailing masters, dismissed for alcohol abuse after just a few months in the navy, had been confirmed drinkers before they ever donned an officer's uniform. Worse yet, it was a problem the pre-1815 navy could not and did not resolve. So threatening had even the suggestion of alcoholic excess become to the navy's leadership that the historian occasionally suspects ship and station commanders who wished to rid themselves of officers troublesome on other grounds were tempted to, and did, label the officer who occasionally overindulged a drunkard in the hope that this charge would bring him down if others did not. So taboo had alcohol abuse become in the eyes of those who made the navy's personnel decisions that, when Sailing Master Robert Cutchin was dismissed in November 1813 on charges of alcoholism brought against him by Hugh G. Campbell, he (unsuccessfully) sought reinstatement by bringing forward documentary proof that he was not an alcoholic, but a confirmed opium user![16]

37. Wild Youth

THINKING OF THE corps of dismissed officers as a number of separate squads—a large group of alcoholics going to ruin at the center of the historian's attention, flanked by smaller but still numerically respectable squads of embezzlers and deserters, with little cadres of sadists, status violators, and sexual offenders almost overlooked because of their small numbers—may cause one to miss a thread that unites many of them. The pre-1815 U.S. social order seems to have embraced a sizable corps of middle-class and upper-middle-class adolescents and postadolescents whose alcohol abuse and embezzling and fighting and destructiveness were manifestations of an inability to fit in comfortably with that established social order.

"The repeated complaints made to me by almost every officer of this ship against Midshipman Phineas Masters induces me to believe that his resignation cannot otherwise than be acceptable," John Rodgers wrote the secretary of the navy from *Constitution* in October 1809. "Mr. Masters's extreme youth alone (being only fourteen years of age) has thus long caused my forbearance; for, although his whole conduct, since his first joining this ship, has been but one tissue of vicious impropriety, I had hoped until now that the force of example and further experience might effect a change. This belief is now at an end, as I believe it to be as utterly impossible to teach him *even* a sense of propriety as it would be to turn night into day."[1] What was an adolescent like Masters doing in the officer corps in the first place?

Part of the answer may be seen in the story of an earlier midshipman, John Harris of Baltimore. Late in 1801 John's father, David Harris, the cashier of the branch bank of the United States at Baltimore, appealed for the reinstatement of his son, who had been discharged under the Peace Establishment Act. The father cited these grounds: "He appears so partial to that turbulent and boisterous life as to prefer it to the calmer and more tranquil scenes of [a] private one. . . . I presume you know enough of my circumstances to conclude that the pay can be no object, but as he is so volatile and wild that I cannot yet restrain him within the bounds of domestic order and regularity, I would prefer his being in the navy to that of a private ship, as the more honorable and preferable school." The naval leadership was inclined to see the John Harrises of the world as equally unsuited to the strict discipline of the navy as they were to the calmer and more tranquil scenes of private life. Robert Smith told young Harris's father that John had been discharged from the navy because of negative fitness reports by his former commanding officer, Thomas Truxtun; but if even one of the officers with whom John had formerly served would recommend his reinstatement, Smith would consider the application. None could be found.[2]

Many parents and other relatives assumed that the corps of midshipmen was a place of last resort to send adolescents who lacked the self-discipline, or who could not be coerced, to function in a nondisruptive way in the home, the school, or the countinghouse. The navy's strict discipline was supposed to be able to effect what those other agencies had failed to do: make the wild boy a useful member of society. Such last-resort hopes were understandable. They were also chimeras. The corps of midshipmen had never been intended to be an institution for the reform of wayward adolescents, and it was not effective in that role. A young gentleman with a track record of trouble in the worlds of home, school, and business was most unlikely to turn into a successful midshipman. Such hopeless cases were prone to show their true colors within their first few months of active duty and to find themselves ending their naval careers just as unsuccessfully as they had terminated their previous life ventures.

William Burley, Jr., was between twenty-four and twenty-five years of age and had never been to sea when he was appointed a midshipman late in 1813. The advanced age for a midshipman's appointment, which age may have been concealed from the Navy Office, did not bode well. Burley was a native of Beverly, Massachusetts, and his father was a sufficiently prominent Republican to have been offered an appointment as a federal commissioner of bankruptcy for the Massachusetts district early in President Jefferson's first term.[3] The future midshipman completed preparatory school at Phillips Andover between 1800 and 1805, then enrolled at Harvard as a member of the class of 1809. So far as the records show, Burley's freshman year at Cambridge was successful, his only recorded infractions of the rules being to have been caught reading at public worship on two different occasions. As a sophomore things changed for the worse. On 25 November 1806 the Harvard faculty records report that young Burley "was concerned in a scene of disorder, to the great disturbance of the college, particularly in breaking windows, bursting the doors of some of the students, and assaulting the windows of a college officer, and in setting up a ladder at the window of another officer, who was absent, with the apparent intention of forcibly entering his chambers. . . . When detected by a college officer, instead of returning to his chamber and desisting from further disorder, he proceeded in a daring manner to assault and break the windows of said officer." As a punishment Burley was immediately suspended and ordered to pursue his studies privately, under the direction of a local clergyman, in the rural quiet of Hampton Falls, New Hampshire, without enjoying any of the normal college vacations.

Burley remained on his good behavior while in exile at Hampton Falls; in August 1807 Harvard agreed to readmit him to his normal class standing. The pattern of behavior that had first appeared in his sophomore year soon reasserted itself. Faculty records for the latter part of 1807 and the year 1808 are peppered with references to Burley being fined for "making an indecent noise and disturbance the last night"; for being absent from classes; for neglecting forensics; for neglect of English composition; for cutting a seat at the time of public worship. Finally, halfway through William Burley's senior year the Harvard faculty decided that they had had enough, and when "it appeared that Burley, a member of the senior class, was guilty of violently assaulting and breaking a window of a college officer in the night" of 27 December 1808, he was immediately suspended and never subsequently applied for readmission.[4]

Except for the negative knowledge that he did not go to sea, how William Burley, Jr., occupied himself during the five years between his dismissal from Harvard in December 1808 and his appointment as a midshipman in November 1813 is unknown, though he may well be the "Burleigh of Beverly" whom a Salem clergyman describes as "sent to Cambridge [i.e., Harvard], was too irregular to finish his course, was put under Judge [Joseph] Story for law, sold his books and played away the money, and enlisted a common soldier."[5] Neither do records survive to show who recommended him for the naval appointment or what they said in his favor. Midshipman Burley was ordered to *Wasp* early in the year 1814, but by 21 April Master Commandant Johnston Blakeley was asking that the new midshipman be removed from under his command because of drunkenness and neglect of duty. It was not Burley's first offense. Blakeley had warned him and counseled him; each time Burley had promised to do better. Now Blakeley's patience was at an end. Isaac Hull, the station commander at Portsmouth, New Hampshire, to whom Blakeley reported, was largely self-educated. Alike impressed with Burley's Harvard credentials and ignorant of his disciplinary record at Cambridge, Hull proposed to give him yet another chance: "Midshipman Burley is a young man of family, well educated, and has no other habit [than drinking] that will prevent his making a promising officer. . . . He promises much, and I have reason to hope that he will yet be an honor to the service." Secretary Jones was skeptical: "Burley's respectable family and liberal education are but an aggravation of his offense. However, Sir, as you appear to think he may be reclaimed, I am willing to try the experiment; but unless a speedy and thorough reformation shall take place, you will report him to this department in order that the service may be freed from his vicious example."

Burley's problems were beyond his power to control, and there was probably nowhere he could have turned for effective help. On 28 April 1814, less than a week after Hull had urged Jones to give Burley another opportunity, and even before Jones could reply to Hull's letter, Sailing Master Nathaniel Stoodly was reporting to Hull that Midshipman Burley "has been in a state of inebriation for three days, nor is there any hopes at present of his reform. He appears to have no command over himself, and to have given himself entirely up to Bacchus." Dismissed immediately, Burley crossed Portsmouth Harbor to the little village of New Castle, New Hampshire, where he sobered up enough to realize the horrible fate of the habitual alcoholic and to send off a final, and fruitless, appeal to Hull.

> When I promised an alteration of my conduct, I meant strictly to have observed it. I did not mean to deceive you by promising what I did not intend to perform. The reflection on the disgrace of it and the consequent ruin that will ensue have made me suffer so severely that I can confidently assure you, Sir, should you permit [me] to return to duty, a similar indiscretion will not again occur. I am not so lost to a sense of shame, nor so destitute of honorable feeling as to reiterate assertions I did not conceive to be strictly true. It would

be ungrateful in me not to acknowledge my having been warned of the consequences of persisting in such a course of conduct by some of my superior officers. To know that I have been treated with unusual lenity and to reflect that I have abused the confidence reposed in me adds keenness to the stings of remorse. Bitterly do I regret that my friends should suffer from my folly and shameful conduct. That is to me the most painful consideration. I shall be ashamed to look my parents and my sisters in the face. I can neither return home nor write to them. And I have not the means of stopping here. My situation is to the last degree desperate. Upon your generosity to excuse me, permit me, Sir, to rely. I am sensible strict justice would condemn me. I pretend not to offer an apology or palliation for faults so shameful. I know that I can control myself, governed as I shall be by the resolution of desperation. I will observe the most rigid temperance. Excuse me, Sir, for troubling you with this application, but I am fully aware of the consequences of an unsuccessful result. Although I deserve punishment, I cannot bear to return to the bosom of my acquaintance and become "a mark to the world" for scorn to point her slow and moving finger at—or, what is worse, an object of its pity. I should prefer exile or death.

From that letter until his death in Beverly, Massachusetts, on 2 October 1821, at the age of thirty-two, there is no record of William Burley, Jr. What the imagination suggests those last seven and a half wretched years must have been like is graphic enough without any documentary description of the sordid reality. When the Burley family genealogy was published in 1880 all record of the existence of William Burley, Jr., was carefully suppressed.[6]

Inherent Vicious Propensities

Considering the amount of time and energy they had to spend coping with them, the navy's leaders had surprisingly little to say about why there were so many wild youths whose behavior barred them from a useful role in the navy or anywhere else in American society. Neither did they speculate on what made them that way. Senior officers apparently made a distinction in their minds between "the common levities of youth," over which they were prepared to "throw a veil," and the behavior of other young men in whom the "disposition to do wrong is innate." Secretaries of the navy, if the opinion of Robert Smith may be taken as representative, shared the view that some young men were, because of natural factors beyond their control, essentially and incorrigibly bad. "The influences of the most correct education," he told Bishop John Carroll, "are too often destroyed by inherent vicious propensities." To this class-without-hope they consigned the wild youth.[7]

One out of every four officers who left the corps before February 1815 did so as a result of dismissal or involuntary resignation. More than half of the dismissed were midshipmen. Although precise numbers are impossible to assign, David Harris might have been describing any one of a high proportion of these dismissed midshipmen when he said of his son, John, "he is so volatile and wild that I cannot yet restrain him within the bounds of domestic order and regularity." Why did young men who were incapable of self-discipline and impervious to external control constitute such a substantial element in the corps of midshipmen? Two answers are possible and, from the historical evidence available, it cannot be said which is the more correct. One could argue that in any society a certain proportion of the adolescents and postadolescents are violent, inclined to alcohol or drug abuse, unable to subordinate themselves to external or internal discipline, psychologically maladjusted to a greater or lesser degree, and destined for lives that society usually labels as failures. This position taken, one might further argue that the officer corps saw a higher proportion of such young men than were to be found in American society at large, because the navy was viewed as the place of last resort where parents sent the problem youth in the hope that strict naval discipline might succeed where all other efforts had failed. Evidence abounds to support this supposition.

One can just as convincingly contend that the years (1794–1815) in which the navy's officer corps was formed were, for reasons not yet fully understood, particularly difficult ones for young men in the United States; that during those two decades a disproportionately large segment of American youth was unwilling or unable to conform its conduct to the norms expected by adult society of the day. It is almost certainly not a coincidence that the years in which the navy was experiencing so much difficulty with turbulent and unsuitable midshipmen were the same years that saw American higher education racked by college riots and rebellions, disorders that extended from 1798 through 1812 and were at their most intense during the years 1798–1802 and 1805–1808.[8] The navy's records, while they furnish abundant, detailed evidence about the behavior of the disruptive young man of 1794–1815, offer only suggestive—not conclusive—proof that his numbers may have been greater, his problems more deeply rooted, and his manifestation of those problems more violent than at other periods in U.S. history. Why was this so? The navy's records offer no hint.

The presence of so many Phineas Masterses, John Harrises, and William Burleys had a measurable impact on the character of the corps of midshipmen. Its seemingly negative toll took the form of high attrition among the navy's apprentice officers (Table 45). Between 1802 and 1809 some 414 midshipmen for whom definite dates of appointment and termination are on record entered the officer corps. Two out of every five of these young men (41.3 percent) were no longer members of the corps two and a half years after appointment. The first thirty months of service were a time of ruthless weeding out. Some midshipmen tried the navy and found it or themselves wanting; more were discovered to be wild boys, bad officer timber, and were sent packing. At first, it appears a sad and wasteful scene. So much effort expended by senior officers on young men who had no business in the officer corps, including many whose tragically self-destructive careers could only be watched with a helpless feeling of fatal inevitability. But, from another perspective, the intense attrition process was healthy for the navy itself. Somewhere between two and a half and three years of service attrition began to slow down. The young men who remained were mostly the promising ones, the navy's future. Two out of every five midshipmen (42.0 percent) completed the five years of service considered optimal for promotion to lieutenant. Among the 174 who remained for the five full years, more than three-quarters (136 or 78.2 percent) were actually commissioned as lieutenants. The pre-1815 navy enjoyed the luxury of inducting large numbers of young men, testing them in the naval environment, and retaining only those who were the most capable and the most promising. Small wonder that the midshipmen of 1802–1809 who survived so arduous a winnowing became the junior officers who performed remarkably in the War of 1812.

What would become of the dismissed problem midshipman? Would he eventually find himself and a useful role in the American social order? Nineteen-year-old William Alexander Duer was, in the summer of 1800, a midshipman of about one year's standing and attached to the frigate *Adams* operating in West Indian waters. Son of William Duer—the former assistant secretary of the treasury under Alexander Hamilton, bankrupt when his extensive private speculations collapsed, dead in debtor's prison in May 1799—young Duer abandoned legal studies at the height of the Quasi-War with France to accept an appointment in the navy. Evening of 16 June 1800 found *Adams* anchored at Martinique; as Lieutenant Francis Harman Ellison later reported to *Adams*'s captain,

> John M. Duncan, midshipman, came upon deck about half past seven p.m. and alleged a complaint against Mr. D[uer]: that he had stabbed him in the thigh with his dirk. I went below, when Mr. D[uer] observed that he was only playing. I replied it was very singular play, and request[ed] him to desist, or words to that amount. About half an hour afterwards . . . Mr. John Livingston came and informed me that unless I went below immediately Mr. Duer would certainly murder Duncan. On going below I found Mr. Duncan holding Duer. I separated them and told Mr. Duer unless he desisted immediately I should be compelled to confine him. He instantly made an attempt to draw his dirk, which fortunately had been rescued from him by Mr. Duncan. He then gave me a blow on the face with so much violence as to drive a tooth down my throat. I immediately seized him and called for the master-at-arms and lieutenant [of] marines. The lieutenant [of] marines and surgeon, Dr. [George] Davis, came in a few minutes, and, as they were entering, I received a second blow on the nose. I then ordered the master-at-arms to get me handcuffs and shackles— Mr. Duer exclaiming that I was a damned cowardly rascal and that he would murder me. During the time that the master-at-arms was getting the irons and confining him, I received several blows from him, accompanied with continual invectives that he would murder me while I slept—that he would murder the party, the damned clan, that was against him. Invectives of the same kind were also used against the above-mentioned gentlemen, the lieutenant [of] marines and surgeon. Such, Sir, were the circumstances which compelled me to degrade an officer so far as to confine him hands and feet.

Secretary Stoddert ordered Midshipman Duer to stand trial by court martial on charges pressed by Lieutenant Ellison. Dismissal appeared the almost certain outcome. At that point young Duer's mother, Lady Catherine Duer (the daughter of William Alexander, Lord Stirling, the Revolutionary War general from New Jersey), began working on Stoddert and her old acquaintance President John Adams, begging that her son be allowed to resign rather than stand trial. The president, unwilling or unable to say no to Lady Kitty, urged Stoddert to accept the resignation of "this unhappy youth," and threw most of the blame on *Adams*'s commander, Richard V. Morris, for not controlling the amount of wine consumed by the midshipmen's mess at dinner. Released from the navy in September 1800, William A. Duer resumed his law studies, was admitted to the New York bar in 1802, practiced for a time at New Orleans, returned to New York and served in the State Assembly from 1814 till 1820, was appointed a judge of the New York Supreme Court in 1822, and served until 1829, when he resigned to become president of Columbia College. After health problems compelled Duer to give up the Columbia presidency, he retired to Morristown, New Jersey, where he took up the life of a country gentleman and lesser man of letters until death finally caught up with him in May 1858.[9]

It would be easy to draw a totally wrong conclusion from the story of William Alexander Duer and to assume that many a wild youth, finally forced to come to terms with himself through the shock of dismissal from the officer corps, was able to make his subsequent life as satisfying and successful in its own way as William A. Duer made his. It is impossible to trace the later lives of a sufficient number of the dismissed to answer, with absolute certainty, the question, What became of these problem midshipmen? Perhaps the very difficulty of tracing them is itself the answer. What evidence exists suggests that William A. Duer was an almost unique exception. For the rest, lives like these lay waiting:

Midshipman Ebenezer Clough, Jr., dismissed in April 1814 in consequence of alcohol abuse and because he "will never make an officer or a *gentleman*; his manners and habits are coarse and vulgar and his associates of the lowest class," died less than a year later at age twenty-two.[10] When Midshipman Charles Fox Sherburne, son of the U.S. district judge for New Hampshire, resigned under pressure in July 1813, that outcome was described as an event "by which the service has got clear of an infamous character." This unsatisfactory end to his naval career might well have been anticipated; just twelve months earlier his father had admitted that Charles, who had lasted only one year at Dartmouth College, is "young, unusually ardent and impetuous, and requires the advice and control of a cool and experienced guide." One way or another young Sherburne acquired enough knowledge of law to be admitted to the bar and survived until 1838, in which year he died at Columbus, Georgia, "from wounds inflicted with a sword-cane in a rencontre."[11] In August 1808 David Porter dismissed acting midshipman Robert A. Grant for alcohol abuse and persistent crossing of status lines to fraternize with enlisted men. Eight months later he was "now in the situation best suiting his capacity, to wit, as waiter in a common grogshop."[12] At St. Marys, Georgia, Midshipman John Davies resigned to avoid a court martial, then enlisted in the marine corps as a fifer.[13] Midshipman Samuel Brittin, described by the officer corps' premier status snob, Alexander Murray, as "the son of an obscure tavern keeper and perfectly uneducated, as well as an idle, worthless fellow," was dismissed in June 1809 for swindling Philadelphia merchants. When last definitely heard from, he "has proved himself the worst of *rascals* and now rambles about the country, where he is not known, swindling and committing various trespasses under the garb of his uniform, and still passes himself off as an officer in the navy." Then he disappears, no one knows where.[14]

Finally, there is this story. Midshipman William C. Davis, the son of Massachusetts solicitor general Daniel Davis, was permitted to resign in January 1809 after he was caught stealing geese at Portland, Maine, and admitted his guilt. Davis's commanding officer, Lieutenant Charles Morris, urged the acceptance of his resignation "in consideration of his parents and of his connections, who are numerous and very respectable." When Davis next turns up in the records, two and a half years later, it is in a letter from one David Reed, whose return address identifies him as an inmate of the New York State Prison. Davis had gone from geese to more ambitious projects:

A certain William Davis, formerly a midshipman in the state service (and known on board the Argus) came to my house one evening and informed me that he was keeping a vessel belonging to Philadelphia, that he had mislaid the keys of her, and that some rigging was on the deck which he was fearful would be lost before the morning if not secured, and requested me that I would let him stow it away in my store for the present. I readily consented to it, not suspecting but what he told me concerning it was the truth. But the next news I heard of it was that it was stolen, that he was apprehended for it, and some enemies of mine informed the authority that they saw me assisting to get it into my house, and that I must have certainly known it was stolen. I was accordingly apprehended and tried with Davis on the same charge, and both was found guilty. I received a sentence of seven years' confinement at hard labor in this prison, but he, in consequence of the interference of some friends with His Excellency the Governor, obtained a pardon from the offense and never came here at all.

Whether Davis's close call with hard labor in the state penitentiary cured his habit of attaching himself to other people's property or whether his father had to keep rescuing him from the consequences of his own acts is not known. He was thirty-four when he died in the summer of 1823.[15]

Wild Boys Revalorized

Is anyone prepared for the next twist in the tale of the wayward? Many of the dismissed midshipmen sooner or later reentered the navy as seamen or petty officers. No systematic search of all the surviving pay- and muster rolls has been attempted in quest of downwardly mobile ex-midshipmen, but certain names have leaped out of rolls being scanned for other purposes. A name-by-name check would undoubtedly turn up more. Midshipman Seth Burnham Alby, the seventeen-year-old ward of Boston navy agent Amos Binney, resigns on the Lake Ontario station in February 1814, alleging for his reasons "an utter dislike to the naval service, in which I am not calculated to shine as an officer, and my dislike to a seafaring life in general." To which text Isaac Chauncey adds the exegesis, "I will only observe that the service is fortunately got rid of a *bad boy*. Although he has talents, he does not possess a single good principle. He has been five or six times arrested since he has been on this station." Alby soon enough changes his mind—or his tune—about seafaring life and, after a fruitless attempt to get reinstated as a midshipman, serves as a seaman in *Sylph* and *Jones* on Lake Ontario until his guardian finally secures him a lieutenant's commission in the artillery in November 1814.[16] A few weeks after Alby hands in his resignation, Midshipman Jacob M. Jacobs, who began his naval career as captain's clerk to James Lawrence in 1810, resigns rather than face a court martial on the Lake Ontario station. Fifteen months later he reappears on the station's rolls as a purser's steward, a berth he continues to hold for seven and a half years.[17] On 3 May 1813 William Jones tells Midshipman Stephen Wilson, "Your habitual intemperance is such as to require your removal from the service of the United States." A year and a half passes, and former officer Wilson turns up on the rolls of the Norfolk station as master's mate, having perhaps gone privateering in the interim. He finishes out the War of 1812 in the master's mate rating, is discharged, and, when he dies at Norfolk in the late spring of 1822, the newspaper notice promotes him posthumously to "formerly a lieutenant of the U.S. Navy."[18]

Midshipman Robert Conkling entered the navy with a glowing recommendation: Robert and his brother "are of reputable family and connection of high worth, and from what I can learn are of considerable genius. I have no hesitation in a belief that from industry and attention they will render themselves worthy . . . and in due time, when occasion shall offer, rather than become a blemish to their profession, add to the luster of your navy." Brave words and high hopes, but within a year Robert Conkling is asking permission to resign rather than face a court martial on charges of repeated drunkenness. Not too long thereafter he drops out of sight and, when his family finally traces his whereabouts, it is to learn that he is serving as a master's mate in Gunboat No. 163 on the New Orleans station. The family promptly secures Secretary Hamilton's order for a discharge and hopes Robert will come home to St. Marys County, Maryland; but the discharge is too late. Robert Conkling died of yellow fever at the naval hospital in New Orleans on 9 September 1811.[19] For disobeying orders by leaving *Constellation* clandestinely on 17 June 1804 in order to fight a duel after Captain Hugh G. Campbell has pointedly refused him permission to go ashore, a court martial sentences George Washington Liggett to dismissal, although he is actually permitted to submit his resignation instead. Nine years later his father, merchant George Liggett of Baltimore, reports that the son was serving as a seaman in the brig *Vixen* at the time of her capture by *Southampton* in November 1812 and has just been exchanged as a prisoner of war. Liggett the son has not been home to see his father in six years. "He has been a wild youth," the father admits, but he has not given up all hope. "He may be of service to himself and family, as he already has been to his country." Hope must turn to disappointment: muster rolls record the death of George W. Liggett, seaman, on board the ship *Alert* on the New York station in February 1814.[20]

And then there was Ephraim Rowland Blaine. In November 1804 Blaine, a midshipman since March 1800 and then serving in *Essex*, was found guilty by a court martial of "disrespectful conduct towards the government of the United States" and sentenced to be dismissed from the navy because of the "infamy and pernicious tendency of his conduct." His offense? Perhaps not a little under the influence of shore-leave ardent spirits, Blaine had told *Essex*'s carpenter, Persifor Taylor, that "we were inferior in every point to England, spoke in the most derisive manner of America and its government, declaring passionately that the Americans were capable of teaching the English nothing better than blackguardism and democracy."

"Why do you serve a country of which you have such a despicable opinion?" asked Midshipman Melancthon Woolsey, who had overheard Blaine's tirade.

"I do not intend to serve it long!"

Midshipman Arthur Sinclair had been a silent observer, one who waited "to see to what lengths [Blaine] would go and what the real character of the man was." He soon found out. "Mr. Woolsey then asked him if he did not know that the majority of the people of the U[nited] States were styled democrats, and that the executive and all the heads of department were the choice of the people. He replied that we had a parcel of foreigners in our service as heads, and particularized Mr. Gallatin, [secretary of the treasury], who he abused most shamefully, and finally concluded by saying that two-thirds of the people of the U[nited] States were damned rascals and blackguards."

With his dismissal for violating too blatantly the corps' self-imposed rule, *the cloth has no politics*, Blaine disappears from the records for five and a half years. He surfaces briefly at New Orleans in the summer of 1810, having, in the interim, acquired a scar on his left thigh from a gunshot wound, then turns up in the frigate *President* in the post of gunner's yeoman in July 1811. In March 1812 he is made acting gunner. On 21 June *President*, flying the broad pennant of John Rodgers, sails from New York on the first cruise of the War of 1812; on 23 June the British frigate *Belvidera* is sighted, is engaged in a running fight, and finally escapes; on 26 June ex-midshipman Ephraim Rowland Blaine, thirty-one years old, son of the commissary general of the Continental army and acting gunner of the U.S. Frigate *President*, falls overboard from the main chains. *President* heaves to, a boat is hastily lowered, but Blaine cannot be saved, nor his body found.[21]

Epilogue: Captain Hull Goes Shopping and Decides to Take a Risk

EARLY A CENTURY and three-quarters has passed since former secretary of the navy William Jones conceded puzzlement as to whether officers who received their professional training entirely in the navy performed better than peers who began their careers in the merchant service. An astute historian studied the War of 1812 and reported that he, too, was baffled. Paul Hamilton's competence was widely questioned. There were all those stories about his drinking. How was it, asked J.C.A. Stagg, that "a department so poorly run could perform so creditably in the War [of 1812]"? Might it have been because the Navy Office was unable to control the navy's officers very closely? Owing to "the weakness of naval administration in this respect, commanders appear to have had a good deal of latitude in . . . determining their operations. This might have allowed greater play for the professionalism of many naval officers, thus making possible some outstanding individual performances."[1]

History certainly ought to challenge Stagg's premise that the Navy Office was "so poorly run." Such an assertion ignores the strengths Paul Hamilton did bring to the job, the effective work done by predecessors Benjamin Stoddert and Robert Smith in setting the navy's traditions, and the infrastructure of experienced clerks and accountants who ran much of the department's day-to-day business. These dissents aside, Stagg's speculation has something in common with the earlier ruminations of William Jones. Both thinkers had an intuitive grip on the correct answer; both failed to ask the right questions.

Recall the missions the navy was called upon to perform during much of the nineteenth century: execution or support of the national government's foreign policy and protection of the commercial activities of the nation's citizens, missions implemented hundreds or thousands of miles from Washington. Remember also the communications environment in which the navy operated. Reporting an event to the Navy Office and receiving the secretary's reply was a matter of days, or weeks, or months. Under such conditions the nation needed intelligent naval officers, men generally informed of the government's policies and intentions, who could exercise initiative to act effectively and wisely with a minimum of day-by-day direction. If there were "outstanding individual performances" by the navy's officers in the War of 1812, it was not because of the "weakness of naval administration," but because that administration was effective in light of the constraints that distance and time imposed. For a decade and a half the nation's and the navy's civilian leadership had labored to develop officers who could perform outstandingly under just such conditions. The naval histories of the two World Wars, among others, are replete with evidence that the ability of central naval authority to intervene in and to control operations via high-speed communications does not necessarily result in more effective decision making or action at the scene of battle than when the man on the spot is left to act according to his best judgment—provided the man on the spot is up to the job.

A familiar incident from the opening weeks of the War of 1812 goes to the heart of the matter. On 12 July 1812 Isaac Hull's *Constitution* cleared the Chesapeake capes under orders to meet the squadron of Commodore John Rodgers at New York; but Rodgers had already departed New York, had encountered *Belvidera* and let her escape, and was by then far out into the Atlantic. What Hull met instead was a powerful British squadron. Was the ignominious capture of one of the U.S. Navy's finest frigates to set the tone for the war? Through the magnificent seamanship of Captain Hull, the first lieutenant, Charles Morris, and Sailing Master John Cushing Aylwin, *Constitution* escaped a seemingly inevitable fate. Although cut off from New York by the British squadron, Hull eventually put into Boston (27 July) and promptly reported his arrival to Washington. He also went right to work filling the frigate's storerooms, for *Constitution* had sailed from Annapolis with only an eight-week supply of stores, which her captain had expected to fill out to full cruising requirements after a short run to New York. "I have directed the [navy] agent to work night and day until [the provisions] are furnished." Hull had every legitimate reason to push the business. The geography of Boston harbor was such that *Constitution* could readily have been blockaded by a superior British force, for whose sails Hull squinted apprehensively to seaward each day. Daily, too, he visited the post office and the navy agent's or sent an officer there in anticipation of instructions from Washington. None appeared.

By 2 August the fickle wind had swung round to the southwest so that *Constitution* was at last able to run out of Boston harbor. Her storerooms were full. The town was alive with reports of either individual British warships or the entire British squadron close at hand. A last check of the post office was made, but still no letters for Isaac Hull. The captain announced that he would put to sea, and run between Georges Bank and Cape Sable and from there to the Newfoundland Banks. Perhaps he could intercept a small convoy bound to England; possibly he would meet Commodore Rodgers. One last task remained to be done: mail a letter to Secretary Hamilton explaining his reasons for sailing without waiting for orders from Washington, two and a half closely written pages of rationale, echoing a similar letter dispatched five days earlier. He was "at a loss how to proceed." By sailing "[I] shall take a responsibility on myself that I should wish to avoid." But "I shall act as at this moment I believe you would order me to do, was it possible for me to receive orders from you." And a good deal more in the same vein.[2] Then he sailed away to encounter a British frigate named *Guerriere*.

Hull's apologetic letter to Hamilton was truthful as far as it went, but was it the whole story? Almost certainly not. The captain probably suspected—and

Isaac Hull
U.S.N.
July 28th 1842

☞ Of the late Commodore Hull it is said,
that he was the first man of any nation who took
an English frigate in fair and single fight.

*In 1842, the last summer of his life, Isaac Hull visited Saratoga Springs, New York.
The commodore's health was failing, perhaps more rapidly than those who met him realized.
He was never a skinny man, and weight had become an increasing problem with the years.
His latest command at sea proved the unhappy denouement to a distinguished career, a
troubled time marked by bitter quarrels with younger subordinates. But for silhouettist
Auguste Edouart all that mattered not. Here was the man who, thirty years before, had
captured* Guerriere *in the first uncertain weeks of naval war with the British giant.
There was still time, in the soft twilight of summer in upstate New York, for one final life
portrait of a nation's hero.* National Portrait Gallery, Washington, D.C.

may even have known off the record—that orders had left Washington on 28 July for him to turn *Constitution* over to William Bainbridge, orders that were delayed in the mail like many another letter before and since. (One can almost hear Hull's *Woosh!* of relief each day the mail arrives without the dreaded letter from the Navy Office and he hurries preparations for sea even faster.) The captain's letters to Hamilton explain and reexplain the situation to the point that the historian wonders, Just what is *Constitution*'s commander up to that he is trying to present in so favorable a light? Only the day before Hull had told his father that once he sailed "I may not return for some time," a determination nowhere hinted in the apologetic letters to Secretary Hamilton.[3] Buried in the accountant of the navy's massive archive of settled accounts, among monstrous stacks of vouchers sent in by Boston navy agent Amos Binney, is a telltale invoice.[4] On 29 July Captain Hull had gone shopping for charts in Boston. *Cape Florida to the Banks. Gulf of St. Lawrence. Boston Bay. Long Island Sound to New York.* Nothing to attract special notice among these. But . . . *The Spanish Main? Demerara? Cayenne? Brazil? Río de la Plata? Atlantic Coast of Africa!* Where was this man going? For how long did he plan to disappear into the Atlantic?

Isaac Hull never admitted, perhaps even to himself, his real intentions as *Constitution* sailed from Boston that August morning. His decisive, if professionally perilous, act displayed the initiative, the sound judgment, and the moral courage that made a Benjamin Stoddert or a Robert Smith or a Paul Hamilton swell up with justified pride and satisfaction. When *Constitution* met *Guerriere* on the afternoon of 19 August 1812, the outcome of the battle, with its unmeasurable contribution to immediate national self-esteem and to the navy's tradition for the next two centuries, was a result toward which the officer corps of the U.S. Navy and its civilian leadership had been working for more than eighteen years. The qualities Isaac Hull displayed in 1812 were ones Thomas Truxtun had articulated at the navy's beginnings: those of the true sea officer.

Appendix

TABLE 1
Size of the Officer Corps, 1800–1815, According to Actual Census

	1 July 1800	1 Feb. 1802	1 Jan. 1805	1 June 1807	1 Jan. 1810	1 Jan. 1813	14 Feb. 1815
Captains	31[a]	12	10	13	13	16	30
Masters commandant	10	0	8	9	8	10	20
Lieutenants	114	31	22	71	70	70	150
Midshipmen	379	150	186	150	255	488	482
Sailing masters	29	14	16	14	54	198	208
Surgeons	33	12	20	21	25	32	53
Surgeon's mates	32	11	14	17	23	43	75
Pursers	38	12	19	19	24	38	47
Chaplains/ schoolmasters	8	3	5	3	6	12	15
Captain's clerks	18	3	6	5	13	22	34
	692	248	306	322	491	929	1,114

a. Includes five commanders of galleys.

TABLE 2
Midshipmen of 1800, 1804–1805, 1809, 1812, and 1814: States of Residence

	Number	Percent[a]
New Hampshire	14	1.7
Vermont	2	0.2
Massachusetts[b]	82	10.0
Rhode Island	28	3.4
Connecticut	17	2.1
	143	17.4
New York	82	10.0
New Jersey	25	3.0
Pennsylvania	114	13.9
Delaware	21	2.5
	242	29.4
Maryland	122	14.9
District of Columbia	43	5.2
Virginia	124	15.1
	289	35.2
North Carolina	32	3.9
South Carolina	54	6.5
Georgia	18	2.2
	104	12.6
Ohio	3	0.4
Kentucky	14	1.7
Tennessee	6	0.7
Mississippi Territory	3	0.4
Louisiana	18	2.2
	44	5.4
Known-state appointees	822	
Foreign nationals	2	
States of residence unknown	61	6.9[c]
All appointees	885	

a. Of all known-state appointees.
b. Includes District of Maine.
c. Of all appointees.

TABLE 3

Midshipmen: States of Residence

	1800		1804–1805		1809		1812		1814	
	Number	Percent[a]	Number	Percent[a]	Number	Percent[a]	Number	Percent[a]	Number	Percent[a]
New Hampshire	1	0.6	1	0.9	1	0.6	9	4.2	2	1.3
Vermont	0	0.0	0	0.0	0	0.0	1	0.5	1	0.6
Massachusetts[b]	21	12.7	5	4.5	14	7.7	28	13.2	14	9.2
Rhode Island	9	5.5	0	0.0	2	1.1	7	3.3	10	6.5
Connecticut	7	4.2	1	0.9	4	2.2	0	0.0	5	3.3
New York	38	23.0	7	6.3	21	11.6	45	21.2	32	20.9
New Jersey	13	7.9	9	8.1	19	10.5	29	13.7	12	7.8
Pennsylvania	33	20.0	13	11.7	17	9.4	20	9.4	31	20.3
Delaware	6	3.7	2	1.8	4	2.2	4	1.9	5	3.3
Maryland	57	34.6	27	24.3	48	26.5	58	27.4	52	34.0
District of Columbia	18	10.9	4	3.6	13	7.2	19	8.9	14	9.2
Virginia	29	17.6	25	22.6	23	12.7	31	14.6	16	10.4
North Carolina	7	4.2	5	4.5	8	4.4	3	1.4	9	5.9
South Carolina	7	4.2	5	4.5	20	11.1	12	5.7	10	6.5
Georgia	3	1.9	1	0.9	4	2.2	3	1.4	7	4.6
Ohio	0	0.0	1	0.9	0	0.0	18	8.5	26	17.0
Kentucky	0	0.0	0	0.0	6	3.2	4	1.9	2	1.3
Tennessee	1	0.6	0	0.0	0	0.0	2	0.9	4	2.6
Mississippi Territory	0	0.0	0	0.0	1	0.6	1	0.5	3	2.1
Louisiana	0	0.0	0	0.0	9	5.0	8	3.8	1	0.6
Known-state appointees	165		111		181		212		153	
Foreign nationals	0		2		0		0		0	
States of residence unknown	16	8.8[c]	8	6.6[c]	4	2.2[c]	20	8.6[c]	13	7.8[c]
All appointees	181		121		185		232		166	

a. Of all known-state appointees.
b. Includes District of Maine.
c. Of all appointees for year.

475

TABLE 4

Midshipmen: Ages at Appointment

	1800 (N = 64)	1804–1805 (N = 43)	1809 (N = 87)	1812 (N = 140)	1814 (N = 146)	All years (N = 480)
Youngest man appointed	9	10	11	2	11	2
Oldest man appointed	26	25	29	27	30	30
Mean age at appointment	17.6	17.4	17.6	16.7	17.8	17.4
Age at first quartile	15	15	15	15	16	15
Median age at appointment	17	18	17	17	17	17
Age at third quartile	19	20	19	19	20	19
Percent of appointees for whom ages are known	35.4	35.5	47.0	60.3	88.0	54.2

TABLE 5
Percentage of Midshipman Appointments
Meeting the Navy Department's Age Criteria

Age at time of appointment	1800	1804–1805	1809	1812	1814	All years
11 and younger	1.6	2.3	3.5	7.9	0.7	3.5
12–18	67.2	62.8	65.5	65.0	63.0	64.6
19 and older	31.2	34.9	31.0	27.1	36.3	31.9

TABLE 6
Chaplains: Length of Service

	Number	Percent	Cumulative percentage
1–12 months	24	48.0	48.0
13–24 months	10	20.0	68.0
25–36 months	7	14.0	82.0
37–48 months	3	6.0	88.0
49+ months	6	12.0	100.0
	50[a]		

a. Eight chaplains, the exact length of whose service has not been determined, are omitted from this calculation.

TABLE 7
Chaplains: Ages at Appointment
(N = 25[a])

Youngest man	19.0
Oldest man	59.0
Mean age	28.7
Median age	26.0
Age at first quartile	23.0
Age at third quartile	32.0
Most common age	26.0 (6 cases)
Percent of appointees for whom ages are known	43.1

a. One man, of known age, was twice appointed a chaplain.

TABLE 8
Confinement as Punishment:
Edward Preble and Theodore Hunt Compared

	Preble Constitution	*Hunt* Hornet
Months covered by record	6	8
Number of enlisted men (including petty officers) potentially subject to punishment	342	168
Total number of confinements	13	22
Number of individuals confined	13	19
Number of repeat offenders	0	2
Percent of individuals at risk actually confined	3.8	11.3
Minimum confinement (days)	1	1
Maximum confinement (days)	20	22
Mean confinement (days)	11.6	6.1
Median confinement (days)	13.0	4.0
Percent of those confined who were also flogged	53.8	27.3
Selected primary offenses for which men were confined:		
Alcohol-related	6	5
Desertion	3	3
Theft	1	0
Neglect of duty	3	0
Fighting	0	9
Seditious behavior	0	2

TABLE 9
Flogging on the Captain's Authority:
Lashes Awarded per Instance of Punishment, All Cases Cumulated

Number of lashes awarded	Number of instances	Percent of all lashes awarded	Cumulative percentage of all lashes awarded
6–10	39[a]	12.7	12.7
12	157	51.1	63.8
15–18	8	2.6	66.4
24	66	21.5	87.9
30–39	22[b]	7.2	95.1
48	6	2.0	97.1
60	7	2.3	99.4
100	1	0.3	99.7
136	1	0.3	100.0
	307		

a. Of these, 23 instances were 6-lash punishments and 8 were for 9 lashes.
b. Of these, 16 instances were 36-lash punishments.

479

TABLE 10
Flogging on the Captain's Authority, 1799–1815

	Argus/Nautilus *William M. Crane*	Constitution *Silas Talbot*	Constitution *Edward Preble*	Enterprize *David Porter*
Total number of enlisted men/ petty officers potentially subject to punishment	255	Not certain[a]	373	113
Period covered by record of punishments	13 Oct 1811– 15 July 1812 (277 days)	5 June 1799– 5 Sept 1800 (459 days)	14 Aug 1803– 17 Sept 1804 (401 days)	21 Aug 1805– 17 Nov 1806 (454 days)
Number of floggings recorded	7	21	45	22
Number of above floggings for which the number of lashes is not recorded	0	0	0	6
Number of individuals flogged	7	16	39	15
Portion of enlisted men/petty officers flogged one or more times	2.7%	Not certain[a]	10.5%	13.3%
Total lashes given, all recorded punishments	204	222	966	186
Maximum number of lashes given one man	48	12	36	24
Minimum number of lashes given one man	24	6	6	6
Mean number of lashes given	29.1	10.6	21.5	11.6
Median number of lashes given	24	12	24	12
Most common number(s) of lashes given (modal number)	24 (5 cases)	12 (16 cases)	24 (20 cases) 12 (16 cases)	12 (12 cases)

a. Because of the fragmentary state of *Constitution*'s muster rolls for this period.
b. Because of instances in which the names of individuals flogged are not given.
c. In two cases *Sylph*'s log records only that all hands were called to witness punishment. For purposes of this tabl◗ and a subsequent tabulation it is assumed that (1) one man was punished on each occasion, and (2) one was a firs◗ time offender and the other a repeat offender.

Hornet *Isaac* *Chauncey*	Hornet *John H.* *Dent*	Hornet *James* *Biddle*	John Adams *Isaac* *Chauncey*	President *William* *Bainbridge*	Sylph *Melancthon* *T. Woolsey*
140	164	111	122	463	211
18 Oct 1805–	9 Mar 1806–	14 Jan–	30 Oct 1804–	28 May 1809–	18 Aug 1813–
8 Mar 1806	8 Dec 1807	15 July 1815	25 Feb 1805	12 Apr 1810	20 Apr 1814
(142 days)	(640 days)	(183 days)	(119 days)	(320 days)	(246 days)
15	39	7	15	21	49
0	7	0	0	3	6
14	Not certain[b]	5	12	Not certain[b]	28[c]
10.0%	Not certain[b]	4.5%	9.8%	Not certain[b]	13.3%
450	958+	84	427	160	696
60	100	24	136	12	48
9	12	8	6	6	6
30.0	29.9	12.0	28.5	8.9	16.2
24	24	12	24	7.5	12
24 (3 cases)	24 (13 cases)	8 (3 cases)		12 (8 cases)	
36 (3 cases)	12 (9 cases)	12 (3 cases)	24 (5 cases)	6 (7 cases)	12 (30 cases)

TABLE 11
Repeat Offenders Punished by Flogging:
Selected Ships, 1799–1815

	Total number of individuals flogged	Number of individuals flogged more than once	Percent who were repeat offenders	Most common number(s) of lashes awarded
Argus/Nautilus (Crane)	7	0	0.0	24
Constitution (Talbot)	16	5	31.3	12
Constitution (Preble)	39	6	15.4	24
Enterprize (Porter)	15	6	40.0	12
Hornet (Chauncey)	14	1	7.1	24/36
Hornet (Biddle)	5	2	40.0	8/12
John Adams (Chauncey)	12	3	25.0	24
Sylph (Woolsey)	28	12	42.9	12

TABLE 12
Offenses for Which Enlisted Men and Petty Officers
Were Convicted by Courts Martial, 1799–1815

	Number of convictions	Percentage of all convictions
Desertion	94	74.0
Mutiny/sedition	23[a]	18.1
Theft/fraud	6	4.7
Murder/attempted murder	2	1.6
Cowardice	1	0.8
Quarreling	1	0.8
	127	
Uncertain	1	
	128	

a. Two additional men, convicted on another primary charge, were also convicted of mutiny/sedition as a secondary charge.

TABLE 13
Executed Flogging Sentences by Courts Martial,
1799–1815

Sentences executed	111
Total lashes awarded	8,814
Maximum sentence (lashes)	320
Minimum sentence (lashes)	6
Mean sentence (lashes)	79.4
Median sentence (lashes)	72
Most common sentence (lashes)	100

TABLE 14
Executed Flogging Sentences Awarded by Courts Martial, 1799–1815: Desertion vs. Mutiny/Sedition

	Desertion	Mutiny/ sedition
Sentences executed	84	18
Total lashes awarded	5,940	2,328
Maximum sentence (lashes)	270	320
Minimum sentence (lashes)	6	70
Mean sentence (lashes)	70.7	129.3
Median sentence (lashes)	50	100
Most common sentence (lashes)	100	100

TABLE 15
Promotions: Rank Attained before 1 June 1815

Rank at initial appointment	Lieutenant	Master commandant	Captain
Midshipman	259	46	21[a]
Sailing master	28[b]	0	0
Lieutenant		12	13[c]
Master commandant			1
	287	58	35

a. Two of these twenty-one were promoted directly from lieutenant to captain without ever holding the rank of master commandant.
b. Includes two Quasi-War master's mates promoted directly to lieutenant.
c. Six of these thirteen were promoted directly from lieutenant without ever holding the rank of master commandant.

TABLE 16
Lieutenants: Ages at Promotion from Midshipman

	May 1799– Feb. 1801	Apr. 1802– Jan. 1807[a]	Aug. 1807– May 1812	Jan. 1813– May 1815[b]	May 1799– May 1815
Youngest man	17	20	19	16	16
Oldest man	32	35	30	32	35
Mean age	21.6	23.3	23.9	21.9	22.6
Age at first quartile	20	21	22	20	21
Median age	21.0	22.0	23.5	22.0	22.0
Age at third quartile	23	25	26	23	24
Number promoted	25	70	46	118	259
Percent for whom ages known	64.0	68.6	73.9	83.1	75.7

a. No new lieutenants were created between February 1801 and April 1802.
b. No new lieutenants were created between May 1812 and January 1813.

TABLE 17
Masters Commandant: Ages at Promotion from Lieutenant

	May 1804– July 1812[a]	Mar. 1813– Mar. 1815[b]	Mar. 1799– Mar. 1815
Youngest man	22	27	22
Oldest man	47	38	47
Mean age	29.8	30.2	29.9
Age at first quartile	26	28	28
Median age	29.0	30.0	29.0
Age at third quartile	32	31	31
Number promoted	23	30	58
Percent for whom ages known	87.0	86.7	81.0

a. Inadequate data exist to calculate ages of masters commandant promoted March 1799–February 1800; no new masters commandant were created between February 1800 and May 1804.
b. No new masters commandant were created between July 1812 and March 1813.

TABLE 18
Captains: Ages at Promotion[a]

	1798– 1800	1804– July 1812[b]	Oct. 1812– Feb. 1815	1798– Feb. 1815
Youngest man	26	25	28	25
Oldest man	43	54	44	54
Mean age	33.5	33.2	31.9	32.7
Age at first quartile	26	29	29	29
Median age	33.0	32.5	31.0	32.0
Age at third quartile	41	34	33	34
Number promoted	8	10	17	35
Percent for whom ages known	75.0	100.0	88.2	88.6

a. Includes eight men promoted directly from lieutenant to captain.
b. No new captains were created between November 1800 and May 1804.

TABLE 19
Years of Service between Appointment and Promotion

	Midshipman to lieutenant	Lieutenant to master commandant	Midshipman to master commandant	Master commandant to captain	Midshipman to captain
Shortest period of service	0.56	0.65	6.05	0.57	6.06
Longest period of service	11.78	11.93	16.42	8.09	15.94
Mean period of service	5.56	6.19	12.59	3.00	14.33
First quartile	4.46	5.50	12.09	1.60	14.20
Median period of service	5.76	6.55	13.40	1.93	14.79
Third quartile	6.87	7.62	13.95	5.25	15.33
Number of men	259	58	46[a]	27	21

a. The difference between this and the previous column is accounted for by twelve men promoted master commandant who entered the navy at the rank of lieutenant.

TABLE 20
Lieutenants: Years of Service as Midshipman before Promotion

	May 1799– Feb 1801	Apr. 1802– Jan. 1807	Aug. 1807– May 1812	Jan. 1813– May 1815
Shortest period of service	0.56	3.38	5.12	2.76
Longest period of service	2.53	8.49	10.04	11.78
Mean period of service	1.55	6.67	6.68	5.33
Median period of service	1.48	6.93	6.16	5.15
Number of men	25	70	46	118

TABLE 21
Masters Commandant: Years of Service as
Lieutenant before Promotion

Less than	Number	Percent	
1 year	2	3.4	
2 years	3	5.2	
3 years	0	0.0	
4 years	2	3.4	
5 years	4	6.9	
6 years	8	13.8	
7 years	22	38.0	67.3%
8 years	9	15.5	
9 years	4	6.9	
10 years	3	5.2	
11 years	0	0.0	
12 years	1	1.7	
	58		

TABLE 22
Masters Commandant: Years of Service as Lieutenant before Promotion

	Mar. 1799– Feb. 1800	May 1804– July 1812[a]	Mar. 1813– May 1815
Shortest period of service	0.66	3.82	3.26
Longest period of service	1.77	9.28	11.93
Mean period of service	1.14	6.23	7.00
Median period of service	1.27	5.79	6.55
Number of men	5	23	30

a. No new masters commandant were created between February 1800 and May 1804.

TABLE 23
Captains: Years of Service as Master
Commandant before Promotion

Less than	Number	Percent	
1 year	1	3.7 ⎫	
2 years	15	55.6 ⎬	70.4%
3 years	3	11.1 ⎭	
4 years	1	3.7	
5 years	0	0.0	
6 years	1	3.7	
7 years	5	18.5	
8 years	0	0.0	
9 years	1	3.7	
	27		

TABLE 24
Captains: Years of Service as Master Commandant before
Promotion

	1804– July 1812[a]	Oct. 1812– Feb. 1815
Shortest period of service	1.93	0.57
Longest period of service	8.09	6.86
Mean period of service	4.69	2.23
Median period of service	6.20	1.66
Number of men	9	16

a. The number of men (2) promoted from master commandant to captain during the Quasi-War with France was too small for inclusion as a column in this table.

TABLE 25
Sailing Masters Appointed 24 July 1797–6 February 1815 by Year of Appointment

	Number appointed	Percent of all masters	Cumulative percentage
1797	2	0.4	0.4
1798	14	2.8	3.2
1799	32	6.3	9.5
1800	14	2.8	12.3
1801	7	1.4	13.7
1802	3	0.6	14.3
1803	6	1.2	15.5
1804	2	0.4	15.9
1805	6	1.2	17.1
1806	2	0.4	17.5
1807	15	3.0	20.5
1808	4	0.8	21.3
1809	54	10.7	32.0
1810	3	0.6	32.6
1811	9	1.8	34.4
1812	176	34.8	69.2
1813	78	15.4	84.6
1814	71	14.0	98.6
1815	7	1.4	100.0
	505		

TABLE 26
Midshipmen and Sailing Masters: Ages at Appointment

	Midshipmen (N = 480)	Masters (N = 171)
Youngest man appointed	2	19
Oldest man appointed	30	64
Mean age	17.4	31.2
Age at first quartile	15	24
Median age	17	29
Age at third quartile	19	36
Percent of appointees for whom ages are known	54.2	33.9

TABLE 27
Sailing Masters: Ages at Appointment
(N = 171)

Age	Number	Percent
19	2	1.2
20–29	86	50.3
30–39	55	32.2
40–49	19	11.1
50 and older	9	5.2

TABLE 28
Midshipmen and Sailing Masters: States of Residence

	Midshipmen		Masters	
	Number	Percent[a]	Number	Percent[a]
New Hampshire	14	1.7	5	1.2
Vermont	2	0.2	0	0.0
Massachusetts[b]	82	10.0	66	16.3
Rhode Island	28	3.4	17	4.2
Connecticut	17	2.1	13	3.2
	143	17.4	101	24.9
New York	82	10.0	62	15.3
New Jersey	25	3.0	6	1.5
Pennsylvania	114	13.9	80	19.7
Delaware	21	2.5	1	0.2
	242	29.4	149	36.7
Maryland	122	14.9	58	14.3
District of Columbia	43	5.2	15	3.7
Virginia	124	15.1	35	8.6
	289	35.2	108	26.6
North Carolina	32	3.9	11	2.7
South Carolina	54	6.5	26	6.4
Georgia	18	2.2	7	1.7
	104	12.6	44	10.8
Ohio	3	0.4	0	0.0
Kentucky	14	1.7	0	0.0
Tennessee	6	0.7	1	0.2
Mississippi Territory	3	0.4	0	0.0
Louisiana	18	2.2	3	0.8
	44	5.4	4	1.0
Known-state appointees	822		406	
Foreign nationals	2		0	
States of residence unknown	61	6.9[c]	99	19.6[c]
All appointees	885		505	

a. Of all known-state appointees.
b. Includes District of Maine.
c. Of all appointees.

TABLE 29

Annual Compensation of Officers of the U.S. Navy, 1797–1817

	Captain, ship of 32 + guns	Captain, ship of 20–31 guns	Master commandant	Lieutenant commanding small vessel	Lieutenant[a]	Surgeon	Sailing master[a], purser, or chaplain	Surgeon's mate	Midshipman[a,b]	Captain's clerk[b]
Act of 1 July 1797										
Base pay per year	$ 900.00				$480.00	$600.00	$480.00	$360.00	$228.00	$300.00
Extra rations per day[c]	5				2	1	1	1	0	0
Annual cash value of rations @ $100.80 per extra ration[d]	504.00				201.60	100.80	100.80	100.80	0.00	0.00
Total annual compensation	1,404.00				681.60	700.80	580.80	460.80	228.00	300.00
As amended by Act of 25 February 1799										
Base pay per year	$1,200.00	$900.00	$720.00	$600.00	$480.00	$600.00	$480.00	$360.00	$228.00	$300.00
Extra rations per day[c]	7[e]	5[e]	4[e]	3	2	1	1	1	0	0
Annual cash value of rations @ $100.80 per extra ration[d]	705.60	504.00	403.20	302.40	201.60	100.80	100.80	100.80	0.00	0.00
Total annual compensation[f]	1,905.60	1,404.00	1,123.20	902.40	681.60	700.80	580.80	460.80	228.00	300.00
1 May 1801–31 December 1813										
Base pay per year	$1,200.00	$900.00	$720.00	$600.00	$480.00	$600.00	$480.00	$360.00	$228.00	$300.00
Annual cash value of rations @ $72.00 per extra ration[d]	504.00	360.00	288.00	216.00	144.00	72.00	72.00	72.00	0.00	0.00
Total annual compensation[f]	1,704.00	1,260.00	1,008.00	816.00	624.00	672.00	552.00	432.00	228.00	300.00
1 January 1814 and after[g]										
Base pay per year	$1,200.00	$900.00	$720.00	$600.00	$480.00	$600.00	$480.00	$360.00	$228.00	$300.00

Annual cash value of rations @ $90.00 per extra ration[d]	630.00	450.00	360.00	270.00	180.00	90.00	90.00	90.00	0.00	0.00
Total annual compensation[f]	1,830.00	1,350.00	1,080.00	870.00	660.00	570.00	690.00	450.00	228.00	300.00

Hardship pay (lakes stations), 18 April 1814–22 February 1817

Base pay per year	$1,500.00	$1,125.00	$900.00	$750.00	$600.00	$600.00	$750.00	$450.00	$285.00	$375.00
Annual cash value of rations @ $90.00 per extra ration[d]	630.00	450.00	360.00	270.00	180.00	90.00	90.00	90.00	0.00	0.00
Total annual compensation[f]	2,130.00	1,575.00	1,260.00	1,020.00	780.00	690.00	840.00	540.00	285.00	375.00

Officer not on active duty after 3 March 1801

Total annual compensation[f]	$600.00	$450.00	$360.00	$240.00	$240.00	$300.00	$300.00	$180.00	$114.00	$0.00[h]

a. Midshipmen acting as lieutenants by appointment from the Navy Department, or whose appointments as such had been confirmed by the department, received the compensation of lieutenants (Accnt LS 10:380: Thomas H. Gilliss to George S. Wise, 16 Aug. 1813). Midshipmen commanding gunboats received the same compensation as sailing masters (OSW 8:152: Robert Smith, Circular to Commanding Officers, 26 Oct. 1808; 8:158: Smith to Rodgers, 7 Nov. 1808). Midshipmen rated as master's mates were paid $20 per month (ASP Nav Aff 1:641).

b. The pay of midshipmen and captain's clerks was not specified by law, but was discretionary with the secretary of the navy; rates established by the Navy Department may conveniently be seen in ASP Nav Aff 1:641.

c. Each officer on active duty was expected to draw one ration. The cash conversion value shown in the adjacent column applies only to the additional rations, beyond that one, allowed by law to certain officers. The number of extra rations attached to particular ranks did not change for the balance of the period covered by this table; hence, this column is omitted after the act of 25 Feb. 1799.

d. Naval pay was calculated on the basis of twelve months of thirty days per month. Partial months were estimated as fractions of thirty (Accnt LS 5:33: Thomas Turner to Abraham Cordrey, 22 Sept. 1804). Throughout this table the cash value of the extra rations is calculated as a 360-day year.

e. Commencing 25 Feb. 1799 any officer commanding a squadron on separate service was entitled to double rations during the continuance of his command.

f. Commencing 1 Sept. 1799 monthly pay was subject to a deduction of 20 cents per month toward the creation of marine hospitals under the terms of "An Act in Addition to 'An Act for the Relief of Sick and Disabled Seamen,'" 2 Mar. 1799. Because of its small size, this deduction ($2.40 per year) has not been shown in the calculation of total yearly compensation.

g. These rates of compensation remained in force throughout the period covered by this book and were altered at various dates in later years, a history that may be followed in Homans, under the index entry "Pay."

h. Captain's clerks were not retained on half-pay when not on active duty.

TABLE 30
Selected Prize Money Distributions

	Frolic, captured by Wasp and subsequently recaptured; congressional appropriation = $25,000 [a]	Falcon, British schooner captured by President; captors' share = $17,875.00; agent's commission = $830.75; distribution = $17,044.25 [b]	British squadron, Lake Erie; congressional appropriation = $255,000 [c]	Levant, captured by Constitution and subsequently recaptured; congressional appropriation = $25,000.00; agent's costs and commission = $1,789.00; distribution = $23,211.00 [d]	Algerian vessels captured by the U.S. squadron; Constellation's portion = $16,868.33 [e]	Same; Torch's portion = $3,743.63 [e]
Squadron commodore	None		$12,750.00	None	$843.42	$187.18
Captain/master commandant	$3,750.00	$2,492.19	7,140.00	$3,481.65	1,686.83	374.36
Lieutenant/sailing master	416.67	196.51	2,295.00	290.13	240.98	124.79
Surgeon, purser, boatswain, gunner, etc.	312.50	142.91	1,214.29	232.11	240.98	93.59
Midshipman, surgeon's mate, captain's clerk, senior petty officer	243.06	68.77	811.35	126.93	95.22	54.60
Junior petty officer, e.g., quartermaster, quarter gunner	208.33	53.11	447.39	51.81	75.31	93.59
Seaman, ordinary seaman, boy	98.32	14.00	214.89	22.19	20.57	15.79

a. ASP Nav Aff 1:564–565.
b. RFP, Ser 2: Account of Charles W. Goldsborough, agent for the distribution of the money, 25 Dec. 1824.
c. ASP Nav Aff 1:563, 566–572.
d. Accts (N) #4627: "Scheme of Distribution of prize money for the capture of the Levant"; SF, XZ: "Pay Roll for Twenty five thousand dollars granted by Act of Congress to the Crew of United States frigate Constitution . . . for the capture of His Britannic Majesty's Ship Levant. . . ."
e. Accnt LR: L.W. Tazewell, Abstract of account as prize agent, enclosed in Tazewell to Constant Freeman, 9 July 1822.

TABLE 31
Prize Money from the Capture of Enemy Vessels:
Quasi-War with France and the War of 1812 Compared
(Captors' Awards Only)

	Quasi-War	1812
Total, all prizes	$239,125	$1,612,376
Largest award	80,275	309,990
Smallest award	94	72
Mean award	2,952	19,426
Median award	1,049[a]	2,908

a. Cases of known proceeds only; median of all prizes, including estimated prize proceeds, is $1,000.

TABLE 32
Commanding Officers Earning More than $500 in Prize Money from the
Capture of Armed Vessels during the Quasi-War with France

	Total prize money @ 10%	Number of paying prizes	Annual pay and rations[a]	Prize money as multiple of pay and rations
Thomas Truxtun	$8,772	3	$1,906	4.6
George Little	4,518[b]	6	1,404	3.2
John Shaw	1,530[c]	6	902	1.7
Hugh G. Campbell	1,139[c]	10	1,123	1.0
Thomas Tingey	785[d]	4	1,404	0.6
Moses Brown	698	4	1,404	0.5
Benjamin Hillar	691[e]	5	1,123[f]	0.6
William Cowper	688[e]	1	1,123	0.6
David Jewett	634	1	1,123	0.6

a. Does not include double rations while serving as squadron commodore or while on independent service.
b. Includes one small prize estimated at $100.
c. Includes one prize estimated at $1,000.
d. Includes three prizes estimated at $1,000 each.
e. Includes two prizes estimated at $1,000 each.
f. Pay subsequent to his 8 February 1800 promotion to master commandant; some prize money was earned while his annual pay and rations were $902.

TABLE 33
Commodores and Captains Earning $10,000 or More in Prize Money during the War of 1812

	As squadron commodore	As commander of single vessel	Total[a]
Stephen Decatur	$ 99	$30,000	$30,099
Thomas Macdonough	22,807	0	22,807
John Rodgers	11,484	8,259	19,743
Charles Stewart	0	14,744	14,744
Isaac Chauncey	14,484+[b]	0	14,484+[b]
Lewis Warrington	0	12,855	12,855
William Bainbridge	3,776	7,500	11,276
Samuel Evans	0	10,290	10,290

a. Because of the changes in compensation rates during the War of 1812 (Table 29), no attempt is made here to calculate total earnings as a multiple of pay and rations.

b. Chauncey's 5 percent as squadron commodore only ($12,750 from Lake Erie battle); how Chauncey may have shared in prize money earned by captures on Lake Ontario in which his own ship may have participated directly is unknown.

TABLE 34
Pursers: Ages at Initial Appointment

Youngest man appointed	19
Oldest man appointed	77
Mean age at appointment	28.1
Age at first quartile	23.0
Median age at appointment	27.0
Age at third quartile	29.5
Number of pursers of known age	53
Percent of all pursers for whom ages are known	43.1

TABLE 35
Pursers: States of Residence at Appointment

	1798–1800		1803–1814		1798–1814	
	Number	Percent[a]	Number	Percent[a]	Number	Percent[a]
New England states	14	36.8	10	14.9	24	22.9
New York, New Jersey, Pennsylvania, Delaware	8	21.1	17	25.4	25	23.8
Maryland, District of Columbia, Virginia	14	36.8	34	50.7	48	45.7
North Carolina, South Carolina, Georgia	2	5.3	3	4.5	5	4.7
Western states and territories	0	0.0	3	4.5	3	2.9
Known-state appointees	38		67		105	
States of residence unknown	14	26.9[b]	4	5.6[b]	18	14.6[b]
All appointees	52		71		123	

a. Of all known-state appointees.
b. Of all appointees for period.

TABLE 36
Slop Purchases by *Argus* Enlisted Men, 20 March–26 June 1805

	Boys (N=8)	Ordinary seamen (N=35)	Seamen (N=38)	Petty officers (N=13)
Monthly wage range	$5–7	$6–8	$10–12	$17–19
Total purchases				
Minimum	$ 0.22	$ 0.00	$ 0.00	$ 2.95
First quartile	0.89	4.00	7.85	6.03
Median	8.44	9.75	12.75	10.00
Third quartile	15.34	14.75	18.73	15.75
Maximum	23.65	30.80	35.15	25.85
Cash balances due after purchases				
Minimum	$−4.25	$−4.93	$−2.82	$35.58
First quartile	5.96	7.80	14.22	41.53
Median	10.40	15.87	19.58	48.20
Third quartile	18.51	21.87	24.48	51.78
Maximum	19.18	25.87	36.65	55.25

TABLE 37
Pursers' Profits

Article	As calculated by John Rodgers before circular of 6 June 1809[a]				As calculated by John Rodgers after circular of 6 June 1809[a]		As calculated by Paul Hamilton[b]			
	Amount per man per year	Cost to purser	Price to enlisted man	Profit (dollars)	Price to enlisted man[c]	Profit (dollars)[c]	Amount per man per year	Cost to purser	Price to enlisted man	Profit (dollars)[d]
Tea	10 pounds	$10.00	$20.00	$10.00	$15.00	$ 5.00	4 pounds	$3.20	$4.80	$1.60
Sugar	80 pounds	8.00	20.00	12.00	12.00	4.00	25 pounds	3.12	4.68	1.56
Tobacco	26 pounds	3.38	13.00	9.62	5.70[e]	1.90	10 pounds	2.00	3.00	1.00
Soap	52 pounds	6.50	13.00	6.50	8.12	1.63	20 pounds	2.00	2.50	0.50
Tin pots	3	0.90	1.50	0.60	1.13	0.23	2	0.40	0.50	0.10
Spoons	3	0.33	0.60	0.27	0.41	0.08	2	0.12	0.15	0.03
Mustard	2 bottles	0.30	1.00	0.70	0.38	0.08	1 bottle	0.20	0.25	0.05
Chocolate	4 pounds	1.00	2.00	1.00	1.25	0.25	4 pounds	0.80	1.00	0.20
Knives	4	0.80	2.00	1.20	1.00	0.20	2	0.40	0.50	0.10
Combs	4	0.50	1.00	0.50	0.63	0.13	2	0.20	0.25	0.05
Brushes	3	0.45	0.90	0.45	0.56	0.11	2	0.40	0.50	0.10
Ribbon	1 yard	0.02	0.04	0.02	0.03	0.01	1 yard	0.04	0.05	0.01
Profit per man per year				$42.86		$13.62				$5.30

a. RFP, LB 1808–1809: John Rodgers to Paul Hamilton, 23 June 1809, "Statement A" and "Statement B."
b. Cong LB 2:108–111: Paul Hamilton to John Randolph, 3 Apr. 1812, enclosing "Paper A."
c. Fractions rounded to the nearest whole cent.
d. Percentages as per the regulations of 1809.
e. For reasons unexplained, Rodgers changes the purser's cost for this one article to $3.80 in his after–6 June 1809 table.

TABLE 38
Actual Cost of Slops, from the Books of Purser James R. Wilson[a]

Article	Rodgers's 1809 estimate	Wilson's 1809–10 actual	Hamilton's 1812 estimate	Wilson's 1811–12 actual	Wilson's 1812–13 actual
Tea	$1.00/lb	0.82	0.80	1.00	1.60
Sugar	0.10/lb	0.12	0.12	0.13	0.17
Tobacco	0.13/lb	0.20	0.20	0.20	0.20
Soap	0.13/lb	0.10	0.10	0.10	0.10
Tin pots	0.30 ea ⎱	0.25	⎧0.20⎱	0.38	0.38
Spoons	0.11 ea ⎰		⎩0.06⎰		
Mustard	0.15/ea	0.12	0.20	0.12	0.12
Chocolate	0.25/lb	0.20	0.20	0.27	0.27
Knives	0.20 ea	0.15	0.20	0.19	0.32
Combs	0.13 ea	0.16	0.10	0.12	0.12
Brushes	0.15 ea	0.35	0.20	0.35	0.35
Ribbon	0.02/yd	not listed	0.02	not listed	not listed

a. Accts (A) Wilson, James R.: Costs and prices of articles issued, 1809/10–1812/13.

TABLE 39
Officers Whose Service Ended before 14 February 1815

	Number	Percent of all officers separated before 14 Feb. 1815	Percent of all officers for whom a manner of termination can be assigned (N=1,517)
Died in service	331	18.5	21.8
Discharged in reductions of force	336	18.8	22.2
Resigned	616	34.4	40.6
Dismissed	234	13.1	15.4
Service terminated; reasons not specified in records	143	8.0	
Precise date and cause of separation from service unknown	128	7.2	
	1,788		

497

TABLE 40
Causes of Death, September 1797–February 1815

	Number	Percent of deaths with known cause (N=247)
Enemy action	48	19.5
Lost with ship	67	27.1
Accident	19	7.7
Duel	18	7.3
Suicide	6	2.4
Natural causes	89	36.0
Cause of death unknown	84	
	331	

TABLE 41
Causes of Death, September 1797–February 1815, with the Unknown-cause Deaths Distributed Proportionately to Suicide, Accident, and Natural-causes Categories

	Number	Percent of all deaths
Enemy action	48	14.5
Lost with ship	67	20.3
Accident	33	10.0
Duel	18	5.4
Suicide	10	3.0
Natural causes	155	46.8
	331	

TABLE 42
**Officers Whose Service Ended before 14 February 1815, Modified to Show
Probable Number of True Resignations and Dismissals**

	Number	Percent of all officers for whom a manner of termination can be assigned (N = 1,517)
Died in service	331	21.8
Discharged in reductions of force	336	22.1
True resignations	462	30.5
Dismissals, including resignations to avoid dismissal	388	25.6
	1,517	

TABLE 43
Ranks of Officers Dismissed, December 1798–February 1815

	Number	Percent of all officers dismissed
Captains	3	0.9
Masters commandant	1	0.3
Lieutenants	31	9.6
Midshipmen	179	55.6
Sailing masters	75	23.3
Surgeons	9	2.8
Surgeon's mates	11	3.4
Pursers	5	1.6
Chaplains/schoolmasters	5	1.6
Captain's clerks	3	0.9
	322	

TABLE 44
Ranks of Officers Dismissed on Charges Involving Alcohol Abuse, December 1798–February 1815

	Number	Percent of all officers dismissed for alcohol abuse	Rank as percentage of officers dismissed, all causes, Dec. 1798–Feb. 1815 (N = 322)
Captains	0	0.0	0.9
Masters commandant	0	0.0	0.3
Lieutenants	9	10.2	9.6
Midshipmen	50	56.8	55.6
Sailing masters	21	23.9	23.3
Surgeons	2	2.3	2.8
Surgeon's mates	2	2.3	3.4
Pursers	3	3.4	1.6
Chaplains/schoolmasters	1	1.1	1.6
Captain's clerks	0	0.0	0.9
	88		

TABLE 45
Length of Service: Midshipmen Who Received Initial Appointments, 1802–1809

	Number	Percent of all appointed	Cumulative percentage
0–6 months	36	8.7	8.7
7–12 months	38	9.2	17.9
13–18 months	39	9.4	27.3
19–24 months	34	8.2	35.5
25–30 months	24	5.8	41.3
31–36 months	15	3.6	44.9
37–42 months	14	3.4	48.3
43–48 months	10	2.4	50.7
49–54 months	16	3.9	54.6
55–60 months	14	3.4	58.0
60+ months	174	42.0	100.0
	414		

Bibliographic Essay: Discovering the Navy's Officers, 1794–1815

Because the chapter notes that follow cannot tell the full story of the sources on which this book is based, some general remarks on those materials are appropriate. Both text and data tables are derived from biographical profiles, compiled over a period of nearly twenty years, for each of the 2,902 identifiable men who entered the officer corps of the U.S. Navy between 5 June 1794 and 13 February 1815. An individual profile may contain information derived from one source or from twenty sources. The notes document most of the specific statements made in the text; but to indicate the basis for each number in every table, to enumerate all the sources for a one-paragraph summary of an officer's life, would be an impossible task.

A. Registers of Officers

The necessary first step was to establish a roster of all the individuals who served as officers in the pre-1815 navy. For the years 1794 through 1807 the task was easy. Accurate lists prepared by the staff of the Navy Department's Office of Naval Records and Library were published in [1] U.S. Office of Naval Records and Library, *Naval Documents Related to the Quasi-War between the United States and France* (Washington, D.C.: U.S. Govt. Print. Off., 1935–38) 7:315–363; and [2] U.S. Office of Naval Records and Library, *Register of Officer Personnel United States Navy and Marine Corps and Ships' Data, 1801–1807* (Washington, D.C.: U.S. Govt. Print. Off., 1945). After 1807, when one loses the guidance of the Office of Naval Records and Library, defining the roster of officers becomes a more difficult assignment. The only published register is [3] Edward W. Callahan, *List of Officers of the Navy of the United States and of the Marine Corps from 1775 to 1900* (New York: L.R. Hamersly, 1901). It is better than no list at all, but not much. Names are misspelled, occasionally grotesquely so; typographical errors abound; incorrect dates of appointment, promotion, and termination are given; data on some officers are incomplete; other officers are entered two or three times, rather than being shown as the same individual once or twice reappointed; finally, all dates shown are those of the official commission or warrant, which may vary widely from the actual date of the appointment or promotion in question.

All post-1807 names and dates of appointment, promotion, or termination were verified against the manuscript source from which Callahan's list was derived: [4] National Archives, Record Group 24, Abstracts of Service Records of Naval Officers, vols. A through E (1798–1817) (National Archives Microfilm Publication M-330, reels 1–3). Although this is an improvement over Callahan, it is still far from being a complete or wholly accurate personnel record. In the mood of administrative slackness that overtook the Navy Department in the latter years of Paul Hamilton's tenure as secretary of the navy, maintenance of the record became increasingly haphazard, and the pressures of wartime conditions after June 1812 only made matters worse. Officers died; resignations were accepted; the incompetent or the supernumerary received summary dismissals. All too often such facts were not recorded in the official register. Moreover, the Abstracts of Service record none of the acting appointments, principally of midshipmen and sailing masters, made by local commanders and never officially confirmed by the Navy Department.

The single best source for identifying officers not recorded in Callahan and the Abstracts of Service was [5] National Archives, Record Group 45, Muster Rolls and Pay Rolls of Vessels and Stations. A few additional pay- and muster rolls, not duplicated in this series, were found in Record Group 217, Fourth Auditor Accounts, Alphabetical and Numerical Series [38, 39]. All told, the surviving muster rolls and payrolls, supplemented by other sources, yielded the names and service records of several hundred officers who are not listed in the Abstracts of Service Records or in Callahan. Even so, it must be emphasized that the 2,902 identifiable officers who entered the navy between 5 June 1794 and 13 February 1815 do not equal the total number of men who actually served. An absolutely complete and accurate list of all serving officers could only be established if the pay- and muster rolls of all pre-1815 ships and shore stations were still in existence. A useful collateral source for verifying some data on officers whose appointments or promotions required Senate confirmation is [6] U.S. Congress, Senate, *Journal of the Executive Proceedings*, vols. 1–2 (Washington, D.C., 1828; reprinted, New York: Johnson Reprint, 1969); for initial appointments the nominee's state of residence is usually given. Finally, concerning one small subset of officers who served in the 1808–15 period there is an excellent published register: [7] U.S. Bureau of Naval Personnel, *United States Navy Chaplains, 1778–1945: Biographical and Service-Record Sketches*, compiled under the direction of Clifford Merrill Drury (Washington, D.C., 1948); this is based on a thorough search of all available records and is virtually complete.

B. Manuscript Records of the Federal Government

Once a list of serving officers, with their ranks and dates of appointment and termination, had been established, flesh and blood were necessary to raise them up again as living human beings. In this task the manuscript official records of the navy, supplemented by those of other federal departments and agencies and all preserved in the National Archives at Washington, proved to be the most valuable source. Not all the federal records cited in the notes are discussed in the paragraphs that follow, only those relatively unfamiliar to naval historians or ones for which some explication seemed appropriate.

The three best-known series of incoming correspondence read are, in the order of their importance for this book and with the inclusive dates: [8] Letters Received by the Secretary of the Navy from Captains, 1 January 1805–31 March 1815 (National Archives Microfilm Publication M-125, reels 1–43); [9] Letters Received by the Secretary of the Navy from Masters Commandant, 9 April 1804–30 December 1815 (Microfilm Publication M-147, reels 1–6); and [10] Letters Received by the Secretary of the Navy from Officers below the Rank of Master Commandant, 29 April 1802–28 February 1815 (Microfilm Publication M-148, reels 1–14). Of the three series, the first two were especially useful for the evaluative comments by senior officers regarding their junior subordinates, and for the mass of material they contain on disciplinary problems within the officer corps. It was the rare naval officer who could resist the temptation to indulge, at some point in his career when he felt himself slighted by the Navy Department, in an autobiographical recapitulation of his services; the third series cited above, commonly known as the Officers' Letters, is a rich source of these self-serving autobiographies. It is also from this series, with its applications for furlough and reports of readiness for duty, that one can develop a grasp of the extent and importance of merchant voyages in officer training before the War of 1812.

A series of incoming letters often slighted by the historian of naval operations is vital for the social historian in search of the officer corps of 1794–1815. The seventy-two volumes of [11] Miscellaneous Letters Received by the Secretary of the Navy, 3 January 1801–28 June 1815 (National Archives Microfilm Publication M-124, reels 1–72), contain a mass of applications and recommendations for officer appointments as well as letters from parents and political sponsors seeking to promote their children's or their protégés' careers. The Miscellaneous Letters also include a high number of acceptances of appointments and resignations by officers.

Other series of incoming letters of special value were as follows:

[12] Letters from Officers Accepting, Declining, and Resigning Appointments and Stating Places of Birth and Residence, 1804–26 (1 vol.); [13] Letters of Resignation from Officers, 1810–25 (2 vols.); [14] Letters of Resignation from Officers, 1803–25 (1 vol.); and [15] Letters of Resignation from Officers, 1812–33 (1 vol.). This series of five chronologically overlapping volumes revealed officers' stated reasons for resigning from the corps. A substantial number of additional letters of resignation will be found in the first four series of incoming letters [8, 9, 10, and 11] described above.

[16] Acceptances of Appointments by Officers, 1804–23 (3 vols.); [17] Acceptances of Appointments by Officers, 1809–39 (3 vols., with the volume that contained names beginning with *C* and *D* apparently lost); [18] Acceptances of Appointments by Midshipmen, 1810–14 (1 vol.); and [19] Acceptances of Appointments by Officers, 1812–16 (2 vols.). A large number of similar letters of acceptance will be found bound in the Miscellaneous Letters [11] series. Although purely formal documents, these acceptances are useful in establishing the full form and correct spelling of names, and for discovering the places of residence of appointees. Commencing late in 1813, midshipmen's acceptances usually specified their ages.

Among the several series of outgoing letters from the office of the secretary of the navy special mention should be made of [20] Letters Sent by the Secretary of the Navy to the President Relative to Appointment of Officers and Various Other Subjects, 1798–1820 (1 vol.), which is particularly useful during Benjamin Stoddert's tenure as secretary of the navy and during the early years of his successor, Robert Smith. A valuable feature, in view of the deficiencies of other appointment records to be discussed below, was Smith's practice—unfortunately discontinued at the end of 1804—of submitting to President Jefferson for his information lists of proposed midshipman appointments, with a statement of states of residence and the names of recommenders. [21] Letters Sent by the Secretary of the Navy to Officers, 16 March 1798–30 April 1817 (National Archives Microfilm Publication M-149, reels 1–12), constitute a series so familiar to naval historians as to need no description here other than to note that the addresses to which the letters of initial appointment recorded therein were sent often offered the only clues to the geographical origins of appointees.

Although the Board of Navy Commissioners was not established until 1815, some of the Commissioners' records look backward to earlier years and are valuable for understanding the officer corps of 1794–1815. The massive files accumulated between 1815 and 1842 have, until quite recently, been almost entirely neglected by naval historians. This is surprising, because the most superficial examination of these volumes reveals how essential they are to understanding the history of the navy between the War of 1812 and the Mexican War.

The single most valuable discovery among the records of the Commissioners was the [22] Register of Officers of the Navy, May 1815–June 1821 (1 vol.). This volume had its origins in a realization that, save for the inadequate Abstracts of Service Records of Naval Officers [4], the Navy Department of 1815 possessed no systematic personnel dossiers on its serving officers. The resulting 29 April 1815 circular from the president of the Board of Navy Commissioners, Commodore John Rodgers, to commanding officers of ships and stations directed, "You will be pleased to transmit to the Board of Navy Commissioners a roll of all the commission and warrant officers under your command, exhibiting their names, grade, dates of commissions and warrants, periods of service, vessels or stations served in as far as you can ascertain it, age, and remarkable conduct, whether good or bad" (Library of Congress, Rodgers Family Papers, Ser 3A, 2d ser.). The replies, covering some six hundred officers below the rank of captain, were summarized under each subject's name in the alphabetical register, and the volume was kept up to date by subsequent fitness reports received over the next six years. Unfortunately, the original reports, which were often considerably more detailed than the summaries in the Register, have been dispersed. Of the thirty reports that can be identified from the Register as having been made in 1815, this historian has been able to locate and use the following (including four from 1817–18) in these repositories:

New York Public Library, U.S. Navy Miscellaneous Box, 1776–1820 [23]:
Arthur Sinclair to John Rodgers, 2 June 1815.

Franklin D. Roosevelt Library, Hyde Park, N.Y., Naval History Manuscript Collection [24]:
Alexander Murray, "A Descriptive Return of Officers Attached to the Philada. Station," 5 May 1815.
Samuel Angus, "A Roll of all the Commissioned, & Warranted Officers, attach'd to the U.S. Corvette John-Adams, under my Command," 9 May 1815.

National Archives, Record Group 45, Miscellaneous Letters [11]:
John Rodgers, "Report of the Qualifications of the Commissioned and
Warrant Officers of the U.S.F. President," 10 March 1814.
National Archives, Record Group 45, Muster Rolls and Pay Rolls of Vessels and
Stations [5]:
Erie: Charles G. Ridgely to John Rodgers, 19 May 1815, enclosing "Roll of
Commissioned and Warrant Officers of the U.S. Ship Erie."
Lake Erie: [Arthur Sinclair], "Descriptive Roll of Commissioned & Warrant
Officers, Erie Station," 2 June 1815.
Gosport: John Cassin to John Rodgers, 8 May 1815.
Independence: William M. Crane to John Rodgers, 2 June 1815, enclosing
"Muster Roll of Officers on Board United States Ship Independence
Captain Crane," 27 May 1815.
New Orleans: Daniel T. Patterson to Board of Navy Commissioners, 19
July 1815, enclosing Daniel T. Patterson to B.W. Crowninshield, 10
February 1815. Daniel T. Patterson to John Rodgers, 3 February 1818.
Philadelphia: Alexander Murray, "A List of Officers & Men attached to the
Philada. Station," 5 January 1817.
Saranac: John H. Elton, "Return of the Commissioned and Warranted
Officers attached to the United States Brig Saranac," 22 December
1815.
Spark: Thomas Gamble to John Rodgers, [5 May 1815], enclosing "A Roll
of the Commissioned and Warrant Officers belonging to the United
States Hermaphrodite Brig Spark under my command," 5 May 1815.
National Archives, Record Group 45, Subject File [26], Class NA:
[Alexander J. Dallas], "Roll of Officers on board the U.S. Schr. Spitfire
with the Dates of their Warrants & vessels or Stations on which they
have served," [4 May 1815].
Wolcott Chauncey to John Rodgers, 5 May 1815, enclosing "A list of
commissioned and warrant officers on board the U.S. Schooner Torch
under my command."
National Archives, Record Group 45, Subject File, Class NI:
Thomas Macdonough to John Rodgers, 6 May 1815.
Thomas Tingey to Rodgers, 9 May 1815.
Charles C.B. Thompson to Rodgers, 28 July 1815.
Thomas Tingey to Rodgers, 31 December 1817.
Melancthon T. Woolsey to Rodgers, 23 February 1818.

Between 1924 and 1942 the Navy Department's Office of Naval Records
and Library gathered a mass of loose papers from its own files, from those of
other offices of the Navy Department, and from private donors. To them it
added documents from the deteriorating bound volumes in its custody, which
volumes it disassembled. The resulting whole was then rearranged either
according to the geographical location in which the event described in the
document took place or according to the topic with which the document deals,
but in either case without regard to the original groupings of the papers. Those
two vast series, running to nearly four hundred shelf feet of archive boxes, are
known respectively as the [25] Area File (National Archives Microfilm Publication M-625) and the [26] Subject File. Of the two, the Area File is the more
familiar to naval historians, but because its focus is primarily on operations, it
contains relatively little of importance for the social historian. The Subject File
proved more fruitful terrain, but it is vast—upward of 800 boxes—and difficult
to use. Papers most valuable for the historian of the officer corps are to be
found in the 158 boxes of class N (Personnel), with materials for the present

book being drawn principally from subclasses NA (rolls and lists of personnel), NI (fitness reports), NJ (discipline), and NN (applications for appointment).

One group of official records was so essential to the writing of this book that it merits an extended discussion at this point, even though the discussion will roam beyond the boundaries of Record Group 45. Each applicant for an appointment in the navy was expected to furnish, in addition to his own letter of application, supporting letters of recommendation. Papers pertaining to any particular applicant were grouped in a small bundle by one of the clerks in the Navy Office and assigned a file number roughly corresponding to the order in which the applications were received; the applicant's name and file number were then recorded in a register of applicants, which was arranged according to type of appointment sought and/or state of residence. Application dossiers constitute far and away the single most important source for the historian of the officer corps. They provide information on some or all of these matters: identity and status of parents, applicant's age, place of residence, education, political affiliation, relationships with persons already in the navy, and life before joining the officer corps. Unfortunately, this rich historical source has met with a strange and somewhat mysterious fate. The nature of the surviving and missing records may be most clearly understood by considering them in their chronological periods:

1794–1800: Some thirty-four applications for appointment in the navy or marine corps during these years survive among the records kept by the Navy Department. Originally these were bound as volume 1 of the series described above as Miscellaneous Letters Received by the Secretary of the Navy [11]. Sometime before the creation of the National Archives, and while the records were still in the custody of the Office of Naval Records and Library, this volume was broken up and the contents distributed to the Area File [25] and the Subject File [26]. Apparently all of the letters of application and recommendation once in this volume are now to be found in Subject File, Class NN, Box 277. Sixteen additional application dossiers are located in National Archives, Record Group 59, Letters of Application and Recommendation during the Administration of John Adams [40]. This combined total of fifty applications is all that now remains of the eight hundred or more application dossiers that were on file in the Navy Office by the close of the Quasi-War with France.

1801–1807: Practically no letters of application or recommendation survive for the first seven years of Robert Smith's tenure as secretary of the navy, although it would appear that an additional thirteen hundred to fifteen hundred applications reached the secretary's desk during those seven years. This absence is particularly distressing, inasmuch as Smith's appointees were the heart of the junior officer corps by the War of 1812. The only exceptions to this lack are the few retained file copies of letters of recommendation among the private papers of certain recommenders—Edward Preble for one—and the fewer than half-dozen dossiers for naval appointments now to be found in National Archives, Record Group 59, Letters of Application and Recommendation during the Administration of Thomas Jefferson [41].

1808–1815: Commencing in 1808, applications and recommendations become plentiful, although the file is incomplete. When the Navy Department began binding its retrospective files of incoming letters in the 1820s, many of the application dossiers were incorporated in the series now known as Miscellaneous Letters Received by the Secretary of the Navy [11]. For no discernible reason, other dossiers, in no way distinguishable from those in the Miscellaneous Letters, remained tied in bundles in their original numerical sequences. These latter dossiers have now become sadly scattered. Many can be found in Subject File [26], Class NN. Others have been integrated into the [27] ZB File, a biographical section of the Subject File never transferred to the National Archives, and which remains in the custody of the Early Records Section of the Naval Historical Center at the Washington navy yard. Some of the documents in these two collections of dossiers are charred around the edges, thereby suggesting that a portion of the dossiers may have been destroyed by fire at some time in the nineteenth century.

Those application dossiers now incorporated into the Subject File and the ZB File have at least remained part of the public record. An unknown proportion of the original application files has become scattered across the land and is now to be found in libraries, historical societies, and the files of private collectors. Nearly one hundred applications from the 1808–15 period stuck to the fingers of Gideon Welles during one of his two tenures at the Navy Department and are now located in volume 1 of the [28] Gideon Welles Papers, at the Library of Congress. A more serious dispersal of application dossiers seems to have occurred in the late nineteenth or early twentieth century, while the records were still in the custody of the Navy Department. A person or persons unknown apparently systematically pilfered the application dossiers for letters with collector value and sold them on the autograph market. The consequence is that there exists hardly a library or a historical society in the land that does not have documents that were once part of the appointment dossiers. These are readily identifiable by their file numbers, their contents, and the fact that they are addressed to one of the secretaries of the navy. Substantial groups of such recommendations are to be found in [29] Miscellaneous Manuscripts Collection, New-York Historical Society, New York City; [30] Albert L. Butler Autograph Collection, Connecticut Historical Society, Hartford; and [31] Manuscripts Department, Alderman Library, University of Virginia, Charlottesville.

Special attention must be drawn to the [32] U.S. Department of the Navy Collection at the Duke University Library, Durham, North Carolina. This is a mass of incoming official correspondence that was at one time part of the four major series of such papers described above [8, 9, 10, and 11] and that became separated from them in a now-unknown manner. No naval historian in search of papers not present in the central files at the National Archives can afford to ignore this collection. It is especially rich in letters of recommendation.

Record Group 24: Records of the Bureau of Naval Personnel

Two obscure volumes housed here are of great value to the social historian. On 18 March 1842 the U.S. Senate directed the secretary of the navy to prepare a tabular statement showing the length of sea service and other duty performed by all commissioned officers and passed midshipmen currently on the navy register (U.S. Congress, Senate, *Journal*, 27th Cong., 2d Sess. [Serial 394], p. 231). In order to compile the required data the secretary was compelled to ask each living officer to fill out printed forms. Twenty-one officers who began their professional careers before 1815 judged that these forms were utterly inadequate to represent their services to the nation or impossible to complete accurately because of lost personal papers. These twenty-four used the occasion to submit extensive autobiographical statements, which will be found in [33]

Letters from Officers Transmitting Statements of Their Service, June 1842–December 1844.

Record Group 217: Records of Accounting Officers of the Treasury Department

Here are found the archives of the accountant of the navy (after 3 March 1817, the fourth auditor of the treasury). These have scarcely been used by naval historians, but they are a tremendously important source for the pre-1815 years. In contrast to the situation with respect to the secretary of the navy's records, incoming correspondence files survive intact from the establishment of the accountant's office in 1798. Important documents originally addressed to the secretary of the navy were often sent downstairs to the accountant because of their accounting implications. Such letters were then filed or bound with the accountant's records. One accountant of the navy, Thomas Turner, served for almost the entire period covered in this book; because he died in office, some personal letters, which he would otherwise have removed from the files, were later bound with his official incoming correspondence.

The arrangement of the accountant's correspondence is simpler than that for the records of the office of the secretary of the navy. There are four principal series, which were read for the years indicated: [34] Letters Received by the Accountant of the Navy (later Fourth Auditor of the Treasury), March 1795–June 1824 (83 vols.); [35] Letters Sent by the Accountant of the Navy (later Fourth Auditor of the Treasury), May 1800–October 1824 (19 vols.), with the first volume of this series, covering the period September 1798–May 1800, housed in Record Group 45; [36] Executive Letters Received by the Accountant of the Navy (later Fourth Auditor of the Treasury), 1801–29 (1 vol.); and [37] Executive Letters Sent by the Fourth Auditor of the Treasury, vol. 1 (April 1820–November 1826).

Of nearly equal importance for the social historian are the Fourth Auditor Settled Accounts. These are divided into an [38] Alphabetical Series and a [39] Numerical Series, but originally constituted one numerical sequence. The accounts now filed alphabetically were apparently separated from the numerical series because they were individually bulkier, but there is no hard-and-fast rule to determine in which series a particular account will be found. No accounts finally settled before 3 March 1817 survive. All those adjusted and settled in the office of the accountant of the navy before the year 1812 were destroyed when the British burned the government buildings at Washington on 24 August 1814 (Letters Sent by the Accountant of the Navy: Thomas Turner to Joseph Reed, 16 December 1814). Accounts settled between 1812 and 3 March 1817—that is, before the reorganization of the accounting activities of the federal government—were lost in a fire that destroyed the Treasury building on 31 March 1833 (Lyle J. Holverstott, "Treasury Records and the Treasury Building Fire of March 31, 1833," March 1940, p. 7; typescript report on file in the Central Search Room, National Archives). The latter loss is less extensive than might appear at first blush. Because of the accounting backlog that developed during and after the War of 1812, many wartime accounts and some from earlier years had not been settled by 3 March 1817 and thus survive. However, with minor exceptions such as Melancthon T. Woolsey, it is pointless for the historian to waste time looking for the accounts of any important naval figure for the Quasi-War, Barbary Wars, or pre–War of 1812 years. All such accounts were reduced to ash and charred paper a century and a half ago. Those accounts that do survive are of great value to the social historian, to the material historian concerned with ship construction and the equipment of ships, and even to the historian of operations. The rigorous accounting rules in force required that all receipts and vouchers be specific and detailed, and important correspondence was often filed with the accounts as supporting evidence.

Record Group 59: Records of the Department of State

Seven related series of documents are pertinent to the history of the navy's pre-1815 officers: [40] Letters of Application and Recommendation during the Administration of John Adams, 1797–1801 (National Archives Microfilm Publication M-406; 3 reels); [41] Letters of Application and Recommendation during the Administration of Thomas Jefferson, 1801–1809 (Microfilm Publication M-418; 12 reels); [42] Letters of Application and Recommendation during the Administration of James Madison, 1809–17 (Microfilm Publication M-438; 8 reels); [43] Letters of Application and Recommendation during the Administration of James Monroe, 1817–25 (Microfilm Publication M-439; 19 reels); [44] Letters of Application and Recommendation during the Administration of John Quincy Adams, 1825–29 (Microfilm Publication M-531; 8 reels); [45] Letters of Application and Recommendation during the Administration of Andrew Jackson, 1829–37 (Microfilm Publication M-639; 27 reels); and [46] Letters of Application and Recommendation during the Administrations of Martin Van Buren, William Henry Harrison, and John Tyler, 1837–45 (Microfilm Publication M-687; 35 reels).

The earliest series were the most useful, and each successive series became progressively less fruitful. Applications for the full spectrum of federal offices will be found in the first two series. Thereafter the Applications and Recommendations become steadily more focused on appointments directly under the control of the Department of State. The two first series contain a substantial number of applications for naval appointments; later series, while including an occasional letter from a serving officer, are primarily interesting for correspondence from former naval officers seeking or holding consular and similar appointments under the Department of State. The first three series are also an excellent source of information about the fathers of midshipmen appointed during the years covered by this book. Indeed, the letters by and about fathers in the Applications and Recommendations may have been more valuable than the letters from and concerning the officers themselves. Applications and recommendations for office during Washington's presidency constitute [47] Series 7 of the George Washington Papers in the Manuscript Division, Library of Congress. Their content and usefulness to the social historian are similar, though on a reduced scale, to those of the papers for the Adams, Jefferson, and Madison administrations in Record Group 59.

Another file in Record Group 59, the [48] List of U.S. Consular Officers, 1789–1939 (National Archives Microfilm Publication M-587), was employed to establish such service by former or future naval officers. The List of U.S. Consular Officers is useful and accurate for dates of appointment but must, in many cases, be supplemented by data from other sources to discover length and termination of service.

Record Group 26: Records of the United States Coast Guard

[49] U.S. Revenue Marine, Register of Officers, 1791–1870, records pre- and postnaval service in revenue cutters by officers of the navy. This register suffers from inadequacies similar to those that characterize the Navy Department's Abstracts of Service Records [4] and the State Department's List of U.S. Consular Officers [48]. It is not a complete roster, and if it is necessary to determine the exact dates of a revenue cutter officer's service, other sources— the applications for revenue cutter posts in the appointment files for the Washington, Adams, and Jefferson administrations [47, 40, 41] and the accounts and vouchers of individual collectors of customs (who paid the revenue cutter officers) in [50] Record Group 217, Miscellaneous Treasury Accounts of the First Auditor of the Treasury (National Archives Microfilm Publication M-235)—will, as often as not, have to be used. The various rosters of officers in [51] Horatio Davis Smith, *Early History of the United States Revenue Marine Service or United States Revenue Cutter Service, 1789–1849*, ed. by Elliot Snow (Washington, D.C., 1932) are also occasionally helpful.

C. Demographic Records of the American and British Governments

Files maintained by the various federal collectors of customs (National Archives, Record Group 36: Records of the Bureau of Customs) in connection with seamen's protective certificates, federally issued identification documents granted to native-born and naturalized American mariners, are a fertile source for data on ages, places of birth (or residence), and physical descriptions (including distinguishing marks, old wounds, or tattoos) for naval officers who also sailed in the merchant service and who applied for such a paper. On the seamen's protective certificates generally and their value as a source of social history, see Ira Dye's landmark study [52] "Early American Merchant Seafarers," American Philosophical Society *Proceedings* 120(1976):331–360. All such records as have thus far come to light at the National Archives were examined during the research for this book. In approximate descending order of usefulness they were (with the years examined): [53] Seamen's Protective Certificate Applications, Philadelphia, 1796–1818; [54] Register of Seamen, Baltimore, 1808–16; [55] Proofs of American Citizenship, New Orleans, 1804–16; [56] Abstracts of Seamen's Protective Certificates, New York, 1815; [57] Abstracts of Seamen's Protective Certificates, Boston, 1815; and [58] Proofs of American Citizenship, Alexandria, D.C., 1803–11.

Similar records from two New England ports are located at the Archives Branch of the Federal Archives and Records Center, Waltham, Massachusetts. They were (with dates examined): [59] Registers of Seamen, New London, 1796–1804, 1803–18; [60] Register of American Seamen, New Haven, 1796–1802, in Journal of the Collector of Customs, New Haven, 1763–1802; and [61] Register of American Seamen, New Haven, 1803–16.

Demographic data, comparable to those recorded in connection with the American seamen's protective certificates, were collected by the British authorities for all American prisoners of war, including officers, who fell into their hands during the War of 1812. These records are now housed at the Public Record Office, London, as: [62] Adm 103/90–91: General Entry Book of American Prisoners-of-War at Dartmoor Prison; [63] Adm 103/190: General

Entry Book of American Prisoners-of-War at Jamaica; [64] Adm 103/268–269: General Entry Book of American Prisoners-of-War at Plymouth; [65] Adm 103/343: General Entry Book of American Prisoners-of-War at Portsmouth; [66] Adm 103/573: General Entry Book of American Prisoners-of-War on Parole at Jamaica, 28 August 1812–30 March 1815; and [67] Adm 103/625: Account of French Prisoners-of-War Who Have Died at Halifax (includes information on American prisoners of war as well). All such prisoner-of-war records were examined from the microfilm copies in the possession of Ira Dye. One similar British prisoner-of-war record is in the Public Archives of Canada, Record Group 8, I, "C" Series, vols. 694A–694B: [68] General Entry Book of American Prisoners of War at Quebec (microfilm publication reels C-3233 and C-3234).

D. *Genealogies, Local Histories, Vital Records*

Beyond the manuscript official records of the federal government the most valuable sources of social data on the members of the officer corps were family genealogies, town and county histories, and published collections of vital records, notably, in the latter category, those for the Massachusetts towns. From these sources were collected places and dates of birth; identity of and status information regarding parents; relationships by blood or marriage with other officers of the navy; marriages; places and dates of death; and (occasionally) clues to pre- and postnaval careers. Genealogies and local histories were most helpful for persons whose familial and geographical origins lay north and east of the Mason-Dixon line. With notable exceptions, especially in South Carolina, southern genealogies were disappointing, and helpful local histories almost nonexistent. Regardless of the side of the Pennsylvania-Maryland border on which an officer's origins lay, it was almost always necessary to establish from the manuscript official records two or three facts about him before a search of genealogies, local histories, or vital records could be undertaken with any reasonable prospect of finding data. There were simply too many people with identical names to confuse one's search. Widespread and continuing interest in matters genealogical has produced an impressive array of bibliographies and other finding aids to such materials that may be consulted in all major libraries supporting genealogical and local history research. Because such finding aids are continually being updated or replaced by better ones, no attempt is made to list them here.

E. *Obituaries*

Newspaper obituary notices were a fruitful source for information about members of the officer corps, particularly in light of the Navy Department's erratic practice when it came to recording the deaths of junior officers in the Abstracts of Service Records [4]. Indexes to newspaper obituary notices found especially helpful were: [69] American Antiquarian Society, *Index of Obituaries in Massachusetts Centinel and Columbian Centinel, 1784–1840* (5 vols.; Boston: G.K. Hall, 1961); [70] Joseph Gavitt, comp., *American Deaths and Marriages, 1784–1829* [microfilm of a card file at the New York State Library, Albany] (2 reels; New Orleans, La.: Polyanthos, 1976); [71] H.R. McIlwaine, ed., *Index to Obituary Notices in the Richmond Enquirer from May 9, 1804, through 1828, and the Richmond*

Whig from January, 1824, through 1838 (Baltimore, Md.: Genealogical Publishing Co., 1974); and [72] "Biographical Notes from the *Maryland Gazette,* 1800–1821," contributed by George A. Martin, *Maryland Historical Magazine* 42(1947):160–183, 270–297.

In addition to obituary notices for which there are published indexes, student research assistants searched all issues of the [73] Washington *Daily National Intelligencer* from 1840 through 1860 in quest of obituaries of naval officers or former naval officers. Some earlier years and earlier issues of the *Daily National Intelligencer* were spot-checked for death notices and obituary sketches of particular individuals.

F. Academy and College Records

These provided not only information on the educational experiences of the future naval officers who could be traced therein, but often data on ages, places of residence, and (occasionally) parents as well. Published and manuscript records are here grouped in one alphabetical sequence by the name of the institution.

[74] Boston Latin School Association. *Catalogue of the Boston Public Latin School, Established in 1635.* With an Historical Sketch, prepared by Henry F. Jenks. Boston, 1886.

[75] Bowdoin College. *General Catalogue of Bowdoin College and the Medical School of Maine: A Biographical Record of Alumni and Officers, 1794–1950.* Brunswick, Maine, 1950.

[76] Brown University. *Historical Catalogue, 1764–1904.* Providence, R.I., 1905.

[77] Brown University. *Historical Catalogue, 1764–1934.* Providence, R.I., 1936. Gives full details only for those "who were not represented by adequate biographies" in [76].

[78] Easterby, James Harold. *A History of the College of Charleston, Founded 1770.* [Charleston, S.C.], 1935. Includes (pp. 278–289) lists of students, 1790–1836.

[79] Columbia University. Committee on General Catalogue. *Columbia University Officers and Alumni, 1754–1857.* Comp. Milton Halsey Thomas. New York: Columbia University Press, 1936. One of the best and most helpful of the alumni catalogs.

[80] Chapman, George T. *Sketches of the Alumni of Dartmouth College.* Cambridge, Mass.: Riverside Press, 1867.

[81] Dartmouth College. *General Catalogue of Dartmouth College and the Associated Schools, 1769–1900.* Hanover, N.H., 1900. Graduates only.

[82] Dartmouth College. *Dartmouth College and Associated Schools General Catalogue, 1769–1940.* Hanover, N.H., 1940. Unlike [81], lists nongraduates as well as graduates.

[83] Reed, George Leffingwell, ed. *Alumni Record, Dickinson College.* Carlisle, Pa., 1905. Includes nongraduates.

[84] Georgetown University Archives. Annual list of Georgetown College students, compiled from the account books by the archives staff (typescript).

[85] Georgia. University. *Catalogue of the Trustees, Officers, Alumni, and Matriculates, from 1785 to 1906.* Athens, Ga.: E.D. Stone Press, 1906.

[86] Hampden-Sidney College. *General Catalogue of the Officers and Students, 1776–1906*. Richmond, Va.: Whillet & Shepperson [1908].

[87] Harvard University. *Quinquennial Catalogue of the Officers and Graduates, 1636–1925*. Cambridge, Mass., 1925.

[88] Matthews, Albert. "Tentative Lists of Temporary Students at Harvard College, 1639–1800." Colonial Society of Massachusetts *Publications* 17(1913–14):271–285. Nongraduates; after 1800 similar information must be culled year by year from Admissions Book, vol. 1, in [89] below.

[89] Harvard University Archives. Admissions Book, vol. 1; Faculty Records, vols. 4, 6–8; Corporation Records, vols. 3–4; Overseers' Records, vol. 4; Quinquennial File; Class of 1800: Class Book; Class of 1814: Secretary's File; George Goldthwait Ingersoll, Record of the Class of 1815; R.M. Hodges, "Records of the Class of 1815"; Harvard College "Necrology," Boston *Daily Advertiser*, Extra, 21 July 1855; *Necrology, 1869–1872* (Cambridge, Mass., 1872); Hector Orr, Commonplace Book, 1789–1804; John Langdon Sibley, Private Journal and Letters Received.

[90] *Sibley's Harvard Graduates: Biographical Sketches of Those Who Attended Harvard College*, vol. 1–. Boston: Massachusetts Historical Society, 1873–.

[91] Fisher, Samuel Herbert. *Litchfield Law School, 1774–1833: Biographical Catalogue of Students*. [New Haven, Conn.:] Yale University Press, 1946.

[92] Maryland. University. School of Medicine. *Catalogue of the Alumni, 1807–1877*. Baltimore, Md.: Kelly, Piet, 1877.

[93] North Carolina. University. *Alumni History*. 2d ed. Durham, N.C.: General Alumni Association, 1924. Includes nongraduates.

[94] Pennsylvania. University. General Alumni Society. *General Alumni Catalogue, 1917*. [Philadelphia, 1917]. Graduates only.

[95] Pennsylvania. University. Society of the Alumni. *Biographical Catalogue of the Matriculates of the College . . . 1749 1893*. Philadelphia, 1894. Includes nongraduates as well as graduates.

[96] University of Pennsylvania Archives. Medical School Matriculation Register.

[97] Carpenter, Charles Carroll. *Biographical Catalogue of the Trustees, Teachers, and Students of Phillips Academy, Andover, 1778–1830*. Andover, Mass.: The Andover Press, 1903.

[98] Phillips Exeter Academy. *General Catalogue of the Officers and Students, 1783–1903*. Exeter, Mass.: The News-Letter Press, 1903.

[99] Alexander, Samuel Davies. *Princeton College during the Eighteenth Century*. New York: A.D.F. Randolph, [1872].

[100] Princeton University. *General Catalogue, 1746–1906*. Princeton, N.J., 1908. Graduates only.

[101] Princeton University Archives. Chronological card file of nongraduates.

[102] McLachlan, James, and Harrison, Richard A. *Princetonians, 1748– : A Biographical Dictionary*. Princeton, N.J.: Princeton University Press, 1976–.

[103] Rutgers University. *Catalogue of the Officers and Alumni of Rutgers College (Originally Queen's College) in Brunswick, N.J., 1766 to 1916*. Comp. Rev. John Howard Raven. Trenton, N.J.: State Gazette Pub. Co., 1916.

[104] "Alumni Register Issue, 1793 thru 1960," St. John's College (Annapolis) *Bulletin*, vol. 13, no. 3 (September 1961).

[105] St. Mary's Seminary. *Memorial Volume of the Centenary of St. Mary's Seminary of St. Sulpice, Baltimore, Md., 1791–1891*. Baltimore: J. Murphy, 1891. Includes (pp. 79–158) a list of students at St. Mary's College, which closed in 1852.

[106] South Carolina. University. *Roll of Students of South Carolina College, 1805–1905*. Andrew Charles Moore, comp. Columbia, S.C.: State Co., 1905.

[107] South Carolina University. South Caroliniana Library. University of South Carolina (South Carolina College) Alumni Records; collected by Professor Andrew Charles Moore for his publication *Roll of Students of South Carolina College* [106] (typescript).

[108] Leavy, William. "Roll of Students of Transylvania University, Mostly during My Stay from Summer of 1803 to October 1811." Kentucky State Historical Society *Register* 41(1943):49–55.

[109] Transylvania College Library. Manuscript card file of students.

[110] Union College. *Catalogue of the Officers and Alumni . . . from 1797 to 1884*. Albany, N.Y.: C. Van Benthuysen, 1884. Includes both graduates and non-graduates.

[111] Vermont. University. *Catalogue of the Officers of Government and Instruction, the Alumni and Other Graduates . . . 1791–1890*. Burlington, Vt.: Free Press Association, 1890.

[112] Vermont. University. *General Catalogue, 1791–1900*. Burlington, Vt.: Free Press Association, 1901.

[113] Washington and Lee University. *Catalogue of the Officers and Alumni, 1749–1888*. Baltimore, Md.: J. Murphy, 1888.

[114] Washington and Lee University. *Alumni Directory, 1749–1970*. Lexington, Va., 1971.

[115] Westford Academy. *General Catalogue of Trustees, Teachers, and Students, 1792–1895*. Westford, Mass., 1912.

[116] U.S. Congress. House. Select Committee on the Subject of the Military Academy at West Point. *Military Academy—West Point*. Washington, D.C.: Blair & Rives [1837?]. (24th Cong., 2d Sess., House Report no. 303 [Serial 306].) Includes (pp. 42–101) a complete register of all cadets admitted to that date.

[117] William and Mary College. *A Provisional List of Alumni, Grammar School Students, Members of the Faculty, and Members of the Board of Visitors, from 1693 to 1888*. Richmond, Va.: Division of Purchase and Printing, 1941.

[118] Williams College. *General Catalogue of the Officers, Graduates, and Non-graduates*. Williamstown, Mass., 1930.

[119] Yale University. *Catalogue of the Officers and Graduates, 1701–1924*. New Haven, Conn., 1924.

[120] Yale University. Annual printed catalogs of the officers and students, 1776, 1783, 1792, 1794, 1803, 1808–13. Title varies; some earlier issues are in Latin and list one class only. Essential for discovering nongraduates.

[121] Dexter, Franklin Bowditch. *Biographical Sketches of the Graduates of Yale College,* [1701–1815]. New York, 1885–1912.

Notes

Abbreviations Employed in the Notes

Abst of serv	Abstracts of Service Records of Naval Officers, RG 24, NA
Accnt Exec LR, 1801–29	Executive Letters Received by the Accountant of the Navy (later Fourth Auditor of the Treasury), 1801–29, RG 217, NA
Accnt Exec LS	Executive Letters Sent by the Fourth Auditor of the Treasury, RG 217, NA
Accnt LR	Letters Received by the Accountant of the Navy (later Fourth Auditor of the Treasury), RG 217, NA
Accnt LS	Letters Sent by the Accountant of the Navy (later Fourth Auditor of the Treasury), RG 217, NA
Accnt LS 1798–1800	Letters Sent by the Accountant of the Navy, September 1798–May 1800, RG 45, NA
Accnt Misc	Miscellaneous Letters Received and Other Papers of the Accountant of the Navy (Green Box), RG 217, NA
Accts (A)	Fourth Auditor Settled Accounts, Alphabetical Series, RG 217, NA
Accts (N)	Fourth Auditor Settled Accounts, Numerical Series, RG 217, NA
Adams Mss	Adams Family Papers, MassHS
AF	Area File of the Naval Records Collection, 1775–1910, RG 45, NA
AGO LR	Letters Received by the Adjutant General's Office (War Department), RG 94, NA
Allen Letters	"Letters of William Henry Allen, 1800–1813," *Huntington Library Quarterly* 1(1937/38):101–132, 203–243
Appmt LB	Letters Sent by the Secretary of the Navy to the President Relative to Appointment of Officers and Various Other Subjects, 1798–1820, RG 45, NA
Appmt Papers AJ	Letters of Application and Recommendation during the Administration of Andrew Jackson, 1829–37, RG 59, NA

Appmt Papers JA	Letters of Application and Recommendation during the Administration of John Adams, 1797–1801, RG 59, NA
Appmt Papers JQA	Letters of Application and Recommendation during the Administration of John Quincy Adams, 1825–29, RG 59, NA
Appmt Papers Madison	Letters of Application and Recommendation during the Administration of James Madison, 1809–17, RG 59, NA
Appmt Papers Monroe	Letters of Application and Recommendation during the Administration of James Monroe, 1817–25, RG 59, NA
Appmt Papers TJ	Letters of Application and Recommendation during the Administration of Thomas Jefferson, 1801–1809, RG 59, NA
Argus orders, 1811	William M. Crane, Rules and Regulations for the Internal Government of the U.S. Sloop *Argus*, October 1811, in Journal kept on board *Argus* and *Nautilus*, October 1811–July 1812, RG 45, NA
ASP	U.S. Congress, *American State Papers: Documents, Legislative and Executive, of the Congress of the United States* (Washington, D.C., 1832–61): Class VI. Naval Affairs (ASP Nav Aff); Class X. Miscellaneous (ASP Misc)
Barron Mss	James Barron and Samuel Barron Papers, Earl Gregg Swem Library, College of William and Mary, Williamsburg, Virginia
Barry Corres	John Barry, Original Public and Private Correspondence (Collection of John Sanford Barnes), NYHS
Boerum	William Boerum, "Private Journal Kept since my Commencement in the Navy," January–July 1815, U.S. Military Academy Library, West Point, New York
Butler Coll	Albert L. Butler Autograph Collection, ConnHS
BW	U.S. Office of Naval Records and Library, *Naval Documents Related to the United States Wars with the Barbary Powers* (Washington, D.C., 1939–45)
CL	Letters Received by the Secretary of the Navy from Captains ("Captains' Letters"), RG 45, NA
CMR	Records of General Courts-Martial and Courts of Inquiry of the Navy Department, RG 125, NA
Commandants & Agents LB	Letters Sent by the Secretary of the Navy to Commandants and Navy Agents, RG 45, NA
Cong LB	Letters Sent by the Secretary of the Navy to Congress, RG 45, NA
ConnHS	Connecticut Historical Society, Hartford
Constitution orders, 1809	John Rodgers, Orders and Regulations for the Government of the United States Frigate Constitution, Addressed to the First Lieutenant and the Other Commissioned, Warrant, and Petty Officers under My Command, 1809, USNAM
Cooper's Hist extra illus	James Fenimore Cooper, *History of the Navy of the United States of America*; extra illustrated by John S. Barnes, NYHS
DAB	*Dictionary of American Biography* (New York: Scribner, 1928–)
Dexter LB	Daniel S. Dexter Letterbook, September 1811–November 1813, RG 45, NA

Duke	Duke University Library, Durham, North Carolina
EPP	Edward Preble Papers, LC
Evans	Charles Evans, *American Bibliography: A Chronological Dictionary of All Books, Pamphlets, and Periodical Publications Printed in the United States of America,* [1639–1800]. (Chicago, etc., 1903–59)
FDRL, Naval Mss	Naval History Manuscript Collection of Franklin D. Roosevelt, Franklin D. Roosevelt Library, Hyde Park, New York
Frederick Rodgers Coll	Papers of Commodore John Rodgers owned by the late Frederick Rodgers of New York City
Gilliam Letters	"Letters of Henry Gilliam, 1809–1817," *Georgia Historical Quarterly* 38(1954):46–66
GLB	Miscellaneous Letters Sent by the Secretary of the Navy ("General Letterbook"), RG 45, NA
GW Mss	George Washington Papers, LC
Hamilton Papers	Alexander Hamilton, *Papers*; ed. Harold C. Syrett [and others] (New York, 1961–87)
Harvard Univ Arch	Harvard University Archives, Cambridge, Massachusetts
HEHL	Henry E. Huntington Library and Art Gallery, San Marino, California
Homans	U.S. Laws, statutes, etc. *Laws of the United States in Relation to the Navy and Marine Corps, to the Close of the Second Session of the Twenty-sixth Congress.* Comp. and arranged by Benjamin Homans (Washington, D.C., 1841)
HR	Records of the U.S. House of Representatives, RG 233, NA
HSPa	Historical Society of Pennsylvania, Philadelphia, Pennsylvania
Humphreys Journal	A.Y. Humphreys, Journal Kept on Board the Frigate *Constitution*, December 1814–March 1815, Lilly
Independence orders, 1815	*General Orders, U.S.S. Independence, 1815* (Washington, D.C.: Naval Historical Foundation, 1969)
Izard Family Papers	Izard Family Papers, LC
JEP	U.S. Congress, Senate, *Journal of the Executive Proceedings* (Washington, D.C., 1828–)
JM Mss	James Madison Papers, LC
Kennon Letters	"Kennon Letters," *Virginia Magazine of History and Biography* 31(1923):185–206, 296–313; 32(1924):76–87, 159–174, 265–280, 344–350; 33(1925):65–75, 268–282; 34 (1926): 120–129, 220–231, 322–338; 35(1927):13–21, 287–292; 36 (1928):170–174, 231–238, 363–370; 37 (1929):46– 51, 143–153, 261–268, 335–338; 38 (1930):157–166, 366–371; 39(1931):46–52; 40 (1932):63–69, 159–165
LB	Letterbook
LC	Manuscript Division, Library of Congress, Washington, D.C.

Lewis Mss	William Lewis Letters in Conway Whittle Family Papers, Earl Gregg Swem Library, College of William and Mary, Williamsburg, Virginia
Lilly	Lilly Library, Indiana University, Bloomington, Indiana
M&PR	Muster Rolls and Pay Rolls of Vessels and Stations, RG 45, NA (usually cited as T829:[roll number] from version in NA Microfilm Publication T-829)
Madison & General Pike orders, 1813–14	William M. Crane, Regulations for the Internal Government of the U.S. Ships *Madison* and *General Pike*, December 1813–July 1814, New York State Historical Association, Cooperstown
MassHS	Massachusetts Historical Society, Boston
McKee, *Edward Preble*	Christopher McKee, *Edward Preble: A Naval Biography, 1761–1807* (Annapolis, Md.: Naval Institute Press, 1972; reprinted, New York: Arno Press, 1980)
MCL	Letters Received by the Secretary of the Navy from Masters Commandant, RG 45, NA
MdHS	Maryland Historical Society, Baltimore
MeHS	Maine Historical Society, Portland
Misc Mss	Miscellaneous Manuscripts
Misc Treas Accts	Miscellaneous Treasury Accounts of the First Auditor of the Treasury, RG 217, NA
ML	Miscellaneous Letters Received by the Secretary of the Navy, RG 45, NA
Murray LB	Alexander Murray Letterbook, May 1799–December 1805, RG 45, NA
NA	U.S. National Archives, Washington, D.C.
Narrative statements of service	Letters from Officers Transmitting Statements of Their Service, June 1842–December 1844, RG 24, NA
Nav Hist Soc	Naval History Society Collection, NYHS
NCR	Board of Navy Commissioners, Register of Officers of the Navy, May 1815–June 1821, RG 45, NA
NHF	Naval Historical Foundation Manuscripts, LC
NYHS	New-York Historical Society, New York City
NYPL	Manuscript Division, New York Public Library, New York City
OL	Letters Received by the Secretary of the Navy from Officers below the Rank of Master Commandant ("Officers' Letters"), RG 45, NA
OSW	Letters Sent by the Secretary of the Navy to Officers ("Officers, Ships of War"), RG 45, NA
Parsons Diary	Usher Parsons, "A Diary Kept During the Expedition to Lake Erie, under Captain O.H. Perry," September 1812–December 1814, Rhode Island Historical Society, Providence
PMS	Peabody Museum, Salem, Massachusetts

President orders, 1809	William Bainbridge, "General Orders for the Government of the U.S. Frigate President," ca. 1809–10, in Alexander S. Wadsworth, Journal, Frigate *Chesapeake*, 9–27 May 1807, MeHS
President orders, ca. 1812	John Rodgers, "Standing General Orders" for the frigate *President*, 1810–14 (Amn 34901), Rodgers Mss
Private LB	Confidential Letters Sent by the Secretary of the Navy ("Private Letters"), RG 45, NA
QW	U.S. Office of Naval Records and Library, *Naval Documents Related to the Quasi-War between the United States and France* (Washington, D.C., 1935–38)
Register of Suits	Solicitor of the Treasury, Register of Suits against Sundry Persons, RG 206, NA
Resignations	Letters of Resignation from Officers, RG 45, NA
RFP	Rodgers Family Papers, LC
RG	Record Group, NA
RG 15	Records of the Veterans Administration, NA
RG 24	Records of the Bureau of Naval Personnel, NA
RG 36	Records of the Bureau of Customs, NA
RG 39	Records of the Bureau of Accounts (Treasury), NA
RG 45	Naval Records Collection of the Office of Naval Records and Library, NA
RG 46	Records of the United States Senate, NA
RG 52	Records of the Bureau of Medicine and Surgery, NA
RG 59	General Records of the Department of State, NA
RG 94	Records of the Adjutant General's Office, NA
RG 125	Records of the Office of the Judge Advocate General (Navy), NA
RG 127	Records of the United States Marine Corps, NA
RG 206	Records of the Solicitor of the Treasury, NA
RG 217	Records of Accounting Officers of the Treasury Department, NA
RG 233	Records of the United States House of Representatives, NA
Roche Letters	"*Constitution* in the Quasi-War with France: The Letters of John Roche, Jr., 1798–1801," *American Neptune* 27(1967): 135–149
Rodgers Mss	Commodore John Rodgers Papers, HSPa
Rutledge Mss	John Rutledge Papers, Southern Historical Collection, University of North Carolina at Chapel Hill Library
SEN	Records of the United States Senate, RG 46, NA
SF	Subject File, RG 45, NA (individual classes within the subject file are identified by two-letter codes, e.g., SF, NN)
Shaw & Shoemaker	Ralph R. Shaw and Richard H. Shoemaker, *American Bibliography: A Preliminary Checklist for 1801–1819* (New York, 1958–83)
Shaw Mss	John Shaw Papers, NHF

Skiddy	William Skiddy, "The ups & downs of a sea life—from 1805," G.W. Blunt White Library, Mystic Seaport, Mystic, Connecticut
Somers Mss	Richard Somers Manuscripts, Gloucester County Historical Society, Woodbury, New Jersey
Spence Mss	Spence-Lowell Collection, HEHL
Talbot Mss	Silas Talbot Papers, G.W. Blunt White Library, Mystiç Seaport, Mystic, Connecticut
TJ Mss	Thomas Jefferson Papers, LC
USMC LR(B)	Letters Received by the Commandant of the Marine Corps, 1798–1817 (bound volumes), RG 127, NA
USMC LR(L)	Letters Received by the Commandant of the Marine Corps, 1799–1818 (loose records in boxes), RG 127, NA
USN Misc	U.S. Navy Miscellany, LC
USNAM	U.S. Naval Academy Museum, Annapolis, Maryland
USND Coll	U.S. Department of the Navy Collection, Duke
Wadsworth Mss	Henry Wadsworth, Journal, June 1802–September 1803, and letters, 1796–1804, Longfellow National Historic Site, Cambridge, Massachusetts
Welles Mss	Gideon Welles Papers, LC
WLCL	William L. Clements Library, University of Michigan, Ann Arbor
Wm Jones Mss	Uselma Clark Smith Collection, William Jones Papers, HSPa
Woolsey Journal	Melancthon T. Woolsey, Journal kept on board Frigates *Boston, Adams, New York*, and *Chesapeake*, September 1801–July 1803 (private collection)
ZB File	ZB File (formerly part of SF), Early Records Section, Naval Historical Center, Washington, D.C.

Introduction: The Bafflement of William Jones

1. HSPa, Wm Jones Mss: "Comparative view of Officers raised in the Navy with those raised in the Merchant Service."

2. The reasons for including or excluding certain ranks as officers for the purposes of this book will be discussed in Chapter 3. An officer is defined to have entered the navy and to be eligible for inclusion herein if he was offered and accepted an appointment. Once an officer formally accepted, he was entitled to draw pay from the date of acceptance, even though there were some individuals who accepted appointments, drew pay, but never performed any active duty. Persons who applied for and were offered appointments but then declined them are not considered to have been members of the officer corps.

Part One: Building the Corps

1. At Headquarters

1. Estimated from the file numbers originally assigned to the surviving May–June 1798 applications for appointment in SF, NN. Such numbers were assigned to applications in roughly the chronological order in which they were received, with the Navy Department simply continuing the numbering sequence begun by the War Department in 1794.

2. Officers officially appointed by the War Department before 18 June 1798 as recorded in Abst of serv, vol. A. The fifty-nine embraced six captains, fifteen lieutenants, twenty-one midshipmen, three sailing masters, four surgeons, five surgeon's mates, and five pursers.

3. Two books document this continuity well: Jennings B. Sanders, *Evolution of Executive Departments of the Continental Congress, 1774–1789* (Chapel Hill: University of North Carolina Press, 1935; reprinted, Gloucester, Mass.: Peter Smith, 1971), and Harry M. Ward, *The Department of War, 1781–1795* (Pittsburgh, Pa.: University of Pittsburgh Press, 1962).

4. OSW 1:434: Charles W. Goldsborough to Thomas Calvert, 27 Mar. 1799; Cornelius William Stafford, *The Philadelphia Directory for 1800* ([Philadelphia]: William W. Woodward, 1800), p. 28 (second sequence of numbered pages).

5. Misc Treas Accts #29,564, voucher 15: on 25 June 1814 Elizabeth Colbert was paid for "Scowering & cleaning three Rooms of the Secretary of the Navy & offices . . . Passage & Stairs."

6. Noble E. Cunningham, *The Process of Government under Jefferson* (Princeton, N.J.: Princeton University Press, 1978), p. 39; Charles O. Paullin, "Washington City and the Old Navy," Columbia Historical Society *Records* 33–34(1932):167, 175; HSPa, Wm Jones Mss: Benjamin Homans to William Jones, [Mar. or Apr. 1813]. For a late-nineteenth-century photograph of the Six Buildings, apparently little changed in general appearance since the days of the Navy Department's sojourn there, see Allen C. Clark, *Greenleaf and Law in the Federal City* (Washington, D.C., 1901), p. 141. U.S. Public Buildings Service, *Executive Office Building* (Washington, D.C.: U.S. Govt. Print. Off., 1970) [Historical Study No. 3], and U.S. Executive Office of the President, Office of Administration, *The Old Executive Office Building: A Victorian Masterpiece* (Washington, D.C., 1984), cover well the earlier War Office building on the same site and provide excellent illustrations.

7. HEHL, Spence Mss: Keith Spence to Mary Spence, 26 Apr. 1800.

8. GLB 1:334: Benjamin Stoddert to John Rutledge, Jr., 12 Oct. 1798; Harvard University, Houghton Library: Stoddert to James McHenry, 5 Jan. 1801. The best biographical summary of Stoddert's life will be found in Michael A. Palmer, *Stoddert's War: Naval Operations during the Quasi-War with France, 1798–1801* (Columbia: University of South Carolina Press, 1987), esp. pp. 10–14; useful supplementary information: *A Biographical Dictionary of the Maryland Legislature, 1635–1789*, Edward C. Papenfuse [and others] (Baltimore, Md.: Johns Hopkins University Press, 1979–85) 2:780–782.

9. Adams Mss, reel 396: Samuel Smith to [John Adams?], 19 Oct. 1799. The most recent sketch of Smith's life, with a comprehensive bibliography, is in Richard A. Harrison, *Princetonians, 1776–1783: A Biographical Dictionary* (Princeton, N.J.: Princeton University Press, 1981), pp. 342–352; in common with much writing about Smith, Harrison's work fails to appreciate the extent of Smith's achievement and success as secretary of the navy.

10. Noble E. Cunningham, ed., "The Diary of Frances Few, 1808–1809," *Journal of Southern History* 29(1963):348, 352.

11. NYHS, Isaac Chauncey LB, 1805–1806: Chauncey to John Stricker, 2 Mar. 1806; for similar opinions see McKee, *Edward Preble*, pp. 106, 350.

12. Accnt LR: Benjamin Stoddert to Thomas Turner, 10 Mar. 1809.

13. Harvard University, Houghton Library: undated clipping, "The Late Robert Smith," from an unidentified newspaper, pasted to Robert Smith to Anna Sanders, 10 Dec. 1836.

14. NYHS, Nav Hist Soc Misc Mss: William Bainbridge to David Porter, 29 Jan. 1810; LC, David Porter Mss: Porter to Samuel Hambleton, 18–19 July 1809 [i.e., 1810]; *Biographical Directory of the South Carolina House of Representatives*, ed. Walter B. Edgar (Columbia: University of South Carolina Press, 1974–) 3:299–301.

15. David Porter to Samuel Hambleton, 28 Feb. 1812, printed in David D. Porter, *Memoir of Commodore David Porter* (Albany, N.Y., 1875), p. 100; LC, David Porter Mss: Porter to Hambleton, 4 Oct. 1812; Irving Brant, *James Madison, Commander in Chief, 1812–1836* (Indianapolis, Ind.: Bobbs-Merrill, 1961), pp. 125–126, and sources cited p. 546; J.C.A. Stagg, the most recent scholar to address the question of Hamilton's departure from office (*Mr. Madison's War: Politics, Diplomacy, and Warfare in the Early American Republic, 1783–1830* [Princeton, N.J.: Princeton University Press, 1983], pp. 289–290), draws on congressional sources to document Hamilton's perceived drinking problem. Stagg also stresses Hamilton's incompetence to handle the job, but does not delve far into the specifics of that incompetence.

16. Linda Maloney, "The War of 1812: What Role for Sea Power?" in *In Peace and War: Interpretations of American Naval History, 1775–1978*, ed. Kenneth J. Hagan (Westport, Conn.: Greenwood, 1978), pp. 53–54. For contemporary support for this explanation of Hamilton's drinking see Appmt Papers JQA: Nathanael G. Maxwell to Henry Clay, 1 Nov. 1826, and Benjamin Henry Latrobe, *Correspondence and Miscellaneous Papers*, ed. John C. Van Horne and Lee W. Formwalt (New Haven, Conn.: Yale University Press, 1984–88) 3:360, 372, 481.

17. HSPa, Wm Jones Mss: William Bainbridge to William Jones, 1 Mar. 1813.

18. HSPa, Wm Jones Mss: [Robert T. Spence], "The Navy," newspaper clipping enclosed in Spence to William Jones, [19] Nov. [1814].

19. JM Mss: Charles W. Goldsborough to James Madison, 7 Jan. 1813; OSW 10:311: William Jones to William Bainbridge, 19 Mar. 1813.

20. HSPa, Wm Jones Mss: James Ewell to William Jones, 9 Mar. 1813; Jones to Ewell, 10 Mar. 1813; DAB 6:229.

21. WLCL, Perry Papers: William S. Rogers to O.H. Perry, 2 Dec. 1812; RG 46, Records of Executive Proceedings of the Senate, Executive Nominations and Accompanying Papers (SEN 13B–A2): Papers Respecting the Nomination of Paul Hamilton to be Commissioner of Loans for South Carolina.

22. HSPa, Wm Jones Mss: Jonathan Roberts to William Jones, 28 Dec. 1812; Brant, *Madison, Commander in Chief*, pp. 125–126; Stagg, *Mr. Madison's War*, p. 290.

23. HSPa, Wm Jones Mss: William Jones to [Eleanor] Jones, 8 Mar. 1813. Jones is the subject of three related studies by Edward K. Eckert: *The Navy Department in the War of 1812* (Gainesville: University of Florida Press, 1973); "William Jones: Mr. Madison's Secretary of the Navy," *Pennsylvania Magazine of History and Biography* 96(1972):167–182; "Early Reform in the Navy Department," *American Neptune* 33(1973):231–245.

24. HSPa, Wm Jones Mss: William Jones to [Eleanor] Jones, 23 Jan. 1813.

25. USS *Constitution* Museum, Boston Naval Shipyard, Charlestown, Mass.: Charles Stewart to William Tudor, Jr., 22 May 1815.

26. FDRL, Naval Mss: O.H. Perry to Samuel Hambleton, 13 Apr., 22 Apr. 1814; WLCL, Perry Papers: Hambleton to Perry, 5 Apr., 12 Apr. 1814. A congruent civilian opinion: Benjamin H. Latrobe, *Correspondence and Miscellaneous Papers* 3:480–481.

27. Linda McKee [Maloney] amply demonstrates this liability of Jones's in relation to the construction of the navy's first 74s in her Ph.D. dissertation, *Captain Isaac Hull and the Portsmouth Navy Yard, 1813–1815* (Ann Arbor: University Microfilms, 1968), esp. ch. 2, "Building the *Washington.*"

28. WLCL, Perry Papers: Samuel Hambleton to Perry, 31 Mar. 1814.

29. Eckert, "William Jones: Mr. Madison's Secretary of the Navy," pp. 179–182, has a good discussion of Jones's money problems.

30. RFP, Ser 2: Robert T. Spence to John Rodgers, 17 Jan. 1815; WLCL, Charles Morris Papers: Thomas Tingey to Morris, 15 Mar. 1815.

31. GLB 5:273–274: Robert Smith to C.W. Goldsborough, 1 Apr. 1802; Cong LB 1: Paul Hamilton to John W. Eppes, 17 Dec. 1810; HSPa, Wm Jones Mss: E.W. DuVal to William Jones, 27 Sept. 1813.

32. An example of one of these slips of paper may be seen in CL: Edward Preble to Robert Smith, 1 Nov. 1806.

33. GLB 4:527–533: C.W. Goldsborough to Robert Smith, 4 Sept., 7 Sept., 8 Sept., 10 Sept. 1801.

34. OSW 7:292: Robert Smith to Thomas Tingey, 22 Jan. 1807; 9:500: C.W. Goldsborough to John Rodgers, 7 Nov. 1811.

35. Thomas Ewell, *Conclusion of the Evidence of the Corruption of the Chief Clerk of the Navy Department* [Washington, D.C., 1813], p. 2. The secretary's private office in the War Office building had a second door by which the secretary or his counterparts from other departments could enter or leave without going through the chief clerk's office (Lilly, War of 1812 Mss: Luke Wheeler to L.W. Tazewell, 22 Mar. 1813).

36. USMC LR(L): Benjamin Homans to Franklin Wharton, 20 Nov. 1813.

37. Misc Treas Accts #29,186, 29,564, and 31,389 (contingent accounts of Benjamin Homans for 13 Apr. 1813 through 31 Dec. 1815) are good examples of these types of expenditures.

38. For one such case see LC, David Porter Mss: Porter to Samuel Hambleton, 29 Sept. 1811; NYHS, Misc Mss: Hambleton to Porter, 12 May 1812.

39. Alice B. Keith, ed., *The John Gray Blount Papers* (Raleigh, N.C.: State Department of Archives and History, 1952–) 1:391, 501–502, 2:24, 386, 436, 439, 3:279–280, 321–322, 423, 455; Hamilton Papers 7:140, 148; GW Mss: Abishai Thomas to George Washington, 2 Aug. 1790.

40. HEHL, Spence Mss: Keith Spence to Mary Spence, 25 Dec. 1800.

41. RG 15, Letters Sent by the Commissioners of the Navy Pension Fund, 23 Dec. 1800–27 Sept. 1816, passim.

42. *Columbian Centinel* (Boston), 8 Dec. 1804.

43. OSW 8:248, 346, 486, 525 give the dates when Goldsborough exercised authority as acting secretary.

44. LC, David Porter Mss: Porter to Samuel Hambleton, 18–19 July 1809 [i.e., 1810].

45. RFP, Ser 3A: C.W. Goldsborough to John Rodgers, 9 Apr. 1815.

46. For the Goldsborough-Ewell quarrel see (with the first five items listed in order of publication) Thomas Ewell, "THAT sense of duty which impels every man to cry out . . . ," 11 Jan. 1813 (LC, Rare Book and Special Collections Division, Broadsides, portfolio 190, no. 22); Charles W. Goldsborough, "DR. THOMAS EWELL, SIR,—Your kind publication of yesterday has just been handed to me . . . ," 12 Jan. 1813 (broadside; Hagley Museum and Library, Greenville, Del.); Ewell, "THE Subscriber owes it to his detestation of slandering and to his regard for truth . . . ," [n.d.] (LC, Rare Book and Special Collections Division, Broadsides, portfolio 190, no. 22); Goldsborough, *To The Public*, 22 Jan. 1813 (28-page pamphlet, Hagley Museum and Library); Ewell, *Conclusion of the Evidence of the Corruption of the Chief Clerk of the Navy Department* [Washington, D.C., 1813] (16-page pamphlet in LC, Rare Book and Special Collections Division, Toner Collection); "The Switch: A Very Short Poem—Consisting of One Canto, Occasioned by a Late Rupture between Two Subaltern Agents in the Navy Department," 18 Jan. [1813] (broadside in HSPa, Wm Jones Mss); JM Mss: C.W. Goldsborough to James Madison, 18 June 1814, 8 Mar. 1815; HSPa, Wm Jones Mss: Goldsborough to William Jones, 15 Feb. 1813; NYHS, Cooper's Hist extra illus: Goldsborough to John Bullus, 15 Feb. 1813.

47. Respecting Goldsborough's dismissal and subsequent attempts to clear his name, see HSPa, Wm Jones Mss: William Jones to C.W. Goldsborough, 27 Feb. 1813; Goldsborough to Jones, 28 Feb. 1813; Jones, "Notes" regarding Goldsborough's dismissal, [ca. 28 Feb. 1813]; Goldsborough to Jones, 8 Mar. 1813; Jones to Mrs. [Eleanor] Jones, 22 Mar. 1813; Goldsborough to Jones, 15 May 1814; JM Mss: Goldsborough to James Madison, 18 June 1814, 8 Mar. 1815; RFP, Ser 3A: Goldsborough to John Rodgers, 9 Apr. 1815.

48. *Daily National Intelligencer* (Washington), 16 Dec. 1843.

49. HSPa, Wm Jones Mss: Elbridge Gerry to James Monroe, 10 Feb. 1813; MassHS, Thomas Jefferson Manuscripts: Thomas Jefferson to [Levi Lincoln], 25 Mar. 1807; Appmt Papers TJ (Isaac Cox Barnet file): Benjamin Homans to Jefferson, 10 Aug. 1801; Appmt Papers Madison: Orchard Cook to [James Madison], 17 June 1812; Homans to Monroe, 25 July 1812; JM Mss: C.W. Goldsborough to Madison, 18 June 1814; LC, Benjamin Homans Mss: Benjamin Homans IV, "A Brief Sketch of the Life of Benjamin Homans—1765–1823"; Mary Lee Mann, ed., *A Yankee Jeffersonian: Selections from the Diary and Letters of William Lee of Massachusetts, Written from 1796 to 1840* (Cambridge: Harvard University Press, 1958), pp. 3–9, 253; *The Boston Directory* (Boston: John West, 1803); *The Boston Directory* (Boston: Edward Cotton, 1805); *The Boston Directory* (Boston: E. Cotton, 1807); *The Boston Directory* (Boston: E. Cotton, 1809).

50. WLCL, Perry Papers: Samuel Hambleton to O.H. Perry, 31 Mar. 1814.

51. WLCL, Perry Papers: Samuel Hambleton to O. H. Perry, 12 Apr. 1814. On DuVal generally, see HSPa, Wm Jones Mss: Edward W. DuVal to William Jones, 26 Feb., 27 Sept. 1813; Benjamin Homans to Jones, 30 Sept. 1813; PMS, Crowninshield Mss: Jones to James Madison, 22 Dec. 1814; Jones to B.W. Crowninshield, 26 Dec. 1814; DuVal to Crowninshield, 16 Feb., 20 Feb. 1815; WLCL, Perry Papers: Samuel Hambleton to O.H. Perry, 1 Feb., 22 Feb. 1815; Appmt Papers Madison: DuVal to [?], 12 Apr. 1815; Gabriel Duvall to James Monroe, 5 Feb. 1817. DuVal's departure from the Navy Office: Cong LB 2:445 and ASP Misc 2:351. For amply full materials on DuVal's later career as the federal Cherokee agent in Arkansas Territory see vols. 19–21 of Clarence

Edwin Carter, ed., *Territorial Papers of the United States* (Washington, D.C.: U.S. Govt. Print. Off., 1934–).

52. WLCL, Perry Papers: Samuel Hambleton to O.H. Perry, 19 Apr. 1815.

53. Charles O. Paullin, *Paullin's History of Naval Administration, 1775–1911* (Annapolis, Md.: U.S. Naval Institute, 1968), p. 164.

54. There is no readily available and accurate roster of the civilian office staff of the Navy Department at this period. One had to be constructed for this book. It is based primarily on the quarterly salary vouchers in Misc Treas Accts. Because some salary vouchers are missing, these had to be supplemented from other sources. Beginning with calendar year 1806, Congress required that each department and office submit a list of clerks employed and the compensation paid them. Lists for the secretary of the navy's office will be found in Cong LB 1–2. The list for 1809 was not copied in Cong LB, but may be found in RG 233, Records of the House of Representatives, Reports, Navy Department 1(5th Cong., 3d Sess.–12th Cong., 1st Sess.):308–309. A retrospective report, showing clerks and compensation for the years 1799–1801, was submitted to the House on 26 Mar. 1802 by Robert Smith; it will be found in the same volume, pp. 85–93. Lists of clerks in the accountant of the navy's office, not to be found in one of the above series, may be seen in Accnt LS 9:271 (1811) and 13:5 (1815). Occasional references to clerk employment were found in several of the series of official records described in the bibliographical essay to the present volume.

55. Cong LB 1:134: Robert Smith to John Randolph, 8 Dec. 1803; Paul Hamilton to John W. Eppes, 17 Dec. 1810; GLB 4:529: C.W. Goldsborough to Smith, 7 Sept. 1801.

56. Cong LB 1: Robert Smith to Uriah Tracy, 29 Mar. 1806.

57. Cong LB 1: Paul Hamilton to John W. Eppes, 17 Dec. 1810; Cong LB 2:148, 150–151: William Jones to Burwell Bassett, 2 Feb. 1813; Jones to Speaker of the House, 6 Feb. 1813.

58. Cong LB 1: Paul Hamilton to John W. Eppes, 17 Dec. 1810. One would possess more detail about the daily operations of the Navy Office if the "standing regulations" for its operations, issued by William Jones in 1813, could be located. The existence of the regulations is documented by a letter from Benjamin Homans to B.W. Crowninshield, 13 Aug. 1818: The clerks in the Navy Office "have written instructions to govern them, every part of their duty specifically assigned to them, and the standing regulations of the office *all signed* by the secretary of the navy, five years ago" (PMS, Crowninshield Mss). The present historian has not been able to locate a copy in NA, in HSPa: Wm Jones Mss, or in LC: Benjamin Homans Papers.

59. For example, PMS, Crowninshield Mss: William Jones to B.W. Crowninshield, 26 Dec. 1814.

60. Appmt Papers JQA: Nathanael G. Maxwell to Henry Clay, 1 Nov. 1826; ML: Maxwell to William Jones, 10 Sept. 1813; Richard K. Showman, ed., *Papers of General Nathanael Greene* (Chapel Hill: University of North Carolina Press, 1976–) 1:14.

61. For Anderson see esp. Appmt Papers Monroe: Samuel T. Anderson to James Monroe, 20 Feb. 1821; ML: Anderson to William Jones, 29 Mar. 1813.

62. HSPa, Wm Jones Mss: Benjamin Homans to William Jones, [Mar. or Apr. 1813].

63. Samuel Poultney Todd and John N. Todd, both pursers in the U.S. Navy, were the sons of James Todd, the brother of Mrs. Madison's first husband, John Todd, Jr. (d. 1793). (Nancy P. Spears, Archivist, Friends Historical Library of Swarthmore College, to Christopher McKee, 2 Sept. 1988, summarizing records of the Philadelphia Monthly Meeting of the Society of Friends; JM Mss: Samuel P. Todd to James Madison, 13 Mar. 1809.)

64. Misc Treas Accts #29,186, voucher 21 (account of William Worthington), refers to "Mr. Maxwell's room" among the secretary's suite of offices on the second floor of the War Office building.

65. HSPa, Wm Jones Mss: Benjamin Homans to William Jones, [Mar. or Apr. 1813].

66. There is no single description of the messenger's duties; they can best be reconstructed from the office contingent accounts in Misc Treas Accts #29,186, 29,564, and 31,389. This historian has not been able to determine the relationship between George and Joseph Sutherland.

67. For examples see Frederick Rodgers Coll: Charles W. Goldsborough to John Rodgers, 26 Nov. 1810, franked by Secretary of State Robert Smith, and Goldsborough to Rodgers, 5 Nov. 1811, franked by Secretary of War William Eustis.

68. The first clerk to report for work in the accountant's office (William Exley) commenced his duties 12 Sept. 1798; Winder's earliest recorded official letter is dated 17 Sept. 1798 (Accnt LS 1798–1800:1).

69. *Biographical Dictionary of the Maryland Legislature* 2:903–904; GW Mss: William Vans Murray to George Washington, 21 Jan. 1795; John Henry to Washington, 24 Feb. 1795; MdHS, James McHenry Papers: William Hindman to McHenry, 12 Aug. 1798; GLB 1:110–111: Benjamin Stoddert to William Winder, 2 Aug. 1798; 2:319: Stoddert to Winder, 28 Aug. 1799.

70. Accnt LS 1798–1800:54–56: William Winder to Benjamin Stoddert, 18 Jan. 1799; Accnt LS 2:93, 110, 177: Thomas Turner to Stoddert, 18 July 1800; Turner to W.W. Burrows, 24 July 1800; Turner to J. & E. Watson, 8 Sept. 1800; 3:52, 346, 455–456: Turner to Stephen Higginson & Co., 26 Apr. 1801; Turner to Comptroller of the Treasury, 28 Nov. 1801; Turner to Robert Smith, 17 Mar. 1802.

71. John B. Larner, "List of Principal Municipal Authorities of the Cities of Washington, Georgetown and the District of Columbia," Columbia Historical Society *Records* 23(1920):182; JEP 1:288–289.

72. Accnt LR: Samuel Smith to [Thomas Turner], 2 July 1801.

73. Lilly, War of 1812 Mss: Luke Wheeler to Littleton W. Tazewell, 22 Mar. 1813; HSPa, Wm Jones Mss: Benjamin Homans to William Jones, [Mar. or Apr. 1813].

74. The decline in Thomas Turner's health may be followed in Accnt LS 9:195, 491: Turner to Thomas T. Tucker, 24 Aug. 1811, 14 Aug. 1812; 10:298, 330, 364: Thomas H. Gilliss to George Harrison, 19 June 1813; Gilliss to William Jones, 8 July 1813; Turner to Tucker, 2 Aug. 1813; 13:56, 65, 72: Gilliss to Timothy Pickering, 29 Feb. 1816; Gilliss to John H. Fawn, 9 Mar. 1816; Gilliss to Samuel Robertson, 14 Mar. 1816; Accnt LR: Turner to Gilliss, 7 Aug. 1813; James Biddle to Turner, 18 Mar. 1814.

75. *Daily National Intelligencer* (Washington), 15 Feb., 22 Feb. 1851; *Biographical Dictionary of the Maryland Legislature* 2:903–904.

76. Accnt LS 5:218: Thomas Turner to Samuel Hambleton, John Macdaniel, [and] John Craven, 30 Sept. 1805.

Notes to Pages

77. Accnt LS 10:205: Thomas Turner to Langdon Cheves, 6 Mar. 1813; 10:165: Turner, List of clerks employed in the office of the accountant during 1812, 3 Feb. 1813; 11:48: Turner, "Estimate of monies necessary to be appropriated for the Office of the Accountant of the Navy for the year 1814," 23 Nov. 1813; Accnt LR: Cheves to Turner, 6 Mar. 1813; Accnt Exec LR, 1801–29: William Jones to Turner, 24 June 1813.

78. Accnt LS 10:501–508: Thomas Turner, "A list of the unsettled Accounts in the Office of the Accountant of the Navy," 6 Dec. 1813.

79. From the surviving records it is impossible to determine the date on which Joseph Sutherland was appointed.

80. Accnt LS 4:176: Thomas Turner to Alexander Dow, 11 Mar. 1803.

81. The precise relationship among the three Macdaniels of the accountant's office has not been established; at least two of them were brothers.

82. Accnt LS 8:512: "A Statement exhibiting the names of the Clerks employed in the office of the Accountant of the Navy for the year 1810," 10 Jan. 1811.

83. Cf. Accnt LS 10:501–508: "A list of the unsettled Accounts in the Office of the Accountant of the Navy," 6 Dec. 1813, particularly 10:507.

2. A Ranked Society

1. SF, NA: Quarter Bill of *Constitution*, ca. Dec. 1812.

2. For examples of chaplains performing the first two duties see CL: Alexander Murray, Journal of a cruise in the U.S. Frigate *Adams*, 9 July–17 Dec. 1805, at 24 Aug., and FDRL, Naval Mss: Charles Stewart, Journal kept on board the U.S. Frigate *Constitution*, 31 Dec. 1813–16 May 1815, at 16 Jan. 1814.

3. OSW 11:191: William Jones to Joseph Bainbridge, 14 Jan. 1814, GLB 3:526: Benjamin Stoddert to Thomas Turner, 21 Aug. 1800. When the building of four 74-gun ships was authorized in Jan. 1813, their congressionally specified complements of officers included both a chaplain and a schoolmaster (Homans, p. 91). However, no schoolmasters were actually appointed for the 74s before the end of the War of 1812.

4. For the captain's clerk's uniform see OL: Benedict I. Neale to William Jones, 19 May 1813. By law the captain's clerk was a petty officer (cf. Homans, pp. 31, 34, 91); however, there is abundant evidence that his de facto status was equivalent to a midshipman's.

5. OL: Charles A. Budd to Paul Hamilton, 11 Feb. 1811.

6. Commandants & Agents LB 1:529: William Jones to John Cassin, 29 Oct. 1813; also GLB 12:240: Jones to [Richard Rush], Attorney General of the U.S., 8 Nov. 1814; RG 45, Letters Received by the Secretary of the Navy from the Attorney General: Rush to Jones, 11 Nov. 1814; OSW 11:454: Jones to Arthur Sinclair, 11 Nov. 1814.

7. For example, Michael Lewis, *A Social History of the Navy, 1793–1815* (London: Allen & Unwin, 1960), p. 23. Lewis, in common with most other writers on the British navy, leaves the term *gentleman* undefined.

8. See Christopher McKee, "Foreign Seamen in the United States Navy: A Census of 1808," *William and Mary Quarterly*, 3d ser., 42(1985):385.

9. HEHL, Spence Mss: Keith Spence to Mary Spence, 15 Dec. 1800; Resignations, 1803–25: Thomas J.H. Cushing to Paul Hamilton, 5 Mar. 1810;

Accts (N) #6973: John W. Dorsey to "Dear Francis," 19 June 1827; CL: Thomas Shields to Stephen Decatur, 27 Nov. 1810, enclosed in Decatur to Hamilton, 28 Dec. 1810; Accnt LR: J.B. Cheshire to Robert Smith, 21 Jan. 1806 [i.e., 1807].

3. Counting the Corps

1. Homans, pp. 31–32, 34–35, 37.

2. TJ Mss: Robert Smith to Thomas Jefferson, 19 Apr. 1805; ASP Nav Aff 1:152–153.

3. Homans, p. 77.

4. Homans, pp. 84–85; Dumas Malone, *Jefferson the President: Second Term, 1805–1809* (Boston: Little, Brown, 1974), pp. 647–648; Craig L. Symonds, *Navalists and Antinavalists: The Naval Policy Debate in the United States, 1785–1827* (Newark: University of Delaware Press, 1980), pp. 137–143.

5. Homans, p. 89. On 2 Jan. 1813 Congress authorized four ships of 74 guns (none of which actually got to sea before the end of the War of 1812) and specified the number of officers authorized for each (Homans, p. 91). Fifteen months later (16 Apr. 1814) an act directing the appointment of four captains and twelve lieutenants for a separate flotilla service became law (Homans, pp. 98–99). Neither of these actions resulted in any general restatement of the size and composition of the naval establishment, which remained subject to administrative discretion and available appropriations.

6. For the Navy Department's official counts of the numbers of officers it thought it had in the various ranks during the pre-1815 years see Charles W. Goldsborough, *An Original and Correct List of the United States Navy* (Washington, D.C., 1800) [Evans #37529], pp. 13–28; ASP Misc 1:314–317 (Feb. 1802); ASP Nav Aff 1:152–153 (Dec. 1805), 171 (Dec. 1807); SF, NA: Manuscript register of officers of the navy and marine corps, ca. 1808–Mar. 1809; ASP Nav Aff 1:255–263 (Feb. 1812), 300–305 (Feb. 1814), 347–352 (Nov. 1814). Between early 1802 and the eve of the War of 1812 there is a high degree of agreement between the numbers of naval officers recorded in the Navy Department's official registers and those discovered by actual census of the corps. In the Quasi-War with France and even more so during the War of 1812 the combined effect of an increased number of acting appointments by ship, squadron, and station commanders and of decreased attention to the maintenance of accurate personnel rosters in the Navy Office was a divergence between the official roll and reality. Particularly in the War of 1812 substantially more officers were actually employed on the navy's ships and stations than one would ever imagine from examining the official roster.

4. Places Much Sought

1. GLB 12:103: William Jones to C.J. Ingersoll, 7 Feb. 1814; Thomas Jefferson, *Writings*, ed. P.L. Ford (New York, 1892–99) 8:178.

2. As, for example, ML: Anthony New to Robert Smith, 5 Nov. 1808.

3. ML: Robert Brent to Paul Hamilton, 14 Aug. 1811; Charles Boarman, [Sr.], to Brent, 13 Aug. 1811; Charles Boarman, [Jr.], to Brent, 13 Aug. 1811. The "immortal and intrepid Major Boarman" to whom young Charles refers was his ancestor William Boreman (or Boarman) (ca. 1630–1709), an upwardly mobile early Catholic immigrant to Maryland. Mariner, planter, land speculator, and Indian trader, Boreman held a variety of civil offices, including sheriff of St. Marys County and member of the lower house of the Maryland Assembly;

he was captain and major in the provincial military and fought with the Calvert forces on the losing side in the battle of the Severn against the Puritans (1655). By the time of his death Boreman, who had probably arrived in Maryland with little else but the clothes he was wearing, had acquired approximately seventy-five hundred acres of land (*A Biographical Dictionary of the Maryland Legislature, 1635–1789*, Edward C. Papenfuse [and others] [Baltimore, Md.: Johns Hopkins University Press, 1979–85] 1:148; C.F. Thomas, *Genealogy of the Boarman Family* [Baltimore, Md., 1897], pp. 5–14).

4. Endorsements on (in the order quoted) ML: Israel Smith to Robert Smith, 21 Feb. 1809 (bound at 10 Mar.); Winslow Foster to Paul Hamilton, 27 Feb. 1811; OL: Benjamin P. Kissam to Paul Hamilton, 29 Nov. 1812; ML: John Buchanan to Robert Smith, 18 Nov. 1808; ZB File (Willis M. Green): William P. Duval to William Jones, 1 Mar. 1814; ML: Henry Denison to Hamilton, 7 May 1811.

5. GLB 7:55: Robert Smith to David Thomas, 3 Feb. 1804; SF, NA (Box 193): Register of applicants, [1809].

6. For example, GLB 9:262: Robert Smith to Theodorus Bailey, 24 Aug. 1808. Bailey, a former Republican congressman and senator, was the postmaster at New York City.

7. GLB 12:51, 100, 103, 105–106: William Jones to Jotham Post, Jr., 17 Dec. 1813; Jones to Pierce Butler, 3 Feb., 7 Feb. 1814; Jones to C.J. Ingersoll, 7 Feb. 1814.

8. GLB 9:262: Robert Smith to Theodorus Bailey, 24 Aug. 1808; 7:55: Smith to David Thomas, 3 Feb. 1804.

9. The dispersal of many of the original application files (see pp. 506–507), the fact that the more prominent the recommender the more likely his letter is to have disappeared from the files into the autograph market, the likelihood that several recommenders from different status categories might unite in a recommendation, and the occasional difficulty presented by a recommender who straddles two status categories make precise quantification of recommenders a dubious proposition. However, the sample of 885 midshipmen employed as the basis for Chapters 5 through 11 yields the following approximate proportions, which may be regarded as acceptably accurate: four midshipmen in ten were appointed on the recommendation of, or through, a member of Congress; two in ten on the recommendation of an officer of the navy; one in ten through a Washington-based federal officeholder, whether cabinet level, below cabinet level, or member of the Supreme Court. Federal appointees outside Washington—customs officials, navy agents, postmasters, district judges, etc.—recommended one midshipman out of every ten appointed. The remaining two-tenths of the midshipman appointees came recommended by a variety of party notables, state officials, worthy citizens, and clergymen.

10. For instance, GLB 9:107: Robert Smith to John Pope, 14 Jan. 1808.

11. For evidence of the existence of the "private list" or "special list" see, for example, the endorsements on ML: William D. Beall to Robert Smith, 18 Nov. 1808; William Fleming to Philip Norborne Nicholas, 31 Mar. 1809; Thomas W. McCall to A.Y. Nicoll, 24 Aug. 1812.

12. NYHS, Albert Gallatin Mss: Robert Smith to Albert Gallatin, 7 June 1805.

13. Columbia University Libraries, De Witt Clinton Papers: Clinton to Robert Smith, 1 Nov. 1805; GLB 8:72–73: Smith to Clinton, 4 Nov. 1805; ML:

Peter Quackenbos to Smith, 22 July 1807; see also GLB 7:136: Smith to Bishop John Carroll, 24 Apr. 1804.

14. GLB 7:129, 209: Robert Smith to John Stricker, 21 Apr. 1804; Smith to Mountjoy B. Luckett, 16 June 1804.

15. ML: Ferdinand Fairfax [and] George Hite to Robert Smith, 5 July 1806; GLB 8:196: Smith to Fairfax and Hite, 8 July 1806; OL: Joseph Bainbridge to Smith, 10 Aug. 1807.

16. GLB 9:156, 230: Robert Smith to John Morrow, 16 Mar. 1808; Smith to G.W. Johnson, 17 June 1808; OSW 2:221: Benjamin Stoddert to James Sever, 22 July 1799.

17. R.C. Anderson, "British and American Officers in the Russian Navy," *Mariner's Mirror* 33(1947):17–27.

18. GLB 7:222–223: Robert Smith to Meriwether Jones, 28 June 1804; 9:24–25: Smith to Eliza P. Law, 21 Aug. 1807; OSW 11:111: William Jones to Robert T. Spence, 9 Oct. 1813.

19. ML: Samuel L. Mitchill to Paul Hamilton, 15 Aug. 1812.

20. GLB 3:354: Benjamin Stoddert to Jonathan Trumbull, 9 May 1800; 9:58: Robert Smith to Jonathan Mason, 29 Oct. 1807; TJ Mss: Smith to Thomas Jefferson, 3 Sept. 1806.

21. GLB 9:103: Robert Smith to John Clopton, 7 Jan. 1808; Resignations, 1803–25: John Fendall to Smith, 24 Dec. 1807; MCL: John H. Dent to Smith, 29 Dec. 1807.

22. Cf. the anonymous editorial comments on this subject, possibly planted or inspired by the Navy Office, in *National Intelligencer* (Washington), 22 Oct. 1812.

23. GLB 9:308: Robert Smith to Daniel D. Tompkins, 12 Dec. 1808.

24. OSW 1:394: Benjamin Stoddert to Moses Tryon, 7 Feb. 1799.

25. GLB 8:40: Robert Smith to Dr. R. Goldsborough, 26 Aug. 1805; OSW 7:13: Smith to Isaac Chauncey, 16 Sept. 1805. As no one knew better than Robert Smith, many of the officers appointed failed to meet the defined standards by a wide margin. The point here is the ideal sought, not the reality too often encountered.

26. Douglass Adair, "Fame and the Founding Fathers," in *Fame and the Founding Fathers: Essays by Douglass Adair,* ed. Trevor Colbourn (New York: Norton, 1974), pp. 3–26; the quotation is from pp. 11–12, but the importance of the entire essay as a key to understanding the mind of the pre-1815 naval officer cannot be overstated.

27. GLB 1:179: Benjamin Stoddert to Stephen Higginson, 28 Aug. 1798; OSW 1:355–356: Stoddert to John Barry, 7 Dec. 1798; GLB 1:346, 440: Stoddert to Robert Oliver, 15 Oct. 1798; Stoddert to James Simons, 13 Dec. 1798; LC, Alexander Hamilton Mss: Stoddert to Hamilton, 1 Jan. 1799 [1800?].

28. GLB 1:180–181: Benjamin Stoddert to Thomas Pinckney, 28 July 1798; 2:142: Stoddert to John C. Jones, 1 June 1799; OSW 1:394: Stoddert to Moses Tryon, 7 Feb. 1799.

29. GLB 4:501–502: Robert Smith to William Hunter, 20 Aug. 1801; OSW 6:520–521: Smith to Alexander Murray, 1 Mar. 1805.

30. Many examples of this practice could be listed. See, as typical, OSW 1:204–205, 244: Benjamin Stoddert to Samuel Barron, 19 Sept., 8 Oct. 1798.

31. WLCL, Perry Papers: Christopher G. Champlin to Christopher R. Perry, 8 June 1798.

32. GŁB 1:223, 341: Benjamin Stoddert to Josiah Parker, 8 Sept., 15 Oct. 1798.

33. GLB 1:274: Benjamin Stoddert to Gibbs & Channing, 25 Sept. 1798.

34. GLB 1:326: Benjamin Stoddert to Benjamin Goodhue, 9 Oct. 1798.

35. OSW 2:309: Benjamin Stoddert to William Bainbridge, 28 Aug. 1799; GLB 3:344: Stoddert to Edward Burgess, 3 May 1800. The last direct appointment to a promotion-track rank higher than midshipman was that of Lieutenant Seymour Potter, 15 Aug. 1800. This was an isolated instance; the last group of direct appointments was made in Feb. 1800. I do not here consider a handful of direct appointments of lieutenants to command gunboats made by Robert Smith in 1804–1805. This policy was almost immediately abandoned in favor of naming sailing masters to such commands; the lieutenants so appointed were quickly eased out of the navy.

36. GLB 5:260: Robert Smith to John Clopton, 12 Apr. 1802; 10:3: Paul Hamilton to John S. Codgell, 17 May 1809.

37. HSPa, Wm Jones Mss: William Bainbridge to William Jones, 2 Sept. 1813.

38. CL: Isaac Chauncey to William Jones, 1 Apr., 14 June 1813; Private LB: Jones to Chauncey, 3 July 1813.

39. During his tenure as secretary William Jones attempted to stop the practice of acting appointments of midshipmen by ship or squadron commanders without prior approval of the secretary of the navy (Commandants & Agents LB 1:479: Jones to William Bainbridge, 18 Aug. 1813; OSW 11:192: Jones to Johnston Blakeley, 14 Jan. 1814). At least one senior captain protested (HSPa, Wm Jones Mss: Bainbridge to Jones, 2 Sept. 1813). A few of the more junior, and vulnerable, commanding officers complied (MCL: John Orde Creighton to Jones, 9 Jan. 1814). As far as this historian can determine from an examination of the muster rolls and other appointment records, most commanding officers ignored Jones's regulation as one more attempt by an unpopular secretary to impose unwelcome control over an area that had formerly been left to their discretion. The secretary was far away; it took him a long time to catch up with what a commanding officer might be doing. The practice of captains and commodores appointing acting midshipmen flourished unabated through the War of 1812 and at least into the war with Algiers that followed.

40. Accnt LR: George Little to Thomas Turner, 1 Mar. 1802.

Part Two: A Corps of Young Gentlemen

1. Individual surgeons and surgeon's mates are mentioned from time to time in this book, but no attempt has been made to compile a composite profile. Harold D. Langley is writing a comprehensive study of early naval medical men, an effort that the present historian does not wish to duplicate or parallel.

2. TJ Mss: Thomas Jefferson to Elizabeth Chamberlayne, 24 Nov. 1805.

3. *Year of appointment* reflects the time at which the young man in question actually began serving as a midshipman, whether it was under a warrant issued by the Navy Office or an acting appointment granted by a ship or station commander.

Numbers of identified midshipmen appointed in other years were 1798 (88), 1799 (234), 1801 (12), 1802 (14), 1803 (25), 1806 (44), 1807 (13), 1808 (43), 1810 (69), 1811 (138), 1813 (71), 1 Jan.–13 Feb. 1815 (22); total, 773.

Accordingly, the 885 midshipmen in the vertical samples used constitute 53.4 percent of all 1,658 identified midshipmen appointed between 16 Mar. 1798 and 13 Feb. 1815.

5. Geography

1. Geographical origins can be discovered for 93 percent of the 885 midshipmen studied. Records are most complete for the midshipmen of 1809, least accurate for 1800.

2. Of the 885 midshipmen studied, only two were noncitizens, both of them acting midshipmen from one or another of the Mediterranean countries who served in U.S. warships during the Tripolitan War.

3. In the interest of reducing confusion both the Territory of Orleans and its successor, the State of Louisiana, are referred to by the latter name.

4. Census of 1810 data from Adam Seybert, *Statistical Annals . . . of the United States of America* (Philadelphia, 1818), p. 22.

5. ML: John Kittredge to Robert Smith, 1 Mar. 1809.

6. OSW 2:221: Benjamin Stoddert to James Sever, 22 July 1799.

7. SF, NA (Box 193).

8. TJ Mss: Thomas Jefferson to Robert Smith, 17 Aug. 1805; OSW 9:440: Paul Hamilton to John Shaw, 28 Aug. 1811.

9. TJ Mss: Thomas Jefferson to Robert Smith, 13 July 1804; Smith to Jefferson, 15 July 1804.

10. Seybert, *Statistical Annals*, p. 47, where the limitations of the data on urban centers are explained as well.

6. Time

1. Throughout this book statements respecting ages should be assumed to be accurate plus or minus one year. Among the sample of 885 midshipmen a precise date of birth can be discovered for approximately one-third (36.0 percent) of the 480 for whom any age information is known. When the Navy Office sought the ages of the officers, the replies often took the form used by acting midshipman John M. Cotter, who told the Board of Navy Commissioners on 25 May 1815, "My age is 17 year" (ZB File). For purposes of age calculations 25 May 1798 is assumed to be Cotter's date of birth. (More than half [53.3 percent] of the midshipman ages have been established in this manner.) If a month and a year of birth are known, the 15th of the month is assumed to be the day of birth; similarly, when only a year of birth is known, 30 June is arbitrarily taken as the day and month of birth. The evasive formulation occasionally found in the records that so-and-so "is in the sixteenth year of his age" is uniformly assumed to mean that the person was between fifteen and sixteen years old, not between sixteen and seventeen. Examples can be found that support either interpretation of this phrase; the one selected here reduces the risk of age inflation.

2. James Durand, *An Able Seaman of 1812* (New Haven, Conn.: Yale University Press, 1926), pp. 37–38.

3. Among the 480 entering midshipmen for whom ages are known, a definite termination date can be established for 450; of these, 288 were between twelve and eighteen when appointed, and 145 were nineteen or older.

7. Kin

1. No attempt is made in the notes to this or other chapters to identify the individual city directories from which information has been culled. Dorothea

N. Spear, *Bibliography of American Directories through 1860* (Worcester, Mass.: American Antiquarian Society, 1961; reprinted, Westport, Conn.: Greenwood Press, 1978), provides an excellent guide to such sources; the actual directories are reproduced in the microform collections of early American imprints found in most major research libraries.

2. ML: Nathaniel Thayer to Paul Hamilton, 13 Sept. 1812.

3. James McLachlan, *Princetonians, 1748–1768: A Biographical Dictionary* (Princeton, N.J.: Princeton University Press, 1976), pp. 372–375; J.G.B. Bulloch, *A History of the Glen Family of South Carolina and Georgia* ([Washington, D.C.], 1923), pp. 46–51.

4. Appmt Papers TJ: John Randall to Albert Gallatin, 1 Oct. 1804.

5. As John Downes ascended the social scale, his father's status may have slipped a little lower; he is almost certainly the Jesse Downes, boatman, residing at 74 Broad Street, Boston, in 1813. For additional evidence of the elder Downes's modest position in society see Daniel T.V. Huntoon, *History of the Town of Canton, Norfolk County, Massachusetts* (Cambridge, Mass., 1893), p. 451.

6. Appmt Papers TJ: Elizabeth Chamberlayne to Thomas Jefferson, 8 Nov., 18 Dec. 1805.

7. Accnt LR: Ben. Leverett to Constant Freeman, 16 Oct. 1822; Appmt Papers TJ: William Barton to Thomas Jefferson, 22 Oct. 1802.

8. CL: Alexander Murray to [Charles W. Goldsborough], 14 Mar. 1809; Murray to Paul Hamilton, 26 June 1809.

9. *Biographical Directory of the South Carolina House of Representatives* (Columbia, S.C., 1974–) 3:642–644.

10. ML: Thomas Blount to Robert Smith, 23 Feb. 1809.

11. Appmt Papers Madison: Isaac Hite to [James Madison], 22 Feb. 1809; Welles Mss: Thomas Tingey to Mordecai Booth, 13 Feb. 1815.

12. William Bradford Browne, *The Babbitt Family History, 1643–1900* (Taunton, Mass., 1912), p. 105

13. However, the evidence that can be deduced from Carl E. Prince, *The Federalists and the Origins of the U.S. Civil Service* (New York: New York University Press, 1977), passim, suggests that naval parents were not different from that segment of society examined by Prince.

14. Appmt Papers TJ: Meriwether Jones to James Madison, 13 Mar. 1801; JEP 1:464–466.

15. Appmt Papers TJ: Meriwether Jones to Thomas Jefferson, 26 Oct. 1805.

16. *The Enquirer* (Richmond, Va.), 19 Aug., 22 Aug. 1806; the latter issue contains a long obituary on Jones.

17. Register of Suits 1:19; SF, XA: George W. Smith to Albert Gallatin, 9 Feb. 1810; C.W. Coleman, "Genealogy of the Smith Family of Essex County, Virginia," *William and Mary Quarterly*, [1st ser.], 6(1897/98):41–52; *Biographical Directory of the Governors of the United States, 1789–1978* (Westport, Conn.: Meckler, 1978) 4:1629–1630.

18. ML: Richard Adams, John Adams, [and] Samuel Y. Adams to [?], 9 Mar. 1812; Richard Lee Smith to Paul Hamilton, 18 June 1812.

19. Appmt Papers AJ: Richard E. Parker to Martin Van Buren, 8 May 1829.

20. Leonard F. Guttridge and Jay D. Smith, *The Commodores* (New York: Harper & Row, 1969; reprinted, Annapolis, Md.: Naval Institute Press, 1984) is an excellent example of this approach.

21. HSPa, Wm Jones Mss: William Jones to [Eleanor] Jones, 10 Feb. 1813.

22. In tracing the Tingey connection the historian is greatly assisted by a fine article, Lewis D. Cook, "William Murdoch (1705–1761) of Philadelphia and His Descendants: Murdoch, Beale, Sweers, Tingey, Kelly, Wingate, Craven, Dulany, Crosby, and Duffield," *Pennsylvania Genealogical Magazine* 16(1948):39–74, as well as the same author's "Three Craven Family Records," *Genealogical Magazine of New Jersey* 21(1946):57–64.

23. GLB 10:403: Paul Hamilton to William Caton, 16 Oct. 1811.

24. ConnHS, Butler Coll: O.H. Perry to Robert Smith, 26 Nov. 1808; ML: Perry to Paul Hamilton, 15 July 1811; AF, A-7: Perry to Nathanael G. Maxwell, 15 July 1811.

25. Haverford College Library, Charles Roberts Autograph Collection: O.H. Perry to David Porter, "Saty. morng." [3 Dec. 1814].

26. Charles Morris, *Autobiography* (Boston, 1880), pp. 19, 20, 25, 40.

27. Quoted in McKee, *Edward Preble*, p. 224.

8. School

1. For sources of information on midshipmen's attendance at educational institutions see section F, "Academy and College Records," in the bibliographical essay. These rosters will not be cited individually in the notes that follow, because the source that supports a particular statement in the text should be readily identifiable in the bibliography.

2. ML: John Avery to Peterson Goodwyn, 17 June 1812; MCL: Jacob Jones to Paul Hamilton, 19 Sept. 1812.

3. Lawrence A. Cremin, *American Education: The Colonial Experience, 1607–1783* (New York: Harper & Row, 1970), esp. pp. 499–516; *American Education: The National Experience, 1783–1876* (New York: Harper & Row, 1980), esp. pp. 371–413.

4. Cremin, *American Education: The Colonial Experience,* p. xiii.

5. MassHS, C.E. French Coll: Charles Stewart to William Jones, 30 June 1814; Resignations, 1810–25: Henry Dearborn to B.W. Crowninshield, 24 Oct. 1816.

6. OL: Arthur Sinclair to Paul Hamilton, 21 Aug. 1810.

7. ML: Nathaniel Thayer to Paul Hamilton, 13 Sept. 1812.

8. For example, Adams Mss, reel 393: William Hunt to John Adams, 11 Mar. 1799.

9. The best list of U.S. colleges of this period is Appendix A ("The Fifty-two Degree-Granting Institutions of Higher Learning Chartered between 1636 and 1820") in Jurgen Herbst, *From Crisis to Crisis: American College Government, 1636–1819* (Cambridge: Harvard University Press, 1982), pp. 244–253.

10. ML: R.S. Steele to Paul Hamilton, 28 Jan. 1813.

11. MCL: Arthur Sinclair to Paul Hamilton, 20 Feb. 1810.

12. As can readily be verified by reading the sketches in any of the later volumes of *Sibley's Harvard Graduates: Biographical Sketches of Those Who Attended Harvard College* (Boston, 1873–).

13. For academies, in addition to Cremin, see also Joseph F. Kett, *Rites of Passage: Adolescence in America, 1790 to the Present* (New York: Basic Books, 1977), pp. 18–20.

14. James Strong, *An Eulogium . . . upon the Late Lieut. Com. Allen* (New York: W. Grattan, 1822), pp. 3–4.

15. Cremin, *American Education: The Colonial Experience*, p. 505.

16. RG 45, Acceptances, 1809–39: Thomas H. Bowyer to Paul Hamilton, 27 Jan. 1812.

17. Good examples of the latter would be David Porter's description of his visit to Leptis Magna, in "Sketch of the Barbary States," *Analectic Magazine* 7(1816):110–113, or ex-midshipman James Biggs's *History of Don Francisco de Miranda's Attempt to Effect a Revolution in South America, in a Series of Letters by a Gentleman Who Was an Officer under That General* (Boston: Oliver and Munroe, 1808).

9. Work

1. Harvard Univ Arch, Class of 1814, Secretary's File (HUD 214:505): Elbridge Gerry, [Jr.], to Thomas W. Phillips, 27 Dec. 1852.

2. Lewis Mss: William Lewis to James Lewis, 17 Apr. 1801; William Lewis to [Elizabeth Herndon], 13 Oct. 1803.

3. Appmt Papers TJ: Overton Carr, [Sr.], to [Thomas Jefferson], 27 Mar. 1804; ML: Robert Brent to Paul Hamilton, 1 Apr. 1812, enclosing Thomas W. Pairo to Brent, 31 Mar. 1812.

4. Hamilton Papers 22:283.

5. ML: John Mason to Paul Hamilton, 26 Mar. 1812, enclosing Henry Dunlap [and others] to Hamilton, 18 Mar. 1812.

6. ML: Seth B. Alby to Paul Hamilton, 12 May 1812; M&PR: Arthur Sinclair, "Descriptive Roll of Commissioned & Warrant Officers, Erie Station," 2 June 1815 (T829:16).

7. MCL: Robert T. Spence to William Jones, 25 July 1813.

8. ML: John Kelly to Thomas Tingey, 17 Dec. 1812; Lewis D. Cook, "William Murdoch (1705–1761), of Philadelphia, and His Descendants," *Pennsylvania Genealogical Magazine* 16(1948):46, 53, 56.

9. ML: Charles Collins to Jeremiah B. Howell, 24 June 1812; J W Simonds to Langdon Cheves, 28 Apr. 1812.

10. NYHS, Nav Hist Soc Misc Mss: Arthur Sinclair to B.W. Crowninshield, 23 Dec. 1816.

11. James F. Zimmerman, *Impressment of American Seamen* (New York: Columbia University, 1925), pp. 259–275.

12. CL: Stephen Decatur to Robert Smith, 17 Nov. 1807.

13. OSW 10:54: Paul Hamilton to Stephen Decatur, 13 June 1812; ML: Edward Carter to Hamilton, 16 Sept. 1812; M&PR: *United States*, 1809–14 (T829:127), fols. 85, 154; *Columbian Centinel* (Boston), 3 Feb. 1813.

14. RG 45, Acceptances, Midshipmen, 1810–14: James Terry to William Jones, 22 July 1814; John Greaton to Benjamin Homans, 19 Dec. 1814; Duke, USND Coll: Charles G. Ridgely to B.W. Crowninshield, 12 Apr. 1816.

15. MCL: Jacob Jones to Paul Hamilton, 19 Dec. 1812; ML: M.D. Dougherty to Hamilton, [n.d., bound at 2 May 1812]; Charles Stewart to Hamilton, 23 May 1812; Robert Patton to Hamilton, 30 May 1812; CL: Thomas Macdonough to William Jones, 20 Sept. 1814.

10. Politics

1. ML: Eph. Vansant to Philip Reed, 28 Feb. 1809.

2. ML: Joel Abbot to James M. Varnum, 24 Sept. 1812; Varnum to Paul Hamilton, 7 Oct. 1812; Westford Academy, *General Catalogue of Trustees, Teachers, and Students, 1792–1895* (Westford, Mass., 1912), pp. 7, 27.

3. ML: Michael Leib to Paul Hamilton, 20 Aug. 1812.

4. Wadsworth Mss: Journal, 1802–1803, entry for 17 June 1803.

5. In an unsigned, undated memorandum for President Jefferson prepared late in 1801 or early in 1802 (TJ Mss, fol. 42199 [reel 25 of the 1976 microfilm edition]) Secretary of War Henry Dearborn reported the political affiliations of "officers of the navy" as Republican, seven; Federalist, seventy. Such numbers clearly cannot include midshipmen and perhaps exclude one or two other ranks as well. None of the seventy-seven individuals is identified.

6. Lilly, War of 1812 Mss: Paul Hamilton to Caesar A. Rodney, 27 July 1810.

7. TJ Mss: Robert Smith to Thomas Jefferson, 28 Nov. [1803]; Jefferson endorsed Smith's letter "Thom," but William H. Thom, the sole midshipman of that name, never served in a schooner.

8. ML: Philip R. Thompson to Robert Smith, 12 Apr. 1806.

9. ML: Samuel Smith to William Jones, 12 Aug. 1813; Jacob Lewis to Jones, 31 Oct. 1813; Joshua Barney to Jones, 4 Apr. 1814; see also CL: Charles Gordon to William Jones, 29 May 1814.

10. ML: Nathaniel F. Williams to William Doughty, 17 Nov. 1813; Paul Beck to William Jones, 8 Dec. 1813.

11. A handful of examples to the contrary can be found at the very beginnings of the Quasi-War naval expansion, while the navy was still administered by Secretary of War James McHenry, who was, in turn, being closely advised by the highly partisan Alexander Hamilton (Appmt Papers JA: Hoysteed Hacker to Theodore Foster, 11 May 1798, and QW 1:102; also McKee, *Edward Preble*, pp. 55–56, and Linda M. Maloney, *The Captain from Connecticut: The Life and Naval Times of Isaac Hull* [Boston: Northeastern University Press, 1986], pp. 16–17). After the Navy Department was established as a separate entity the statement made in the text holds true for the balance of the 1798–1815 years.

12. Isaac Hull to William Bainbridge, 11 Apr. 1808, quoted in Maloney, *Captain from Connecticut*, p. 127.

13. HSPa, Gratz Coll: William Bainbridge to David Porter, 13 June 1815.

11. Why

1. ZB File: George N. Hollins to Samuel Smith, 8 Feb. 1814.

2. "Autobiography of Commodore George Nicholas Hollins, C.S.A.," *Maryland Historical Magazine* 34(1939):228–243, quoted passage at p. 228.

3. ML: Thomas Tingey to Robert Smith, 2 Mar. 1809; Tunis Craven to Smith, 2 Mar. 1809.

4. Duke, USND Coll: Daniel Davis to Josiah Quincy, 27 Jan. 1808.

5. HSPa, Wm Jones Mss: Richard Dale to William Jones, 29 July 1813.

6. ML: Robert Anderson to Paul Hamilton, 18 Apr. 1812.

7. Talbot Mss: Sarah Connolly to Silas Talbot, 12 June 1799.

8. Henry Clay, *Papers*, ed. James F. Hopkins [and others] (Lexington: University of Kentucky Press, 1959–) 1:666; AGO LR File #7871: George Walker to Richard Cutts, 8 Jan. 1815.

9. Kennon Letters 32:81 (2 Aug. 1809).

10. Accnt LR: Ben. Leverett to Constant Freeman, 16 Oct. 1822.

11. ZB File: Christopher Ellery to William Jones, 27 Feb. 1814.

12. ML: Nicholas Brewer to [Paul Hamilton?], 23 June 1811.

13. MCL: David Porter to Paul Hamilton, 18 Sept. 1810; Jack D.L. Holmes and Raymond J. Martinez, "The Naval Career of Lawrence Rousseau," *Louisiana History* 9(1968):341–354.

14. ML: Richard Hall to Robert Brent, 31 Mar. 1812.

Part Three: A Society within Wooden Walls

12. Eye of the Novice

1. OSW 8:375; for a sample of the printed form letter see Accts (A) Archer, Richard C.: Paul Hamilton to Archer, 18 May 1809.

2. RG 45, Acceptances, 1804–23.

3. Lewis Mss: William Lewis to Edward Herndon, 29 Aug. 1802.

4. Izard Family Papers: Ralph Izard, Jr., to Alice Izard, 28 May [i.e., June], 6 July 1801.

5. Izard Family Papers: Ralph Izard, Jr., to Alice Izard, 7 Oct. 1801.

6. Lewis Mss: William Lewis to Edward Herndon, 29 Aug. 1802; see also MCL: David Porter to Paul Hamilton, 12 Aug. 1811.

7. Allen Letters 104 (26 June 1800).

8. *President* orders, ca. 1812, article 72, and orders respecting marines, articles 4, 5, 6, 7, and 9; *Independence* orders, 1815, article 34.

9. The best evidence for the practice seen by this historian is to be found in Purser Benjamin F. Bourne's receipt roll for the 1815 cruise of *Peacock* in Accts (A). Therein Lieutenant John Percival and Midshipmen William H. Baldwin, Allen Griffin, Israel Israel, Jr., Robert Ritchie, and William T. Rodgers may be seen purchasing duck frocks and, especially, duck trousers in quantities not dissimilar from their enlisted shipmates in *Peacock*. See also *Constitution*'s slop book, 1803–1804, in M&PR: *Constitution* Pay Roll, 1803–28, vol. 1 (T829:95), fols. 22–38.

10. *President* orders, 1809, article 21.

11. *President* orders, 1809, article 5; *President* orders, ca. 1812, articles 16 and 81; *Argus* orders, 1811, article 30; *Independence* orders, 1815, article 32; AF, A-7: John Orde Creighton, orders, Newport, R.I., 28 Sept. 1814.

12. *Constitution* orders, 1809, article 76; Woolsey Journal, 1801–1803, entry of 15 Jan. 1802; RG 24, *John Adams*, Log, entries for 6 and 11 July 1810.

13. Lewis Mss: William Lewis to Garritt Minor, 14 Nov. 1802.

14. Effie Gwynn Bowie, *Across the Years in Prince George's County* (Richmond, Va.: Garrett and Massie, 1947), p. 199.

15. Boerum, 29 Jan. 1815.

16. Boerum, 13 Feb., 27 Feb., 10 May, 4 Feb., 1 Feb., 18 Mar., 22 Apr., 9 Feb., 28 May 1815.

17. Boerum, 29 June 1815.

18. Skiddy. The midshipmen mentioned by name were Joseph E. Smoot, Thomas A. Tippett, and Ira Titus. The other midshipmen in *Hornet* during this cruise were William Boerum, Adam Kuhn, and Samuel B. Phelps (M&PR: *Hornet*, 1805–19 [T829:99], fols. 118–127).

19. Comparison of Skiddy's memoirs with contemporary records such as Boerum and RG 24, *Hornet*, Log, 24 Jan.–22 June 1815, shows Skiddy's recollections to be remarkably accurate; in this instance, compare *Hornet*'s log for 27 Jan. 1815, which substantiates Skiddy's memories.

20. QW 1:155; Roche Letters 138–139; EPP: Gentlemen of the Wardroom to Edward Preble, 21 July, 29 July, 5 Aug., 12 Aug., 18 Aug., 26 Aug., 9 Sept. 1804; Officers of the Gunroom to Preble, 29 Apr., 10 June 1804; Talbot Mss: Gentlemen of the Wardroom to Silas Talbot, 4 Aug., 11 Aug. 1799; Skiddy, in account of Equator crossing quoted above; Woolsey Journal, 1801–1803, entry for 4 Aug. 1802; Accnt LR: Alexander Murray to Thomas Turner, 8 Feb. 1810.

21. Woolsey Journal, 1801–1803, entry for 17 July 1802.

22. *President* orders, ca. 1812, articles 58, 87, 91; *Argus* orders, 1811, articles 8, 46; Murray LB: Alexander Murray to Ambrose Shirley, 22 Aug. 1800.

23. Woolsey Journal, 1801–1803, entry for 4 Aug. 1802. Tourism by American naval officers, particularly in Mediterranean ports, is described more fully in McKee, *Edward Preble*, passim.

24. Woolsey Journal, 1801–1803, entries for 4–5 July 1802.

25. Woolsey Journal, 1801–1803, entry for 4 Aug. 1802.

26. Kennon Letters 33:278–281 (4 May 1812).

13. Midshipman to Lieutenant

1. *President* orders, ca. 1812, "Exercise of Cannon"; RFP, LB 1808–1809: John Rodgers to Charles Ludlow, 1 Apr. 1809. A goodly number of watch, quarter, and station bills of the pre-1815 navy survive. The discussion that follows is based on the most elaborate of these, HSPa, Rodgers Mss: Quarter Bill, Boarding Bill, Watch Bill, Order of Mooring and Unmooring, Order of Reefing and Hoisting Topsails, Order of Tacking and Wearing, and Mess Roll, U.S. Frigate *Congress*, 1804 (Amn 300). Also consulted were HSPa, Rodgers Mss: Quarter Bill, etc., U.S. Frigate *John Adams*, 1802–1803 (Amn 300); SF, NA: Quarter Bill of *Constitution*, 1812, at time of battle with *Java*; USN Misc: "Quarter Bill, U.S.F.U.S.," in Memo Book, *United States* Frigate, 1809.

2. *Argus* orders, 1811, article 27.

3. Practice varied greatly, depending on the organizational preferences of the captain regarding the distribution of midshipmen to the divisions. According to the quarter bills cited in note 1 above, John Rodgers assigned only one midshipman to assist the lieutenant at each division of guns, distributing the others to the tops and braces in time of battle; Stephen Decatur, in *United States*, allocated one lieutenant and three midshipmen to a division; Bainbridge went into battle with *Java* with five midshipmen quartered in each division, one for every pair of guns.

4. *President* orders, ca. 1812, articles 71, 88, and "Exercise of Cannon."

5. *President* orders, ca. 1812, articles 42, 67–68; *Argus* orders, 1811, articles 9, 13; *Madison & General Pike* orders, 1813–14, articles 12, 30; *Independence* orders, 1815, article 50.

6. *Argus* orders, 1811, articles 9, 28; *Madison & General Pike* orders, 1813–14, articles 3, 30; *Independence* orders, 1815, article 50; Roche Letters 139.

7. Izard Family Papers: Ralph Izard, Jr., to Alice Izard, 12 Aug. 1801; *Argus* orders, 1811, article 8.

8. *President* orders, ca. 1812, article 93.

9. *Madison & General Pike* orders, 1813–14, article 23; *President* orders, ca. 1812, articles 54, 93; *Argus* orders, 1811, article 42.

10. Summer was officially defined as the period from 22 Mar. through 21 Sept.; the balance of the year was winter (*President* orders, ca. 1812, article 26).

11. Just how terrifying the fear of fire and explosion were in a wooden ship may be measured by the fact that, of the hundred-plus articles in John Rodgers's standing general orders for *President*, thirteen dealt in detail with fire prevention and control, more than for any other single aspect of shipboard life (*President* orders, ca. 1812, articles 26–30, 35–37, 72, 77, 82, 83, and "General Orders in Case of Fire").

12. *Argus* orders, 1811, article 16; *Madison* & *General Pike* orders, 1813–14, articles 7, 20; NYHS, Cooper's Hist extra illus: Samuel Barron to John Cassin, 14 Sept. 1801.

13. *President* orders, ca. 1812, articles 4, 47, 93; *Argus* orders, 1811, articles 6, 42.

14. Lewis Mss: William Lewis to Garritt Minor, 31 Mar. 1803.

15. MCL: Lewis Warrington to William Jones, 2 Oct. 1813; OL: Arthur Sinclair to Paul Hamilton, 24 Feb. 1810.

16. NYHS, Misc Mss: Charles Morris to Lemuel Morris, 20 July 1810, is an interesting explanation of this point; Morris tells why he declined John Rodgers's invitation to become *President*'s first lieutenant.

17. *President* orders, ca. 1812, article 64.

18. Dexter LB: Daniel S. Dexter to Robert Spedden, 2 June, 5 June 1813; Dexter to Isaac McKeever, 7 June 1813.

19. *Independence* orders, 1815, p. 20.

20. RFP, LB 1808–1809: John Rodgers to Charles Ludlow, 1 Apr. 1809.

21. *President* orders, ca. 1812, articles 39, 56, 63–64, 92; *Argus* orders, 1811, articles 5, 17, 18, 33; RG 24, *John Adams*, Log, 29 May 1810; RFP, John Rodgers Journal, Frigate *President*, 1812–14, entries for 11–12 May 1813; *Independence* orders, 1815, pp. 14–15. The daily routine in a frigate of this era is described in McKee, *Edward Preble*, pp. 214–219.

22. NYHS, Misc Mss: Charles Morris to Lemuel Morris, 6 Jan. 1808. Morris's allusion to John Gilpin refers to William Cowper's 1782 ballad "The Diverting History of John Gilpin," in which the protagonist's borrowed horse runs away with him.

14. Two Enemies

1. Lilly: Humphreys Journal, Jan. 1815.

2. Howard I. Chapelle, *History of the American Sailing Navy* (New York: Norton, 1949), pp. 188–189, 547; U.S. Naval History Division, *Dictionary of American Naval Fighting Ships* (Washington, D.C., 1959–81) 5:26; OL: Arthur Sinclair to Paul Hamilton, 4 Jan., 8 Jan., 16 Jan. 1811. The account of the Dec. 1811–Jan. 1812 voyage of *Nautilus* is based principally on these sources: MCL: Arthur Sinclair to Paul Hamilton, 19 Jan. 1811 [i.e., 1812]; CMR 3:0993–1021: Court of Inquiry into the Conduct of Arthur Sinclair, 15–18 Sept. 1812; M&PR: Muster rolls, *Nautilus*, Jan.–Dec. 1811, Jan.–July 1812 (T829:196), fols. 127–146; CL: John Rodgers to Hamilton, 8 Jan., 17 Jan. 1812; OSW 9:542: Hamilton to Rodgers, 18 Jan. 1812; 9:550: Hamilton to Sinclair, 29 Jan. 1812; NHF, Porter Family Coll: David Porter to Samuel Hambleton, 20 Jan. 1812.

3. Wadsworth Mss: Journal, 1802–1803, ca. Apr. 1803; GLB 7:147: Robert Smith to John Campbell, 27 Apr. 1804; 8:112: Smith to John Stricker, 30 Jan. 1806; OL: Walter Winter to Smith, 4 May 1805, [n.d., received 20 May 1805], 12 Jan. 1806, 19 Apr., 18 May, 29 Oct. 1807; Arthur Sinclair to Paul Hamilton, 24 Feb. 1810; ML: John Mun to Smith, 25 Jan. 1806; OSW 8:131: Smith to Winter, 14 Aug. 1808.

4. SF, NI: Thomas Macdonough to John Rodgers, 6 May 1815; OL: Charles A. Budd to Paul Hamilton, 11 Feb. 1811.

5. MCL: Arthur Sinclair to Paul Hamilton, 20 Mar. 1812.

6. At the subsequent court of inquiry Sinclair proved that this incident did not take place when Winter said it had, which does not establish that it possessed no basis in fact. Winter, short on sleep and food, like everyone else, probably had the time sequence confused.

7. The only source for events after 27 Dec. is Sinclair's report of 19 Jan. 1812 (MCL); this is rather imprecise on dates during the latter part of the voyage. Dates stated in the text and reconstructed from Sinclair's report could be off a day or so either way.

8. Some partial exceptions are Midshipman Henry Gilliam on the *Constitution-Guerriere* battle and Midshipman Robert T. Spence on the explosion of Gunboat No. 9 off Tripoli (quoted pp. 399–400); Purser Samuel Hambleton's narrative of the battle of Lake Erie (MdHS, Hambleton Diary, Mar. 1813–Oct. 1814, entry for 12 Oct. 1813); Surgeon Usher Parsons's various writings on the Lake Erie conflict, especially his *Brief Sketches of the Officers Who Were in the Battle of Lake Erie* (Albany, N.Y.: J. Munsell, 1862); Midshipman David Geisinger's account of the combat between *Wasp* and *Reindeer*, 28 June 1814, in USN Misc: Geisinger Journal, 2 May–23 Sept. 1814; and the "Autobiography of Commodore George Nicholas Hollins, C.S.A.," *Maryland Historical Magazine* 34(1939):229–231, for the *President-Endymion* battle.

9. Dudley Pope, *Life in Nelson's Navy* (Annapolis, Md.: Naval Institute Press, 1981), p. 151.

Part Four: To Make a Sea Officer

1. HEHL, MH 122: Thomas Truxtun to James McHenry, 3 Mar. 1797; see also the important letter from Robert Smith to Edward Preble, 2 Aug. 1803, printed in McKee, *Edward Preble*, pp. 131–132.

2. This is simply a restatement of Bernard Bailyn's definition of education— "one thinks of education not only as formal pedagogy but as the entire process by which a culture transmits itself across the generations"—in his *Education in the Forming of American Society* (Chapel Hill: University of North Carolina Press for the Institute of Early American History and Culture, 1960), p. 14.

15. The Young Officer's Best Teachers

1. CL: William Bainbridge to Robert Smith, 4 May 1808; Isaac Hull to Charles W. Goldsborough, 27 Apr. 1809; Hull to Paul Hamilton, 23 July 1809; Bainbridge to Hamilton, 25 Sept., 7 Nov. 1809, 29 Jan. 1810; OL: Jacob Jones to Hamilton, 2 Nov. 1809; OSW 8:514: Goldsborough (for Hamilton) to John Rodgers or William Bainbridge, 13 Oct. 1809.

2. For example MCL: David Porter to Paul Hamilton, 23 July 1810; CL: Hugh G. Campbell to Charles W. Goldsborough, 17 July 1809; Campbell to Hamilton, 22 July 1810; ML: Thomas Macdonough to Charles Jarvis, 24 Dec. 1813, enclosed in Jarvis to William Jones, 10 Jan. 1814.

3. Narrative Statements of Service: W. Branford Shubrick to A.P. Upshur, 16 Aug. 1842.

4. ML: Susan Jackson to Robert Smith, 31 Oct. 1808. See also, for similar sentiments, CL: William Bainbridge to William Jones, 24 Sept. 1813; MCL:

Charles Gordon to Paul Hamilton, 28 June 1812; ML: Buckner Thruston to Smith, 28 Feb. 1809; W.J. Gunning to Hamilton, 4 June 1810; Arthur Breese to Hamilton, 4 Apr. 1811; Thomas McCall to Charles Tait, 20 Apr. 1812; John S. Sherburne to Hamilton, 3 July 1812; RG 45, Acceptances, 1809–39: James C. Pickett to Hamilton, 1 July 1812; John Hatfield to Hamilton, 25 Nov. 1812.

5. See two remarkable and complementary accounts: Narrative Statements of Service: Thomas ap C. Jones to Secretary of the Navy, 24 Apr. 1844, and the long obituary notice of Jones in *Daily National Intelligencer* (Washington), 1 June 1858. Jones concluded his 1844 statement, "To narrate all the incidents of tempest, disease, rencounters with smugglers and pirates, and of war during that period would fill a volume, which, at this time, would be considered a romance."

6. CL: Alexander Murray to Paul Hamilton, 11 Aug. 1812.

7. CL: Alexander Murray to Robert Smith, 21 Mar., 29 Apr. (enclosing Murray to Bernard Henry, 28 Apr.), 13 June 1808; Frederick Rodgers Coll: Murray to John Rodgers, 28 Apr. 1808; OSW 8:104: Smith to Murray, 16 June 1808; RG 45, Letters Sent by the Secretary of the Navy to Officers Commanding Gunboats, Dec. 1803–Dec. 1808:288–289, 298: Smith to Murray, 31 Mar., 20 Apr. 1808.

8. OSW 6:472: Robert Smith to Samuel Barron, 2 June 1804.

9. Thomas Truxtun, "A Short Account of the Several General Duties of Officers of Ships of War, from an Admiral down to the Most Inferior Officer," in his *Remarks, Instructions, and Examples Relating to the Latitude & Longitude . . .* (Philadelphia: T. Dobson, 1794), pp. xvii–xviii.

10. Resignations, 1803–25: George W. Spotswood to [Robert Smith], 11 May 1803.

11. Of many references that could be cited, the following are representative of the Navy Department's policy on encouraging merchant voyaging: OSW 5:144: Robert Smith to James S. Higinbotham, 28 July 1801; 6:229–230, 260: Smith, Circular to Charles Jones and ten other midshipmen, 28 July 1803; Smith to Andrew Sterett, 8 Dec. 1803; 7:87, 96, 186, 241, 250: Smith to John M. Gardner, 13 Mar. 1806; Smith to Anthony Y. Denton, 26 Mar. 1806; Smith to Seth Nicholson, 14 July 1806; Smith to William Peters, 8 Oct. 1806; Smith to Turner McGlauhon, 27 Oct. 1806.

12. Estimated from officers' furloughs to serve in the merchant marine noted in U.S. Office of Naval Records and Library, *Register of Officer Personnel, United States Navy and Marine Corps, and Ships' Data, 1801–1807* (Washington, D.C., 1945). The numbers are 567 officers, of whom 132 (23.3 percent) are identified as furloughed for merchant service. No great faith should be pinned on these deceptively precise numbers. This source overlooks a small number of men who were naval officers during the years under discussion. Some officers, known from other records to have received furloughs during which they made merchant voyages, are not so noted. However, there is no reason to question that the true proportion falls somewhere between one-fifth and one-quarter of all officers.

13. HSPa, Connaroe Papers: James Biddle to William Bainbridge, 19 Apr. 1808.

14. Lewis Mss: William Lewis to John B. Nicolson, 18 Apr. 1812.

15. OL: John M. Funck to Robert Smith, 22 Apr. 1807; ML: George Harrison to Smith, 8 July 1807.

16. CL: John Rodgers to Robert Smith, 8 July 1808.

17. One officer reported "several voyages" without giving a clue as to the exact number.

18. Roche Letters 147 (24 Feb. 1801).

19. ML: Thomas English to Robert Smith, 30 Jan. 1808; RG 45, Acceptances, Midshipmen, 1810–14: English to Paul Hamilton, 20 July 1810; OL: M. Yarnall to Hamilton, 11 Jan. 1811; James Reilly to Hamilton, 25 June 1811; John J. Yarnall to Hamilton, 16 Jan. 1812; CL: John Rodgers to Hamilton, 15 Sept. 1812.

20. The precise figures on the capacities in which merchant voyages were made are master, 7+; mate, 14; before the mast, 9; supercargo, 1; unknown, 43; total, 74+.

21. OL: Charles Wergman, Certificate re William Peters, 8 Feb. 1809; Abst of serv, vol. C, for Peters's return in *Hornet*, Dec. 1807; OL: Joseph L. Biggs to Paul Hamilton, 28 June 1811; William C. Beard to Hamilton, 9 Sept. 1809; Fitz Henry Babbit to Hamilton, 18 May 1811; Jesse D. Elliott to William Jones, 28 Mar. 1813.

22. OL: William P. Adams to Robert Smith, 26 June 1807; Frederick Rodgers Coll: Henry S. Newcomb to John Rodgers, 14 Mar. 1811.

16. Setting the Norm

1. In his *Remarks, Instructions, and Examples Relating to the Latitude & Longitude* (Philadelphia: T. Dobson, 1794), Appendix, pp. xi–xxiii.

2. NYHS, Isaac Chauncey LB, 1805–1806: Isaac Chauncey to Thomas Truxtun, 4 Aug. 1805.

3. USNAM.

4. QW 1:299, 572; *President* orders, 1809, articles 4, 10; Wadsworth Mss: Thomas Truxtun, "To the Midshipmen of the Navy and Particularly Those Who Serve with Me," ca. Mar. 1802.

5. QW 1:572–573; 2:325; Wadsworth Mss: Truxtun, "To the Midshipmen of the Navy," ca. Mar. 1802; Murray LB: Alexander Murray to Midshipmen of the *Insurgente*, 8 Aug. 1799.

6. QW 1:302; Wadsworth Mss: Truxtun, "To the Midshipmen of the Navy," ca. Mar. 1802; Truxtun, "A Short Account of the Several General Duties of Officers of Ships of War," in *Remarks, Instructions, and Examples*, Appendix, p. xviii.

7. OSW 7:13: Robert Smith to Isaac Chauncey, 16 Sept. 1805.

8. USNAM: Thomas Truxtun to Thomas Robinson, Jr., 18 Apr. 1799; Murray LB: Alexander Murray to Midshipmen of the *Insurgente*, 8 Aug. 1799; Murray to Officers of the Wardroom, 7 Feb. 1800; Wadsworth Mss: Truxtun, "To the Midshipmen of the Navy," ca. Mar. 1802; *President* orders, 1809, article 5; *Argus* orders, 1811, articles 28, 42; *President* orders, ca. 1812, article 16; *Independence* orders, 1815, p. 23.

9. For example, OSW 2:19: Benjamin Stoddert to C.R. Perry, 8 May 1799; 5:332: Robert Smith to Thomas Truxtun, 8 Feb. 1802; CL: Hugh G. Campbell to Paul Hamilton, 20 Oct. (bound at 9 Oct.), 9 Dec., 20 Dec. 1809; RG 45, Journal kept on board *Argus* and *Nautilus*, Oct. 1811–July 1812, at 8 Mar. 1812; NYPL: "Journal kept on board the U.S. vessel of war Frolic, Joseph Bainbridge, commander, of 18 guns," 20 Feb.–20 Apr. 1814, at 6 Mar. 1814.

10. Homans, pp. 59–69.

11. This historian questions that the entire act would have been read at Sunday muster. There was little point in boring the ship's company with articles devoted to administrative detail. Indeed, reading such somnolence-inducing paragraphs would have weakened the impact of articles detailing responsibility, order, crime, and punishment. To judge from the marginal marks in Edward Preble's copy of "An Act for the Better Government of the Navy of the United States" (MeHS, Preble Mss) it was his practice to read section 1, articles 1 through 28, 31–32, 38, 41–42, section 4, and sections 7–9. Most of the sections he read publicly (or had read) dealt with disciplinary matters. However, in the light of his own punishment practice (McKee, *Edward Preble*, pp. 221–224, and Chapter 21 of this book), it is significant that he omitted from the public reading section 1, article 30, which limited an officer's power to punish an enlisted man on his own authority, including the prohibition on the infliction of more than twelve lashes.

12. U.S. War Department, *Marine Rules and Regulations* ([Philadelphia]: John Fenno, 1798 [Evans #34893]; reprinted unaltered, Boston: Printed by Manning & Loring, for William T. Clapp, 1799 [Evans #36544]); U.S. Navy Department, *Naval Regulations, Issued by Command of the President of the United States of America, January 25, 1802* (Washington, D.C., 1802 [Shaw & Shoemaker #3374]; reprinted, with minor changes and corrections, Washington, D.C.: For the Navy Office, 1809 [Shaw & Shoemaker #19018]; reprinted again, Washington, D.C.: For the Navy Office, 1814 [not recorded in Shaw & Shoemaker, but a copy is held by the U.S. Naval Academy Library, Annapolis]). The British ancestor is Great Britain, Privy Council, *Regulations and Instructions Relating to His Majesty's Service at Sea, Established by His Majesty in Council* (13th ed.; London, 1790). The extent to which officers and leaders of the pre-1815 U.S. Navy were familiar with the much more extensive and heavily revised product of the British navy of the wars of the French Revolution and Empire, its *Regulations and Instructions Relating to His Majesty's Service at Sea, Established by His Majesty in Council* (London: W. Winchester and Son, 1808), cannot be determined. There was a definite cultural lag between the two navies in these matters. The 1808 *Regulations and Instructions* did heavily influence U.S. Navy Department, *Rules, Regulations, and Instructions for the Naval Service of the United States; Prepared by the Board of Navy Commissioners of the United States, with the Consent of the Secretary of the Navy, in Obedience to an Act of Congress Passed Seventh February 1815* (Washington, D.C.: Printed by E. DeKrafft, 1818 [Shaw & Shoemaker #46605]), the code that replaced the *Naval Regulations* of 1802.

The 1798 U.S. *Marine Rules and Regulations* were compiled by Secretary of War James McHenry late in 1797 or early in 1798; they may be his greatest administrative legacy to the U.S. Navy. Before submitting the manuscript to President John Adams for final approval McHenry circulated it to Captains John Barry and Thomas Truxtun, who made changes and additions (Adams Mss, reel 387: John Barry [and] Thomas Truxtun to James McHenry, 2 Feb. 1798). By mid-Mar. 1798 the manuscript regulations had been approved by the president and were ready to be printed (RG 45, Correspondence on Naval Affairs when the Navy Was under the War Department, Oct. 1790–June 1798: McHenry to Samuel Nicholson, 14 Mar. 1798), appearing soon thereafter as a 56-page pamphlet.

Not later than mid-Nov. 1801 Robert Smith had in hand a manuscript draft of a new version of the rules and regulations (the future *Naval Regulations* of

1802), which he circulated successively to Captains John Barry, Thomas Truxtun, Richard V. Morris, and Alexander Murray for comments, alterations, and additions between 13 Nov. and 24 Dec. 1801 (OSW 5:265–266: Robert Smith, letters to Barry, Truxtun, Morris, and Murray, 13 Nov. 1801; Murray LB: Murray to Smith, 24 Dec. 1801). The printed version was ready for distribution by early Feb. 1802 (OSW 5:332: Smith to Truxtun, 8 Feb. 1802). Who compiled the basic draft of the 1802 *Naval Regulations*? An educated guess is Captain Thomas Tingey who (1) lived in Washington; (2) had the confidence of Robert Smith and President Jefferson; (3) is known to have owned copies of the British *Regulations and Instructions* (Accnt LR: Tingey to Thomas Turner, 25 July 1800); and (4) was, significantly, not among those to whom the manuscript was sent for comment.

17. Mentors and Challenges

1. For a more extended discussion of this point see Christopher McKee, "Edward Preble and the 'Boys': The Officer Corps of 1812 Revisited," in *Command under Sail: Makers of the American Naval Tradition, 1775–1850*, ed. James C. Bradford (Annapolis, Md.: Naval Institute Press, 1985), pp. 71–96.

2. C.O. Paullin in DAB 13:357–358; "Life of Commodore Murray," *Port Folio,* 3d [i.e., 4th] ser., 3(1814):399–409; MdHS, Murray Family Papers: Alexander Murray to Magnus Murray, 12 Apr. 1799 (an autobiographical statement; the best single source) and 18 July 1818; SF, NN: Alexander Murray to George Washington, 3 May 1794, and supporting recommendations in the same file; GLB 2:175: Benjamin Stoddert to Jacob Read, 13 June 1799; CL: Alexander Murray to Robert Smith, 1 Jan., 4 July 1807; to Paul Hamilton, 17 Oct. 1812; to William Jones, 22 Jan. 1813; to B.W. Crowninshield, 16 Jan. 1815; Accnt LR: Alexander Murray to Thomas Turner, 18 Apr. 1807; NYHS, Albert Gallatin Mss: Alexander Murray to Gallatin, 14 Aug. 1807; PMS: John Rodgers to B.W. Crowninshield, 11 Feb. 1815; HSPa, Wm Jones Mss: Manuel Eyre to Jones, 17 Mar. 1813; McKee, *Edward Preble*, passim, esp. pp. 107–113, 224n; William Bell Clark, *Gallant John Barry* (New York: Macmillan, 1938), p. 318; Clark, *Lambert Wickes, Sea Raider and Diplomat* (New Haven, Conn.: Yale University Press, 1932), pp. 11–13, 120; for the relationship among Murray, the Nicholson brothers, and Wickes see Byam Kerby Stevens, *Genealogical-Biographical Histories of the Families of Stevens, Gallatin, and Nicholson* (New York, 1911), pp. 30–31; it is uncertain whether Wickes was a blood relative of Murray's; the latter's aunt was definitely one of the wives of Lambert's father, Samuel.

3. Harvard University, Houghton Library: O.H. Perry to Samuel R. Marshall, 19 Sept. 1805; NYHS, Cooper's Hist extra illus: Perry to Hugh G. Campbell, 21 Dec. 1813. For the conflicting opinions of young subordinates regarding Campbell see Izard Family Papers: Ralph Izard, Jr., to Alice Izard, 21/27 Oct., 12 Nov. 1802 (unfavorable); Woolsey Journal, 1801–1803, entry of 14 Nov. 1802 (favorable); BW 2:271: P.N. O'Bannon to William Ward Burrows, 10 Sept. 1802; USMC LR(L): same to same, 15 Dec. 1802 (unfavorable, then favorable); Barron Mss: Arthur Sinclair to James Barron, 18 Sept. 1805 (favorable).

4. The brief obituary of Campbell in Washington's *Daily National Intelligencer,* 13 Nov. 1820, says, "A proper biographical notice of the deceased veteran will probably be presented to the public by the hand of a friend." If

this intention was carried into execution, the present historian has been unable to locate where it was published. Campbell's will (May 1820) is in South Carolina Archives, Columbia: South Carolina Wills Transcripts 34:399–401; the inventory of his goods and chattels, including 324 bottles of undrunk madeira, his pew in Charleston's St. Paul's Church, and seven black slaves, is in South Carolina Inventories F:351–352 at the same agency.

5. HSPa, Society Miscellaneous Collection: Hugh G. Campbell to Jones & Clark, 21 Mar. 1801; HSPa, Wm Jones Mss: William Johnson, Jr., to William Jones, 23 Oct. 1813; GLB 4:322: Samuel Smith to Jones, 2 May 1801; CL: Campbell to Charles W. Goldsborough, 18 Mar. 1809; Campbell to Jones, 28 Nov. 1813.

6. CL: Hugh G. Campbell to Paul Hamilton, 24 July 1809, 26 Mar. 1810. Hamilton strongly supported his fellow South Carolinian's efforts; cf. his endorsement on the letter of 26 Mar. 1810 and OSW 8:469–470, 535: Hamilton to Campbell, 3 Aug., 18 Nov. 1809.

7. CMR 2:0002–0022; Accnt LR: John B. Cheshire to Robert Smith, 21 Jan. 1806 [i.e., 1807]; CL: Hugh G. Campbell to Smith, 3 Oct. 1806.

8. NYHS, Cooper's Hist extra illus: Samuel Barron to John Cassin, 26 Aug. 1801; Barron to [Midshipmen of *Philadelphia*], 31 Mar. 1802; Barron to Lieutenants of *Philadelphia*, 28 July 1802; see also Barron to Westwood T. Mason, 24 Aug. 1801; Barron to James Nicholson, 24 Aug. 1801; Barron to Charles Wilson, 28 Sept. 1801; Barron to John R. Fenwick, 6 Jan. 1802; the pages of Barron's order book from which these citations are taken have been rebound in chaotic order.

9. Woolsey Journal, 1801–1803, entries for 14 Mar.–24 May 1802, passim.

10. CL: Charles Stewart to William Jones, 5 Mar. 1813, and enclosures; OSW 10:344: Jones, note, 13 Apr. 1813, to letter dismissing Rogers.

11. CL: Charles Gordon to William Jones, 10 Mar. 1814; John Cassin to Jones, 21 Mar. 1814.

12. CL: William Bainbridge to Thomas Turner, 12 Oct. 1813 (bound at 12 Oct. 1814).

13. Elizabeth Donnan, ed., *Documents Illustrative of the History of the Slave Trade to America* (Washington, D.C., 1930–35) 3:88, 99–100, 360; Appmt Papers TJ: Daniel McNeill to [Thomas Tingey], 6 Dec. 1806.

14. Woolsey Journal, 24 Jan., 14 Mar. 1802.

15. Izard Family Papers: Ralph Izard, Jr., to Alice Izard, 15 Sept. 1801, 21/27 Oct. 1802.

16. USMC LR(L): Anthony Gale to W.W. Burrows, 16 Dec., 23 Dec. 1800; USMC LR(B): John R. Fenwick to Burrows, 27 June 1802.

17. McKee, *Edward Preble*, pp. 101–102; Woolsey Journal, 3 Jan., 16 Jan., 20 Jan., 28 Jan., 15 Mar., 1 Apr., 12–13 May, 24 May 1802; Somers Mss: Richard Somers, [Memorandum respecting *Boston*'s departure from Málaga without Purser Wadsworth and other officers, n.d.].

18. Woolsey Journal, 10 May 1802; Accnt LS 4:100–102: Thomas Turner to Robert Smith, 28 Oct. 1802; Turner to Charles Wadsworth, 1 Nov. 1802; Accnt LR: Smith to Turner, 29 Oct. 1802; Daniel McNeill to Turner, 6 Nov. 1802.

19. Izard Family Papers: Ralph Izard, Jr., to Alice Izard, 12 Nov. 1802.

20. Appmt Papers TJ: Daniel McNeill to [Thomas Tingey], 6 Dec. 1806; Frederick Rodgers Coll: Ralph Izard, [Jr.], to John Rodgers, 9 July 1808.

21. ZB File: George C. Logan to John B. Heffernan, 6 July 1953; McNeill's will (26 May 1829) is in South Carolina Archives, Columbia: South Carolina Wills Transcripts 39:1158–1161; the inventory of his personal effects, including thirteen slaves, will be found in South Carolina Inventories H:20 at the same agency.

18. A School in Every Frigate

1. *Columbian Centinel* (Boston), 15 June, 22 June 1799; *J. Russell's Gazette* (Boston), 20 June, 24 June, 27 June 1799.

2. QW 6:177.

3. GLB 2:146: Benjamin Stoddert to John C. Jones, 1 June 1799; CL: Isaac Chauncey to William Jones, 30 Nov. 1814; OL: Cheever Felch to B.W. Crowninshield, 17 Feb. 1815; MCL: Robert T. Spence to William Jones, 6 Oct. 1813; NHF, Shaw Mss, LB 1810–12: M.B. Carroll to D.T. Patterson, 17 July 1810; HSPa, Rodgers Mss, Amn 300, "Miscellaneous Orders": John Rodgers to [Samuel Evans], 17 July 1804. Useful comparative information on British practices is found in F.B. Sullivan, "The Naval Schoolmaster during the Eighteenth Century and the Early Nineteenth Century," *Mariner's Mirror* 62(1976):311–326.

4. RFP, Ser 3A: Gardner Thomas to John Rodgers, 6 Mar. 1815.

5. Harvard Univ Arch: Quinquennial File (HUG 300); Admissions Book 1 (UA III:15.5.2); J.L. Sibley, Private Journal, 27 Apr. 1848 (HUG 1791.72.10); Sibley, Letters Received 2:74; Faculty Records 7:52, 92, 106, 119, 134, 143, 156, 168, 174, 178; Corporation Records 4:596; CL: Stephen Cassin to Arthur Sinclair, 1 Oct. 1823, enclosed in Sinclair to Secretary of the Navy, 2 Oct. 1823; ML: David P. Adams to Paul Hamilton, 23 Jan., 8 Apr. 1811; James Lawrence to Hamilton, 26 Jan. 1811; Thomas McClanahan to Hamilton, 22 Nov. 1811; OSW 9:424: Hamilton to Adams, 15 Aug. 1811; NCR; Adams's charts illustrating *Essex*'s cruise in the Pacific are in NYHS, Cooper's Hist extra illus, vol. 2, pt. 2.

6. Harvard Univ Arch, Hector Orr, Commonplace Book, 1789–1804 (HUD 789.67): Orr to [Richard] Derby, 28 July 1799; Admissions Book 1; Faculty Records 6:242, 264–265, 266, 294, 299–300, 305, 327, 352; EPP, Rufus Low, Journal, Frigate *Essex*, 1799–1800, entry for 17 Oct. 1800; *Essex*, Stores, 1799–1801: "Inventory & Sales of the Effects of Mr. Jason Howard deceased," 17 Oct. 1800.

7. George Chandler, *The Chandler Family: The Descendants of William and Annis Chandler* (2d ed.; Worcester, Mass.: Charles Hamilton, 1883), pp. 202–203, 418–419, but note that the letter from Samuel Chandler to his mother, printed therein, should correctly be dated 31 Jan. 1802; Harvard Univ Arch: Admissions Book 1; Faculty Records 4:69, 106, 109, 125–127, 129; Quinquennial File; Samuel Chandler to John Barry, 21 Apr. 1800, quoted, from an unlocated original, in Martin I.J. Griffin, *Commodore John Barry* (Philadelphia, 1903), p. 405; NYHS, Barry Corres: Chandler to John Barry, 27 Aug. 1800; OSW 5:26: Samuel Smith to Chandler, 1 June 1801; 5:384, 395: Robert Smith to Chandler, 9 Apr., 20 Apr. 1802; Accnt LR: Benjamin Stoddert to Thomas Turner, 13 May 1800; Thomas Truxtun to Turner, 3 Mar. 1802; Chandler to Robert Smith, 17 Apr. 1802.

8. Homans, p. 34; GLB 2:146: Benjamin Stoddert to John C. Jones, 1 June 1799; 3:526: Stoddert to Thomas Turner, 21 Aug. 1800; OSW 11:191: William Jones to Joseph Bainbridge, 14 Jan. 1814.

9. See, for example, Joseph F. Kett, *Rites of Passage: Adolescence in America, 1790 to the Present* (New York: Basic Books, 1977), pp. 48–50.

10. HSPa, Rodgers Mss, Amn 300, "Miscellaneous Orders": Rodgers to [Samuel Evans], 17 July 1804; M&PR: *Congress,* 1799–1814 (T829:79), fols. 112, 127.

11. TJ Mss: Thomas Jefferson to Elizabeth Chamberlayne, 24 Nov. 1805; OL: Robert Thompson to Robert Smith, 13 Jan. 1807. The latter document makes it sound as though the measure was formally introduced: "the Bill which you presented Congress last session." However, there survives no evidence of such a bill in either the printed or the manuscript records of the Ninth Congress.

12. For Thompson and his role see HSPa, Thomas Truxtun LB, 1800–1801: Truxtun to Benjamin Stoddert, 14 Nov. 1800; Truxtun to Officers of the Gun Room Mess, 12 Nov. 1800; Eugene S. Ferguson, *Truxtun of the Constellation* (Baltimore, Md.: Johns Hopkins Press, 1956), p. 210; QW 6:530–531; Izard Family Papers: Ralph Izard, Jr., to Alice Izard, 2 Dec. 1802; OSW 6:229–230: Robert Smith, Circular to Charles Jones [and ten other midshipmen], 28 July 1803; 6:244, 249: Smith to John Cassin, 13 Oct., 1 Nov. 1803; 6:284: Smith to Robert Thompson, 24 Jan. 1804; 7:193: Smith to Thompson, 23 July 1806; 7:330: Smith to Thomas Tingey, 9 Mar. 1807; 7:373, 381: Smith to Thompson, 27 Apr., 4 May 1807; 9:31, 214–215: Paul Hamilton to John Rodgers, 6 Feb., 26 Oct. 1810; OL: Thompson to Smith, 13 Jan., 26 Mar., 27 Apr., 27 July, 4 Nov. 1807; Thompson to Hamilton, 19 Sept. 1810 (bound at 19 Sept. 1809); CL: Rodgers to Smith, 25 Mar., 28 July 1808; RFP, LB 1807–1808: Rodgers to Jacob Jones, 14 Apr. 1808; LB 1809–1810: Rodgers to Thompson, 23 May 1810.

13. The best biographical sketch of Hunter is that in Richard A. Harrison, *Princetonians, 1769–1775: A Biographical Dictionary* (Princeton, N.J.: Princeton University Press, 1980), pp. 225–229; for Hunter's later years this needs to be supplemented by Appnt Papers Monroe: Andrew Hunter to James Monroe, Aug. 1819, and by the sources cited in the notes that follow.

14. ML: Andrew Hunter to William Jones, [n.d., but bound at 24 Mar. 1813]. Abst of serv, vol. D, was used to determine the length of time that midshipmen studied with Hunter, which is assumed to be the span between the date a midshipman was ordered under Hunter's tuition till he was ordered on active duty on shipboard or furloughed. This, the only available method for discovering the length of such study, is open to a number of criticisms; there is, for example, no way to prove that a midshipman was present and studying the whole while. The figures in the text should be regarded as generally indicative but hardly precise.

15. OL: Andrew Hunter to Paul Hamilton, 6 Dec., 12 Dec. 1811, 28 Feb., 16 Mar., 15 May, 29 May, 8 June, 22 June, 27 June (two letters), 18 July, 30 Sept., 5 Oct., 25 Nov. 1812; Hunter to William Jones, 29 June 1813 (bound at 17 Mar. 1814); ML: John M. Hepburn to Jones, 27 Aug. 1813.

16. GLB 10:301–302: Paul Hamilton to William Helms, 21 Feb. 1811; 11:55: Hamilton to George Harrison, 14 Mar. 1812; OSW 9:430: Hamilton to Andrew Hunter, 21 Aug. 1811; 10:38, 210: Hamilton to Hunter, 14 May, 24 Nov. 1812; OL: Hunter to Hamilton, 30 Apr. 1811, 11 Mar., 16 May, 27 Nov. 1812; ML: Hunter to Helms, 22 Feb. 1811; Hunter to William Jones, [n.d., but bound at 24 Mar. 1813].

17. CL: Isaac Chauncey to William Jones, 30 Nov. 1814; OL: Cheever Felch to B.W. Crowninshield, 17 Feb. 1815; WLCL, Chew Papers: Felch to Thomas J. Chew, 13 Jan. 1814 [i.e., 1815].

18. RFP, Ser 3A/2: Arthur Sinclair to William Reed, 12 Dec. 1814; ML: Charles Tait to B.W. Crowninshield, 19 Jan. 1815; Cong LB 2:354, 422: Crowninshield to Tait, 23 Jan. 1815, 17 Feb. 1816; PMS, Crowninshield Mss: Thomas Tingey to Crowninshield, 23 Jan. 1815; RFP, Ser 2: [Cheever Felch], "On the Expediency of a Naval Academy," [1815?]; RG 45, Letters Sent by the Board of Navy Commissioners to the Secretary of the Navy 1:82: John Rodgers [and] David Porter to Crowninshield, 25 Nov. 1815.

19. Learning to Be a Navy

1. OSW 2:326: Benjamin Stoddert to William Cowper, 2 Sept. 1799; CL: Arthur Sinclair to John Rodgers, 17 June 1810, enclosed in Rodgers to Paul Hamilton, 20 June 1810.

2. QW 1:111.

3. HEHL, MH 122: Thomas Truxtun to James McHenry, 3 Mar. 1797.

4. ML: Benjamin Smith to [Charles W. Goldsborough], 19 Mar. 1809, enclosing Thomas N. Gautier to Benjamin Smith, 8 Feb. 1809; George C. Clitherall to Paul Hamilton, 24 Mar. 1810; *Dictionary of North Carolina Biography*, ed. William S. Powell (Chapel Hill: University of North Carolina Press, 1979–) 2:289.

5. OSW 6:265–266: Robert Smith to John P. Lovell, 20 Dec. 1803; CL: John Rodgers to Smith, 22 May 1806, enclosing David Porter to Rodgers, 17 May 1806; BW 6:454.

6. Roche Letters 138 (19 June 1798).

7. For a particularly good account of one future U.S. naval officer's experience of impressment, see "Biographical Sketch of the Late Lieutenant Aylwin," *Analectic Magazine* 3(1814):54–61.

8. PMS, Crowninshield Mss: John Rodgers to B.W. Crowninshield, 11 Feb. 1815; HEHL, HR 12: William Bainbridge to David Porter, 5 Nov. 1803; NYHS, Misc Mss: Charles Morris to Noadiah Morris, 29 Sept. 1808.

9. In addition to what follows, see also the discussion of Preble's shipboard library in McKee, *Edward Preble*, pp. 219–221; Preble's is the only pre-1815 inventory of an officer's personal library discovered by this historian.

10. London, 1797; Talbot Mss: Cyrus Talbot to Silas Talbot, 12 Jan. 1800.

11. Five editions, London, 1787–1811.

12. CL: Isaac Chauncey to Robert Smith, 25 Jan. 1808, for example. Four editions of McArthur's work were published in London between 1792 and 1813; American naval officers probably used the 2d (1805) or the 3d (1806).

13. Washington City: William Duane, 1805; ML: Duane to Paul Hamilton, 12 Nov. 1811; distribution of copies to newly appointed midshipmen began with 19 Mar. 1805 and was discontinued with appointments made on and after 16 Jan. 1809 (OSW 6:542, 8:189).

14. MCL: John Smith to Robert Smith, 29 July 1807; McKee, *Edward Preble*, pp. 71–72; EPP: Roger Curtis, [Standing regulations for the squadron at the Cape of Good Hope], 16 Jan.–27 Feb. 1800; Commissioners for Taking Care of Sick and Wounded Seamen, *Instructions for Navy Surgeons* (bound at 18 Jan. 1800); Home Popham, *The Marine Vocabulary; or, Telegraphic Signals* (Calcutta: Printed at the Honorable Company's Press, 1801).

20. Leaders

1. CMR 5:0187: "A list of the different classes and the number of persons in each class composing the crew of the Constitution on her sailing from Boston [and] when she returned"; M&PR: *Vixen, Warren, & Wasp*, 1806–36 (T829:136), fol. 233.

2. For more detailed figures and analysis see Ira Dye, "Early American Merchant Seafarers," American Philosophical Society *Proceedings* 120(1976): 331–360; Dye, "The Tattoos of Early American Seafarers, 1796–1818," American Philosophical Society *Proceedings* 133(1989):520–554; Harold D. Langley, "The Negro in the Navy and Merchant Service—1798–1860," *Journal of Negro History* 52(1967):273–286; W. Jeffrey Bolster, " 'To Feel like a Man': Black Seamen in the Northern States, 1800–1860," *Journal of American History* 76(1989/ 90):1173–1199; Christopher McKee, "Foreign Seamen in the United States Navy: A Census of 1808," *William and Mary Quarterly*, 3d ser., 42(1985):383– 393. Through the publication of N.A.M. Rodger's *The Wooden World: An Anatomy of the Georgian Navy* (Annapolis, Md.: Naval Institute Press, 1986) it is now possible to compare the demographic profile of U.S. seafarers with the most relevant foreign group, British mariners, albeit for a slightly earlier period, the Seven Years' War; the emphasis of Rodger's excellent book is heavily on the enlisted man. Another fine work on before-the-mast mariners of a slightly earlier period, one that is superlative on subjective and psychological issues, is Marcus Rediker, *Between the Devil and the Deep Blue Sea: Merchant Seamen, Pirates, and the Anglo-American Maritime World, 1700–1750* (New York: Cambridge University Press, 1987).

3. Alexander S. Mackenzie, *Life of Commodore Oliver Hazard Perry* (New York, 1840) 1:189.

4. MCL: David Porter to Paul Hamilton, 9 Aug. 1811.

5. MCL: Thomas Robinson to Secretary of the Navy, 26 Apr., May 1809.

6. Frederick Rodgers Coll: S.H. Bullus [and twelve others] to John Rodgers, 5 June 1810.

7. CL: William Bainbridge to William Jones, 25 Sept. 1813.

8. Accts (N) #1656: John Downes to Robert M. Rose, 21 Oct. 1809.

9. Accts (N) #546: George W. Rodgers to William Knight, 24 Mar. 1815; Accts (N) #1062: Rodgers to Thomas Turner, 17 Feb. 1815; QW 7:223.

10. Frederick Rodgers Coll: Joseph E. Smith to John Rodgers, 8 July 1808; Rodgers's advice, if he gave it in writing, has not been located.

11. Rhode Island Historical Society, Providence: Usher Parsons, "A Diary Kept during the Expedition to Lake Erie under Captain O.H. Perry," 24 Sept. 1812–10 Dec. 1814, entries for 1 and 3 Oct. 1812.

12. Accts (N) #878: Nelson Webster to John L. Cummings, 26 May 1814; Cummings, account with the United States, [6 June 1814].

13. Truxtun, *Remarks, Instructions, and Examples Relating to the Latitude & Longitude* (Philadelphia: T. Dobson, 1794), Appendix, p. xvii.

14. *President* orders, 1809, articles 8 and 13; *President* orders, ca. 1812, article 13; *Argus* orders, 1811, article 42.

15. CL: Isaac Chauncey to Benjamin Homans, 5 Jan. 1815.

16. OSW 1:142–143: Benjamin Stoddert to Isaac Phillips, 9 Aug. 1798; ML: Joshua Barney to William Jones, 4 Aug. 1814; *President* orders, 1809, articles 4 and 10; *President* orders, ca. 1812, articles 7 and 10.

17. CL: Hugh G. Campbell to Samuel Elbert, 24 Mar. 1810.

18. *Madison & General Pike* orders, 1813–14, article 21; *President* orders, ca. 1812, article 9; *Argus* orders, 1811, article 43.

19. CL: John Rodgers to Paul Hamilton, 10 Nov. 1810.

20. CL: William Bainbridge to William Jones, 10 June 1813.

21. Usher Parsons, *Brief Sketches of the Officers Who Were in the Battle of Lake Erie* (Albany, N.Y.: J. Munsell, 1862), p. 9.

22. Wadsworth Mss: Thomas Truxtun, "To the Midshipmen of the Navy, and Particularly Those Who Serve with Me," ca. Mar. 1802.

23. QW 7:2.

24. *Life in Letters: American Autograph Journal* (American Autograph Shop, Merion Station, Pa.) 6(1941):81–84.

25. CMR 3:0225–0268; CL: Thomas Tingey to Paul Hamilton, 15 Nov. 1810, enclosing Tingey to Beekman V. Hoffman, 14 Nov. 1810.

26. Samuel Leech, *Thirty Years from Home; or, A Voice from the Main Deck* (London: H.G. Collins, 1851), pp. 102, 104, 125, 133, 148.

27. Narrative Statements of Service: Edmund P. Kennedy to A.P. Upshur, 15 June 1842; OL: undated statement by Christopher Gadsden and Charles W. Goldsborough, bound between 22 and 24 Apr. 1810; MCL: Robert T. Spence to William Jones, 14 Oct. 1813; CL: John H. Dent to Jones, 9 June 1813, enclosing Kennedy to Dent, 5 June 1813; Accnt LR: Kennedy to Constant Freeman, 6 Dec. 1820.

28. CL: John Rodgers to Paul Hamilton, 14 Sept. 1811; CMR 3:0334–0351, 0362–0365; OSW 9:255–257: Hamilton to Rodgers, 31 Dec. 1810.

29. For Creighton's continued physical abuse of enlisted men see the Nov. 1811 court martial of seaman Edward Jones (CMR 3:0755–0776). His postwar bad relations with subordinate officers are summarized in James E. Valle, *Rocks & Shoals: Order and Discipline in the Old Navy, 1800–1861* (Annapolis, Md.: Naval Institute Press, 1980), pp. 258–261.

21. Sanctions

1. CMR 3:0094–0100, 0111–0114. For Jealous's earlier courts martial see USNAM, *Spitfire* Log, 1 Dec. 1805–18 Aug. 1806, entries for 1 Dec. 1805, 31 Jan., 19 Feb., 25 Feb. 1806, and CMR 2:0774–0777.

2. There have been few historical studies of the practice of corporal punishment in the U.S. military forces. Harold D. Langley, *Social Reform in the United States Navy, 1798–1862* (Urbana: University of Illinois Press, 1967), esp. pp. 131–206, is an outstanding exception; his presentation of actual punishment practice is subordinate to his primary theme, the campaign to abolish flogging. Myra C. Glenn, *Campaigns against Corporal Punishment: Prisoners, Sailors, Women, and Children in Antebellum America* (Albany: State University of New York Press, 1984), is another work of the first stature, especially noteworthy for its integration of naval antiflogging sentiment with parallel social movements of the period and for its exploration of the shared mindset that produced these related crusades. Glenn is almost entirely concerned with the years after 1815. Both her book and, to a lesser extent, Langley's tend to accept antiflogging polemical tracts as primary sources of information on actual practice, a method

that is clearly open to bias. Valle's *Rocks & Shoals* is based on the court martial transcripts (CMR) to the virtual exclusion of all other sources; moreover, the author uses the traditional, and sometimes misleading, military charges as his organizing categories, rather than building his structure on the actual behavior covered by these often intentionally vague umbrellas.

Useful quantified material on corporal punishment in the contemporaneous U.S. Army is similarly scarce. Richard C. Knopf, "Crime and Punishment in the Legion, 1792–1793," Historical and Philosophical Society of Ohio *Bulletin* 14(1956):232–238, is the notable exception. Knopf's data and conclusions permit some rewarding comparisons with naval practice. One does, however, wish that Knopf had provided a broader spectrum of data on army flogging sentences and that he had made clearer distinctions between officer and enlisted offenses. John S. Hare's older "Military Punishments in the War of 1812," American Military Institute *Journal* 4(1940):225–239, is primarily descriptive of the variety of punishments in use in the 1812–15 land forces, a number of which make naval practice appear enlightened and humane! Hare has made no attempt to quantify the different punishments, save in the case of death sentences (p. 238); under this rubric comparison with the far more lenient navy is instructive. Edward M. Coffman's treatment of enlisted discipline and corporal punishment in *The Old Army: A Portrait of the American Army in Peacetime, 1784–1898* (New York: Oxford University Press, 1986), esp. pp. 196–200, is primarily anecdotal and descriptive, with only occasional snatches of quantified data.

The British naval experience in corporal punishment is highly relevant, because the U.S. Navy drew many of its traditions from its English-speaking counterpart. It would be difficult to overpraise Dudley Pope's *The Black Ship* (London: Weidenfeld and Nicolson, 1963). Pope's treatment of corporal punishment, esp. pp. 59–70, 332–337, is noteworthy in many ways, not the least of which is that Pope was the first scholar to search logbooks systematically for data on actual punishment practice. John D. Byrn's excellent *Crime and Punishment in the Royal Navy: Discipline on the Leeward Islands Station, 1784–1812* (Aldershot: Scolar Press, 1989) provides fascinating quantitative data that make possible a detailed comparison of British and American practice. In both its sophistication and its rigor Byrn's methodology is far superior to Valle's in *Rocks & Shoals*. Byrn's book is crippled, however, by one major flaw: failure (e.g., Table 1 [p. 58] and esp. Table 2 [p. 68]) to segregate data on officers and enlisted men. No bibliography of this subject would be complete without a mention of a strange volume, Scott Claver's *Under the Lash: A History of Corporal Punishment in the British Armed Forces* (London: Torchstream Books, 1954). Easily criticized as a scissors-and-pastepot compendium, it contains a substantial, if heterogeneous, body of information not to be found elsewhere between one pair of covers. *Under the Lash* suffers from undisciplined organization and an absence of critical and quantitative evaluation that make it impossible, for example, to determine whether a particular incident is a singular, an extreme, or a typical practice. At once useful, insightful, thought-provoking, and frustrating, *Under the Lash* has provided some of the most useful clues for the present chapter.

Publication of Robert W. Fogel and Stanley L. Engerman's *Time on the Cross: The Economics of American Negro Slavery* (Boston: Little, Brown, 1974) provoked a spirited debate over, among other issues, the appropriate quantitative methods for measuring slave floggings and, indeed, whether comparative quantitative assessments have any valid role in analyzing so allegedly reprehensible a practice. The best summary discussion of the whole subject is in Herbert G. Gutman, *Slavery and the Numbers Game: A Critique of Time on the Cross* (Urbana: University of Illinois Press, 1975), pp. 14–41, the notes to which volume provide a bibliography of the subject to that time. Another useful critique of *Time on the Cross* is Richard Sutch, "The Treatment Received by American Slaves: A Critical Review of the Evidence Presented in *Time on the Cross*," *Explorations in Economic History* 12(1975):335–438, esp. (on flogging) pp. 339–344.

3. CMR 3:0186–0198.

4. Conveniently reprinted in QW 7:462–473 and in Homans, pp. 59–69.

5. Samuel F. Holbrook, *Threescore Years: An Autobiography* (Boston, 1857), p. 113.

6. *Argus* orders, 1811, article 44; *Madison & General Pike* orders, 1813–14, articles 25 and 28; *Independence* orders, 1815, p. 20.

7. McKee, *Edward Preble*, p. 224.

8. MeHS, Edward Preble Mss: *Constitution*'s Daily Reports of Prisoners, Jan.–June 1804.

9. Preble's longest recorded confinement of a seaman, fifty days for attempted desertion, occurred before the period covered by the surviving master-at-arms reports and is known only because it is mentioned in EPP: *Constitution* Log, 9 Dec. 1803.

10. RG 24, *Hornet* Logs, 28 July 1805–1 Nov. 1811. The only information recorded in the *Constitution* master-at-arms morning reports not present in the *Hornet*'s log are the identities of the officers ordering the confinement.

11. Holbrook, *Threescore Years*, pp. 97–98.

12. CL: Proceedings of a court of inquiry held on board *Enterprize* at Charleston, S.C., 15 June 1814, enclosed in John H. Dent to William Jones, 17 June 1814.

13. For a detailed composite description of post-1815 floggings see Langley, *Social Reform in the United States Navy*, pp. 139–141, supplemented by the visual representation of the same scene in John Haskell Kemble, ed., *Sketches of California and Hawaii by William H. Meyers, Gunner, U.S.N., aboard the United States Sloop-of-War Cyane, 1842–1843* (San Francisco: Book Club of California, 1970), plate 2.

14. Claver, *Under the Lash*, p. 113.

15. Detroit Public Library, Burton Historical Collection, Woolsey Family Papers: Log, U.S. Schooner *Sylph*, 18 Aug. 1813–20 Apr. 1814.

16. CMR 4:0024.

17. EPP: *Constitution* Log, 21 May 1803–28 Oct. 1804; *John Adams* Log, 30 Oct. 1804–25 Feb. 1805; LC, David Porter Mss: *Enterprize* Log, 21 Aug. 1805–17 Nov. 1806; NYHS: *Constitution* Log, 6 Dec. 1798–20 Oct. 1800; NYPL: *Frolic* Journal, 20 Feb.–20 Apr. 1814; HSPa, Dreer Collection: Fitz Henry Babbit, *Argus* Journal, 5 May 1808–22 May 1810; Detroit Public Library, Burton Historical Collection, Woolsey Family Papers: *Sylph* Log, 18 Aug. 1813–20 Apr. 1814; Melancthon T. Woolsey, Journal kept on board Frigates *Boston, Adams, New York,* and *Chesapeake,* 22 Sept. 1801–23 July 1803 (private collection); RG 45: Journal kept on board *Argus* and *Nautilus,* 13 Oct. 1811–15 July 1812; Gunboat No. 110 Log, 14 July 1812–6 July 1813; RG 24: *Constitution* Logs, 17 June 1810–13 Dec. 1812; *Hornet* Logs, 28 July 1805–1 Nov. 1811 and 24 Jan.–

22 June 1815; *John Adams* Logs, 16 May 1809–18 Aug. 1815; *President* Log, 28 May 1809–12 Apr. 1810; *Wasp-Argus-Hornet* Log, 20 July 1809–6 Nov. 1813.

18. The figures that follow were derived by dividing the total number of floggings for each ship and captain in Table 10 by the number of enlisted men and petty officers at risk in that ship and that number in turn by the total days covered by the record of punishments; the resulting number was then multiplied by the median number of men at risk, all vessels (164), and the median number of days (299) covered by the punishment records. Because the number of men at risk in *Constitution* under Silas Talbot is not known, he is not included in the figures given in the text.

19. RG 24, *Hornet* Log, 24 Jan.–22 June 1815, may be checked against United States Military Academy Library, West Point: William Boerum, "Private Journal Kept since my Commencement in the Navy," 14 Jan.–15 July 1815. All punishments listed in Boerum are also noted in the log; the official log includes several punishments not reported by Midshipman Boerum.

20. CL: John H. Dent to William Jones, 4 Oct. 1814.

21. CMR 1 through CMR 6, plus the following trials known from other sources: (1) Patrick Doran (May 1802) in SF, NO; (2) William Perry, John Reeson, Richard Sinnet, and Philip Wady (Dec. 1805) in RFP, Ser 2, Box 24; (3) Peter Jealous and William Marshall (Feb. 1806) in USNAM, *Spitfire* Log, 19 Feb., 25 Feb. 1806; (4) John Williams (Sept. 1807) in LC, USN Misc, *Chesapeake* Log, 17 Sept., 24 Sept. 1807; (5) George Dailey (Jan. 1810) in *President* Log, 19 Jan. 1810; and (6) John Bowen (Apr. 1811) in *Enterprize* Log, 24–25 Apr. 1811.

22. But, let it be underlined, not *entirely* complete. For example, on 24 Apr. 1811 the log of *Enterprize* records, "This day a court martial was held on John Bowen for desertion." The next day, "agreeable to the sentence of a court martial, John Bowen (quartermaster) was reduced to an ordinary seaman and received one hundred lashes, fifty of which he received on board the Constellation." No transcript of this trial is preserved among the Navy Department's records. How many other such cases could be discovered by assiduous searching cannot be surmised; but it is doubtful that more cases would alter the statistical profile here presented.

23. BW 5:61–70; M&PR: *Hornet*, 1805–19 (T829:99), fols. 2–9.

24. There exists no analytical study of desertion in the U.S. Navy, but the historian of the American force can learn much from the informed, sensitive, and sophisticated analysis of the British navy's desertion problems in N.A.M. Rodger's "Stragglers and Deserters from the Royal Navy during the Seven Years' War," *Bulletin of the Institute of Historical Research* 57(1984):56–79.

25. In the case of one of the seventeen punishments in excess of 100 lashes (John Williams, who received 168 lashes on 24 Sept. 1807) it is not clear from the skimpy record whether he was punished for desertion or for mutiny/sedition.

26. CMR 5:0623.

27. CMR 2:0939–0943, 0945.

28. Commandants & Agents LB 1:528–529: William Jones to John Cassin, 29 Oct. 1813.

29. Michael R. Weisser, *Crime and Punishment in Early Modern Europe* (Atlantic Highlands, N.J.: Humanities Press, 1979), pp. 138–142; Michael Stephen Hindus, *Prison and Plantation: Crime, Justice, and Authority in Massachusetts and*

South Carolina, 1767–1878 (Chapel Hill: University of North Carolina Press, 1980), pp. 93–95; Arthur N. Gilbert, "Military and Civilian Justice in Eighteenth-Century England: An Assessment," *Journal of British Studies* vol. 17, no. 2 (Spring 1978):41–65.

30. CMR 1:0062–0076. Because *Eagle* was operating in the West Indies, a court martial, not a civil court, had jurisdiction in the case.

31. In Massachusetts, between 1780 and 1810, virtually all individuals (92.9 percent) convicted of murder were actually executed (Hindus, *Prison and Plantation,* p. 103).

32. CMR 5:0321–0328.

33. CMR 5:0870–0872.

34. Pope, *The Black Ship,* p. 69 and elsewhere, for example.

35. CMR 5:0886–0887.

36. CMR 3:0755–0776, 0780; M&PR: *President,* 1800–1813 (T829:72), fol. 425.

37. CMR 2:0516–0539; HSPa: F.H. Babbit, *Argus* Journal, 25 Nov. 1808; M&PR: *Argus,* 1803–13 (T829:23), fol. 57.

38. CMR 3:0661–0665; M&PR: *United States,* 1809–14 (T829:126), fols. 78, 80.

39. CMR 3:0661–0662, 0666–0668; M&PR: *United States,* 1809–14 (T829:126), fol. 135; M&PR: *Vixen, Warren, & Wasp,* 1806–36 (T829:136), fol. 248.

22. The *Hermione* Phobia

1. The story of the *Hermione* mutiny is the subject of Dudley Pope's *The Black Ship* (London: Weidenfeld and Nicolson, 1963), a classic to which no summary here can do justice.

2. QW 5:506; EPP: William Ash to Edward Preble, 28 Aug. 1800.

3. BW 4:203, 226–227; CMR 1:0887–0894. It is doubtful that Quinn ever received the full 244-lash balance of his sentence. *President*'s muster roll shows that he was "drum'd ashore" on 30 June, five days after the flogging Darby describes (M&PR: *President,* 1800–1813 [T829:72], fol. 210). This would hardly have allowed time for Quinn to recover and receive additional increments of his flogging.

4. SF, HF: Transcript from *Connecticut Gazette and Commercial Intelligencer* (New London), 23 Apr. 1800; QW 5:404–405, 408.

5. NYHS, Misc Mss: Richard Somers to William Jonas Keen, 13 Aug. 1800.

6. For example CMR 3:0428–0441 (Samuel McClarey and John Loring), 3:0669–0674 (Joseph R. Sherburn), and 3:0755–0776 (Edward Jones).

7. FDRL: Charles Stewart, Journal kept on board the U.S. Frigate *Constitution,* 31 Dec. 1813–16 May 1815.

8. CL: Hugh G. Campbell to Robert Smith, 14 Oct. 1807, enclosing Charles Ludlow to Campbell, 9 June 1807; James Durand, *An Able Seaman of 1812* (New Haven, Conn.: Yale University Press, 1926), pp. 32–35, gives a seaman's perspective on the incident, a version that agrees in essential details with Ludlow's; BW 6:557; OSW 7:540: Smith to Campbell, 1 Dec. 1807.

9. Rea, p. 16.

10. Rea, pp. 3–4.

11. CMR 2:0805–0806, 0808.

12. CMR 4:0931.

13. Richard Sutch, "The Treatment Received by American Slaves: A Critical Review of the Evidence Presented in *Time on the Cross*," *Explorations in Economic History* 12(1975):342; emphasis added in the penultimate sentence.

14. J.R. Dinwiddy, "The Early Nineteenth-Century Campaign against Flogging in the Army," *English Historical Review* 97(1982):308–331; E.E. Steiner, "Separating the Soldier from the Citizen: Ideology and Criticism of Corporal Punishment in the British Armies, 1790–1815," *Social History* 8(1983):19–35; John S. Hare, "Military Punishments in the War of 1812," American Military Institute *Journal* 4(1940):230, 236, 238; Edward M. Coffman, *The Old Army: A Portrait of the American Army in Peacetime, 1784–1898* (New York: Oxford University Press, 1986), pp. 196–197; Harold D. Langley, *Social Reform in the United States Navy, 1798–1862* (Urbana: University of Illinois Press, 1967), pp. 152–153; U.S. Laws, Statutes, etc., *United States Statutes at Large* (Boston, etc., 1845 to date) 4:647–648.

15. Commandants & Agents LB 1:547–548: William Jones to William Bainbridge, 12 Jan. 1814; for a similar earlier statement by a secretary of the navy, see OSW 9:66: Paul Hamilton to Isaac Hull, 8 Apr. 1810.

16. On this precise point see the evidence cited by Herbert G. Gutman with respect to slave flogging (*Slavery and the Numbers Game: A Critique of Time on the Cross* [Urbana: University of Illinois Press, 1975], p. 39). Similar evidence from the U.S. Army can be found in the 1795 journal of Joseph Gardner Andrews (*A Surgeon's Mate at Fort Defiance*, ed. Richard C. Knopf [Columbus: Ohio Historical Society, 1957], p. 16) wherein he reports the existence, at Post Vincennes, of the "Damnation Club," the requirement for membership in which "was to be ever ready to receive one hundred lashes, if it might be the means of procuring a pint of whiskey for the good of said society."

17. Theodore C. Mason, *Battleship Sailor* (Annapolis, Md.: Naval Institute Press, 1982), pp. 19–20, or James J. Fahey, *Pacific War Diary, 1942–1945* (Boston: Houghton Mifflin, 1963), p. 314, or numerous other examples that could be cited.

Part Six: Competing for Honor

1. This is true as theory and is certainly the way participants subjectively view the structure, but there have been many exceptions to the theoretical model. In the pre-1815 U.S. Navy the number of captains always exceeded the number of masters commandant, even though the former was the more exalted rank. For more recent examples of the same phenomenon see Morris Janowitz, *The Professional Soldier: A Social and Political Portrait* (Glencoe, Ill.: Free Press, 1960), pp. 65–67.

2. This date, rather than 14 Feb. of the same year, has been selected so as to include in the story of promotion a number of advancements that were in process as the War of 1812 came to an end.

23. Discovering Merit

1. OSW 2:70, 76–78: Benjamin Stoddert to Silas Talbot, 28 May, 29 May 1799; 2:309–309a: Stoddert to William Bainbridge, 28 Aug. 1799; Appmt LB: Stoddert to John Adams, 30 May 1799, 11 Aug. 1800.

2. OSW 6:154: Robert Smith to Daniel T. Patterson, 30 May 1803. For other representative statements of Smith's policy, see OSW 5:383: Smith to

Charles Ludlow, 8 Apr. 1802; 7:389–390: Smith to Jonathan Thorn, 12 May 1807; GLB 5:281: Smith to Thomas Tillinghast, 26 Apr. 1802; 7:359: Smith to Richard Peters, 11 Mar. 1805; 7:399: Smith to [Samuel] White, 10 Apr. 1805; 8:315: Smith to J.W. Walker, 4 Mar. 1807; Appmt LB: Smith to Thomas Jefferson, 14 Feb. 1809.

3. GLB 7:359: Robert Smith to Richard Peters, 11 Mar. 1805.

4. OSW 11:151–152: William Jones to Thomas T. Webb, 17 Nov. 1813; see also Private LB: Jones to Isaac Chauncey, 30 Apr. 1814.

5. Jones's views on promotion-by-merit are contained primarily in three letters from which the single, coherent statement in the preceding paragraphs has been woven: OSW 11:24–26: William Jones to Robert T. Spence, 26 July 1813; 11:87–90: Jones to James Renshaw, 15 Sept. 1813; Cong LB 2:186–187: Jones to Joseph Anderson, 30 July 1813.

6. OSW 5:465–467: Robert Smith, General Order, 18 Aug. 1802; Smith to John Barry, Richard Dale, or William Bainbridge, 19 Aug. 1802; Smith to Barry, 19 Aug. 1802. For the report of one early examining board see Accnt LR: John Barry to Robert Smith, 24 Feb. 1803.

7. As will be explained more fully in note 9, the dates of commissioning lieutenants, and consequently their relative seniority, are muddled in U.S. Office of Naval Records and Library, *Register of Officer Personnel, United States Navy and Marine Corps, and Ships' Data, 1801–1807* (Washington, D.C., 1945). Based on the correct information in Abst of serv, these nine midshipmen were the only ones actually promoted and commissioned as lieutenants between the time Benjamin Stoddert left office (at the end of Mar. 1801) and Jan. 1807:

Name	Nominal date as lieutenant	Date actually commissioned
Abner Woodruff	1 Apr. 1802	4 Mar. 1803
Theodore Hunt	4 Apr. 1802	4 Mar. 1803
Michael B. Carroll	10 Apr. 1802	4 Mar. 1803
Benjamin Smith	14 Apr. 1802	4 Mar. 1803
James B. Decatur	20 Apr. 1802	4 Mar. 1803
Charles Ludlow	22 Apr. 1802	22 Apr. 1802
Samuel Elbert	4 Mar. 1803	4 Mar. 1803
William M. Livingston	6 Mar. 1803	6 Mar. 1803
George W. Reed	10 Mar. 1803	10 Mar. 1803

8. BW 4:138–139; 5:139, 533; OSW 6:477–478: Robert Smith to Arthur Sinclair, 9 June 1804; Frederick Rodgers Coll: Samuel Barron to John Rodgers, 10 Nov. 1804, with results of examinations noted; same to same, [n.d.], enclosing Smith to Barron, 1 June 1804; John M. Gardner to Rodgers, 11 Nov. 1804; Barron Mss: Benjamin Turner to Barron, 6 Nov. 1804; CL: Rodgers to Smith, 20 Aug. 1805.

9. OSW 7:198: Robert Smith to Benjamin F. Read and Daniel T. Patterson, 29 July 1806; 7:303–304: Smith to Edward Preble, 7 Feb. 1807, and similar letters of the same date to eight other commanding officers; 7:362–363: Smith, Circular to Lieutenants, 20 Apr. 1807. In addition to the sixty-one commissions dated Jan.–Mar. 1807, James Lawrence was given a commission backdated to 6 Apr. 1802. No lieutenant's commissions were actually delivered by the Navy

Office between 10 Mar. 1803 and 20 Apr. 1807. As has already been mentioned (note 7), the data in U.S. Office of Naval Records and Library, *Register of Officer Personnel, 1801–1807,* respecting dates of commissions as lieutenants are not entirely accurate. From that volume it would appear that five men (James Biddle, Seth Cartee, Joseph J. Maxwell, Peter S. Ogilvie, and Sybrant Van Schaick) all held commissions dated 18 May 1804. However, as Abst of serv, vol. C, makes clear, none of the 18 May 1804 commissions was ever issued; all were returned to the Navy Office by John Rodgers. By the time the sixty-two lieutenant's commissions were issued, Cartee, Maxwell, and Ogilvie were dead; none was ever a commissioned lieutenant. Van Schaick, who had passed the examination with flying colors, had fallen under a cloud. Robert Smith did not include his name in the list of lieutenant nominations sent to the Senate on 7 Jan. 1807 (JEP 2:47), and Van Schaick rather pitifully resigned his warrant and acting lieutenant's commission in person at the Navy Office on 9 July (Abst of serv, vol. C; Resignations, 1803–25: Van Schaick to Smith, 9 July 1807). The correct date of James Biddle's commission as lieutenant is 11 Feb. 1807. To complete the roster of significant errors in the dates of lieutenant's commissions in *Register of Officer Personnel,* William M. Crane should be 20 Jan. 1807, *not* 20 July 1803, the date of his appointment as an acting lieutenant; John D. Henley is 31 Jan. 1807; James S. Higinbotham ought to be 18 Mar. 1807; to George Mann's record there should be added: lieutenant, 26 Mar. 1807.

10. Appmt LB: Benjamin Stoddert to John Adams, 25 May 1799.

11. GLB 7:399: Robert Smith to [Samuel] White, 10 Apr. 1805; also GLB 7:359: Smith to Richard Peters, 11 Mar. 1805.

12. MCL: James Biddle to William Jones, 12 July 1813.

13. CL: Alexander Murray to [Robert Smith], Jan. 1806.

14. OSW 11:24–26: William Jones to Robert T. Spence, 26 July 1813.

15. HSPa, Wm Jones Mss: Undated memorandum beginning, "The records of the department being deficient in the important and necessary information in relation to the individual qualifications. . . ." In 1815 Jones's plan was actually put into effect by the Board of Navy Commissioners, who continued their register (NCR) until about 1821. By that date it was apparent that the secretary of the navy was going to permit the commissioners no effective role in personnel decisions, and the register was allowed to lapse.

16. Alexander S. Mackenzie, *Life of Commodore Oliver Hazard Perry* (New York, 1843) 2:72.

24. Impatient Youth

1. OSW 11:136: William Jones to John Rodgers, 2 Nov. 1813.

2. Izard Family Papers: Ralph Izard, Jr., to Alice Izard, 27 Aug. 1801.

3. FDRL, Naval Mss: David Conner to Rachel Conner, 5 Oct. 1813.

4. TJ Mss: Robert Smith, Memorandum for Thomas Jefferson on the bill for establishing a naval militia, received 14 Nov. 1805; GLB 8:315: Smith to J.W. Walker, 4 Mar. 1807; 8:54: Smith to James Gamble, 5 Oct. 1805; Appmt LB: Smith to Thomas Jefferson, 14 Feb. 1809.

5. It should be remembered that any age statement could be in error by as much as plus or minus one year; see Chapter 6, note 1, for a detailed discussion of the age data used in this book.

6. The possibility of a one-year error in either direction should again be noted; this historian's subjective impression is that such a possibility is unlikely to affect the conclusion in this case.

7. CL: John Rodgers to William Jones, 14 Oct. 1813.

8. OSW 11:136: William Jones to John Rodgers, 2 Nov. 1813.

9. SF, NI: Thomas Macdonough to John Rodgers, 6 May 1815.

10. Any person wishing to examine the evidence in detail can readily repeat the exercise here described with the aid of the registers of officers listed in the bibliographical essay, section A, taking into consideration the corrections recorded in notes 7 and 9 to Chapter 23.

11. OSW 11:88–89: William Jones to James Renshaw, 15 Sept. 1813.

12. MCL: John Shaw to Robert Smith, 17 July 1806 (two letters), 21 Aug. 1807; CL: Shaw to Paul Hamilton, 19 Feb. 1810. As was his practice, Smith maintained total silence regarding the reasons for this decision.

13. CL: John Cassin to Paul Hamilton, 14 Oct. 1812; ML: John Rodgers to Robert Smith, 20 Aug. 1805; Burwell Bassett to Hamilton, 14 Dec. 1812, enclosing Robert Henley to Bassett, 20 Nov. 1812; SF, NI: Thomas Macdonough to Rodgers, 6 May 1815.

25. Promotion Blues

1. Barron Mss: Edward O'Brien to Samuel Barron, 7 May 1804; OSW 6:423: Robert Smith to O'Brien, 11 May 1804.

2. BW 6:120–121, 126, 164; Resignations, 1803–25: Andrew Sterett to Robert Smith, 29 June 1805.

3. CL: Oliver H. Perry to William Jones, 16 Oct. 1813, and Jones's endorsement thereon.

4. Charles Morris, *Autobiography* (Boston, 1880), pp. 59, 61; JEP 2:327–333; RG 46, Papers Relative to Nominations: Memorials of James Lawrence, 22 Oct. 1812, and Charles Ludlow, [n.d.]; CL: William Bainbridge to Paul Hamilton, 8 Oct. 1812; MCL: Arthur Sinclair to Hamilton, 7 Oct. 1812; Lawrence to Hamilton, 10 Oct. 1812; Joseph Tarbell to Hamilton, 3 Nov. 1812; Ludlow to William Jones, 17 Mar. 1813; Sinclair to Jones, 23 Mar. 1813; William M. Crane to Jones, 28 Apr. 1813; OL: Ludlow to Hamilton, 29 Oct. 1812; Daniel T. Patterson to Hamilton, 10 Nov. 1812; ML: Ludlow to Hamilton, 24 Aug. 1811; OSW 10:389: Jones to Ludlow, 1 May 1813; USNAM: Lawrence to Thomas Tingey, 3 Oct. 1812.

5. Narrative statements of service: Francis H. Gregory, [autobiographical narrative, ca. 1842]; CL: Isaac Chauncey to William Jones, 23 Aug. 1813, enclosing Gregory to Chauncey, 23 Aug. 1813; Chauncey to Jones, 5 Apr., 20 June (two letters) 1814; Private LB: Jones to Chauncey, 28 June 1814.

6. Lewis Mss: William Lewis to Edward Herndon, 25 Sept. 1805.

7. GLB 5:252, 261, 281: Robert Smith to Christopher Raymond Perry, 8 Apr. 1802; Smith to James Nicholson, 12 Apr. 1802; Smith to Thomas Tillinghast, 26 Apr. 1802; 6:136, 179: Smith to [Christopher] Ellery, 1 Mar. 1803; Smith to Perry, 29 Mar. 1803.

8. MCL: Daniel T. Patterson, Memorial to William Jones, 30 Nov. 1813; OL: Patterson to Paul Hamilton, 10 Nov. 1812.

9. Cong LB 2:186–187: William Jones to Joseph Anderson, 30 July 1813.

10. Accnt LR: John Shaw to Danièl S. Dexter, 16 Nov. 1812.

11. Dexter LB: Daniel S. Dexter to James Brown, 14 Nov., 29 Nov. 1813; Dexter to Thomas B. Robertson, 29 Nov. 1813; AF, A-8: Dexter to Senate of the United States, [29 Nov. 1813].

12. MCL: Daniel T. Patterson, Memorial to William Jones, 30 Nov. 1813.

26. Mortification's Berth

1. CL: John Rodgers to William Jones, 23 Mar. 1813.

2. OSW 5:465: Robert Smith, General Order, 18 Aug. 1802, with emphasis added.

3. ML: John G. Cowell to Paul Hamilton, 24 Sept. 1812.

4. BW 5:477.

5. Adams Mss, reel 397: Robert Harrison to John Adams, 11 Jan. 1800.

6. OL: Jonathan D. Ferris to William Jones, 26 Feb. 1813.

7. James Fenimore Cooper, *History of the Navy of the United States of America* (2d ed.; Philadelphia, 1840) 2:280n; David C. Bunnell, *Travels and Adventures, during Twenty-three Years of a Sea-faring Life* (Palmyra, N.Y., 1831), p. 107; James Fenimore Cooper, ed., *Ned Myers; or, A Life before the Mast* (Philadelphia, 1843), pp. 73–74; Talbot Mss: James Trant to Silas Talbot, 6 June, 29 Aug. 1798; OSW 1:446: Benjamin Stoddert to Richard V. Morris, 5 Apr. 1799; Accnt LR: Trant to Thomas Turner, 14 Apr. 1802; OL: Trant to Robert Smith, 14 Feb. 1808; Trant to Paul Hamilton, 8 Apr. 1812; Trant to William Jones, 21 May, 5 Dec. 1814; CL: Isaac Chauncey to Hamilton, 9 Feb. 1812; RFP, Ser 3A: Trant to John Rodgers, 12 May 1815. With respect to Trant's age this narrative follows the information he gave when taken prisoner during the War of 1812 (Public Archives of Canada, Ottawa: General Entry Book of American Prisoners of War at Quebec, 1812–15, entry #1068), which would make him fifty years old in Sept. 1813, rather than the sixty-six years of age that newspaper obituaries made him at the time of his death (*Columbian Centinel* [Boston], 16 Sept. 1820).

8. GLB 9:315: Robert Smith to D.B. Williams, 23 Dec. 1808; see also 9:336: Smith to Tobias E. Stansbury, 28 Jan. 1809.

9. GLB 10:3: Paul Hamilton to John S. Cogdell, 17 May 1809.

10. OSW 10:288: William Jones to Stephen Decatur, 3 Mar. 1813; the "regulation" was in Jones's head, not on paper.

11. OSW 11:71: William Jones to William Harper, 1 Sept. 1813.

12. For example SEN 13A-G14: Memorial of Edward F. Howell [and ninety-eight other midshipmen] to Senate of the United States, received 16 Jan. 1815.

13. ML: Henry Henry to Robert Smith, 1 Oct., 17 Dec. 1808 (both bound at 30 Sept.); Luke Tiernan to Smith, 30 Sept. 1808; Theodorick Armistead to Paul Hamilton, 4 July 1812; Alexander McKim to Hamilton, 9 July 1812; Tiernan to Hamilton, 9 July 1812; Joseph Tarbell to B.W. Crowninshield, 13 Mar. 1815; CL: John Cassin to Secretary of the Navy, 7 Jan. 1815; SF, NA: Wolcott Chauncey to John Rodgers, 5 May 1815, enclosing "A list of commissioned and warrant officers on board the U.S. Schooner Torch under my command"; Narrative statements of service: Henry Henry to Abel P. Upshur, 26 Sept. 1842; *Daily National Intelligencer* (Washington), 29 July 1857.

14. *Daily National Intelligencer* (Washington), 17 Nov. 1855.

15. Excluded from these calculations are the four midshipmen (Alexander C. Harrison, Edward N. Cox, James Lawrence, and Humphrey Magrath) who held sailing master's warrants before progressing to lieutenant.

16. CL: Stephen Decatur to William Jones, 23 Feb. 1813; OL: John D. Sloat to William Jones, 20 Mar. 1813; ML: William Henry Allen to Jones, 22 Apr. 1813; OSW 10:288, 381: Jones to Stephen Decatur, 3 Mar., 28 Apr. 1813.

Part Seven: Money and the Officer

1. Accnt LS 1798–1800:13: William Winder to Gibbs & Channing, 10 Oct. 1798.

27. Cash Rewards of Service

1. Homans, pp. 35, 45–46; Cong LB 1:20–24: Benjamin Stoddert to Josiah Parker, 9 Feb. 1799. Technically the law of 1 July 1797 and its pay rates expired on 3 Mar. 1799; the limitations on certain officer salaries stated therein were not explicitly continued by Congress, seemingly because Congress and the Navy Department, busy fighting a series of wars, failed to notice that the legal authorization for the salaries had expired. Salaries actually paid continued to be those specified in the acts of 1 July 1797 and 25 Feb. 1799. In Feb. 1814 William Jones, as part of a larger review of the legal basis for naval compensation, discovered the defect and brought it to the attention of Congress (Cong LB 2:236–237: William Jones to John Gaillard, 1 Mar. 1814). As a consequence, authorization for naval salaries below the rank of lieutenant commanding a small vessel was restated in an act of 18 Apr. 1814 (Homans, pp. 100–101), but the salaries themselves were not changed from those specified in the act of 1 July 1797.

2. [Instructions to commanders and pursers with respect to the method of keeping the books and accounts of the vessels (2d printing)], pp. 13–14 ("Provision Account").

3. GLB 2:46: Benjamin Stoddert to Gibbs & Channing, 11 Apr. 1799; Cong LB 1:20–24: Stoddert to Josiah Parker, 9 Feb. 1799.

4. OSW 1:56: Benjamin Stoddert to Charles Wadsworth, 22 June 1798; Accnt LS 3:59: Thomas Turner to Isaac Garretson [and other pursers], 1 May 1801; Private LB: William Jones to Isaac Chauncey, 18 Mar. 1814.

5. OSW 3:85: Benjamin Stoddert to David Ross, 30 Nov. 1799, for an example of an officer furloughed without pay and rations.

6. Homans, p. 72; Cong LB 1:74–75: Benjamin Stoddert to Chairman of the Committee on Naval Affairs for the 2d Session of the 6th Congress, 12 Jan. 1801.

7. Accnt LS 4:390, 399, 6:486–487: Thomas Turner to Samuel Barron, 5 Mar., 24 Mar. 1804, 15 Apr. 1808.

8. Homans, pp. 101, 107; SEN 13A-G8: William M. Crane to William Jones, 8 Feb. 1814, enclosing Crane [and twenty-four others] to Senate and House of Representatives, 8 Feb. 1814; Private LB: Jones to Isaac Chauncey, 18 Apr. 1814; OSW 11:286–287: Jones to Arthur Sinclair [and] Thomas Macdonough, 18 Apr. 1814.

9. RG 45, Letters Sent by the Board of Navy Commissioners to the Secretary of the Navy 1:484–486: John Rodgers to Smith Thompson, 10 Jan. 1821.

10. So far as this historian is aware the practice is discussed only twice in the official records of the pre-1815 navy: (1) CL: Thomas Tingey to Robert

Smith, 19 May 1808; endorsement by Thomas Turner on muster roll enclosed with above letter; [Charles W. Goldsborough], unsigned and undated memorandum bound with the Tingey letter; Commandants & Agents LB 1:25: Smith to Tingey, 25 May 1808; and (2) Accnt LS 7:189: Turner to Alexander Murray, 23 Nov. 1808.

11. For examples of officers who enlisted their slaves and drew their pay see Accnt LR: David Porter, Sr., to Thomas Turner, 25 Sept., 28 Sept., 1 Oct. 1805; Alexander Murray to Turner, 16 May 1809.

12. HSPa, Wm Jones Mss: William Jones to [Eleanor] Jones, 21 Mar. 1813.

13. Accnt LR: Thomas H. Gilliss [and other clerks] to Thomas Turner, [21 Oct. 1815], enclosing a comparative statement of the cost of living in the District of Columbia, 1812–13 vs. 1815.

14. CL: Edward Preble to Robert Smith, 7 June 1805.

15. CL: John Rodgers to Robert Smith, 25 May 1808, enclosing Wolcott Chauncey [and thirteen other midshipmen] to Rodgers, 14 May 1808, and endorsement by Thomas Turner.

16. FDRL, Naval Mss: David Conner to Rachel Conner, 25 Nov. 1811. At $52 a month ($624 per year) Conner is including the cash value of both of his rations.

17. OL: Nathaniel Haraden to Paul Hamilton, 22 Nov. 1809; CL: Isaac Hull to Hamilton, 29 May 1809.

18. MCL: Thomas Robinson to Paul Hamilton, 1 July 1809.

19. CL: William Bainbridge to Paul Hamilton, 17 Mar. 1810 (bound at 17 Mar. 1812); Samuel Barron to Hamilton, 19 Mar. 1810; OSW 9:127: Hamilton to Barron, 7 July 1810.

20. Murray LB: Alexander Murray to William Eustis, 15 Dec. 1803; Murray to Nicholas R. Moore, 11 Dec. 1803. In the end nothing came of the officer corps attempt, sustained over the better part of a decade, to persuade Congress to (1) return the cash value of the ration to 28 cents; (2) allow full rations in addition to half-pay to officers not on active duty; (3) grant additional rations to masters commandant; (4) increase the pay of midshipmen; and (5) provide pensions to the widows or orphans of officers killed in action. For that reason the story of their lobbying campaign is not related in this book. It may be reconstructed from BW 3:201, 211–212; Cong LB 1:136–138: Robert Smith to Eustis, 24–26 Dec. 1803; Accnt LS 4:390, 399: Thomas Turner to Samuel Barron, 5 Mar., 24 Mar. 1804; Accnt LR: Murray to Turner, 18 May 1806; *Annals of Congress* 13.1046, 1048; HR 11A-F6.1: *To the Honorable Senate and House of Representatives of the United States, in Congress assembled: The Memorial of the undersigned Officers of the Navy of the United States,* 21 Jan. 1808 (three copies, two manuscript, one printed, with different signatures and with the legislative history endorsed thereon); HR 11A-B1: "A Bill in relation to the pensions and rations of the officers of the Navy," 28 Dec. 1810 (actually the bill of 7 Feb. 1810, with the date only changed); U.S. Congress (11th, 3d Sess., 1810–11), House of Representatives, *A Bill in Relation to the Pensions and Rations of the Officers of the Navy* [Washington, D.C., 1810; Shaw & Shoemaker #21607]; *Annals of Congress* 18:1651, 2251; 20:1207–1208; 21:1378–1379; 22:473, 860–862; *National Intelligencer* (Washington), 20 Dec. 1810 (for House action of 19 Dec.); ASP Nav Aff 1:182–184; Cong LB 1: Paul Hamilton to Joseph Anderson, 6 June 1809; CL: John Rodgers to Smith, 16 Jan. 1808; William Bainbridge to Hamilton, 23 May 1809; RFP, LB 1811–12: Rodgers to Burwell Bassett, 11

Feb. 1811; RFP, Ser 3A: Thomas Tingey to Rodgers, 21 Nov. 1809; Ser 3A/2: Bainbridge to Rodgers, 1 Apr. 1811; Isaac Chauncey to Rodgers, 10 Dec. 1811; Frederick Rodgers Coll: Murray to Rodgers, 28 Apr. 1808; [Charles W. Goldsborough to Rodgers, ca. June 1809]; NYHS, Isaac Hull LB, Mar. 1814–Mar. 1815: Hull to David Daggett, 19 Nov. 1814. No copy of the measure introduced in the House on 21 Apr. 1808, namely a bill in addition to the act entitled "An act supplementary to the act entitled 'An act providing for a Naval Peace Establishment and for other purposes'" (*Annals of Congress* 18:2251), can now be found among the records of Congress; presumably the file copy was pulled and reworked as the bill introduced on 7 Feb. 1810.

28. Big Money

1. These are the handful of references to freight found by the present historian: GLB 2:271: Benjamin Stoddert to Joseph Ball, 3 Aug. 1799; 3:57: Stoddert to Alexander Baring, 9 Dec. 1799; 4:25: Stoddert to Samuel Smith, 19 Sept. 1800; OSW 3:35–36: Stoddert to Alexander Murray, 12 Nov. 1799; 4:434: Samuel Smith to Henry Geddes, 10 Apr. 1801; 9:512: Paul Hamilton to James Lawrence, 26 Nov. 1811; Ipswich and East Suffolk Record Office, Ipswich, England, James Lawrence Letterbook, Feb. 1809–Jan. 1813: Lawrence to Hamilton, 29 Nov., 30 Nov. (two letters) 1811; Lawrence to Mr. Pappilion [and similar letters to others], 30 Nov. 1811; MCL: John Rodgers to Lawrence, 12 Nov. 1811, enclosed in Lawrence to Hamilton, 5 Dec. 1811; RFP, Ser 3A/2: Lawrence to Rodgers, 21 Nov. 1811; Isaac Chauncey to Rodgers, 10 Dec. 1811; Frederick Rodgers Coll: John Bullus to Rodgers, 30 Nov. 1811.

2. Homans, pp. 67–68. This was the prize money distribution in force after 1 June 1800. The earlier "Act for the Government of the Navy of the United States," 2 March 1799, under which the Quasi-War prize money was distributed through 31 May 1800, had significantly different provisions, which may be seen in detail in Homans, pp. 55–56.

3. A significant share of credit for the financial rewards showered on the victors in this battle belongs to Purser (and squadron prize agent) Samuel Hambleton. His lobbying efforts in Washington on behalf of the victors may be followed in detail in WLCL, Perry Papers: Samuel Hambleton to O.H. Perry, 31 Mar., 4 Apr., 5 Apr., 12 Apr., 5 May, 16 May, 26 May, 2 June 1814.

4. Brown University, John Hay Library, Parsons Family Papers: Pliny Hayes, Jr., to Usher Parsons, 23 Apr. 1814.

5. There exists no one-place source for prize money earned from the capture of French armed vessels during the Quasi-War. A list of all such prizes is in QW 7:372–373. Because the Commissioners of the Navy Pension Fund were keenly interested in collecting the fund's half of any prize money, their records are the best source for discovering how much was earned by individual ships and captains. The most comprehensive record is the "Abstract of Monies pertaining to the fund for Navy pensions & half pay, being the United States proportion of the proceeds of the Sales of French Armed Vessels &c., captured by the Vessels of War of the U. States" at the end of RG 15, Letters Sent by the Commissioners of the Navy Pension Fund, Dec. 1800–Sept. 1816. Information on the proceeds of other prizes can be discovered by digging through the volumes of QW. Even after combing these two sources, the historian still has only a partial record of prize money earned during the war. In all, some ninety-two vessels were captured on the grounds that they were French armed

ships. Of these at least eleven apparently earned no prize money for the captors. One was sunk; the others were either judged by the courts not to be lawful prizes or were restored under the terms of the peace treaty of 30 Sept. 1800. Among the remaining eighty-one prizes the actual cash proceeds can be discovered (or accurately estimated) for fifty-nine (72.8 percent). In order to carry out the analysis of prize money presented in the text, some means had to be settled upon for handling the one-quarter of the cases in which sale figures are unknown. The median captors' share of those prizes the actual sale prices of which are known is $1,049; and the values immediately adjacent to the median are $1,027 and $1,064. Using these figures as a guide, the captors' (and the Pension Fund's) shares of those prizes for which actual sale figures are not available have been estimated at $1,000 in each instance of missing data. Using this method of estimation makes the Pension Fund's share of all Quasi-War prizes $149,400, a figure sufficiently consistent with the known capital of the Navy Pension Fund to inspire reasonable confidence in the method of estimation. (For the capital of the Pension Fund see ASP Nav Aff 1:73, 80–82, 103–104, 112, 124–125, 143, 156, 178, bearing in mind that it required several years of effort by the Commissioners of the Navy Pension Fund to find and collect all the money due to the Fund.) The weakness of the method is that in those cases in which a substantial proportion of the prizes made by a particular captain must be estimated, the possibility exists of substantial error in stating the prize money earned by that captain. Wherever such an estimate-induced error may exist in the text, a warning is given.

With War of 1812 prize money the problem is the opposite of the one for the Quasi-War. Using ASP Nav Aff 1:299, 374, 380–395, 416–427, 535–582, 895–897, supplemented by *The Naval War of 1812: A Documentary History,* ed. William S. Dudley (Washington, D.C.: Naval Historical Center, 1985–) 1 (for 1812 prizes); Charles Lee Lewis, *The Romantic Decatur* (Philadelphia, 1937), pp. 131–132 (for *Macedonian*); Linda M. Maloney, *The Captain from Connecticut: The Life and Naval Times of Isaac Hull* (Boston: Northeastern University Press, 1986), p. 234 (for *Boxer*); and RFP, Ser 2, Account of Charles W. Goldsborough, agent for the distribution of prize money, 25 Dec. 1824 (for *Falcon*), it is possible to calculate, with an acceptable degree of accuracy, the total amount of prize money earned by the captors from all prizes taken in the War of 1812. In contrast to the Quasi-War situation, no missing prize money amounts had to be supplied by estimation; however, the various lists and documents in ASP Nav Aff 1 are, in many cases, deficient in the names of capturing vessels and their commanding officers, as well as dates of capture. Numerous, but far from all, of these gaps may be filled from information in the War of 1812 prize list in George F. Emmons, *The Navy of the United States* (Washington, D.C., 1853), pp. 56–75.

6. Inability to identify, in the present state of historical knowledge, the names of the commanding officers who made a significant number of the War of 1812's smaller prizes, as well as the difficulty of calculating the total number of officers commanding the navy's numerous gunboats during that conflict, make it impossible to carry out a parallel analysis for the War of 1812's commanding officers.

7. Thomas Tingey's purported earnings are based on so many estimated prizes (three out of four) that they should perhaps be wholly disregarded. His

general aptitude for financial gain makes this historian suspect that the real total was probably higher.

8. Library Company of Philadelphia (collections housed at HSPa): Thomas Truxtun–Charles Biddle Letters, esp. Truxtun's letters of 13 July, 26 July, 28 Nov. 1799, 3 Aug. 1800, 4 Jan., 30 Apr., 14 May, 15 June, 14 July 1801, 6 Mar., 7 Mar. 1802, 17 Nov. 1804 (the last enclosing Truxtun to Jones & Clark, 17 Nov. 1804).

9. Albert Gleaves, *James Lawrence* (New York, 1904), pp. 172–175.

10. The rules for calculating salvage accruing to naval vessels were established and changed twice during the Quasi-War, then remained fixed for the balance of the pre-1815 period. They will be found detailed in U.S. Laws, Statutes, etc., *United States Statutes at Large* 1:574–575 (28 June 1798), 716 (2 Mar. 1799); 2:16–18 (3 Mar. 1800).

11. QW 6:276a. Inadequate data have been discovered on salvage earnings from which to attempt to calculate an estimated median award or to form any idea of the range of such awards.

12. QW 5:563.

29. Money Men

1. For guidance in coping with this mass of paperwork the purser's primary reliance was on the "instructions to commanders and pursers with respect to the method of keeping the books and accounts of the vessels" which were issued by the accountant of the navy as a printed pamphlet. This is one of the scarcest of the early naval imprints. There were two printings, neither of which bore a title page or any indication of the issuing office; both carry the title *General Muster Book* at the head of the first page of text. Drafting of the instructions was begun by or under William Winder and completed by or under Thomas Turner. The manuscript version was reviewed, and in some degree revised, by Thomas Tingey, who drew on his experience in the British navy. The earlier of the two editions appears to have been printed at Washington or Georgetown, D.C., sometime between 25 July and 13 Oct. 1800, on paper watermarked 1799 (Accnt LS 1798–1800:267, 272: William Winder to Ebenezer Bushnell, 23 Nov. 1799; Winder to Thomas J. Chew, 2 Dec. 1799; Accnt LS 2:88, 231: Thomas Turner to William Bainbridge, 17 July 1800; Turner to Alexander Murray, 13 Oct. 1800; Accnt LR: Thomas Tingey to Turner, 25 July 1800). It numbers twenty pages and the title, *General Muster Book,* is set in gothic type. Only one copy has been thus far located, that in the Houghton Library at Harvard University. No definite evidence exists to establish the date of the second printing, although from the text it is clear that it antedates the 3 Mar. 1817 reorganization of the office of the accountant of the navy to that of fourth auditor of the treasury. The second printing is readily identified by its twenty-six pages, a result of its being set in larger type than the 1800 imprint. Textual differences between the two printings are insignificant. Two copies of the second printing have been located, one at the New York Public Library (like the first printing, it is cataloged as U.S. Navy Dept., *General Muster Book*) and the other in Accts (A) Box 3059.

2. Accnt LR: James R. Wilson to Thomas Turner, 7 Aug. 1813; George M. Wilson to Turner, 17 Apr., 1 Aug. 1814; George S. Wise to Turner, 16 May 1814; Accnt LS 12:124: Turner to Harriet B. Wilson, 30 Mar. 1815; Accnt

Exec LS 80: Constant Freeman to Smith Thompson, 8 Mar. 1821; OL: George M. Wilson to William Jones, 29 July 1814; Philadelphia Maritime Museum: Isaac Hull to Thomas J. Chew, 14 Nov. 1812.

3. GLB 2:307: Benjamin Stoddert to Jeremiah Yellott, 23 Aug. 1799.

4. No new pursers were appointed between mid-July 1814 and the end of the War of 1812. Only initial appointments are here counted; if a purser was discharged and later recalled to active duty, only the first appointment is tallied.

5. Typical lists of slops available from pursers include NYHS, Nav Hist Soc Misc Mss: "Prices of Slops &c the property of Charles Wadsworth Purser Frigate U States as affixed by Commodore [John] Barry," July 1799 (an unusually elaborate supply); Accts (A) Martin, John: "A Statement of Slop Clothing received and expended on board the United States Ship President," 18 Feb. 1801; *Constitution* slop book, 1803–1804, in M&PR: *Constitution* Pay Roll, 1803–28, vol. 1 (T829:95), fols. 22–38; Accts (A) Wilson, James R.: Booklet showing costs and prices of slops, 1809/10–1812/13; Accts (A) Garretson, Isaac: "Survey of Slops & Stores remaining in the Pursers department on board the United States Frigate President," 16 Jan. 1810; Accts (A) Magrath, Humphrey: Receipt roll for slops, U.S. Brig *Viper*, 30 June 1811; Accts (A) Halsey, James M.: "Slops expended on board the U.S. Frigate President from the 20th Octr. 1813"; "Slops recd. from May 1814 to 20 May 1815"; "Slop statement of the cost and prices to be charged at on board the U.S. Frigate Guerriere," [1814].

6. *President* orders, ca. 1812, article 55; *Madison* & *General Pike* orders, 1813–14, article 5; see also *Argus* orders, 1811, article 10.

7. Accnt LR: Alexander Murray to Thomas Turner, 16 May, 23 May 1809; Accnt LS 7:384–385: Turner to Murray, 19 May 1809.

8. CL: Hugh G. Campbell to Robert Smith, 28 July 1806.

9. M&PR: *Argus,* 1803–13 (T829:23), fols. 1–12 (payroll) and 18–40 (issue book).

10. Sample lists of Quasi-War slops as provided by navy agents: Accts (A) Allen, Moses: "Account of Purser's stores supplied to the U.S. Frigate Boston . . . by the Committee for building said Frigate," 24 July 1799, and Accts (A) Alline, Benjamin: "An Account of Slops Distributed on board Herald . . . to the 13 July 1799."

11. Quasi-War slop policies may be followed in GLB 1:81: Benjamin Stoddert to Jeremiah Yellott, 24 July 1798; 1:321–322: Stoddert to Nicholas Johnson, 9 Oct. 1798; 1:423: Stoddert to Robert Gill, 5 Dec. 1798; 2:210: Stoddert to Yellott, 21 June 1799; 2:394–395: Stoddert to Joseph Waters [and] Nicholas Johnson, 10 Oct. 1799; 3:379: Stoddert to James & Ebenezer Watson, 21 May 1800; 4:5–6, 58: Stoddert to George Harrison, 1 Sept., 6 Oct. 1800; OSW 3:314–315: Stoddert to James Key, 29 Mar. 1800; 4:331: Stoddert to Henry Geddes, 5 Dec. 1800; Accnt LS 1798–1800:318, 337: Thomas Turner to Thomas J. Chew, 8 Feb. 1800; Turner to Joseph Hooper, 19 Feb. 1800; Accnt LS 2:268, 359: Turner to James S. Deblois, 1 Nov. 1800; Turner to Gill, 27 Jan. 1801.

12. GLB 4:58, 110: Benjamin Stoddert to George Harrison, 6 Oct., 11 Nov. 1800.

13. GLB 4:515: Robert Smith to Thomas Turner, 1 Sept. 1801; Accnt LS 3:376: Turner to Smith, 24 Dec. 1801; *Naval Regulations* (1802), "Regulations Respecting Slops."

14. Cong LB 2:108–109: Paul Hamilton to John Randolph, 3 Apr. 1812; OSW 6:454: Robert Smith to Charles Wadsworth [and other pursers], 28 May 1804; 6:462–463: Smith to Samuel Barron [and other captains], 30 May 1804; 6:465–469: Smith to Barron [and other captains], 31 May 1804; 7:43: Smith to Barron, 21 Nov. 1805; 7:270: Smith to Samuel Hambleton, 6 Dec. 1806; Accnt LS 6:437: Thomas Turner to Thomas N. Gautier, 16 Feb. 1808; 7:147–148: Turner to Murray, 16 Sept. 1808; CL: Hugh G. Campbell to Smith, 28 July 1806; OL: Timothy Winn [and] Noadiah Morris to Smith, 8 Apr. 1806; Barron Mss: Gwinn Harris to Barron, 12 May 1805; for a partial accounting for slop purchases made by one Barron squadron purser see Accts (A) Harris, Gwinn: Harris to Smith, 31 May 1804, with invoices and receipts enclosed. The only direct references to congressional investigation into slop sales found by this historian are in Smith's letters of May 1804 cited above; it was presumably part of the House Ways and Means Committee's general examination of naval accounting practices, for which see *Annals of Congress* 13:1011.

15. SF, NJ.

16. Cong LB 2:108–109: Paul Hamilton to John Randolph, 3 Apr. 1812; Accnt Exec LR, 1801–29: Hamilton to Thomas Turner, 30 May [1809]; ML: Turner to Hamilton, 30 May 1809; OSW 8:385–386: Hamilton, Circular, 6 June 1809; 8:458–459: Hamilton, Circular, 27 July 1809; 10:31: Hamilton to Thomas Shields, 7 May 1812; 10:58: Hamilton to Samuel Hambleton, 15 June 1812; Accnt LS 7:420–421: Turner, Circular to Pursers, 7 June 1809; 8:349: Turner to Timothy Winn, 30 July 1810; 11:454: Turner to James M. Halsey, 20 Dec. 1814; Accnt LR: Winn to Turner, 23 July 1810; Thomas H. Gilliss to Robert Ormsby, 7 June 1813; John Shaw, Circular [to officers under his command], 8 July 1813; CL: Alexander Murray to Hamilton, 16 June 1809; MCL: David Porter to Hamilton, 10 Sept. 1809, enclosing Hambleton to Porter, 8 Sept. 1809; OL: Shields to Hamilton, 21 July 1811; Robert Ormsby to William Jones, 9 June 1813, and important endorsement by T.H. Gilliss; RFP, LB 1808–1809: John Rodgers to C.S. Huntt, 12 June 1809; Rodgers to Hamilton, 23 June 1809, with "Statement A" and "Statement B."

17. OL: Timothy Winn [and] Noadiah Morris to Robert Smith, 8 Apr. 1806.

18. In June 1803 Purser Keith Spence estimated his annual net profit as purser of the frigate *Philadelphia* at $1,500 per year (HEHL, Spence Mss: Keith Spence to Mary Spence, 8 June 1803), closer to Hamilton's than to Rodgers's figure.

30. Poisoning the Rats

1. Accnt LS 8:107–137: "A Statement of the nature and amount of extra allowances to officers of the Navy," 1 Apr. 1801–4 Mar. 1809.

2. The involved history of the Committee of Investigation may be followed in these sources: RG 206, Letters Received by the Solicitor of the Treasury from the Navy Department, 1815–38: Charles W. Goldsborough to Samuel L. Southard, 20 Dec. 1824 (an excellent brief history of the committee); *Annals of Congress* 20:61–73, 163, 448; 23:345, 353–355; U.S. Congress, House, Committee of Investigation of the State of the Treasury, *Report (in Part) from the Committee Appointed on the 31st Ult. to Inquire Whether Monies Drawn from the Treasury since the 4th March 1801 Have Been Faithfully Applied to the Object for Which They Were Appropriated, and Whether the Same Have Been Regularly Accounted for . . . June*

27th, 1809 (Washington, D.C.: R.C. Weightman, 1809) [Shaw & Shoemaker #19033]; HR 11A-C9.4: John Randolph to Albert Gallatin, 3 June 1809; ML: Randolph to Paul Hamilton, 29 Nov. 1811 (and enclosed list of questions), 5 Feb. 1812; Cong LB 1: Hamilton to Randolph, 7 June, 17 June 1809; Hamilton to Daniel Sheffey, 12 Feb. 1810; 2:76: Hamilton to Sheffey, 4 Dec. 1811; 2:88–93: Hamilton to Randolph, 6 Feb. 1812, and enclosures; 2:104–108: Hamilton to Randolph, 17 Mar. 1812; 2:108–111: Hamilton to Randolph, 3 Apr. 1812, and Enclosure A; GLB 11:31, 35–36: Hamilton to Thomas Turner, 28 Jan. 1812, and enclosure; Accnt LS 7:429–448: Turner to Hamilton, 16 June 1809, and enclosed papers; 8:100–137: Turner to Hamilton, 15 Dec. 1809, and enclosed papers; 9:279–280: "Questions By the Committee of Investigation to the Accountant of the Navy, and his answers," 13 Jan. 1812; 9:332–333: "Statement showing the respective balances in the hands of Pursers attached to Stations, per their returns, and the balances standing to the debit of Pursers, attached to vessels, remaining to be accounted for," 9 Mar. 1812; 9:335–337: T.H. Gilliss, "Explanations to sundry requisitions made by the Committee of Investigation," 9 Mar. 1812; Accnt LR: Randolph to Turner, 9 Jan. 1812; NYHS, Misc Mss: Samuel Hambleton to David Porter, 21 Nov. 1811.

3. The origins of the legislation mandating Senate confirmation of pursers would be a mystery without a series of letters from Samuel Hambleton revealing the real story: NYHS, Misc Mss: Hambleton to David Porter, 9 Nov. 1811, 22 Feb., 25 Feb., 13 Apr. 1812; other sources include ML: James Lloyd to Paul Hamilton, 24 Feb., 15 Apr. 1812; GLB 11:76: Hamilton to Thomas Newton, 24 Apr. 1812; Accnt LS 9:362–364: "Statement showing the respective balances in the hands of Pursers attached to stations per their returns, and the balances standing to the debit of Pursers attached to vessels remaining to be accounted for, with the date of their last settlement," 16 Apr. 1812; *Annals of Congress* 23:164–166, 929; ASP Nav Aff 1:255–264; JEP 2:250, 257, 258.

31. The Perils of Accountability
1. Accnt LS 10:185–186: Thomas Turner to Isaac Chauncey, 15 Feb. 1813, replying to Accnt LR: Chauncey to Turner, 4 Feb. 1813, provides an excellent discussion of this, but examples could be multiplied. The present chapter generalizes from extensive reading in the records of the accountant of the navy from 1798 through the 1820s; citations are intended only as specific examples, not comprehensive listings of sources.

2. The records of the accountant of the navy (later fourth auditor of the treasury) in RG 217 are replete with material on the financial operations and all too frequent financial collapses of U.S. navy agents.

3. See Accnt Exec LS 209–210: Constant Freeman to Samuel L. Southard, 22 Nov. 1823, for a good example of the comptroller of the treasury's authority to overrule both the accountant and the secretary of the navy on a particular expenditure.

4. Accnt LS 2:365: Thomas Turner to George Harrison, 29 Jan. 1801.

5. Accnt LS 6:222: Thomas Turner to Clement S. Huntt, 29 May 1807; 3:105: Turner to John Mantz, 29 May 1801.

6. Detroit Public Library, Burton Historical Collection, Woolsey Mss.

7. Accnt LS 1798–1800:309–310: Thomas Turner to Stephen Higginson & Co., 30 Jan. 1800; Accnt LS 3:87: Turner to Henry Geddes, 20 May 1801; 4:7: Turner to James Watson, 31 May 1802; 7:237: Turner to M.T. Woolsey, 18 Jan. 1809.

8. Accnt LS 4:400–403: Thomas Turner to Christopher Ellery, 27 Mar. 1804, enclosing "Abstract of charges by Capt. Perry in his accounts against the Department not admitted" and "Statement of Captain Perry's account pr. Settlement of this day."

9. 21st Congress, 2d Session, House of Representatives, Document No. 17 (Serial 206); such congressional documents are hereafter cited as Serial 206/17, etc. The threads of individual officer debts have been traced through the annual lists of unpaid balances on the books of the accountant of the navy (after Mar. 1817 the fourth auditor of the treasury) in ASP Finance 1:803–809 (1802); U.S. Comptroller of the Treasury, *Letter from the Comptroller of the Treasury, Transmitting a Statement of the Accounts in the Treasury, War and Navy Departments, Which Have Remained More Than Three Years Unsettled, or on Which Balances Appear to Have Been Due More Than Three Years Prior to the Thirtieth of September Last . . . December 1, 1809* (Washington, D.C.: A. & G. Way, 1809) [Shaw & Shoemaker #18919]; *Letter from the Comptroller of the Treasury, Transmitting a Statement of the Accounts in the Treasury, War and Navy Departments, Which Have Remained More Than Three Years Unsettled, or on Which Balances Appear to Have Been Due More Than Three Years Prior to the Thirtieth of September Last . . . December 11th, 1810* (Washington, D.C.: R.C. Weightman, 1810) [Shaw & Shoemaker #21675]; *Letter from the Comptroller of the Treasury, Transmitting a Statement of the Accounts in the Treasury, War and Navy Departments, Which Have Remained More Than Three Years Unsettled, or on Which Balances Appear to Have Been Due More Than Three Years Prior to the Thirtieth of September Last . . . November 11, 1811* (Washington, D.C.: A. & G. Way, 1811) [Shaw & Shoemaker #24153]; Accnt LS 10:68–83 (1812), 11:464–483 (1814), 12:479–498 (1815), 14:102–117 (1816), 15:160–181 (1817), 16:1–12 (1818); Accnt Exec LS 43–59 (1820), 115–135 (1821), 259–299 (1823), 347–376 (1824); Serial 133/42 (1825), 154/135 (1826), 170/25 (1827), 184/8 (1828), 195/10 (1829), 206/17 (1830), 217/41 (1831), 235/135 (1832), 254/13 (1833), 272/54 (1834), 286/16 (1835), 302/37 (1836), 321/2 (1837), 346/30 (1838), 364/28 (1839), 382/10 (1840), 402/93 (1841), 423/198 (1842), 444/275 (1843), 466/145 (1844), 500/123 (1846), 521/68 (1847). Details of individual balances due, how they were incurred, and attempts to collect them are, in many cases, extensively recorded in Accnt LR and Accnt LS. Actual statements of accounts and supporting vouchers, as well as pertinent correspondence, may often be found in Accts (A) or Accts (N). The government's attempts to collect these debts by legal action can be traced in RG 206, Solicitor of the Treasury, Register of Suits against Sundry Persons, vols. 1, 3, and 4; rich supporting detail on the suits and related debts will be found in three series of the solicitor's incoming correspondence in RG 206: Letters Received from U.S. District Attorneys, Marshals, and Clerks of Court; Letters Received from the Auditor of the Navy Department (Fourth Auditor); and Letters Received from the Navy Department.

10. For purser-debtors see, in addition to the sources just cited, two lists with more extensive notes in Accnt LS 17:25–27 (1 Mar. 1820) and Accnt Exec LS 221–227 (5 Feb. 1824). Pursers' detailed vouchers, to the extent that they survive, are almost always found in Accts (A).

11. Accnt LR: Thomas Johnston to Constant Freeman, 14 Sept. 1819, enclosed in Johnston to Freeman, 24 May 1820.

12. Amos Kendall, Fourth Auditor of the Treasury, letter of transmittal, 21 Dec. 1830, covering the 1830 list of persons with unsettled naval balances in Serial 206/17. For an example of creatively conjuring a credit to wipe out a

small balance against a long-dead officer, see Accts (N) #6569 (Jonathan Church).

13. RG 206, Letters Received by the Solicitor of the Treasury from U.S. District Attorneys, Marshals, and Clerks of Court: New Hampshire: Daniel Humphreys to Stephen Pleasonton, 26 Oct. 1823; Massachusetts: George Blake to Pleasanton, 6 Nov. 1823.

14. For example, Homans, pp. 196, 197, 206, 212, 217.

15. Serial 225/301: [Report of the Committee on Claims on the petition of] Charles Ludlow, 1 Feb. 1832, but note therein, pp. 2–4, Amos Kendall to Levi Woodbury, 25 Jan. 1832, denying that any real loss had been incurred and explaining how such treasury note discounts had been refunded to pursers and other disbursing agents in an extralegal manner in the years immediately after the War of 1812.

16. Register of Suits 1:35; in addition to the material on Darby's case running through the sources cited in notes 9 and 10, see RG 45, Letters Received by the Secretary of the Navy from the Attorney General, 1807–25: William Wirt to Samuel L. Southard, 23 July 1824.

17. OSW 3:76: Benjamin Stoddert to James Key, 23 Nov. 1799; 4:257: Stoddert to Robert Lewis, 27 Oct. 1800; Accnt LR: Lewis to Stoddert, 19 May 1800; George Harrison to Thomas Turner, [13 Dec.], 20 Dec. 1804; Accnt LS 4:249: Turner to Lewis, 11 June 1803; Turner to Harrison, 10 June 1803; 4:258: Turner to Harrison, 23 June 1803; 5:48, 73: Turner to Harrison, 24 Oct., 17 Dec. 1804; 5:88: Turner to Gabriel Duvall, 9 Jan. 1805; AF, A-7: Turner to Duvall, 18 Oct. 1806, enclosing Harrison to Turner, 15 Oct. 1806; Register of Suits 1:16.

18. See, for example, the charges against Silas Dinsmoor in Accnt LR: Wilson Jacobs to Samuel Smith, 7 May 1801.

19. CL: Hugh G. Campbell to William Jones, 11 Nov. 1814.

20. OSW 12:31, 81A, 128, 193, 325, 327: B.W. Crowninshield to Hugh G. Campbell, 9 Feb., 28 Mar., 22 May 1815; Benjamin Homans to Robert T. Spence, 22 Aug. 1815; Homans to John Hulburd, 24 May 1816; Crowninshield to Campbell, 28 May 1816; CL: Campbell to Crowninshield, 9 June 1816; Accnt LS 11:17: Thomas Turner to N.W. Rothwell, 27 Dec. 1813; 13:452: Constant Freeman to John P. White, 7 Nov. 1816; Accnt LR: Charles Snell to [Secretary of the Navy], 26 May 1815, with pencil note by Homans; RG 206, Letters Received by the Solicitor of the Treasury from U.S. District Attorneys, Marshals, and Clerks of Court: Delaware, 1803–95: George Read, Jr., to Stephen Pleasonton, 16 Nov. 1824; Delaware Hall of Records, Dover, New Castle County Probate Records: Rothwell, Inventory of goods and chattels, 21 Aug. 1818; Settlements with administrators of Rothwell's estate, 6 Oct. 1819, 6 Dec. 1821. At the time of Rothwell's death his goods and chattels consisted of four horses, a watch, his table silver, some personal jewelry, clothing, two portable desks, a liquor case, four trunks, and his portrait, the whole appraised at $304.75. Money raised from the sale of these was inadequate to reimburse even the creditors who submitted claims before that made by the United States.

21. CL: Stephen Decatur to Robert Smith, 24 May 1808; MCL: P.C. Wederstrandt to Smith, 2 Aug. 1808; OSW 8:86: Smith to Decatur, 30 May 1808; Accnt LS 7:427: Thomas Turner to Robert Henley, 12 June 1809.

22. Homans, pp. 87, 90.

23. RG 39, Navy Pursers' Surety Bonds: Spence, Groeme Keith, 10 May 1814.

24. OSW 11:314–315: William Jones to Isaac Garretson [and nine other pursers], 19 May 1814.

25. Accnt LS 12:171: Thomas Turner to Amos Binney, 28 Apr. 1815; Accnt LR: Binney to Turner, 24 Oct. 1815.

26. Accnt LS 11:223: Thomas Turner to George Harrison, 31 May 1814; Accnt LR: Harrison to Turner, 2 June, 12 June, 14 June 1814.

27. U.S. Laws, Statutes, etc., *United States Statutes at Large* 1:441–442 (3 Mar. 1795), 512–516 (3 Mar. 1797), 561–562 (6 June 1798); 3:399 (3 Mar. 1817).

28. Accnt LS 5:175–176: Thomas Turner to Peter Trezevant, 18 June 1805; 6:40, 331, 9:26: Turner to Gabriel Duvall, 1 Nov. 1806, 28 Sept. 1807, 28 Feb. 1811; 16:354, 374: Constant Freeman to Edward Jones, 18 Aug. 1819; Freeman to Trezevant, 6 Sept. 1819; 20:412: Tobias Watkins to Trezevant, 11 Sept. 1824; Accnt Exec LS 234–235: Thomas H. Gilliss to Samuel L. Southard, 9 Mar. 1824; Accnt LR: Trezevant to Benjamin Stoddert, 21 Jan. 1800; RG 206, Letters Received by the Solicitor of the Treasury from U.S. District Attorneys, Marshals, and Clerks of Court: South Carolina: Thomas Parker to Joseph Anderson, 15 Dec. 1819; Register of Suits 1:18; HR 18A-F2.1: Trezevant to House of Representatives, 31 Jan. 1824; John T. Trezevant, *The Trezevant Family in the United States* (Columbia, S.C., 1914), pp. 17–23.

29. ML: James Turner to Robert Smith, 1 Mar. 1809; Nathaniel Macon to Smith, 1 Mar. 1809; James Turner to Secretary of the Navy, 16 June 1809; James Hamilton to Macon, 16 Jan. 1811; Theodore Hunt to Edwin T. Satterwhite, 30 Jan. 1811; Willis Alston [and] James Cochran to [Paul Hamilton], 25 Feb. 1811; CMR 4:0401–0406: Court of inquiry into the loss of the books, accounts, and papers of Purser Edwin T. Satterwhite, 27 May 1813; Accnt LS 10:304–306: Thomas H. Gilliss to William Jones, 24 June 1813; 11:88–89: Thomas Turner to Jones, 22 Feb. 1814, enclosing detailed statement of Satterwhite's account; 12:249: Thomas Turner to Joseph Reed, 8 June 1815; 14:221: Constant Freeman, Certificate, 28 Apr. 1817; Accnt Exec LR, 1801–29: Jones to Thomas Turner, 22 Feb. 1814; OSW 11:36–37: Jones to Satterwhite, 5 Aug. 1813; 11:305: Jones to Satterwhite, 29 Apr. 1814; 12:32: B.W. Crowninshield to Edward Cutbush, 11 Feb. 1815; RG 52, Washington Navy Yard Hospital, Register of Patients, 1812–40: Record of Satterwhite's admission (12 Feb. 1815) and discharge (12 Mar. 1815); Cong LB 2:233–234: Jones to Stevenson Archer, 24 Feb. 1814; GLB 12:148: Jones to Thomas Turner, 5 Apr. 1814; 12:149: Jones to Richard Rush, 13 Apr. 1814; RG 45, Letters Received by the Secretary of the Navy from the Attorney General, 1807–25: Rush to Jones, 14 Apr. 1814; RG 217, Fourth Auditor Journals 8:210 (10 May 1814); Accts (N) #39: Final settlement with Satterwhite, 5 Apr. 1817; Homans, p. 211.

Part Eight: Pathology of a Profession

1. OL: William Jasper to Paul Hamilton, 23 Nov. 1811; ML: Robert Jasper to William Jones, 26 Apr. 1814; GLB 12:156: Jones to Robert Jasper, 30 Apr. 1814.

2. For an interesting case of the latter practice, involving Lieutenant David Ross, see FDRL, Naval Mss: Ross to John Barry, 7 May 1799; OSW 3:85: Benjamin Stoddert to Ross, 30 Nov. 1799; 5:367: Robert Smith to Ross, 25

Mar. 1802; ML: Stoddert to Charles W. Goldsborough, 10 Jan. 1807, enclosing Ross to Smith, 22 Sept. 1806.

32. The President of Terrors

1. Woolsey Journal, 13 July 1802. A different version of this chapter was published as "The Pathology of a Profession: Death in the United States Navy Officer Corps, 1797–1815," *War & Society* 3(1985):1–25.

2. RFP, LB 1807–1808: John Rodgers to Michael McBlair, 8 June 1808; RFP, LB 1808–1809: Rodgers to Mrs. [Susan] Jackson, 11 July 1809; Allen Letters 218 (14 Oct. 1807); CL: Arthur Sinclair to William Jones, 2 Dec. 1814; McKee, *Edward Preble*, p. 354.

3. Alexander S. Mackenzie, *Life of Stephen Decatur* (Boston, 1848), p. 218.

4. One officer, Jonathan Thorn, had been killed by hostile Indians on the Northwest Coast in June 1811; at the time of his death Thorn was commander of the merchant vessel *Tonquin*.

5. *Shannon*'s June 1813 defeat of *Chesapeake* (7 deaths); Preble's attacks on Tripoli (6); *Pelican*'s Aug. 1813 capture of *Argus* (3); Perry's Sept. 1813 victory at Lake Erie (3); Macdonough's Sept. 1814 defeat of the British fleet on Lake Champlain (3); and *President*'s standoff with *Endymion* (3—or 4, if one includes R.S. Dale).

6. ASP Nav Aff 1:291; Amos A. Evans, "Journal Kept on Board the United States Frigate 'Constitution,' 1812," *Pennsylvania Magazine of History and Biography* 19(1895):477–480; size of *Constitution*'s ship's company from SF, NA: Quarter bill of *Constitution*, ca. Dec. 1812.

7. Gilliam Letters 61 (7 Sept. 1812); BW 4:352.

8. RG 24, *United States* Log, 17 Aug. 1812.

9. CL: O.H. Perry to Paul Hamilton, 1 Oct. 1812 (misbound at 23 Nov. 1813).

10. CL: Hugh G. Campbell to Paul Hamilton, 22 Oct. 1811.

11. CL: Charles Gordon to William Jones, 10 Mar. 1814.

12. Chesapeake Bay Maritime Museum, Saint Michaels, Md., Samuel Hambleton, New Orleans Station Letterbook, 1807–11: Hambleton to Philip Marshall, 23 Mar. 1810.

13. ZB File: William P.H. Smith to John Mason, 19 Nov. 1813, 8 Feb. 1814; Lewis Condict to Mason, 7 Mar. 1814; CL: Isaac Chauncey to William Jones, 17 Oct. 1814.

14. James E. Valle, *Rocks & Shoals: Order and Discipline in the Old Navy, 1800–1861* (Annapolis, Md.: Naval Institute Press, 1980), p. 88, citing as his authority for the second figure Allan R. Bosworth, *My Love Affair with the Navy* (New York: Norton, 1969), p. 79, who in turn apparently got it from Charles O. Paullin, "Dueling in the Old Navy," U.S. Naval Institute *Proceedings* 35(1909):1157. The last-named gives, in his otherwise excellent article, no basis for his much too low figure for death from enemy action.

15. Barron Mss: James Barron to Samuel Barron, 28 Jan. 1803.

16. CL: John Rodgers to Robert Smith, 7 Aug. 1808.

17. ZB File: McKenzie, Allen.

18. CL: Arthur Sinclair to William Jones, 2 Dec. 1814; John Rodgers to Paul Hamilton, 17 Oct. 1810.

19. BW 2:293–296, 311.

20. OL: Joseph H. Nicholson to Robert Smith, 28 Feb. 1805.

21. OSW 8:571: Paul Hamilton to Stephen Decatur, 11 Dec. 1809.

22. OSW 11:470: William Jones to John T. Ritchie, 30 Nov. 1814.

23. BW 2:308. Smith decided that no judicial proceedings against Lawson were possible.

24. As can be seen from Table 39 there were probably 10 suicides among the 331 deaths in the officer corps, Sept. 1797–Feb. 1815, or 3.0 percent of the total deaths. In Portsmouth, N.H., 1801–20, suicide accounted for only 0.54 percent of all deaths; the figure for Boston, 1811–20, is 0.34 percent. Extrapolated figures for Portsmouth, 1801–11, 1818–20, would give a crude suicide rate of 9.8 persons per 100,000 population (J. Worth Estes, *Hall Jackson and the Purple Foxglove: Medical Practice and Research in Revolutionary America, 1760–1820* [Hanover, N.H.: University Press of New England, 1979], pp. 108–109). In Philadelphia, 1839–45, the crude average annual suicide rate per 100,000 population was 5.0 (Roger Lane, *Violent Death in the City: Suicide, Accident, and Murder in Nineteenth-Century Philadelphia* [Cambridge: Harvard University Press, 1979], pp. 13–34; figures for 1839–45 at p. 15). All of these figures predict a much lower incidence of suicide than is found among naval officers, 1797–1815. Apart from the tendency to conceal suicide in reporting mortality among the civilian population, it needs to be recalled that the naval figures are for elite white males (the social group, as Lane demonstrates, most prone to suicide in the nineteenth century) in their young adult years, while the Portsmouth, Boston, and Philadelphia figures are for the population at large. If data on death among elite white males aged 15 to 38 among the civilian population in the first two decades of the nineteenth century could be isolated, it is possible that they might be found to be as suicide-prone as their naval officer contemporaries.

25. ML: George Harrison to Robert Smith, 23 Apr. 1807; CL: Stephen Decatur to Smith, 17 Jan. 1808.

26. Resignations, 1803–25: Humphrey Magrath to Robert Smith, 15 Mar. 1804; CL: Arthur Sinclair to William Jones, 6 May, 30 May 1814; OL: Ezekiel Salomon to Jones, 20 June 1814; Edmund P. Kennedy to Jones, 15 July 1814; ML: Stephen Kingston to B.W. Crowninshield, 12 Mar. 1815; Accnt LR: Sinclair to [Thomas Turner?], 30 May 1814; Sinclair to Turner, 13 June 1814; Salomon to Turner, 13 July 1814; WLCL, Perry Papers: Samuel Hambleton to O.H. Perry, 5 May, 12 July 1814.

27. Talbot Mss: Cyrus Talbot to Silas Talbot, 4 Feb. 1801; Richard Somers, *Letters and Papers*, comp. and ed. Frank H. Stewart (Woodbury, N.J., 1942), p. 16.

28. The total number of officer deaths from tuberculosis would be fifteen if all of the nine cases described as consumption or lingering illness, but the symptoms of which are unrecorded, were added to the six known cases of tuberculosis. In Portsmouth, N.H., and Boston, Mass., tuberculosis was the cause of more than 20 percent of deaths in the 1801–20 period—21.7 percent and 22.27 percent respectively (Estes, *Hall Jackson and the Purple Foxglove*, pp. 100–101).

29. ML: Archibald McAllister to Robert Smith, 14 Oct. 1807, 6 Feb. 1808; Accnt LR: Thomas G. McAllister to Smith, July [1808]; Archibald McAllister to Smith, 23 Jan. 1809; *Columbian Centinel* (Boston), 4 Mar. 1809; Mary Catherine McAllister, *Descendants of Archibald McAllister of West Pensboro Township, Cumberland County, Pa., 1730–1898* (Harrisburg, 1898), p. 71.

33. Shrinking the Corps

1. HSPa, Wm Jones Mss: William Jones to Lloyd Jones, 27 Feb. 1813; OSW 10:299: William Jones to Jacob Lewis, 13 Mar. 1813.

2. GLB 1:506: Benjamin Stoddert to Alexander Hamilton, 1 Feb. 1799; Hamilton Papers 22:468–469; HSPa, Rodgers Mss, LB 1799–1803: John Rodgers to Stoddert, 20 Nov. 1799.

3. Captains (17), masters commandant (6), lieutenants (51), midshipmen (136), sailing masters (17), surgeons (15), surgeon's mates (16), pursers (27), chaplains/schoolmasters (3), and captain's clerks (10). The number of officers who departed the navy permanently as a result of the Peace Establishment Act was certainly higher than these 298. There is ample evidence that the Quasi-War ships carried acting officers, chiefly midshipmen, whose identities cannot be established from surviving records, but there exists no accurate means of estimating the number of such unknown officers. Captain's clerks are certainly underrepresented in the above enumeration, and possibly chaplains/schoolmasters as well.

4. OSW 4:456: Samuel Smith to William Flagg, 15 Apr. 1801.

5. Rutledge Mss: Samuel Smith to John Rutledge, Jr., 12 May 1801; for the incoming administration's attitude toward political affiliations in the land force see Theodore J. Crackel, *Mr. Jefferson's Army: Political and Social Reform of the Military Establishment, 1801–1809* (New York: New York University Press, 1987), esp. ch. 2, "A Chaste Reformation."

6. CMR 1:0688.

7. QW 4:28, 293; Accnt LR: Daniel Hawthorn to Benjamin Stoddert, 15 Dec. 1800; GLB 2:437: Stoddert to Samuel Chase, Jr., 29 Oct. 1799.

8. QW 6:472–473, 559; see also Samuel Eliot Morison, *"Old Bruin": Commodore Matthew C. Perry, 1794–1858* (Boston: Little, Brown, 1967), pp. 21–24. The text of the C.R. Perry court of inquiry and voluminous related papers will be found in CMR 1:0177–0433. Important supporting documents are also in HSPa, Boudinot Papers: Joseph Boss III to Benjamin Stoddert, 28 July 1800; L.J. Dugas to [Stoddert], 13 Aug. 1800; Simeon Martin, Jr., to Stoddert, 22 Aug. 1800; John L. Boss to Stoddert, 24 Aug. 1800; and in Talbot Mss: John L. Boss to Silas Talbot, 24 Aug., 1 Sept. 1800.

9. Only those individuals who were pensioned under laws in force at the close of the War of 1812 and whose names were placed on the pension rolls before 1819 are included in the discussion of the naval officer pensioners. In the 1820s and 1840s, but more particularly in the 1830s, the names of at least thirty other officers, most of them still on active duty, were added to the pension rolls for disabilities sustained before 14 Feb. 1815. They are not counted or considered here, because the story of their pensioning belongs to the social history of a later navy.

10. OSW 4:73: Benjamin Stoddert to Patrick Fletcher, 14 July 1800; RG 15, War of 1812 Pension Application Files, Navy Invalid #171: Fletcher to Stoddert, 16 July 1800; John D. Smith, Certificate, 14 Sept. 1801.

11. OSW 3:366½, 367: Benjamin Stoddert to Thomas Robinson, 16 Apr. 1800; Stoddert to James F. Goelet, 16 Apr. 1800; RG 15, Old Wars Pension Application Files, Navy Invalid #638: Thomas Robinson, Certificate, 26 Feb. 1805; Robert Thorn, Certificate, 1 Mar. 1805; Richard V. Morris, Certificate, 23 Mar. 1805; SEN 14A-G8: Sarah Goelet to Senate and House of Representatives, 22 Jan. 1816.

12. ML: Isaac Baldwin to B.W. Crowninshield, 20 Jan. 1815; RG 15, War of 1812 Pension Application Files, Navy Widow #62: Isaac Baldwin to Benjamin Homans, 1 Dec. 1815; Elizabeth Baldwin to Homans, 25 July 1816.

13. RG 15, Old Wars Pension Application Files, Navy Invalid #1615: Nathaniel T. Weems to Robert Smith, 18 Oct. 1808; Appmt Papers Madison: Weems to Smith, 14 Dec. 1810.

14. RG 15, War of 1812 Pension Application Files, Navy Widow #1347: Smith Thompson to William Harris Crawford, 2 Apr. 1822; Pension Certificate, 24 July 1817.

15. RG 15, War of 1812 Pension Application Files, Navy Invalid #1480: Joshua Barney, Certificate, 2 Jan. 1818; University of Virginia, Alderman Library, Manuscripts Department: William McCoy to [Benjamin W. Crowninshield?], 8 Feb. 1815.

16. RG 15, War of 1812 Pension Application Files, Navy Invalid #1303: Samuel R. Trevett, Certificate, [1815].

34. Departure Voluntary—and Otherwise

1. ML: Jaqueline B. Harvie to Paul Hamilton, 23 Apr. 1812.

2. Resignations, 1810–25: Edward N. Thayer to William Jones, 26 Feb. 1814; John Larkin to Jones, 31 Dec. 1813; Resignations, 1803–25: James Macay to Smith, 18 Nov. 1803; John Mott to Smith, 25 Jan. 1806; Resignations, 1810–25: Charles O. Cannon to Jones, 23 Jan. 1813.

3. OL: Jacob Jones to Paul Hamilton, 27 Mar. 1810.

4. CL: John Rodgers to Paul Hamilton, 26 Jan. 1811, enclosing Theodore C. Van Wyck to Rodgers, 23 Jan. 1811.

5. Kennon Letters 32:279.

6. Resignations, 1810–25: Joseph Smith to William Jones, 9 Feb. 1813.

7. Resignations, 1810–25: George Coggeshall to George Parker, 4 Nov. 1813.

8. Appmt Papers TJ: James Taylor to [James Madison], 22 Sept. 1806; William D.S. Taylor to Madison, 24 Sept. 1806; JM Mss: Richard Taylor to Madison, 3 Mar. 1805; W.D.S. Taylor to Madison, 17 Jan. 1807; Richard Taylor to Madison, 25 Jan. 1808.

9. JM Mss: Ambrose Spencer to James Madison, 18 Apr. 1812.

10. Charles Morris, *Autobiography* (Boston, 1880), pp. 50–51.

11. MassHS, William Eustis Mss: Frederick Baury to William Eustis, 15 July 1810; ML: Baury to Paul Hamilton, 15 July 1810.

12. MCL: Thomas Robinson to Paul Hamilton, 1 July 1809.

13. Resignations, 1804–26: Peter Leonard to Robert Smith, 14 Mar. 1805; EPP: Leonard to Edward Preble, 4 Sept. 1806; Preble to Smith, 6 Oct. 1806; Leonard to Preble, 4 Nov. 1806.

35. Exit the Unwanted

1. OSW 11:176: William Jones to Hugh G. Campbell, 20 Dec. 1813.

2. CMR 1:0920–0921: Richard Dale to Benjamin Stoddert, 28 Sept. 1800.

3. CL: John Rodgers to Charles W. Goldsborough, 23 Mar. 1809, enclosing James T. Leonard to Rodgers, 22 Mar. 1809; CMR 2:0779–0786: Maddox court martial, 11–12 Apr. 1809; OSW 8:328: Goldsborough to Joshua Maddox, 2 May 1809.

4. CL: Hugh G. Campbell to Paul Hamilton, 15 Feb. 1811.

5. CL: John R. Grayson to Hugh G. Campbell, 13 Mar. 1813; MCL: Samuel Elbert to John H. Dent, 16 Feb. 1808, and St. Clair Elliott to Dent, 11 Feb. 1808, enclosed in Dent to Robert Smith, 17 Feb. 1808; OL: Elbert to Smith, 28 Jan. 1808; Archibald B. Lord to Theodore Hunt, 28 Apr. 1809, enclosed in Hunt to Charles W. Goldsborough, 28 Apr. 1809; CMR 3:[0446–0469]: Thompson court martial, 4–5 Mar. 1811; CL: T.N. Gautier to Thomas Riddle, [n.d.], enclosed in Dent to Jones, 18 Feb. 1813.

6. CMR 1:0631.

7. RFP, Ser 2: Court martial of William Reed, Jr., 12–15 Aug. 1805. The transcript of the same trial in CMR 1 is hopelessly chaotic and mutilated. Neither transcript contains a copy of Reed's 20 July 1805 letter to John Rodgers, the official grounds for his court martial. One supposes it was not too different from the earlier one in Frederick Rodgers Coll: William Reed, Jr., to John Rodgers, 13 July 1805.

8. CMR 1:0624–0631.

9. CMR 1:0146, 0150–0151: Moses Tryon to Richard V. Morris, 22 June 1800.

10. CL: Isaac Chauncey to Paul Hamilton, 3 May 1812.

11. CL: Samuel Elbert [and others] to Hugh G. Campbell, 6 July 1812, enclosed in Campbell to Paul Hamilton, 8 July 1812.

12. CMR 5:0744–0749, 0758.

13. OL: Thomas N. Gautier to Samuel C. Armour, 10 Mar. 1812.

14. Cf. James E. Valle, *Rocks & Shoals: Order and Discipline in the Old Navy, 1800–1861* (Annapolis, Md.: Naval Institute Press, 1980), pp. 165–175; Arthur N. Gilbert, "Buggery and the British Navy, 1700–1861," *Journal of Social History* 10(1976/77):72–98; Gilbert, "The *Africaine* Courts-Martial: A Study of Buggery and the Royal Navy," *Journal of Homosexuality* 1(1974):111–122. N.A.M. Rodger in *The Wooden World: An Anatomy of the Georgian Navy* (Annapolis, Md.: Naval Institute Press, 1986), pp. 80–81, provides a useful balance to Gilbert's perspective on the issue.

15. OL: John R. Sherwood [and] Lewis B. Page to Stephen Decatur, 23 Mar. 1812; CL: Decatur to Paul Hamilton, 24 Mar. 1812; OSW 9:588: Hamilton to Decatur, 28 Mar. 1812.

16. McKee, *Edward Preble*, p. 153.

17. SF, NO: File of documents, "Case of Midshipman Philip Philibert," 1813–15; Accnt Misc: Philibert to [Secretary of the Navy], 14 Apr. 1815; OSW 12:57, 129, 186: B.W. Crowninshield to Daniel T. Patterson, 10 Mar., 16 May 1815; Benjamin Homans to Patterson, 14 Aug. 1815; M&PR: New Orleans Station & *Viper*, 1805–26 (T829:149), fol. 115.

18. CL: John Rodgers to Robert Smith, 31 July 1808; Frederick Rodgers Coll: Smith to Rodgers, 6 Aug. 1808; RFP, LB 1808–1809: Rodgers to Smith, 10 Aug. 1808.

19. CL: Hugh G. Campbell to William Jones, 25 Mar. 1814.

20. CMR 2:0825–0916.

21. CMR 3:0118–0129 (Magruder); 3:0130–0156 (Peters); these cases are well covered in Valle, *Rocks & Shoals*, pp. 177–178.

22. CMR 4:0820–0902; CL: Isaac Chauncey to William Jones, 16 Apr. 1813.

23. The practice of officers keeping women on board their commands was alive and well in late 1814 when certain officer veterans of David Porter's

Pacific adventures in *Essex*, temporarily attached to Gunboat No. 98 at New York, "usually" had "two or three women" living with them in the cabin (Samuel F. Holbrook, *Threescore Years: An Autobiography* [Boston, 1857], p. 82).

24. MCL: St. Clair Elliott to John H. Dent, 11 Feb. 1808, and Samuel Elbert to Dent, 16 Feb. 1808, enclosed in Dent to Robert Smith, 17 Feb. 1808.

25. MCL: Samuel Evans to Paul Hamilton, 18 Sept. 1809.

26. OL: T.N. Gautier to William Jones, 7 Apr. 1813.

27. CL: Isaac Hull to Paul Hamilton, 1 Apr. 1810.

28. GLB 4:307–308, 314: Abishai Thomas to Daniel Ludlow, 27 Apr. 1801; Samuel Smith to Ludlow, 29 Apr. 1801; OL: James Lawrence to Robert Smith, 10 Feb. 1807; Rutledge Mss: William Ward Burrows to John Rutledge, [Jr.], 29 Apr. 1801.

29. SF, NN: John Adams to Benjamin Stoddert, 23 Sept. 1800, enclosing Jesse V. Lewis to Adams, 14 Sept. 1800; GLB 4:40, 149: Stoddert to John Hopkins, 26 Sept. 1800; Stoddert to Stephen Higginson & Co., 6 Dec. 1800; Accnt LR: Thomas Johnston to Thomas Turner, 3 May 1800; Higginson & Co. to Turner, 20 Aug. 1800; Gibbs & Channing to Turner, 13 Sept. 1800; Lewis to Stoddert, 3 Mar. 1801; Accnt LS 2:196: Turner to Gibbs & Channing, 23 Sept. 1800; 3:220: Turner to Jacob Sheafe, 17 Aug. 1801.

30. Many examples could be cited, but see especially the case of Midshipman William Charles Neill: CL: Alexander Murray to Paul Hamilton, 1 July 1809, enclosing Benedict I. Neale to John M. Gardner, 30 June 1809; OL: Neale to William Jones, 19 May 1813.

31. JM Mss: Paul Hamilton to James Madison, 11 Sept. 1811; NYHS, Misc Mss: Samuel Hambleton to David Porter, 17 Oct. 1811; George T. Chapman, *Sketches of the Alumni of Dartmouth College* (Cambridge, Mass.: Riverside Press, 1867), p. 141; Dartmouth College, *General Catalogue, 1769–1940* (Hanover, N.H., 1940), p. 99; Dartmouth College Archives, Alumni folders: Joseph A. Smith to John M. Comstock, 5 Mar. 1886.

36. Foremost of Crimes

1. PMS, Crowninshield Mss: John Rodgers to B.W. Crowninshield, 11 Feb. 1815.

2. MCL: John Smith to Robert Smith, 10 Aug. 1808; ML: Nathaniel Fanning to Robert Smith, 5 Aug. 1805; CL: Hugh G. Campbell to Robert Smith, [ca. 30] Sept. 1805; John Rodgers to Robert Smith, 23 Aug. 1808 (bound at 12 Oct.); Rodgers to Paul Hamilton, 22 Nov. 1809, enclosing Henry S. Newcomb to Rodgers, 8 Oct. 1809; MCL: John H. Dent to Hamilton, 14 May 1809, enclosing Jesse Wilkinson to Theodore Hunt, 9 May 1809. For more on William B. Maxwell's short, unhappy life see *Dictionary of Georgia Biography*, ed. Kenneth Coleman and Charles S. Gurr (Athens: University of Georgia Press, 1983) 2:699–700.

3. GLB 1:445: Stoddert to Thomas Martin, 20 Dec. 1798; OSW 3:367: Stoddert to James F. Goelet, 16 Apr. 1800; Paul Hamilton's endorsement on CL: William Bainbridge to Hamilton, 20 Dec. 1809; CMR 5:0085: Sentence on James William Forrest, Apr. 1814.

4. RG 45, Letters Sent by the Board of Navy Commissioners to the Secretary of the Navy 1:218: Commissioners' comments, 26 Dec. 1817, on the secretary's list of proposed promotions; OL: James Lawrence to Paul Hamilton, 28 July,

1 Aug. 1809; Usher Parsons, *Brief Sketches of the Officers Who Were in the Battle of Lake Erie* (Albany, N.Y.: J. Munsell, 1862), p. 11; CMR 1:0438, 0443.

5. The paragraphs that follow draw heavily on the analysis in W.J. Rorabaugh's splendid *The Alcoholic Republic: An American Tradition* (New York: Oxford University Press, 1979). Some critics have questioned the evidence Rorabaugh marshals to demonstrate the extent of alcohol abuse in the United States between 1790 and 1830. The navy's experience strongly supports Rorabaugh's thesis, not his critics' caveats. Data for annual per capita consumption of alcohol are from Rorabaugh's Table A1.2 (p. 233), supplemented for 1976–85 by data supplied by the U.S. National Clearinghouse for Alcohol and Drug Information, Rockville, Md. Figures since 1970 are based on the U.S. population aged fourteen and older, rather than fifteen and older.

6. GLB 8:172: Robert Smith to Elie Williams, 31 May 1806. On 21 Apr. 1806 the navy had 1,300 enlisted men on active duty (ASP Nav Aff 1:155) and perhaps 310 officers. The forty-five thousand gallons almost certainly included grog rations for dockyard workers (and possibly for the marine corps) as well as for the uniformed naval personnel.

7. EPP: "Bill of stores purchased at Boston for the use of the Cabin & for the accommodation of Coln. Lear & family as passengers for Algiers," 26 July 1803. Preble's settled accounts for his Mediterranean command no longer exist, hence the uncertainty regarding his eventual reimbursement.

8. Accts (A) Attwood, M.C.: "A TABLE of the component parts of the ration allowed in the navy of the United States," 30 Mar. 1809. This was a printed document issued by the accountant's office to pursers; a later version, dated 1 Jan. 1814, is in Accts (A) Halsey, James M.

9. BW 5:508.

10. CL: Stephen Decatur to Robert Smith, 22 July 1807.

11. GLB 8.172. Robert Smith to Elie Williams, 31 May 1806; 9:182: Smith to John Bullus, 12 Apr. 1808; 11:292: William Jones to Bullus, 31 May 1813; Commandants & Agents LB 1:14: Smith to Thomas Tingey, 12 Apr. 1808; J.F. Cooper, *Jack Tier; or, The Florida Reef* (Boston: Houghton Mifflin, [1884]), p. 380.

12. MCL: David Porter to Robert Smith, 29 Aug. 1808; Porter to Paul Hamilton, 9 Aug., 3 Nov. 1809, enclosing Porter to William Sim, 1 Nov. 1809; ML: Joseph Kent to Hamilton, 4 Dec., 18 Dec. 1811; Accnt LR: John Hague to Thomas Turner, 21 July 1812; CL: Joseph Tarbell to William Jones, 16 Dec. 1813.

13. OL: Thomas Macdonough to John T. Drury, 12 Nov. 1814, enclosed in Drury to William Jones, 1 Dec. 1814.

14. RFP, Ser 3A/2: Charles W. Goldsborough to John Rodgers, 13 Mar. 1809; CL: Rodgers to Goldsborough, 16 Mar., 4 May 1809, the latter enclosing Edward Trenchard to Rodgers, 19 Apr. 1809; OSW 8:369–370: Paul Hamilton to Isaac Hull, 27 May 1809; ML: J. [or I.] Parker to Hamilton, 10 June 1809; Joseph Tilden to Hamilton, 21 June 1809, 19 Feb. 1810; GLB 10:149–150: Hamilton to Tilden, 27 Feb. 1810.

15. *Federal Gazette and Baltimore Daily Advertiser*, 3 June 1808.

16. CL: Hugh G. Campbell to William Jones, 23 Oct. 1813; John Hulburd to Campbell, 5 Jan. 1814, enclosed in Campbell to Jones, 14 Jan. 1814.

37. Wild Youth

1. CL: John Rodgers to Paul Hamilton, 7 Oct. 1809.

2. Accnt LR: David Harris to Robert Smith, 17 Nov. 1801; GLB 6:260, 270–271: Smith to John A. Hanna, 14 May 1803; Smith to Samuel Sterett, 24 May 1803.

3. Appmt Papers TJ: William Burley, [Sr.], to James Madison, 27 July 1802. The elder Burley declined the offer.

4. Harvard Univ Arch: Faculty Records 7:389, 413; 8:8, 12–14, 17, 59, 72, 75, 83, 87, 94, 115, 130, 141, 143, 158, 160, 167, 173–174.

5. William Bentley, *Diary* (Salem: Essex Institute, 1905–14; reprinted, Gloucester, Mass.: Peter Smith, 1962) 4:159.

6. CL: Isaac Hull to William Jones, 23 Apr. 1814, enclosing Johnston Blakeley to Hull, 21 Apr. 1814; Hull to Jones, 27 Apr. 1814, enclosing Nathaniel Stoodly to Hull, 28 Apr. 1814; William Burley, Jr., to Hull, 6 Apr. [i.e., May] 1814, enclosed in Hull to Jones, 7 May 1814; Commandants & Agents LB 2:60: Jones to Hull, 30 Apr. 1814; Charles Burleigh, *The Genealogy of the Burley or Burleigh Family of America* (Portland, Me., 1880), pp. 17–18, 33.

7. MdHS, Murray Family Papers: Alexander Murray to Magnus Murray, 12 Apr. 1799; CL: Hugh G. Campbell to Robert Smith, 21 Jan. 1806; OL: Arthur Sinclair to Charles W. Goldsborough, 17 Oct. 1809; GLB 7:136: Smith to Bishop John Carroll, 24 Apr. 1804.

8. For the college turmoil of 1798–1812 see Joseph F. Kett, *Rites of Passage: Adolescence in America, 1790 to the Present* (New York: Basic Books, 1977), pp. 51–59, and Steven J. Novak, *The Rights of Youth: American Colleges and Student Revolt, 1798–1815* (Cambridge: Harvard University Press, 1977).

9. DAB 5:486–488; CMR 1:0144–0145: Francis H. Ellison to Richard V. Morris, 17 June 1800; OSW 4:131, 135: Benjamin Stoddert to Morris, 12 Aug. 1800; Stoddert to William A. Duer, 12 Aug. 1800; GLB 3:508: Stoddert to Lady Catherine Duer, 31 July 1800; QW 6:221.

10. CL: Isaac Hull to William Jones, 23 Apr. 1814, enclosing James E. Carr to Johnston Blakeley, 19 Apr. 1814; *Columbian Centinel* (Boston), 22 Feb. 1815.

11. CL: William Bainbridge to William Jones, 24 July 1813; ML: John S. Sherburne to Paul Hamilton, 3 July 1812; *Columbian Centinel* (Boston), 28 Apr. 1838.

12. MCL: David Porter to Robert Smith, 24 Mar. 1809, enclosing Charles C.B. Thompson to Porter, 4 Aug. 1808.

13. CL: Hugh G. Campbell to William Jones, 27 Feb. 1813.

14. CL: Alexander Murray to Paul Hamilton, 26 June, 31 Aug., and [9 Sept.] 1809.

15. OL: Charles Morris to Robert Smith, 28 Jan. 1809; Frederick Rodgers Coll: David Reed to John Rodgers, 11 June 1811; *Columbian Centinel* (Boston), 4 July 1823.

16. Resignations, 1810–25: Seth B. Alby to William Jones, 15 Feb. 1814; CL: Isaac Chauncey to Jones, 15 Mar. 1814; OL: Alby to Jones, 17 Feb. 1814; M&PR: *Jones*, 1814–18 (T829:16).

17. CL: Isaac Chauncey to William Jones, 16 Apr. 1814; M&PR: Sackets Harbor Station, 1812–26 (T829:18).

18. OSW 10:391: William Jones to Stephen Wilson, 3 May 1813; M&PR: Norfolk Station, 1807–38 (T829:157), fol. 61; *Columbian Centinel* (Boston), 5 June 1822.

19. ML: William D. Beall to Robert Smith, 18 Nov. 1808; OL: Charles Ludlow to John Rodgers, 13 Dec. 1809; OSW 9:421: Paul Hamilton to John Shaw, 8 Aug. 1811; CL: Shaw to Hamilton, 13 Sept. 1811.

20. CMR 1:1048–1052; Resignations, 1803–25: George W. Liggett to Robert Smith, 6 July 1804; ML: George Liggett to William Jones, 28 June 1813; Public Record Office, London: ADM 103/190, General Entry Book of American Prisoners-of-War at Jamaica, prisoner #373; M&PR: New York Station, 1813–28 (T829:154), fol. 16.

21. CMR 19:1024–1038; RG 36: Proofs of American Citizenship, New Orleans (3 July 1810); M&PR: *President*, 1800–1813 (T829:72), fols. 373, 425; RFP: M.C. Perry, Journal kept on board *President*, 19 Mar. 1811–25 July 1813, entry for 26 June 1812.

Epilogue: Captain Hull Goes Shopping and Decides to Take a Risk

1. J.C.A. Stagg, *Mr. Madison's War: Politics, Diplomacy, and Warfare in the Early American Republic, 1783–1830* (Princeton, N.J.: Princeton University Press, 1983), p. 289.

2. CL: Isaac Hull to Paul Hamilton, 28 July, 2 Aug. 1812.

3. Linda M. Maloney, *The Captain from Connecticut: The Life and Naval Times of Isaac Hull* (Boston: Northeastern University Press, 1986), p. 181.

4. Accts (A) Binney, Amos: Bemis & Eddy invoice, 29 July 1812.

Index

About the Author

Christopher McKee is Samuel R. and Marie-Louise Rosenthal Professor and Librarian of the College at Grinnell College, Iowa. He is the author of *Edward Preble: A Naval Biography, 1761–1807* (Naval Institute Press, 1972). In 1990/91 Mr. McKee held the Secretary of the Navy's Research Chair in Naval History at the Naval Historical Center in Washington, D.C.

The **Naval Institute Press** is the book-publishing arm of the U.S. Naval Institute, a private, nonprofit professional society for members of the sea services and civilians who share an interest in naval and maritime affairs. Established in 1873 at the U.S. Naval Academy in Annapolis, Maryland, where its offices remain today, the Naval Institute has more than 100,000 members worldwide.

Members of the Naval Institute receive the influential monthly magazine *Proceedings* and discounts on fine nautical prints, ship and aircraft photos, and subscriptions to the quarterly *Naval History* magazine. They also have access to the transcripts of the Institute's Oral History Program and get discounted admission to any of the Institute-sponsored seminars regularly offered around the country.

The Naval Institute's book-publishing program, begun in 1898 with basic guides to naval practices, has broadened its scope in recent years to include books of more general interest. Now the Naval Institute Press publishes more than forty new titles each year, ranging from how-to books on boating and navigation to battle histories, biographies, ship and aircraft guides, and novels. Institute members receive discounts on the Press's more than 375 books.

Full-time students are eligible for special half-price membership rates. Life memberships are also available.

For a free catalog describing the Naval Institute Press books currently available, and for further information about U.S. Naval Institute membership, please write to:

Membership & Communications Department
U.S. Naval Institute
Annapolis, Maryland 21402

Or call, toll-free, (800) 233-USNI. In Maryland, call (301) 224-3378.

THE NAVAL INSTITUTE PRESS

A GENTLEMANLY AND HONORABLE PROFESSION

The Creation of the U.S. Naval Officer Corps, 1794–1815

Designed by Pamela L. Schnitter

Set in Baskerville
by Maryland Composition Company, Inc.
Glen Burnie, Maryland

Printed on 50-lb. Antique Cream
and bound in Joanna Arrestox and Papan Homespun
with text-matching endsheets
by The Maple-Vail Book Manufacturing Group
Binghamton, New York